Red Hat® Linux® Networking and System Administration

Red Hat® Linux® Networking and System Administration

Terry Collings and Kurt Wall

M&T Books

Wiley Publishing, Inc.

Red Hat® Linux® Networking and System Administration

Published by
M&T Books
An imprint of Wiley Publishing, Inc.
909 Third Avenue
New York, NY 10022
www.wiley.com

For general information on our other products and services or to obtain technical support, please contact our Customer Care Department within the U.S. at 800-762-2974, outside the U.S. at 317-572-3993, or fax 317-572-4002.

Wiley also publishes its books in a variety of electronic formats. Some content that appears in print may not be available in electronic books.

Library of Congress Cataloging-in-Publication Data:

Library of Congress Control Number: 2001093591
ISBN: 0-7645-3632-X
Manufactured in the United States of America
10 9 8 7 6 5 4 3

> LIMIT OF LIABILITY/DISCLAIMER OF WARRANTY: WHILE THE PUBLISHER AND AUTHOR HAVE USED THEIR BEST EFFORTS IN PREPARING THIS BOOK, THEY MAKE NO REPRESENTATIONS OR WARRANTIES WITH RESPECT TO THE ACCURACY OR COMPLETENESS OF THE CONTENTS OF THIS BOOK AND SPECIFICALLY DISCLAIM ANY IMPLIED WARRANTIES OF MERCHANTABILITY OR FITNESS FOR A PARTICULAR PURPOSE. NO WARRANTY MAY BE CREATED OR EXTENDED BY SALES REPRESENTATIVES OR WRITTEN SALES MATERIALS. THE ADVICE AND STRATEGIES CONTAINED HEREIN MAY NOT BE SUITABLE FOR YOUR SITUATION. YOU SHOULD CONSULT WITH A PROFESSIONAL WHERE APPROPRIATE. NEITHER THE PUBLISHER NOR AUTHOR SHALL BE LIABLE FOR ANY LOSS OF PROFIT OR ANY OTHER COMMERCIAL DAMAGES, INCLUDING BUT NOT LIMITED TO SPECIAL, INCIDENTAL, CONSEQUENTIAL, OR OTHER DAMAGES.

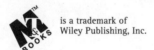

About the Authors

Terry Collings has been working in the computer field since 1981 and has experience in all types of operating systems and their associated hardware. He has industry certifications in Novell, TCP/IP, MS Windows, and Unix. Terry's full-time job is at Muhlenberg College in Allentown, PA, where he is the school's Instructional Technologist. His main function in this position is assisting faculty in the use of computer technology to augment their classroom presentations. He is also the system administrator for the school's online course content management software. Terry also teaches a wide range of computer and technology-related courses in the evenings at Allentown Business School. Terry has been a technical editor for several Hungry Minds, Inc., books and is the co-author of the *Linux Bible*. He can be reached at `collings@muhlenberg.edu`.

Kurt Wall first touched a computer in 1980 when he learned FORTRAN on an IBM mainframe of forgotten vintage; things have only gotten better since then. These days, Kurt is a full-time Linux and Unix author, editor, consultant, and programmer. He has written five books about Linux and Unix programming and system administration, is working on his sixth, and is the technical editor for over a dozen other Linux- and Unix-related titles. Currently, Kurt works from his home in Indianapolis. He can be reached via e-mail at `kwall@kurtwerks.com`.

Credits

CONTRIBUTING WRITERS
Viktorie Navratilova
Dennis Powell
Brandon Wiley

ACQUISITIONS EDITOR
Terri Varveris

PROJECT EDITOR
Martin V. Minner

TECHNICAL EDITORS
Joel Lee
Matt Hayden
Sandra Moore

COPY EDITOR
Marti Paul

RED HAT PRESS LIAISON
Lorien Golaski, Red Hat
Communications Manager

PROJECT COORDINATOR
Dale White

**GRAPHICS AND PRODUCTION
SPECIALISTS**
Beth Brooks
Sean Decker
Melanie DesJardins
Jeremey Unger

QUALITY CONTROL TECHNICIANS
Laura Albert
Luisa Perez
Carl Pierce
Marianne Santy

SENIOR PERMISSIONS EDITOR
Carmen Krikorian

MEDIA DEVELOPMENT SPECIALIST
Greg Stephens

MEDIA DEVELOPMENT COORDINATOR
Marisa Pearman

COVER DESIGN
Michael Freeland

COVER PHOTO
Hulton Getty

PROOFREADING AND INDEXING
TECHBOOKS Production Services

This book is dedicated to the victims and heroes of September 11, 2001.

Preface

Red Hat Linux is the most popular distribution of Linux currently in use. Red Hat Linux has shown itself to be a robust, reliable operating system that can run on a variety of hardware, from personal computers to large mainframes. Linux in general, and Red Hat Linux in particular, is a very powerful operating system that can be used at the enterprise level as a full-fledged server, as well as at the workstation level for typical user applications. For those of us dissatisfied with the reliability of other commercially available operating systems, Red Hat Linux is a pleasant alternative.

How This Book Is Organized

This book is divided into five parts. Each part covers a specific area of functionality in a typical Red Hat Linux system.

Part I – Red Hat Linux System and Network Administration Defined

This part describes the duties of a system administrator. Chapter 1 explains some of the more common tasks, such as installing servers and application software, managing user accounts, and backing up and restoring files. Many more topics are covered in this chapter. Chapter 2 details the steps involved in planning and building a network and planning for security and disaster recovery. Chapter 3 takes you through the steps required to install Red Hat Linux on a local system as well as on a remote system. Chapter 4 gives an explanation of the Red Hat Linux file system and storage devices. Chapter 5, the last chapter in Part I, lists the system and network configuration files and their uses.

Part II – Red Hat Linux Network Services

This part of the book is where you learn about the networking services available in Red Hat Linux. Chapter 6 gives an explanation of the TCP/IP protocol suite and how to configure it on your system. Chapter 7 tells how to configure the Network File System (NFS) for sharing files with other Linux or Unix computers on your network. Chapter 8 provides a description of the Network Information System (NIS) as well as configuration instructions. If you have computers running Microsoft operating systems, Chapter 9 is where you find instructions for connecting your Red Hat Linux network to the Windows network. The final chapter in this part, Chapter 10, tells you how to connect your Red Hat Linux network to computers running the Apple operating system.

Part III – Red Hat Linux Internet Services

Internet services are somewhat different from network services used on an internal network. Chapter 11 begins this part by explaining Internet services, and includes a discussion of the xinetd and TCP wrappers configuration files.A fundamental part of using the Internet is the ability to enter a domain name and have it converted into an IP number that is the actual address of a computer. The name-to-number conversion is done by the Domain Name System (DNS), which is covered in Chapter 12. Chapter 13 describes the File Transfer Protocol (FTP) and gives installation and configuration instructions. Sending and receiving e-mail has become so common that it's hard to remember the time before we had it. Chapter 14 explains mail services and its configuration. Last, but not least, you find an explanation of setting up a Web server. Chapter 15 covers Apache, one of the most popular Web servers in use.

Part IV – Red Hat Linux System Maintenance

The goal of this part of the book is to provide a fundamental understanding of the tasks required to maintain your system and ensure that it runs optimally. Chapter 16 explains the Red Hat Network, a service available from Red Hat that you can use to keep your system current. You can register your systems with Red Hat and then receive notifications of updated or new software that can be installed. Chapter 17 discusses upgrading and customizing the kernel for your specific needs. Chapter 18 tells you how to use the command line to perform all of your system administrative tasks. If you want to use scripts to automate some of your work, Chapter 19 is where you find out how to do it. Chapter 20 deals with monitoring the performance of your system. Creating users and groups is a basic part of system maintenance, and Chapter 21 describes this process. Chapter 22 details the steps necessary to back up your file system and use the backups to restore your system. The final chapter in this part, Chapter 23, gives instructions on installing and upgrading software packages.

Part V – Security and Problem Solving

A critical area of concern for system administrators is maintaining a secure system. Most of the chapters in this part deal with security, beginning with Chapter 24, which covers security basics. Chapter 25 addresses local, or *host-based,* security. In Chapter 26 you find an explanation of firewalls and Internet security and the risks you may encounter from outside connections. Chapter 27 looks at ways to monitor a Red Hat Linux system for attempted, potential, and actual security compromises using the tools available in a standard Red Hat Linux installation. The last chapter in this part, Chapter 28, lists problems you may encounter during normal operation of your system and the steps to take to solve the problems discussed.

How to Use This Book

Our intention for this book is to cover the Red Hat Linux operating system in enough detail to provide the answers that you need. The book is divided into the parts previously discussed to make it easy for you to go to the specific part for the topic you need to learn about. You can use the book as a reference for whatever you need to know about a particular topic.

Using this book's icons

Watch for the following margin icons to help you get the most out of this book:

 Tips provide special information or advice.

 Caution icons warn you of a potential problem or error.

 This icon directs you to related information in another section or chapter.

 A Note highlights an area of interest or special concern related to the topic.

 This icon points you toward related material on the book's CD-ROM.

Conventions

This book uses the following conventions for explanations of how to do things on your computer:

◆ *Italic type* introduces new technical terms. It also indicates replaceable arguments that you should substitute with actual values – the context makes clear the distinction between new terms and replaceable arguments.

◆ **Bold type** shows a command you type in.

◆ `Monospaced text` distinguishes commands, options, and arguments from surrounding explanatory content.

◆ Keys to press in combination are shown like this example: Ctrl+Alt+Delete means to press all three keys at the same time.

◆ The term *click* means to press the left mouse button once. *Double-click* means to press the left button twice in quick succession. *Right click* means to press the right mouse button once. *Drag* means to hold down the left mouse button and move the mouse while holding down the button.

Terry Collings's Acknowledgments

Until I started writing books, I never realized how many people are involved with producing a book like this and how much work they do. The first person I want to thank is my coauthor, Kurt Wall. Kurt is the reason I became involved with working on Linux books when I was asked to technical edit a Linux book several years ago. Since then, Kurt and I have collaborated on other projects, most recently this book.

I also want to acknowledge the hard work of Viktorie Navratilova, Dennis Powell, and Brandon Wiley who stepped in and wrote several chapters for me when I was out with a medical problem. Their help was a significant contribution to the completion of this book.

A special thank-you goes out to Terri Varveris, my acquisitions editor at Hungry Minds. Terri is a wonderful person to work with and is one of the nicest people I have ever known. She is also responsible for choosing our project editor, Marty Minner. Marty is very organized and he makes sure we do our jobs, but in a nice way that makes him a pleasure to work with. Finally, thanks to our copy editor, technical editors, and production staff at Hungry Minds for their efforts in ensuring that our work is technically accurate as well as grammatically correct and properly presented.

Finally, I would like to thank my wife Nancy for all her support and encouragement. She is my true inspiration.

Kurt Wall's Acknowledgments

Like Terry, I appreciate the work of Viktorie, Dennis, and Brandon in helping Terry and me complete this book when Terry became ill. Thanks to Terri Varveris for giving me the chance to write about Linux, something I truly enjoy doing — Terri, let's do this again. Here's a vigorous nod to Marty Minner, who deftly managed the day-to-day details of converting raw manuscript into a finished book — every author should have such a capable, patient, and witty project editor. Kudos as well to the rest of the team at Hungry Minds who labored to make this book a reality.

I would be remiss if I failed to thank Terry Collings for inviting me to participate in this book — he may yet decide that I didn't do him any favors by getting him involved in writing books. I look forward to another opportunity to work with him.

I would like to extend my deepest thanks to and appreciation of the mission and members of Mount Tabor Lutheran Church in Salt Lake City — their service and example kept me going in dark, trying times.

Contents at a Glance

Contents

Part I

Red Hat Linux System and Network Administration Defined

IN THIS PART:

This part introduces the system administrator's duties. The chapters in this part discuss planning a network, installing Red Hat Linux, and working with the Red Hat Linux file system and configuration files.

Chapter 1

Duties of the System Administrator

IN THIS CHAPTER

- ◆ The Linux system administrator
- ◆ Installing and configuring servers
- ◆ Installing and configuring application software
- ◆ Creating and maintaining user accounts
- ◆ Backing up and restoring files
- ◆ Monitoring and tuning performance
- ◆ Configuring a secure system
- ◆ Using tools to monitor security

LINUX IS A MULTIUSER, multitasking operating system from the ground up, and in this regard the system administrator has flexibility — and responsibility — far beyond those of other operating systems. Now, Red Hat has employed innovations that extend these duties even for the experienced Linux user. In this chapter, we look at those requirements.

The Linux System Administrator

Linux involves much more than merely sitting down and turning on the machine. Often you hear talk of a "steep learning curve," but that discouraging phrase can be misleading. Instead, Linux is quite different from the most popular commercial operating systems in a number of ways, and while it is no more difficult to learn than other operating systems, it is likely to seem very strange even to the experienced administrator of some other system. In addition, the sophistication of a number of parts of the Red Hat Linux distribution has increased by an order of magnitude, so even an experienced Linux administrator is likely to find much that is new and unfamiliar. Fortunately, there are new tools designed to make system administration easier than it has ever been before.

Make no mistake: Every computer in the world has a system administrator. It may be — and probably is — that the majority of system administrators are probably those who decided what software and peripherals were bundled with the machine when it was shipped. That status quo remains because the majority of users who acquire computers for use as appliances probably do little to change the default values. But the minute a user decides on a different wallpaper image or adds an application that was acquired apart from the machine itself, he or she has taken on the mantle of system administration.

Such a high-falutin' title brings with it some responsibilities. No one whose computer is connected to the Internet, for instance, has been immune to the effects of poorly administered systems, as demonstrated by the Distributed Denial of Service (DDoS) and e-mail macro virus attacks that have shaken the online world in recent years. The scope of these acts of computer vandalism (and in some cases computer larceny) would have been greatly reduced if system administrators had a better understanding of their duties.

The Linux system administrator is more likely to understand the necessity of active system administration than are those who run whatever came on the computer, assuming that things came from the factory properly configured. The user or enterprise that decides on Linux has decided, too, to assume the control that Linux offers, and the responsibilities that this entails.

By its very nature as a modern, multiuser operating system, Linux requires a degree of administration greater than that of less robust home market systems. This means that even if you are using a single machine connected to the Internet by a dial-up modem — or not even connected at all — you have the benefits of the same system employed by some of the largest businesses in the world, and will do many of the things that the IT professionals employed by those companies are paid to do. Administering your system does involve a degree of learning, but it also means that in setting up and configuring your own system you gain skills and understanding that raise you above mere "computer user" status. The Linux system administrator does not achieve that mantle by having purchased a computer but instead by having taken full control of what his or her computer does and how it does it.

You may end up configuring a small home or small office network of two or more machines, perhaps including ones that are not running Linux. You may be responsible for a business network of dozens of machines. The nature of system administration in Linux is surprisingly constant, no matter how large or small your installation. It merely involves enabling and configuring features you already have available.

By definition, the Linux system administrator is the person who has "root" access, which is to say the one who is the system's "super user" (or root user). A standard Linux user is limited as to the things he or she can do with the underlying engine of the system. But the "root" user has unfettered access to everything — all user accounts, their home directories, and the files therein; all system configurations; and all files on the system. A certain body of thought says that no one should ever log in as "root," because system administration tasks can be performed more easily and safely through other, more specific means, which I discuss in due course.

The system administrator has full system privileges, so the first duty is to know what you're doing lest you break something.

 By definition, the Linux system administrator is the person who has "root" access, which is to say the one who is the system's "super user."

The word "duties" implies a degree of drudgery; in fact, they're a manifestation of the tremendous flexibility of the system measured against responsibility to run a tight installation. These duties do not so much constrain the system administrator as free him or her to match the installation to the task. But all are likely employed to some degree in every system. Let's take a brief look at them.

Installing and Configuring Servers

In the Linux world, the word "server" has a meaning that is broader than you might be used to. For instance, the standard Red Hat Linux graphical user interface (GUI) requires a graphical layer called XFree86. This is a server. It runs even on a stand-alone machine with one user account. It must be configured. (Fortunately, Red Hat Linux has made this a simple and painless part of installation on all but the most obscure combinations of video card and monitor; gone are the days of anguish configuring a graphical desktop.)

Likewise, printing in Linux takes place only after you have configured a print server. Again, this has become so easy as to be nearly trivial.

In certain areas the client-server nomenclature can be confusing, though. While you cannot have a graphical desktop without a server, you can have World Wide Web access without a Web server, file transfer protocol (FTP) access without running an FTP server, and Internet e-mail capabilities without ever starting a mail server. You may well want to use these servers, all of which are included in Red Hat Linux, but then again you may not. And whenever a server is connected to other machines outside your physical control, there are security implications — you want users to have easy access to the things they need, but you don't want to open up the system you're administering to the whole wide world.

 Whenever a server is connected to machines outside your physical control, security issues arise. You want users to have easy access to the things they need, but you don't want to open up the system you're administering to the whole wide world.

Linux distributions used to be shipped with all imaginable servers turned on by default. This was a reflection of an earlier, more polite era in computing, when people did not consider vandalizing other people's machines to be good sport. But the realities of a modern, more dangerous world have dictated that all but essential servers are off unless specifically enabled and configured. This duty falls to the system administrator. You need to know what servers you need and how to employ them, and to be aware that it is bad practice and a potential security nightmare to enable services that the system isn't using and doesn't need. Fortunately, the following pages show you how to carry out this aspect of system administration easily and efficiently.

Installing and Configuring Application Software

This may seem redundant, but it's crucial that the new Linux system administrator understand two characteristics that set Linux apart from popular commercial operating systems: The first is the idea of the root or super user, and the second is that Linux is a multiuser operating system. Each user has (or shares) an account on the system, be it on a separate machine or on a single machine with multiple accounts.

One reason that these concepts are crucial is found in the administration of application software — productivity programs.

While it is possible for individual users to install some applications in their home directories — drive space set aside for their own files and customizations — these applications are not available to other users without the intervention of the system administrator. Besides, if an application is to be used by more than one user, it probably needs to be installed higher up in the Linux file hierarchy, which is a job that can be performed by the system administrator only. (The administrator can even decide which users may use which applications by creating a "group" for that application and enrolling individual users into that group.)

New software packages might be installed in /opt, if they are likely to be upgraded separately from the Red Hat Linux distribution itself; by so doing, it's simple to retain the old version until you are certain the new version works and meets expectations. Some packages may need to go in /usr/local or even /usr, if they are upgrades of packages installed as part of Red Hat Linux. (For instance, there are sometimes security upgrades of existing packages.) The location of the installation usually matters only if you compile the application from source code; if you use a Red Hat Package Manager (RPM) application package, it automatically goes where it should.

Configuration and customization of applications is to some extent at the user's discretion, but not entirely. "Skeleton" configurations — administrator-determined default configurations — set the baseline for user employment of applications. If there are particular forms, for example, that are used throughout an enterprise, the system administrator would set them up or at least make them available by adding them to the skeleton configuration. The same applies, too, in configuring user desktops and in even deciding what applications should appear on user desktop menus. Your company may not want the games that ship with modern Linux desktops to be available to users. And you may want to add menu items for newly installed or custom applications. The system administrator brings all this to pass.

Creating and Maintaining User Accounts

Not just anyone can show up and log on to a Linux machine. An account must be created for each user and — you guessed it — no one but the system administrator may do this. That's simple enough.

But there's more, and it involves decisions that either you or your company must make. You might want to let users select their own passwords, which would no doubt make them easier to remember, but which probably would be easier for a malefactor to crack. You might want to assign passwords, which is more secure in theory but which increases the likelihood that users will write them down on a conveniently located scrap of paper — a risk if many people have access to the area where the machine(s) is located. You might decide that users must change their passwords periodically, and you can configure Red Hat Linux to prompt users to do so.

And what to do about old accounts? Perhaps someone has left the company. What happens to his or her account? You probably don't want him or her to continue to have access to the company network. On the other hand, you don't want to simply delete the account, perhaps to discover later that essential data resided nowhere else.

To what may specific users have access? It might be that there are aspects of your business that make World Wide Web access desirable, but you don't want everyone spending their working hours surfing the Web. If your system is at home, you may wish to limit your children's access to the Web, which contains sites to which few if any parents would want their children exposed.

These issues and others are parts of the system administrator's duties in managing user accounts. Whether the administrator or his or her employer establishes the policies governing them, those policies should be established — if in an enterprise, preferably in writing — for the protection of all concerned.

Backing Up and Restoring Files

Until equipment becomes absolutely infallible, and until people lose their desire to harm the property of others (and, truth be known, until system administrators become perfect), there is a need to back up important files so that in the event of a failure of hardware, security, or administration, the system can be up and running again with minimal disruption. Only the system administrator may do this.

(Because of its built-in security features, Linux may not allow users to be able even to back up their own files to floppy disks.)

Again, knowing that file backup is your job is not enough. You need to formulate a strategy for making sure your system is not vulnerable to catastrophic disruption. And it's not always obvious. If you have a high-capacity tape drive and several good sets of restore diskettes, you might make a full system backup every few days. If you are managing a system with scores of users, you might find it more sensible to back up user accounts and system configuration files, figuring that reinstallation from the distribution CDs would be quicker and easier than getting the basics off a tape archive. (Don't forget the applications you've installed separate from your Red Hat Linux distribution, especially including anything heavily customized!)

Once you've decided *what* to back up, you need to decide *how frequently* you want to perform backups and whether you wish to maintain a series of incremental backups – adding only the files that have changed since the last backup – or multiple full backups, and *when* these backups are to be performed – do you trust an automated, unattended process? Or, if you have input as to the equipment used, do you want to use a redundant array of independent disks, or RAID, which is to say multiple hard drives all containing the same data as insurance against the failure of any one of them, in addition to other backup systems. (A RAID is not enough, because hard drive failure is not the only means by which a system can be brought to a halt.)

Conversely, you do not want to become complacent or to foster such an attitude among users. Part of your strategy should be the maintenance of perfect backups without ever needing to resort to them. This means encouraging users to keep multiple copies of their own important files, all in their home directories, so that you are not being asked to mount a backup so as to restore a file that a user has corrupted. (And if the system is stand-alone, you as your own system administrator might want to make a practice of backing up configuration and other important files.)

The chances are that even if you're working for a company, you'll make these decisions – all your boss wants is a system that works perfectly, all the time. Backing up is only half the story, too. You need to formulate a plan for bringing the system back up in the event of a failure. Such a plan extends to areas outside the scope of this book. Sometimes hardware failures are so severe that the only solution is replacing the hard drive, replacing everything *except* the hard drive, or even restoring from backup to a whole new machine.

TIP   Backing up is only half the story. You need to formulate a plan for bringing the system back up in the event of a failure.

Monitoring and Tuning Performance

The default installation of Red Hat Linux goes a long way toward capitalizing on existing system resources. But there is no "one size fits all" configuration, and Linux is infinitely configurable or close to it.

On a modern stand-alone system, Linux is going to be pretty quick, and if it isn't, there's something wrong — something that is up to the system administrator to fix. But you might want to squeeze that one last little bit of performance out of your hardware. Or you might have a number of people using the same fileserver, mail server, or other shared machine, in which case seemingly small improvements in system performance can mean a lot.

System tuning is an ongoing process aided by a variety of diagnostic and monitoring tools. Some performance decisions are made at installation time, while others are added or tweaked later. A good example is the use of the hdparm utility, which can increase throughput in IDE drives considerably — but for some high-speed modes a check of system logs will show that faulty or inexpensive cables can, in combination with hdparm, produce an enormity of nondestructive but system-slowing errors.

Proper monitoring allows you to detect a misbehaving application that might be consuming more resources than it should or failing to exit completely on close. Through the use of system performance tools you can determine when hardware — such as memory, added storage, or even something as elaborate as a hardware RAID — should be upgraded for more cost-effective use of a machine in the enterprise or for complicated computational tasks such as three-dimensional rendering.

Possibly most important, careful system monitoring and diagnostic practices give you an early heads-up when a system component is showing early signs of failure, so that any potential downtime can be minimized. Combined with the resources for determining which components are best supported by Red Hat Linux, performance monitoring can result in replacement components which are far more robust and efficient in some cases.

And in any case, careful system monitoring plus wise use of the built-in configurability of Linux allows you to squeeze the best possible performance from your existing equipment, from customizing video drivers to applying special kernel patches to simply turning off unneeded services to free memory and processor cycles.

To squeeze the best performance from your equipment, monitor your system carefully and use Linux's built-in configurability wisely.

Configuring a Secure System

If there is a common thread in Linux system administration, something that is a constant presence in everything you do, it is the security of the computer and data integrity.

What does this mean? Well, just about everything. The system administrator's task, first and foremost, is to make certain that no data on the machine or network are likely to become corrupted, whether by hardware or power failure, by misconfiguration or user error (to the extent that the latter can be avoided), or by malicious or inadvertent intrusion from elsewhere. It means doing all the tasks described throughout this chapter well and with a full understanding of their implication, and it means much more.

No one involved in computing can have failed to hear of the succession of increasingly serious attacks upon machines connected to the Internet. The majority of these have not targeted Linux systems, but that doesn't mean that Linux systems have been entirely immune, either to direct attack or to the effects of attacks on machines running other operating systems. In one Distributed Denial of Service (DDoS) attack aimed at several major online companies, many of the "zombie" machines – those which had been exploited so that the vandals could employ thousands of machines instead of just a few – were running Linux that had not been patched to guard against a well-known security flaw. In the various "Code Red" attacks of the summer of 2001, Linux machines themselves were invulnerable, but the huge amount of traffic generated by this "worm" infection nevertheless prevented many Linux machines from getting much Web-based work done for several weeks, so fierce was the storm raging across the Internet. And few Internet e-mail users have gone without receiving at least some "SirCam" messages – nonsensical messages from strangers with randomly selected files from the strangers' machines attached. While this infection did not corrupt Linux machines as it did those running a different operating system, anyone on a dial-up connection who had to endure the download of several megabytes of infected mail would scarcely describe himself or herself as unaffected by the attack.

Depending on how and to what a Linux machine is connected, the sensitivity of the data it contains and the uses to which it is put, security can be as simple as turning off unneeded services, monitoring the Red Hat Linux security mailing list to make sure that all security advisories are followed, and otherwise engaging in good computing practices to make sure the system runs robustly. Or it can be an almost full-time job involving levels of security permissions within the system and systems to which it is connected, elaborate firewalling to protect not just Linux machines but machines that, through their use of non-Linux software, are far more vulnerable, and physical security – making sure no one steals the machine itself!

For any machine that is connected to any other machine, security means hardening against attack and making certain that no one is using your machine as a platform for launching attacks against others. If you are running Web, ftp, or mail servers, it means giving access to those who are entitled to it while locking out everyone else. It means making sure that passwords are not easily guessed and not made available to unauthorized persons, that disgruntled former employees no longer have access to the system, and that no unauthorized person may copy files from your machine or machines.

Security is an ongoing process — it has been said that the only really secure computer is one that contains no data and that is unplugged from networks and even power supplies, has no keyboard attached, and resides in a locked vault. While that is theoretically true, it also implies that security diminishes the usefulness of the machine, don't you think? So your job as a system administrator is to strike just the right balance between maximum utility and maximum safety, all the while bearing in mind that confidence in a secure machine today says nothing about the machine's security tomorrow.

In the pages that follow, you'll learn about the many tools that Red Hat Linux provides to help you guard against intrusion, even to help you prevent intrusion into non-Linux machines that may reside on your network. Linux is designed from the beginning with security in mind, and in all of your tasks you should maintain that same security awareness.

TIP Your job as a system administrator is to strike the right balance between maximum utility and maximum safety, all the while bearing in mind that confidence in a secure machine today says nothing about the machine's security tomorrow.

Using Tools to Monitor Security

Crackers — people who, for purposes of larceny or to amuse themselves, like to break into other people's computers — are a clever bunch. If there is a vulnerability in a system, they will find it. Fortunately, the Linux development community is quick to find potential exploits and to find ways of slamming shut the door before crackers can enter. Fortunately, too, Red Hat is diligent in making available new, patched versions of packages in which potential exploits have been found. So your first and best security tool is making sure that whenever a security advisory is issued, you download and install the repaired package. This line of defense can be annoying, but it is nothing compared to rebuilding a compromised system.

And as good as the bug trackers are, sometimes their job is reactive. Preventing the use of your machine for nefarious purposes and guarding against intrusion are, in the end, your responsibility alone. Again, Red Hat Linux equips you with tools to detect and deal with unauthorized access of many kinds. As this book unfolds, you'll learn how to install and configure these tools and how to make sense of the warnings they provide. Pay careful attention to those sections and do what they say. If your machine is connected to the Internet, you will be amazed at the number of attempts that are made to break into your machine. And you'll be struck by how critical an issue security is.

Summary

As you, the system administrator, read this book, bear in mind that your tasks are ongoing and that there is never a machine that is completely tuned, entirely up-to-date, and utterly secure for very long. The pace of Linux development is breathtaking, so it's important that you keep current in the latest breakthroughs. This book gives you the very best information as to the Red Hat Linux distribution you're using and tells you all you need to know about getting the most from it. But more than that, you should read it with an eye toward developing a Linux system administrator's point of view, an understanding of how the system works as opposed to the mere performance of tasks. As the best system administrators will tell you, system administration is a state of mind.

Chapter 2

Planning the Network

WHILE YOU CAN set up a Red Hat Linux network on the fly, your time will be spent most efficiently if you plan your network. Preparation reduces confusion not just now but in the future, makes provision for expansion later on, and assures that you make the best use of system resources. Although setting up a huge network of hundreds of nodes requires planning beyond the scope of this chapter, here we explore the fundamentals of planning and preparing for your new network installation.

Deciding What Kind of Network You Need

Linux is, by definition and right out of the box, a network operating system. It is also nearly infinitely configurable, meaning that you can tailor a network to meet your precise needs. That is a tremendous strength, but it can also be very daunting when compared to systems that are more limited in possibilities — as the philosopher James Burnham said, where there is no alternative, there is no problem.

Before you install Red Hat Linux on anything other than a stand-alone box just to take a look at it, you would be well-advised to consider what kind of network you want to install, what it will be used for, what kinds of connections to the outside world it will have, and whether it is something you're likely to expand later.

Questions to ask include:

◆ What services do you wish to provide within your local network?

◆ Will your network be made up entirely of Linux machines, or will boxes running other operating systems be connected to it?

◆ What devices (printers, scanners, DSL or cable modem or even T-1 connections) do you plan to share?

◆ Do you intend to host a Web site or an FTP site?

◆ What security implications do you foresee?

◆ How many machines will make up your network?

It makes sense for you to start making notes, and to begin by answering these questions. The details of setting up your network can be found elsewhere in this book. But careful planning now lets you chart a clear path to a quick and efficient network and, perhaps even more important, helps you make sure that your network is secure from both internal and external mischief.

To learn more about setting up your network, see Chapters 6–10.

For example, many people are now using DSL or cable Internet service and wish to set up small networks purely to allow sharing of such a broadband connection. A permanent Internet connection demands that you pay more attention to security, which in turn means making sure that you do not accidentally have any easily exploited services running. If the network includes easily exploited operating systems, security becomes even more of a concern. Perhaps you will decide to set up a firewall on your Linux machine (or even set up a Linux box solely for firewall purposes). Or you might decide to employ one of the firewall-gateway-router network appliances that are gaining popularity and simply attach a hub to the appliance and attach each machine on the "network" to that hub. Such a network may not be big, but it may be all that you need or want.

A good rule of thumb is to provide the services your network needs, and *only* those it needs.

But you may, and probably do, want to do more. Even if your needs are modest at first, adding services is a simple thing to do in Red Hat Linux. You will likely want some features, such as printer sharing, from the beginning, however.

Before you do anything else, you need to decide the "topology" of your network — how machines are connected — and whether you want a peer-to-peer or client/server network. These details matter, because on one hand you can overbuild your network so that your equipment won't be used efficiently, or on the other hand you can underestimate the demands on the network, resulting in one or more machines slowing down to near uselessness.

Understanding topologies

Your network will probably be one of the first two (at least to start) of the following four commonly used topologies:

Star Topology — You can think of this system as resembling a power strip with various devices that require electricity plugged into it. But in this case, instead of a power strip you have a network hub, and instead of devices needing electricity you have devices needing and providing data. These devices might include computers, network-equipped printers, cable or DSL modems, a local network backbone, or even other hubs. Star topology networks are connected by "twisted pair" cabling, which looks a great deal like the cabling used in modular phone systems. Star networks have more conductors and terminate in connectors called RJ-45s, while your phone is connected with RJ-11s. You may have up to 1,024 "nodes" — discrete machines or devices — on a star topology network, at speeds of up to 100MB per second. The newest networking technology provides even faster speeds. Figure 2-1 shows an example of a star topology network.

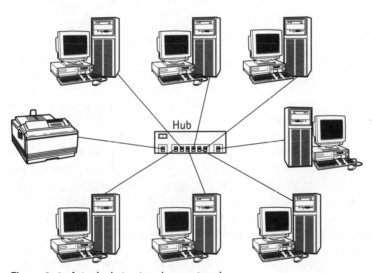

Figure 2-1: A typical star topology network

Bus Topology — If star topology resembles a power strip with many devices plugged into it, bus topology physically resembles strings of Christmas tree lights, hooked together one after another. Of course, on your network, there will be a lot more going on than what happens on a string of lights. But on a bus topology network, one machine is plugged to the next, which is plugged to the next, and so on. Bus topology is held together by coaxial or "thin Ethernet" cable, familiar at least in general form to anyone involved in amateur radio or anyone who has ever hooked up cable television. With this kind of topology, each end of the chain is specifically terminated by use of a "terminating resistor." Bus topology networks are limited to 30 machines, and, while considered highly reliable, their potential bandwidth (data-handling capacity) is limited to 10MB per second. Figure 2-2 shows a typical bus topology network.

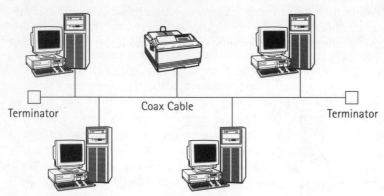

Figure 2-2: A typical bus topology network

Ring Topology – Imagine those Christmas tree lights again, but this time have the end of the string plugged into its beginning, creating a loop. Popularized by IBM's Token Ring system, ring networks are relatively difficult to set up, but do offer high bandwidth. Figure 2-3 shows a typical ring topology network.

Tree Topology – You almost certainly won't undertake this system at the outset, but you should know about it anyway. A tree network involves a high-speed "backbone" which is connected in the fashion of bus topology, but instead of connecting individual machines, it connects groups of star topology subnetworks.

Your choice of networks will be determined, possibly, by equipment that you already have. If you are setting up a new network, speed, ease of configuration, and relatively low cost all argue in favor of a star topology network. Figure 2-4 shows a typical tree topology.

Client/server or peer-to-peer?

You need also to decide whether you're going to set up a client/server or peer-to-peer network.

In a *client/server* network, machines are dedicated to performing a variety of functions, in some ways like the old mainframe/dumb terminal days. You might, for instance, have a print server that handles print jobs for every computer on the network – a highly useful arrangement if, for example, yours is an enterprise that prepares many invoices, contracts, or other documents. Or you might have a file server, whose sole purpose is to serve up "boilerplate" documents or the contents of a huge database, or to be the repository of a big project on which many people are working. If your enterprise has an online presence, you may wish to dedicate one (or more) machines as a Web site server, and perhaps one or more machines as an FTP (file transfer protocol) server, so that people may download (or even upload) files. You'll probably need some kind of mail server to handle both external e-mail and messages sent within the network itself. Clients are machines connected to such a network that are not servers but that instead rely on network services provided by the server machines. Clients are usually full, freestanding workstations, although it is possible to connect dumb terminals — monitor, keyboard, pointing device — to such a network in some circumstances. In order to use the services provided by the server(s), clients need to have accounts on the desired server(s) and must log in to those accounts.

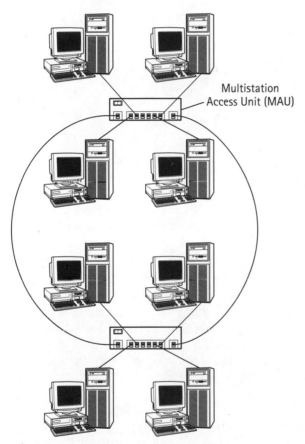

Multistation
Access Unit (MAU)

Figure 2-3: A typical ring topology network

A *peer-to-peer* network resembles a client/server network in that the machines are wired to each other and that some services are shared. But in a peer network, those shared items — a CD reader, perhaps, or a printer — reside on machines that are also used for other purposes. If you have a very small, low traffic network, a peer-to-peer system might be for you, because it requires no dedicated server machine(s). Peer networking can prove impractical for high-volume operations, because, for instance, multiple big print jobs can keep the poor soul whose printer is shared from getting much else done, so heavy can be the load on his or her system.

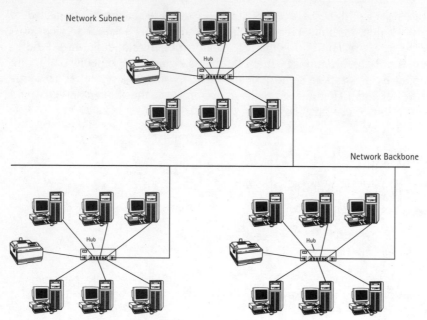

Figure 2-4: A typical tree topology network

What's in the mix?

If you are only a little bit familiar with Red Hat Linux, your exposure to it probably has been industry press reports dealing with its suitability as a server operating system — and there is no doubt that for this purpose it is superb. Please don't make the mistake of thinking, though, that this is *all* it is good for. Red Hat Linux comes with a full range of powerful and secure (by industry standards, although security is a process, not a state of being) server applications. But it also comes with powerful, attractive, and easy to use graphical desktops and a wide range of productivity applications, communications tools, and, yes, even amusements, which make it an ideal client or peer operating system as well.

Still, it might be that your network is a mixed marriage of machines of different architectures and operating systems. You may have a graphics design department that would sooner paint with their fingers on a cave wall than use anything other than a Macintosh. You may have legacy applications, boilerplate documents, or client (paying customer as opposed to class of computer) relations that require you to keep one or more Windows machines around. In these cases, you may well choose to have a client/server arrangement, with a good, secure Red Hat Linux box serving as a firewall between your network and the outside world, a mail server (it is now easy with Linux to filter out e-mail attachments of the sort that have caused so much disruption of Windows networks in recent years), a Web server if you have a presence in that milieu, and even perhaps a print server.

Many peer functions can be performed on a mixed network, but your job as a system administrator is much easier if you undertake the more straightforward client/server approach with a mixed installation. Additionally, if your network includes machines running Windows and is connected to the Internet, you would be irresponsible not to set up a firewall and let Linux handle Web, FTP, and mail service. History has shown that Linux is more secure in its fundamental architecture, but beyond that, there are thousands of eyes constantly searching for and fixing potential security exploits. Red Hat Linux is often first to make these fixes available, usually before the exploits are known to the cracker crowd.

 TIP If your network includes machines running Windows and is connected to the Internet, set up a firewall and let Linux handle your Web, FTP, and mail services.

A client/server network is very much like a small Internet, meaning that just about any machine can connect to it and make use of its services, irrespective of its architecture or operating system.

Determining system requirements

Depending on the kind of network you choose, you need, of course, computers, plus any other devices you intend to connect to the hub (if you're using a star-topology network), plus an appropriate and supported Ethernet card for each machine — two for your firewall machine, because it will have one line in from the outside world and one line out to the rest of your network — as well as the appropriate cabling and, if you go the recommended star topology route, a hub or hubs sufficient to support the network.

Red Hat Linux support for a broad range of Ethernet cards is excellent. Still, there are some factors you need to take into consideration. First, if you have old, eight-bit Ethernet adapters, now is the time to replace them. They are slow and often difficult to configure. Good, 100Mbps cards are now quite inexpensive, and this is probably not an area where a slow card that's slightly cheaper is a good long-term economy. Be sure to check the Red Hat hardware database at `http://www.redhat.com/support/hardware/` before buying new cards — in fact, it's a good idea to check it to make sure that the ones you have are supported, if you're upgrading to Red Hat Linux. (You needn't do this for Windows machines connected to an existing network, because as long as they're properly configured for use with Windows, and as long as you continue to use Windows with them, they will work on your network, even though it's served by Red Hat machines. Of course, if you have eight-bit or old, slow peer network cards and you're going to star architecture, you'll need to replace them, too.)

TIP If you have old, eight-bit Ethernet adapters, now is the time to replace them.

At this stage, too, you need to decide which headaches you're willing to accept and which ones might more sensibly be placed elsewhere. An example of this is Web and FTP hosting. For a few dollars per month, you can arrange for your Web site (and FTP site, if you have one) to be hosted by a large and secure commercial concern. Although it's fun to host your own site, it may be much more cost effective to outsource those duties. The best ones have strict security rules – assigned passwords and administrator access by SSH or other highly secure methods only – and have very high bandwidth and professional administration. With such an arrangement, you can still have your own domain and still have your own local mail server, with mail downloaded from your hosting company. (Your own SMTP mail server for outgoing mail can remain on a local machine.) For many smaller companies, the cost is more than covered by the ability to use a low cost cable or DSL service whose terms of use prohibit Web and FTP servers, meaning that you can gain an extra level of professional service at no cost – quite a bargain. Of course, if your enterprise is of sufficient size that you have a T-1 line and a huge server farm, there's little gain in not doing your own hosting.

Planning and Implementing Security

The importance of computer security simply cannot be overstated. Practically every day there are new stories of systems large and small that have been cracked by vandals and other criminals. Enterprises have been held hostage as criminals threatened to release the credit card numbers of thousands or hundreds of thousands of customers. Not long ago, the entire Internet was slowed drastically because hundreds of thousands of machines, many whose owners weren't even aware that they were running Web server software, were hijacked by a series of increasingly vicious and efficient "worm" programs and were put to work trying to corrupt other machines. The attack grew to the point where there were so many machines at work scanning the Internet for potential victims that much of the Internet's bandwidth – practically all of it in some places – was consumed. A system administrator who allows machines under his or her control to be vulnerable to this kind of attack when there is an alternative – which there is – ought to be fired.

Addressing external and internal threats

The threats from the outside world are very real and very frightening, and the extent to which data on your network are safe from prying eyes or random acts of destruction is entirely up to you. But your concerns cannot stop there. While cracker attacks get all the press, there are security concerns just as real, found within your own network. And this is true whether your network is a 500-node affair in an enterprise or a three-node home network.

Imagine the damage that a disgruntled employee could do — or, for that matter, a child disappointed at being grounded. Imagine what harm a dishonest employee could bring about, upon gaining access to company accounts or company secrets — or a troubled teenager who finds your credit card number (which you should *never* put on your computer. *Never.* Just don't, as much as some companies, interested in their bottom line and not your financial security, would have you do so).

Though less exciting before the fact, there is also the security issue of a user who simply makes a mistake that but for the presence of security safeguards could destroy crucial data or, conceivably, bring down the system.

Take advantage of all the multiple lines of defense available, no matter the size of your network (even if you have a single stand-alone system that is physically accessible to others or that is connected to the Internet). Otherwise, you would be right in assuming that anything on your network (or the machines on it) is accessible to anyone else who is a little bit determined to get at it. Part V of this book deals with security issues in great detail, but much of your security policy needs to be established now, before you've installed the network.

To learn more about security, see Chapters 24–27.

Formulating a security policy

What should your security policy consist of? Well, a number of things:

AN EFFECTIVE PASSWORD POLICY

Although the method brings grumbles from users, assigned, random passwords made up of a combination of numbers and capital and lowercase letters, all with no discernable meaning, are safest. (This procedure includes, most especially, the root account password.)

Who has access to what? Red Hat Linux allows you to create special groups and assign users to them. This means that some users might have access to devices such as CD burners and modems, while others may not. You may have sensitive situations in which you do not want users to send files or even carry them from the building on a floppy disk. You can provide increased security by use of groups. You needn't necessarily set this up first thing, but it's important to plan for and good to keep in mind.

GENERAL SECURITY RULES

A server that isn't running cannot be used to crack your system. If you're not using a server application, don't run it. Change all passwords periodically. Be prompt in removing network access of any employee who is discharged. Employ intrusion detection software, and check your logs regularly for anything unusual.

SECURITY UPDATES

Are you subscribed to the Red Hat Linux security mailing list? (Find it at http://www.redhat.com/mailing-lists/linux-security/index.html.) Have you established a procedure for making sure that every security update is downloaded and installed?

AN APPROPRIATE FIREWALL SYSTEM

If yours is a stand-alone box on a broadband connection, the bare minimum is an Internet firewall-gateway-router appliance plus use of iptables. If you are running a Web site, you'll probably want to set up a separate firewall machine. (The more experienced administrator could go so far as to create a custom firewall on a bootable CD, then boot the firewall machine from that CD. It is impossible to install a root kit on a CD, and the machine can have a hard drive for logging purposes.)

Security is a process — a matter of constantly outwitting people who wish your network ill. Red Hat Linux goes a long way toward helping you beat crackers to the punch, but it's up to you to make sure that your machine is not just buttoned up tightly today, but continues to be secure tomorrow and the day after.

Planning for Recovery from Disasters

Rare is the professional system administrator who hasn't been awake and at work for an entire weekend recovering from some tremendous mishap. And rare is the owner of a stand-alone machine who hasn't spent frantic hours trying with varying degrees of success to recover from a catastrophic failure of hardware, software, or execution.

System administrators who plan their network well may not be able to prevent disasters entirely, but they greatly reduce the likelihood of such events taking place, and make complete or near-complete recovery a quick and orderly process.

Planning for recovery ideally involves considering everything bad that can possibly happen and figuring out a way around it. But that which is ideal often does not coincide with that which is practical, especially when it involves spending money to guard against an infinitesimal likelihood. Fortunately, the things that save you from likely disasters save you from most unlikely ones, too.

Just as security planning requires attention to threats from outside and inside the network, there are two parts to disaster planning. The first is doing everything you can to prevent a catastrophe from taking place.

Only you, or other administrators at your organization, know how important your system is and how much money is budgeted to keep it running. But the chances are good that an uninterruptible power supply (UPS) that keeps the network up at least long enough to save and close open files and shuts down the system in an orderly fashion will fit within the available funds. (A good UPS system is especially useful if your enterprise has a generator backup that kicks on in the event of power failure, because generators do not always start instantly and when they do, the electricity provided is not always clean enough for computer use. A battery backup can protect you from both of these potential problems – and if your enterprise is important enough to have an emergency generator, it's probably important enough to keep the network running.)

Redundancy is also important. Make sure in your plans that no critical data are kept on just one machine. Then, in the event of a machine failure, a replacement machine with a copy of your critical data can be put online very quickly. This is some but not all of the theory of RAID (redundant array of independent disks) systems, in which multiple hard drives in the same machine contain the same data. RAID is good protection in the event that any one drive fails (the best RAIDs allow hot-swapping of drives, so a replacement can be added without bringing the system down), but it also allows for much faster data access, making it especially useful for file server machines. Don't be lulled into complacency by a RAID, though – there are computer failure modes that can render the entire system useless.

Renegade electricity is one of the worst enemies of system reliability. Little power strips with surge suppression are better than nothing, but more robust power conditioning is needed if really important equipment and data are to be protected. In fact, all lines from the outside world that attach to your computer or its peripherals should be protected, be they phone lines or a cable or DSL connection. Likewise, the peripherals themselves should be on protected circuits.

A regular – daily or better – backup scheme should be formulated, with one set of backups stored in a safe place off site as protection against loss of data in the event of fire, flood, tornado, or other physical disaster. One way of making this process relatively painless, albeit an expensive one, is to rent storage from a commercial concern whose business is just that: storing other people's data. The best of these are very responsive and very secure.

In keeping with Murphy's law, the worst failures and calamities take place at the worst possible times – just before the rollout of a new product, just as the monthly billing is scheduled to go out, in the middle of the worst blizzard in 10 years, or while most of the computer staff is on vacation or out sick. You'll need to establish an emergency response policy that takes these examples, and there are many others, into account. This may involve convincing your employer of the necessity of sufficient staff to guard against such horrors, or even the employment of an outside firm to augment your own staff in the event of an especially ill-timed disaster. If your company follows the latter route, it's well worth the investment of time and money to make sure that the outside firm's representatives tour and learn your network on a day when everything is cooking along happily.

Of course, some of this planning is far more elaborate than anything you're likely to undertake if you have only a small household network or a very small office; on the other hand, if you're in a very large enterprise, data security and system integrity involve issues and procedures far beyond the scope of this book. Everything mentioned in this section, however, can be scaled to fit any network.

Write It Down — Good Records Can Save Your Job

A very important part of network planning is to put it all down on paper and to save that paper. Working out your network's design is best done by actually diagramming the network, perhaps making multiple diagrams that explore different strategies. When you settle on a design, you should do a more formal diagram; it is a good idea to save the discarded designs as well, perhaps with a note on each explaining why it wasn't chosen. Formalizing the network design and saving the discarded ideas is useful for several reasons: it is good material to bolster your decisions in case you're second-guessed; it demonstrates that you considered all the possibilities; and the formal diagram is a valuable tool should someone need to administer the system in your absence.

A written security policy is essential in the enterprise, and not a bad idea even for a home network. But there is a second security file you should keep, a full security log. Such a record might begin by detailing what security measures you have designed into the system. It should include copies of any security notices you have received, as well as an initialed notation of when the recommended security patch was applied. If log files show an attempted crack of your network, hard copies of the relevant portions should be kept there, too.

When users or management complain about how you have the system so tight that it seems inconvenient even for them to log in, there's nothing like the ability to prove that the system is regularly under attack — and it will be, by port scanners and others — to demonstrate the wisdom of tight security. A very big company has made huge amounts of money by putting user convenience over security, and many companies have paid a high price for adopting it. Your Red Hat Linux system costs a very small amount of user inconvenience in exchange for greatly enhanced system security. It's useful to be able to prove that the threat is real.

A security log is also the place to keep copies of any security-related e-mail messages from within the company, from log listings of employees who have decided to "go exploring" (which is sometimes but not always a sign of bad intent) to exchanges with management over the implementation of new security features. This file is not something for general consumption, but it's very important. Keep a copy locked away at work, and it wouldn't hurt to keep a copy safely off site, too.

To learn more about writing a security policy, see Chapter 24.

While your security log should include details of actions you have taken to prevent disaster and actions you have recommended in that regard, your plan of action in the event of a catastrophe should also be committed to paper and should be well known and easily available. If you are the sole administrator, it is far better to work out your plan of action calmly and ahead of the time it's needed, which of course you will have done. But under the stress of an actual emergency, it is easy to forget important aspects. Having a specific plan on paper, right in front of you, is a big help and a great stress reliever. Your action plan should be sufficiently detailed so that if the disaster takes place while you are away, any competent system administrator can use it to bring the system back up. If you are part of a larger computer department, include the assignments of others in restoring the system. In either case, someone who is completely trusted and who is never on vacation at the same time you are should know root's password. Alternately, the password can be placed in a sealed envelope inside the company safe — the one time that it is allowable to put a password on paper.

 Keep a hard copy of your security log in a safe place!

We're all happy with the idea of the paperless office, but until computers become perfectly reliable, paper — as a roadmap indicating where you are and how you arrived there — will be necessary.

Summary

In this chapter you learned the importance of planning your network before you begin to construct it, discovered some of the options available to you, and found out some of the reasons why you might choose one over another. You learned that network security is a never-ending task made easier by careful planning, and that threats can come both from outside the network and from among its users. Working to prevent catastrophic failures and having a plan to recover from them is something you've learned to do. And you now know the importance of putting it all on paper as you go along.

Chapter 3

Installing Red Hat Linux

IN THIS CHAPTER

◆ Exploring your PC's components

◆ Checking for supported hardware

◆ Starting the installation

◆ Configuring Red Hat Linux installation

◆ Selecting packages to install

◆ Using KickStart

THIS CHAPTER explains the steps necessary to install Red Hat Linux on a single system, and how to use Red Hat's KickStart installation program. The KickStart installation program can be used to automate the installation process for server and client installations on one or more computers. You begin by making a list of your PC's hardware. You use this hardware inventory later when you begin the installation.

 If you purchase an official Red Hat Linux boxed set, you are eligible for installation support from Red Hat. Also, an online installation manual is available on the Red Hat Web site at www.redhat.com/support/manual.

Exploring Your PC's Components

Before installing Red Hat Linux, you should compile a list of the hardware components in your computer. Linux supports different types of hardware through software components called *device drivers*, similar to other operating systems. A driver is required for each type of peripheral device, and depending on the age of your hardware, a driver may not be available. If your hardware is current, meaning less than two years old, the drivers you need are probably available and included with the distribution. If you need a driver that is not included with the distribution, searching the Internet usually provides you with a solution.

You can install and run Red Hat Linux even if no Linux drivers are available for certain devices. Of course these devices do not function, but this may not be a problem for you depending on the device. To be able to install Red Hat Linux, you must have a compatible processor, bus type, floppy disk, hard disk, video card, monitor, keyboard, mouse, and CD-ROM drive. If you are planning to use a graphical user interface (GUI) such as GNOME or KDE, you must ensure that XFree86 (the X Window System for Linux) supports the mouse, the video card, and the monitor. Nearly all devices made within the last two years are supported.

The following sections briefly describe the PC hardware supported by Red Hat Linux. Your hardware list should contain information about the hardware described here before you begin to install Red Hat Linux on your PC.

Processor

The *central processing unit (CPU)* or just *the processor* is an integrated circuit chip that performs nearly all the control and processing functions in the PC. Red Hat Linux runs on an Intel 80386 processor or newer, as well as compatibles made by AMD or Cyrix. However, you probably don't want to use any processor older than a Pentium class processor. Red Hat Linux also supports motherboards with multiple processors with the *symmetric multiprocessing (SMP)* Linux kernel.

Bus

The *bus* provides the electrical connection between the processor and its peripherals. Several types of PC buses exist. The most recent is the *Peripheral Component Interconnect (PCI)* bus, and it is found on all current production motherboards. Another is the *Industry Standard Architecture (ISA)* bus, formerly called the AT bus because IBM introduced it in the IBM PC-AT computer in 1984. Other buses include Extended Industry Standard Architecture (EISA); VESA local (VL-bus); and Micro Channel Architecture (MCA). Red Hat Linux supports all of these buses.

Memory

Referred to as *random-access memory* or *RAM*, memory is not a consideration in determining compatibility. For good performance though, you need at least 32MB of RAM for a workstation, and even more for a server. If you are planning to run the X Window System to be able to use a GUI on the PC, you need even more memory because the X Window System manages the graphical interface through an X server, which is a large program that needs a lot of memory to run efficiently.

If you are buying a new PC, it probably comes with 64MB or more RAM. If you can afford it, buy as much RAM as you can, because the more RAM a system has, the more efficiently it runs multiple programs (because the programs can all fit in memory). Red Hat Linux can use a part of the hard disk as virtual memory. Such disk-based memory, called *swap space*, is much slower than physical memory.

Video card and monitor

If you are not planning to use the X Window System, any video card works. Red Hat Linux supports all video cards in text mode. If you are planning to use the X Window System, be sure to find a video card that is supported by *XFree86,* which is the Red Hat Linux version of the X Window System. You can save yourself a lot of aggravation if your video card is supported by XFree86.

Your choice of monitors is dependent on your use of the X Window System. For text mode displays, typically used on servers, any monitor will do. If you are setting up a workstation, or using the X Window System on your server, choose a monitor that supports the display resolution you use. Resolution is expressed in terms of the number of picture elements, or *pixels*, horizontally and vertically (such as 1024×768).

XFree86's support for a video card depends on the *video chipset* — the integrated circuit that controls the monitor and causes the monitor to display output. You can find out the name of the video chipset used in a video card from the card's documentation.

Your video card's name may not be in the list at the Red Hat site. The important thing to note is the name of the video chipset. Many popular video cards made by different manufacturers use the same video chipsets. Look for the name of the video chipsets listed at the Red Hat site. In nearly all cases, the Red Hat Linux installation program automatically detects the video chipset as it sets up the X Window System.

Hard drive

Red Hat Linux supports any hard drive that your PC's *basic input/output System (BIOS)* supports as long as the system BIOS supports the hard drive without any additional drivers. To be able to boot Red Hat Linux from a large hard drive (any drive with more than 1,024 cylinders), the Linux Loader (LILO), the Linux kernel, and the LILO configuration files must be located in the first 1,024 cylinders of the drive. This is because the Linux Loader uses BIOS to load the kernel and the BIOS cannot access cylinders beyond the first 1,024.

For hard drives connected to your PC through a *SCSI (Small Computer System Interface)* controller card, Red Hat Linux must have a driver that enables the SCSI controller to access and use the hard drive.

As for the size (storage capacity) of the drive, most new systems seem to have 8 to 10GB of capacity. You should buy the highest capacity drive that you can afford.

Floppy disk drive

Linux drivers use the PC BIOS to access the floppy disk drive, so any floppy disk drive is compatible with Red Hat Linux. The Red Hat Linux installation program can be started from the CD-ROM if your PC has one and is able to boot from it. If not, you have to boot Red Hat Linux from a floppy disk drive during the installation, so you need a high-density 3.5-inch (1.44MB capacity) floppy disk drive. You can also avoid booting from a floppy if you can boot your PC under MS-DOS (not an MS-DOS window under Windows 95/98/2000), and you can access the CD-ROM from the DOS command prompt.

Keyboard and mouse

Red Hat Linux supports any keyboard that already works with your PC. The mouse, however, needs explicit support in Red Hat Linux. You need a mouse if you want to configure and run XFree86, the X Window System for Linux. Red Hat Linux supports most popular mice, including the commonly found PS/2-style mouse. Red Hat Linux also supports touch pad devices, such as ALPS GlidePoint, as long as they are compatible with one of the supported mice.

SCSI controller

The Small Computer System Interface, commonly called *SCSI* (and pronounced *scuzzy*), is a standard way of connecting many types of peripheral devices to a computer. SCSI is used in many kinds of computers, from high-end UNIX workstations to PCs. Typically, you connect hard drives and CD-ROM drives through a *SCSI controller*. To use a SCSI device on your PC, you need a SCSI controller card that plugs into one of the connector slots on your PC's bus.

A single SCSI controller supports device addresses 0 through 7, with 7 usually assigned to the controller itself. This means that you can connect up to seven SCSI devices to your PC. (With SCSI 2 you can connect up to 14 devices.) If you want to access and use a SCSI device under Linux, you have to make sure that Red Hat Linux supports your SCSI controller card.

CD-ROM drive

CD-ROM (compact disc read-only memory) drives are popular because each CD-ROM can hold up to 650MB of data, a relatively large amount of storage compared with a floppy disk. CD-ROMs are reliable and inexpensive to manufacture. Vendors can use a CD-ROM to distribute a large amount of information at a reasonable cost. This book provides Red Hat Linux on CD-ROMs, so you need a CD-ROM drive to install the software.

Sound card

If you are configuring a server, you probably aren't too interested in playing sounds. But, with Red Hat Linux, you can play sound on a sound card to enjoy multimedia programs and games. If you have a sound card, you can also play audio CDs. Nearly all sound cards available today are supported.

Network card

A network interface card (NIC) is necessary if you connect your Red Hat Linux PC to a local area network (LAN), which is usually an Ethernet network. If you are configuring a server, you certainly want to configure a network card. Red Hat Linux supports a variety of Ethernet network cards. ARCnet and IBM's token ring network are also supported. Check the hardware list on the Red Hat site to see if your NIC is supported. Nearly all NICs currently in use are supported.

For any Red Hat Linux PC connected to a network, you need the following information:

- The PC's host name

- Domain name of the network

- Internet Protocol (IP) address of the PC (or, if the IP address is provided by a DHCP server, the server's address)

- Gateway address

- IP address of name servers

Checking for Supported Hardware

To check if Red Hat Linux supports the hardware in your PC, follow these steps:

1. Make a list of the make, model, and other technical details of all hardware installed in your PC. Most of this information is in the manuals that came with your hardware. If you don't have the manuals, and you already have an operating system on the PC, you may be able to obtain this information from that operating system.

2. Next, go to the Red Hat Web site at http://www.redhat.com/hardware. Compare your hardware list to the list of hardware that the latest version of Red Hat Linux supports. If the components listed earlier are supported, you can prepare to install Red Hat.

Creating the Red Hat Boot Disk

To boot Red Hat Linux for the first time and start the Red Hat Linux installation program, you need a Red Hat boot disk. For this step, you should turn on your PC without any disk in the A: drive and then run Windows as usual.

You do not need a boot disk if you can start your PC under MS-DOS — not an MS-DOS window in Windows 95 — and access the CD-ROM from the DOS command prompt. If you run Windows 95/98, restart the PC in MS-DOS mode. However, you may not be able to access the CD-ROM in MS-DOS mode because the startup files — AUTOEXEC.BAT and CONFIG.SYS — may not be configured correctly. To access the CD-ROM from DOS, you typically must add a CD-ROM driver in `CONFIG.SYS` and add a line in `AUTOEXEC.BAT` that runs the MSCDEX program. Try restarting your PC in MS-DOS mode and see if the CD-ROM can be accessed.

The Red Hat boot disk starts your PC and the Red Hat Linux installation program. After you install Red Hat Linux, you no longer need the Red Hat boot disk (except when you want to reinstall Red Hat Linux from the CD-ROMs).

The Red Hat boot disk contains an initial version of the Red Hat Linux installation program that you use to start Red Hat Linux, prepare the hard disk, and load the rest of the installation program. Creating the Red Hat boot disk involves using a utility program called `RAWRITE.EXE` to copy a special file called the Red Hat Linux *boot image* to a disk.

To create the Red Hat boot disk under Windows, follow these steps:

1. Open an MS-DOS window (select Start → Programs → MS-DOS Prompt).

2. In the MS-DOS window, enter the following commands at the MS-DOS prompt. (Author's comments are in parentheses and your input is in boldface):

   ```
   d:    (use the drive letter for the CD-ROM drive)
   cd \dosutils
   rawrite
   Enter disk image source file name: \images\boot.img
   Enter target diskette drive: a
   Please insert a formatted diskette into drive A: and press -
   ENTER- :
   ```

3. As instructed, you should put a formatted disk into your PC's A: drive and then press Enter. `RAWRITE.EXE` copies the boot-image file to the disk.

When the DOS prompt returns, remove the Red Hat boot disk from the A: drive and label it as a Red Hat boot disk.

Starting the Red Hat Linux Installation

To start the Red Hat Linux installation, put the Red Hat boot disk in your PC's A: drive and restart your PC. The PC loads Red Hat Linux from the boot disk and begins running the Red Hat installation program. The Red Hat installation program controls the installation of the operating system.

Be sure to place the first installation CD-ROM in the CD-ROM drive after you start the PC. The installation program looks for the Red Hat Linux CD-ROMs to start the installation in graphical mode. If the installation program can't find the CD, the installation program starts in text mode and prompts for the CD-ROM.

A few moments after you start the boot process, an initial screen appears. The screen displays a welcome message and ends with a `boot:` prompt. The welcome message tells you that more information is available by pressing one of the function keys F1 through F5.

If you want to read the help screens, press the function key corresponding to the help you want. If you don't press any keys after a minute, the boot process proceeds with the loading of the Linux kernel into the PC's memory. To start booting Red Hat Linux immediately, press Enter. After the Linux kernel loads, it automatically starts the Red Hat Linux installation program. This, in turn, starts the X Window System, which provides a graphical user interface for the installation.

You should have all the configuration information explained earlier in this chapter before you begin, and if the installation program detects your hardware, installing Red Hat Linux from the CD-ROM on a fast (200 MHz or better) Pentium PC should take 30 to 40 minutes.

During the installation, the Red Hat installation program tries to determine the hardware in your PC and alters the installation steps as required. For example, if the installation program detects a network card, the program displays the appropriate network configuration screens. If a network card is not detected, the network configuration screens are not displayed. So, depending on your specific hardware, the screens you see during installation may differ from those shown in this section.

If you run into any problems during the installation, refer to Chapter 28 to learn how to troubleshoot common installation problems.

You go through the following steps before moving on to disk setup and installation:

1. The installation program starts the X Window System and displays a list of languages in a graphical installation screen. Use your mouse to select the language you want and then click the Next button to proceed to the next step.

In the graphical installation, each screen has online help available on the left side. You can read the help message to learn more about what you are supposed to select in a specific screen.

2. The installation program displays a list of keyboard types, as shown in Figure 3-1. Select a keyboard model that closely matches your PC's keyboard. If you don't see your keyboard model listed, select one of the generic models: Generic 101-key PC or Generic 104-key PC. (Newer keyboards with the Windows keys match this model.) Next, select a keyboard layout that depends on your language's character set (for example, English in the United States). Finally, select the Enable dead keys option if the language you select has special characters that must be composed by pressing multiple keys in sequence. For the English language, you can safely select the Disable dead keys option.

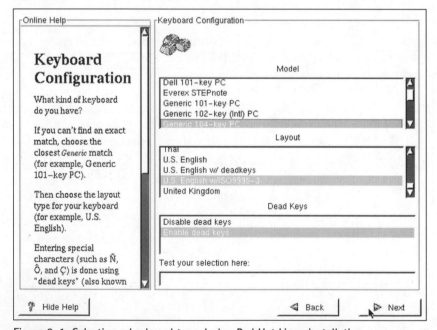

Figure 3-1: Selecting a keyboard type during Red Hat Linux installation

3. The installation program displays a screen (see Figure 3-2) from which you can configure the mouse in your system. The various mouse types are listed in a tree structure organized alphabetically by manufacturer. You need to know your mouse type and whether it is connected to the PC's serial port or the PS/2 port. If your mouse type appears in the list, select

it. Otherwise, select a generic mouse type. Most new PCs have a PS/2 mouse. Finally, for a two-button mouse, you should select the Emulate 3 Buttons option. Because many X applications assume that you use a three-button mouse, you should select this option. On a typical two-button mouse, you can simulate a middle-button click by pressing both buttons simultaneously. On a Microsoft Intellimouse, the wheel acts as the middle button.

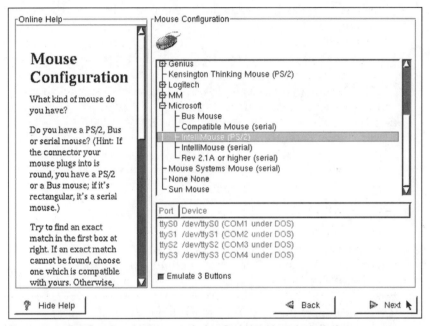

Figure 3-2: Configuring your mouse during Red Hat Linux installation

If you select a mouse with a serial interface, you are asked to specify the serial port where the mouse is connected. For COM1, specify /dev/ttyS0 as the device; for COM2, the device name is /dev/ttyS1.

4. The installation program displays a welcome message that provides some helpful information, including a suggestion that you access the online manuals at http://www.redhat.com. Click the Next button to proceed to the next step.

5. The installation program displays a screen asking if you want to install a new system or upgrade an older Red Hat installation.

For a new installation, the installation program requires you to select the installation type — *Workstation*, *Server*, *Laptop*, or *Custom*. The Workstation, Server, and Laptop installations simplify the installation process by partitioning the disk in a predefined manner. A Workstation-class installation deletes all currently existing Linux-related partitions. A Server-class installation deletes all existing disk partitions, including any existing Windows partitions. A Laptop-class installation includes additional packages for PCMCIA support. For maximum flexibility (so you can specify how the disk is used), select the Custom installation.

The next major phase of installation involves partitioning the hard disk for use in Red Hat Linux.

Partitioning the Hard Disk for Red Hat Linux

Red Hat Linux requires you to partition and prepare a hard disk before you can install Red Hat Linux. For a new PC, you usually do not perform this step, because the vendor normally takes care of preparing the hard disk and installing Windows and all other applications on the hard disk. Because you are installing Red Hat Linux from scratch, however, you have to perform this crucial step yourself. As you see in the following sections, this task is just a matter of following instructions.

The Red Hat Linux installation program offers you several choices for partitioning your hard drive. You can choose to have the installation program automatically partition your disk, you can choose to use Disk Druid, or you can use fdisk. For this installation, you will choose Disk Druid, a utility program that enables you to partition the disk and, at the same time, specify which parts of the Linux file system you want to load on which partition.

Before you begin to use Disk Druid to partition your disk, you need to know how to refer to the disk drives and partitions in Linux. Also, you should understand the terms *mount points* and *swap partition*. In the next three sections, you learn these terms and concepts and then proceed to use Disk Druid.

Naming disks and devices

If you are experienced with Unix or Linux, this section and the two following are quite basic to you. If you are already familiar with Unix and Linux file systems and naming conventions, skip to the section titled "Preparing Disk Partitions for Red Hat Linux." The first step is to understand how Red Hat Linux refers to the various disks. Linux treats all devices as files and has actual files that represent each device. In Red Hat Linux, these *device files* are located in the /dev directory. If you are new to Unix, you may not yet know about Unix filenames. But you learn more as you continue to use Red Hat Linux. If you know how MS-DOS filenames work, you find that Linux filenames are similar. However, they have two exceptions: they do not use drive letters (such as A: and C:), and they substitute the slash (/) for the MS-DOS backslash (\) as the separator between directory names.

Because Linux treats a device as a file in the /dev directory, the hard disk names start with /dev. Table 3-1 lists the hard disk and floppy drive names that you may have to use.

TABLE 3-1 HARD DISK AND FLOPPY DRIVE NAMES

Name	Description
/dev/hda	First Integrated Drive Electronics (IDE) hard drive (the C: drive in DOS and Windows) connected to the first IDE controller as the master drive.
/dev/hdb	Second (IDE) hard drive connected to the first IDE controller as the slave drive.
/dev/hdc	First (IDE) hard drive connected to the second IDE controller as the master drive.
/dev/hdd	Second (IDE) hard drive connected to the second IDE controller as the slave drive.
/dev/sda	First Small Computer System Interface (SCSI) drive.
/dev/sdb	Second SCSI drive.
/dev/fd0	First floppy drive (the A: drive in DOS).
/dev/fd1	Second floppy drive (the B: drive in DOS).

TIP When Disk Druid displays the list of partitions, the partition names take the form hda1, hda2, and so on. Linux constructs each partition name by appending the partition number (1 through 4 for the four primary partitions on a hard disk) to the disk's name. Therefore, if your PC's single IDE hard drive has two partitions, notice that the installation program uses hda1 and hda2 as the names of these partitions.

Mounting a file system on a device

In Red Hat Linux, you use a physical disk partition by associating it with a specific part of the file system. This arrangement is a hierarchical directory — a *directory tree.* If you have more than one disk partition (you may have a second disk with a Linux partition), you can use all of them in Red Hat Linux under a single directory tree. All you have to do is decide which part of the Linux directory tree should be located on each partition — a process known in Linux as *mounting a file system on a device.* (The disk partition is a device.)

The term *mount point* refers to the directory you associate with a disk partition or any other device.

Suppose that you have two disks on your PC, and you have created Linux partitions on both disks. Figure 3-3 illustrates how you can mount different parts of the Linux directory tree (the *file system*) on these two partitions.

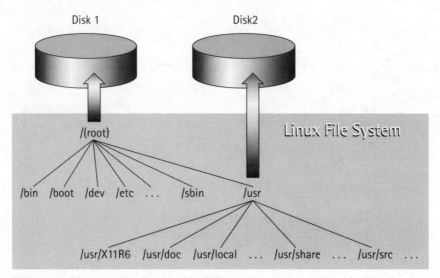

Figure 3-3: Mounting the Red Hat Linux file system on two disk partitions

Understanding the swap partition

Most advanced operating systems support the concept of *virtual memory*, in which part of your system's hard disk functions as an extension of the physical memory (RAM). When the operating system runs out of physical memory, it can move (or swap out) the contents of currently unneeded parts of RAM to make room for a program that needs more memory. When the operating system needs to access anything in the swapped-out data, it has to find something else to swap out and then it swaps in the required data from disk. This process of swapping data back and forth between the RAM and the disk is also known as *paging*.

Because the disk is much slower than RAM, the system's performance is slower when the operating system has to perform a lot of paging. However, virtual memory enables you to run programs that you otherwise can't run.

Red Hat Linux supports virtual memory and can make use of a swap partition. When you create the Linux partitions, you should also create a swap partition. With the Disk Druid utility program, described in the next section, creating a swap partition is easy. Simply mark a partition type as a swap device and Disk Druid performs the necessary tasks.

Preparing disk partitions for Red Hat Linux

After you select Custom installation, a screen prompts you for the method you want to use to partition the disk — the choices are the Linux `fdisk` program or Disk Druid. You should select Disk Druid and click the Next button. You should then see the Disk Druid screen (as shown in Figure 3-4).

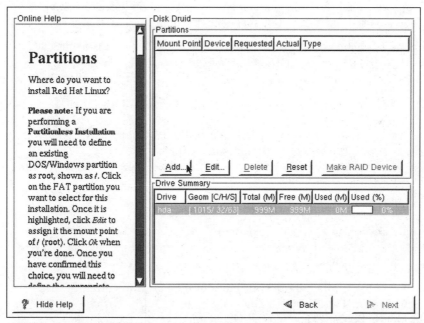

Figure 3-4: The Disk Druid screen from the Red Hat Linux installation program

Before beginning to partition the drive, consider exactly how you want to create the partitions. Most people typically create one partition on the drive to be used as the root partition. This works well in most cases, but it can cause some problems. If the root directory should become full, the system could crash. Many times the partition fills because of system logging, e-mail, and print queue files. These files are all written to the /var directory by default, so it would be a good idea to create a separate partition for /var to prevent the root directory from filling up with system logs, e-mail, and print files. You might also want to create a separate partition for your user's directories if you have a large number of users.

Disk Druid gathers information about the hard drives on your system and displays a list of disk drives in the lower part of the screen and the current partition information for one of the drives in the Partitions list in the upper part. For each partition, Disk Druid shows five fields:

- ◆ **Mount Point** indicates the directory where the partition will be mounted. For example, if you have only one partition for the entire Linux file system, the mount point is the root directory (/). For the swap partition, this field shows <Swap>. If this field appears as <not set>, you have to specify a mount point. To do so, select the partition and click the Edit button.

- ◆ **Device** refers to the partition's device name. For example, hda1 is the first partition on the first IDE drive.

- ◆ **Requested** field shows how much space the partition has. For example, if the partition has 256MB of space, this field appears as 256M.

- ◆ **Actual** field shows the amount of disk space the partition is using. Usually, the Requested and Actual fields are the same, but they may differ for partitions that can grow in size.

- ◆ **Type** field shows the partition's type, such as Linux Native or DOS.

If there are no partitions defined, the table in the Partitions list is empty. You have to add new partitions by clicking the Add button.

You perform specific disk setup tasks in Disk Druid through the five buttons that run across the middle of the screen. Specifically, the buttons perform the following actions:

- ◆ **Add** enables you to create a new partition, assuming there is enough free disk space available. When you click this button, another dialog box appears in which you can fill in information necessary to create a partition.

- ◆ **Edit** enables you to alter the attributes of the partition currently highlighted in the Partitions list. You make changes to the current attribute in another dialog box that appears when you click the Edit button.

- ◆ **Delete** removes the partition currently highlighted in the Partitions list.

- ◆ **Reset** causes Disk Druid to ignore any changes that you may have made.

- ◆ **Make RAID Device** sets up a *RAID (Redundant Array of Independent Disks)* device — a technique that combines multiple disks to improve reliability and data transfer rates. There are several types of RAID configurations. This button is active only if your system has the hardware necessary to support a RAID device.

Exactly what you do in Disk Druid depends on the hard drives in your PC and the partitions they already have. For this discussion, I assume that you are using the entire hard drive space for the Red Hat installation.

SETTING UP THE PARTITIONS

To prepare a new hard drive to install Red Hat Linux, you have to perform the following steps in Disk Druid:

1. Create a new partition for the Linux file system. To do this, press the Add button on the Disk Druid screen. You should see a dialog box (refer to Figure 3-5) where you can fill in / as the mount point and enter the size in megabytes. To compute the size, simply subtract the size of the swap space (32MB or the amount of RAM in your PC, whichever is more) from the original size of the partition. Select the OK button to complete this step and return to the Disk Druid screen. If you are planning to create a separate partition for /var or /home, be sure to subtract these amounts from the root partition.

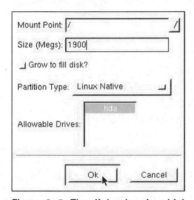

Figure 3-5: The dialog box in which you fill in the attributes of a new partition

2. Create another new partition and set it as a Linux swap space. To do this, click the Add button in the Disk Druid screen (see Figure 3-4). In the dialog box (see Figure 3-5), enter the size of the partition. Click the list of partition types and use the mouse to select Linux Swap as the type. When you do so, the text <Swap Partition> appears in the Mount Point field. Next, click the OK button to define the new partition and return to the Disk Druid screen.

3. After making the changes, click the Next button in the Disk Druid screen to proceed to the next installation step.

SELECTING PARTITIONS TO FORMAT

After you finish specifying the partitions in Disk Druid, the Red Hat installation program displays a screen (see Figure 3-6) listing the partitions that you may have to format for use in Linux. If you have only one disk partition for Red Hat Linux, the list shows only one partition.

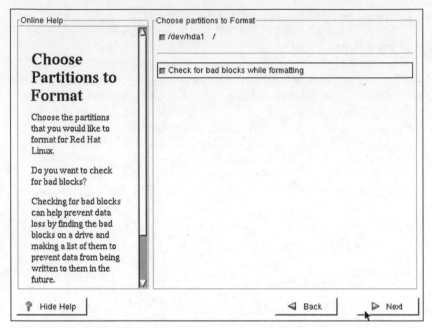

Figure 3-6: Selecting partitions to format for use in Red Hat Linux

To format the partition, click the button next to the partition's name. You should also click the button next to the item marked Check for bad blocks while formatting so that the formatting process marks any areas of the disk that may be physically defective.

If you have multiple disk partitions mounted on different directories of the Linux file system and you are upgrading an existing installation, you do not have to format any partitions in which you want to preserve existing data. For example, if you have all user directories on a separate disk partition mounted on the /home directory, you do not have to format that partition.

You have now completed the disk preparation phase of the installation. The installation program performs the actual formatting of the partitions after it asks for some more configuration information, including the packages you want to install.

Configuring Red Hat Linux Installation

After you prepare the disk partitions with Disk Druid and specify which partitions to format, the installation program moves on to some configuration steps. The typical configuration steps are:

◆ Install LILO/GRUB

◆ Configure the network

◆ Set the time zone

◆ Set the root password and add user accounts

◆ Configure password authentication

The following sections guide you through each of these configuration steps.

Installing the Boot Loader

The Red Hat installation program displays the Boot Loader Configuration screen (see Figure 3-7), which asks you where you want to install the boot loader. A boot loader is a program that resides on your disk and starts Red Hat Linux from the hard disk. Red Hat version 7.2 provides two choices of boot loaders, LILO and GRUB. Previous versions of Red Hat offered only LILO. LILO stands for Linux Loader, and GRUB stands for Grand Unified Bootloader.

The first button on this screen asks if you want to create a boot disk. This is different from the installation boot disk; you can use this disk to boot your Linux system if the Linux kernel on the hard disk is damaged or if the boot loader does not work. The Create boot disk button is selected by default and you should leave it that way. Later on, the installation program prompts you to insert a blank floppy into your PC's A: drive.

The GRUB boot loader is selected as the default choice on this screen. If you desire, you can choose to install LILO instead of GRUB by selecting the appropriate radio button, or you can choose not to install any boot loader. If you choose not to install one of the boot loaders, you should definitely create a boot disk. Otherwise, you can't start Red Hat Linux when you reboot the PC.

The next part of the Boot Loader Configuration screen gives you the option of installing the boot loader in one of two locations:

◆ Master Boot Record (MBR), which is located in the first sector of your PC's hard disk

◆ First sector of the partition where you loaded Red Hat Linux

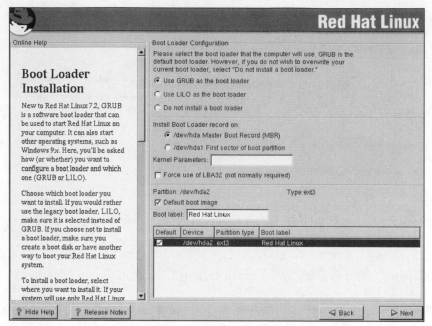

Figure 3-7: The Boot Loader Configuration screen enables you to specify where to install the boot loader and whether to create a boot disk.

You should install the boot loader in the MBR, unless you are using another operating system loader such as System Commander or OS/2 Boot Manager. The screen includes a text field labeled Kernel parameters that enables you to enter any special options that Red Hat Linux may need as it boots. Your need for special options depends on what hardware you have.

The remainder of the Boot Loader Configuration screen gives you the option to select the disk partition from which you want to boot the PC. A table then lists the Linux partition and any other partitions that may contain another operating system. If your system has a Linux partition and a DOS partition (that actually has Windows 95/98 installed on it), the table shows both of these entries. Each entry in that table is an operating system that the boot loader can boot.

After you install the boot loader, whenever your PC boots from the hard disk, the boot loader runs and displays a screen showing the operating systems that you can boot. You may move the highlight bar to the name of an operating system to boot. (The Boot label column in the table in the bottom right section of Figure 3-7 shows the names you may enter at the boot loader prompt). If the list shows two entries labeled linux and dos, choose linux to boot Linux and dos to boot from the DOS partition (which should start Windows 95/98, if that's what you have installed on that partition).

When rebooting the PC, if you enter nothing at the boot loader screen, the boot loader waits for a few seconds and boots the default operating system. The default operating system is the one with a check mark in the Default column in Figure 3-7. In this case, Linux is the default operating system.

All of the instructions in this section are for your information if you choose to change any of the default settings. You can essentially accept the default selections on this screen and click the Next button to proceed to the next configuration step.

Configuring the network

If the Linux kernel detects a network card, the Red Hat installation program displays the Network Configuration screen (see Figure 3-8), which enables you to configure the local area network (LAN) parameters for your Linux system.

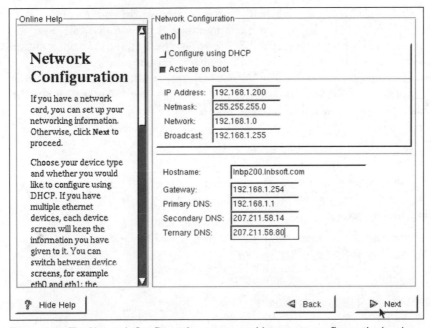

Figure 3–8: The Network Configuration screen enables you to configure the local area network.

This step is not for configuring the dial-up networking. You need to perform this step if your Linux system is connected to a TCP/IP LAN through an Ethernet card.

If the Red Hat installation program does not detect your network card and you have a network card installed on the PC, you should restart the installation and type expert at the boot prompt. Then you can manually select your network card. See Chapter 28 for more information on troubleshooting.

The Network Configuration screen (Figure 3-8) displays tabbed dialog boxes — one for each network card installed on your system and detected by the Linux kernel. These tabs are labeled eth0, eth1, and so on. If your system has only one Ethernet card, you see only the eth0 tab. Figure 3-8 has only one tab. Each tab offers two choices for specifying the IP (Internet Protocol) address for the network interface:

◆ Use DHCP — Click the button labeled Configure using DHCP if your PC obtains its IP address and other network information from a *Dynamic Host Configuration Protocol (DHCP)* server.

◆ Provide static IP address — Fill in the necessary network-related information manually.

You should select DHCP only if a DHCP server is running on your local area network. If you choose DHCP, your network configuration is set automatically and you can skip the rest of this section. You should leave the Activate on boot button selected so that the network is configured whenever you boot the system.

To provide static IP address and other network information, you have to enter certain parameters for TCP/IP configuration in the text input fields that appear on the Network Configuration screen (refer to Figure 3-8).

The Network Configuration screen asks for the following key parameters:

◆ IP address of the Ethernet interface

◆ The host name for your Linux system. (For a private LAN, you can assign your own host name without worrying about conflicting with any other existing systems on the Internet.)

◆ IP address of the *gateway* (the system through which you might go to any outside network)

◆ IP address of the primary name server

◆ IP address of a secondary name server

◆ IP address of a ternary name server

If you have a private LAN (one that is not directly connected to the Internet), you may use an IP address from a range designated for private use. Common IP addresses for private LANs are the addresses in the range 192.168.1.1 through 192.168.1.254. Chapter 6 provides more in-depth information about TCP/IP networking and IP addresses.

After you enter the requested parameters, click the Next button to proceed to the next configuration step.

Setting the time zone

After completing the network configuration, you have to select the *time zone* — the difference between the local time and the current time in Greenwich, England, which is the standard reference time. The time zone is also known as *Greenwich Mean Time (GMT)* or UTC, which was selected by the International Telecommunication Union (ITU) as a standard abbreviation for *Coordinated Universal Time*. The installation program shows you the Time Zone Selection screen (see Figure 3-9) from which you can select the time zone, either in terms of a geographic location or as an offset from the UTC. Figure 3-9 shows the selection of a time zone based on UTC offset.

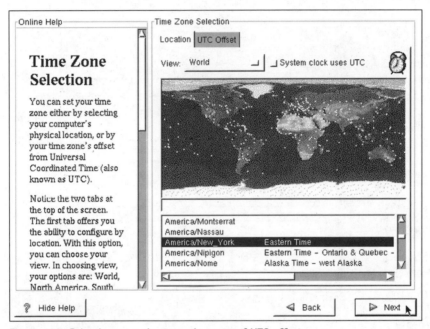

Figure 3-9: Selecting your time zone in terms of UTC offset

Notice that there are two tabs on the Time Zone Selection screen — Location and UTC Offset. Initially, the screen shows the Location tab. This tab enables you to pick a time zone by simply clicking your geographic location. As you move the mouse over the map, the currently selected location's name appears in a text field. If you want, you can also select your location from a long list of countries and regions. If you live on the East Coast of the United States, for example, select USA/Eastern. Of course, the easiest way is to simply click Eastern USA on the map.

If the world view of the map is too large for you to select your location, click the View button on top of the map. A drop-down list of views appears with several choices. You can then click the view appropriate for your location.

The other way to set a time zone is to specify the time difference between your local time and UTC. Click the UTC Offset tab to select the time zone this way.

For example, if you live in the eastern part of the United States, select UTC-05:00 as the time zone. The –05:00 indicates that the eastern part of the U.S. is five hours behind the UTC time. This tab also enables you to activate Daylight Saving Time, which applies to the USA only. After you select your time zone, click the Next button to proceed to the next configuration step.

Setting the root password and add user accounts

After completing time zone selection, the installation program displays the Account Configuration screen (see Figure 3-10) in which you set the root password and add one or more user accounts.

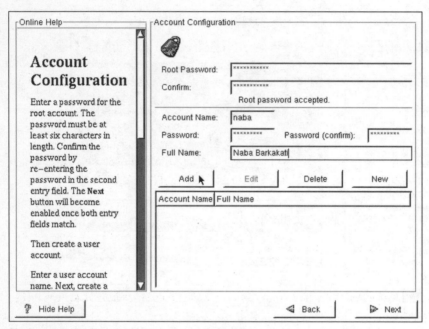

Figure 3-10: Setting the root password and adding other user accounts

The root user is the *superuser* in Linux. Because the superuser can do anything in the system, you should assign a password that you can remember — but that others cannot guess easily. Typically, make the password at least eight characters long, include a mix of letters and numbers, and (for good measure) throw in some special characters such as + or *. Remember the password is also case sensitive.

Type the password on the first line and then reenter the password on the next line. Each character in the password appears as an asterisk (*) on the screen for security reasons. Both entries must match before the installation program accepts the password. The installation program displays a message when it accepts the root password. After you type the root password twice, you might also want to add one or more user accounts.

To add a user account, fill in the Account Name, Password, and Full Name fields and then click the Add button. The new account information then appears in the table underneath the Add button. You do not have to add all the user accounts at this time. Later on, you can use the Linuxconf tool (which comes with Red Hat) to add more user accounts.

You must enter the root password before you can proceed with the rest of the installation. After you do so and add any other user accounts you need, click the Next button to continue with the installation.

Configuring password authentication

The installation program displays the Authentication Configuration screen, shown in Figure 3-11, from which you can configure the password authentication options. You can enable or disable several options. Of these, the first two are already selected:

◆ **Enable MD5 passwords:** Select this option to enable users to use long passwords of up to 256 characters instead of the standard password that can be, at most, eight characters long. Note that *MD5* refers to *Message Digest 5*, an algorithm developed by RSA, Inc. to compute the digest of the entire data of a message. Essentially, MD5 reduces a message to a digest consisting of four 32-bit numbers.

◆ **Enable shadow passwords:** This option causes the /etc/psswd file to be replaced by /etc/shadow, which only the superuser (root) can read. This option provides an added level of security.

You should use these default settings for increased system security.

Beneath the password options, four tabs on this screen allow the user to configure options for NIS, LDAP, Kerberos 5, and SMB.

The NIS tab screen is already displayed and offers the option of enabling NIS. If you choose to enable NIS, you can then choose the name of the domain to which your system is a member. You can also choose to send a broadcast message to search for an NIS server on your network. If you choose not to send a broadcast message, you can enter the name of a specific server.

Chapter 8 explains the installation and configuration of the Network Information Service (NIS). Chapters 24 and 26 provide information about network security and its implementation.

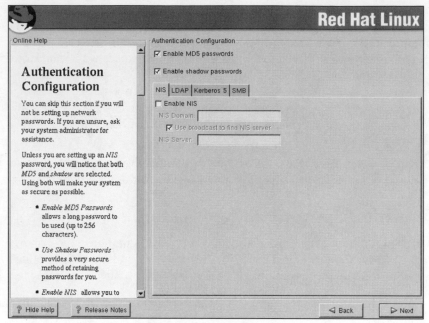

Figure 3-11: The Authentication Configuration screen

Use the LDAP tab to set options for Lightweight Directory Access Protocol (LDAP). With LDAP, you can organize information about users on your system into an LDAP directory that can be used for system authentication. From the LDAP screen you can enable LDAP and set the following options:

◆ LDAP Server – Specify the IP address of an LDAP server on your network

◆ LDAP Base DN – Search for user information by using its Distinguished Name (DN)

◆ Use TLS lookups – Send encrypted user names and passwords to an LDAP server before authentication

The Kerberos 5 tab opens the Kerberos 5 configuration screen. You can use Kerberos 5 to provide secure network authentication services for your network. You can enable Kerberos 5 from this screen and set the following options:

◆ Realm – Enables you to choose to access a network running Kerberos 5

◆ KDC – With this option, you can access a Key Distribution Center (KDC) to obtain a Kerberos ticket

◆ Admin server – Using this option, you can access a server running the Kerberos 5 admin program

The final tab on the Authentication Configuration screen is SMB. Server Message Block (SMB) is the protocol used on Microsoft networks for file sharing. Clicking on the SMB tab opens the SMB configuration screen, where you can enable SMB and choose the following options:

◆ SMB server — Shows the name of the SMB server you will use

◆ SMB workgroup — Shows the name of the workgroup containing the SMB server or servers

After you have finished setting your configuration options on the Authentication Configuration screen, click the Next button to proceed to the next configuration step.

Selecting the Package Groups to Install

After you complete the key configuration steps, the installation program displays a screen from which you can select the Red Hat Linux package groups that you want to install. After you select the package groups, you can take a coffee break while the Red Hat installation program formats the disk partitions and copies all selected files to those partitions.

Red Hat uses special files called *packages* to bundle a number of files that make up specific software. For example, all configuration files, documentation, and binary files for the Perl programming language come in a Red Hat package. You use a special program called *Red Hat Package Manager (RPM)* to install, uninstall, and get information about packages. Chapter 23 shows you how to use RPM. For now, just remember that a package group is made up of several Red Hat packages.

Figure 3-12 shows the Package Group Selection screen with the list of package groups that you can elect to install. An icon, a descriptive label, and a radio button for enabling or disabling identify each package group.

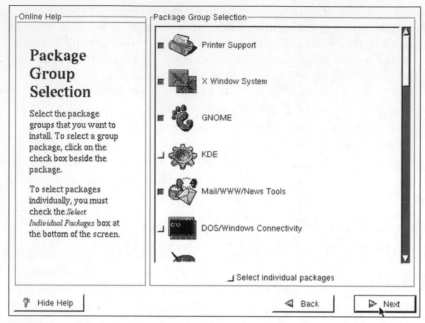

Figure 3-12: GUI screen from which you select the components to install

Some of the components are already selected, as indicated by the pressed-in buttons. This is the minimal set of packages that Red Hat recommends for installation for the class of installation (Workstation, Server, or Custom) you have chosen. You can, however, choose to install any or all of the components. Use the mouse to move up and down in the scrolling list, and click the mouse on an entry to select or deselect that package group.

In an actual Red Hat Linux installation, you install exactly those package groups that you need. Each package group requires specific packages to run. The Red Hat installation program automatically checks for any package dependencies and shows you a list of packages that are required but that you have not selected. In this case, you should install the required packages. You should install only the packages you think you will need immediately after starting the system. Installing too many packages could expose your system to security risks. You can always add packages later.

Because each package group is a collection of many different Red Hat packages, the installation program also gives you the option to select individual packages. If you select the item labeled Select individual packages, which appears below the list in Figure 3-12, and then click the Next button, the installation program takes you to other screens where you can select individual packages. If you are installing Red Hat Linux for the first time, you really do not need to go down to this level of detail to install specific packages. Simply pick the components that you think you need from the screen shown in Figure 3-12. After you select the components you want, click the Next button to continue with the rest of the installation.

You can always install additional packages later with the RPM utility program, described in Chapter 23.

Completing the Installation

After you complete the key configuration steps and select the components to install, the installation program configures the X Window System. The installation program uses an X server with minimal capability that can work on all video cards. In this step, the installation program prepares the configuration file that the X server uses when your system reboots. You can choose not to configure the X Window System by checking the appropriate box.

The installation program tries to detect the monitor and displays the X Configuration screen (see Figure 3-13) with the result, whether or not it succeeds.

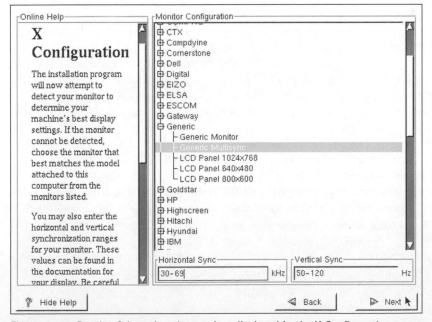

Figure 3-13: Result of detecting the monitor displayed in the X Configuration screen

If the installation program displays a wrong monitor or a generic one as the choice, you should enter a range of values for the two parameters that appear along the bottom of the screen:

◆ **Horizontal Sync** – the number of times per second the monitor can display a horizontal raster line, in kilohertz (KHz). A typical range might be 30–64 KHz.

◆ **Vertical Sync** – how many times per second the monitor can display the entire screen, in hertz (Hz). Also known as *vertical refresh rate*, the typical range is 50–90 Hz.

Typically, the monitor's documentation includes all this information. Other places to get information about your monitor include your Microsoft Windows setup, your system's Windows driver, your computer vendor's Web site, or the Norton System Information tool.

 Do not specify a horizontal synchronization range that is beyond the capabilities of your monitor. A wrong value can damage the monitor.

After selecting the monitor, the installation program tries to detect the video card and displays the result in a screen. The detected card appears as the selected item in a long list of video cards. If you know the exact name of the video card or the name of the video chipset used in the video card, select that item from the list.

On the same screen where you view and select the video card, you may also turn on the graphical login by clicking the button labeled Use Graphical Login. By doing so you get a graphical login screen when you reboot the system.

After you finish selecting X configuration options, click the Next button. The installation program displays an informative message telling you that a log of the installation is in the /tmp/install.log file. That file essentially lists all the Red Hat packages that are installed in your system. You can review the install log later and keep the file for future reference. The content of the install log depends on the exact packages you choose to install.

Click the Next button to proceed with the installation. The Red Hat installation program formats the disk partitions and then installs the packages. As it installs packages, the installation program displays a status screen showing the progress of the installation with information such as the total number of packages to install, the number installed so far, an estimated amount of disk space needed, and an estimated time remaining to install. The time required for installation of the packages is dependent on the number of packages you have selected and the speed of your system.

After all the packages are installed, the installation program displays a screen that prompts you to insert a blank floppy into your PC's A: drive. This floppy is the emergency boot disk that you can use to start Red Hat Linux if something happens to the hard disk or you do not install the LILO or GRUB.

Insert a blank floppy into your PC's A: drive and click the Next button. The installation program copies the Linux kernel and some other files to the floppy. After preparing the boot disk, the installation program displays a message informing you that installation is complete.

 Inserting a blank floppy into your PC's A: drive destroys all data on the floppy.

You are then instructed to remove the floppy from drive A: before exiting the installation program. Label the floppy as a boot disk, and save it in a safe place in case you need it in the future. Then click the Exit button to reboot your PC. When it finishes rebooting, you should get the Red Hat Linux graphical login screen if you chose this option, otherwise, you see the terminal login prompt.

Using KickStart

As a system administrator, one of your jobs is installing and configuring Red Hat on server and client computers. This could be a time-consuming job if you have many servers and clients to administer. To make your job easier, there is a program available to automate the Red Hat installation process. This program is called KickStart. With KickStart you can create and store configuration files for your server or client installations and then use these files to perform your installations and upgrades. Installations and upgrades can be done from a local CD-ROM or using NFS. If you are installing across the network, you need to have a DHCP server for each network segment.

The file that is used by KickStart to read the configuration information for the automated installation is called ks.cfg. The ks.cfg file can be located on a boot disk or on a network installation server. A sample KickStart configuration file, named sample.ks, is located in the /doc directory of the Red Hat Installation CD. This file is a plain text file that can be edited with any text editing program. You can use the sample file and make modifications as necessary for your installation. Here are some rules that you need to follow when modifying or creating your own file.

- ◆ Items must be listed in a specific order.

- ◆ Only required items have to be included in the file.

- Skipping a required item causes the installation program to prompt you for the missing information. The installation continues after the missing item is specified.

- Lines starting with a pound sign ("#") are treated as comments and are ignored.

- The following items are required in the order listed:

  1. language

  2. network

  3. installation method (cdrom or nfs)

  4. device specification (if the device is required for the installation)

  5. keyboard

  6. noprobe (optional)

  7. zerombr (yes or no; clears the MBR)

  8. part (required for installs)

  9. installation or upgrade (choose one)

  10. mouse (for configuring the mouse)

  11. timezone (for setting the time zone)

  12. xconfig (for configuring the X Window system)

  13. auth (configures password security and NIS)

  14. LILO configuration

  15. %page (specify packages to be installed here)

 If you are performing an upgrade, the ks.cfg file needs to contain only the installation method, the device specification, the keyboard type, the word *upgrade*, and LILO.

KickStart files are split into three sections: commands, package list, and scripts. The format of the file is:

```
1. <command section>
2. any combination of %pre, %post, or %packages
3. <install class>
```

The file must be ended by a post section as shown. If you want to run any scripts after the installation, include them after the post command.

KickStart Commands

The commands shown in the previous section are described next. For a complete listing of KickStart commands, you can go to the Red Hat Web site and look at the Red Hat 7 Reference Guide. The commands shown next are from this source.

Auth — Authentication Options

auth (required) — Sets up the authentication options for the system. It's similar to the authconfig command that can be run after the install. By default, passwords are normally encrypted and are not shadowed.

◆ --enablemd5 — Use md5 encryption for user passwords.

◆ --enablenis — Turns on NIS support. By default, --enablenis uses whatever domain it finds on the network. A domain should almost always be set by hand (via --nisdomain).

◆ --nisdomain — NIS domain name to use for NIS services.

◆ --nisserver — Server to use for NIS services (broadcasts by default).

◆ --useshadow — Use shadow passwords.

◆ --enableldap — Turns on LDAP support in /etc/nsswitch.conf, allowing your system to retrieve information about users (UIDs, home directories, shells, and so forth) from an LDAP directory. Use of this option requires that the nss_ldap package be installed. You must also specify a server and a base DN (distinguished name).

◆ --enableldapauth — Use LDAP as an authentication method. This option enables the pam_ldap module for authentication and password changing, using an LDAP directory. Use of this option requires that the nss_ldap package be installed. You must also specify a server and a base DN.

◆ --ldapserver= — The name of the LDAP server used if you specified either --enableldap or --enableldapauth. This option is set in the /etc/ldap.conf file.

◆ --ldapbasedn= — The DN in your LDAP directory tree under which user information is stored. This option is set in the /etc/ldap.conf file.

◆ --enablekrb5 — Use Kerberos 5 for authenticating users. Kerberos itself has no notion of home directories, UIDs, or shells, so if you enable Kerberos you still need to enable LDAP, NIS, or Hesiod if you want to avoid having to use the /usr/sbin/useradd command to make their accounts known to this workstation. Use of this option requires the pam_krb5 package to be installed.

◆ --krb5realm — The Kerberos 5 realm your workstation belongs to.

◆ --krb5kdc — The KDC (or KDCs) that serve requests for the realm. If you have multiple KDCs in your realm, separate their names with commas (,).

◆ --krb5adminserver — The KDC in your realm that is also running kadmind. This server, which can be run only on the master KDC if you have more than one, handles password changing and other administrative requests.

◆ --enablehesiod — Enable Hesiod support for looking up user home directories, UIDs, and shells. More information on setting up and using Hesiod on your network is in /usr/share/doc/glibc-2.x.x/ README.hesiod, which is included in the glibc package. Hesiod is an extension of DNS that uses DNS records to store information about users, groups, and various other items.

◆ --hesiodlhs — The Hesiod LHS (left-hand side) option, set in /etc/ hesiod.conf. This option is used by the Hesiod library to determine the name to search DNS for when looking up information, similar to LDAP's use of a base DN.

◆ --hesiodrhs — The Hesiod RHS (right-hand side) option, set in /etc/ hesiod.conf. This option is used by the Hesiod library to determine the name to search DNS for when looking up information, similar to LDAP's use of a base DN.

bootloader

bootloader (required) [1] — Specifies how the boot loader should be installed and whether the bootloader should be LILO or GRUB.

◆ append — Specifies kernel parameters.

◆ location= — Specifies where the boot record is written. Valid values are the following: mbr (the default), partition (installs the boot loader on the first sector of the partition containing the kernel), or none (do not install the boot loader).

◆ password=mypassword — If using GRUB, sets the GRUB bootloader password to mypassword. This should be used to restrict access to the GRUB shell where arbitrary kernel options can be passed.

◆ md5pass=mypassword — If using GRUB, similar to --password except mypassword should be the password already encrypted.

◆ useLilo — Use LILO instead of GRUB as the boot loader.

◆ linear — If using LILO, use the linear LILO option; this is only for backward compatibility (and linear is now used by default).

◆ nolinear — If using LILO, use the nolinear LILO option; linear is the default.

◆ lba32 — If using LILO, force use of lba32 mode instead of autodetecting.

clearpart

clearpart (optional) — Removes partitions from the system, prior to creation of new partitions. By default, no partitions are removed.

◆ linux — Erases all Linux partitions.

◆ all — Erases all partitions from the system.

◆ drives [1] — Specifies which drives to clear partitions from.

◆ initlabel [1] — Initializes the disk label to the default for your architecture (msdos for x86 and gpt for Itanium). The installation program does not ask if it should initialize the disk label if installing to a brand new hard drive.

device --opts

device (optional) — On most PCI systems, the installation program autoprobes for Ethernet and SCSI cards properly. On older systems, and some PCI systems, KickStart needs a hint to find the proper devices, however. The device command tells Anaconda to install extra modules.

◆ --opts — Options to pass to the kernel module. Note that multiple options may be passed if put in quotes.

driverdisk

driverdisk (optional) — Driver disks can be used during KickStart installations. You need to copy the driver disk's contents to the root directory of a partition on the system's hard drive. Then use the driverdisk command to tell the installation program where to look for the driver disk.

◆ driverdisk <partition> [--type <fstype>]

<partition> is the partition containing the driver disk.

◆ type — File system type (for example, vfat, ext2, or ext3).

firewall

firewall (optional) — Firewall options can be configured in KickStart. This configuration corresponds to the Firewall Configuration screen in the installation program.

- firewall [--high | --medium | --disabled] [--trust <device>] [--dhcp] [--ssh]   [telnet] [--smtp] [--http] [--ftp] [--port <portspec>].

- Levels of security — You can choose one of the following levels of security: high, medium, disabled.

- trust <device> — If you list a device here, such as eth0, then all traffic coming from that device goes through the firewall. To list more than one device, use --trust eth0, --trust eth1. Do not use a comma-separated format such as --trust eth0, eth1.

- Allow incoming — Enabling these options allow the specified services to pass through the firewall: --dhcp, --ssh, --telnet, --smtp, --http, --ftp.

- port <portspec> — You can specify that ports be allowed through the firewall using the port:protocol format. For example, if you want to allow IMAP access through your firewall, you can specify imap:tcp. You can also specify numeric ports explicitly; for example, to allow UDP packets on port 1234 through, specify 1234:udp. To specify multiple ports, separate them with commas.

install

install (optional) — Tells the system to install a fresh system rather than to upgrade an existing system. This is the default mode.

Installation methods

You must use one of the these commands to specify what type of KickStart is being done:

NFS

Install from the NFS server specified.

- --server <server> — Server from which to install (hostname or IP).

- --dir <dir> — Directory containing the Red Hat installation tree.

For example:

```
nfs --server <server> --dir <dir>
```

CD-ROM

Install from the first CD-ROM drive on the system. For example:

```
cdrom
```

HARD DRIVE

Install from a Red Hat installation tree on a local drive, which must be either VFAT or ext2.

◆ `--partition` `<partition>` — Partition to install from (such as, sdb2).

◆ `--dir` `<dir>` — Directory containing the Red Hat installation tree.

For example:

```
Harddrive -partition <partition> --dir <dir>
```

URL

Install from a Red Hat installation tree on a remote server via FTP or HTTP. For example:

```
url --url http://<server>/<dir>
url --url ftp://<username>:<password>@<server>/<dir>
```

interactive

`interactive` (optional) [1] — Uses the information provided in the KickStart file during the installation, but allows for inspection and modification of the values given. You will be presented with each screen of the installation program with the values from the KickStart file. Either accept the values by clicking Next or change the values and click Next to continue. See also the section titled "autostep."

keyboard

`keyboard` (required) — Sets system keyboard type.

language

`lang` (required) — Sets the default language for the installed system. The language you specify is used during the installation as well as to configure any language-specific aspect of the installed system. For example, to set the language to English, the KickStart file should contain the following line:

```
Lang en_US
```

lilo

`lilo` (replaced by `bootloader`) — Specifies how the boot loader should be installed on the system. By default, LILO installs on the MBR of the first disk, and installs a dual-boot system if a DOS partition is found (the DOS/Windows system boots if the user types dos at the `LILO:` prompt).

The lilo section is provided only for backward compatibility. You should use bootloader, discussed earlier in this section.

- --append `<params>` — Specifies kernel parameters.
- --linear — Uses the linear LILO option; this is for backward compatibility only (and linear is now used by default).
- --location — Specifies where the LILO boot record is written. Valid values are mbr (default), partition (installs the boot loader on the first sector of the partition containing the kernel), or none, which prevents any boot-loader from being installed.

lilocheck

lilocheck (optional) — If lilocheck is present, the installation program checks for LILO on the MBR of the first hard drive, and reboots the system if it is found — in this case, no installation is performed. This can prevent KickStart from reinstalling an already installed system.

mouse

mouse (required) — Configures the mouse for the system, both in GUI and text modes. Options are:

- --device `<dev>` — Device the mouse is on (such as --device ttyS0).
- --emulthree — If present, the X Window System uses simultaneous left+right mouse buttons to emulate the middle button (should be used on two-button mice).

If the mouse command is given without any arguments, or if it is omitted, the installation program attempts to autodetect the mouse (which works for most modern mice).

network

network (optional) — Configures network information for the system. If network is not given, and the KickStart installation does not require networking (in other words, it's not installed over NFS), networking is not configured for the system. If the installation does require networking, Anaconda assumes that the install should be done over eth0 via a dynamic IP address (BOOTP/DHCP), and configures the final, installed system to dynamically determine its IP address. The `network` command configures the networking information for the installation for network kickstarts as well as for the final, installed system.

◆ `--bootproto` — One of `dhcp`, `bootp`, or `static` (defaults to DHCP, and `dhcp` and `bootp` are treated the same). Must be `static` for static IP information to be used.

◆ `--device <device>` — Used to select a specific Ethernet device for installation. Note, using `--device <device>` is not effective unless the KickStart file is a local file (such as `ks=floppy`), since the installation program configures the network to find the KickStart file. Example:

```
network -bootproto dhcp -device eth0
```

◆ `--ip` — IP address for machine to be installed.

◆ `--gateway` — Default gateway, as an IP address.

◆ `--nameserver` — Primary name server, as an IP address.

◆ `--netmask` — Netmask for the installed system.

◆ `--hostname` — Hostname for the installed system.

The three methods of network configuration are:

◆ DHCP

◆ BOOTP

◆ static

The DHCP method uses a DHCP server system to obtain its networking configuration. As you might guess, the BOOTP method is similar, requiring a BOOTP server to supply the networking configuration.

The static method requires that you enter all the required networking information in the KickStart file. As the name implies, this information is static, and is used during the installation, and after the installation as well.

To direct a system to use DHCP to obtain its networking configuration, use the following line:

```
network -bootproto dhcp
```

To direct a machine to use BOOTP to obtain its networking configuration, use the following line in the KickStart file:

```
network -bootproto bootp
```

The line for static networking is more complex, as you must include all network configuration information on one line. You need to specify:

◆ IP address

◆ netmask

◆ gateway IP address

◆ name server IP address

Keep in mind two restrictions if you use the static method:

◆ All static networking configuration information must be specified on *one* line; you cannot wrap lines using a backslash, for example.

◆ You can specify only one name server here. However, you can use the KickStart file's %post to add more name servers, if needed.

partition

part (required for installs, ignored for upgrades) – Creates a partition on the system. Partition requests are of the form:

```
part <mntpoint> --size
<size> [--grow] [--onpart
<partc>] [--ondisk
<disk>] [--onprimary
<N>] [--asprimary <N>]
```

The <mntpoint> is where the partition is mounted, and must be of the following forms:

/<mntpoint>

(i.e. /, /usr, /home)

◆ swap – The partition is used as swap space.

◆ raid.<id> – The partition is used for software RAID (see the raid command later).

◆ --size <size> – Sets the minimum size for the partition.

◆ --grow – Tells the partition to grow to fill available space (if any), or up to maximum size setting.

◆ --maxsize <size> – Sets the maximum partition size when the partition is set to grow.

◆ `--noformat` — Tells the installation program not to format the partition; for use with the `--onpart` command.

◆ `--onpart <part>` or `--usepart <part>` — Tells the installation program to put the partition on the *already existing* device *<part>*. For example, partition `/home --onpart hda1` puts `/home` on `/dev/hda1`, which must already exist.

◆ `--ondisk <disk>` — Forces the partition to be created on a particular disk. For example, `--ondisk.sdb` puts the partition on the second disk on the system.

◆ `--onprimary <N>` — Forces the partition to be created on primary partition *<N>* or fail. *<N>* can be 1 through 4.

◆ `--asprimary <N>` — Forces auto allocation as a primary partition *<N>* or fail. *<N>* can be 1 through 4.

◆ `--bytes-per-inode=<N>` — *<N>* represents the number of bytes per inode on the file system when it is created. It must be given in decimal format. This option is useful for applications where you want to increase the number of inodes on the file system.

◆ `--type=<X>` — Sets partition type to *<X>*, where *<X>* is a numerical value.

All partitions created are formatted as part of the installation process unless `--noformat` and `--onpart` are used.

raid

`raid` (optional) — Assembles a software RAID device. This command is of the form:

```
raid <mntpoint> --level <level> --device mddevice><partitions*>
```

The `<mntpoint>` is the location where the RAID file system is mounted. If it is `/`, the RAID level must be 1 unless a boot partition (`/boot`) is present. If a boot partition is present, the `/boot` partition must be level 1 and the root (`/`) partition can be any of the available types. The `<partitions*>` (which denotes that multiple partitions can be listed) lists the RAID identifiers to add to the RAID array.

◆ `level <level>` — RAID level to use (0, 1, or 5).

◆ `device <mddevice>` — Name of the RAID device to use (such as md0 or md1). RAID devices range from md0 to md7, and each may be used only once.

◆ `spares=N [1]` — Specifies that there should be *N* spare drives allocated for the RAID array. Spare drives are used to rebuild the array in case of drive failure.

- ◆ `fstype [1]` — Sets the file system type for the RAID array. Valid values are ext2, ext3, swap, and vfat.

- ◆ `noformat [1]` — Do not format the RAID array.

The following example shows how to create a RAID level 1 partition for /, and a RAID level 5 for /usr, assuming there are three SCSI disks on the system. It also creates three swap partitions, one on each drive.

```
part raid.01 --size 60 --ondisk sda
part raid.02 --size 60 --ondisk sdb
part raid.03 --size 60 --ondisk sdc
part swap --size 128 --ondisk sda
part swap --size 128 --ondisk sdb
part swap --size 128 --ondisk sdc
part raid.11 --size 1 --grow --ondisk sda
part raid.12 --size 1 --grow --ondisk sdb
part raid.13 --size 1 --grow --ondisk sdc
raid / --level 1 --device md0 raid.01 raid.02 raid.03
raid /usr --level 5 --device md1 raid.11 raid.12 raid.13
```

reboot

`reboot` (optional) — Reboot after the installation is complete (no arguments). Normally, KickStart displays a message and waits for the user to press a key before rebooting.

rootpw

`rootpw` (required) — Usage: rootpw [--iscrypted] $\langle password \rangle$
Sets the system's root password to the $\langle password \rangle$ argument.

- ◆ `--iscrypted` — If this is present, the password argument is assumed to already be encrypted.

skipx

`skipx` (optional) — If present, X is not configured on the installed system.timezone.

timezone

`timezone` (required) — Usage: timezone [--utc] $\langle timezone \rangle$
Sets the system time zone to $\langle timezone \rangle$, which may be any of the time zones listed in `timeconfig`.

- ◆ `--utc` — If present, the system assumes the hardware clock is set to UTC (Greenwich Mean) time.

upgrade

upgrade (optional) — Tells the system to upgrade an existing system rather than install a fresh system.

xconfig

xconfig (optional) — Configures the X Window System. If this option is not given, the user needs to configure X manually during the installation, if X was installed; this option should not be used if X is not installed on the final system.

- ◆ --noprobe — Don't probe the monitor.
- ◆ --card <card> — Use card <card>; this card name should be from the list of cards in Xconfigurator. If this argument is not provided, Anaconda probes the PCI bus for the card.
- ◆ --monitor <mon> — Use monitor <mon>; this monitor name should be from the list of monitors in Xconfigurator. This is ignored if --hsync or --vsync is provided; if no monitor information is provided, the monitor is probed via plug-and-play.
- ◆ --hsync <sync> — Specifies the horizontal sync frequency of the monitor.
- ◆ --vsync <sync> — Specifies the vertical sync frequency of the monitor.
- ◆ --defaultdesktop=(GNOME or KDE) — Sets the default desktop to either GNOME or KDE (and assumes that GNOME and/or KDE has been installed through %packages).
- ◆ --startxonboot — Use a graphical login (runlevel 5) for the installed system.

zerombr — Partition table initialization

zerombr (optional) — If zerombr is specified, and yes is its sole argument, any invalid partition tables found on disks are initialized. This destroys all of the contents of disks with invalid partition tables. This command should be used as:

zerombr yes

%packages — Package Selection

Use the %packages command to begin a KickStart file section that lists the packages you'd like to install (this is for installations only, as package selection during upgrades is not supported).

Packages can be specified by component or by individual package name. The installation program defines several components that group together related packages. See the RedHat/base/comps file on any Red Hat Linux CD-ROM for a list of components. The components are defined by the lines that begin with a number followed by a space, and then the component name. Each package in that component is then listed, line-by-line. Individual packages lack the leading number found in front of component lines.

Additionally, you may run across three other types of lines in the `comps` file:

- Architecture-specific lines (alpha:, i386:, and sparc64:)

  If a package name begins with an architecture type, you need only type in the package name, not the architecture name. For example:

  For `i386: netscape-common` you need to use only the `netscape-common` part for that specific package to be installed.

- Lines beginning with ?.

  Lines that begin with a ? are specific to the installation program. You do not have to do anything with these types of lines.

- Lines beginning with `-hide`.

  If a package name begins with `--hide`, you need to type in only the package name, minus the `--hide`. For example:

  For `--hide KDE Workstation` you need to use only the `KDE Workstation` part for that specific package to be installed.

In most cases, it's necessary to list only the desired components and not individual packages. Note that the `Base` component is always selected by default, so it's not necessary to specify it in the `%packages` section.

For example:

```
%packages
@ Networked Workstation
@ C Development
@ Web Server
@ X Window System
bsd-games
```

As you can see, components are specified, one to a line, starting with an @ symbol, a space, and then the full component name as given in the `comps` file. Specify individual packages with no additional characters (the `bsd-games` line in the preceding example is an individual package).

You can also direct the KickStart installation to use the workstation- and server-class installations (or choose an everything installation to install all packages). To do this, simply add *one* of the following lines to the `%packages` section:

```
@ Gnome Workstation
@ KDE Workstation
@ Server
@ Everything
```

%pre — Pre-Installation Configuration Section

You can add commands to run on the system immediately after the ks.cfg has been parsed. This section must be at the end of the KickStart file (after the commands) and must start with the %pre command. Note that you can access the network in the %pre section; however, name service has not been configured at this point, so only IP addresses will work.

%post — Post-Installation Configuration Section

You have the option of adding commands to run on the system once the installation is complete. This section must be at the end of the KickStart file and must start with the `%post` command. Note, you can access the network in the `%post` section; however, *name service* has not been configured at this point, so only IP addresses work.

Starting a KickStart Installation

To begin a KickStart installation, you must boot the system from a Red Hat Linux boot disk, and enter a special boot command at the boot prompt. If the KickStart file resides on the boot disk, the proper boot command is:

```
boot: linux ks=floppy
```

If, on the other hand, the KickStart file resides on a server, the appropriate boot command is:

```
boot: linux ks
```

Anaconda looks for a KickStart file if the `ks` command line argument is passed to the kernel. The ks command can take a number of forms:

◆ `ks=floppy` — The installation program looks for the file `ks.cfg` on a VFAT file system on the floppy in drive `/dev/fd0`.

◆ `ks=hd:<device>/<file>` — The installation program mounts the file system on `<device>` (which must be VFAT or ext2), and looks for the KickStart configuration file as `<file>` in that file system (for example, `ks=hd:sda3/mydir/ks.cfg`).

◆ `ks=file:/<file>` — The installation program tries to read the file `<file>` from the file system; no mounts are done. This is normally used if the KickStart file is already on the `initrd` image.

◆ `ks=nfs:<server:>/<path>` — The installation program looks for the KickStart file on the NFS server `<server>`, as file `<path>`. The installation program uses DHCP to configure the Ethernet card.

◆ `ks=cdrom:/<path>` —The installation program looks for the KickStart file on CD-ROM, as file `<path>`.

◆ `ks` — When `ks` is specified without additional command line parameters, the DHCP bootServer field of the configuration file is used to obtain the name of the NFS server. This information is also used to configure the Ethernet card using DHCP, and to find the location of the KickStart file. The KickStart file can be found in one of three locations:

■ If the bootfile starts with a /, and DHCP is configured, the installation program looks in the root directory on the NFS server for the bootfile.

■ If the bootfile does not start with a /, and DHCP is configured, the installation program looks in the `/kickstart` directory on the NFS server for the file.

■ When no bootfile is listed, the IP address of the PC receiving the installation is checked for the file.

Summary

In this chapter you learned about installing Red Hat Linux. First you learned about the hardware on your system, and then you made a list of your components. Then you checked the Red Hat Web site to find out if your hardware was compatible with Red Hat Linux. You learned how to install Red Hat Linux on a single computer. Finally, you learned about the Red Hat program called KickStart. Using KickStart, you can automate the installation procedure for client and server PCs on your network.

Chapter 4

Red Hat Linux File System

IN THIS CHAPTER

◆ Understanding the Red Hat Linux file system structure

◆ Using file system commands

◆ Working with Linux-supported file systems

◆ Linux disk management

THIS CHAPTER BEGINS with a description of the Red Hat Linux file system structure and an explanation of the directories and the files they contain. Following the look at the file system structure are the file system commands, essential to proper file system management. In addition to the native Linux file system, Red Hat Linux supports many other file system types. This chapter explains the other file system types and ends with a discussion of Linux disk management.

Understanding the Red Hat Linux File System Structure

Understanding the organization, or layout, of the Red Hat Linux file system is one of the most important aspects of system administration. For administrators, programmers, users, and installed software, knowing how and where the files are stored on the system is critical for proper system operation. A standard should be in place that specifies locations for specific types of data. Fortunately, Red Hat has chosen to follow the standards outlined in the Filesystem Hierarchy Standard (FHS). This section briefly explains the FHS and its relevance to proper system administration. For the complete standard, refer to `http://www.pathname.com/fhs`.

The FHS provides specific requirements for the placement of files in the directory structure. Placement is based on the type of information contained in the file. Basically two categories of file information exist: shareable or unshareable, and variable or static. Shareable files are files that can be accessed by other hosts, and unshareable files can be accessed only by the local system. Variable files contain information that can change at any time on their own, without anyone actually changing the file. A log file is an example of such a file. A static file contains information that does not change unless a user changes it. Program documentation and

71

binary files are examples of static files. Figure 4-1 shows the organization of the file system on a typical Red Hat Linux system. Following the figure is an explanation of each directory and the types of files it may contain.

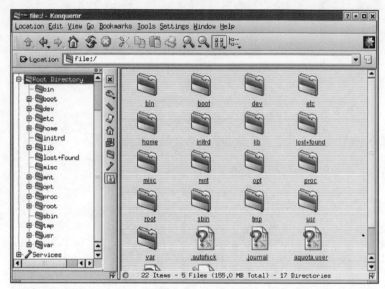

Figure 4-1: The file system organization for a typical Red Hat Linux system

As shown in the illustration, the Red Hat Linux file system is organized in a flat, hierarchical file system. Linux's method of mounting its file systems in a flat, logical, hierarchical method has advantages over the file system mounting method used by Windows. Linux references everything relative to the root file system point /, whereas Windows has a different root mount point for every drive.

If you have a /usr partition that fills up in Linux, you can create another file system called /usr/local and move your /usr/local data from /usr to the new file system definition. This practice frees up space on the /usr partition, and is an easy way to bring your system back up to a fully functional state.

This trick wouldn't work on a Windows machine, because Windows maps its file locations to static device disk definitions. You would have to change programs' file references from c:\ to d:\, and so forth. Linux's file system management is another good reason to use Linux on your production servers instead of Windows.

The / directory

The / directory is called the *root* directory and is typically at the top of the file system structure. In many systems, the / directory is the only partition on the system and all other directories are mounted under it. Figure 4-1 shows a file system with the / directory mounted as the only partition, with all other directories mounted beneath it. The primary purpose of the / directory is booting the system, and to correct any problems that might be preventing the system from booting. According to the FHS, the / directory must contain, or have links to, the following directories:

◆ bin — This directory contains command files for use by the system administrator or other users. The bin directory can not contain subdirectories.

◆ boot — On Red Hat systems, this is the directory containing the kernel, the core of the operating system. Also in this directory are files related to booting the system, such as the bootloader.

◆ dev — This directory contains files with information about devices, either hardware or software devices, on the system.

◆ etc — This directory and its subdirectories contain most of the system configuration files. If you have the X Window System installed on your system, the X11 subdirectory is located here. Networking related files are in the subdirectory sysconfig. Another subdirectory of etc is the skel directory, which is used to create files in users' home directories when the users are created.

◆ home — This directory contains the directories of users on the system. Subdirectories of home will be named for the user to whom they belong.

◆ lib — The shared system files and kernel modules are contained in this directory and its subdirectories.

◆ mnt — This directory is the location of the mount point for temporary file systems, such as a floppy or CD.

◆ opt — This directory and its subdirectories are often used to hold applications installed on the system.

◆ proc — Information about system processes is included in this directory.

◆ root — This is the home directory of the root user. Don't confuse this with the / directory, which has the same name.

◆ sbin — Contained in this directory are system binaries used by the system administrator or the root user.

◆ tmp — This directory contains temporary files used by the system.

◆ usr — This directory is often mounted on its own partition. It contains shareable, read-only data. Subdirectories can be used for applications, typically under /usr/local.

◆ var — Subdirectories and files under var contain variable information, such as system logs and print queues.

Using File System Commands

Most of the commands a Unix user needs to know are related to manipulating files on the system. Files control everything on the system, so they are very important. Each of the following subsections discusses a useful file system command that every system administrator should know about, and what they do.

ls

ls is probably the most commonly used Unix command. It lists information about files on the system. By default ls shows you the names of unhidden files in the current directory. You can use several additional options with ls to show you all sorts of detailed aspects of a file as well. Because ls has so many options, few system administrators know them all.

A common usage of ls is ls-la, which lists files in a longer format, and lists all files, including hidden files.

cp

cp is Unix's copy command. The syntax of cp is pretty basic and is just like any other operating system's file copy command.

To copy filename-a to filename-b, type: **cp filename-a filename-b**.

It is said that the reason Unix commands are so short is because Unix was first used on a PDP-11, which had a keyboard whose keys were very hard to press, so keystrokes were kept to a minimum.

rm

rm is Unix's remove command. To remove a file, type **rm filename**.

rm plays a large part in Unix mythology because every Unix administrator dreads having someone with root privileges type **rm -rf /*** on their system.

mv

mv is the move command. If moving files within a file system, mv operates more like a rename than a move, because just the logical name and logical location are changed. If a file is moved across file systems, mv copies the file over first and then removes it from the old location.

To move filename-a to filename-b, type **mv filename-a filename-b**.

chown

chown changes the user or group ownership of a file or directory. Maintaining proper file ownership helps ensure that only the people who own the file have access to it, since world accessible permissions can be severely limited without inhibiting the use of the file to its rightful owner.

To change ownership of a file to username ben, type **chown ben filename**.

chgrp

chgrp changes only the group ownership of a file or directory. To set the group ownership of a file to group admin, type **chgrp admin filename**.

chmod

This command changes file access permissions, handy when you want to limit who can and cannot read, write or execute your files. Permissions that can be modified with this command are write access, read access, and executable access for the user owner, the group owner, and all users on the system (world access).

chmod also determines if the program text should be saved on the swap device and whether or not the command should be run under the user ID of the owner or under the group ID of the group owner.

chmod has two methods of changing filename permissions. One way is the numeric method, which sets the user, group and world permissions at once. In this method, 4 represents read, 2 represents write, and 1 represents execute. So if you set a file's permissions to 444, you are setting it to be only readable to user, group, and world owners. If you add the numbers together you can add more file permissions. So to make a file writeable (4), readable (2), and executable (1) by user, and not accessible in any way to anybody else, you set it to permissions number 700. That breaks down to (4+2+1) for user, and no permissions for group or world, hence the two 0's. To change a file's permissions to 700, type **chmod 700 filename**.

The other way to specify chmod permissions is the character flag method, which changes only the attributes you specify. The letters used to change owner permissions are u for user, g for group, and o for other. To indicate the permissions mode, r is for read, w is for write, and x stands for execute. The + and – signs are used to indicate if the permission is being added or removed from the file. For example, to add readable and writeable permissions to filename-a for the user who owns it, type **chmod u+rw filename-a**.

chmod does not change the permissions of symbolic links, but instead it changes the file permissions of the symbolic link's target file.

chattr

chattr enables you to set special access attributes on files. You can set files to repress updating the access time, or set files to be append-only, immutable, or undeletable. You can also use chattr to make sure that a secure deletion is done. chattr works on only ext2 and ext3 file systems.

Some of the file attributes that can be changed with this command are immutable, secure deletion, and append only. To make a file immutable, type **chattr +I filename**.

ln

ln creates hard or symbolic links between files. These links are useful in many different situations where you don't want to copy a file to many different locations. You may want to save disk space, or ensure that you have the same version of the file in two different locations on a system.

Symbolic links come in handy when compiling and installing new kernels, since you can keep two different vmlinuz files with two different names in your /boot directory and choose which one to boot by making a symlink between vmlinuz and the specific vmlinuz kernel version file you want to boot. Then make a reference to the /boot/vmlinuz symlinks in your lilo.conf file.

Hard links cause two different filenames to share the same inode. This means the hard links and the target file are basically two names for the same file. If you delete the hard link, you also delete the target file. Hard links cannot be made to directories, and they cannot be made across file systems.

Symbolic links are much more common than hard links because of their flexibility. A symbolic link is really a special file type that references another file. When you try to open the symbolic link, the kernel passes the operation onto the target file. However when you remove the symbolic link, only the symbolic link file is removed and the target file remains unaffected. Symbolic links can be made to directories and across file systems

To create a symbolic link called mailalias pointing to a program named pine, type **ln –s pine mailalias**.

symlinks

This is a symbolic link maintenance utility. It checks for things like symlink sanity and dead symbolic links. symlinks is especially useful for people who maintain FTP sites and CD-ROM distributions.

Links are classified as either relative, absolute, dangling, messy, lengthy, or other_fs. Relative symlinks are defined as symlinks that are linked to other files by a relative path such as ../../ instead of listing the absolute path relative to a file system mount point, such as /usr/local/. Absolute symlinks point to a file whose path includes a file system mount point. Dangling symlinks point to a file that no longer exists. Messy symlinks contain dots or slashes in the path that aren't necessary. These can be cleaned up when symlinks is run with the -c flag. Lengthy links use ../ more than is necessary for specifying the file location. Symlinks classified as other_fs are those whose target file is on a different file system than the source of the symlink.

To clean up a directory's symbolic links, type **symlinks –c directoryname**.

The -c option converts absolute symlinks to relative links, so that the symlinks remain valid no matter what mount point the file system is mounted on. This option cleans up messy links and shortens lengthy links.

stat

This command tells you the status of a specified file or file system. In order to run this command you don't need to have access rights to the file, but you do need to be able to search all the directories in the path leading up to the file location.

stat gives you lots of detailed information about a file, such as device number, inode number, access rights, number of hard links, owner user ID and name, owner group ID and name, device type, total file size, number of allocated blocks for the file, IO block size, last access time, last modification time, and — last but not least — last changed time.

If the -f flag is used, the following information is also displayed: file system type, file system block size, number of blocks in the file system, free blocks, free blocks for nonroot users, total number of inodes, number of free inodes, and the maximum length of filenames.

To see the status of a file, type **stat filename**.

lsof

lsof is a very handy tool that lists what files are open on your system, and what active process is holding them open. This command lists all files held open both by local system processes and network services.

lsof can list open files by user or by process. You can give lsof a filename or a directory name, and it tells you what process is holding it open. This information is especially helpful if you need to edit a file, but you can't because something is holding the file open for writing and blocking all other programs from editing it.

Open files tracked by lsof can be more than standard Unix files. They can also be directories, character special files, block special files, libraries, executing text references, streams, Internet sockets, NFS files, or Unix domain sockets. `lsof` can show you status only on files on which you have permissions to run the `stat` system function.

To see what process is holding a lock on a file, type **lsof filename**.

mknod

This command enables you to create block and character device files and named pipes.

macutil

This is a Linux to Mac file system conversion suite that contains the packages listed next.

MACUNPACK

`macunpack` extracts files from a Macintosh MacBinary archive, usually a `.bin` file.

HEXBIN

`hexbin` takes in Macintosh binhex files and converts them to a Unix readable format.

MACSAVE

This utility reads Macintosh MacBinary files from standard input, and writes them to a file.

MACSTREAM

This utility takes in a series of files and combines them into a MacBinary stream and outputs them to standard out.

BINHEX

`binhex` takes in files and outputs them in BinHex 4.0 format to standard out. By default this utility takes in MacBinary format files.

TOMAC

`tomac` reads in files and sends them to a Macintosh computer using the XMODEM protocol.

FROMMAC

`frommac` receives files from a Macintosh computer and stores them in the current directory in MacBinary format.

Working With Linux—Supported File Systems

Linux is a very flexible operating system that has a long history of interoperability with other systems on a number of different hardware platforms. A consequence of this friendliness to other operating systems is that Linux can read and write to several different file systems that originated with other operating systems much different from Linux. This section details the different file systems supported and where they originated.

One reason that Linux supports so many file systems is because of the design of its Virtual File Systems (VFS) layer. The VFS layer is a data abstraction layer between the kernel and the programs in userspace that issues file system commands.

 Programs that run inside the kernel are in *kernelspace*. Programs that don't run inside the kernel are in *userspace*.

The VFS layer avoids duplication of common code between all file systems. It provides a fairly universal backward compatible method for programs to access all of the different forms of file support. Only one common, small API set accesses each of the file system types, to simplify programming file system support.

Standard disk file systems

Support for these file systems come standard in Red Hat Linux. They are compiled into the kernel by default. If for some reason your kernel does not currently support these file systems, a kernel recompile with the proper options turned on should enable you to access all these file systems.

MINIX

minix holds an important spot in Linux history, since Torvalds was trying to make a better minix than minix. He wanted to improve upon the 16-bit minix kernel by making a better 32-bit kernel that did everything that minix did and more. This historical connection is the main reason why minix file system support is available in Linux.

One reason to run a minix file system is that it has less metadata overhead than ext2, and so it is a preferable choice for boot and rescue disks. Rescue disks made with older versions of Red Hat Linux use a minix file system.

EXT2

ext2 has become the standard file system for Linux. It is the next generation of the ext file system. The ext2 implementation has not changed much since it was introduced with the 1.0 kernel back in 1993. Since then there have been a few new features added. One of these was sparse super blocks, which increases file system performance.

ext2 was designed to make it easier for new features to be added, so that it can constantly evolve into a better file system. Users can take advantage of new features without reformatting their old ext2 file systems. ext2 also has the added bonus of being designed to be POSIX compliant. New features that are still in the development phase are access control lists, undelete, and on-the-fly compression.

ext2 is flexible, can handle file systems up to 4TB large, and supports long file-names up to 1,012 characters long. In case user processes fill up a file system, ext2 normally reserves about 5 percent of disk blocks for exclusive use by root so that root can easily recover from that situation. Modern Red Hat boot and rescue diskettes now use ext2 instead of minix.

EXT3

The extended 3 file system is a new file system introduced in Red Hat 7.2. ext3 provides all the features of ext2, and also features journaling and backward compatibility with ext2. The backward compatibility enables you to still run kernels that are only ext2 aware with ext3 partitions.

You can upgrade an ext2 file system to an ext3 file system without losing any of your data. This upgrade can be done during an update to Red Hat 7.2.

ext3 support comes in kernels provided with the Red Hat 7.2 distribution. If you download a kernel from somewhere else, you need to patch the kernel to make it ext3 aware, with the kernel patches that come from the Red Hat ftp site. It is much easier to just stick with kernels from Red Hat.

ext3's journaling feature speeds up the amount of time it takes to bring the file system back to a sane state if it's not been cleanly unmounted (that is, in the event of a power outage or a system crash).

Under ext2, when a file system is uncleanly mounted, the whole file system must be checked. This takes a long time on large file systems. ext3 keeps a record of uncommitted file transactions and applies only those transactions when the system is brought back up.

A cleanly unmounted ext3 file system can be mounted and used as an ext2 file system. This capability can come in handy if you need to revert to an older kernel that is not aware of ext3. The kernel sees the ext3 file system as an ext2 file system.

ext3's journaling feature involves a small performance hit to maintain the file system transaction journal. Therefore it's recommended that you use ext3 mostly for your larger file systems, where the ext3 journaling performance hit is made up for in time saved by not having to run `fsck` on a huge ext2 file system.

REISERFS

The Reiser file system is a journaling file system designed for fast server performance. It is more space efficient than most other file systems, because it does not take up a minimum of one block per file. If you write a bunch of really small files to disk, reiserfs squeezes them all into one block instead of writing one small file to one block like other file systems do. Reiserfs also does not have fixed space allocation for inodes, which saves about 6 percent of your disk space.

SYSTEMV

Linux currently provides read support for SystemV partitions, and write support is experimental. The SystemV file system driver currently supports AFS/EAFS/EFS, Coherent FS, SystemV/386 FS, Version 7 FS, and Xenix file systems.

UFS

ufs is used in Solaris and early BSD operating systems. Linux provides read support, and write support is experimental.

FAT

FAT is one of a few different file systems used with Windows over the years. Almost every computer user has used FAT at one time or another, since it was the sparse base operating system at the heart of all Windows operating systems.

FAT was originally created for QDOS and used on 360K (double density, double sided) floppy disks. Its address space has since been extended from 12 bit to 32 bit, so it can handle very large file systems. Nowadays it's possible to create FAT file systems over a terabyte in size.

 Do not confuse a FAT file system with a FAT32 file system. They are named similarly, but are two different beasts!

NTFS

NTFS is the next generation of HPFS. It comes with all business versions of Microsoft operating systems beginning with Windows NT. Unlike FAT, it is a b-tree file system, meaning it has a performance and reliability advantage over FAT.

HPFS

The High Performance File System first came with OS/2 Version 1 created by Microsoft. It's the standard OS/2 file system. Since OS/2 usage has dropped off significantly, HPFS has become a relatively uncommon file system.

HFS

The Hierarchical File System is used with older versions of Mac OS. Macintosh-formatted files have two parts to them: a data fork and a resource fork. The resource fork contains Macintosh operating system-specific information such as dialog boxes and menu items. The data fork contains the meat of the file data. The data fork is readable by Unix.

Linux to Macintosh file conversion tools are available bundled in the `macutils` package. The tools included in that package are: `macunpack`, `hexbin`, `macsave`, `macstream`, `binhex`, `tomac`, and `frommac`. See the previous section called "Important File System Commands" to read more about these tools.

The modern Mac OS file system, `hfs+`, is currently not supported under Linux.

HFS is a different file system than HP-UX HFS. HP-UX HFS is a non-journaled file system format available on HP-UX systems.

Nonstandard Linux file systems

Support for these file systems needs to be explicitly compiled into the Linux kernel, since kernel support for them is not configured by default.

IBM JFS

IBM JFS is an easy to use journaling file system created by IBM. It is designed for high-throughput server environments. This is the same file system that will be provided in AIX version 5l. Linux support for JFS was written by IBM. IBM has contributed quite a bit of code to the Linux cause, and is a staunch supporter of Linux. They have also decided to make Linux their main server file system in the future.

SGI XFS

SGI's Extended File System (XFS) is SGI's newest file system for all Silicon Graphics systems, from workstations to their supercomputer line (before they sold that line to Terra computers.) It has been available for use on Linux since May 2001.

XFS is designed for high performance. It rapidly recovers from system crashes and can support extremely large disk farms (it can handle files as large as a million terabytes.) It is one of a very few journaling file systems that has a proven track record in production environments for several years now.

Its other features include access control lists, volume management, guaranteed rate I/O, and journaling for faster recovery. XFS can be backed up while still in use, which comes in handy since it reduces system administration time. This is a fast file system, and now you can read it with your Red Hat Linux machine.

FREEVXFS

VxFS is the Veritas file system developed by the Veritas Corporation. It is used in SCO UnixWare, HP-UX, Solaris, and other systems. Some of its features include access control lists, journaling, online backup, and support for files up to 2TB large.

Three different versions of VxFS are in use. Version 1 is the original VxFS that is not commonly used anymore. Version 2 includes support for filesets and dynamic inode allocation. Version 4 is the latest version, and it supports quotas and large files.

GNU utilities available for Linux called VxTools can read VxFS versions 2 and 4. The tools included in the VxTools package are `vxmount`, `vxumount`, `vxls`, `vxcat`, `vxidump`, `vxcd`, and `vxpwd`. Currently there is only read support in Linux for VxFS file systems.

GFS

GFS is Sistina's Global File System. It is a clustered journaling file system for SANs that enables multiple servers to have read/write access to a single file system on shared SAN devices.

GFS is scalable, since storage devices and servers can be added without taking the system down or taking the disks offline. It also makes a single image of all the data in the SAN, so that if a server fails it can be removed and replaced while the load is rebalanced amongst the remaining servers.

In a proper cluster setup, all nodes in the cluster share the same storage devices through a fiber channel, SCSI hookup, or network block device. Each node sees the file system as being local to their machine, and GFS synchronizes files across the cluster. GFS is fully symmetric, so there is no server that is a bottleneck or single point of failure. GFS uses regular Unix-style file semantics.

Memory file systems and virtual file systems

These file systems do not exist on disk in the same way that traditional file systems do. They either exist entirely in system memory, or they are virtual because they are an interface to system devices, for example.

CRAMFS

`cramfs` is designed to cram a file system onto a small ROM, so it is small, simple, and able to compress things well. The largest file size is 16MB, and the largest file system size is 256MB.

Since `cramfs` is so compressed, it isn't instantly updateable. The `mkcramfs` tool needs to be run to create or update a `cramfs` disk image. The image is created by compressing files one page at a time, so this enables random page access. The metadata is not compressed, but it has been optimized to take up much less space than other file systems. For example, only the low 8 bits of the gid are stored. This saves space but also presents a potential security issue.

TMPFS

`tmpfs` is structured around the idea that whatever is put in the /tmp file system is accessed again shortly. `tmpfs` exists solely in memory, so what you put in temp doesn't persist between reboots.

Creating /tmp as an in-memory file system is a performance boost. Creating /tmp as an in-memory file system is done in Solaris since the overhead of Solaris is very large. Creating /tmp as an in-memory file system hasn't been done before in Linux because the ext2 file system has pretty good performance already. But for those who feel that they need the performance gains of storing /tmp in memory, this option is now available in Linux.

RAMFS

ramfs is basically cramfs without the compression.

ROMFS

This is a read-only file system that is mostly used for the initial RAM disks of installation disks. It was designed to take up very little space, so you could fit a kernel and some useful code into a small boot disk, without having the file system overhead taking up too much precious space in memory or on the disk.

The kernel on the disk has only this file system linked into it, and then it can load any modules it needs later, after bootup. After the kernel is loaded, it can call other programs to help determine what SCSI drivers are needed, if any, or what IDE or floppy drives should be accessed after bootup. This method is perfect for rescue diskettes or installation diskettes, where all that is really required is that a very bare minimum kernel be loaded into memory, so after initial boot it can then load from CD-ROM whatever ext2 modules or other drivers are necessary to mount the system's regular drives.

The romfs file system is created with a program called genromfs.

PROC

proc is a virtual file system that acts as an interface to the kernel's internal data structures. proc can be used to get detailed information about a system's hardware and to change kernel parameters at run time. Even the process listing command, ps, gets its information from the proc file system. The kernel parameters can be changed with the sysctl command.

PROC SOFTWARE INFORMATION   The /proc directory contains a great deal of information about your currently running system software. If you look at the /proc directory on Linux, you see one subdirectory for each process running on the system. The subdirectories are named after the process's ID (PID) number. Each of those subdirectories has several standard files, and each of them gives you a different set of information.

The status file in those proc directories contains process status in human readable format. So if you want to see the status of your ssh server, you first need to know the ssh server's PID number. You can find this number in a few different ways. One easy way is to look at a process listing and grep for the string "ssh". The output should look like the lines below:

```
[vnavrat@buffy vnavrat]$ ps -elf | grep ssh
140 S root       933     1  0 69   0   -   664 do_sel Oct23 ?        00:00:01
/usr/sbin/sshd
140 S root     14807   933  0 69   0   -   882 do_sel 18:36 ?        00:00:00
/usr/sbin/sshd
000 S vnavrat 14883 14808  0 71   0   -   434 pipe_w 18:52 pts/10    00:00:00
grep ssh
```

The process table contains multiple hits for ssh, since there is a master sshd process, and one sshd process is spawned for each ssh session currently open. The first line is the master sshd server process. You can tell because its parent process ID is 1, also known as the init process that spawns all processes at boot time, and is responsible for re-spawning important server processes that die during runtime. The second line is an ssh daemon handling an incoming ssh connection, evident because it lists the previous ssh process as its parent. The final line lists the grep process that you just ran, so you can disregard that line.

You should look at the status of the master ssh daemon, which, as you saw previously, is running with a PID of 933. So cd to the /proc/933 directory, and take a look at the status file in that directory. The output appears below:

```
[vnavrat@buffy vnavrat]$ less /proc/933/status
Name:    sshd
State:   S (sleeping)
Pid:     933
PPid:    1
TracerPid:      0
Uid:     0       0       0       0
Gid:     0       0       0       0
FDSize: 32
Groups:
VmSize:     2656 kB
VmLck:         0 kB
VmRSS:      1236 kB
VmData:      116 kB
VmStk:        16 kB
VmExe:       240 kB
VmLib:      2176 kB
SigPnd: 0000000000000000
SigBlk: 0000000000000000
SigIgn: 8000000000001000
SigCgt: 0000000000016005
CapInh: 0000000000000000
CapPrm: 00000000fffffeff
CapEff: 00000000fffffeff
```

Other useful files in the /proc/PID directory and their contents are:

cmdline — contains the process's command line arguments

cpu — contains the current and last CPU on which the process was executed

cwd — contains a link to the process's current working directory

environ — contains values of the process's environmental variables exe — contains a link to the process's executable

fd — a directory that contains all the process's file descriptors

maps — contains memory maps to the process's executables and library files

mem — contains the memory held by this process

root — contains a link to the root directory of the process

stat — contains the process status

statm — contains the process memory status information

status — contains the process status in human readable format

PROC HARDWARE INFORMATION   As mentioned previously, the /proc directory also contains some useful hardware information. This information comes in handy when you compile a new kernel. If you've forgotten the specific details about your hardware, you can look through the files in the /proc directory to get information about what's installed and running on your Linux machine.

If you suspect that you're having hardware problems due to an IRQ conflict, you can also see your hardware's interrupts by looking at the /proc/interrupts file.

The interrupts file from my desktop machine at work is shown below. Each number corresponds to an IRQ. The acronyms at the end of the IRQ listing are NMI (Non-Maskable Interrupt), LOC (Local Interrupt Counter of the internal APIC of each CPU), and ERR. ERR is a counter that starts out at 0 at boot time and is incremented each time there is an error in the IO-APIC bus. The IO-APIC bus connects the CPUs in an SMP system. When an error happens, the information is immediately retransmitted, so you shouldn't worry too much about a moderate number of errors in this field.

```
[vnavrat@buffy vnavrat]$ less /proc/interrupts
          CPU0
  0:    9720704        XT-PIC  timer
  1:      30515        XT-PIC  keyboard
  2:          0        XT-PIC  cascade
  5:    9869566        XT-PIC  Crystal audio controller
  8:          1        XT-PIC  rtc
 11:    1233943        XT-PIC  usb-uhci, eth0
 12:     682220        XT-PIC  PS/2 Mouse
 14:      77739        XT-PIC  ide0
 15:    2694731        XT-PIC  ide1
NMI:          0
LOC:    9720557
ERR:          0
MIS:          0
```

In the main /proc directory, quite a few files contain detailed information on your system hardware. The kind of details listed are things such as what hardware it is, the model, and the manufacturer.

Below is the contents of the cpuinfo file in proc. This tells you what kind of processor you have, and most importantly, how fast it is.

```
[vnavrat@buffy vnavrat]$ less /proc/cpuinfo
processor       : 0
vendor_id       : GenuineIntel
cpu family      : 6
model           : 7
model name      : Pentium III (Katmai)
stepping        : 3
cpu MHz         : 498.479
cache size      : 512 KB
fdiv_bug        : no
hlt_bug         : no
f00f_bug        : no
coma_bug        : no
fpu             : yes
fpu_exception   : yes
cpuid level     : 2
wp              : yes
flags           : fpu vme de pse tsc msr pae mce cx8 apic sep mtrr
pge mca cmov
pat pse36 mmx fxsr sse
bogomips        : 992.87
```

Some important /proc files are

/proc/cpuinfo — contains info about the CPU

/proc/interrupts — tells you what interrupts are in use

/proc/scsi — tells you what kind of SCSI adapter is installed

/proc/parport — contains info about the parallel ports on your system

/proc/tty — contains info about ttys that are available and in use

/proc/apm — contains advanced power management information

/proc/bus — a directory that contains bus-specific information

/proc/devices — lists available character and block devices

/proc/dma — lists used DMS channels

/proc/filesystems — lists supported file systems

/proc/fs — contains file system parameters

/proc/ide — directory that contains information about the IDE subsystem

/proc/ioports — contains information about system I/O port usage

/proc/modules — contains a list of currently loaded modules

/proc/net — contains networking information

/proc/uptime — contains the system uptime

/proc/version — contains the system version

/DEV/PTS

/dev/pts is a lightweight version of devfs. Instead of having all the device files supported in the virtual file system, it provides support for only virtual pseudo terminal device files. /dev/pts was implemented before devfs.

DEVFS

The Device File System (devfs) is another way to access "real" character and block special devices on your root file system. The old way used major and minor numbers to register devices. devfs enables device drivers to register devices by name instead.

Linux Disk Management

This section explains some basics about disk partitioning and disk management under Linux. To see how your Linux disks are currently partitioned and what file systems are on them, look at the /etc/fstab file.

Below you can see what a simple /etc/fstab file looks like:

```
[vnavrat@buffy vnavrat]$ more /etc/fstab
LABEL=/              /                    ext3     defaults          1 1
LABEL=/boot          /boot                ext3     defaults          1 2
/dev/sda1            /dos                 auto     noauto,owner      0 0
LABEL=/home          /home                ext3     defaults          1 2
/dev/fd0             /mnt/floppy          auto     noauto,owner      0 0
LABEL=/tmp           /tmp                 ext3     defaults          1 2
LABEL=/usr           /usr                 ext3     defaults          1 2
LABEL=/var           /var                 ext3     defaults          1 2
none                 /proc                proc     defaults          0 0
none                 /dev/shm             tmpfs    defaults          0 0
none                 /dev/pts             devpts   gid=5,mode=620    0 0
/dev/sda5            swap                 swap     defaults          0 0
/dev/cdrom           /mnt/cdrom           iso9660  noauto,owner,kudzu,ro 0
0
```

To see how your Linux disks are currently partitioned and what file systems are on them, look at the /etc/fstab file.

Partitioning an x86 machine

When partitioning an x86 PC, you need to be mindful of the limitations present in the x86 architecture. You are allowed to create 4 primary partitions. Primary partitions are the only partitions that are bootable. You can create more partitions if you make logical partitions.

Logical partitions are set into a primary partition. So if you choose to make logical partitions, you are allowed to make only three primary partitions for operating system use, and the fourth partition is dedicated to hosting the logical partitions.

Mounting other OS partitions/slices

Not only can Linux read other operating systems' file systems, it can also mount disk drives from other systems and work with their partition tables. However, it is necessary to compile two options into the kernel to do this. You must have the file system support and the file partitioning support turned on in the kernel. Usually file system support is compiled as a module by default, but disk partition support usually has to be explicitly compiled.

Some common partitioning schemes that Linux supports are: x86 partitions, BSD disklabel, Solaris x86, Unixware, Alpha, OSF, SGI, and Sun.

Mounting other operating systems' partitions is helpful if you need to put a Sun hard disk into a Linux machine, for example. You may need to do this if the original Sun system has gone bad, and you need to recover the information that was on its disk, or if it's the target of a forensic computer crime investigation, and you need to copy the disk contents to another machine to preserve evidence. This method takes advantage of the fact that copying a large amount of data is much faster across a SCSI connection than across a network.

If you need to copy a large amount of raw disk data across a network, you can use the Network Block Daemon, which enables other machines to mount a disk on your machine as if it were on their machine.

When running the Network Block Daemon, make sure that you have the appropriate partition support compiled into the kernel.

Metadevices

Metadevices are virtual block devices that are made up of other block devices. An example of a metadevice is a disk array that makes many disks look like one large disk. When a disk that's mounted as a regular block device dies, then the data on it becomes unavailable. If a disk dies in a metadevice, the metadevice is still up. As long as the criteria are met for the minimum number of working devices in the metadevice, the metadevice still functions.

LOGICAL VOLUMES

Logical Volume Manager (LVM) enables you to be much more flexible with your disk usage than you can be with conventional old-style file partitions. Normally if you create a partition, you have to keep the partition at that size indefinitely.

For example, if your system logs have grown immensely, and you've run out of room on your /var partition, increasing a partition size without LVM is a big pain. You would have to get another disk drive, create a /var mount point on there too, and copy all your data from the old /var to the new /var disk location. With LVM in place, you could add another disk, and then assign that disk to be part of the /var partition. Then you'd use the LVM file system resizing tool to increase the file system size to match the new partition size.

Normally you might think of disk drives as independent entities, each containing some data space. When you use LVMs, you need a new way of thinking about disk space. First you have to understand that space on any disk can be used by any file system. A Volume Group is the term used to describe various disk spaces (either whole disks or parts of disks) that have been grouped together into one volume.

Volume groups are then bunched together to form Logical volumes. Logical volumes are akin to the historic idea of partitions. You can then use a file system creation tool such as fdisk to create a file system on the logical volume. The Linux kernel sees a logical volume in the same way it sees a regular partition.

Some Linux tools for modifying logical volumes are pvcreate for creating physical volumes, vgcreate for creating volume groups, vgdisplay for showing volume groups, and mke2fs for creating a file system on your logical volume.

RAID 1 IN SOFTWARE

RAID stands for Redundant Array of Independent Disks. RAID 1, known as disk mirroring, is a redundant RAID disk mode. A mirror of the first disk is kept on the other disks. If all disks crash but one, all data can still be recovered. To work properly, RAID1 needs two or more disks, and zero or more spare disks.

RAID 5 IN SOFTWARE

RAID 5 combines the ability to use a large number of disks while still maintaining some redundancy. It uses three or more disks, and spare disks are optional. The final RAID 5 array contains the combined file size of all disks except one. The equivalent of one disk's worth of space is taken up by the parity information, which is written evenly across all the disks.

   A RAID 5 array can survive one disk loss, but if more than one disk fails, all data is lost.

RAID IN HARDWARE

The principles of the software RAID levels also apply to hardware RAID setups. The main difference is that in hardware RAID the disks have their own RAID controller with built-in software that handles the RAID disk setup, and I/O. To Linux, the hard RAID interface is transparent, so the hardware RAID disk array looks like one giant disk.

STORAGE AREA NETWORKS

A Storage Area Network (SAN) is a high availability, high performance disk storage structure that enables several systems to store their partitions on the same large disk array. A server handles this large disk array and also such things as disk failover and regular information backup. This system provides reliable storage and fast access, since the servers are connected to the disk array through a SCSI link or through a fiber channel.

Summary

Linux supports many file systems. It supports those from other operating systems, remote file systems, memory file systems, CD-ROM file systems, virtual file systems, and metadevice file systems.

   This makes Linux very good at managing and accessing any file or file systems that you may ever come across in a multiplatform environment.

Chapter 5

Red Hat System Configuration Files

IN THIS CHAPTER

◆ Becoming familiar with the system configuration files

◆ Becoming familiar with the network configuration files

◆ Managing the init scripts

THIS CHAPTER describes the file system and configuration files in a typical Red Hat Linux server.

The system configuration files in the /etc directory are the first places a system administrator goes after installing a system to set it up. The /etc directory is probably the most often visited directory by a system administrator after their own home directory and /var/log.

All of the systemwide important configuration files are found either in /etc or in one of its many subdirectories. An advantage to keeping all system configuration files under /etc is that it's easier to restore configurations for individual programs, as opposed to having all the system's configurations rolled up into a monstrous registry hive like some operating systems.

 Be vigilant that your files in /etc are only modifiable by appropriate users. Generally this means being modifiable only by root.

Because these files are so important and their contents so sensitive (everything from users' hashed passwords to the host's ssh key are stored in /etc), it is important to keep the file permissions set properly on everything in /etc. Almost all files should be owned by root, and *nothing* should be world writable. Most files should have their file permissions set to user readable and writable, and group and world readable, like this:

```
-rw-r--r--    1 root     root         172 Aug  6 02:03 hosts
```

Some notable exceptions are files such as /etc/shadow, where users' hashed passwords are stored, and /etc/wvdial.conf, which stores dial-up account names and passwords. These files' permissions should be set to owned by root, and read by root only, like this:

```
-rw-------    1 root      root         1227 Sep  2 13:52 /etc/shadow
```

The /etc/sysconfig directory contains configuration scripts written and configured by Red Hat and Red Hat administration tools. /etc/sysconfig contains both system and networking configuration files. Putting these files in /etc/sysconfig distinguishes them from other /etc configuration files not designed by Red Hat. You should keep these files in a separate directory so that the risk of other developers writing configuration files with the same names and putting them in the same place as existing config files, is reduced.

Examining the System Configuration Files

The Red Hat system configuration files can fall within a few different functions. Some specify system duties, such as logging and automatically running programs with cron. Some set default configurations for important programs such as sendmail and Bash. And many other system configuration files are responsible for arranging the appearance of the system, such as setting the colors that show up when a directory listing is shown, and what banners pop up when someone logs in. This section discusses the more important system configuration files on your Red Hat Linux system.

Systemwide shell configuration scripts

These files determine the default environment settings of system shells and what functions are started every time a user launches a new shell.

The files discussed next are located in /etc. These configuration files affect all shells used on the system. An individual user can also set up a default configuration file in their home directory that affects only their shells. This ability is useful in case the user wants to add some extra directories to their path, or some aliases that only they use.

When used in the home directory, the names are the same, except they have a . in front of them. So /etc/bashrc affects bash shells systemwide, but /home/kelly/.bashrc effects only the shells started by user kelly.

SHELL CONFIG SCRIPTS: BASHRC, CSH.CSHRC, ZSHRC
Bashrc is read by bash, csh.cshrc is read by tcsh, and zshrc is read by zsh. These files are read every time a shell is launched, not just upon login, and they

determine the settings and behaviors of the shells on the system. These are places to put functions and aliases.

PROFILE This file is read by all shells except tcsh and csh upon login. Bash falls back to reading it if there is no bash_profile. Zsh looks for zprofile, but if there is none, it reads profile as well. Listing 5-1 shows a typical /etc/profile.

Listing 5-1: A typical /etc/profile

```
# /etc/profile

# System wide environment and startup programs
# Functions and aliases go in /etc/bashrc

if ! echo $PATH | /bin/grep -q "/usr/X11R6/bin" ; then
  PATH="$PATH:/usr/X11R6/bin"
fi

PATH=$PATH:/sbin:/usr/sbin:/usr/local/sbin

ulimit -S -c 1000000 > /dev/null 2>&1
if [ `id -gn` = `id -un` -a `id -u` -gt 14 ]; then
        umask 002
else
        umask 022
fi

USER=`id -un`
LOGNAME=$USER
MAIL="/var/spool/mail/$USER"

HOSTNAME=`/bin/hostname`
HISTSIZE=1000

if [ -z "$INPUTRC" -a ! -f "$HOME/.inputrc" ]; then
        INPUTRC=/etc/inputrc
fi

export PATH USER LOGNAME MAIL HOSTNAME HISTSIZE INPUTRC

for i in /etc/profile.d/*.sh ; do
        if [ -x $i ]; then
                . $i
        fi
done

unset i
```

profile is a good place to set paths because it is where you set environmental variables that are passed on to child processes in the shell. If you want to change the default path of your shells in profile, modify the following line:

```
PATH=$PATH:/sbin:/usr/sbin:/usr/local/sbin
```

Do not add too many paths to this line, because users can set their own paths using a .profile in their home directories. More default paths than are necessary can pose a security risk. For example, a user named katie may want to run her own version of pine that she keeps in her home directory.

In that case, she may want to have /home/$USER or /home/katie at the beginning of her path so that when she types **pine**, the version in her home directory is found by the shell first, before finding the copy of pine in /usr/bin/pine. Generally, putting /home/$USER or any other directory whose contents are not controlled by root in /etc/profile is not a good idea.

The reason for this warning is because a rogue user or cracker could compile a backdoor, a way to enter the system unexpectedly, or corrupted version of a program and somehow get it in a user's home directory, perhaps even by mailing it to them. If users' paths are set to check their home directories first, then they may think they are running a system program, but instead are unknowingly running an alternate version.

On the other hand, if this path modification is set only in katie's .profile, then only she runs this risk. She should also be aware of this risk since she has to do the extra step of adding this path modification herself.

Another useful variable to change in the system profile is the number of user commands saved in the .history file in their home directory. This command history is especially useful, since you can scroll up through your previous commands by using the up and down arrows. To change the number of commands saved in the .history file, modify this line:

```
HISTSIZE=1000
```

BASH, TCSH, ZSH AND THEIR CONFIG FILE READ ORDERS
The shells read a couple different configuration files when starting up. It is good to know which files are read in what order, so that you know where to set variables that will only apply to certain users.

BASH   bash reads the following files on startup: /etc/profile, ~/.bash_profile, ~/.bash_login, and ~/.profile. Upon logout, bash reads ~/.bash_logout.

TCSH   tcsh reads the following files when starting up: /etc/csh.cshrc, and then /etc/csh.login. After these come the config files in the user's home directory: ~/.tcshrc (or if not present, then ~/.cshrc), ~/.history, ~/.login, ~/.cshdirs.

ZSH   zsh reads the following when starting up: /etc/zshenv, ~/.zshenv, /etc/zprofile, ~/.zprofile, /etc/zshrc, ~/.zshrc, and /etc/zlogin. Nonlogin shells also read ~/.bashrc. Upon logout, zsh reads the ~/.zlogout and /etc zlogout files.

System environmental settings

The files discussed in this section deal with system environmental settings.

MOTD

This file contains the message that users see every time they log in. It's a good place to communicate messages about system downtime and other things that users should be aware of. On the other hand, you can put amusing quotes here to entertain your users. Usually the motd contains a message like:

```
Welcome to Generic University's Unix mail system.
This system is monitored. Unauthorized use prohibited.
System downtime scheduled this Sunday night from 10pm to 1am.
```

TIP   The motd file is a plain text file, but variables can be placed into the script to customize what users see when they log in. You can customize the output based on the user group, user type, or user ID number.

DIR_COLORS

Red Hat Linux enables you to view file listings in color, as long as you are using a terminal program that supports colors. This file specifies which colors should be used to display what kinds of files. By default, executable files are green, directories are dark blue, symlinks are light blue, and regular files are white.

ISSUE

Whatever is in this file shows up as a prelogin banner on your console. By default, this file tells what version of Red Hat is running on the system, and the kernel version.

The default file looks like this:

```
Red Hat Linux release 7.2 (Enigma)
Kernel \r on an \m
```

So when you log in you see this message:

```
Red Hat Linux release 7.2 (Enigma)
Kernel 2.4.10 on an i686
```

ISSUE.NET

This file generally contains the same thing as /etc/issue. It shows up when you attempt to telnet into the system. Because it shows up to people who are connecting to your system over the Internet, you should change this message to include a warning such as "Access is being monitored. Unauthorized access is prohibited." Displaying this warning is a good practice because if you want to prosecute intruders, it helps your case to show that you warned them that unauthorized access was prohibited.

ALIASES

The file /etc/mail/aliases is the e-mail aliases file for the sendmail program. By default it contains many system account aliases. The aliases file sends mail for all the basic system accounts such as bin, daemon, and operator, to root's mailbox. In sendmail versions 8.11.4 and later, this file is in /etc/mail/aliases.

Other common e-mail aliases that people make, for example, send all of root's mail to the user who commonly acts as root. So if Taleen acts as root most of the time, she can alias root's mailbox to her mailbox. This way she doesn't need to log in as root to read important system mail.

To do this she'd put the following line in the aliases file:

```
root:        taleen
```

Or if she wants to send all root mail to her account on a remote machine, the line would read:

```
root:        taleen@buffy.xena.edu
```

Whenever you make changes to this file, you need to run the newaliases command to have the changes take affect in sendmail.

DUMPDATES

If you do backups with dump, this file is important to you. dumpdates stores information about the last system backup that was done. This data helps determine what kind of backup should be done next time dump runs. It stores the name of the last file system that was backed up, the backup increment level, and the time and date it was last run.

FSTAB

fstab contains important information about your file systems, such as what file system type the partitions are, where they are located on the hard drive, and what mount point is used to access them.

This information is read by vital programs, such as mount, umount, and fsck. mount runs at start time and mounts all the file systems mentioned in the fstab file, except for those with noauto in their line. If a partition you want to access is not listed in this file, you have to mount it manually. This can get tedious, so it's better to list all of your file systems in the `fstab`. However, you should not put nfs file systems into the `fstab` file.

When `fsck` is run at bootup it also checks all the file systems listed in `fstab` for consistency. It then fixes those file systems that are corrupted, usually because they were not umounted properly when the system crashed or suddenly lost power. File systems with an `fs_passno` value of 0 (the number in the last column) are not checked at boot time. As you can see in Listing 5-2, almost all file systems are checked at startup except for the floppy drive, which is not checked by `fsck` at bootup.

The `fstab` line has six fields, and each field represents a different configuration value. The first field describes the remote file system. The second field is the mount point used to access the file system. The third field describes the file system type. The fourth field is the place for any mount options you may need. The fifth field is 0 or 1 to determine if dump backs up this file system. The final field sets the order in which fsck checks these file systems.

Listing 5-2: A typical fstab file

```
# LABEL=/             /                   ext3     defaults                1 1
# LABEL=/boot         /boot               ext2     defaults                1 2
/dev/hda5             /                   ext3     defaults                1 1
/dev/hda2             /boot               ext2     defaults                1 2
/dev/fd0             /mnt/floppy          auto     noauto,owner            0 0
none                 /proc               proc     defaults                0 0
none                 /dev/shm            tmpfs    defaults                0 0
none                 /dev/pts            devpts   gid=5,mode=620          0 0
/dev/hda3            swap                swap     defaults                0 0
/dev/hda1            /mnt/dos            vfat     noauto                  0 0
/dev/cdrom           /mnt/cdrom          iso9660  noauto,owner,kudzu,ro 0 0
/dev/cdrom1          /mnt/cdrom1         iso9660  noauto,owner,kudzu,ro 0 0
/SWAP                swap                swap     defaults                0 0
```

LILO.CONF

LILO is the boot time LInux LOader. At boot time it gives you the option of booting into different operating systems and even into different kernel versions of the Linux operating system.

The information on where operating systems should be loaded from, and which one is started by default is stored in lilo.conf. Whenever this file is changed, lilo must be run again in order for changes to take effect. If there is anything wrong with the syntax of `lilo.conf`, lilo alerts you to that problem when you run it again.

As you can see in Listing 5-3, the `lilo.conf` file is pretty simple. The first section contains general information, such as which drive is the boot drive (boot=/dev/hda), and how many tenths of a second the LILO prompt should be displayed on the screen (timeout=50, which is 5 seconds). In this `lilo.conf`, the operating system booted by default is linux (default=linux).

After the initial general preferences section you will see the boot images section. lilo.conf enables up to 16 boot images to be defined. The first image defined here is the default linux image that boots with the vmlinuz-2.4.9-ac10 kernel. Its root file system is located on the first IDE disk on the fifth partition, at /dev/hda5.

The second image defined is the Windows boot partition. If you type DOS (label=DOS) at the LILO prompt, you boot into this Windows installation. As you can see, Windows is installed on the first partition of the first IDE disk (/dev/hda1).

Listing 5-3: The lilo.conf file

```
boot=/dev/hda
map=/boot/map
install=/boot/boot.b
prompt
timeout=50
message=/boot/message
linear
default=linux

image=/boot/vmlinuz-2.4.9-ac10
        label=linux
        read-only
        root=/dev/hda5
        append="hdd=ide-scsi"

other=/dev/hda1
        optional
        label=DOS
```

GRUB.CONF

grub stands for the modest acronym GRand Unified Bootloader. It is a new boot-time operating system loader that Red Hat 7.2 encourages you to use as the default boot loader instead of lilo.

A big difference between lilo and grub is that lilo usually offers a simple text interface, while grub offers a much more elaborate graphical interface. When you make a change to lilo.conf, you must rerun lilo, but when you change grub.conf, you do not have to rerun grub. At boot time they both operate in the same fashion, giving you a basic choice between which installed kernels you want to run.

Here is a typical grub.conf file:

```
# grub.conf generated by anaconda
#
# Note that you do not have to rerun grub after making changes to
        this file
# NOTICE:  You have a /boot partition.  This means that
```

```
#        all kernel and initrd paths are relative to /boot/, eg.
#        root (hd0,1)
#        kernel /vmlinuz-version ro root=/dev/sda8
#        initrd /initrd-version.img
#boot=/dev/sda
default=0
timeout=10
splashimage=(hd0,1)/grub/splash.xpm.gz
title Red Hat Linux (2.4.16)
        root (hd0,1)
        kernel /vmlinuz-2.4.16 ro root=/dev/hda5 hdd=ide-scsi
title Red Hat Linux (2.4.9-13)
        root (hd0,1)
        kernel /vmlinuz-2.4.9-13 ro root=/dev/hda5 hdd=ide-scsi
        initrd /initrd-2.4.9-13.img
title DOS
        rootnoverify (hd0,0)
        chainloader +1
```

As you can see, the default=0 line indicates that the first kernel section (2.4.16) should be booted by default. grub starts its counting at 0 instead of 1. The title line contains the label that will be shown in the boot menu for that kernel. The root line specifies that Linux will be booted off the first hard drive. The kernel line indicates the kernel's location on the file system.

In the DOS title section, notice that grub is calling a chain loader to be used for loading DOS. This is because grub doesn't support loading DOS. grub uses a chain loader to load any operating system that it doesn't support.

CRON FILES

cron is a daemon that executes commands according to a preset schedule that a user defines. It wakes up every minute and checks all cron files to see what jobs need to be run at that time. cron files can be set up by users or by the administrator to take care of system tasks. Basically a user edits their crontab file by telling cron what program they'd like run automatically and how often they'd like it to be run.

User crontab files are stored in /var/spool/cron/. They are named after the user they belong to. System cron files are stored in the following subdirectories of /etc directory:

cron.d

cron.daily

cron.hourly

cron.monthly

cron.weekly

crontab in the /etc directory is sort of the master control file that is set up to run all the scripts in the cron.daily directory on a daily basis, all the scripts in the cron.hourly directory on an hourly bases, and so on with cron.monthly and cron.weekly.

cron.d is where system maintenance files that need to be run on a different schedule than the other /etc cron files are kept. By default, a file in cron.d called sysstat runs a system activity accounting tool every 10 minutes, 24 x 7.

 Chapter 20 explains the cron command in more detail.

SYSLOG.CONF

The syslog daemon logs any notable events on your local system. It can store these logs in a local file or send them to a remote log host for added security. It can also accept logs from other machines when acting as a remote log host. All these options and more, such as how detailed the logging should be, are set in the syslog.conf file.

Listing 5-4 is an excerpt that demonstrates the syntax and logic of the syslog.conf file. The first entry specifies that all messages that are severity level info or higher should be logged in the /var/log/messages file.

Also indicated by the first entry is that any mail, news, private authentication, and cron messages should be logged elsewhere. Having separate log files makes it easier to search through logs if they are separated by type or program. The lines following this one specify the other places where those messages should be logged.

Authentication privilege messages are somewhat sensitive information, so they are logged to /var/log/secure. That file can be read by root only, whereas /var/log/messages is sometimes set to be readable by everyone, or at least has less stringent access control. By default, /var/log/messages is set to be read by root only as well.

All mail messages are logged to /var/log/maillog, and cron messages are saved at /var/log/cron. uucp and critical-level news daemon log messages are saved to /var/log/spooler. All of these log files are set by default to be readable by root only. Emergency messages are sent to all the log files listed in the syslog.conf file, including to the console.

Listing 5-4: An excerpt from the /etc/syslog.conf file

```
# Log anything (except mail) of level info or higher.
# Don't log private authentication messages!
*.info;mail.none;news.none;authpriv.none;cron.none
/var/log/messages

# The authpriv file has restricted access.
```

```
authpriv.*                                              /var/log/secure

# Log all the mail messages in one place.
mail.*                                                  /var/log/maillog


# Log cron stuff
cron.*                                                  /var/log/cron


# Everybody gets emergency messages
*.emerg                                                           *


# Save news errors of level crit and higher in a special file.
uucp,news.crit                                          /var/log/spooler
```

LD.SO.CONF

This configuration file is used by ldconfig. ldconfig configures dynamic linker run-time bindings. It contains a listing of directories that hold shared libraries. Shared library files typically end with .so, whereas static library files typically end with .a, indicating they are an archive of objects.

You may need to edit this file if you've installed a program that has installed a shared library to a different library directory that is not listed in the ld.so.conf file. In this case you get an error at runtime that the library does not exist.

An additional troubleshooting step to take in that case is to run ldd on the executable in question, which prints shared library dependencies. The output would look something like this:

```
[root@buffy lib]# ldd /bin/bash
/bin/sh: error while loading shared libraries: libtermcap.so.2:
cannot open shared
 object file: No such file or directory
```

To fix this problem, confirm that you do have the correct library installed, and add its directory to the ld.so.conf file, so that it will be found. You can see a default listing of library directories in Listing 5-5.

Listing 5-5: A typical ld.so.conf file

```
/usr/lib
/usr/kerberos/lib
/usr/X11R6/lib
/usr/lib/mysql
/usr/local/lib
/usr/local/lib/oms/plugins
```

Continued

Listing 5-5 *(Continued)*

```
/usr/i486-linux-libc5/lib
/usr/lib/sane
/usr/lib/qt-1.45/lib

/usr/lib/qt-3.0.0/lib
/usr/lib/qt-2.3.1/lib


/usr/lib/wine
```

LOGROTATE.CONF

`logrotate.conf` and the files within `logrotate.d` determine how often your log files are rotated by the logrotate program. logrotate can automatically rotate, compress, remove, and mail your log files. Log files can be rotated based on size or on time, such as daily, weekly, or monthly.

As you can see from the `default logrotate.conf` file shown in Listing 5-6, most of the options set for how and when to rotate the system logs are pretty self-explanatory.

For every program that has a separate log rotation configuration file in `logrotate.d`, and uses `syslogd` for logging, there also has to be a corresponding entry for that program in `syslog.conf`. This is because syslog needs to save log entries for these programs in separate files so that their log files can be rotated independently from one another.

Listing 5-6: The logrotate.conf file

```
# see "man logrotate" for details
# rotate log files weekly
weekly

# keep 4 weeks worth of backlogs
rotate 4

# create new (empty) log files after rotating old ones
create

# uncomment this if you want your log files compressed
#compress

# RPM packages drop log rotation information into this directory
include /etc/logrotate.d

# no packages own lastlog or wtmp -- we'll rotate them here
/var/log/wtmp {
```

```
monthly
create 0664 root utmp
rotate 1
}
```

System configuration files in the /etc/sysconfig directory

The system configuration files in the /etc/sysconfig directory are quite varied. These files set the parameters used by many of the system hardware devices, as well as the operation of some system services. The files discussed in this section are only a few of the many files in this directory.

APMD

apmd contains configuration information for the advanced power management daemon to follow. This is most useful for laptops rather than servers, since it contains lots of settings to suspend your linux machine, and restore it again.

Some settings in this file include when you should be warned that battery power is getting low, and if Linux should synch with the hardware clock when the machine comes back from suspend mode.

CLOCK

This file contains information on which time zone the machine is set to, and whether or not it is using Greenwich Mean Time for its system clock time.

AMD

amd is the file system automounter daemon. It automatically mounts an unmounted file system whenever a file or directory within that file system is accessed. File systems are automatically unmounted again after a period of disuse.

This file is where you would add amd options to be run every time by amd. Options include specifying where amd activity should be logged, and specifying how long amd should wait before umounting an idle file system.

UPS

This file contains information on what UPS is attached to your system. You can specify your UPS model, to make it easier for the Linux system to communicate with your UPS when the UPS needs to shut down the system.

Examining the Network Configuration Files

This section discusses the following topics:

◆ Files to change when setting up a system or moving the system

◆ Starting up network services from xinetd

◆ Starting up network services from the rc scripts

◆ Other important network configuration files in the `/etc/sysconfig` directory

Files to change when setting up a system or moving the system

Whenever you set up a system to work on a new network, either because you've just installed Red Hat or you're moving the machine from one location to another, a set of files need to be modified to get it working on the new network.

You need to:

◆ Set up the IP addresses of your network interfaces. Make changes to:

`/etc/sysconfig/network-scripts/ifcfg-eth0`

`/etc/sysconfig/network-scripts/ifcfg-eth1`

◆ Set up the hostname of your machine. Make changes to:

`/etc/sysconfig/network`

`/etc/hosts`

◆ Set up a default gateway. Make changes to:

`/etc/default-route`

◆ Set up the DNS servers to reference. Make changes to:

`/etc/resolv.conf`

◆ Make a local file of hostname to IP address mappings. Make changes to:

`/etc/hosts`

◆ Set up the device order from which hostnames are looked up. Make changes to:

`/etc/nsswitch.conf`

Chapter 12 explains the Domain Name System (DNS) and how to set it up on your network.

TIP Red Hat Linux provides a handy graphical tool for configuring your network settings called the Red Hat Network Administration tool, or neat. Start up neat while in X-Windows, and enjoy an interface very similar to the Windows control panel for networks.

SETTING UP THE IP ADDRESS

The first thing you should do is set an IP address on your network interfaces. This step provides your computer with an identity on the network. If you haven't set the IP address already in the installation process, you need to edit the configuration files by hand.

To set the IP address on your first Ethernet interface eth0, edit the /etc/syscon-fig/network-scripts/ifcfg-eth0 file. A copy of this file is shown in Listing 5-7.

Insert your interface's IP address on the line that says:

```
IPADDR="192.168.1.10"
```

You should also check that the rest of the lines look alright, but pay special attention to the following two lines:

```
BROADCAST=192.168.1.255
NETMASK="255.255.255.0"
```

Listing 5-7: The /etc/sysconfig/network-scripts/ifcfg-eth0 file

```
DEVICE="eth0"
BOOTPROTO="none"
BROADCAST=192.168.1.255
IPADDR="192.168.1.10"
NETMASK="255.255.255.0"
NETWORK=192.168.1.0
ONBOOT="yes"
USERCTL=no
IPXNETNUM_802_2=""
IPXPRIMARY_802_2="no"
IPXACTIVE_802_2="no"
IPXNETNUM_802_3=""
IPXPRIMARY_802_3="no"
IPXACTIVE_802_3="no"
IPXNETNUM_ETHERII=""
IPXPRIMARY_ETHERII="no"
IPXACTIVE_ETHERII="no"
```

Continued

Listing 5-7 *(Continued)*

```
IPXNETNUM_SNAP=""
IPXPRIMARY_SNAP="no"
IPXACTIVE_SNAP="no"
```

SETTING UP THE HOSTNAME

Once you've picked your hostname, you need to put it into two different places: /etc/sysconfig/network and /etc/hosts.

In /etc/sysconfig/network, shown next, change the line that says:

```
HOSTNAME="buffy"
```

This is the /etc/sysconfig/network file:

```
NETWORKING=yes
HOSTNAME="buffy"
GATEWAY="192.168.1.1"
GATEWAYDEV="eth0"
FORWARD_IPV4="yes"
```

You also need to modify the /etc/hosts file. Change the first line in the file, which would look something like this:

```
127.0.0.1       buffy     localhost.localdomain localhost locala localb localc
```

SETTING UP A DEFAULT GATEWAY

Now that you've given your machine an identity on the network, you need to tell it where to send all its traffic. Ideally this would be a switch or a router that takes all your traffic in the direction of the Internet and the rest of your network, otherwise known as your default gateway.

This setting rarely changes, unless you've moved your machine to a different part of the network. It is very important that it is correct. Change the /etc/default-route file to contain just the IP address of the gateway, like this:

```
192.168.1.1
```

SETTING UP THE DNS SERVERS

Now you should be able to communicate with the other hosts on the network. However you won't be able to talk to them unless you know their IP addresses, because you haven't set up what DNS servers you should reference to map hostnames to IP addresses.

The program that resolves hostnames to IP addresses reads a file called resolv.conf, so you need to put your DNS server IP addresses there. Generally you need one nameserver, but you can include up to three, if you'd like. Specifying more than one name server is important. If the first one on the list is not responding, your computer tries to resolve against the next one on the list, until it finds one that is responding.

Edit /etc/resolv.conf to contain a list of nameservers, like so:

```
nameserver 1.2.3.4
nameserver 1.2.3.5
nameserver 1.2.3.6
```

MAKING A LOCAL FILE OF HOSTNAME TO IP ADDRESS MAPPINGS

Linux gives you the ability to store a list of hostnames and their corresponding IP addresses in /etc/hosts, so that you don't have to look them up in DNS every time you use them. While you shouldn't do this with every hostname you ever use, one of the advantages gained by configuring often-used hostnames in this way includes the ability to alias a fully qualified hostname to a shorter version of itself. So instead of typing out **ssh foo.xena.edu** every time you want to ssh to that machine, you can just type **ssh foo**, and have it connect to the same host.

Another useful example occurs if you're monitoring several servers' network services from a monitoring host. If you're monitoring ssh connectivity to certain servers, for example, and your DNS server stops responding, then the monitoring software may report that all your hosts are down. This happens because the monitoring software tries to connect to the server via its hostname, and gets no response because DNS is not providing it with an IP address to connect to. In this case it looks like your whole network fell over, when the real problem is that your DNS service is not responding properly.

To keep this kind of scenario from happening, you should put the hostnames and IP addresses of all your monitored servers in /etc/hosts. This way, your monitoring software looks into /etc/hosts to get the proper IP addresses, instead of relying on DNS.

The only caveat to keep in mind when putting hosts in /etc/hosts is that if the hostname's IP address changes for whatever reason, the hosts file does not automatically update to reflect that change. If you start getting connection errors when connecting to a host in the /etc/hosts file, you should do an nslookup on the host and update your /etc/hosts file accordingly.

Your /etc/hosts file should contain IP address to hostname mappings that follow this format:

```
IP_address canonical_hostname aliases
```

So that the lines look like this:

```
192.168.1.66    foo.xena.edu      foo
192.168.1.76    buffy.xena.edu    buffy
152.2.210.81    sunsite.unc.edu   sunsite
```

SETTING UP THE DEVICE ORDER FROM WHICH HOSTNAMES ARE LOOKED UP

Now that you've set up your DNS servers and hosts file, you need to tell your Linux server which method it should use first to look up hostnames.

The place to set up this configuration is in the `/etc/nsswitch.conf` file. Edit the following line:

```
hosts:       files nisplus dns
```

The order of the words *files*, *nisplus*, and *dns* determines which method is checked first. Files refers to the `/etc/hosts` file, nisplus refers to any nisplus servers you may have on your network, and dns refers to any DNS servers you have set up your machine to reference.

As you can see in Listing 5-8, the `/etc/nsswitch.conf` file contains some other useful settings. Other useful settings are the following two lines, which specify whether the server should authenticate users off the local password file or off the network's NIS plus service:

```
passwd:      files nisplus
shadow:      files nisplus
```

Listing 5-8: The /etc/nsswitch.conf file

```
#
# /etc/nsswitch.conf
#
# An example Name Service Switch config file. This file should be
# sorted with the most-used services at the beginning.
#
# The entry '[NOTFOUND=return]' means that the search for an
# entry should stop if the search in the previous entry turned
# up nothing. Note that if the search failed due to some other reason
# (like no NIS server responding) then the search continues with the
# next entry.
#
# Legal entries are:
#
#       nisplus or nis+       Use NIS+ (NIS version 3)
#       nis or yp             Use NIS (NIS version 2), also called YP
#       dns                   Use DNS (Domain Name Service)
#       files                 Use the local files
#       db                    Use the local database (.db) files
#       compat                Use NIS on compat mode
#       hesiod                Use Hesiod for user lookups
#       [NOTFOUND=return]     Stop searching if not found so far
#
```

```
# To use db, put the "db" in front of "files" for entries you want to be
# looked up first in the databases
#
# Example:
#passwd:     db files nisplus nis
#shadow:     db files nisplus nis
#group:      db files nisplus nis

passwd:      files nisplus
shadow:      files nisplus
group:       files nisplus

#hosts:      db files nisplus nis dns
hosts:       files nisplus dns

# Example - obey only what nisplus tells us...
#services:   nisplus [NOTFOUND=return] files
#networks:   nisplus [NOTFOUND=return] files
#protocols:  nisplus [NOTFOUND=return] files
#rpc:        nisplus [NOTFOUND=return] files
#ethers:     nisplus [NOTFOUND=return] files
#netmasks:   nisplus [NOTFOUND=return] files

bootparams: nisplus [NOTFOUND=return] files

ethers:      files
netmasks:    files
networks:    files
protocols:   files nisplus
rpc:         files
services:    files nisplus

netgroup:    files nisplus

publickey:   nisplus

automount:   files nisplus
aliases:     files nisplus
```

Starting up network services from xinetd

xinetd is Red Hat 7.1's replacement for inetd. xinetd is started on bootup, and listens on ports designated in the /etc/xinetd.conf for incoming network connections. When a new connection is made, xinetd starts up the corresponding network service.

You should disable any unnecessary services from being started from `xinetd` as part of securing your machine. The way to do this is to edit that service's configuration file. `xinetd`'s main configuration file is `/etc/xinetd.conf`. At the end of the `xinetd.conf` file is a line that indicates that all the files in the `/etc/xinetd.d` are also included in the configuration. This means that you need to go through the files in that directory as well in order to turn off any services you don't want.

So, to disable telnet, you would look in `/etc/xinetd.d` for a file called 'telnet'. The `telnet` file is shown in Figure 5-9. Edit the line in the config file that says disable = no, and change that to disable = yes, as it appears in Listing 5-9. Once that line is set to disable = yes, the service is disabled and does not start up the next time you boot up.

Listing 5-9: The telnet config file in the xinetd.d directory

```
/etc/xinetd.d/telnet

# default: on
# description: The telnet server serves telnet sessions; it uses \
#       unencrypted username/password pairs for authentication.
service telnet
{
        flags           = REUSE
        socket_type     = stream
        wait            = no
        user            = root
        server          = /usr/sbin/in.telnetd
        log_on_failure  += USERID
        disable         = yes
}
```

An automated tool, called `chkconfig`, manages what services are started from `xinetd` and the rc scripts. You can read more about chkconfig in the section called "Managing rc Scripts Using chkconfig."

Starting up network services from the rc scripts

Network services that are not started out of `xinetd` are started out of the rc scripts at boot time. Network services started at the default boot level 3 (multiuser networked mode) are started out of the `/etc/rc3.d` directory. If you look in that directory, you should see a file with the name of the service you want to stop or start. The script to start the service starts with an S, and the kill script starts with a K.

So for example, ssh is started from `/etc/rc3.d  /S55sshd`, and killed upon shutdown from `/etc/rc6.d/K25sshd`. Runlevel 6 is the shutdown level, so that's why its kill script is located in the `rc6.d` directory.

Detailed information on managing all of the services started at boot time can be found in the section "Managing the init Scripts."

Other important network configuration files in the /etc/sysconfig directory

You can use the files listed in this section to create routes to other hosts, either on your own network, or on outside networks. You also can use these files to set up firewall rules for your network to either allow or disallow connections to your network.

STATIC-ROUTES

If you want to set up some static routes on your machine, you can do so in the static-routes file. This config file has lines that follow the format of:

```
network-interface net network netmask netmask gw gateway
```

IPTABLES

iptables is the next generation Linux firewall. It supercedes the ipchains firewall. It can use ipchains rules as a component of its firewall filtering, but iptables and ipchains cannot be run at the same time.

This is the file where the iptables rules are stored. iptables syntax is very similar to the ipchains syntax, which is briefly explained by the following example.

IPCHAINS

ipchains is a Linux firewall that is now being superceded by iptables. The GUI interface that configures the ipchains firewall rules is firewall-config. The ipchains rules are stored in the ipchains file.

When you install Red Hat, it asks if you would like to set up a host-based firewall. If you select a medium or heavy security host-based firewall, a default set of ipchains rules installs according to your preferences.

The following is a simplified configuration file. The gist of this configuration is that all incoming traffic to privileged ports (those below 1024) is dropped except for ssh traffic. The first line accepts all traffic from the loopback interface. The second line accepts all incoming TCP traffic to the ssh port. The third line drops all incoming TCP traffic to ports between 1 and 1024. The last line drops all incoming UDP traffic to ports between 1 and 1024.

```
-A INPUT -i lo -j ACCEPT
-A INPUT -p tcp --dport 22 -p tcp -j ACCEPT
-A INPUT -p tcp -s ! 192.168.1.0/24 --dport 1:1024 -j DROP
-A INPUT -p udp -s ! 192.168.1.0/24 --dport 1:1024 -j DROP
```

Network configuration files in /etc/sysconfig/network-scripts

You can use the files in this directory to set the parameters for the hardware and software used for networking. The scripts contained here are used to enable network interfaces and set other network related parameters.

IFCFG-NETWORKINTERFACENAME

A few files fall into this specification. Red Hat specifies a separate configuration file for each network interface. In a typical Red Hat install you might have many different network interface config files that all follow the same basic syntax and format.

You could have ifcfg-eth0 for your first Ethernet interface, ifcfg-irlan0 for your infrared network port, ifcfg-lo for the network loop-back interface, and ifcfg-ppp0 for your PPP network interface.

IFUP AND IFDOWN

These files are symlinks to `/sbin/ifup` and `/sbin/ifdown`. In future releases, these symlinks might be phased out. But for now, these scripts call any other necessary scripts from within the network-scripts directory. These should be the only scripts you call from this directory.

You call these scripts with the name of the interface that you want to bring up or down. If these scripts are called at boot time, then "boot" is used as the second argument. For instance, to bring your Ethernet interface down and then up again after boot, you would type:

```
ifup eth0
ifdown eth0
```

Managing the init Scripts

This section discusses the following topics:

- ◆ Managing rc scripts by hand
- ◆ Managing rc scripts using `chkconfig`

Init scripts determine what programs start up at boot time. Red Hat and other Unix distributions have different runlevels, so there are a different set of programs that are started at each runlevel.

Usually Red Hat Linux starts up in multiuser mode with networking turned on. These are some of the other runlevels available:

- ◆ 0 – Halt
- ◆ 1 – Single-user mode
- ◆ 2 – Multiuser mode, without networking
- ◆ 3 – Full multiuser mode
- ◆ 4 – Not used
- ◆ 5 – Full multiuser mode (with an X-based login screen)
- ◆ 6 – Reboot

The system boots into the default runlevel set in /etc/inittab (see List-ing 5-10).

 In Red Hat Linux, the default boot level is 3. When booting into an X-windows login, the default boot level is 5.

Listing 5-10: A default /etc/inittab file

```
#
# inittab        This file describes how the INIT process should set up
#                the system in a certain run-level.
#
# Author:        Miquel van Smoorenburg, <miquels@drinkel.nl.mugnet.org>
#                Modified for RHS Linux by Marc Ewing and Donnie Barnes
#


# Default runlevel. The runlevels used by RHS are:
#   0 - halt (Do NOT set initdefault to this)
#   1 - Single user mode
#   2 - Multiuser, without NFS (The same as 3, if you do not have networking)
#   3 - Full multiuser mode
#   4 - unused
#   5 - X11
#   6 - reboot (Do NOT set initdefault to this)
#
id:5:initdefault:

# System initialization.
si::sysinit:/etc/rc.d/rc.sysinit

l0:0:wait:/etc/rc.d/rc 0
l1:1:wait:/etc/rc.d/rc 1
l2:2:wait:/etc/rc.d/rc 2
l3:3:wait:/etc/rc.d/rc 3
l4:4:wait:/etc/rc.d/rc 4
l5:5:wait:/etc/rc.d/rc 5
l6:6:wait:/etc/rc.d/rc 6

# Things to run in every runlevel.
ud::once:/sbin/update
```

Continued

Listing 5-10 *(Continued)*

```
# Trap CTRL-ALT-DELETE
ca::ctrlaltdel:/sbin/shutdown -t3 -r now

# When our UPS tells us power has failed, assume we have a few minutes
# of power left.  Schedule a shutdown for 2 minutes from now.
# This does, of course, assume you have powerd installed and your
# UPS connected and working correctly.
pf::powerfail:/sbin/shutdown -f -h +2 "Power Failure; System Shutting Down"

# If power was restored before the shutdown kicked in, cancel it.
pr:12345:powerokwait:/sbin/shutdown -c "Power Restored; Shutdown Cancelled"

# Run gettys in standard runlevels
1:2345:respawn:/sbin/mingetty tty1
2:2345:respawn:/sbin/mingetty tty2
3:2345:respawn:/sbin/mingetty tty3
4:2345:respawn:/sbin/mingetty tty4
5:2345:respawn:/sbin/mingetty tty5
6:2345:respawn:/sbin/mingetty tty6

# Run xdm in runlevel 5
# xdm is now a separate service
x:5:respawn:/etc/X11/prefdm -nodaemon
```

Managing rc scripts by hand

If you want to configure what services are started at boot time, you need to edit the rc scripts for the appropriate runlevel. The default runlevel is 3, which is full multi-user mode. So to change what services are started in the default runlevel, you should edit the scripts found in /etc/rc3.d.

When you look at a directory listing of the rc directories, notice that the files either start with S or K. The files that start with S are startup files, and the files that start with K are kill files. The S scripts are run in the numerical order listed in their filenames.

Note that case is important. Scripts that do not start with a capital S do not run upon startup. So one good way to keep scripts from starting up at boot time without deleting them is to rename the file with a small s at the beginning instead of a capital S. This way you can always put the script back into the startup configuration by capitalizing the initial letter.

When the system starts up, it runs through the scripts in the rc directory of the runlevel it's starting up in. So when the system starts up in runlevel 3, it runs the scripts in the /etc/rc3.d directory.

Looking at the directory listing included in Listing 5-11, you can see that the first few services start in this order: kudzu, reconfig, iptables, and network. That is because their scripts are named S05kudzu, S06reconfig, S08iptables, and S10network, respectively.

Kudzu is called first because it detects new hardware. Reconfig runs to put into effect any changes made with the chkconfig tool. Iptables then starts up the built-in firewall. Network then brings up the system's network interfaces. As you can see, the order in which these services are started makes a lot of sense, and their order is enforced by the way their rc startup scripts are named.

Listing 5-11: A directory listing of the r3.d directory

```
[root@buffy rc3.d]# ls
K05innd          K20rwhod        K50xinetd    K74ypserv    K92ipvsadm    S60lpd
K08vmware        K25squid        K54pxe       K74ypxfrd    K92upsd       S83iscsi
K09junkbuster    K28amd          K55routed    K75gated     K96irda       S90crond
K10fonttastic    K30mcserv       K61ldap      K75netfs     S05kudzu      S90xfs
K12mysqld        K30sendmail     K65identd    K84bgpd      S06reconfig   S91atalk
K15gpm           K34yppasswdd    K65kadmin    K84ospf6d    S08iptablesS95anacron
K15httpd         K35smb          K65kprop     K84ospfd     S10network    S97rhnsd
K15postgresql    K35vncserver    K65krb524    K84ripd      S12syslog     S99linuxconf
K16rarpd         K40mars-nwe     K65krb5kdc   K84ripngd    S17keytable   S99local
K20bootparamd    K45arpwatch     K73ypbind    K85zebra     S20random     S99wine
K20nfs           K45named        K74apmd      K86nfslock   S28autofs
K20rstatd        K46radvd        K74nscd      K87portmap   S40atd
K20rusersd       K50snmpd        K74ntpd      K91isdn      S55sshd
K20rwalld        K50tux          K74ups       K92ipchains  S56rawdevices
[root@buffy rc3.d]#
```

The S scripts are started in this order until they have all been started. When the system shuts down, the corresponding K, or kill scripts are run to shut down the services started from the rc directory. In general, every S script should have a corresponding K script to kill the service at shutdown.

If you can't find the corresponding K script in the startup directory, it is probably located in the shutdown directory. When the system is shut down, it enters runlevel 6. So most of the K scripts are in /etc/rc6.d. A typical /etc/rc6.d directory listing is shown in Listing 5-12.

Listing 5-12: The file contents of the /etc/rc6.d directory

```
[root@buffy rc6.d]# ls
K00linuxconf    K16rarpd        K34yppasswdd    K55routed    K74nscd      K85zebra
K03rhnsd        K20bootparamd   K35atalk        K60atd       K74ntpd      K86nfslock
K05anacron      K20iscsi        K35smb          K60crond     K74ups       K87portmap
K05innd         K20nfs          K35vncserver    K60lpd       K74ypserv    K88syslog
K05keytable     K20rstatd       K40mars-nwe     K61ldap      K74ypxfrd    K90network
K08vmware       K20rusersd      K44rawdevices   K65identd    K75gated     K91isdn
```

Continued

Listing 5-12 *(Continued)*

```
K09junkbuster   K20rwalld      K45arpwatch    K65kadmin    K75netfs     K92ipchains
K10wine         K20rwhod       K45named       K65kprop     K80random    K92ipvsadm
K10xfs          K25squid       K46radvd       K65krb524    K84bgpd      K95kudzu
K12mysqld       K25sshd        K50snmpd       K65krb5kdc   K84ospf6d    K95reconfig
K15gpm          K28amd         K50tux         K72autofs    K84ospfd     K96irda
K15httpd        K30mcserv      K50xinetd      K73ypbind    K84ripd      S00killall
K15postgresql   K30sendmail    K54pxe         K74apmd      K84ripngd    S01reboot
```

If you ever need to restart a service that's started from an rc directory, an easy way to do it properly is to run its startup script with the restart option. This procedure enables all the proper steps to be followed (configuration files read, lock files released, and so forth) when the service starts up again. So to restart syslog, for example, run the following command from the rc directory:

```
[root@buffy rc3.d]# ./S12syslog restart
Shutting down kernel logger:                               [  OK  ]
Shutting down system logger:                               [  OK  ]
Starting system logger:                                    [  OK  ]
Starting kernel logger:                                    [  OK  ]
```

Managing rc scripts using chkconfig

Red Hat 7.2 comes with a useful tool called chkconfig. It helps the system administrator manage rc scripts and xinetd configuration files without having to manipulate them directly. It is inspired by the chkconfig command included in the IRIX operating system.

Type **chkconfig --list** to see all the services chkconfig knows about, and whether they are stopped or started in each runlevel. An abridged example output is shown in the following listing. The chkconfig output can be a lot longer than that listed here, so be prepared to pipe it through less or more.

The first column is the name of the installed service. The next seven columns each represent a runlevel, and tell you whether that service is turned on or off in that runlevel.

Since xinetd is started on the system whose chkconfig output is excerpted, at the end of chkconfig's report is a listing of what xinetd started services are configured to begin at boot time. The listing is abridged, since a lot of services can be started from xinetd, and there's no need to show all of them.

Listing 5-13 shows how chkconfig can be an effective tool for handling all your network services and controlling which ones get started up at boot time. This is the output of chkconfig --list:

Listing 5-13: Output from chkconfig --list

```
atd            0:off    1:off    2:off    3:on     4:on     5:on     6:off
rwhod          0:off    1:off    2:off    3:off    4:off    5:off    6:off
keytable       0:off    1:on     2:on     3:on     4:on     5:on     6:off
nscd           0:off    1:off    2:off    3:off    4:off    5:off    6:off
syslog         0:off    1:off    2:on     3:on     4:on     5:on     6:off
gpm            0:off    1:off    2:on     3:off    4:off    5:off    6:off
kudzu          0:off    1:off    2:off    3:on     4:on     5:on     6:off
kdcrotate      0:off    1:off    2:off    3:off    4:off    5:off    6:off
lpd            0:off    1:off    2:on     3:on     4:on     5:on     6:off
autofs         0:off    1:off    2:off    3:on     4:on     5:on     6:off
sendmail       0:off    1:off    2:on     3:off    4:off    5:off    6:off
rhnsd          0:off    1:off    2:off    3:on     4:on     5:on     6:off
netfs          0:off    1:off    2:off    3:off    4:off    5:off    6:off
network        0:off    1:off    2:on     3:on     4:on     5:on     6:off
random         0:off    1:off    2:on     3:on     4:on     5:on     6:off
rawdevices     0:off    1:off    2:off    3:on     4:on     5:on     6:off
apmd           0:off    1:off    2:on     3:off    4:off    5:off    6:off
ipchains       0:off    1:off    2:off    3:off    4:off    5:off    6:off

<snip>

xinetd based services:
        rexec:  off
        rlogin: off
        rsh:    off
        chargen:        off
        chargen-udp:    off
        daytime:        off
        daytime-udp:    off
        echo:   off
        echo-udp:       off
        time:   off
        time-udp:       off
        finger: off
        ntalk:  off
        talk:   off
        telnet: off
        wu-ftpd:        on
        rsync:  off
        eklogin:        off
        gssftp: off
        klogin: off
```

To turn a service off or on using chkconfig, use this syntax:

```
chkconfig servicename off|on|reset
```

So to turn off the ftp daemon turned on previously, type:

```
chkconfig wu-ftpd off
```

To turn on xinetd, type:

```
chkconfig xinetd on
```

Run `chkconfig --list` again to see if the service you changed has been set to the state you desire. Changes you make with chkconfig take place the next time you boot up the system.

Summary

All systemwide configuration files are located in `/etc`. So if you want to change something across the system, look in `/etc` and its subdirectories first. If you're at a loss in terms of figuring out which configuration file you need to edit, try grepping for keywords in `/etc`.

To change configuration variables for one or a few users, you can usually edit configuration files within the individual users' home directories. Most configuration files in home directories start with a . so you need to look for them with the `ls -a` command.

Be mindful of configuration file permissions, to ensure that unauthorized parties cannot modify them. Flat out instant root access for unauthorized parties is one possible outcome of a modified configuration file. A more likely outcome is that a configuration file modification would make it easier for a system compromise to take place.

You can either edit startup files by hand, or by using one of Red Hat Linux's useful system administration tools such as chkconfig. You should at least know the format of the startup files and where they are, so that if automatic tools can't do the job for some reason, you can always change things yourself.

Part II

Red Hat Linux Network Services

IN THIS PART:

This part provides a detailed discussion of the network services available in Red Hat Linux. The chapters explain the TCP/IP protocol suite, the Network File System, and the Network Information System. This part also explains how to connect your Red Hat Linux network to Windows and Apple networks.

Chapter 6

TCP/IP Networking

IN THIS CHAPTER

- ◆ TCP/IP explained

- ◆ Understanding network classes

- ◆ Setting up a network interface card (NIC)

- ◆ Understanding subnetting

- ◆ Working with Classless InterDomain routing (CIDR)

- ◆ Working with Gateways and routers

- ◆ Configuring DHCP

- ◆ Configuring a point-to-point protocol (PPP) connection

- ◆ Configuring IP masquerading

THIS CHAPTER provides an overview of the TCP/IP protocols as they apply to networking with Red Hat Linux. TCP/IP is complex and many books have been written on this topic alone. If you want to learn more about TCP/IP, a good place to start is to use one of the Internet search engines to search for this topic on the Internet. After the description of TCP/IP, this chapter explains how to configure such a network in a Red Hat Linux environment.

TCP/IP Explained

TCP/IP is an acronym for Transmission Control Protocol/Internet Protocol, and refers to a family of protocols used for computer communications. TCP and IP are just two of the separate protocols contained in the group of protocols developed by the Department of Defense, sometimes called the DoD Suite, but more commonly known as TCP/IP.

In addition to Transmission Control Protocol and Internet Protocol, this family also includes Address Resolution Protocol (ARP), Domain Name System (DNS), Internet Control Message Protocol (ICMP), User Datagram Protocol (UDP), Routing Information Protocol (RIP), Simple Mail Transfer Protocol (SMTP), Telnet and many others. These protocols provide the necessary services for basic network functionality, and you will take a closer look at them for a better understanding of how the network works.

To be able to send and receive information on the network, each device connected to it must have an address. The address of any device on the network must be unique and have a standard, defined format by which it is known to any other device on the network. This device address consists of two parts:

◆ the address of the network to which the device is connected

◆ the address of the device itself – its node or host address

Devices that are physically connected to each other (not separated by routers) would have the same network number but different node, or host numbers. This would be typical of an internal network at a company or university. These types of networks are now often referred to as *intranets*.

The two unique addresses I've been talking about are typically called the *network layer* addresses and the *Media Access Control (MAC)* addresses. Network Layer addresses are IP addresses that have been assigned to the device. The MAC address is built into the card by the manufacturer and refers to only the lowest level address by which all data is transferred between devices.

Now that you know a little about addressing, you need to learn how the address, and also the data, is transmitted across the network. This transfer is accomplished by breaking the information into small pieces of data called packets or datagrams. Why is it necessary to use packets instead of just sending the entire message as one long stream of data? There are two reasons for this – sharing resources and error correction.

Let's look at the first, sharing resources. If two computers are communicating with each other, the line is busy. If these computers were sharing a large amount of data, other devices on the network would be unable to transfer their data. When long streams of data are broken into small packets, each packet is sent individually, and the other devices can send their packets between the packets of the long stream. Since each packet is uniquely addressed and has instructions on how to reassemble it, it does not matter that it arrives in small pieces.

The second reason for breaking the data into packets is error correction. Because the data is transmitted across media that is subject to interference, the data can become corrupt. One way to deal with the corruption is to send a checksum along with the data. A checksum is a running count of the bytes sent in the message. The receiving device compares its total to the total transmitted. If these numbers are the same, the data is good; but if they are different, either the checksum or the data itself is corrupt. The receiving device then asks the sender to resend the data. By breaking the data into small packets, each with its own checksum, it is easier to ensure that a good message arrives, and if not, only a small portion needs to be resent instead of the entire message.

In the description of packets, I mentioned unique addressing and reassembly instructions. Because packets also contain data, each is made up of two parts, the *header,* which contains the address and reassembly instructions, and the *body,* which contains the data. Keeping all this information in order is the *protocol.* The protocol is a set of rules that specifies the format of the package and how it is used.

Understanding Network Classes

As stated earlier, all addresses must have two parts, the network part and the node, or host, part. Addresses used in TCP/IP networks are four bytes long, called IP addresses, and are written in standard dot notation, which means a decimal number separated by dots. For example, 192.168.1.2. The decimal numbers must be within the numeric range of 0 to 255 to conform to the one-byte requirement. IP addresses are divided into classes with the most significant being classes A, B, and C depending on the value of the first byte of the address. Table 6-1 shows valid numbers for these classes.

TABLE 6-1 NETWORK CLASSES AND THEIR IP NUMBER RANGE

Class	First Byte
Class A	0–127
Class B	128–191
Class C	192–233

The reason for the class division is to enable efficient use of the address numbers. If the division were the first two bytes to the network part as shown in Table 6-1 and the last two bytes to the host part, then no network could have more than 2^{16} hosts. This would be impractical for large networks and wasteful for small networks.

There are a few ways to assign IP addresses to the devices depending on the purpose of the network. If the network is internal, an intranet, not connected to an outside network, any class A, B, or C network number can be used. The only requirement is choosing a class that allows for the number of hosts to be connected. Although this is possible, in the real world this approach would not allow for connecting to the Internet.

A more realistic approach would be to register with one of the domain registration services and request an officially assigned network number. An organization called the InterNIC maintains a database of all assigned network numbers to ensure that each assignment is unique. After obtaining a network number, the host numbers may be assigned as required. Nearly all IP devices require manual configuration; you will look at assigning IP addresses later when you actually set up your own network. You have now seen that each device has a unique network and node address which is called an IP address. Earlier this was described as the Network Layer address. You also read about the Media Access Control, or MAC, address. The MAC address was defined as the lowest level at which communication occurs. On an Ethernet network, this address is also called the Ethernet Address. This is the address that is ultimately necessary for transmission of data. For transfer to happen, the IP address must be mapped to the Ethernet address of the device. The mechanism that makes this possible is Address Resolution Protocol or ARP.

To determine the Ethernet address of a node on the same network, the sending device sends an ARP request to the Ethernet broadcast address. The Ethernet broadcast address is a special address to which all Ethernet cards are configured to "listen." The ARP request, containing the sender's IP and Ethernet addresses, as well as the IP address it is looking for, asks each device for the Ethernet address that corresponds to a particular IP address. The device whose address matches the request sends a reply to the sender's Ethernet address. The sender is then able to send its data to the specific address it received in response to its ARP request. This process works for sending data between devices on the same network, but what about sending data to devices on different networks? For this you need a router.

Routers enable networks not physically connected to each other to communicate. A router must be connected physically to each network that wants to communicate. The sending node must be able to send its request to a router on its own network, and the receiving node must also be on a network connected to a router. The sending node sends its request to the router on its network. This router is typically called the *default gateway*, and its address must be manually configured in the sending node's configuration files. You will learn how to do this later in this chapter in the "Gateways and Routers" section.

The router receives the request from the sending node and determines the best route for it to use to transmit the data. The router has an internal program, called a *routing table*, which it uses to send the data, either to another router if the other network is not directly connected, or directly to the other network. If the destination network can not be found in the routing table, then the packet is considered undeliverable and is dropped. Typically if the packet is dropped, the router sends an ICMP Destination Unreachable message to the sender.

Routing tables can be manually configured or acquired dynamically. *Manual configuration* means that it is necessary for whoever is setting up the router to provide all the information about other networks and how to reach them. This method is impractical because of the size of the file required and constantly changing information.

Dynamic acquisition means that the router sends a message using the Routing Information Protocol (RIP). RIP enables routers to share details with other routers concerning networks and their locations.

Ultimately, the purpose of everything you have looked at so far — packets, IP addresses, and routing — is to give users access to services such as printing, file sharing, and e-mail.

You have had a brief look at the IP part of the TCP/IP family of protocols and have arrived at TCP. Transmission Control Protocol is encapsulated in IP packets and provides access to services on remote network devices. TCP is considered to be a stream-oriented reliable protocol. The transmission can be any size because it is broken down into small pieces as you have already seen. Data that is lost is retransmitted, and out-of-order data is reordered. The sender is notified about any data that cannot be delivered. Typical TCP services are File Transfer Protocol (FTP), Telnet, and Simple Mail Transfer Protocol (SMTP).

Setting Up a Network Interface Card (NIC)

Every Red Hat Linux distribution includes networking support and tools that can be used to configure your network. In this section you'll learn how to configure a computer for connection to an internal and external network.

Even if the computer is not connected to outside networks, an internal network functionality is required for some applications. This address is known as the loopback and its IP address is 127.0.0.1. You should check that this network interface is working before configuring your network cards. To do this, you can use the ifconfig utility to get some information. If you type ifconfig at a console prompt, you will be shown your current network interface configuration. Figure 6-1 illustrates the output of the ifconfig command.

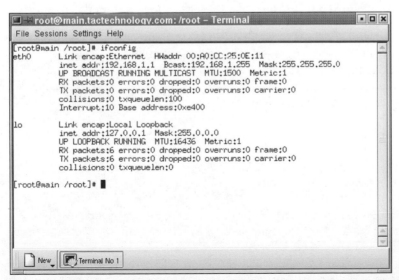

Figure 6-1: The ifconfig utility shows the current network interface configuration.

TIP   Make sure the loopback (IP address 127.0.0.1) is working before you begin to configure your network cards.

If your loopback is configured, the `ifconfig` shows a device called lo with the address 127.0.0.1. If this device and address are not shown, you can add the device by using the `ifconfig` command as follows:

```
ifconfig lo 127.0.0.1
```

You then need to use the `route` command to give the system a little more information about this interface. For this you type:

```
route add -net 127.0.0.0
```

You now have your loopback set up and the `ifconfig` command shows the device lo in its listing.

Configuring the network card

Configuring a network card follows the same procedure as configuring the loopback interface. You use the same command, `ifconfig`, but this time use the name 'eth0' for an Ethernet device. You also need to know the IP address, the netmask, and the broadcast addresses. These numbers vary depending on the type of network being built. For an internal network that never connects to the outside world, any IP numbers can be used, however there are IP numbers typically used with these networks. Table 6-2 shows the IP numbers that are usually used for such networks.

TABLE 6-2 RESERVED NETWORK NUMBERS

Network Class	Netmask	Network Addresses
A	255.0.0.0	10.0.0.0–10.255.255.255
B	255.255.0.0	172.16.0.0–17.31.255.255
C	255.255.255.0	192.168.0.0–192.168.255.255

If you are connecting to an existing network, you must have its IP address, netmask, and broadcast address. You also need to have the router and domain name server addresses.

In this example, you configure an Ethernet interface for an internal network. You need to issue the command:

```
ifconfig eth0 192.168.1.1 netmask 255.255.255.0 broadcast 192.168.1.255
```

As shown in Figure 6-2, this results in the creation of device eth0 with a network address of 192.168.1.1, a netmask of 255.255.255.0 and a broadcast address of 192.168.1.255. A file is created in /etc/sysconfig/network-scripts called ifcfg-eth0. A listing of this file would show the information that you just entered. The line onboot=yes tells the kernel to configure this device at system startup.

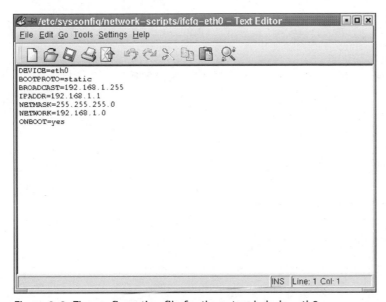

Figure 6-2: The configuration file for the network device eth0

Configuring an internal network

Now you have a network device configured for one computer. To add additional computers to your network you need to repeat this process on the other computers you want to add. The only change is that you need to assign a different IP address. For example, the second computer on your network could have the address 192.168.1.2, the third could have 192.168.1.3, and so on.

This section does not cover the physical requirements for building a network — cabling, hubs, and so forth. A good source for this information is a book titled *Network Plus* by David Groth.

In addition to configuring the network cards on each of the computers in the network, three files on each computer need to be modified. These files are all located in the /etc directory and they are:

- /etc/hosts.conf
- /etc/hosts
- /etc/resolv.conf

The /etc/hosts.conf file contains configuration information for the name resolver and should contain the following:

```
order hosts, bind                                                    multi on
```

This configuration tells the name resolver to check the /etc/hosts file before attempting to query a nameserver and to return all valid addresses for a host found in the /etc/hosts file instead of just the first.

The /etc/hosts file contains the names of all the computers on the local network. For a small network, maintaining this file is not difficult, but for a large network keeping the file up to date is often impractical. Figure 6-3 shows a network containing three computers. The first two addresses, localhost and 192.168.1.3, are the same computer, and the other two addresses represent different computers on the same network. In most networks, the IP addresses are assigned dynamically, and this file would just show the loopback interface and the localhost name.

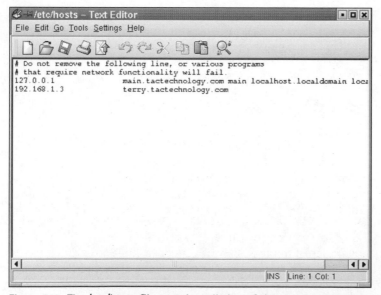

Figure 6-3: The /etc/hosts file contains a listing of the computers on your network.

The /etc/resolv.conf. file provides information about nameservers employed to resolve host names. Figure 6-4 shows a typical resolv.conf file listing.

Chapter 12 discusses Domain Name Servers (DNS).

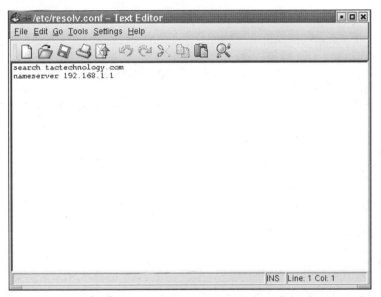

Figure 6-4: The /etc/resolv.conf file contains a listing of the domain and nameservers on the network.

Understanding Subnetting

You have learned how easy it is to build an internal network, but now you need to learn how to connect to the outside world. A few more steps accomplish outside connection, including configuring a router, obtaining an IP address, and actually making the connection. You begin with obtaining an IP address and subnetting.

Earlier in this chapter you saw that IP addresses used on the Internet are assigned by the InterNIC. Now you will take a closer look at the makeup of IP addresses and how they can be extended through subnetting.

IP numbers are not assigned to hosts, they are assigned to network interfaces on hosts. Even though many computers on an IP network have a single network interface and a single IP number, a single computer can have more than one network interface. In this case, each interface would have its own IP number.

TIP   It is also possible to assign more than one IP address to a single NIC. This is
accomplished using the **ifconfig** and **route** commands. To add another IP
address, 192.168.1.4, to eth0 issue these commands:

```
ifconfig eth0:0 192.168.1.4
route add -host 192.168.1.4 dev eth0
```

The first command binds the IP address to the virtual interface eth0:0 and
the second command adds a route for the address to the actual device eth0.

Even though this is true, most people refer to host addresses when referring to an
IP number. Just remember, this is simply shorthand for the IP number of this particular interface on this host. Many devices on the Internet have only a single interface and thus a single IP number.

In the current (IPv4) implementation, IP numbers consist of 4 (8-bit) bytes for a
total of 32 bits of available information. This system results in large numbers, even
when they are represented in decimal notation. To make them easier to read and
organize, they are written in what is called dotted quad format. The numbers you
saw earlier in this chapter were expressed in this format, such as the internal network IP address 192.168.1.1. Each of the four groups of numbers can range from 0
to 255. The following shows the IP number in binary notation with its decimal
equivalent. If the bit is set to 1 it is counted, and if set to zero it is not counted.

```
  1  +  1  +  1  +  1  +  1  +  1  +  1  +  1
128 + 64 + 32 + 16 +  8  +  4  +  2 +  1 = 255
```

The binary notation for 192.168.1.1 would be:

```
11000000.10101000.00000001.00000001
```

The dotted quad notation from this binary is:

```
(128+64) = 192.(128+32+8) = 168.(1)=1.(1) = 1
```

The leftmost bits of the IP number of a host identify the network on which the
host resides; the remaining bits of the IP number identify the network interface.
Exactly how many bits are used by the network ID and how many are available to
identify interfaces on that network is determined by the network class. Earlier you
learned that there are three classes of networks and you saw how they are composed
in Table 6-1.

Class A IP network numbers use the left quad to identify the network, leaving
3 quads to identify host interfaces on that network. Class A addresses always have
the farthest left bit of the farthest left byte a zero, so there are a maximum of 128
class A network numbers available, with each one containing up to 33,554,430
possible interfaces.

The network numbers 0.0.0.0, known as the default route, and 127.0.0.0, the loopback network, have special meanings and cannot be used to identify networks. You saw the loopback interface when you set up your internal network. You'll look at the default route when you set up your connection to the Internet. So if you take these two network numbers out, there are only 126 available class A network numbers.

Class B IP network numbers use the two left dotted quads to identify the network, leaving two dotted quads to identify host interfaces. Class B addresses always have the farthest left bits of the left byte set to 10. This leaves 14 bits left to specify the network address giving 32,767 available B class networks. Class B networks have a range of 128 to 191 for the first of the dotted quads, with each network containing up to 32,766 possible interfaces.

Class C IP network numbers use the left three quads to identify the network, leaving the right quad to identify host interfaces. Class C addresses always start with the farthest left 3 bits set to 1 1 0 or a range of 192 to 255 for the farthest left dotted quad. This means that there are 4,194,303 available Class C network numbers, each containing 254 interfaces.

IP addresses are also set aside for internal networks, as you saw in Table 6-2.

Interpreting IP numbers

IP numbers can have three possible meanings. The first of these is an address of a network, which is the number representing all the devices that are physically connected to each other. The second is the broadcast address of the network, which is the address that enables all devices on the network to be contacted. Finally, the last meaning is an actual interface address. Look at a Class C network for an example. For a Class C network:

◆ 192.168.3.0 is a Class C network number

◆ 192.168.3.42 is a host address on this network

◆ 192.168.3.255 is the network broadcast address

When you set up your Ethernet device, eth0, you used the `ifconfig` utility to pass some information that was written to the `ifcg-eth0` file. One of these parameters was the network mask. The network mask is more properly called the *subnetwork mask*. However, it is generally referred to as the *network mask*, or *subnet mask*. The determining factor in subnetting is the network mask and how it is understood on a local network segment. In setting up your network card you used a netmask of 255.255.255.0. In this case all the network bits were set to one and the host bits were set to zero. This is the standard format for all network masks. Table 6-2 shows the network masks for the three classes of networks.

You should remember two important things about the network mask. The network mask affects only the interpretation of IP numbers on the same network segment, and the network mask is not an IP number, it is used to modify how IP numbers are interpreted by the network.

The network mask affects only the interpretation of IP numbers on the same network segment.

A subnet enables you to use one IP address and split it up so that it can be used on several physically connected local networks. This is a tremendous advantage, as the number of IP numbers available is rapidly diminishing. You can have multiple subnetted networks connected to the outside world with just one IP address. By splitting the IP address, it can be used on sites which need multiple connectivity, but eliminates the problems of high traffic and difficult manageability.

The other advantages to subnetting are that different network topologies can exist on different network segments within the same organization, and overall network traffic is reduced. Subnetting also enables increased security by separating traffic into local networks.] There is a limit to the number of subnets that can be created simply based on the number of times a given number can be divided. Tables 6-3, 6-5, and 6-6 show the possible numbers of subnets and hosts that can exist.

Before you subnet your network

Before you can subnet your network, you need to make some choices and gather some information.

First you need to decide the number of hosts on each of your subnets so you can determine how many IP addresses you need. Earlier in this chapter you set up an Ethernet interface using the reserved internal Class C network number 192.168.1.0. You will continue to use this number for the subnetting example.

Every IP network has two addresses that cannot be used — the network IP number itself and the broadcast address. Whenever you subnetwork the IP network you are creating additional addresses that are unusable. For each subnet you create, two addresses are unusable, the subnet's network IP address and its broadcast address. Every time you subnet you are creating these two unusable addresses, so the more subnets you have, the more IP addresses you lose. The point is, don't subnet your network more than necessary.

 Don't subnet your network more than necessary.

Next you need to determine the subnetwork mask and network numbers. The network mask for an IP network without subnets is simply a dotted quad that has all the "network bits" of the network number set to '1' and all the host bits set to '0'.

So, for the three classes of IP networks, the standard network masks are shown in Table 6-2.

Subnetworking takes one or more of the available host bits and makes them appear as network bits to the local interfaces. If you wanted to divide your Class C network into two subnetworks, you would change the first host bit to one, and you would get a netmask of 11111111.11111111.11111111.10000000 or 255.255.255.128. This would give you 126 possible IP numbers for each of our subnets. Remember that you lose two IP addresses for each subnet. If you want to have four subnetworks, you need to change the first two host bits to ones, and this would give you a netmask of 255.255.255.192. You would have 62 IP addresses available on each subnetwork. Table 6-3 shows the subnets, the subnet masks, and the available hosts for your Class C network.

TABLE 6-3 CLASS C SUBNETS AND SUBNET MASKS

Number of Bits	Number of Subnets	Subnet Mask	Number of Hosts
1	2	255.255.255.128	126
2	4	255.255.255.192	62
3	8	255.255.255.224	30
4	16	255.255.255.240	14
5	32	255.255.255.248	6
6	64	255.255.255.252	2

Now all you need to do is assign the appropriate numbers for the network, the broadcast address, and the IP addresses for each of the interfaces and you're nearly done. Table 6-4 shows these numbers for subnetting your Class C network into two subnets.

TABLE 6-4 CREATING TWO SUBNETS FOR A CLASS C NETWORK ADDRESS

Network	Netmask	Broadcast	First IP	Last IP
192.168.1.0	255.255.255.128	192.168.1.127	192.168.1.1	192.168.1.126
192.168.1.128	255.255.255.128	192.168.1.255	192.168.1.129	192.168.1.254

Creating subnets for Class A and B networks follows the same procedure as that shown for Class C networks. Table 6-5 shows the subnets for a Class A network, and Table 6-6 shows the subnets for a Class B network.

TABLE 6-5 CLASS A SUBNETS AND SUBNET MASKS

Number of Bits	Number of Subnets	Subnet Mask	Number of Hosts
2	2	255.192.0.0	4194302
3	6	255.224.0.0	2097150
4	14	255.240.0.0	1048574
5	30	255.248.0.0	524286
6	62	255.252.0.0	262142
7	126	255.254.0.0	131070
8	254	255.255.0.0	65534
9	510	255.255.128.0	32766
10	1022	255.255.192.0	16382
11	2046	255.255.224.0	8190
12	4094	255.255.240.0	4094
13	8190	255.255.248.0	2046
14	16382	255.255.252.0	1022
15	32766	255.255.254.0	510
16	65534	255.255.255.0	254
17	131070	255.255.255.128	126
18	262142	255.255.255.192	62
19	524286	255.255.255.224	30
20	1048574	255.255.255.240	14
21	2097150	255.255.255.248	6
22	4194302	255.255.255.252	2

TABLE 6-6 CLASS B SUBNETS AND SUBNET MASKS

Number of Bits	Number of Subnets	Subnet Mask	Number of Hosts
2	2	255.255.192.0	16382
3	6	255.255.224.0	8190
4	14	255.255.240.0	4094
5	30	255.255.248.0	2046
6	62	255.255.252.0	1022
7	126	255.255.254.0	510
8	254	255.255.255.0	254
9	510	255.255.255.128	126
10	1022	255.255.255.192	62
11	2046	255.255.255.224	30
12	4094	255.255.255.240	14
13	8190	255.255.255.248	6
14	16382	255.255.255.252	2

Classless InterDomain Routing (CIDR)

CIDR was invented several years ago to keep the Internet from running out of IP addresses. The class system of allocating IP addresses can be very wasteful. Anyone who could reasonably show a need for more than 254 host addresses was given a Class B address block of 65,533 host addresses. Even more wasteful was allocating companies and organizations Class A address blocks, which contain over 16 million host addresses! Only a tiny percentage of the allocated Class A and Class B address space has ever been actually assigned to a host computer on the Internet.

People realized that addresses could be conserved if the class system was eliminated. By accurately allocating only the amount of address space that was actually needed, the address space crisis could be avoided for many years. This solution was first proposed in 1992 as a scheme called *supernetting*. Under supernetting, the class subnet masks are extended so that a network address and subnet mask could, for example, specify multiple Class C subnets with one address. For example, if you needed about a thousand addresses, you could supernet 4 Class C networks together:

```
192.60.128.0   (11000000.00111100.10000000.00000000)  Class C subnet address
192.60.129.0   (11000000.00111100.10000001.00000000)  Class C subnet address
192.60.130.0   (11000000.00111100.10000010.00000000)  Class C subnet address
192.60.131.0   (11000000.00111100.10000011.00000000)  Class C subnet address
-----------------------------------------------------------
192.60.128.0   (11000000.00111100.10000000.00000000)  Supernetted Subnet address
255.255.252.0  (11111111.11111111.11111100.00000000)  Subnet Mask
192.60.131.255 (11000000.00111100.10000011.11111111)  Broadcast address
```

In this example, the subnet 192.60.128.0 includes all the addresses from 192.60.128.0 to 192.60.131.255. As you can see in the binary representation of the subnet mask, the network portion of the address is 22 bits long, and the host portion is 10 bits long.

Under CIDR, the subnet mask notation is reduced to simplified shorthand. Instead of spelling out the bits of the subnet mask, the number of 1s bits that start the mask are simply listed. In the example, instead of writing the address and subnet mask as

```
192.60.128.0, Subnet Mask 255.255.252.0
```

the network address is written simply as:

```
192.60.128.0/22
```

This address indicates starting address of the network, and number of 1s bits (22) in the network portion of the address. If you look at the subnet mask in binary you can easily see how this notation works.

```
(11111111.11111111.11111100.00000000)
```

The use of a CIDR-notated address is the same as for a Class address. Class addresses can easily be written in CIDR notation (Class A = /8, Class B = /16, and Class C = /24).

It is currently almost impossible for you, as an individual or company, to be allocated your own IP address blocks. You will be told simply to get them from your ISP. The reason for this is the ever-growing size of the Internet routing table. Just five years ago, there were less than 5,000 network routes in the entire Internet. Today, there are over 100,000. Using CIDR, the biggest ISPs are allocated large chunks of address space, usually with a subnet mask of /19 or even smaller. The ISP's customers, often other, smaller ISPs, are then allocated networks from the big ISP's pool. That way, all the big ISP's customers, and their customers, are accessible via one network route on the Internet.

CIDR will probably keep the Internet happily in IP addresses for the next few years at least. After that, IPv6, with 128 bit addresses, will be needed. Under IPv6, even careless address allocation would comfortably enable a billion unique IP addresses for every person on earth! The complete details of CIDR are documented in RFC1519, which was released in September of 1993.

 Requests for Comment (RFC) are documents containing information about computer networking and many areas of the Internet. If you want to learn more about RFCs, check out `ftp://ftp.rfc-editor.org/in-notes/rfc2555.txt`.

Gateways and Routers

You have successfully created two subnets from your Class C network, but the individual network segments cannot communicate with each other yet. You still have to configure a path for them and you do this using a router. Earlier in this chapter you learned that a router is necessary for separate networks to communicate with each other. You also learned that each network must be connected to a router in order for this communication to take place. This router that is connected to each network is called its *gateway*.

In Linux, you can use a computer with two network interfaces to route between two or more subnets. To be able to do this you need to make sure that you enable IP Forwarding. All current Linux distributions have IP Forwarding compiled as a module, so all you need to do is make sure the module is loaded. You can check this by entering the following query at a command prompt:

```
cat /proc/sys/net.ipv4/ip_forward.
```

If forwarding is enabled the number 1 is returned, and if not enabled the number 0 is returned.

To enable IP forwarding if it is not already enabled, type the following command:

```
echo "0" > /proc/sys/net/ipv4/ip_forward
```

Continue your setup using the two subnets you previously created with the information in Table 6-4.

Assume that a computer running Linux is acting as a router for your network. It has two network interfaces to the local LANs using the lowest available IP address in each subnetwork on its interface to that network. The network interfaces would be configured as shown in Table 6-7.

TABLE 6-7 NETWORK INTERFACE CONFIGURATION

Interface	IP Address	Netmask
eth0	192.168.1.1	255.255.255.128
eth1	192.168.1.129	255.255.255.128

The network routing it would use is shown in Table 6-8.

TABLE 6-8 NETWORK ROUTING CONFIGURATION

Destination	Gateway	Mask	Interface
192.168.1.0	192.168.1.1	255.255.255.128	eth0
192.168.1.128	192.168.1.129	255.255.255.128	eth1

You're nearly finished now, just one more step. Each computer on the subnet has to show the IP address for the interface that is its gateway to the other network. The computers on the first subnet, the 192.168.1.0 network, would have the gateway 192.168.1.1. Remember that you used the first IP address on this network for the gateway computer. The computers on the second subnet, 192.168.1.128, would use 192.168.1.129 as the gateway address. You can add this information using the route command as follows:

```
route add -net 192.168.1.0 and then
route add default gw 192.168.1.129
```

This command sets up the route for local (internal) routing as well as sets up the external route for our first subnet. You need to repeat the previous commands, substituting the appropriate numbers for the second subnet and any additional subnets. You have now successfully set up two subnets and established communication between them. Next you'll look at connecting to the Internet.

Configuring Dynamic Host Configuration Protocol (DHCP)

So far you have learned to configure a network card and assign it an IP address, subnet mask, broadcast address, and gateway. Using DHCP, you can have an IP address and the other information automatically assigned to the hosts connected to your network. This method is quite efficient and convenient for large networks with many hosts, because the process of manually configuring each host is quite time consuming. By using DHCP, you can ensure that every host on your network has a valid IP address, subnet mask, broadcast address, and gateway, with minimum effort on your part.

You should have a DHCP server configured for each of your subnets. Each host on the subnet needs to be configured as a DHCP client. You may also need to configure the server that connects to your ISP as a DHCP client if your ISP dynamically assigns your IP address.

Setting up the server

The program which runs on the server is dhcpd and is included as an RPM on Red Hat 7.2 installation CD 2. Look for the file dhcp-2.0p15-1.i386.rpm and use the Gnome-RPM (the graphical RPM tool) from the desktop, or use the rpm command from a command prompt to install it.

In Red Hat Linux the DHCP server is controlled by the text file /etc/dhcpd.conf. Here is a sample of a typical setup file. Shown in parentheses is an explanation of the line.

```
default-lease-time 36000; (The amount of time in seconds that the
     host can keep the IP address.)
max-lease-time 100000; (The maximum time the host can keep the IP
     address.)
#domain name
option domain-name "tactechnology.com"; (The domain of the DHCP
     server.)
#nameserver
option domain-name-servers 192.168.1.1; (The IP address of the DNS
     servers.)
#gateway/routers, can pass more than one:
option routers 1.2.3.4,1.2.3.5;
option routers 192.168.1.1; (IP address of routers.)
#netmask
option subnet-mask 255.255.255.0; (The subnet mask of the network.)
#broadcast address
```

```
option broadcast-address 192.168.1.255; (The broadcast address of
    the network.)
#specify the subnet number gets assigned in
subnet 192.168.1.0 netmask 255.255.255.0 (The subnet that uses the
    dhcp server.)
#define which addresses can be used/assigned
range 192.168.1.1 192.168.1.126; (The range of IP addresses that can
    be used.)
```

If this file does not exist on your server, you can create it using a text editor. Be sure to use the proper addresses for your network.

To start the server, run the command dhcpd. To ensure that the dhcpd program runs whenever the system is booted, you should put the command in one of your init scripts.

Configuring the client

First you need to check if the dhcp client is installed on your system. You can check for it by issuing the following command:

```
which dhcpcd
```

If the client is on your system, you will see the location of the file. If the file is not installed, you can find it on Red Hat Installation CD 1. Install the client using the rpm command. After you install the client software, start it by running the command dhcpcd. Each of your clients will now receive its IP address, subnet mask, gateway, and broadcast address from your dhcp server.

Since you want this program to run every time the computer boots, you need to place it in the /etc/rc.local file. Now whenever the system starts, this daemon will be loaded.

Configuring a Point-to-Point Protocol (PPP) Connection

With PPP, you can send TCP/IP using the serial ports on your computers. You are probably already familiar with PPP, as this is the method typically used to connect to the Internet using a modem and telephone line. PPP can also be used to directly connect another computer to the serial port of your server.

On Red Hat 7.1, the protocol is not installed in the kernel, but is a loadable module. You load the PPP module using the modprobe ppp command.

The PPP daemon command pppd has the following format: the command followed by the device name, the port speed, and any options as shown here.

```
pppd serial_device port_speed options
```

This command is started by the `/etc/sysconfig/network-scripts/ifup-ppp` script. This script can be manually edited, or you can use the Internet Dialer to configure it.

Configuring a PPP server

As stated earlier, PPP can be used in conjunction with a modem and telephone line to provide a connection to the Internet as well as a direct serial connection to another PC. Configuring the direct connection for the server requires just one line of code, as follows:

```
pppd /dev/ttyS1 115700 crtscts
```

This command starts the PPP daemon, tells it to use the serial port ttyS1, sets the port speed, and starts the hardware flow control request to send (rts) and clear to send (cts). You should place this line in your `/etc/rc.d/rc.local` script so it loads whenever the system boots.

This is the only configuration that needs to be done for the server, because a direct connection is quite simple. Only two computers connect here, the server and one client. Configuring a server for multiple connections using a modem and dial-up connection is more complex and is explained next.

To configure the server to receive incoming calls, two files need to be modified. First, there needs to be an entry in the `/etc/passwd` file for the users that will be dialing in. Next, you need to create a ppplogin script that sets the user's shell and starts the ppp daemon with the correct parameters when the user starts a dial-up session.

Beginning with the password file, you need an entry similar to the following:

```
terry:x: 722:200:Terry Collings:/tmp:/etc/ppp/ppplogin
```

This entry is similar to others in the `/etc/passwd` file and performs similar functions, such as assigning a working directory (`/tmp` in this example) and the user's shell, which in this case is a script called ppplogin.

The file `/etc/ppplogin` is a script that you must create and will be used by anyone who is dialing into the server. Here is a sample script.

```
#!/bin/sh
mesg -n
stty -echo
exec /sbin/pppd crtscts modem passive auth
```

- ◆ The first line, `#!/bin/sh`, specifies the shell to use to interpret the script.

- ◆ The next line, `mesg -n`, disallows users sending data to the terminal.

- ◆ The third line, `stty -echo`, suppresses the characters typed by the user being returned and displayed on the user's terminal.

- ◆ The last line starts the PPP daemon and sets some parameters for the program.

The first option turns on hardware flow control. The second option tells the daemon to monitor the Data Carrier Detect (DCD) signal from the modem. This option is useful for determining if a connection still exists. The third option tells the system to wait for a Link Control Packet (LCP) from the remote system. The last option is used by PPP to request authentication from the remote system. This security is required by the PPP daemon in addition to the username and password required by the login. PPP uses two kinds of security: Password Authentication Protocol (PAP) and Challenge Handshake Authentication Protocol (CHAP). PAP security is very weak, and you would be better off not using it. I explain CHAP security next.

 Password Authentication Protocol (PAP) security is weak, and you should avoid using it. Use CHAP instead.

CHAP security

The Challenge Handshake Authentication Protocol is implemented by default when using PPP. All configuration for Chap is done using the `/etc/ppp/chap-secrets` file. The `chap-secrets` file is made up of four fields.

- ◆ **client:** The name of the system that initiates the call and must respond to the challenge sent by the server.

- ◆ **server:** The name of the system that sends the challenge.

- ◆ **secret:** A key that is used to encrypt and decrypt the challenge. The server sends a challenge to the client which then encrypts it using the secret key and sends it back to the server. The server uses the key to decrypt the client's response. If the challenge and reply are the same, the client is authenticated.

- ◆ **address:** The IP address or name of the host.

The following is an example file:

```
# client  server    secret    IP address
  terry    main      hellobozo terry.tactechnology.com
  main     terry     youclown  main.tactechnology.com
```

This file would be on the PPP server. This file also needs to be on the PPP client so the client would have the proper information to respond to the server's challenge.

Configuring a PPP client

To configure a PPP client for a direct connection, you need to place the following line of code in the /etc/rc.d/rc.local file of the client computer:

```
pppd /dev/ttyS1 115700 crtscts defaultroute
```

This command is basically the same as the one you used to configure the direct connect server, with the only difference being the default route. The default route sets the server as the router for this client for any connections to the outside.

A PPP connection is a dial-up connection that requires a modem and an analog phone line, and it is by far the most common way to connect to the Internet. You can easily set up a PPP client on a Red Hat Linux system, especially using a graphical method. The Gnome desktop includes a program called RP3 — the Gnome PPP dialer, and KDE includes a program called Internet Dialer.

Setting up a PPP connection

Internet Dialer is part of the K Desktop Environment (KDE), which is included with the Red Hat Linux distribution. Next you set up a PPP connection using Internet Dialer.

Start the Internet Dialer program by selecting the K menu, and then choosing Internet → Internet Dialer. The screen shown in Figure 6-5 appears.

Figure 6-5: The initial Internet Dialer dialog screen

Click Setup to create a new connection. Figure 6-6 shows the dialog box for creating a new connection.

Figure 6-6: The KPPP Configuration screen

Click New to open the New Account setup box as shown in Figure 6-7.

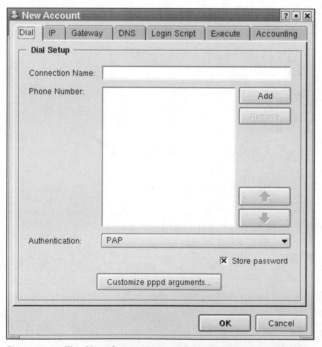

Figure 6-7: The New Account setup box enables you to enter
information about your Internet Service Provider.

When you established your Internet account with your ISP, you should have received setup information. You need to use this information to set up KPPP.

In most cases the default choices work, but it is a good idea to always check them to be sure something is not wrong. Proceed as follows:

1. In the Connection Name box enter a name for this connection.

2. In the Phone Number box enter the number needed to dial your ISP.

3. After you have entered the previous information, click OK. When the Configuration box appears, the Connection Name you chose is shown in the Account Setup section.

4. Select the Device tab. Figure 6-8 shows the Device page.

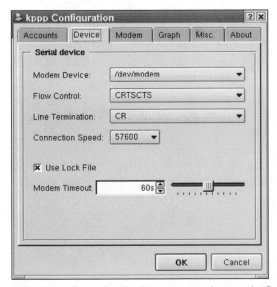

Figure 6-8: Enter details about your modem on the Device page.

Tell KPPP the location of your modem in the Modem Device drop-down box. The default setting here is /dev/modem, and it is a symbolic link to the actual modem device. You should specifically tell the system the location of your modem, which would be /dev/ttyS0 to /dev/ttyS3. TtyS0 corresponds to com1 in the DOS/Windows world, ttyS1 is com2, and so on. So if your modem is installed on com1 in Windows, it would be /dev/ttyS0 in Linux.

The default settings for flow control and line termination usually work, so no change is necessary here.

The Connection Speed should be 115200 for a 56K modem, and 57600 for any other modem.

Next, select the Modem tab. Figure 6-9 shows the Modem page.

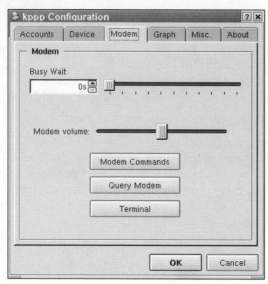

Figure 6-9: The Modem page enables you to set the modem volume and test your configuration.

To set the delay between redial attempts in the event of a busy signal, enter a number in the Busy Wait box. Choose the modem volume by moving the slider bar right to increase and left to decrease.

To see if you chose the correct device for your modem, click the Query Modem button. If your modem is correctly configured, you should see an output box like the one shown in Figure 6-10.

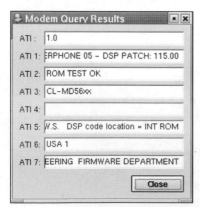

Figure 6-10: The result of the modem query shows that the modem is responding.

If you have chosen the wrong port, you will see a message like the one shown in Figure 6-11. You will have to go back to the Device tab and choose a different port.

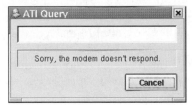

Figure 6-11: The result of the modem query shows that the port is not configured correctly.

When the modem query shows correctly, everything is properly configured. Click the OK button to save your profile. When the initial screen reappears, as shown in Figure 6-5, enter your Login ID and Password in the appropriate boxes and click Connect. If all is well, you will see a screen similar to Figure 6-12.

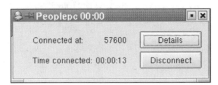

Figure 6-12: A successful connection has been made by Internet Dialer.

If you want to check the status of your connection use the `ifconfig` command as shown in Figure 6-13.

```
[root@main /root]# ifconfig
eth0      Link encap:Ethernet  HWaddr 00:A0:CC:25:0E:11
          inet addr:192.168.1.1  Bcast:192.168.1.255  Mask:255.255.255.0
          UP BROADCAST RUNNING MULTICAST  MTU:1500  Metric:1
          RX packets:0 errors:0 dropped:0 overruns:0 frame:0
          TX packets:0 errors:0 dropped:0 overruns:0 carrier:0
          collisions:0 txqueuelen:100
          Interrupt:10 Base address:0xe400

lo        Link encap:Local Loopback
          inet addr:127.0.0.1  Mask:255.0.0.0
          UP LOOPBACK RUNNING  MTU:16436  Metric:1
          RX packets:26 errors:0 dropped:0 overruns:0 frame:0
          TX packets:26 errors:0 dropped:0 overruns:0 carrier:0
          collisions:0 txqueuelen:0

ppp0      Link encap:Point-to-Point Protocol
          inet addr:63.24.27.70  P-t-P:206.115.156.186  Mask:255.255.255.255
          UP POINTOPOINT RUNNING NOARP MULTICAST  MTU:1524  Metric:1
          RX packets:4 errors:0 dropped:0 overruns:0 frame:0
          TX packets:5 errors:0 dropped:0 overruns:0 carrier:0
          collisions:0 txqueuelen:3

[root@main /root]#
```

Figure 6-13: The ifconfig command shows the PPP connection.

Configuring IP Masquerading

So far you have configured an internal network consisting of two subnets, and you configured a router for connectivity between the networks. Assuming that you made the connection to the Internet through your router, you need to make only a few configuration changes and every computer on your network can connect to the Internet through your one connection. To use a single Internet connection for multiple computers, you need to use *IP masquerading*. IP masquerading enables you to connect a TCP/IP network to the outside world using a single server and a single IP address.

Current Red Hat Linux distributions make IP masquerading available as a module, so you need only load the module and enable the appropriate configuration. You already enabled IP forwarding when you configured your router, so you need to consider only one more item, a utility called iptables, which sets up a simple packet filtering firewall.

To learn about securing your Red Hat Linux system for the Internet, see Chapter 26.

The iptables utility gives you enough protection for now. To set up masquerading, type the following commands:

```
iptables -P forward DENY
iptables -A forward -s 192.168.0.0/24 -j MASQ -d 0.0.0.0/0
```

Those commands are all that needs to be done to enable the firewall rules and to start masquerading.

Of course you want IP masquerading enabled whenever you boot the computer, so it's a good idea to make a script file that enables IP forwarding as well as the iptables utility. This file would ensure that forwarding and masquerading start each time the machine boots.

Be sure to include the command to start IP forwarding (shown earlier in this chapter) as well as the iptables commands shown previously.

Summary

In this chapter you learned about the TCP/IP protocol suite and how it works to enable communication across networks. Then you learned how to configure a network interface card. You used subnetting to create two internal subnetworks and configured a router so the subnetworks could communicate with each other. You set up a Dynamic Host Configuration Protocol server to assign IP addresses to the hosts on the network. You also enabled forwarding and masquerading so that every computer on your internal network could have Internet access.

Chapter 7

The Network File System

IN THIS CHAPTER

- ◆ What is NFS?
- ◆ Configuring an NFS server
- ◆ Configuring an NFS client
- ◆ Tuning NFS
- ◆ Troubleshooting NFS
- ◆ Examining NFS security

RED HAT LINUX SERVERS are often installed to provide centralized file and print services for networks. This chapter explores the nooks and crannies of using NFS, the Network File System, to create a file server.

NFS Overview

NFS, the Network File System, is the most common method for providing file sharing services on Linux and Unix networks. It is a distributed file system that enables local access to remote disks and file systems. Indeed, in a properly designed and implemented NFS environment, NFS's operation is totally transparent to clients using remote file systems. NFS is also a popular file sharing protocol, so NFS clients are available for many non-Unix operating systems, including the various Windows versions, MacOS, VAX/VMS, and MVS.

Understanding NFS

NFS uses a standard client/server architecture. The server portion consists of the physical disks containing shared file systems and several daemons that make the shared file systems (or entire disks, for that matter) visible to and available for use by client systems on the network. This process is normally referred to as *exporting a file system*. Server daemons also provide for file locking and, optionally, quota management on NFS exports. NFS clients simply mount the exported file systems, colloquially but accurately called *NFS mounts*, on their local system just as they would mount file systems on local disks.

The possible uses of NFS are quite varied. For example, many sites store users' home directories on a central server and use NFS to mount the home directory when users log in or boot their systems. Of course, in this case, the exported directories must be mounted as /home/*username* on the local (client) systems, but the export itself can be stored anywhere on the NFS server, say, /exports/users/*username*. Another common scheme is to export public data or project-specific files from an NFS server and to enable clients to mount these remote file systems anywhere they see fit on the local system. Figure 7-1 illustrates both of these examples.

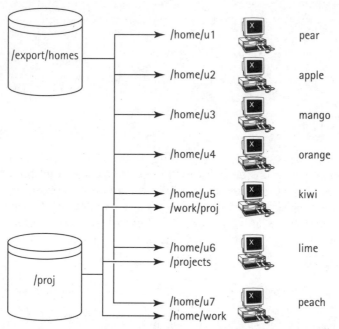

Figure 7-1: Exporting home directories and project-specific file systems

The network shown in Figure 7-1 shows that all the client systems (pear, mango, and so forth) mount their home directories from an NFS server named diskbeast. On diskbeast, the exported file systems are stored in the /exports/homes directory (/exports/homes/u1, /exports/homes/u2, and so on). When users log in to any given system, their home directory is automatically mounted on /home/*username* on that system. So, if the user u1 logs in on pear, /exports/homes/u1 is mounted on pear's file system as /home/u1 (often written in *host:/mount/point* format, for example, pear:/home/u1). If u1 then logs in on mango, too (not illustrated in the figure), mango also mounts /home/u1. Of course, logging in on two systems this way is potentially dangerous because changes to files in the exported file system made from one login session may affect the behavior of the other, but it is also very convenient, in other situations, for such changes to be immediately visible.

Figure 7-1 also shows that three users, u5, u6, and u7, mount a project-specific file system, /proj, also exported from diskbeast, in various locations on their local file systems, kiwi:/work/proj, lime:/projects, and peach:/home/work.

NFS is also used to provide diskless clients, such as X terminals or the slave nodes in a cluster, with their entire file system, including the kernel image and other boot files. Although the examples mentioned illustrate typical NFS usage, NFS can be used in almost any situation requiring transparent local access to remote file systems. In fact, you can use NFS and NIS together to create a highly centralized network environment that makes it easier to administer the network, add and delete user accounts, protect and back up key data and file systems, and give users a uniform, consistent view of the network regardless of where they log in.

Chapter 8 covers NIS in depth.

As you will see in the sections titled "Configuring an NFS Server" and "Configuring an NFS Client," NFS is easy to set up and maintain and pleasantly flexible. Exports can be mounted read-only or in read-write mode. Permission to mount exported file systems can be limited to a single host or to a group of hosts using either host names with the wildcards * and ? or using IP address ranges. Other options enable strengthening or weakening of certain security options as the situation demands.

NFS advantages

Clearly, the biggest advantage NFS provides is centralized administration. It is much easier, for example, to back up a file system stored on a server (such as the /home file system) than it is to back up /home directories scattered throughout the network, on systems that are geographically dispersed, and that might or might not be accessible when the backup is made. Similarly, NFS, especially when used with NIS, makes it trivially simple to update key configuration files, provide access to shared disk space, or limit access to sensitive data. NFS can also conserve disk space and prevent duplication of resources because file systems that change infrequently or that are usually read-only, such as /usr, can be exported as read-only NFS mounts. Likewise, upgrading applications employed by users throughout a network simply becomes a matter of installing the new application and changing the exported file system to point at the new application.

End users also benefit from NFS. When NFS is combined with NIS, users can log in from any system, even remotely, and still have access to their home directories and see a uniform view of shared data. Users can protect important or sensitive data or information that would be impossible or time consuming to recreate by storing it on an NFS mounted file system that is regularly backed up.

NFS disadvantages

NFS has its shortcomings, of course, primarily in terms of performance and security. As a distributed, network-based file system, NFS is sensitive to network congestion. Heavy network traffic slows down NFS performance. Similarly, heavy disk activity on the NFS server adversely affects NFS's performance. In both cases, NFS clients seem to be running slowly because disk reads and writes take longer. If an exported file system is not available when a client attempts to mount it, the client system hangs, although this can be mitigated using a specific mount. An exported file system also represents a single point of failure. If the disk or system exporting vital data or application becomes unavailable for any reason (say, due to a disk crash or server failure), no one can access that resource.

NFS has security problems because its design assumes a trusted network, not a hostile environment in which systems are constantly being probed and attacked. The primary weakness is that the NFS protocol is based on RPC, remote procedure calls, which are one of the most common targets of exploit attempts. As a result, sensitive information should never be exported from or mounted on systems exposed to the Internet, that is, one that is on or outside a firewall. Indeed, security experts generally recommend that NFS not be used across the Internet under any circumstances.

Even inside a firewall, providing all users access to all files might pose greater risks than user convenience and administrative simplicity justify. Care must be taken when exporting directories or file systems to limit access to the appropriate users and also to limit what those users are permitted to do with the data. NFS also has quirks that pose potential security risks. For example, when the root user on a client system mounts an NFS export, you do not want root on the client to have root privileges on the exported file system. By default, NFS prevents this, a procedure called *root squashing*, but a careless administrator might override it.

As you proceed through this chapter, especially in the next section, you learn ways to address some of NFS's shortcomings, or at least how to avoid hitting the potholes that you cannot fix. The final section, "NFS Security," discusses key NFS security weaknesses and the measures you can take to minimize the security risks associated with NFS.

Configuring an NFS Server

Configuring an NFS server boils down to design and implementation. Of these two steps, design is the most important because it ensures that the implementation is transparent to end users and trivial to administer. The implementation is remarkably straightforward. This section highlights the server configuration process, discusses the key design issues to keep in mind, identifies the key files and commands you use to implement, maintain, and monitor the NFS server, and illustrates the process using a typical NFS configuration.

Overview of server configuration

Although the breakdown is somewhat artificial because NFS server configuration is uncomplicated, you can divide server configuration into four steps:

◆ Design

◆ Implementation

◆ Testing

◆ Monitoring

Designing the server consists of deciding what file systems to export to which users and selecting a naming convention and mounting scheme that maintains network transparency. With the design in place, implementation is a matter of configuring the exports and starting the appropriate daemons. Testing, obviously, makes sure that the naming convention and mounting scheme works as designed and identifies potential performance bottlenecks. Monitoring, finally, extends the testing process: you need to ensure that exported file systems continue to be available and that heavy usage or a poorly conceived export scheme does not adversely affect overall performance.

Designing an NFS server

As suggested a moment ago, designing a useful NFS server involves

◆ Selecting the file systems to export

◆ Choosing which users (or hosts) are permitted to mount the exported file systems

◆ Selecting a naming convention and mounting scheme that maintains network transparency and ease of use

◆ Configuring the server and client systems to follow the convention

 See the section titled "Configuring an NFS Client" later in this chapter to learn about configuring the client system.

Alas, there are few general rules to guide the design process, though, because NFS imposes few restrictions beyond what file systems can be exported and because the design of the underlying network, the number and type of servers and clients, and the needs of each site vary. That said, here are some tips and suggestions for designing an NFS server and its exports that ease administrative overhead and reduce user confusion:

◆ Good candidates for NFS exports include any file system that is shared among a large number of users, such as /home, workgroup project directories, shared directories, such as /usr/share, the mail spool (/var/mail), and file systems that contain application binaries and data used by many users on the network. File systems that are relatively static, such as /usr, are also good candidates for NFS exports because there is no need to replicate the same static data and binaries across multiple machines.

◆ Use /home/*username* to mount home directories. This is one of the most fundamental directory idioms in the Unix/Linux world, so disregarding it not only antagonizes users but also breaks a lot of software that presumes user home directories live in /home. Of course, on the server, you have more leeway as to where to store home directories, but see the next suggestion.

◆ Use the same path names on the server and on clients. That is, if an exported file system is named /opt/mysql on the server, it should be mounted as /opt/mysql on the client. This convention not only facilitates transparent access to shared file systems, it also makes it easier to track down problems on the server because you do not have to remember the mapping from an exported file system to a mounted a file system.

◆ Few networks are static, particularly network file systems, so design NFS servers with growth in mind. For example, avoid the temptation to drop all third-party software on a single exported file system because, over time, the file system grows to the point that it needs to be subdivided, leading to administrative headaches when client mounts must be updated to reflect a new set of exports.

◆ Similarly, overall disk and network performance improves if exported file systems are distributed across multiple servers rather than concentrated on a single server. If using multiple servers is not possible, at least try to situate NFS exports on separate physical devices and/or on separate disk controllers. Doing so reduces disk I/O contention.

When identifying the file systems to export, keep in mind the following three rules that restrict how file systems can be exported:

◆ You can export only local file systems and their subdirectories. To express this restriction in another way, you cannot export a file system that is itself already an NFS mount. For example, if a system named diskbeast mounts /home from a server named homebeast, diskbeast cannot re-export /home. Clients wishing to mount /home from homebeast must do so directly.

◆ A subdirectory of an exported file system cannot be exported unless the subdirectory resides on a different physical disk than its parent. For example, suppose `diskbeast`, an NFS server, has the following entry in its `/etc/fstab`:

```
/dev/sda1 /usr/local ext3 defaults 1 2
```

If you export `/usr/local`, you cannot *also* export `/usr/local/devtools` because `/usr/local/devtools` is on the same disk as `/usr/local`.

 NFS *clients* are free to mount `/usr/local` and `/usr/local/devtools` separately because, as you will see in the section titled "Configuring an NFS Client," client systems can mount any subdirectory of an exported file system unless specifically forbidden to do so by export options used in the server's `/etc/exports` file.

If, however, `diskbeast`'s `/etc/fstab` showed the following disk configuration:

```
/dev/sda1 /usr/local          ext3 defaults 1 2
/dev/sdb1 /usr/local/devtools ext3 defaults 1 2
```

you *could* export both `/usr/local` and `/usr/local/devtools` because they reside on different physical disks.

◆ Conversely, the parent directory of an exported subdirectory cannot be exported unless the parent directory resides on a different physical disk. That is, if you export `/usr/local/devtools`, you cannot also export `/usr/local` unless `/usr/local` is on a different disk device than `/usr/local/devtools`. This rule just extends the logic of Rule 2 in the opposite direction.

Key files, commands, and daemons

This subsection discusses the key files, commands, and daemons that make up an NFS server. On most Linux systems these files and programs include the following:

◆ Configuration and status files

- `/etc/exports`
- `/var/lib/nfs/rmtab`

- `/var/lib/nfs/xtab`

- `/etc/hosts.allow`

- `/etc/hosts.deny`

◆ Daemons

- `rpc.portmap`

- `rpc.mountd`

- `rpc.nfsd`

- `rpc.statd`

- `rpc.lockd`

- `rpc.rquotad`

◆ Scripts and commands

- `/etc/rc.d/init.d/nfs`

- `nfstat`

- `showmount`

- `rpcinfo`

- `exportfs`

NFS Server Configuration and Status Files	NFS Server Daemons	NFS Server Scripts and Commands
/etc/exports	rpc.portmap	/etc/rc.d/init.d/nfs
/var/lib/nfs/rmtab	rpc.mountd	nfstat
/var/lib/nfs/xtab	rpc.nfsd	showmount
/etc/hosts.allow	rpd.statd	rpcinfo
/etc/hosts.deny	rpc.lockd	exportfs
	rpc.rquotad	

NFS SERVER CONFIGURATION AND STATUS FILES

The server configuration file is /etc/exports, which contains a list of file systems to export, the clients permitted to mount them, and the export options that apply to client mounts. Each line in /etc/exports has the following format:

```
dir host(options) [host(options)] ...
```

where *dir* is a directory or file system to export, *host* specifies one or more hosts permitted to mount *dir*, and *options* specifies one or more mount options. *host* can be specified as a single name, an NIS netgroup, as a group of hosts using the form address/netmask, or as a group of hosts using the wildcard characters ? and *. Multiple *host(options)* entries are accepted, which enables you to specify different export options depending on the host or hosts mounting the directory.

When specified as a single name, *host* can be any name that DNS or the resolver library can resolve to an IP address. If host is an NIS netgroup, it is specified as @groupname. The address/netmask form enables you to specify all hosts on an IP network or subnet. In this case the netmask can be specified in dotted quad format (/255.255.252.0, for example) or as a mask length (such as /22). You may also specify host using the wildcards * and ?, subject to the caveat that * and ? do not match the dots in a hostname, so that *.kurtwerks.com matches all hosts in the kurtwerks.com domain, but not, for example, hosts in the subdomain guru.kurtwerks.com.

Chapter 8 discusses NIS netgroups in detail.

Consider the following sample /etc/exports file:

```
/usr/local  *.kurtwerks.com(ro)
/home       192.168.0.0/255.255.255.0(rw)
/projects   @dev(rw)
/var/tmp    192.168.0.1(rw)
```

The first line permits all hosts with a name of the format *somehost.* kurtwerks.com to mount /usr/local. The second line permits any host with an IP address in the range 192.168.0.0 to 192.168.0.255 to mount /home. The third line permits any member of the NIS netgroup named dev to mount /projects. The final line permits only the host whose IP address is 192.168.0.1 to mount /var/tmp.

The export options determine the characteristics of the exported file system. Table 7-1 lists valid values for *options*, with the default values appearing in bold face.

TABLE 7-1 /ETC/EXPORTS EXPORT OPTIONS

Option	Description
Secure	Requires client requests to originate from a secure (privileged) port, that is, one numbered less than 1024
Insecure	Permits client requests to originate from unprivileged ports (those numbered 1024 and higher)
Ro	Exports the file system read-only, disabling any operation that changes the file system
Rw	Exports the file system read-write, permitting operations that change the file system
Async	Allows the server to cache disk writes to improve performance
Sync	Forces the server to perform a disk write before the request is considered complete
Subtree_check	If only part of a file system, such as a subdirectory, is exported, subtree checking makes sure that file requests apply to files in the exported portion of the file system
no_subtree_check	Disables subtree_check
Wdelay	Allows the server to delay a disk write if it believes another related disk write may be requested soon or if one is in progress, improving overall performance
no_wdelay	Disables wdelay (must be used with the sync option)
root_squash	Maps all requests from a UID or GID of 0 to the UID or GID, respectively, of the anonymous user (-2 in Red Hat Linux)
no_root_squash	Disables root_squash
all_squash	Maps all requests from all UIDs or GIDs to the UID or GID, respectively, of the anonymous user
no_all_squash	Disables all_squash
Anonuid=uid	Sets the UID of the anonymous account to uid
Anongid=gid	Sets the GID of the anonymous account to gid

The various squash options, and the anonuid and anongid options bear additional explanation. root_squash prevents the root user on an NFS client from having root privileges on an NFS mount. The Linux security model ordinarily

grants root full access to the file systems on a host. However, in an NFS environment, exported file systems are shared resources and are properly "owned" by the
root user of the NFS server, not by the root users of the client systems that mount
them. The root_squash option preserves the Linux security model by remapping
the root UID and GID (0) to that of a less privileged user, -2. The no_root_squash
option disables this behavior, but should not be used because doing so poses significant security risks. Consider the implications, for example, of letting a client
system have root access to the file system containing sensitive payroll information.

The all_squash option has a similar effect to root_squash, except that it
applies to all users, not just the root user. The default is no_all_squash, however,
because most users that access files on NFS exported file systems are already
merely mortal users, that is, their UIDs and GIDs are unprivileged, so they do not
have the power of the root account. Use the anonuid and anongid options to specify the UID and GID of the anonymous user. The default UID and GID of the anonymous user is -2, which should be adequate in most cases.

subtree_check and no_subtree check also deserve some elaboration. When a
file system subdirectory is exported but its parent directory is not, the NFS server
must verify that the accessed file resides in the exported portion of the file system,
a check that is programmatically nontrivial. To facilitate this verification, called a
subtree check, the server stores file location information in the file handle given to
clients when they request a file. In most cases, this is not a problem, but can be
(potentially) troublesome if a client is accessing a file that is renamed or moved
while the file is open, because renaming or moving the file invalidates the location
information stored in the file handle. Disabling the subtree check using no_
subtree_check avoids the problem and has the beneficial side effect of improving
performance, especially on exported file systems that are highly dynamic, such
as /home.

Unfortunately, disabling subtree checking also poses a security risk. The subtree
check routine ensures that files to which only root has access can be accessed only
if the file system is exported with no_root_squash, even if the file itself enables
more general access.

The manual page for /etc/exports (man 5 exports) recommends using
no_subtree_check for /home because it normally experiences a high level of file
renaming and moving. It also recommends leaving subtree checking enabled (the
default) for file systems that are exported read-only, file systems that are largely
static (such as /usr or /var), and file systems from which subdirectories, not the
parent directories, are exported.

Here is a modified version of the /etc/exports file presented earlier.

```
/usr/local  *.kurtwerks.com(ro,secure)
/home       192.168.0.0/255.255.255.0(rw,secure,no_subtree_check)
/projects   @dev(rw,secure,anonuid=600,anongid=600,sync,no_wdelay)
/var/tmp    192.168.0.1(rw,insecure,no_subtree_check)
```

The hosts have not changed, but additional export options have been added. For example, /usr/local is exported read-only (ro) because it does not change, but the other three file systems are exported in read-write (rw) mode. /usr/local, /home, and /project can be accessed only from clients using secure ports (the secure option), but the server accepts requests destined for /var/tmp from any port because the insecure option is specified. For /projects, the anonymous user is mapped to the UID and GID 600, as indicated by the anonuid=600 and anongid=600 options. Note, however, that because only members of the NIS netgroup dev are permitted to mount /projects, only their UIDs and GIDs are remapped. /home and /var/tmp are exported using the no_subtree_check option because they see a high volume of file deletion, renaming, and moving. Finally, the sync and no_wdelay options disable write caching and delayed writes to the /project file system, presumably because the impact of data loss would be significant in the event the server crashes. However, forcing disk syncs in this manner also imposes a performance penalty because the kernel's normal disk caching and buffering heuristics cannot be applied.

Two additional files store status information about NFS exports, /var/lib/nfs/rmtab and /var/lib/nfs/xtab. Each time the rpc.mountd daemon (see the subsection "NFS Server Daemons"), which services mount requests for exported file systems, receives a mount request, it adds an entry to /var/lib/nfs/rmtab. Conversely, when mountd receives a request to unmount an exported file system, it removes the corresponding entry from /var/lib/nfs/rmtab. The following short listing shows the contents of /var/lib/nfs/rmtab on an NFS server that exports /home in read-write mode and /usr/local in read-only mode. In this case, the host with IP address 192.168.0.2 has mounted both exports:

```
$ cat /var/lib/nfs/rmtab
192.168.0.2:/home:0x00000002
192.168.0.2:/usr/local:0x00000001
```

Fields in rmtab are colon-delimited, so it has three fields: the host, the exported file system, and the mount options specified in /etc/exports. Rather than try to decipher the hexadecimal options field, you can read the mount options directly from /var/lib/nfs/xtab. The exportfs command, explored in the subsection titled "NFS Server Scripts and Commands," maintains /var/lib/nfs/xtab, which contains the current table of exported file systems. The following listing shows the contents of /var/lib/nfs/xtab on the system I used for testing this chapter's examples (the output wraps because of page width constraints).

```
$ cat /var/lib/nfs/xtab
/usr/local
192.168.0.2(ro,async,wdelay,hide,secure,root_squash,no_all_squash,su
btree_check,secure_locks,mapping=identity,anonuid=-2,anongid=-2)
/tmp/foo
```

```
192.168.0.2(ro,async,wdelay,hide,secure,root_squash,no_all_squash,su
btree_check,secure_locks,mapping=identity,anonuid=-2,anongid=-2)
/home
192.168.0.2(rw,async,wdelay,hide,secure,root_squash,no_all_squash,su
btree_check,secure_locks,mapping=identity,anonuid=-2,anongid=-2)
```

As you can see in the listing, the format of the `xtab` file mirrors that of `/etc/exports`, except that `xtab` lists the default values for options not specified in `/etc/exports` in addition to the options specifically listed.

The last two configuration files to discuss, `/etc/hosts.allow` and `/etc/hosts.deny`, are not properly part of an NFS server because you can configure an NFS server without them and the server functions perfectly (to the degree, at least, that *anything* ever functions perfectly). However, using the access control features of these files helps enhance both the overall security of the server and the security of the NFS subsystem. They are part of the TCP Wrappers package, which is covered in detail in Chapter 11, so, rather than preempt the discussion of TCP Wrappers, I suggest how to modify these files, briefly explain the rationale, and let you read Chapter 11 to understand the modifications in detail.

First, add the following entries to `/etc/hosts.deny`:

```
portmap:ALL
lockd:ALL
mountd:ALL
rquotad:ALL
statd:ALL
```

These entries deny access to NFS services to all hosts not explicitly permitted access in `/etc/hosts.allow`. Accordingly, the next step is to add entries to `/etc/hosts.allow` to permit access to NFS services to specific hosts. As you will learn in Chapter 11, entries in `/etc/hosts.allow` take the form

daemon:*host_list* [*host_list*] ...

The NFS HOWTO (http://nfs.sourceforge.net/nfs-howto/server.html#CONFIG) discourages use of the ALL:ALL syntax in /etc/hosts.deny. "While this is more secure behavior [than denying access to specific services], it may also get you in trouble when you are installing new services, you forget you put it there, and you can't figure out for the life of you why they won't work."

I respectfully disagree. The stronger security enabled by the ALL:ALL construct in /etc/hosts.deny far outweighs any inconvenience it might pose when configuring new services.

---

daemon is a daemon such as portmap or lockd, and *host_list* is a list of one or more hosts specified as host names, IP address, IP address patterns using wild-cards, or address/netmask pairs. For example, the following entry permits access to the portmap daemon to all hosts in the kurtwerks.com domain:

```
portmap:.kurtwerks.com
```

The next entry permits access to all hosts on the subnetworks 192.168.0.0 and 192.168.1.0

```
portmap:192.168.0. 192.168.1.
```

You need to add entries for each host or host group permitted NFS access for each of the five daemons listed in /etc/hosts.deny. So, for example, to permit access to all hosts in the kurtwerks.com domain, add the following entries to /etc/host.allow:

```
portmap:.kurtwerks.com
lockd:.kurtwerks.com
mountd:.kurtwerks.com
rquotad:.kurtwerks.com
statd:.kurtwerks.com
```

Note that, unlike the syntax of /etc/exports, a name of the form .domain.dom matches all hosts, including hosts in subdomains like .subdom.domain.dom.

NFS SERVER DAEMONS

Providing NFS services requires the services of six daemons: /sbin/portmap, /usr/sbin/rpc.mountd, /usr/sbin/rpc.nfsd, /sbin/rpc.statd, /sbin/rpc.lockd, and, if necessary, /usr/sbin/rpc.rquotad. They are generally referred to as portmap, mountd, nfssd, statd, lockd, and rquotad, respectively. Table 7-2 briefly describes each daemon's function.

TABLE 7-2 NFS SERVER DAEMONS

Daemon	Function
portmap	Enables NFS clients to discover the NFS services available on a given server
mountd	Processes NFS client mount requests
nfsd	Provides all NFS services except file locking and quota management
statd	Implements NFS lock recovery when an NFS server system crashes

Daemon	Function
lockd	Starts the kernel's NFS lock manager
rquotad	Provides file system quota information NFS exports to NFS clients using file system quotas

The NFS daemons should be started in the following order to work properly:

1. portmap

2. nfsd

3. mountd

4. statd

5. rquotad (if necessary)

Notice that the list omits lockd. nfsd starts it on an as-needed basis, so you should rarely, if ever, need to invoke it manually. Fortunately, the Red Hat Linux initialization script for NFS, /etc/rc.d/init.d/nfs, takes care of starting up the NFS server daemons for you. Nevertheless, you might one day find it helpful to know the proper order in which to start the daemons. By default, the startup script starts eight copies of nfsd in order to enable the server to process multiple requests simultaneously. To change this value, make a backup copy of /etc/rc.d/init.d/nfs, edit the script, and change the line that reads

RPCNFSDCOUNT=8

Change the value from 8 to one that suits you. Busy servers with many active connections might benefit from doubling or tripling this number. If file system quotas for exported file systems have *not* been enabled on the NFS server, it is unnecessary to start the quota manager, rquotad, but be aware that the Red Hat initialization script starts rquotad whether quotas have been enabled or not.

Chapter 21 covers file system quotas in detail.

NFS SERVER SCRIPTS AND COMMANDS

Starting and maintaining an NFS server requires surprisingly few commands. Three initialization scripts start the required daemons, /etc/rc.d/init.d/portmap, /etc/rc.d/init.d/nfs, and /etc/rc.d/init.d/nfslock. The exportfs command enables you to manipulate the list of current exports on the fly without needing to edit /etc/exports. The showmount command provides information about clients and the file systems they have mounted. The nfsstat command displays detailed information about the status of the NFS subsystem.

The portmap script starts the portmap daemon, frequently referred to as *the portmapper*, needed by all programs that use RPC, such as NIS and NFS. The Red Hat Linux boot process starts the portmapper automatically, so you rarely need to worry about it, but it is good to know the script exists. Like most startup scripts, it requires a single argument, either start, stop, restart, or status. As you can probably guess, the start and stop arguments start and stop the portmapper, restart restarts it (by calling the script with the start and stop arguments, as it happens), and status indicates whether or not the portmapper is running, showing its PID if it is.

The primary NFS startup script is /etc/rc.d/init.d/nfs. Like the portmapper, it requires a single argument, start, stop, status, restart, or reload. start and stop start and stop the NFS server, respectively. The restart argument stops and starts the server processes in a single command and should be used after changing the contents of /etc/exports. However, it is not necessary to reinitialize the NFS subsystem by bouncing the server daemons in this way. Rather, you can use the script's reload argument, which causes exportfs, discussed shortly, to reread /etc/exports and to re-export the file systems listed there. Both restart and reload also update the time stamp on the NFS lock file used by the initialization script, /var/lock/subsys/nfs. The status argument displays the PIDs of the mountd, nfsd, and rquotad daemons. For example,

```
$ /etc/rc.d/init.d/nfs status
rpc.mountd (pid 4358) is running...
nfsd (pid 1241 1240 1239 1238 1235 1234 1233 1232) is running...
rpc.rquotad (pid 1221) is running...
```

The output of the command confirms that the three daemons are running and shows the PIDs for each instance of each daemon. All users are permitted to invoke the NFS initialization script with the status argument, but all the other arguments (start, stop, restart, and reload) *do* require root privileges.

NFS services also require the file locking daemons lockd and statd. As noted earlier, nfsd starts lockd itself, but you still must start statd separately. Red Hat Linux includes an initialization script for this purpose, /etc/rc.d/init.d/nfslock. It accepts almost the same arguments as /etc/rc.d/init.d/nfs, with the exception of the reload argument (because statd does not require a configuration file).

Thus, if you ever need to start the NFS server manually, the proper invocation sequence is to start the portmapper first, followed by NFS, followed by the NFS lock manager, that is:

```
/etc/rc.d/init.d/portmap start
/etc/rc.d/init.d/nfs start
/etc/rc.d/init.d/nfslock start
```

Conversely, to shut down the server, reverse the start procedure:

```
/etc/rc.d/init.d/nfslock stop
/etc/rc.d/init.d/nfs stop
/etc/rc.d/init.d/portmap stop
```

Because other programs and servers may require portmapper's service, I suggest you let it run unless you drop the system to run level 1 to perform maintenance.

You can also find out what NFS daemons are running using the rpcinfo command with the -p option. rpcinfo is a general purpose program that displays information about programs that use the RPC protocol, of which NFS is one. The -p option queries the portmapper and displays a list of all registered RPC programs. The following listing shows the output of rpcinfo -p on a fairly quiescent NFS server:

```
$ rpcinfo -p
   program vers proto   port
    100000    2   tcp    111  portmapper
    100000    2   udp    111  portmapper
    100011    1   udp    974  rquotad
    100011    2   udp    974  rquotad
    100003    2   udp   2049  nfs
    100003    3   udp   2049  nfs
    100021    1   udp   1031  nlockmgr
    100021    3   udp   1031  nlockmgr
    100021    4   udp   1031  nlockmgr
    100005    1   udp   1055  mountd
    100005    1   tcp   1297  mountd
    100005    2   udp   1055  mountd
    100005    2   tcp   1297  mountd
    100005    3   udp   1055  mountd
    100005    3   tcp   1297  mountd
```

rpcinfo's output shows the RPC program's ID number, version number, the network protocol it is using, the port number it is using, and an alias name for the program number. The program number and name (first and fifth columns) are taken from the file /etc/rpc, which maps program numbers to program names and also lists aliases for program names. At a bare minimum, to have a functioning NFS server, rpcinfo should list entries for portmapper, nfs, and mountd.

The exportfs command enables you to manipulate the list of available exports, in some cases without editing /etc/exports. It also maintains the list of currently exported file systems in `/var/lib/nfs/xtab` and the kernel's internal table of exported file systems. In fact, the NFS initialization script discussed earlier in this subsection uses `exportfs` extensively. For example `exporfs -a` initializes the `xtab` file, synchronizing it with the contents of `/etc/exports`. To add a new export to `xtab` and to the kernel's internal table of NFS exports without editing `/etc/exports`, use the following syntax:

```
exportfs -o exp_opts host:directory
```

`exp_opts`, `host`, and `directory` use the same syntax as that described for `/etc/exports` earlier in the chapter. Consider the following:

```
# exportfs -o async,rw 192.169.0.3:/var/tmp
```

This command exports `/var/tmp` with the `async` and `rw` options to the host whose IP address is `192.168.0.3`. This invocation is exactly equivalent to the following entry in `/etc/exports`:

```
/var/tmp 192.168.0.3(async,rw)
```

A bare `exportfs` call lists all currently exported file systems, and using `-v` lists currently exported file systems with their mount options.

```
# exporfs -v
/home             192.168.0.*(rw,async,wdelay,root_squash)
```

To remove an exported file system, use the `-u` option with `exportfs`. For example, the following command unexports the `/home` file system shown in the previous example.

```
# exportfs -v -u 192.168.0.*:/home
unexporting 192.168.0.*:/home
unexporting 192.168.0.2:/home from kernel
```

The `showmount` command queries the mount daemon, `mountd`, about the status of the NFS server. Its syntax is:

```
showmount [-adehv] [host]
```

Invoked with no options, `showmount` displays a list of all clients that have mounted file systems from the current host. Specify `host` to query the mount daemon on that host, where `host` can be a resolvable DNS host name or, as in the following example, an IP address:

```
# showmount 198.60.22.
Hosts on 198.60.22.2:
hammer.xmission.com
mammon.xmission.com
news.xmission.com
```

Table 7-3 describes the effect of showmount's options:

TABLE 7–3 OPTIONS FOR THE SHOWMOUNT COMMAND

Option	Description
-a	Displays client host names and mounted directories in *host:directory*
-d	Displays only the directories clients have mounted
-e	Displays the NFS server's list of exported file systems
-h	Displays a short usage summary
-v	Displays showmount's version number
--no-headers	Disables displaying descriptive headings for showmount's output

The following examples show the output of showmount executed on an NFS server that has exported /home to the client named rh, which has an IP address of 192.168.0.2, using the following entry in /etc/exports:

```
/home 192.168.0.*(rw)
```

The first command uses the -a option for the most comprehensive output, the second uses the -d option to show only the mounted directories, and the third example uses -e to show the server's export list.

```
# showmount -a
All mount points on luther.kurtwerks.com:
192.168.0.2:/home
# showmount -d
Directories on luther.kurtwerks.com:
/home
# showmount -e
Export list for luther.kurtwerks.com:
/home 192.168.0.*
```

The `showmount` command is most useful on potential NFS clients because they can identify the directories an NFS server is exporting. By the same token, however, this poses a security risk because, in the absence of entries in `/etc/hosts.deny` that forbid access to the portmapper, *any* host can obtain this information from an NFS server.

Example NFS server

This section illustrates a simple but representative NFS server configuration. It exports two file systems. The first is `/home`, which resides on a dedicated disk, `/dev/hdc1`, the first IDE disk on the secondary IDE controller. The second exported file system is `/usr/local`, which is a subdirectory of the `/usr` file system located on the device `/dev/hda5`.

Here are the entries for this configuration in `/etc/exports`:

```
/home 192.168.0.*(rw,no_subtree_check)
/usr/local 192.168.0.*(ro)
```

With the exports configured, start the daemons (the portmapper is already running) using the initialization scripts:

```
# /etc/rc.d/init.d/nfs start
Starting NFS services:                               [  OK  ]
Starting NFS quotas:                                 [  OK  ]
Starting NFS mountd:                                 [  OK  ]
Starting NFS daemon:                                 [  OK  ]
# /etc/rc.d/init.d/nfslock start
Starting NFS file locking services:
Starting NFS statd:                                  [  OK  ]
```

Next, use `rpcinfo -p` to make sure the necessary daemons are running, then finish up with `showmount -a` (or `exportfs -v`) to list the server's NFS exports:

```
# rpcinfo -p
   program vers proto   port
    100000    2   tcp    111  portmapper
    100000    2   udp    111  portmapper
    100011    1   udp    779  rquotad
    100011    2   udp    779  rquotad
    100005    1   udp   1057  mountd
    100005    1   tcp   1053  mountd
    100005    2   udp   1057  mountd
    100005    2   tcp   1053  mountd
    100005    3   udp   1057  mountd
    100005    3   tcp   1053  mountd
    100003    2   udp   2049  nfs
```

```
    100003    3   udp   2049  nfs
    100021    1   udp   1058  nlockmgr
    100021    3   udp   1058  nlockmgr
    100021    4   udp   1058  nlockmgr
    100024    1   udp   1059  status
    100024    1   tcp   1054  status
# showmount -a
All mount points on luther.kurtwerks.com:
192.168.0.2:/home
192.168.0.2:/usr/local
# exportfs -v
/usr/local      192.168.0.*(ro,async,wdelay,root_squash)
/home
192.168.0.*(rw,async,wdelay,root_squash,no_subtree_check)
```

After you have confirmed that the NFS daemons are running and that the exports are available, you are ready to configure one or more NFS clients.

Configuring an NFS Client

Configuring client systems to mount NFS exports is even simpler than configuring the NFS server itself. This section of the chapter provides a brief overview of client configuration, identifies the key files and commands involved in configuring and mounting NFS exported file systems, and shows you how to configure a client to access the NFS exports configured in the previous section.

Overview of client configuration

Configuring a client system to use NFS involves making sure that the portmapper and the NFS file locking daemons statd and lockd are available, adding entries to the client's /etc/fstab for the NFS exports, and mounting the exports using the mount command.

Key files and commands

From an NFS client's perspective, NFS exported file systems are functionally equivalent to local file systems. Thus, as you might expect, you use the mount command at the command line to mount NFS exports on the fly, just as you would a local file system. Similarly, to mount NFS exports at boot time, you should add entries to the file system mount table, /etc/fstab. As a networked file system, NFS is sensitive to network conditions, so the mount command supports special options that address NFS's sensitivities and peculiarities. Table 7-4 lists the major NFS-specific options that mount accepts. For a complete list and discussion of all NFS-specific options, see the NFS manual page (man nfs).

TABLE 7–4 NFS–SPECIFIC MOUNT OPTIONS

Option	Description
rsize=*n*	Sets the NFS read buffer size to *n* bytes (the default is 4096)
wsize=*n*	Sets the NFS write buffer size to *n* bytes (the default is 4096)
timeo=*n*	Sets the RPC transmission timeout to *n* tenths of a second (the default is 7). Especially useful with the soft mount option
retry=*n*	Sets the time to retry a mount operation before giving up to *n* minutes (the default is 10,000)
port=*n*	Sets the NFS server port to which to connect to *n* (the default is 2049)
mountport=*n*	Sets the mountd server port to connect to *n* (no default)
mounthost=*name*	Sets the name of the server running mountd to *name*
bg	Enables mount attempts to run in the background if the first mount attempt times out (disable with nobg)
fg	Causes mount attempts to run in the foreground if the first mount attempt times out, the default behavior (disable with nofg)
soft	Allows an NFS file operation to fail and terminate (disable with nosoft)
hard	Enables failed NFS file operations to continue retrying after reporting "server not responding" on the system, the default behavior (disable with nohard).
intr	Allow signals (such as Ctrl+C) to interrupt a failed NFS file operation if the file system is mounted with the hard option (disable with nointr). Has no effect unless the hard option is also specified or if soft or nohard is specified
tcp	Mount the NFS file system using the TCP protocol (disable with notcp)
udp	Mount the NFS file system using the UDP protocol, the default behavior (disable with noupd)
lock	Enables NFS locking and starts the statd and lockd daemons (disable with nolock)

The most commonly used and useful NFS-specific mount options are rsize=8192, wsize=8192, hard, intr, and nolock. Increasing the default size of the NFS read and write buffers improves NFS's performance. The suggested value is

8192 bytes, but you might find that you get better performance with larger or smaller values. The `nolock` option can also improve performance because it eliminates the overhead of file locking calls, but not all servers support file locking over NFS. As explained in Table 7-5, if an NFS file operation fails, you can use a keyboard interrupt, usually Ctrl+C, to interrupt the operation if the exported file system was mounted with *both* the `intr` and `hard` options. This prevents NFS clients from hanging.

 The section titled "Client Security Considerations" near the end of the chapter suggests several general mount options you can use to improve security on an NFS client.

As with an NFS server, an NFS client needs the portmap daemon to process and route RPC calls and returns from the server to the appropriate port and programs. Accordingly, make sure the portmapper is running on the client system using the portmap initialization script, `/etc/rc.d/init.d/portmap`.

In order to use NFS file locking, both an NFS server and any NFS clients need to run `statd` and `lockd`. As explained in the previous section, the simplest way to accomplish this is to use the initialization script, `/etc/rc.d/init.d/nfslock`. Presumably, you have already started `nfslock` on the server system, so all that remains is to start it on the client system.

Once you have configured the mount table and started the requisite daemons, all that remains is to mount the file systems. Chapter 4 discusses the `mount` command used to mount file systems, so this section shows only the `mount` invocations needed to mount NFS file systems. During the initial configuration and testing, it is easiest to mount and unmount NFS export at the command line. For example, to mount `/home` from the server configured at the end of the previous section, execute the following command as root:

```
# mount -t nfs luther:/home /home
```

You can, if you wish, specify client mount options using `mount`'s `-o` option, as shown in the following example (the command wraps because of page width constraints — you should type it on a single line):

```
# mount -t nfs luther:/home /home -o
rsize=8292,wsize=8192,hard,intr,nolock
```

Alternatively, you can use \ to escape an embedded newline in the command:

```
# mount -t nfs luther:/home /home \
-o rsize=8292,wsize=8192,hard,intr,nolock
```

After satisfying yourself that the configuration works properly, you probably want to mount the exports at boot time. Fortunately, Red Hat Linux makes this easy because the initialization script /etc/rc.d/init.d/netfs, which runs at boot time, mounts all networked file systems automatically, including NFS file systems. It does this by parsing /etc/fstab looking for file systems of type nfs and mounting those file systems.

Example NFS client

The NFS server configured in the previous section exported /home and /usr/local, so I will demonstrate configuring an NFS client that mounts those directories.

1. Clients that want to use both exports need to have the following entries in /etc/fstab:

```
luther:/usr/local /usr/local nfs
rsize=8192,wsize=8192,hard,intr,nolock 0 0
luther:/home       /home       nfs
rsize=8192,wsize=8192,hard,intr,nolock 0 0
```

2. Start the portmapper using the following command:

```
# /etc/rc.d/init.d/portmap start
Starting portmapper:                            [  OK  ]
```

3. Mount the exports using one of the following commands:

```
# mount -a -t nfs
```

or

```
# mount /home /usr/local
```

The first command mounts all (-a) directories of type nfs (-t nfs). The second command mounts only the file systems /home and /usr/local. Verify that the mounts completed successfully by attempting to access files on each file system. If everything works as designed, you are ready to go. Otherwise, read the section titled "Troubleshooting NFS" for tips and suggestions for solving common NFS problems.

Tuning NFS

The subject of performance tuning deserves its own book. Nevertheless, we can provide some general guidelines for improving NFS's performance and offer a few tips for maintaining a responsive NFS environment. As we remarked earlier in this chapter, NFS is sensitive to network performance, more specifically to network congestion and bandwidth problems. As a general rule, if NFS performance starts to degrade, you can be reasonably certain that heavy network traffic is the culprit.

However, NFS traffic, especially at the server, tends to be "bursty," that is, it is characterized by periods of relative quiescence broken up by sharp upward spikes in activity. As a result, tuning efforts need to take into account such uneven access patterns to insure optimal performance under load *and* during less strenuous periods.

Before we discuss specific problems and solutions, here are a few general suggestions that you can apply to improve a system's performance overall and the performance of an NFS server in particular. While most of these tips address a server system, they also have beneficial effects on a client system.

◆ Spread NFS exported file systems across multiple disks and, if possible, multiple disk controllers. The purpose of this strategy is to avoid disk *hot spots*, concentrating I/O operations on a single disk or a single area of a disk. Similarly, distributing disks containing NFS exported file systems on multiple disk controllers reduces the amount of I/O traffic on any single controller, which improves the overall performance of the I/O subsystem.

◆ Replace IDE disks with SCSI disks, and, if you have the budget for it, SCSI disks with FibreChannel disk arrays. IDE disks, even the UDMA variety that operate at 66Mhz, use the system CPU for I/O transfers, whereas SCSI disks do not. This step prevents disk I/O from becoming CPU bound and also takes advantage of SCSI's generally faster performance. FibreChannel, although markedly more expensive than SCSI, offers even faster performance. However, in small shops and for small servers, using FibreChannel is akin to killing gnats with a howitzer.

◆ Consider replacing 10MB Ethernet cards with 100MB Ethernet cards throughout the network. Although only slightly more expensive than their 10MB cousins, 100MB cards offer considerably more throughput per dollar. The faster cards result in better network performance across the board, not just for NFS. Of course, to reap the benefit of 100MB cards, they need to be used on both clients and servers, and the gateways, routers, and switches must be capable of handling 100MB speeds.

◆ Replace hubs with switches. Network hubs, while less expensive than switches, route all network traffic across the same data channel, which can become saturated during periods of heavy activity. Switches, on the other hand, transmit network packets across multiple data channels, reducing congestion and packet collisions and resulting in faster overall throughput.

◆ If necessary, dedicate one or more servers specifically to NFS work. CPU or memory intensive processes, such as Web, database, or compute servers, can starve an NFS server for needed CPU cycles or memory pages.

◆ In extreme cases, resegmenting the network may be the answer to NFS performance problems. The goal with this tip is to isolate NFS traffic on its own segment, again, reducing network saturation and congestion and allocating dedicated bandwidth to NFS traffic.

To diagnose specific NFS performance problems, use the nfsstat command, which prints the kernel's NFS statistics. Its syntax is:

```
nfsstat [-acnrsz] [-o facility]
```

Unfortunately, nfsstat only displays NFS server statistics because the NFS client does not currently accumulate data for use in reports, even though nfsstat includes an option (-c) for reporting client statistics. Table 7-5 explains nfsstat's options.

TABLE 7-5 nfsstat COMMAND OPTIONS

Option	Description
-a	Prints NFS, RPC, and network statistics for NFS clients and servers.
-c	Prints NSF client statistics. This option is not currently supported.
-n	Prints only NFS statistics. By default, nfsstat displays both NFS and RPC information.
-r	Prints only RPC statistics. By default, nfsstat displays both NFS and RPC information.
-s	Prints NFS server statistics. By default, nfsstat displays both server and client statistics.
-z	Resets the kernel's NFS statistics counters to zero. This option is not currently supported.
-o facility	Display statistics for the specified facility.

The facility argument for the -o option enables you to fine tune the type of information nfsstat displays. facility can have one of the following values:

- fh — Displays utilization data on the server's file handle cache, including the total number of lookups and the number of cache hits and misses.

- net — Shows network layer statistics, such as the number of received packets or number of TCP connections.

- nfs — Displays NFS protocol statistics categorized by RPC call.

- rc — Prints utilizatation data on the server's request reply cache, including the total number of lookups and the number of cache hits and misses.

- rpc — Prints general RPC information.

The Linux NFS-HOWTO on the NFS Web page at `http://nfs.sourcefource.net/nfs-howto/`, dedicates an entire section to performance tuning the Linux NFS implementation. Another valuable source of general performance tuning information, not only for NFS but for all varieties of Linux issues, is the Linux Performance Tuning Web site at `http://linuxperf.nl.linux.org/`.

Troubleshooting NFS

In addition to performance degradation, you might encounter other problems with NFS that require resolution. This section discusses some of the typical difficulties system administrators have with NFS and how to resolve them. These tips are only a starting point.

The Linux NFS-HOWTO on the NFS Web page at `http://nfs.sourcefource.net/nfs-howto/` dedicates an entire section to troubleshooting NFS.

First here are some problems that, in reality, are red herrings. Log messages resembling the following are annoying, but harmless:

```
kernel: fh_verify: kwall/users: permission failure, acc=4, error=13
kernel: nfs: server localhost not responding, still trying
kernel: nfs: task 18273 can't get a request slot
kernel: nfs: localhost OK
nfslock: rpc.lockd startup failed
kmem_create: forcing word size alignment - nfs_fh
```

The first message occurs when the NFS `setattr` call fails because an NFS client is attempting to access a file to which it does not have access. This message is harmless, but many such log entries might indicate a systematic attempt to compromise the system. The next three messages represent client attempts to contact the NFS server that are timing out. When such timeouts occur, the NFS client reduces the number of concurrent requests it sends in order to avoid overloading the server, which results in these messages. Although such messages are usually harmless, if they persist, you may want to investigate possible saturation of the network or the NFS server. The `rpc.lockd` startup failure message almost always occurs when older NFS startup scripts try to start newer versions of `rpc.lockd` manually — these attempts fail because the kernel NFS server daemon, `knfsd`, starts the locking daemon automatically. To make the failure message go away, edit the startup scripts and remove statements that attempt to start `lockd` manually. The final error message occurs if the kernel detects that an NFS file handle is 16 bits, rather than 32 bits or a multiple thereof.

Would that all error messages were as harmless as these! A log message resembling the following, while not dire, demands timely attention:

```
nfs warning: mount version older than kernel
```

This message means exactly what it says: the version of the `mount` command that you are using is older than the kernel version. So, the solution is to upgrade the `mount` package in order for mount to recognize any additional options or features of the new kernel.

If you transfer very large files via NFS, and NFS eats all of the available CPU cycles, causing the server to respond at a glacial pace, you are probably running an older version of the kernel that has problems with the `fsync` call that accumulates disk syncs before flushing the buffers. This issue is reportedly fixed in the 2.4 kernel series, so upgrading the kernel may solve the problem.

Similarly, if you execute commands on an NFS exported file system that do not result in large data transfers from server to client (such as an `ls` command) and have no problem, but then experience severe response problems with large data transfers (such as a `cp` command), you may be using `rsize` or `wsize` parameters on the client that are larger than the `rsize` or `wsize` parameters on the server. Reduce these values on the client side to see if performance recovers. Also make sure that the firewall for the client and the server permits fragmented packets to pass through. NFS uses packet fragmentation, so firewalls that deny or drop fragmented packets force constant retransmission of data. Reportedly, this is especially a problem on Linux systems still using the 2.2 packet filter, ipchains. Rewrite the filters to accept fragmented packets, and performance should improve almost immediately.

If you are unable to see files on a mounted file system, check the following items:

◆ Make sure that the file system is, in fact, mounted. Use one of the following commands to verify that the file system is mounted:

```
# cat /proc/mounts
# mount -f
```

Obviously, if the file system is not mounted, mount it.

◆ If the file system is mounted, make sure that another file system is not mounted on top of it. If you *have* layered a file system on top of an export, unmount and remount both, making sure to mount them on separate mount points.

◆ Make sure the client has read privileges to the specified files by verifying the file system permissions on the server, the client's mount point, and that the mount options (in /etc/fstab or specified on the command line) are correct on the client.

If you cannot mount an exported directory, the most common error message is:

```
mount failed, reason given by server: Permission denied
```

This error message means that the server thinks the client does not have access to the specified export. In this case, do one or more of the following:

◆ Review the export specifications in /etc/exports on the server, making sure that they are correct *and* that the client is mounting the export the same way it is exported. For example, an NFS client cannot mount an exported directory read/write (the rw mount option) if that directory is exported from the server read-only (using the ro export option).

◆ On the server, execute the following command:

```
# exportfs -ar
```

This command makes sure that any changes made to /etc/exports since the exports were first exported are updated in the server's exports table and propagated out to NFS clients.

◆ Look at the contents of /var/lib/nfs/xtab to review the complete list of all of the export options applied to a given export. If they are incorrect, edit /etc/exports accordingly and then rerun the exportfs -ar command to update the server's export table with the proper options.

Examining NFS Security

As explained at the beginning of the chapter, NFS has some inherent security problems that make it unsuitable for use across the Internet and potentially unsafe for use even in a trusted network. This section identifies key security issues of NFS in general and the security risks specific to an NFS server and to NFS clients and suggests remedies that minimize your network's exposure to these security risks. Be forewarned, however, that *no* list of security tips, however comprehensive, makes your site completely secure and that plugging NFS security holes does not address other potential exploits.

General NFS security issues

One NFS weakness, in general terms, is the /etc/exports file. If a cracker is capable of spoofing or taking over a *trusted address*, one listed in /etc/exports, then your mount points are accessible. Another NFS weak spot is normal Linux file system access controls that take over once a client has mounted an NFS export: once mounted, normal user and group permissions on the files take over access control.

The first line of defense against these two weaknesses is to use host access control as described earlier in the chapter to limit access to services on your system, particularly the portmapper, which has long been a target of exploit attempts. Similarly, you should put in entries for `lockd`, `statd`, `mountd`, and `rquotad`.

More generally, wise application of IP packet firewalls, using netfilter, dramatically increases NFS server security. netfilter is stronger than NFS daemon-level security or even TCP Wrappers because it restricts access to your server at the packet level. Although netfilter is described in detail in Chapter 26, this section gives you a few tips on how to configure a netfilter firewall that plays nicely with NFS.

First, identify the ports and services NFS uses so that you know where to apply the packet filters. Table 7-6 lists the ports and protocols each NFS daemon (on both the client and server side) use.

TABLE 7-6 PORTS AND NETWORK PROTOCOLS USED BY NFS DAEMONS

Service	Port	Protocols
portmap	111	TCP, UDP
nfsd	2049	TCP, UDP
mountd	variable	TCP, UDP
lockd	variable	TCP, UDP
statd	variable	TCP, UDP
rquotad	variable	UDP

 NFS over TCP is currently experimental on the server side, so you should almost always use UDP on the server. However, TCP is quite stable on NFS clients. Nevertheless, using packet filters for both protocols on both the client and the server does no harm.

Note that `mountd`, `lockd`, `statd`, and `rquotad` do not bind to any specific port, that is, they use a port number assigned randomly by the portmapper (which is one of portmapper's purposes in the first place). The best way to address this variability is to assign each daemon a specific port using the `-p` option and then to apply the packet filter to that port. Regardless of how you configure your firewall, you must have the following rule:

```
iptables -A INPUT -f -j ACCEPT
```

This rule accepts all packet fragments except the first one (which is treated as a normal packet) because NFS does not work correctly unless you let fragments through the firewall. Be sure to read Chapter 26 carefully to configure your NFS server's firewall properly.

Server security considerations

On the server, always use the `root_squash` option in `/etc/exports`. Actually, NFS helps you in this regard because root squashing is the default, so you should not disable it (with `no_root_squash`) unless you have an extremely compelling reason to do so. With root squashing in place, the server substitutes the UID of the anonymous user for root's UID/GID (0), meaning that a *client's* root account cannot even access, much less change, files that only the *server's* root account can access or change.

The implication of root squashing may not be clear, so permit me to make it explicit: all critical binaries and files should be owned by root, not bin, wheel, adm or another nonroot account. The only account that an NFS client's root user cannot access is the server's root account, so critical files owned by root are much less exposed than if they are owned by other accounts.

NFS also helps you maintain a secure server through the `secure` mount option because this mount option is one of the default options `mountd` applies to all exports unless explicitly disabled using the `insecure` option. As you will learn in Chapter 11, ports 1–1024 are reserved for root's use; merely mortal user accounts cannot bind these ports. Thus, ports 1–1024 are sometimes referred to as privileged or secure ports. The secure option prevents a malevolent nonroot user from initiating a spoofed NFS dialogue on an unprivileged port and using it as a launch point for exploit attempts.

Client security considerations

On the client, disable SUID (set UID) programs on NFS mounts using the `nosuid` option. The `nosuid` option prevents a server's root account from creating an SUID root program on an exported file system, logging in to the client as a normal user, and then using the UID root program to become root on the client. In some cases, you might also disable binaries on mounted file systems using the `noexec` option, but this effort almost always proves to be impractical or even counterproductive because one of the benefits of NFS is sharing file systems that contain scripts or programs that need to be executed.

NFS version 3, the version available with Red Hat Linux (well, with version 2.4 of the Linux kernel) supports NFS file locking. Accordingly, NFS clients must run `statd` and `lockd` in order for NFS file locks to function correctly. `statd` and `lockd`, in turn, depend on the portmapper, so consider applying the same precautions for `portmap`, `statd`, and `lockd` on NFS clients that were suggested for the NFS server.

In summary, using TCP wrappers, the `secure`, `root_squash`, and `nosuid` options, and sturdy packet filters can increase the overall security of your NFS setup. However, NFS is a complex, nontrivial subsystem, so it is entirely conceivable that new bugs and exploits will be discovered.

Summary

In this chapter you learned to configure NFS, the Network File System. First, you found a general overview of NFS, its typical uses, and its advantages and disadvantages. Next, you found out how to configure an NFS server, you identified key files and commands to use, and you saw the process with a typical real-world example. With the server configured and functioning, you then learned how to configure a client system to access NFS exported file systems, again using key configuration files and commands and simulating the procedure with a representative example. You also learned how to address NFS performance problems and how to troubleshoot some common NFS errors. The chapter's final section identified potential security problems with NFS and suggested ways to mitigate the threat.

Chapter 8

The Network Information System

IN THIS CHAPTER

- Understanding NIS
- Configuring an NIS server
- Configuring an NIS client
- Strengthening NIS security

A COMMON CHALLENGE facing administrators charged with maintaining a network of Linux machines is how to share information across the network while maintaining that information centrally. The Network Information Service (NIS) is one solution to such a challenge.

Understanding NIS

This chapter describes how to configure NIS services on a network. The Network Information Service distributes information that needs to be shared throughout a Linux network to all machines on the network. NIS was originally developed by Sun Microsystems and known as Yellow Pages (YP), so many commands begin with the letters yp, such as `ypserv`, `ypbind`, and `yppasswd`. Unfortunately for Sun, the phrase "Yellow Pages" was (and is) a registered trademark of British Telecom in the United Kingdom, so Sun changed the name of their Yellow Pages services to Network Information Service. Despite the name change, however, the NIS suite of utilities retained the `yp` prefixes because administrators had become accustomed to them.

The information most commonly distributed across a network using NIS consists of user database and authentication information, such as `/etc/passwd` and `/etc/group`. If, for example, a user's password entry is shared by all login hosts via the NIS password database, that user is able to log in on all login hosts on the network, all hosts, that is, that are running the NIS client programs. However, user authentication databases are not the only use for NIS — any information that needs to be distributed across a network and that can or should be centrally administered

185

is a viable candidate for sharing via NIS. For example, you can use NIS to distribute a company telephone directory or a listing of accounting codes.

 Do not be confused by the use of the word *database*. I use *database* in its general sense to refer to a centralized store of information, not to refer to database management systems such as Oracle or MySQL.

NIS uses a standard client-server architecture arrayed in one of several possible configurations. NIS configurations revolve around the notion of a *domain*. An NIS domain is not the same as an Internet or DNS domain. A *DNS domain name* (more specifically, a fully qualified domain name, or FQDN), as you know, is the official name that uniquely identifies a system to the Internet domain name system. An *NIS domain name* refers to a group of systems, typically on a LAN or on only a subnet of a LAN, that use the same NIS maps. NIS domains are typically used as system management tools, a convenient method for organizing groups of machines that need to access the information shared across a network using a set of common NIS maps.

NIS databases are stored in DBM format, a binary file format based on simple ASCII text files. For example, the files `/etc/passwd` and `/etc/group` can be converted directly to DBM format using an ASCII-to-DBM conversion program named `makedbm`.

Each NIS domain must have at least one system that functions as an NIS server for that domain. An NIS *server* is a centrally-administered repository for information that is shared across the network using NIS. NIS *clients* are programs that use NIS to query designated servers for information that is stored in the servers' databases, which are known as *maps*. NIS servers can be further subdivided into master and slave servers. A *master* server maintains the authoritative copies of the NIS maps.

A *slave* server maintains copies of the NIS databases, which it receives from the master NIS server whenever changes are made to the databases stored on the master. In NIS configurations that use slave servers, the slaves receive copies of the DBM databases, not the ASCII source files. The `yppush` program notifies slave servers of changes to the NIS maps, and then the slaves automatically retrieve the updated maps in order to synchronize their databases with the master. NIS clients do not need to do this because they communicate with their designated server(s) to obtain current information. The rationale for slave servers is to provide redundancy — if the master server is unavailable for some reason, slave servers function as backup servers until the master is again available.

Four NIS topologies are commonly used:

◆ A single domain with a master server, no slave servers, and one or more clients (Figure 8-1)

◆ A single domain with a master server, one or more slave servers, and one or more clients (Figure 8-2)

◆ Multiple domains, each with its own master server, no slave servers, and one or more clients (Figure 8-3)

◆ Multiple domains, each with its own master server, one or more slave servers, and one or more clients (Figure 8-4)

The single domain configurations are the most widely used in most situations. Figure 8-1 illustrates the single domain, single server configuration. Figure 8-2 shows the single domain, multiple server configuration.

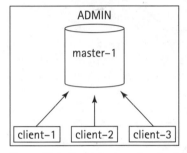

Figure 8-1: A single domain, single server NIS configuration

In Figure 8-1, the single server, master-1, responds to all queries from NIS clients (client-1, client-2, and client-3) and is the sole source of information for the domain, named admin. Figure 8-2 illustrates the same domain but includes a slave server, slave-1. In this case, client-1 and client-2 continue to query the master server, but client-3 communicates with the slave server when performing NIS queries.

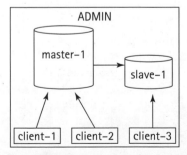

Figure 8-2: A single domain, multiple server NIS configuration

In Figure 8-2, client-3 has not specifically been configured to communicate with the slave server. Rather, it sends out NIS broadcast messages for a given domain and accepts replies from any server authoritative for that domain – the server that "wins" is the server that replies first.

At large sites or in complicated networks, you might find it necessary to have multiple NIS domains. Figures 8-3 and 8-4 illustrate such configurations. Figure 8-3 shows two domains, admin and devel, each with its own master server, master-admin and master-devel. Clients in the admin domain (client-1, client-2, and client-3) communicate only with the master-admin server, and clients in the devel domain (client-4, client-5, and client-6) communicate only with master-devel.

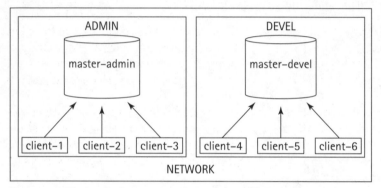

Figure 8-3: The multiple domain, single server NIS configuration

Figure 8-4 illustrates the same setup as Figure 8-3, except that each domain has a slave server, slave-admin and slave-devel, and some of the clients in each domain communicate with the slave servers rather than with the master. As in the single server example, any given client will communicate with the server for its domain that responds the fastest to a broadcast query.

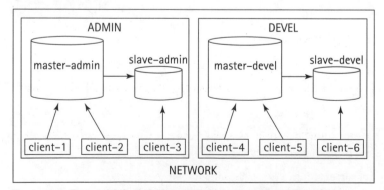

Figure 8-4: The multiple domain, multiple server NIS configuration

An important caveat pertaining to NIS usage needs to be emphasized: a singleton server (one whose function is not duplicated or replicated elsewhere in the network) that relies upon NIS for key data potentially represents a single point of failure. If your network or organization relies on high availability of your network, NIS may not be an acceptable solution for information sharing.

A properly configured NIS setup involves configuring at least one NIS server and one or more NIS clients. If your Red Hat Linux system is going to be part of a network with existing NIS servers, you only need to install and configure the client programs, ypbind, ypwhich, ypcat, yppoll, and ypmatch. The most important program is the NIS client daemon, ypbind. ypbind is usually started from the system's startup procedure. As soon as ypbind is running your system has become an NIS client.

On the other hand, if your Red Hat Linux system is going to be part of a network that does not already have NIS servers in place, you need to configure at least one NIS server, which involves configuring the ypserv client daemon and identifying the files that NIS distributes to client programs and, optionally, to slave servers.

Configuring an NIS Server

The simplest NIS configuration consists of a single NIS server and one or more clients. In this case, NIS server configuration involves the following steps:

1. Setting the NIS domain name.

2. Configuring and starting the server daemon, ypbind.

3. Initializing the NIS maps.

4. Starting the NIS password daemon.

5. Starting the NIS transfer daemon if you use slave servers.

6. Modifying the startup process to start the NIS daemons when the system reboots.

If your NIS configuration also utilizes slave servers, you also need to perform configuration steps on the slave servers.

For more information about NIS configuration, see the NIS HOW-TO at the Linux Documentation Project, `http://www.linuxdoc.org/HOWTO/NIS-HOWTO/index.html`, and the NIS Web pages at `http://www.suse.de/~kukuk/nis/`.

Key files and commands

Table 8-1 lists the commands, daemons, and configurations files used to configure and maintain an NIS server. They are described in greater detail as the text explains how to set up and run an NIS server.

TABLE 8-1 NIS SERVER CONFIGURATION COMMANDS AND FILES

Command	Description
nisdomainname	Sets a system's NIS domain name
ypserv	Handles the primary NIS server duties
ypinit	Builds and installs the NIS databases
yppasswdd	Processes user password changes in an NIS environment
ypxfrd	Speeds up the transfer of large NIS maps from master to slave servers
yppush	Propagates updated NIS maps to slave servers
/var/yp/securenets	Lists hosts permitted to access the NIS maps
/etc/ypserv.conf	Stores runtime configuration options and special host access directives

Setting the NIS domain name

The initial step in configuring an NIS client is to set the NIS domain name. When first configuring the NIS server, the quickest way to set an NIS domain name is to use the nisdomainname command:

```
# nisdomainname nisdomain
```

Replace *nisdomain* with the name of your NIS domain. Next, reissue the nisdomainname command with no arguments to confirm that the NIS domain name was successfully set. These measures to set the NIS domain name are only temporary — the name set will not survive a system reboot. You learn later in this section how to set the NIS domain name permanently.

 You can also use the domainname command to get and set a system's NIS domain name. In fact, you can use one of a number of similarly named commands to do so. See the domainname man page for more information.

Configuring and starting the server daemon

With the NIS domain name set, at least temporarily, you can configure and start the primary NIS server daemon. The key configuration files are /var/yp/securenets and /etc/ypserv.conf. /etc/ypserv.conf is the configuration file for both ypserv, the primary NIS server daemon, and the NIS transfer daemon, ypxfrd. It contains runtime configuration options, called *option lines*, for ypserv, and host access information, called *access rules*, for both ypserv and ypxfrd. The default values in /etc/ypserv.conf, which are shown in Listing 8-1, are sufficient for most NIS server configurations.

Listing 8-1: The Default ypserv.conf File Values for Red Hat Linux

```
dns:no
*:shadow.byname:port:yes
*:passwd.adjunct.byname:port:yes
*:*:none
```

ypserv and ypxfrd read /etc/ypserv.conf when they start and when sent a SIGHUP signal (for example, by kill -HUP). Entries in the file appear one per line. Each line is made up of colon-separated fields defining either an option line or an access rule. An option line has the following format:

option:[yes|no]

option can be either dns or xfr_check_port. dns controls whether or not the NIS server performs a DNS lookup for hosts not listed in the host maps. The default is no. xfr_check_port controls whether or not ypserv runs on a port numbered less than 1024, a so-called *privileged port*. The default is yes. As you can see in the default configuration file, the dns option is no. The absence of xfr_check_port from the configuration file means that ypserv uses a privileged port.

Access rules have the slightly more complicated format:

host:*map*:*security*:*mangle*[:*field*]

◆ *host* — The IP address to match. Wildcards are allowed. For example, the entry `192.168.0.` refers to all IP addresses between 192.168.0.1 and 192.168.0.255.

◆ *map* — The name of a map to match or * for all maps.

◆ *security* — The type of security to use. Can be one of `none`, `port`, `deny`, or `des`. An entry of `none` enables access to *map* for *host* unless *mangle* is set to `yes`, in which case access is denied. `port` enables access if the connection is coming from a privileged port. If *mangle* is set to `yes`, access is enabled, but the password field is mangled. If *mangle* is no, access is denied. `deny` denies the matching host access to this map. `des` requires DES authentication.

◆ *mangle* — The type of port to use. If set to yes, *field* is replaced by x if the requesting port is an unprivileged port. If set to `no`, *field* is not mangled if the requesting port is unprivileged.

◆ *field* — The field number in the map to mangle. The default value if *field* is not specified is 2, which corresponds to the password field in `/etc/group`, `/etc/shadow`, and `/etc/passwd`.

Access rules are tried in order, and all rules are evaluated. If no rule matches a connecting host, access to the corresponding map is enabled.

The most important configuration file is `/var/yp/securenets`, which contains network number and netmask pairs that define the lists of hosts permitted to access your NIS server maps. It contains one entry per line of the form *m.m.m.m n.n.n.n*, where *m.m.m.m* is a netmask and *n.n.n.n* is network number. A host match occurs if the IP address matches the network number and mask. For example, consider a `/var/yp/securenets` with these entries:

```
255.255.255.255 127.0.0.1
255.255.255.0 192.168.0.0
```

The first line indicates that the localhost (IP address 127.0.0.1) is permitted to access the NIS server. The second line specifies that any host with an IP address in the range 192.168.0.1 to 192.168.0.255 is permitted to access the NIS server. All other hosts are denied access.

Before starting the server, make sure the portmapper daemon, `portmap`, is running. NIS requires the portmapper because NIS uses remote procedure calls (RPC). To see if the portmapper is running, you can use the portmapper's initialization script, `/etc/rc.d/init.d/portmap`, or the `rpcinfo` command. If the portmapper is not running, you can easily start it. Using the initialization script, the command to execute and its output, are:

```
# /etc/rc.d/init.d/portmap status
portmap (pid 559) is running...
```

The output indicates the process ID (PID) of the portmapper. On the other hand, if the portmapper is *not* running, the output of the command looks like the following:

```
# /etc/rc.d/init.d/portmap status
portmap is stopped
```

To start the portmapper, execute the following command:

```
/etc/rc.d/init.d/portmap start
Starting portmapper:                              [  OK  ]
```

You can also use the `rpcinfo` command shown next to see if the portmapper is running:

```
# rpcinfo -p localhost
   program vers proto   port
    100000   2   tcp    111  portmapper
    100000   2   udp    111  portmapper
```

Again, if you do not see output indicating that the portmapper is running, use the initialization script shown previously to start the portmapper. Once you have the portmapper started, start the NIS server using the command:

```
# /etc/rc.d/init.d/ypserv start
Starting YP server services:                      [  OK  ]
```

Next, use the following `rpcinfo` invocation to make sure that the server is running:

```
# rpcinfo -u localhost ypserv
program 100004 version 1 ready and waiting
program 100004 version 2 ready and waiting
```

Initializing the NIS maps

Once the NIS server is running, you have to create something for it to serve, which means you need to create the NIS databases on the machine acting as the NIS server. The command for doing so is `ypinit`. `ypinit` builds a complete set of NIS maps for your system and places them in a subdirectory of `/var/yp` named after the NIS domain. As suggested earlier in the chapter, you should have only one master server per NIS domain. All databases are built from scratch, either from information available to the program at runtime, or from the ASCII database files in `/etc`. These files include:

- ◆ `/etc/passwd`
- ◆ `/etc/group`

- ◆ /etc/hosts
- ◆ /etc/networks
- ◆ /etc/services
- ◆ /etc/protocols
- ◆ /etc/netgroup
- ◆ /etc/rpc

To create the NIS databases, execute the command /usr/lib/yp/ypinit -m.

```
# /usr/lib/yp/ypinit -m
```

 TIP   Before initializing the NIS databases, you might want to make backup copies of the source text files shown in the list.

This command uses the -m option to indicate that it is creating maps for the master server.

If you also configure one or more slave NIS servers, you need to make sure that they can successfully communicate with the master server. From each slave server, make sure that ypwhich -m works, which means that the slave servers must also be configured as NIS clients, as described in the section "Configuring an NIS Client." After configuring the slave server as described in that section, execute the command:

```
# /usr/lib/yp/ypinit -s masterhost
```

The -s instructs ypinit to create a slave server using the databases from the master server named masterhost. An NIS database on a slave server is set up by copying an existing database from a running server. masterhost can also be a server on which the NIS maps are current and stable. Your NIS server is now up and running.

Starting the NIS password daemon

Because NIS is used to share authentication information, a method must exist for users to change this information on the NIS server and then to propagate the updated information out to other NIS clients and any slave servers that might be present. Similarly, when new users are added or existing users are deleted, clients and slaves must be notified of the change. The daemon that handles this requirement is yppasswdd. yppasswdd handles password changes and updating other NIS information that depends on user passwords. `yppasswdd` runs only on the NIS master server. Starting the NIS password daemon is a simple matter of executing its initialization script with an argument of start, as shown in the following:

```
# /etc/rc.d/init.d/yppasswdd start
```

Keep in mind that NIS users are not permitted, by default, to change their full name or their login shell. You can enable NIS users to change their login information by starting `yppasswdd` using the `-e chfn` (to allow name changes) or `-e chsh` (to allow login shell changes) options.

Starting the server transfer daemon

`ypxfrd` is used to speed up the transfer of large NIS maps from master to slave servers. Ordinarily, when a slave server receives a message from a master server that there is a new map, the slave starts `ypxfr` to transfer the new map. `ypxfr` reads the contents of a map from the master server one entry at a time. The transfer daemon, `ypxfrd`, speeds up the transfer process by enabling slave servers to copy the master's maps rather than building their own from scratch. As with the password daemon, you run the transfer daemon on the master server only. To start the transfer daemon, execute the command:

```
# /etc/rc.d/init.d/ypxfrd start
```

If you need to update a map, run `make` in the `/var/yp` directory on the NIS master. This command updates a map if the source file is newer, and propagates the new map out to the slave servers, if present.

Starting the NIS servers at boot time

Once you have configured your NIS server, you should make the system changes persistent, which consists of permanently storing the NIS domain name in the network configuration and ensuring that the required daemons (`ypserv`, `yppasswdd`, and, if you use slave servers, `ypxfrd`) start and stop when the system starts and stops.

The first step is permanently saving the NIS domain name. To do this, add the following line to `/etc/sysconfig/network`:

```
NISDOMAIN=nisdomainname
```

Replace `nisdomainname` with the NIS domain name you selected when you initially configured your server. The networking subsystem reads this file at boot time and picks up the domain name to use.

The next step is to run `serviceconf`, the new Red Hat Linux system service configuration tool, to configure the NIS daemons to start at boot time. To do so, type serviceconf (as root) in a terminal window or click Main Menu → Programs → System → Service Configuration on the GNOME panel. The resulting screen should resemble Figure 8-5.

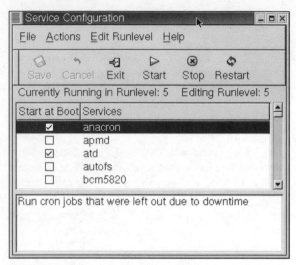

Figure 8-5: The Service Configuration main window

Scroll down to the bottom of the list, and then place check marks in the boxes next to the services you want to start at boot time. In Figure 8-6, for example, yppasswdd and ypserv have been checked, meaning that they start at boot time. Click Save to save your changes, and then click Exit to close serviceconf.

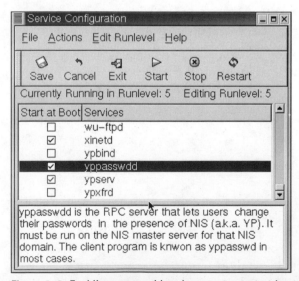

Figure 8-6: Enabling yppaswdd and ypserv to start at boot time

Configuring an example NIS server

This section illustrates the process of setting up a simple master server. The NIS domain name is kurtwerks, running on the server marta.kurtwerks.com, which has an IP address 192.168.0.1. There are no slave servers, and all hosts in the kurtwerks.com DNS domain are permitted to access the NIS server.

1. Set the NIS domain name:

   ```
   # nisdomainname kurtwerks
   # nisdomainname
   kurtwerks
   ```

2. Edit /var/yp/securenets to permit access to the NIS server for the specified hosts. The default configuration enables all hosts to have access (0.0.0.0 0.0.0.0) so change that line to read 255.255.255.0 192.168.0.0. The complete file now resembles the following:

   ```
   255.255.255.255    127.0.0.0
   255.255.255.0      192.168.0.0
   ```

3. Make sure that the portmapper is running:

   ```
   #rpcinfo -p localhost
      program vers proto   port
       100000   2   tcp    111   portmapper
       100000   2   udp    111   portmapper
   ```

4. Start the primary server daemon, ypserv:

   ```
   # /etc/rc.d/init.d/ypserv start
   Starting YP server services:                       [  OK  ]
   ```

5. Confirm that ypserv is running:

   ```
   # rpcinfo -u localhost ypserv
   program 100004 version 1 ready and waiting
   program 100004 version 2 ready and waiting
   ```

6. Initialize the NIS maps:

   ```
   # /usr/lib/yp/ypinit -m

   At this point, we have to construct a list of the hosts which
       will run NIS
   servers.  marta.kurtwerks.com is in the list of NIS server
       hosts.  Please continue to add
   the names for the other hosts, one per line.  When you are
       done with the
   list, type a <control D>.
           next host to add:  marta.kurtwerks.com
   ```

```
          next host to add:
The current list of NIS servers looks like this:

marta.kurtwerks.com

Is this correct?  [y/n: y]   y
We need some  minutes to build the databases...
Building /var/yp/kurtwerks/ypservers...
Running /var/yp/Makefile...
gmake[1]: Entering directory `/var/yp/kurtwerks'
Updating passwd.byname...
Updating passwd.byuid...
Updating group.byname...
Updating group.bygid...
Updating hosts.byname...
Updating hosts.byaddr...
Updating rpc.byname...
Updating rpc.bynumber...
Updating services.byname...
Updating services.byservicename...
Updating netid.byname...
Updating protocols.bynumber...
Updating protocols.byname...
Updating mail.aliases...
gmake[1]: Leaving directory `/var/yp/kurtwerks'
```

7. Start the password daemon, yppasswdd:

   ```
   # /etc/rc.d/init.d/yppaswdd start
   Starting YP passwd services:                      [  OK  ]
   ```

8. Confirm that yppasswd is running:

   ```
   # rpcinfo -u localhost yppasswd
   program 100009 version 1 ready and waiting
   ```

9. Edit /etc/sysconfig/network and add the following line, commenting out or deleting any other line that begins with NISDOMAIN:

   ```
   NISDOMAIN=kurtwerks
   ```

10. Use the Service Configuration tool, as explained earlier, to configure ypserv and yppasswdd to start at boot time.

11. Reboot the server to make sure the daemons start.

If you run slave servers, repeat steps 7 and 8 for the transfer daemon, ypxfrd. Also make sure to set ypxfrd to start at boot time in step 10. Your shiny new NIS master server is now up and running and ready to answer requests from NIS clients.

Configuring an NIS Client

After you have successfully configured at least one master NIS server, you are ready to configure one or more NIS clients. The general procedure for setting up an NIS client involves the following steps:

1. Set the NIS domain name.

2. Configure and start the NIS client daemon.

3. Test the client daemon.

4. Configure the client's startup files to use NIS.

5. Reboot the client.

The following subsections describe these steps in detail and discuss the command and configuration file syntax. Note that there is some overlap between configuring a client and a server, so discussion emphasizes client configuration tasks. The final subsection configures an example NIS client to illustrate the process of setting up a no-frills NIS client system that connects to the server configured at the end of the previous section.

Setting the NIS domain name

The initial step in configuring an NIS client is to set the NIS domain name. As explained in the previous section, execute the following command to set it:

```
# nisdomainname nisdomain
```

As before, replace *nisdomain* with the name of your NIS domain.

Configuring and starting the client daemon

The NIS client daemon, `ypbind` uses a configuration file named `/etc/yp.conf` that specifies which NIS servers clients should use and how to locate them, a process known as *binding* the client to the server. NIS clients can use one of three methods to bind the server, and the type of entry in `/etc/yp.conf` controls how binding takes place. The simplest entry takes the form:

```
ypserver nisserverip
```

This entry tells clients to use the server whose IP address is *nisserverip*. An example of this kind of entry might be:

```
ypserver 192.168.0.1
```

A somewhat more flexible approach enables clients to broadcast a query for the server to contact for a given NIS domain. This method saves tedious editing of client configuration files if (or, perhaps, when) the IP address of the NIS server changes. This entry takes the form shown here, where *nisdomain* is the name of the NIS domain of which the local host is a member.

```
domain nisdomain broadcast
```

An example entry for broadcast clients might resemble the following:

```
domain kurtwerks broadcast
```

Finally, if client systems are members of multiple NIS domains or they can connect to one of several servers for the same NIS domain, the following form enables you to associate a given server with a given NIS domain:

```
domain nisdomain server nisserverip
```

This type of entry in /etc/yp.conf associates the NIS domain *nisdomain* with the NIS server (either master or slave) whose IP address is *nisserverip*. One example of this type of entry might be:

```
domain kurtwerks server 192.168.0.1
domain kurtwerks server 192.168.0.2
domain bookbeast server 192.168.0.2
```

The first two lines identify two servers as the NIS servers for the kurtwerks NIS domain. The second and third lines indicate that the NIS server whose IP address is 192.168.0.2 serves two NIS domains, kurtwerks and bookbeast.

 If the client system can resolve host names to IP addresses without NIS (if, for example, the client runs a caching name server or has an entry in /etc/hosts for the NIS server) you can use a host name instead of an IP address, but your best bet is to use IP addresses in /etc/yp.conf to minimize problems that might arise if name lookup services become inoperable for some reason.

To set the client's NIS servers, you can edit /etc/yp.conf directly or use the authconfig tool, a text mode program for configuring how your system performs user authentication. The following procedure shows you how to use the authconfig program to configure a client system to use NIS:

1. Become the root user and execute the command authconfig in a terminal window. The initial screen should resemble Figure 8-7.

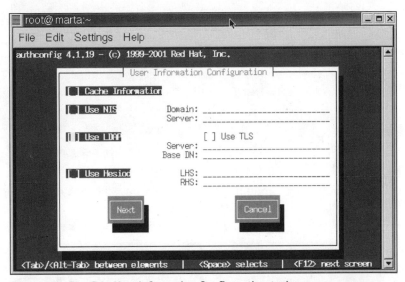

Figure 8-7: The first User Information Configuration tool screen

2. With the cursor positioned in the Cache Information check box, press Space to place an asterisk (*) in the check box. Setting this option causes the client to cache information retrieved from the server, making subsequent NIS lookups considerably faster.

3. Press the Tab key to move the cursor to the Use NIS check box, and then press Space again to place an asterisk in the check box.

4. Press the Tab key to move the cursor to the Domain text box, and then type the NIS domain name.

5. Press the Tab key to move the cursor to the Server text box, and then type the server's IP address. The User Information Configuration Screen should now resemble Figure 8-8.

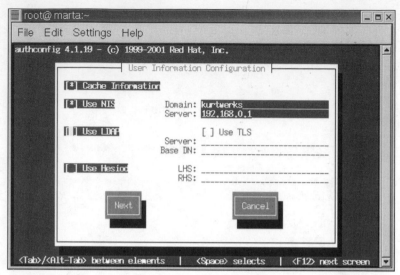

Figure 8-8: The filled out User Information Configuration tool screen

6. Press the Tab key to highlight the Next button, and then press Enter to proceed to the next screen, shown in Figure 8-9.

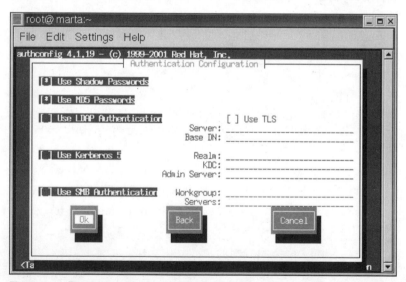

Figure 8-9: The Authentication Configuration screen

7. Press the Tab key until the Ok button is highlighted, and then press Enter to save your changes and exit the `authconfig` tool.

Listing 8-2 shows the contents of /etc/yp.conf after completing the authconfig configuration procedure.

Listing 8-2: authconfig Edits Made to /etc/yp.conf

```
# /etc/yp.conf - ypbind configuration file
# Valid entries are
#
#domain NISDOMAIN server HOSTNAME
#       Use server HOSTNAME for the domain NISDOMAIN.
#
#domain NISDOMAIN broadcast
#       Use  broadcast  on  the local net for domain NISDOMAIN
#
#ypserver HOSTNAME
#       Use server HOSTNAME for the  local  domain.  The
#       IP-address of server must be listed in /etc/hosts.
#
domain kurtwerks server 192.168.0.1
```

NIS client programs, like the NIS servers, require RPC to function properly, so make sure the portmapper is running before starting the client daemon, ypbind. To start the client daemon, execute the following command, which invokes the ypbind initialization script:

```
# /etc/rc.d/init.d/ypbind start
Binding to the NIS domain:                            [  OK  ]
Listening for an NIS domain server.
```

After starting the NIS client daemon, use the command rpcinfo -u localhost ypbind to confirm that ypbind was able to register its service with the portmapper. The output should resemble the following:

```
# rpcinfo -u localhost ypbind
program 100007 version 1 ready and waiting
program 100007 version 2 ready and waiting
```

 If you skip the test procedure outlined in this section, you must at least set the domain name and create the /var/yp directory. Without this directory, ypbind does not start.

Finally, use one of the NIS client commands discussed in the section titled "Key NIS client files and commands" to test whether or not the client and server are communicating properly. For example, use the `ypcat` command to display the contents of the NIS shared password file:

```
# ypcat passwd.byname
```

In order for user lookups to work properly on the client, do not add users whose authentication information will be retrieved using NIS on the client system. Instead, add the following line to the end of /etc/passwd on your NIS clients:

```
+::::::
```

Now, edit /etc/host.conf so that it uses NIS for hostname lookups. By default, the Red Hat Linux host lookup configuration file looks like the following:

```
order hosts,bind
```

Change this line so that it reads:

```
order hosts,nis,bind
```

Lastly, edit /etc/nsswitch.conf to add standard NIS to lookups performed when a user authentication and related information is requested. Change the lines that look like the following:

```
passwd:     files nisplus
shadow:     files nisplus
group:      files nisplus
hosts:      files nisplus
```

Make them look like the following:

```
passwd:     files nis
shadow:     files nis
group:      files nis
hosts:      files nis
```

Configuring the client startup files

As with configuring an NIS server, you must modify some system configuration files and make sure that the client daemon starts and stops as the system starts and stops. In addition to setting the NIS domain name in /etc/sysconfig/network and setting the server information in /etc/yp.conf, you must use the Service Configuration tool to make sure that the client daemon, ypbind, starts at boot time. To do so, start serviceconf as explained in the section on configuring an NIS server, scroll down to the bottom of the services list, and place a check mark beside the ypbind service (see Figure 8-10).

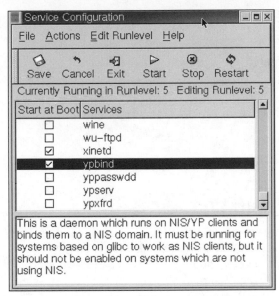

Figure 8-10: Enabling the NIS client daemon to start at boot time

Click Save to save your changes, and then click Exit to close the Service Configuration tool. Finally, reboot the client system and watch the boot messages to ensure that ypbind actually starts. After rebooting the client system, NIS client services is up and running.

Key NIS client files and commands

Table 8-2 lists the key NIS client configuration files and commands and briefly describes their purpose.

TABLE 8-2 NIS CLIENT CONFIGURATION FILES AND COMMANDS

File/Command	Description
ypwhich	Displays the name of the master NIS server
ypcat	Prints the entries in an NIS database
yppasswd	Changes user passwords and information on the NIS server
yppoll	Displays the server and version number of an NIS map
ypmatch	Prints the value of one or more entries in an NIS map

Continued

TABLE 8-2 NIS CLIENT CONFIGURATION FILES AND COMMANDS *(Continued)*

File/Command	Description
/etc/yp.conf	Configures the NIS client bindings
/etc/nsswitch.conf	Configures the system name database lookup
/etc/host.conf	Configures hostname resolution

Testing your NIS configuration

If the preceding configuration steps worked as expected, as they should, you can verify your NIS configuration with a few simple commands. For example, an NIS client configured as described in this chapter should retrieve its password information from the NIS server. So, the following command, executed on an NIS *client*, should print the NIS *server's* password database:

```
# ypcat passwd
nfsnobody:!!:65534:65534:Anonymous NFS User:/var/lib/nfs:/sbin/nologin
bubba:$1$F21EoTOW$32MNfbobZBidGOoSB9mks/:500:500:Bubba:/home/bubba:/bin/bash
marysue:$1$1·nQMOck_$VLfSEARlmgeRHzFHXuThr/:501:501:O. Mary
Sue:/home/marysue:/bin/bash
```

Similarly, you can use the ypmatch command to print a specific piece of information. For example, to print an arbitrary user's NIS password entry, you can use a ypmatch command of the form ypmatch *username* passwd, where *username* is the name of the user in which you are interested. So, to print bubba's password entry, the command is

```
# ypmatch bubba passwd
bubba:$1$F21EoTOW$32MNfbobZBidGOoSB9mks/:500:500:Bubba:/home/bubba:/bin/bash
```

To display marysue's group file entry, likewise, the proper command is

```
# ypmatch marysue group
marysue:!:501:
```

To display a list of the maps the NIS server is sharing, use the command ypcat -x, as shown in the following example:

```
# ypcat -x
Use "ethers"    for map "ethers.byname"
Use "aliases"   for map "mail.aliases"
```

```
Use "services"  for map "services.byname"
Use "protocols" for map "protocols.bynumber"
Use "hosts"     for map "hosts.byname"
Use "networks"  for map "networks.byaddr"
Use "group"     for map "group.byname"
Use "passwd"    for map "passwd.byname"
```

Configuring an example NIS client

This subsection illustrates configuring an NIS client to use the NIS services provided by the NIS server configured earlier in the chapter. As before, the NIS domain name is kurtwerks, running on the server marta.kurtwerks.com, which has an IP address 192.168.0.1.

1. Set the NIS domain name:

```
# nisdomainname kurtwerks
# nisdomainname
kurtwerks
```

2. Edit /etc/yp.conf to identify the default NIS server. The completed configuration file is (without comments):

```
ypserver 192.168.0.1
```

3. Make sure that the portmapper is running:

```
#rpcinfo -p localhost
   program vers proto   port
    100000   2   tcp    111  portmapper
    100000   2   udp    111  portmapper
```

4. Start the primary client daemon, ypbind:

```
# /etc/rc.d/init.d/ypbind start
Binding to the NIS domain:                    [  OK  ]
Listening for an NIS domain server.
```

5. Confirm that ypbind is running:

```
# rpcinfo -u localhost ypbind
program 100007 version 1 ready and waiting
program 100007 version 2 ready and waiting
```

6. Edit /etc/host.conf and add NIS to the services used for hostname lookups. The completed file looks like this:

```
order hosts,nis,bind
```

7. Edit `/etc/nsswitch.conf`, changing the entries that resemble the following:

```
passwd:     files nisplus
shadow:     files nisplus
group:      files nisplus
hosts:      files nisplus
```

Change these entries so that they look like this:

```
passwd:     files nis nisplus
shadow:     files nis nisplus
group:      files nis nisplus
hosts:      files nis nisplus
```

8. Use the Service Configuration tool, as explained earlier, to configure `ypbind` to start at boot time.

9. Reboot the server to make sure that the client daemon starts.

Strengthening NIS Security

In general, the same sorts of security issues that arise with NFS also pose a problem with NIS. Because NIS uses RPC, exploits based on the portmapper may compromise system security. Moreover, because user passwords and other authentication information is transmitted as clear text, *do not* use NIS over the Internet unless you encrypt the transmission using SSH or another IP tunneling or encapsulation scheme. If possible or practical, your NIS domain name should *not* be a name associated with the server's DNS domain name, although this method is a common approach. The rationale for selecting different DNS and NIS domain names is that doing so makes it a little harder for crackers to retrieve the password database from your NIS server. On the server side, the primary security consideration is limiting access to NIS maps using the `/var/yp/securenets` configuration syntax described in the server configuration section of this chapter.

Summary

In this chapter you saw how to configure NIS server and client services on Red Hat Linux. You first learned how to set up and test an NIS server and how to ensure that the NIS server comes up after a system reboot. You also learned how to configure an NIS client to connect to an NIS server for user authentication information.

Chapter 9

Connecting to Microsoft Networks

IN THIS CHAPTER

- Installing Samba
- Configuring the Samba server
- Using Swat
- Configuring the Samba client
- Using a Windows printer from the Linux computer
- Testing the Samba server

IN THIS CHAPTER you learn how to connect a Red Hat Linux network to a Microsoft network. Computers running Windows 95 or greater use a protocol called Server Message Block (SMB) to communicate with each other and to share services such as file and print sharing. Using a program called Samba, you can emulate the SMB protocol and connect your Red Hat Network to a Windows network to share files and printers. The Linux PC icon appears in the Windows Network Neighborhood window, and the files on the Linux PC can be browsed using Windows Explorer.

Installing Samba

Before you can use Samba to connect to the Windows computers, it must first be installed on the Linux PC. All current distributions of Linux include Samba, but it may not have been installed during the system installation. Even if it is has been installed, you should always check for the latest version, to find out if any problems have been fixed by the latest release, and to install it if necessary. To see if Samba is installed on your system, type the following:

```
rpm -q samba
```

If Samba is not installed, the command returns the output shown in Figure 9-1.

209

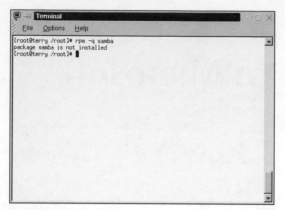

Figure 9-1: The RPM query shows that Samba is not installed on this system.

If Samba is installed, the RPM query returns the version number as shown in Figure 9-2.

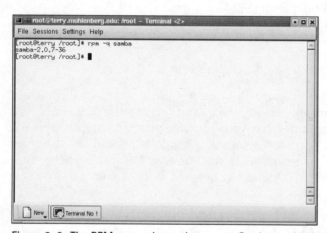

Figure 9-2: The RPM query shows the current Samba version installed on this system.

The latest version of Samba (2.0.7 as of this writing) can be obtained at Samba's Web site located at http://www.samba.org. Follow the instructions at the site for downloading the RPM file for your distribution. After downloading the Samba RPM file, install it as follows ("name of file" is the version number downloaded):

```
rpm -i samba(name of file)
```

If you are unable to download the RPM version, or you want to compile the program yourself, download the file samba-latest.tar.gz. Extract the file using the following command:

```
tar -xfvz samba-latest.tar.gz
```

Change to the directory containing the extracted files (usually /usr/src) and then type

```
./configure
```

Press Enter and wait for the command prompt to return. From the command prompt type

```
make
```

Press Enter and wait for the command prompt to return. Finally, type **install** from the command prompt. If all goes well, Samba is installed when the command prompt returns. Now you need to configure it.

In order for Samba to provide its services, both the Red Hat Linux PC as well as the Windows PC need to be configured. You start with the Red Hat Linux PC and then go to the Windows PC.

 In this chapter I refer to the Red Hat Linux PC as the Samba server and the Windows PC as the Samba client.

Configuring the Samba Server

Beginning with version 2.0 Samba includes a utility called SWAT, the Samba Web Administration Tool. This tool makes setting up Samba very easy. The main Samba configuration file is /etc/smb.conf. SWAT enables you to use a Web browser as the interface to /etc/smb.conf and makes the necessary modifications to this file. While you are using SWAT to make the configuration changes, you will learn more about the smb.conf file. A sample smb.conf file was created during the installation that can be used for reference. You should rename this file because you will create a new smb.conf using SWAT and it will overwrite the original file.

The smb.conf file is divided into several sections, the names of which I show as bracketed subsection titles in the following discussion. Shown next is the smb.conf file from one of the computers on my home network. Refer to this file to see what a section looks like as it is described.

```
# Samba config file created using SWAT
# from localhost (127.0.0.1)
# Date: 2000/05/25 10:29:40
# Global parameters
```

```
[global]
      workgroup = ONE
      netbios name = TERRY
      server string = Samba Server
      security = SHARE
      log file = /var/log/samba/log
      max log size = 50
      socket options = TCP_NODELAY SO_RCVBUF=8192 SO_SNDBUF=8192
      dns proxy = No
      wins support = Yes
      hosts allow = 192.168.1.
      hosts deny = all
[homes]
      comment = Home Directories
      read only = No
[printers]
      comment = All Printers
      path = /var/spool/samba
      guest ok = Yes
      print ok = Yes
      browseable = Yes
[nancy]
      path = /oldwin
      valid users = nancy
      read only = No
      guest ok = no
      browseable = yes
```

[global]

The first section of the smb.conf file is the [global] section. Each section contains a list of options and values in the format:

```
option = value
```

You have hundreds of options and values at your disposal, and you look at the most common ones here. For a complete listing of options refer to the smb.conf man page.

- ◆ **workgroup = ONE** is the name of the workgroup shown in the identification tab of the network properties box on the Windows computer.

- ◆ **netbios name = TERRY** is the name by which the Samba server is known to the Windows computer.

- ◆ **server string = Samba Server** is the name of the Samba server.

- ◆ **security = SHARE** is the level of security applied to server access. Other possible options are user, the default setting; domain; and server. Using share makes it easier to create anonymous shares that do not require authentication, and it is useful when the netbios names of the Windows computers are different from other names on the Linux computer. Server is used if the password file is on another server in the network. Domain is used if the clients are added to a Windows NT domain using smbpasswd, and login requests are by a Windows NT primary or backup domain controller.

- ◆ **log file = /var/log/samba/log** is the location of the log file.

- ◆ **max log size = 50** is the maximum size in kilobytes that the file can grow to.

- ◆ **socket options = TCP_NODELAY SO_RCVBUF=8192 SO_SNDBUF=8192** enables the server to be tuned for better performance. TCP_NODELAY is a default value, the BUF values set send and receive buffers.

- ◆ **dns proxy = No** indicates that the netbios name will not be treated like a DNS name and there is no DNS lookup.

- ◆ **wins support = Yes** is used to tell the Samba server to act as a WINS server.

- ◆ **hosts allow = 192.168.1.** means that requests from this network will be accepted.

- ◆ **hosts deny = all** means that all hosts' requests will be denied.

[homes]

The next section of the `smb.conf` file, [homes], is used to enable the server to give users quick access to their home directories. Refer to the smb.conf man page for a more complete description of how the [homes] section works.

- ◆ **comment = Home Directories** is a comment line

- ◆ **read only = No** specifies that users can write to their directories.

[printers]

This section sets the options for printing.

- ◆ **path = /var/spool/samba** is the location of the printer spool directory.

- ◆ **guest ok = Yes** enables guest access to the printer.

- ◆ **print ok = Yes** enables clients to send print jobs to the specified directory. This option must be set or printing does not work.

- ◆ **browseable = Yes** means that the printer appears in the browse list.

Be sure to have your printer properly configured for your Linux network before you attempt to set it up for use with Windows clients. You need to enter the location of the path to the print spool for the printer you want to use in the smb.conf file.

[nancy]

The last section of this smb.conf file is called [nancy]. This is the computer that my wife uses, so I named this share for her.

- **path = /oldwin** is the path to the directory accessible by nancy.

- **valid users = nancy** specifies the users that can use the shares.

- **read only = No** enables write access to the directory.

- **guest ok = no** prevents guest access.

- **browseable = yes** means that the share is visible in browse lists.

The smb.conf file you have just analyzed was created using the SWAT program as indicated by the comment lines at the beginning of the file. You can also create this file from scratch by entering values for the options shown previously, or by modifying the smb.conf file that is installed along with the program. Remember that you looked at a simple file for a small network. Always refer to the smb.conf man page for complete details about options and values. Next you use SWAT to configure smb.conf.

Using SWAT

Before you can use SWAT, you need to change two files to enable it. The first file is /etc/services. This file is a list of Internet services and their port numbers and protocols. You need to add the following line to /etc/services.

```
Swat  901/tcp
```

Next you need to add a line to /etc/inetd.conf. The inetd daemon runs at system startup and listens for connections at specific ports. The inetd.conf file lists the programs that should be run when the inetd daemon detects a request at one of the ports. You need to add the following line:

```
Swat    stream   tcp      nowait.400      root /usr/sbin/swat swat
```

If you're interested in more details about the line you added, look at the inetd man page. Finally, you need to restart the inetd daemon so it reads the changes you made to `inetd.conf`. To do this, type at the command prompt:

```
killall -HUP inetd
```

Now you can start a Web browser and get ready to run SWAT. Because most distributions include Netscape, use this browser to start SWAT. In the location box, enter the address for localhost and the port number for SWAT as `http://localhost:901`. Doing so opens a dialog box asking for a user ID and password as shown in Figure 9-3.

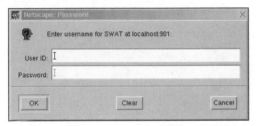

Figure 9-3: After entering the address for localhost and the port number used by SWAT, enter a user ID and password.

You have to be root in order to configure Samba, so enter **root** as the user ID and enter the password for root. The main SWAT screen, as shown in Figure 9-4, appears after entering the user ID and password.

You begin configuring the [globals] section by clicking the GLOBALS icon. The Global Variables page appears as shown in Figure 9-5. The values shown are being read from the `smb.conf` file which already exists on the system. As stated earlier, all systems include a default `smb.conf` which is used by SWAT. The values shown in your file are different from those shown in the figures because I have already made configuration changes.

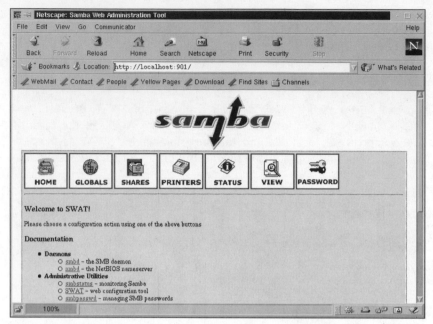

Figure 9-4: The main screen of the SWAT program appears after you enter the login information.

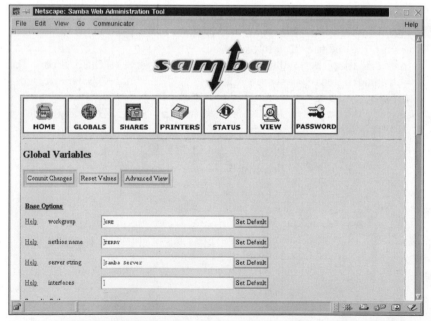

Figure 9-5: The global variables page makes it easy to configure the [globals] section of the smb.conf file.

The Global Variables page is divided into six sections:

- ◆ Base Options
- ◆ Security Options
- ◆ Logging Options
- ◆ Tuning Options
- ◆ Browse Options
- ◆ WINS Options

Figure 9-6 shows the Base and Security Options sections.

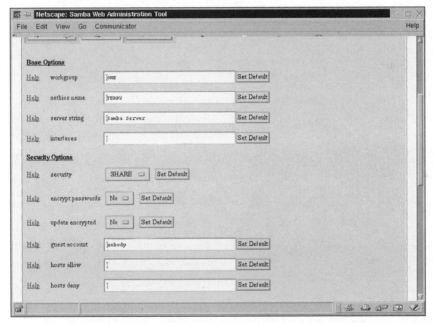

Figure 9-6: The Base and Security Options sections of the Global Variables page of SWAT.

As you can see, the options shown here are the same options you looked at in the smb.conf file. The values shown are the values I previously discussed for my system. To configure Samba for your system, use your own values for the options in these sections. Figure 9-7 shows the remaining sections of the Global Variables page.

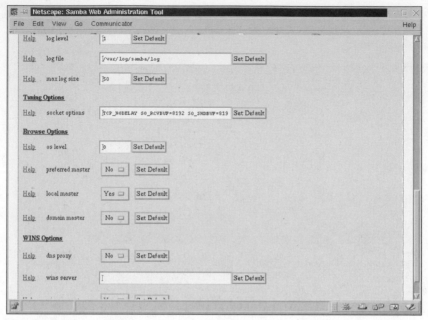

Figure 9-7: The log, tuning, browse, and WINS options of the globals variables page

After you have entered the appropriate values for your system, click Commit Changes (see Figure 9-5) to save them to the file. Next you create shares by clicking the SHARES icon, which opens the Share Parameters page, as shown in Figure 9-8.

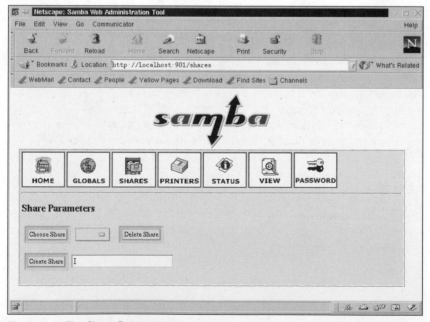

Figure 9-8: The Share Parameters page enables shares to be created and modified.

To create a new share, fill in a name for the share and click the Create Share button. An expanded Share Parameters page, as shown in Figure 9-9, appears.

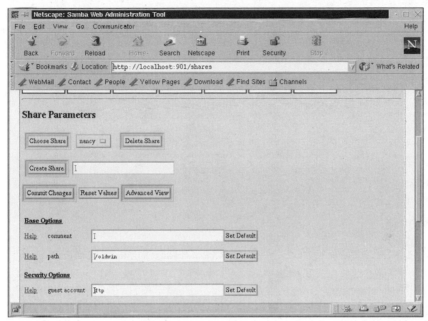

Figure 9-9: The expanded Share Parameters page enables you to enter the configuration information for Windows computers that can access the Samba server.

As seen in figure 9-9, I have entered the appropriate information for the share [nancy], which is my wife's computer that is running Windows 95. The information here is the same as discussed earlier when looking at the smb.conf file. Enter the appropriate information for your computer, and then click Commit Changes to save them to the smb.conf file.

Next you set up a printer that the Windows computer can use. Clicking the PRINTERS icon opens the Printer Parameters page where you can create and modify printer information. This page is similar to the Share Parameters page except you need to create or select a printer rather than a share. To create a new printer, type the name of the printer and click Create Printer. If you already have a printer configured, it is marked with an asterisk and can be selected from the drop-down list. An expanded Printer Parameters page, as shown in Figure 9-10 opens.

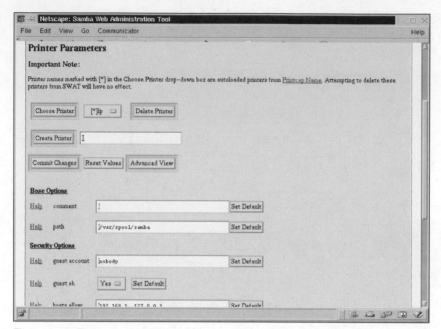

Figure 9-10: The expanded Printer Parameters page shows the name of the printer share you selected.

As seen in Figure 9-10, I have entered the appropriate information for the [printer] share. The information here is the same as discussed earlier when looking at the [printer] section of the smb.conf file. Pay attention to the Important Note at the top of the Printer Parameters page. If you already have a printer configured in Red Hat Linux it is used as the default printer by Samba and it cannot be deleted from the list. Be sure to click Commit Changes to save the information to the smb.conf file.

After the smb.conf is created, you can run a utility called testparm that checks the file for errors. At a command prompt, type **testparm** and if all is well you should see output like that shown in Figure 9-11.

After making changes to the smb.conf file, you must restart Samba services, or start Samba, if it is not running. Starting Samba can be done through SWAT by choosing the STATUS icon. The Server Status page, as shown in Figure 9-12, shows if the Samba daemons are running or not. The two daemons are smbd and nmbd and can be started or restarted by clicking the appropriate buttons.

Figure 9-11: The testparm utility checks the smb.conf file for errors.

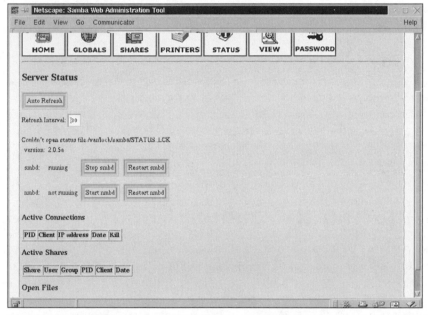

Figure 9-12: The Server Status page shows the current status of the Samba daemons.

You can also start Samba from a command prompt. The command to start Samba is /usr/sbin/samba start or /etc/rc.d/init.d/samba start, depending on your distribution. After starting Samba you can run smbclient on your localhost to get some configuration information. Issue the command

```
smbclient -L localhost
```

Then press Enter at the password request. You should see output similar to that in Figure 9-13.

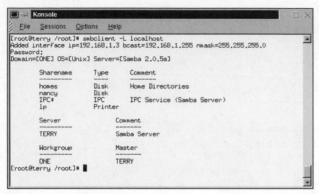

Figure 9-13: Checking the smbclient on your local host gives you Samba configuration information about the server.

The last thing you need to do on the server is create the user that uses the share you created. On my home network, which I used in this example, I called the share [nancy], so I need to create a user called nancy. I typed **useradd nancy** at a command prompt. Then I assigned a password for this account by using the `passwd` command.

Everything is now configured on the server, but you can't connect to any Windows computers yet because you haven't set them up. You do this next.

Configuring the Samba Client

From the Windows desktop click Start, then choose Settings→Control Panel to open the Control Panel window as seen in Figure 9-14.

Figure 9-14: The Windows Control Panel

Double click the Network icon and check for "File and Printer Sharing for Microsoft Networks" and "Client for Microsoft Networks" in the Configuration window showing installed network components. See Figure 9-15.

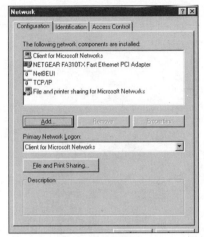

Figure 9-15: The network configuration window lists installed components and enables the installation of others.

If these two items are not installed you must install them, as follows:

1. Click Add.

2. Click Client, and then click Add in the Select Network Component Type box.

3. Click Microsoft, and then click Client for Microsoft Networks in the Select Network Client box.

4. Click OK.

Figure 9-16 shows the process just described.

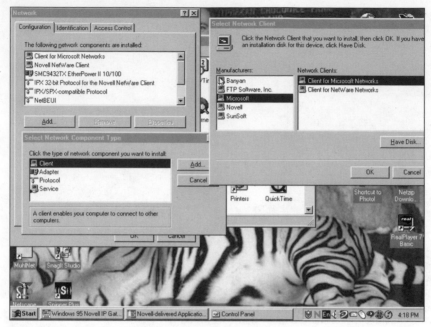

Figure 9-16: Installing Client for Microsoft Networks

To install File and printer sharing for Microsoft Networks:

1. Click Add.

2. Click Service, and then click Add in the Select Network Component Type box.

3. Click Microsoft, and then click File and printer sharing for Microsoft Networks in the Select Network Service box.

4. Click OK.

Figure 9-17 shows the process just described. Restart the computer as required.

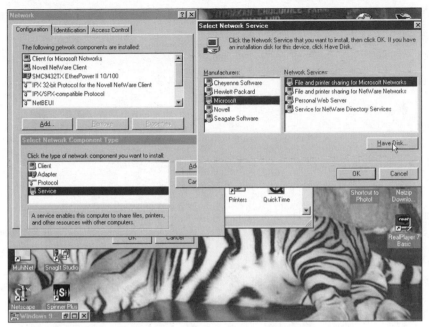

Figure 9-17: Installing File and printer sharing for Microsoft Networks

After the computer restarts, you see a network login window asking for a user-name and password. Click Cancel for now because there are a few more items that need to be set up.

You should now find a Network Neighborhood icon on the desktop.

1. Right click this icon and choose Properties from the drop-down list.

2. In the Network Properties window, click the Identification tab. In this window you enter a computer name and workgroup name, as shown in Figure 9-18.

   These names are what appear when browsing the network. The computer description does not appear in the network browse list.

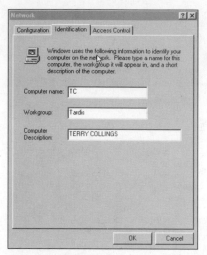

Figure 9-18: The Identification window is where you
enter a name for your computer and its workgroup.

3. Click the Access Control tab and click the Share Level Access Control
   button as shown in Figure 9-19.

4. Click OK.

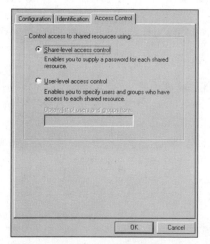

Figure 9-19: Choose Share Level Access Control
in the Access Control window.

5. Click the Configuration tab.

6. Click the File and Print Sharing button.

7. In the File and Print Sharing window (see Figure 9-20), check both options.

8. Click OK.

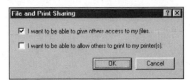

Figure 9-20: Choose both options in the File and
Print Sharing window.

Next the TCP/IP settings need to be configured.

1. Click the TCP/IP listing for the network card in the Network Properties
   window.

2. Click Properties.

3. In the TCP/IP Properties window, click IP Address if it is not already
   selected.

4. Click Specify an IP address, and then fill in the IP address and subnet
   mask for this computer as shown in Figure 9-21.

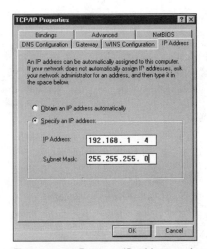

Figure 9-21: Enter an IP address and subnet mask
for the Windows computer.

Assigning an IP address manually works well for a network with a small number of computers. For a network with a large number of computers, it is best to automatically assign IP addresses using Dynamic Host Configuration Protocol (DHCP).

5. Click the WINS Configuration tab, and then select Enable Wins Resolution.

6. Enter the IP address of the Samba server (Linux computer) as the Primary WINS Server (see Figure 9-22).

7. Click OK.

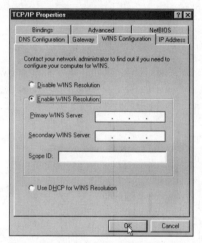

Figure 9-22: Enter the IP address of the Linux computer for the primary WINS server.

8. Click the Bindings tab for the network card and make sure that Client for Microsoft Networks and File and printer sharing for Microsoft Networks are there and checked, as shown in Figure 9-23.

9. Click OK to close the window.

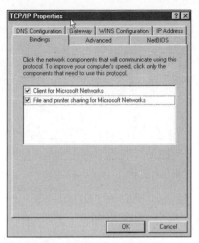

Figure 9-23: Checking the Bindings tab to be
sure the components are there

10. Highlight File and printer sharing for Microsoft Networks in the list from
    the Configuration window.

11. Click the Properties button and then the Advanced button and ensure
    that Browse Master is set to Disable, and LM Announce is set to No (see
    Figure 9-24).

12. Click OK.

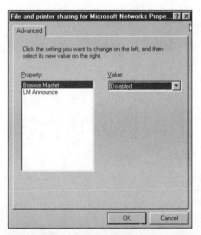

Figure 9-24: Setting the Browse Master and
LM Announce properties

13. Close the Network properties window by clicking OK.

You receive a message asking you to reboot the computer again so Windows can write all the changes you made to the registry.

When the computer has rebooted, open My Computer and right click a drive icon. The pop-up menu now has an entry called Sharing. Clicking this entry opens a window where the name and access type of the shared drive can be entered. See Figure 9-25.

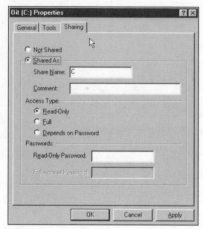

Figure 9-25: Entering the name and access type for the shared drive

If you have a printer connected to your Windows computer that you would like to use from the Linux computer, double-click the Printers icon in My Computer and enable sharing for the printer as described for the disk share. The Windows computer has to be rebooted again, and you need to add some configuration information about the Windows printer to the Linux box. You can do this while the Windows computer is rebooting, as discussed next.

Using a Windows Printer from the Linux Computer

Since all distributions include a printer configuration tool, it is easiest to use this tool to help configure the printer. Red Hat Linux includes printtool, and this is what I use to configure the printer. Type **printtool** at a command prompt and after the program starts, click Add. Then choose SMB/Windows95.NT printer and click OK (see Figure 9-26).

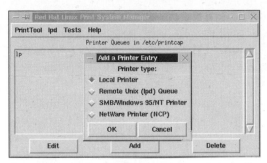

Figure 9-26: Using the Red Hat printtool to configure a Samba printer

 It may be necessary to add an lpt port to the Samba client to enable printing to some networked printers.

A warning box appears regarding passwords and Samba. After reading this warning, click OK to go to the printer entry box. Configuring the printer connected to the Windows computer is very similar to configuring a printer connected to a Linux computer with a few exceptions. The hostname of the print server is the name of the Windows computer. Enter the IP address of the Windows computer in the IP number of Server box, and finally, enter the name of the printer. You can leave the other boxes blank and click OK when finished. See Figure 9-27.

Figure 9-27: Entering the configuration information about the Windows printer

From the printer manager page of printtool, highlight the entry for the printer you just created. Click the tests menu and print the first two test pages (see Figure 9-28).

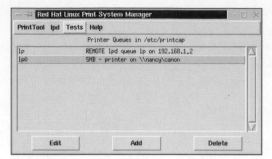

Figure 9-28: Testing the printer configuration of the Windows printer

Testing the Samba Server

Now you are ready to test everything you have done so far. On the Windows computer, double-click Network Neighborhood. In the Network Neighborhood window you should now see a listing for the Windows computer and the shares you made available. The Linux computer should be listed here, and, if you open it, the directories you made available from it are visible.

If you double-click the directory from the Linux computer, you are prompted for a username and password to enter the directories. In this example you created one directory called oldwin, so this is the directory you should see from the browse list.

On the Linux computer you can use the smbclient utility to access the directories on the Windows computer as follows:

```
Smbclient //nancy/directory name
```

Why use Samba instead of NFS?

Earlier you set up the Network File System to enable file sharing across your network. Why didn't you just use NFS to share the Windows files? Well, you could have, but it makes more sense to use Samba to communicate with Windows computers. The Server Message Block (SMB) protocol is how Windows computers communicate with each other. It is the Windows native protocol for sharing files and printers. By using the same protocol, you are ensuring that file and printer sharing operate with a minimum of difficulty.

This utility is very similar to the FTP utility. A list of commands can be obtained by typing **help** at the `smbclient` command prompt.

That's all there is to it. Now you can share files between your Linux and Windows computers.

Summary

In this chapter you learned about the Server Message Block (SMB) protocol. This protocol is used by Windows computers to communicate with each other. You learned about a Linux program called Samba, which emulates the SMB protocol and can be used to connect Linux networks to Windows networks. You installed and configured Samba on a Red Hat Linux server and then configured the Windows clients.

Chapter 10

Connecting to Apple Networks

IN THIS CHAPTER you learn how to connect a Red Hat Linux machine to an Apple network. The Apple network uses a network routing and addressing suite called AppleTalk to communicate between Apple machines. Using a suite of Unix daemons called Netatalk, you can communicate with Apple machines using the various AppleTalk protocols. You can set up file and print sharing between Apple and Linux machines. You can even set up a Red Hat Linux machine as an AppleTalk router.

Understanding AppleTalk

AppleTalk is the Apple standard for personal computer networking. Much as Linux uses NFS and LPR for file and printer sharing, Apple computers use AppleTalk. You need to install and configure AppleTalk for Red Hat Linux in the event that you want to either access the files and printers of an Apple machine from the Red Hat machine, or vice versa. Luckily, AppleTalk is a convenient set of protocols. Almost all aspects of AppleTalk routing are worked out automatically by the AppleTalk routers. Therefore, AppleTalk networks require minimal configuration and maintenance.

AppleTalk addressing

Each AppleTalk address is a network number combined with a node number. A network number is a 16-bit number and so can have a value from 0 to 65536. The range 1 to 65279 is open for arbitrary use, while 65280 to 65534 is reserved for networks which contain no AppleTalk routers. A node number is an 8-bit number with two reserved addresses, allowing for 253 nodes per network.

In the case of a stand-alone network which contains no AppleTalk routers, no configuration of addresses should be necessary. If the default config files are used, the clients and servers in the network amiably resolve their various addresses automatically. If AppleTalk routers are already present in the network, the server can poll the existing routers in order to automatically configure itself. If the server is to be the first AppleTalk router in the network, network numbers must be assigned to the various network interfaces which communicate with the AppleTalk network. This function is controlled by the atalkd program file. Information on configuring this and other daemons can be found in the section "Configuring the Daemons."

Apple zones

AppleTalk zones exist for three reasons: organization of the network, descriptive naming, and access control. They are similar in this way to a hybrid of domain names and HTTP realms. In a small network zones are not very useful. By default, all nodes are contained in the default zone, which is unnamed. In a larger network where organization and access control are issues, you can name zones and define which nodes are in which zones. Each zone can be assigned to multiple networks. Also, each network can be assigned to multiple zones. This flexibility in zone assignment allows for a very flexible system of network organization. However, zones can only contain addresses, not other zones. Since nesting zones is not possible, the namespace is more or less flat.

Zone naming is controlled by the AppleTalk routers. If the Red Hat machine is set up as an AppleTalk router, the zone to network address mappings need to be defined in the atalkd.conf file. Otherwise, each machine simply needs to be configured to specify which zone it is in.

Installing the AppleTalk Software

This section discusses the AppleTalk DDP kernel module, installing Netatalk, Configuring /etc/ services, and configuring Netatalk.

The AppleTalk DDP kernel module

DDP is the AppleTalk datagram protocol (Datagram Delivery Protocol). It is similar to TCP, but uses AppleTalk addresses rather than IP addresses. DDP is only the lowest level of the AppleTalk protocol suite. DDP is included as a kernel module in Red Hat 7.2.

You should first check to see if the DDP module is already running on your system. Execute dmesg | grep -i apple. If any lines are printed that look like this: "AppleTalk 0.18a for Linux NET4.0," the AppleTalk DDP module is already loaded. You can now progress to installing and configuring the Netatalk daemon.

If the DDP module is not already in the kernel, insert it with the command:

```
modprobe appletalk
```

After inserting the kernel module, it is time to install and configure Netatalk.

Installing Netatalk

AppleTalk consists of a whole suite of protocols, such as RTMP, NBP, ZIP, AEP, ATP, PAP, ASP, and AFP. These are application-level protocols corresponding roughly to IP-based application-level protocols such as DHCP and DNS. Only DDP is in the kernel. The rest of the protocols are implemented in user-space daemons and are part of the Netatalk package. Netatalk runs on many variations of UNIX, including Linux. Two versions of Netatalk are available, the official version and a version extensively patched by Adrian Sun and known as netatalk+asun.

The Adrian Sun patches are primarily for supporting AFP 2.2 (AppleShare TCP/IP). The netatalk+asun version is generally preferable. However, the two versions merge in Netatalk1.5.

Netatalk is not included with Red Hat 7.2, but is available from rpmfind.net. The latest stable version of netatalk+asun at the time of this writing is 2.1.3-22. The latest development versions are available from the Netatalk project at http://netatalk.sourceforge.net.

You install the Netatalk package just like any other Red Hat package, as in the following command:

```
rpm -vv -install netatalk+asun-2.1.3-22.rpm
```

Once Netatalk is installed you can configure all of the separate daemons that are included.

Some versions of Netatalk have PAM (Pluggable Authentication Module) support and others do not. The netatalk+asun package includes PAM support. If this is a desirable feature on your system, make sure that you have PAM correctly configured and that you install the netatalk+asun version of the package.

Configuring /etc/services

To use Netatalk under Linux, you need to have entries for the AppleTalk protocols in your /etc/services file. When you install the Netatalk RPM, it automatically appends these entries to your /etc/services file:

```
rtmp            1/ddp           # Routing Table Maintenance Protocol
nbp             2/ddp           # Name Binding Protocol
echo            4/ddp           # AppleTalk Echo Protocol
zip             6/ddp           # Zone Information Protocol
afpovertcp      548/tcp         # AFP over TCP
afpovertcp      548/udp
```

You should not have to modify these entries. However, you might want to check and make sure that they have been successfully added to your /etc/services file.

Configuring Netatalk

The Netatalk RPM package installs the /etc/rc.d/init.d/atalk script which runs the various Netatalk daemons. The atalk script is run automatically during the boot process. You can configure several options that determine which daemons the atalk script launches and how it launches them. The atalk script reads its configuration information from the /etc/atalk/config script. This script sets the following options for how atalk should behave:

AFPD_MAX_CLIENTS
This option determines the maximum number of clients that can connect to the AppleTalk filesharing daemon (afpd) at one time. The default value is 5, which is probably too small for most networks.

ATALK_NAME
This option determines what the NBP name of the local AppleTalk host should be. The default for this option is to run the following shell script command:

```
echo ${HOSTNAME} | cut -d. -f1
```

This command takes the hostname of the machine and uses just the first part. So, for instance, if the hostname for the machine was blanu.net, the NBP name of the AppleTalk host would be set to blanu. This command may not set the NBP name to a desirable value if the hostname of the machine is not set correctly. You can type the command **echo $HOSTNAME** to determine what the hostname of the machine is currently set to.

PAPD_RUN
This option determines whether the Printer Access Protocol Daemon (papd) should be run. The default is yes. You can change it to no if you want to prevent papd from running. You should disable papd if you do not want other computers to be able to access the machine's printers via the AppleTalk network.

AFPD_RUN
This option determines whether the Apple File Protocol Daemon (afpd) should be run. The default is yes. You can change this to no if you want to prevent afpd from running. You should disable afpd if you do not want other computers to be able to access the machine's files via the AppleTalk network.

ATALK_BGROUND
This option determines whether the AppleTalk daemon (atalkd) should run in the background or take control of the executing process. The default value is yes, as the

atalk script normally runs on boot and it is customary to launch daemons in the background. The only reason to change this option to no is if you are going to run atalk manually from the command line.

After you have configured the settings in the /etc/atalk/config file, you can edit the configuration files for the various daemons: atalkd, papd, and afpd.

The atalkd program reads its configuration from /etc/atalk/atalkd.conf. A sample version of this file is automatically installed by the RPM. If for some reason this file is not present when atalkd is run, atalkd attempts to configure all interfaces and then attempts to write a configuration file.

Configuring the Daemons

The primary daemon in the Netatalk suite is atalkd. The atalkd program is responsible for all AppleTalk network services other than DDP (which is, as you know, in the kernel). The atalkd daemon takes care of routing, name registration, name lookup, zone registration, zone lookup, and the AppleTalk Echo Protocol (similar to ping). The atalkd daemon is usually run at boot time. If you install the RPM package, it should automatically be set to run at boot time because the RPM installs the script /etc/rc.d/init.d/atalk. This is the script that should be run to start and stop atalkd and also to cause it to reload its configuration file.

Configuring atalkd

The atalkd configuration file, atalkd.conf, consists of one interface configuration command per line. Lines starting with "#" are considered to be comments and ignored.

Configuring AppleTalk Interfaces

Each AppleTalk interface has a line in the atalkd.conf file specifying all of its configuration parameters. The lines are in the following format:

```
interface [ -seed ] [ -phase number ] [ -net net-range ]
[ -addr address ] [ -zone zonename ]
```

All of the parameters except for the interface name are optional. The interface parameter is the name of the interface to configure. The default configuration file installed by the RPM is actually empty. This is fine because atalkd can automatically discover and configure all local interfaces without any configuration. The only reason to add interfaces to the atalkd.conf file is to specify the optional information about them or to exclude some local interfaces from configuration.

The simplest atalkd.conf file would have just a list of local interfaces, one on each line. You do not have to specify the loopback device interface as it is already configured automatically. Here is an example of a simple configuration file:

```
eth0
eth1
```

This file would have approximately the same effect as an empty configuration file. However, if you want to exclude some local interfaces from being configured by atalkd, excluding them from a nonempty config file should do the trick.

CONFIGURING SEED INFORMATION

The primary use of the `atalkd.conf` file is to specify the seed options for your various interfaces. Although all of the options for interface configuration are optional, if you specify a `-seed` option, all of the rest of the options are then mandatory. The `-seed` directive enables you to specify the seed information for an interface. The `-seed` option does not take a parameter. It only specifies that the rest of the parameters should be considered as seed information and should be overridden by values obtained from the network's routers. If a router on the network disagrees with the seed information provided for an interface, atalkd exits when it is started. If `-seed` is not specified, all of the other specified parameters may be overridden automatically by atalkd when the interface is configured.

CONFIGURING ZONE INFORMATION

The first `-zone` directive in each interface configuration line specifies the default zone for that interface. Of course, each interface can be in multiple zones. The behavior of the default zone depends on the phase. Phase 1 has only one zone, so a different default zone cannot be specified. In Phase II, all routers on the AppleTalk network are configured to use the default zone and must all agree on what the default zone is. Specifying "*" for any `--zone` parameter is a shorthand for specifying that the zone should be the same as the default zone on the first interface. The default zone for a machine is determined by the configuration of the local routers. If you want a service to appear in a zone other than the default zone for the machine, you must configure the service to tell it what zone to be in.

CONFIGURING ROUTING INFORMATION

If you are connecting the Red Hat Linux Netatalk router to an existing AppleTalk network, you must contact the administrators of the AppleTalk network to obtain appropriate network addresses for your network interfaces. The atalkd daemon automatically acts as an AppleTalk router if more than one local interface is configured.

Each interface must be assigned a unique net range. A net range is two network addresses separated by a "-". The interface controls all network addresses in the net range. A network address is between 1 and 65279. The addresses 0 and 65535 are illegal. The addresses 65280 to 65534 are reserved. It is best to use the smallest net range that is still useful. When in doubt omit the `-net` option.

CONFIGURING ADDITIONAL INFORMATION

All of the optional parameters have defaults. The default for -phase is 2. The phase can also be specified on the command line when running atalkd using the −1 and −2 command line options. If -addr is specified but -net is not, a net range of 1 is the default.

Additional configuration

One important issue to consider when configuring the Red Hat system is whether or not to disable papd, the AppleTalk printer daemon. By default, the system is configured to run papd with the default empty config file in /etc/atalk/papd.conf. Since the config file is empty, papd attempts to make accessible to the network all local printers as configured in /etc/printcap to be accessible via AppleTalk and PAP (Printer Access Protocol). This procedure may be undesirable because

- A printer on the Red Hat machine may not be meant for public access. For instance, it might require more expensive toner or paper. Also, it might be in an inaccessible location so that people would not be able to pick up their printouts.

- You may want to separate Linux printers and Apple printers for purposes of load balancing. You may not want everyone to be printing on the Linux printers when there are perfectly good Apple printers going unused.

- If the Red Hat machine is set up to be a client to remote AppleTalk printers, by default, these printers are exposed to AppleTalk as well as the local printers. This situation causes the AppleTalk printers to have two entries, which can be very confusing to users.

In the latter case you can put entries into the papd.conf file for any printers that you want to expose via AppleTalk, excluding remote AppleTalk printers. In the other cases you can simply stop papd from running on boot. That way, no Red Hat printers are exposed via AppleTalk.

The papd program is executed on boot by the /etc/rc.d/init.d/atalk program. This program reads information about what daemons to run from the file /etc/atalk/config. If you want to disable papd from running, you can change the line PAPD_RUN from "yes" to "no."

More information on editing your /etc/atalk/config file is available in the section "Configuring Netatalk."

Configuring AppleTalk file sharing

The afpd program provides an AppleTalk Filing Protocol (AFP) interface to the Linux file system. The afpd program is normally run at boot time by the /etc/ rc.d/init.d/atalk script. The afpd program is useful if you want remote computers to be able to access the files on the Linux machine over the AppleTalk network. If this is not a desirable situation, afpd can be disabled. More information on disabling afpd is available in the section called "Configuring Netatalk." Note that it is not necessary to run afpd in order for the Red Hat machine to access remote file systems over AppleTalk, either on Macs or on other Unix machines, which are running afpd. The Red Hat machine needs only to run afpd to expose its own files to the network.

The afpd program has many command line arguments, all of which are optional. The syntax for calling afpd is as follows:

```
afpd [-d] [-f defaultvolumes] [-s systemvolumes] [-u] [-n nbpname]
 [-c maxconnections] [-g guest] [-G] [-K] [-C] [-A]
```

Table 10-1 describes the arguments used in this syntax.

TABLE 10-1 Arguments Used When Calling AFPD

Argument	Description
-d	Specifies that the daemon not fork, and that a trace of all AFP commands be written to stdout.
-f defaultvolumes	Specifies that defaultvolumes should be read for a list of default volumes to offer, instead of /etc/atalk/AppleVolumes.default.
-s systemvolumes	Specifies that systemvolumes should be read for a list of volumes that all users are offered, instead of /etc/atalk/AppleVolumes.system.
-u	Reads the user's AppleVolumes file first. This option causes volume names in the user's AppleVolumes file to override volume names in the system's AppleVolumes file. The default is to read the system AppleVolumes file first. Note that this option doesn't effect the precedence of filename extension mappings: the user's AppleVolumes file always has precedence.
-n nbpname	Specifies that nbpname should be used for NBP registration, instead of the first component of the hostname in the local zone.

Argument	Description
-c maxconnections	Specifies the maximum number of connections to allow for this afpd. The default is 5.
-g guest	Specifies the name of the guest account. The default is "nobody."
-G, -K, -C, and -A	Causes the server to not offer NoUserAuthent, Kerberos IV, Cleartext Passwrd, and AFS Kerberos logins, respectively. The default is to enable all available login methods.

The afpd program reads several configuration files. The /etc/atalk/afpd.conf file configures options affecting the operation of the daemon. The volumes to share over the network are configured in several files. The /etc/atalk/AppleVolumes.system file is first read. Then, the /etc/atalk/AppleVolumes.default file is read, and the settings are combined with those from /etc/atalk/AppleVolumes.system. If the /etc/atalk/AppleVolumes.default file is not found, the $HOME/AppleVolumes file is read instead. If the $HOME/AppleVolumes file is not found, the $HOME/.AppleVolumes file is read instead. Because afpd is normally run as root, it normally reads /root/AppleVolumes or /root/.AppleVolumes. This automatic behavior can lead to confusing behavior if you try to test afpd manually as a user other than root and no /etc/atalk/AppleVolumes.default file is present. The settings are different when run as root or as another user. However, the /etc/atalk/AppleVolumes.default file is supplied by the RPM, so this is the file that is normally read when afpd is run.

You do not generally have to edit the /etc/atalk/AppleVolumes.default file. This file provides useful default file extension mappings. Changes should generally be made in the /etc/atalk/AppleVolumes.system file as the default version of this file is empty.

The AppleVolumes configuration files contains both volume and extension information. This information is formatted one item per line. The lines have the following syntax:

```
pathname [volumename]
.extension [type] [creator]
```

If the volumename is omitted, the last portion of the pathname is used. If the type is omitted, "????" is used. If the creator is omitted, "UNIX" is used.

Setting up AFP Accounts

With Netatalk, AFP user accounts are the same as Linux user accounts. Therefore you must add user accounts for each AFP user that you want to be able to log in. Authentication of these accounts is done using the standard Linux login authentication mechanism, which checks the password supplied by the user with the password stored in the /etc/passwd file. Note that afpd checks to see if the user has a valid login shell by checking the shell which the user is set to use against the list of shells in the /etc/shells file. If the user is using a shell which is not included in that file, authentication fails.

Configuring AFS to work with AppleTalk

You can set up AppleTalk so that it works with AFS. First you must of course have the AFS server installed and configured properly. You also need Kerberos 4, patch level 10, properly installed and configured in order to do authentication.

Next, add an AFB principal name entry in /etc/svrtab to enable Kerberos authentication. The entry takes the following form:

```
afpserver.NBP_name@realm
```

For example,

```
afpserver.blanu@dnalounge
```

The NBP name must match the Kerberos principal name for authentication to occur. If afpd's default NBP name does not match the site's method for generating principal names, you must use the -n option when running afpd.

Configuring AppleTalk printer sharing

You can configure AppleTalk printers in two ways. You can either access a remote printer over AppleTalk from the Red Hat machine or you can expose the printers accessible to the Red Hat machine so that they are usable to remote computers over AppleTalk. In this section I describe how to make printers on the Red Hat machine accessible over AppleTalk to remote machines. Setting up the Red Hat machine to act as a client to remote printers is presented in the section "Configuring Red Hat as an AppleTalk Client."

The program that exposes local printers over the AppleTalk network is called papd. It is a daemon that communicates over the network using the Printer Access Protocol (PAP). The papd daemon spools print jobs to lpd, the Linux printer daemon. After accepting a print job from the network, papd spools the job into the lpd spool directory and then wakes up the lpd daemon to examine and process the modified printing spool. The management of the spools and the actual process of printing is handled entirely by the lpd daemon.

The papd daemon is usually started at boot time just as atalkd and lpd are. It reads its configuration from the /etc/atalk/papd.conf file. The file is in the same format as the /etc/printcap file which is used for configuring lpd. The name of the entry in the papd.conf file is registered via NBP, the AppleTalk Name Binding Protocol, so that the printer can be accessed remotely using AppleTalk and PAP.

The papd daemon has three optional parameters, as follows:

Parameter	Description
-d	Do not fork or disassociate from the terminal. Write some debugging information to stderr.
-f configfile	Consult configfile instead of /etc/atalk/papd.conf for the configuration information.
-p printcap	Consult printcap instead of /etc/printcap for LPD configuration information.

The papd daemon is launched on boot by the /etc/rc.d/init.d/atalk script. This script is responsible for starting, stopping, and reloading all of the Netatalk daemons. You don't normally have to edit this script. However, since this is where papd is run, this is where optional command line arguments should be placed. Generally you don't have to specify any of papd's optional command line arguments.

The printcap file format enables you to specify capabilities about a printer. Different printers support different capabilities. The following capabilities are supported for AppleTalk printers:

Name	Type	Default	Description
pd	str	".ppd"	Pathname to PPD file
pr	str	"lp"	LPD printer name
op	str	"operator"	Operator name for LPD spooling

The papd.conf file is only for exposing printers over the AppleTalk network. The printers must already be set up to work with lpd by having entries added to the printcap file.

If no configuration file is present, the hostname of the machine is used when the printers are registered with NBP and all other NBP options have default values. If no configuration file is present, papd attempts to expose all printers present in the lapd configuration file /etc/printcap to the network. This method works in most cases, and the configuration file installed by the RPM is in fact empty. The only reason to edit the papd.conf file is to exclude printers from being network accessible or to specify additional or nonstandard information about the printers.

Here is a sample papd.conf file:

```
Mac Printer Spooler::pr=ps:pd=/usr/share/lib/ppd/HPLJ_4M.PPD:op=mcs:
HP Printer::
```

This configuration file sets up two printers which are assumed to already be configured in the /etc/printcap file. The first printer is named "ps" in the printcap file and is exposed to the AppleTalk network via the NBP name "Mac Printer Spooler." It uses the PPD file located in /usr/share/lib/ppd. It specifies that all jobs run on this printer should be owned by the user named "mcs." The second printer is exposed on the network by the NBP name "HP Printer." As all capabilities are omitted from this entry, the defaults are assumed for all options. Since a configuration file exists, printers not included in the configuration file are not exposed to the network via AppleTalk even if they exist in the printcap file.

Configuring Red Hat as an AppleTalk Client

In addition to being an AppleTalk server and router, a Red Hat Linux machine can also be an AppleTalk client. This capability is useful if you're adding a Linux machine to an existing network of Apple machines or integrating a Linux network with an Apple one.

Accessing Apple printers

The first order of business is of course to get Netatalk configured and to run atalkd. Once the Red Hat machine is connected to the AppleTalk network, it is time to choose an Apple Printer to connect to.

Finding the printer's zone

In order to print to an Apple printer, you need to know its zone. The command to find this information is nbplkup. It is used to list all objects in the AppleTalk network along with zone, address, and type information. In order to find the zone for the specific printer you want, you must know its name. Of course, you can browse the available objects using nbplkup if you don't remember the printer's name.

USING NBPLKUP TO FIND APPLETALK OBJECTS

The syntax for the `nbplkup` command is as follows:

```
nbplkup [ -r maxresp ] pattern
```

`nbplkup` uses NBP, the AppleTalk Name Binding Protocol, to find information about AppleTalk objects in the network. The pattern that you supply `nbplkup` with determines which objects it displays information about. The `-r` parameter is used to control how many entries are returned. The default number of entries to return is 1,000.

The syntax for the `nbplkup` pattern is:

```
object:type@zone
```

The object and type field can have a literal value or "=," which acts as a wildcard allowing for any values to match. The zone field can have a literal value or "*," which matches the local zone. The fields can also be omitted individually. If they are omitted, the values for the omitted fields are taken from the NBPLOOKUP environment variable. The format of the environment variable is the same as the command line pattern. Only fields not specified in the command line pattern are taken from NBPLOOKUP. If the omitted fields are not supplied in NBPLOOKUP (because it is not set or it also has omitted fields), they have hard-coded defaults. The default object name is the first component of the machine's hostname as supplied by gethostbyname(). The default type is "AFPServer." The default zone is "*," specifying the local zone.

CHECKING ON THE PRINTER'S STATUS

Once the NBP name of the printer has been determined, you can configure the Red Hat machine to access the printer remotely via AppleTalk. First you should check on the status of the printer to make sure that it is connected and operational. The program to run to do this is called `papstatus`.

THE PAPSTATUS COMMAND

The `papstatus` command is used for reporting the status of a remote AppleTalk printer. It has one required argument which specifies the NBP name of the remote printer. The `papstatus` program is executed as follows:

```
papstatus [ -p nbpname ]
```

Here is an example of the `papstatus` command:

```
papstatus -p "HP Writer"
```

TESTING THE PRINTER

After confirming that the printer is operational on the network, you may find it useful to print a test page using AppleTalk Printer Access Protocol (PAP). The program to do this is called pap.

USING THE PAP COMMAND

The pap command is used to connect to the AppleTalk printer daemon, papd, and to send it files to be printed. The pap program is not normally used directly to print files. Printing is normally done via the Red Hat Linux printing mechanisms which typically use lpd to print files. The lpd program needs to be configured to use pap behind the scenes for printing on remote AppleTalk printers. However, pap can be used directly to test the setup of the printers and the network before lpd has been configured. When the pap command is executed it attempts to make a connection with the remote printer using the AppleTalk Printer Access Protocol.

The syntax for pap is as follows:

```
pap [ -c ] [ -e ] [ -p nbpname ] [ -s statusfile ] [ files ]
```

All of the command line parameters are optional. If no files are specified on the command line, pap reads the file to print from standard input. If no printer is specified on the command line, pap looks in its current working directory for a file called .paprc. If such a file is present, it parses the file to find the NBP name of the printer to print to.

The format of the .paprc file is a list of NBP names. Lines beginning with "#" are assumed to be comments and ignored. If the type portion of the name is omitted, the type defaults to "LaserWriter." If the zone portion of the name is omitted, the zone defaults to the default local zone of the host machine.

The -c option tells pap to tell the printer that it has been waiting forever. If this option is not specified, pap tells the printer how long it has actually been waiting. This option is useful for getting a print job printed immediately, cutting in front of other print jobs. Printers sometimes schedule print jobs so that the ones that have been waiting longer get printed sooner. Therefore, specifying that the print job has been waiting forever enables it to be printed sooner than it would have been otherwise.

The -e option specifies that any messages from the printer which pap might print should be sent to stderr instead of stdout. This option is useful when pap is invoked by another program. When pap is invoked by the psf program, for instance, pap is given this option.

The -s option specifies the file to which the printer status should be written. While pap is waiting for the printer to process the input that is sent to it, it receives messages detailing the status of the print operation. If this option is specified, the file is overwritten to contain the most recent status message received from the printer. If this option is not specified, status messages print to stdout unless the -e option has been specified, in which case they print to stderr. This option is useful when `pap` is invoked from another program. When `pap` is invoked by the psf program, for instance, `pap` is given this option.

Here is an example of `pap`:

```
pap -c -p "HP Writer:LaserWriter@*" testfile.ps
```

This command prints the file "testfile.ps" on the printer named "HP Writer" which is of type "LaserWriter" and is in the local zone, which is designated by the special name "*." The printer is told that the print job has been waiting forever, so the print job is most likely scheduled immediatcly. Note that the default values were used in the NBP name sent to the `pap` command. Thus this command is identical to the command:

```
pap -c -p "HP Writer" testfile.ps
```

Summary

In this chapter you learned about the AppleTalk protocol. This protocol is used by Apple computers to communicate with each other. You learned about a Linux protocol suite called Netatalk which implements the AppleTalk protocols and can be used to connect Linux networks to Apple networks. You installed and configured Netatalk on a Red Hat Linux server and then configured the various daemons that implement AppleTalk file and printer sharing on Linux.

Part III

Red Hat Linux Internet Services

IN THIS PART:

Internet services are somewhat different from network services used on an internal network. This part provides an introduction to Internet services and explains the Domain Name System. This part also provides instructions for configuring FTP services, mail services, and Web servers.

Chapter 11

What are Internet Services?

IN THIS CHAPTER

- ◆ Learning about secure services
- ◆ Learning how to avoid less secure Internet protocols
- ◆ Using your Linux machine as a server
- ◆ Configuring the inetd server
- ◆ Configuring the xinetd server
- ◆ Figuring out which services are started from xinetd, and which are standalone
- ◆ Configuring Linux Firewall Packages

WHAT IS AN INTERNET SERVICE? Basically, an Internet Service can be defined as any service that can be accessed through TCP/IP based networks, whether an internal network (Intranet) or external network (Internet). Actually, TCP and IP are two of the protocols that are included in a group of protocols sometimes known as the *Internet protocols*. Since the two most frequently used or discussed protocols of the suite are TCP and IP, the entire suite is often referred to as just *TCP/IP*. Internet services can be provided through either secure or non-secure TCP/IP connections. Common services are Telnet, FTP, SMTP, HTTP, ICMP, ARP, DNS, ssh, scp, sftp, and others.

The significance of TCP/IP as the basis for these services cannot be overlooked. TCP/IP provides a platform- and operating system-independent protocol for these services. Any computer, running any operating system, can communicate with any other computer on the network if they both use TCP/IP protocols for establishing and maintaining the connection and formatting and transmitting the data.

The availability of a wide range of Internet services makes Linux machines versatile workhorses that can fulfill many different functions in a company's network. This chapter covers the wide range of common services that come standard with every Red Hat Linux 7.2 system.

Chapter 6 explains the TCP/IP suite of protocols. Chapter 13 explains setting up and using FTP. Chapter 14 discusses mail transfer and SMTP. Chapter 15 covers HTTP and setting up an HTTP server.

Secure Services

There are common services, such as telnet and ftp, that were written in the days when everyone trusted everybody else on the Internet. These services send all of their traffic in plain text, including passwords. Plain text traffic is extremely easy to eavesdrop on by anyone between the traffic's source and destination. Since the Internet has exploded in popularity, running insecure services such as these is not a good idea. That's why secure replacements have been developed. These replacements provide stronger authentication controls and encrypt all their traffic to keep your data safe. You should always run secure services instead of insecure services.

ssh

Secure Shell, also known as ssh, is a secure telnet replacement that encrypts all traffic, including passwords, using a public/private encryption key exchange protocol. It provides the same functionality of telnet, plus other useful functions, such as traffic tunneling.

This is what it looks like to ssh into a machine for the first time:

```
[vnavrat@buffy vnavrat$ ssh vnavrat@woolf.xena.edu
The authenticity of host 'woolf.xena.edu (123.456.789.65)'
can't be established.
RSA key fingerprint is
 b2:60:c8:31:b7:6b:e3:58:3d:53:b9:af:bc:75:31:63.
Are you sure you want to continue connecting (yes/no)? yes
Warning: Permanently added 'woolf.xena.edu,123.456.789.65'
(RSA) to the list of known hosts.
vnavrat@woolf.xena.edu's password:
 Welcome to woolf
Unauthorized usage prohibited.  Please check your quotas.
vnavrat:~>
```

Ssh asks you if you want to accept and trust the host key being sent to you as being the real key. This question is asked only once, when you log in to a machine for the first time. After this first login, ssh behaves exactly like telnet — you start ssh, it asks for your password, and then you have a regular terminal screen.

In addition to providing terminal access, ssh tunnels almost any other protocol through it. So it is possible to tunnel POP, rcp, and other protocols through ssh to turn them into encrypted, more secure protocols. With enough imagination and practice, you can make almost anything more secure with ssh.

Here is an example of how to tunnel your mail through ssh in order to keep your password and mail encrypted and secure during transit. In this example, you use POP3 to retrieve your mail from the remote machine buffy.xena.edu. Normally you would tell your POP3 software to connect from your localhost to port 110 (the POP port) of buffy.xena.edu.

But in this example the first step is to configure your POP mailer to connect to port 16510 of your own machine, and put in the password for your account on buffy.xena.edu. The second step is to set up the ssh tunnel, which encrypts and forwards the traffic over the network to buffy.xena.edu's POP port.

To set up the ssh tunnel, type the following at the command line:

```
ssh -N -L 16510:127.0.0.1:110 vnavrat@buffy.xena.edu
```

And voila, you are now sending and receiving your mail through an encrypted ssh tunnel.

scp

Secure Copy, also known as scp, is part of the ssh package. It is a secure alternative to rcp and ftp, because, like ssh, the password is not sent over the network in plain text. You can scp files to any machine that has an ssh daemon running.

The syntax of scp is

```
scp user@host:file1 user@host:file2
```

To copy a file named swords-n-steaks.txt to remote host xena from local host buffy, type

```
[vnavrat@buffy vnavrat]$ scp swords-n-steaks.txt vnavrat@xena:weapons/
vnavrat@xena's password:
swords-n-steaks.txt          100% |*****************************|    54
00:00
```

And to copy a file named nixon-enemies-list.txt from remote host xena to your current directory on local host buffy, type

```
[vnavrat@buffy vnavrat]$ scp vnavrat@xena:nixon-enemieslist.txt .
vnavrat@buffy's password:
nixon-enemies-list.txt       100% |*****************************|    54
00:00
```

sftp

Secure File Transfer Program, also known as sftp, is an FTP client that performs all its functions over ssh.

The syntax for sftp is

```
sftp user@host:file file
```

Less Secure Services

These are insecure services that should not be used, since they trust that the network is absolutely secure. Their secure equivalents should be used instead.

Using these services should be discouraged, because all their traffic is sent over the network in plain text. This means that anyone with a common sniffer such as tcpdump can see every key stroke that is typed in the session, including your users' passwords.

telnet

telnet is a protocol and application that enables someone to have access to a virtual terminal on a remote host. It resembles text-based console access on a Unix machine.

Telnet is an application that's available almost everywhere. Because of this distribution, most beginning Unix users use Telnet exclusively to communicate with other Unix and NT machines. Since all telnet traffic, including passwords, is sent in plain text, the Secure Shell (ssh) command should be used instead, if at all possible. ssh provides an equivalent interface to telnet, with increased features, and most importantly, encrypted traffic and passwords.

This is what it looks like when you log into a machine with telnet:

```
[vnavrat@buffy vnavrat]$ telnet xena
Trying 127.0.0.1...
Connected to xena.
Escape character is '^]'.
Welcome to null.xena.edu
login:
```

ftp

ftp is a ubiquitous file transfer protocol that runs over ports 20 and 21. For transferring software packages from anonymous ftp repositories, such as ftp.red-hat.com, ftp is still the standard application to use. However, for personal file transfers, you should use scp. scp encrypts the traffic, including passwords. Once you have successfully logged on to an ftp server, you can type **help** for a list of available commands. Two important commands to remember are put to move a file from your machine to the remote machine, and get to pull a file from the remote server to your machine. To send multiple files you can use mput, and to retrieve multiple files you can use mget. ls or dir give you a listing of files available for download from the remote side.

 To learn more about FTP commands, see Chapter 13.

rsync

rsync is an unencrypted file transfer program that is similar to rcp. It includes the added feature of allowing just the differences between two sets of files on two machines to be transferred across the network. Because it sends traffic unencrypted, it should be tunneled through ssh. Otherwise don't use it. The rsync server listens on port 873.

rsh

rsh is an unencrypted mechanism to execute commands on remote hosts. Normally you specify a command to be run on the remote host on rsh's command line, but if no command is given, you are logged into the remote host using rlogin. rsh's syntax is

rsh remotehostname remotecommand

rlogin

rlogin is a remote login program that connects your terminal to a remote machine's terminal. rlogin is an insecure protocol, because it sends all information, including passwords, in plain-text. It also enables an implicit trust relationship to exist between machines, so that you can use rlogin without a password.

finger

finger enables users on remote systems to look up information about users on another system. Generally finger displays a user's login name, real name, terminal name, idle time, login time, office location, and phone number. You should disable finger outside of your local network, because user information gathered from it could be used to compromise your system. The finger daemon listens on port 79.

talk and ntalk

Talk and talk are real-time chat protocols. The talk server runs on port 517 and the ntalk server runs on port 518. To send someone else a talk request, type **talk** or **ntalk username@hostname.** If their server is running a talk or ntalk daemon and they are logged in, they will see a message inviting them to chat with you. Talk and ntalk aren't as popular as they once were, since instant messenger clients have become very popular.

Using Your Linux Machine as a Server

The following sections give you an overview of what common server protocols are available on Linux.

http

The most common Web server used on Linux is Apache. Apache is started out of a system's rc scripts. Apache is easily configurable, and its configuration files live in /etc/httpd/conf/. While Apache can be set to listen to many different network ports, the most common port it listens on is port 80.

For more information on installing and configuring the Apache Web server, see Chapter 15.

sshd

The secure shell daemon (sshd) is started out of the system's rc scripts. Its global system configuration files are in /etc/ssh, and users' ssh configuration files are in $HOME/.ssh/. The ssh server listens on port 22.

sshd can be configured to run on an alternate port. Running ssh on a port other than 22 comes in handy if port 22 is being blocked by a firewall. Running ssh on a different port also adds a measure of security through obscurity. Automatic scanners used by hackers will miss that ssh is running on your machine if they don't find it running on the standard port they expect.

ftpd

The FTP daemon uses ports 20 and 21 to listen for and initiate FTP requests. Its configuration files `ftpaccess`, `ftpconversions`, `ftpgroups`, `ftphosts`, and `ftpusers`, are located in the `/etc` directory.

 You can find more information on setting up the FTP daemon in Chapter 13.

dns

The Domain Name Service (DNS), which maps IP addresses to hostnames, is served by the named program on port 53. Its configuration file is `named.conf` in the `/etc` directory.

 To read more about setting up DNS on your Linux machine, see Chapter 12.

The Inetd Server

`inetd` is called an Internet *superserver*. It is launched at boot time, and listens for connections on network sockets. When `inetd` starts up, it checks the `inetd.conf` file to see what services should be running. It then reads the `/etc/services` file to see what ports those services should be running on. Listing 11-1 shows excerpts from a copy of the `/etc/services` file. The `/etc/services` file is a good reference for looking up what ports important network services run on. Be sure to look at the `/etc/services` file if you're wondering what an open port is doing.

The `inetd.conf` file excerpted in Listing 11-2 has most services commented out with # at the beginning of the line so they don't run. Services that are uncommented in this file, such as the following `finger` daemon, run upon `inetd`'s startup:

```
finger   stream  tcp     nowait  nobody  /usr/sbin/tcpd  in.fingerd
```

After `inetd` starts, if there is a connection made on a service port listed (and uncommented) in `inetd.conf`, `inetd` then launches the appropriate network service. Once `inetd` launches a network service, it goes back to listening for more incoming network connections. If there is a connection attempt made on a port that `inetd` or any other network service is not listening to, the Linux kernel responds with a reset packet to close the connection. An advantage of this design is that load is reduced by having one process listen for connections and then spawn new processes when appropriate.

Listing 11-1: Excerpts From a Default /etc/services File

```
# /etc/services:
# $Id: services,v 1.22 2001/07/19 20:13:27 notting Exp $
#
# Network services, Internet style
#
# Note that it is presently the policy of IANA to assign a single
    well-known
# port number for both TCP and UDP; hence, most entries here have
    two entries
# even if the protocol doesn't support UDP operations.
# Updated from RFC 1700, ``Assigned Numbers'' (October 1994).  Not
    all ports
# are included, only the more common ones.
#

<snip>

#
# Each line describes one service, and is of the form:
#
# service-name  port/protocol  [aliases ...]   [# comment]

<snip>

chargen          19/tcp          ttytst sourcechargen     19/udp
        ttytst source
ftp-data         20/tcp
ftp-data         20/udp
ftp              21/tcp
ftp              21/udp
ssh              22/tcp                          # SSH Remote Login Protocol
ssh              22/udp                          # SSH Remote Login Protocol
telnet           23/tcp
telnet           23/udp
# 24 - private mail system
smtp             25/tcp          mail
smtp             25/udp          mail
time             37/tcp          timserver
time             37/udp          timserver
rlp              39/tcp          resource        # resource location
```

```
rlp                39/udp      resource        # resource location
nameserver         42/tcp      name            # IEN 116
nameserver         42/udp      name            # IEN 116
nicname            43/tcp      whois
nicname            43/udp      whois
tacacs             49/tcp              # Login Host Protocol (TACACS)
tacacs             49/udp              # Login Host Protocol (TACACS)
re-mail-ck         50/tcp              # Remote Mail Checking Protocol
re-mail-ck         50/udp              # Remote Mail Checking Protocol
domain             53/tcp      nameserver      # name-domain server
domain             53/udp      nameserver
whois++            63/tcp
whois++            63/udp
bootps             67/tcp                      # BOOTP server
bootps             67/udp
bootpc             68/tcp                      # BOOTP client
bootpc             68/udp
tftp               69/tcp
tftp               69/udp
gopher             70/tcp                      # Internet Gopher
gopher             70/udp
```

Listing 11-2: Excerpts From a Default /etc/inetd.conf File

```
<snip>


# <service_name> <sock_type> <proto> <flags> <user> <server_path>
    <args>
#
# Echo, discard, daytime, and chargen are used primarily for
    testing.
#
# To re-read this file after changes, just do a 'killall -HUP inetd'
#

<snip>

# These are standard services.
#
ftp     stream  tcp     nowait  root    /usr/sbin/tcpd  in.ftpd -l -a
telnet  stream  tcp     nowait  root    /usr/sbin/tcpd  in.telnetd
#
```

Continued

Listing 11-2 *(Continued)*

```
# Shell, login, exec, comsat and talk are BSD protocols.
#
#shell    stream  tcp    nowait  root    /usr/sbin/tcpd  in.rshd
#login    stream  tcp    nowait  root    /usr/sbin/tcpd  in.rlogind
#exec     stream  tcp    nowait  root    /usr/sbin/tcpd  in.rexecd
#comsat   dgram   udp    wait    root    /usr/sbin/tcpd  in.comsat
#talk     dgram   udp    wait    nobody.tty   /usr/sbin/tcpd  in.talkd
#ntalk    dgram   udp    wait    nobody.tty   /usr/sbin/tcpd  in.ntalkd
#dtalk    stream  tcp    wait    nobody.tty   /usr/sbin/tcpd  in.dtalkd
#
# Pop and imap mail services et al
#
#pop-2    stream  tcp    nowait  root    /usr/sbin/tcpd  ipop2d
#pop-3    stream  tcp    nowait  root    /usr/sbin/tcpd  ipop3d
#imap     stream  tcp    nowait  root    /usr/sbin/tcpd  imapd
#
# The Internet UUCP service.
#
#uucp     stream  tcp    nowait  uucp    /usr/sbin/tcpd
/usr/lib/uucp/uucico  -l
```

Xinetd

xinetd is a replacement for inetd, that adds more security and functionality. inetd is the old workhorse of the Linux networking world, and xinetd is an improvement on an important program that has been around for several years. It incorporates new features that have been desired by system administrators for a few years now.

Another great reason to run xinetd is that it can run alongside inetd. You can set up secured and extensively logged services with xinetd, and still be able to run services such as RPC that don't run well with xinetd from inetd.

Essentially, inetd and xinetd behave the same way. They both start at system boot time, and they wait and listen for a connection to come in on the ports to which they are assigned in their conf files. Once a connection request is made, if the service requested requires that a new server be spawned, then both inetd and xinetd spawn a new server and keep listening for new connection requests on the service port.

One of the most notable improvements of xinetd over inetd is that anyone can start network services. With inetd, only root can start a network service, and that restriction leads to a host of security problems.

xinetd supports encrypting plain text services such as the ftp command channel by wrapping them in stunnel.

xinetd also enables you to do access control on all services based on different criteria, such as remote host address, access time, remote host name, and remote host domain. In the past this kind of access control could be accomplished only with tools like tcpwrappers, or firewall software. Even then, tcpwrappers could only reliably control tcp traffic.

xinetd also takes the extra security step of killing servers that aren't in the configuration file and those that violate the configuration's access criteria. It can help prevent Denial of Service (DOS) attacks by limiting normal functions that can cripple the machine if there are too many of them occurring at the same time.

For example, xinetd can limit the amount of incoming connections to the whole machine or from a single host to prevent network overflow attacks. It can limit the number of processes that are forked by a network service. xinetd can also stop a service if it is driving the machine's load up too high, to prevent the machine from being slowed to a crawl because of the incoming network traffic.

Log capabilities have also been improved in xinetd. For each service it runs, it can log the remote user and host address, how long the service has been running, and failed access control attempts.

xinetd is flexible enough to enable you to utilize increased security measures such as chrooted environments.

You may notice that the xinetd.conf file (Listing 11-3) is much shorter than inetd.conf, making it easier to read through and customize. The last line says that all the files in the /etc/xinetd.d directory are read into the xinetd.conf file as well. Each service started by xinetd gets its own dedicated file in the /etc/xinetd.d directory. This way you can tell, with a glance at the xinetd.d file listing, what services are being started by it.

Listing 11-3: The xinetd.conf File

```
#
# Simple configuration file for xinetd
#
# Some defaults, and include /etc/xinetd.d/
defaults
{
        instances               = 60
        log_type                = SYSLOG authpriv
        log_on_success          = HOST PID
        log_on_failure          = HOST
        cps                     = 25 30
}


includedir /etc/xinetd.d
```

The last line of the xinetd.conf shown in Listing 11-3 file shows the directory location of the individual configuration files for the services that use xinetd. Listing 11-4 shows the telnet configuration file that is located in the /etc/xinet.d directory.

Listing 11-4: The xinetd config File Entry Required to Set Up a Chrooted telnet Daemon

```
service telnet_chroot
{
        log_on_success  = HOST PID DURATION USERID
        log_on_failure    = HOST RECORD USERID
          no_access     147.125.11.93
        socket_type     = stream
        protocol        = tcp
          port            = 8000
        wait            = no
        user            = root
        server          = /usr/sbin/chroot
          server_args     = /var/public/servers
    /usr/libexec/telnetd
}
```

Note that, in this example, access is denied to the host whose IP address is 147.125.11.93. Other hosts can be added to this line by separating them by commas, and by using wildcard expressions such as *. `log_on_success` specifies what information is logged upon successful login, and `log_on_failure` specifies what's logged when someone attempts to telnet into the machine and fails.

`xinetd` can read your `inetd.conf` file if it's run through a tool called `itox`. `itox` is included in the official `xinetd` package, which is available from `www.xinetd.org`. If you want to replace `inetd` with `xinetd` on your system, you can run `itox` by typing

```
itox < /etc/inetd.conf > /etc/xinetd.conf
```

In your `inetd.conf` file, if you don't have path names listed for each of your network daemons, that is, you have `in.telnetd` instead of `/usr/sbin/in.telnetd`, you should run the `itox` command with the `-daemon_dir` flag:

```
itox -daemon_dir=/usr/sbin < /etc/inetd.conf > /etc/xinetd.conf
```

If you still use a telnet server on your system, you should be aware that by default `telnetd` does not start up with `xinetd`. In order to start a telnet daemon in `xinetd`, you should use the `groups = yes` option within the `xinetd.conf` file.

Inetd and Xinetd vs. Stand-Alone

Which services are stand-alone, and which are started from inetd or xinetd? Sometimes it can get confusing keeping track of how to start a certain service, or keep it from running in the first place. In order to control a service, you need to know what spawns it. Here is a general listing of what services are spawned from superservers such as `inetd` and `xinetd`, and which are started on their own from `rc` scripts or root.

Inetd- or xinetd-started services

The following services are started from `inetd`, or from `xinetd` on newer systems. Each of these services should ideally have its own file in the `/etc/xinetd.d` directory, so you should look in that directory to enable or disable these services.

`chargen` — random character generator that sends its traffic over tcp

`daytime-udp` — gives you the time over `udp`

`finger` — user information lookup program

`kshell` — restricts user access to the shell

`rlogin` — service similar to telnet, but enables trust relationships between machines

`swat` — Samba Web Administration Tool

`time` — gives you the time

`chargen-udp` — random character generator that sends its traffic over `udp`

`echo` — echoes back all characters sent to it over `tcp`

`gssftp` — kerberized FTP server

`rsh` — remote shell

`talk` — a talk (real-time chat) server

`time-udp` — gives you the time over `udp`

`comsat` — notifies users if they have new mail

`echo-udp` — echoes back all characters sent to it over `udp`

`klogin` — kerberos's answer to `rlogin`

`ntalk` — a talk (real-time chat) server

`rsync` — remote file transfer protocol

`telnet` — telnet server

`wu-ftpd` — an `ftp` server

`daytime` — gives you the time over `tcp`

`eklogin` — encrypting kerberized `rlogin` server

krb5-telnet — kerberized telnet server

rexec — provides remote execution facilities

sgi_fam — file monitoring daemon

tftp — trivial file transfer program

Stand-alone services

These services are started from the rc scripts specifically written for them in the rc directories. You can enable or disable these services from those directories.

apache — Web server

sshd — ssh server

sendmail — mail server

qmail — mail server

postfix — mail server

thttpd — semilightweight Web server

boa — lightweight Web server

named — dns server

xfs — X font server

xdm — X display manager

portmap — maps RPC services to ports

rpc.quotad — serves quota information

knfsd — userspace portion of the NFS daemon

rpc.mountd — NFS mount server

rpc.ypbind — NIS server

squid — Web proxy server

nessusd — penetration testing server

postgresql — database server

mysql — database server

oracle — database server

Linux Firewall Packages

Linux provides a few different mechanisms for system security. One of these mechanisms is Linux's firewall packages. Two of the firewalling packages available are tcp-wrappers and ipchains. tcp-wrappers is a minimalistic packet filtering application to protect certain network ports, and ipchains is a packet filtering firewall. Another important firewall package, called iptables, is not covered in this section.

To read more about iptables and Linux system security, see Chapter 26.

tcp-wrappers

The TCP Wrapper program is a network security tool whose main functions are to log connections made to inetd services and restrict certain computers or services from connecting to the tcp-wrapped computer.

Currently xinetd does many of the same things that tcp-wrappers does. But it's still worth running tcp-wrappers if you're also running inetd, or if you want to use the hosts.allow and hosts.deny configuration files to control access to your computer.

TCP wrappers works only on programs that are started from inetd. So services such as sshd, apache, and sendmail cannot be "wrapped" with tcp-wrappers. tcp-wrappers also cannot be used with udp or rcp services, because these services wait for a short time after a connection is closed to see whether another connections will be initiated soon. These daemons specify the "wait" option in inetd.conf, which is not recognized by the tcp-wrapper program.

You can see whether tcp-wrappers is running by checking to see if /usr/sbin/tcpd is in your process listing. You can see if it's installed on your system by looking at the inetd.conf.

An inetd.conf without tcp-wrappers would look like this:

```
telnet  stream  tcp    nowait  root    ./usr/sbin/in.telnetd in.telnetd
```

An inetd.conf with tcp-wrappers looks like this:

```
telnet  stream  tcp    nowait  root    /usr/sbin/tcpd in.telnetd
```

Once tcp-wrappers is installed on your system, you can specify the ruleset they follow in the config files /etc/hosts.allow and /etc/hosts.deny.

When `inetd` starts up, it looks through `/etc/inetd.conf` to see what network service connections it should start listening for. Then it checks `/etc/services` to discover what port it should listen to. On tcp-wrapped systems, `tcpd` is specified as the service to be started in `inetd.conf` instead of the regular service, as was shown in the second line of the example.

`tcpd` is then called and reads the `/etc/hosts.allow` file to see if the hostname of the computer that's trying to connect is listed there. If it is, the connection is allowed. If it is not, `tcpd` checks `/etc/hosts.deny` to see if there's an entry that matches the hostname. If the hostname is in `/etc/hosts.deny`, the connection is closed. If the hostname of the computer connecting is in neither `/etc/hosts.allow` nor `/etc/hosts.deny`, the connection is allowed to continue by default.

The syntax of an allow or deny rule follows this format:

```
service: hostname : options
```

So to enable all services from your own machine (localhost), use a rule like this in your `hosts.allow` file:

```
ALL: ALL@127.0.0.1 : ALLOW
```

To enable only machines from the `xena.edu` domain to telnet into your machine, use this rule in your `hosts.allow` file:

```
in.telnetd: .xena.edu : ALLOW
```

To deny telnet access to everyone on the Internet (who isn't explicitly mentioned in your `/etc/hosts.allow` file), and then e-mail a report to the root account on that machine that someone attempted a telnet connection, use the following rule in your `hosts.deny` file:

```
in.telnetd:ALL : spawn (echo telnet connection tried from %h %a to %d at `date` | \
tee -a /var/log/tcp.deny.log |mail root@localhost )
```

ipchains

`ipchains` is Linux's built-in IP firewall administration tool. Using `ipchains` enables you to run a personal firewall to protect your Linux machine. If the Linux machine is a routing gateway for other machines on your network, it can act as a packet filtering network firewall if more than one network interface is installed.

For more information on setting up a Linux firewall, see Chapter 26.

Summary

As a general rule, you should endeavor to use programs that encrypt their network traffic, instead of using those that use unencrypted protocols.

If you must use a plain-text protocol like `POP` or `rsync`, wrapping it in `ssh` or `ssl` keeps your passwords and data safe from network listeners. `Ssh` is versatile enough to wrap around almost anything.

In general, most services are started from `inetd.conf` or `xinetd.conf`. If a service you're looking into is not started from there, it is probably being started from the machine's `rc` scripts.

If you ever need to know on which port a network protocol operates, check the `/etc/services` file.

Linux's network capabilities have grown a great deal in the past couple of years. Currently, a properly configured Red Hat server can function as many different network devices — anything from an AppleTalk or Samba server to an LDAP server or firewall. Once you get a grasp of how the servers are started and configured in general, the possibilities of what you can do are nearly endless.

Chapter 12

The Domain Name System

THIS CHAPTER provides information about the Domain Name System (DNS), which is used for name address resolution. In this chapter you learn how the Domain Name System works for finding hosts on TCP/IP networks. You also learn about different types of DNS servers and how to configure them for your own network. After configuring your servers, you'll learn about some diagnostic tools that can be used to check the configuration and performance of your DNS.

Understanding DNS

Name address resolution is, simply stated, the conversion of people friendly names into computer friendly numbers. Remember from Chapter 6 that each interface on the network has an IP address. This address is expressed as a dotted quad group. These groups of numbers present no problem to the computers in the network, but it is very difficult for humans to remember many groups of numbers. So you need to be able to enter names and then have these names converted into numbers. Each time you type a Web site's address into your browser, the Domain Name System (DNS) goes to work. You enter names that are easy for you to remember, and the names are resolved into numbers that computers find easy to understand. Enabling efficient human/machine interaction is the function of name address resolution. In this chapter you learn how to install and configure the Domain Name System, which provides this name address resolution.

First, take a look at domain names and their organization using the domain name tactechnology.com. The first part of this domain name, tactechnology, is the name of the company, institution, or organization. The next part, after the period (dot in today's vernacular) is called the top-level domain. In addition to the com top-level domain, you will find a few others. Table 12-1 shows other top-level domains in the United States.

TABLE 12-1 UNITED STATES TOP-LEVEL DOMAINS

Top-Level Domain	Meaning
com	Typically, a business (for example, `www.tactechnology.com`)
edu	An educational institution (for example, `www.muhlenberg.edu`)
gov	A U.S. government agency (for example, `www.whitehouse.gov`)
mil	A branch of the U.S. military (for example, `www.army.mil`)
net	A network affiliated organization (for example, `www.tellurium.net`)
org	A noncommercial organization (for example, `www.lvcg.org`)
int	An international organization (for example, `www.wipo.int`)
us	The U.S. domain, with each listing as a lower level (for example, `www.state.pa.us`)

Top-level domains in other countries include a two-letter suffix, such as fr for France or su for Switzerland. Not all of the top-level domains are the same as the top-level U.S. domains, but a company in France could be `http://www.frenchcompany.com.fr`.

Large domains may be further broken down into subdomains. For example, the U.S. Department of Justice site is `www.usdoj.gov`. The Justice Department includes many agencies such as the Immigration and Naturalization Service. To find the INS, the usdoj domain contains the subdomain `www.ins.usdoj.gov`. An individual computer in the INS also has a host name, for example Mexico. The complete name for this computer is then `mexico.ins.usdoj.gov`, and you can find its IP address by using the DNS to look it up.

When you type in a host name, your system uses its resources to resolve names into IP addresses. One of these files is `/etc/nsswitch.conf` (nsswitch means name service switch), which contains a line telling the system where to look for host information. Figure 12-1 shows the `/etc/nsswitch` file and the hosts line.

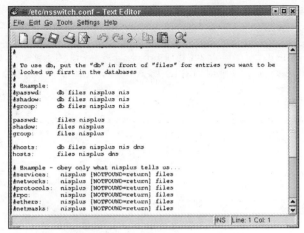

Figure 12-1: The nsswitch.conf file tells the resolver
routines where to look for IP addresses.

The information following the word *host* tells the system to first look at the local
files, then in the NIS database, and finally to use the Domain Name Service (DNS)
to resolve the names into IP numbers. One of the local files searched is the /etc/
hosts file.

Refer to Chapter 6 for more information about the /etc/hosts file.

The hosts file contains IP addresses and host names that you used on your
sample network. So why couldn't you use this file for name resolution? Well, you
could on a small internal network that you controlled and which did not have very
many IP addresses. But, the hosts file is not a manageable solution on a large network, as it is an impossible task to keep it up to date. You could not have control
over every IP address.

After the system looks in the hosts file and fails to find the address, the next file
checked is /etc/resolv.conf. This file contains the IP addresses of computers that
are known as Domain Name Servers, and these are listed in /etc/resolv.conf as
just name servers. Figure 12-2 shows the /etc/resolv.conf file on one of the
computers in the tactechnology.com domain that you have been using for most of
the networking examples.

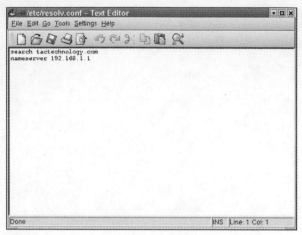

Figure 12-2: The /etc/resolv.conf file points to domain name servers used to resolve IP addresses.

Two name servers are listed in the file shown in Figure 12-2. You could list up to three name servers, but two is all that is required, enabling a connection to one of the name servers in case the other name server is down or not reachable. Don't list more than three name servers, as any over three are ignored.

Installing the Software

So far you have learned about name address resolution and the structure of domains in the United States. Now you learn about the Domain Name System servers that resolve the name into IP numbers. The most common DNS server used in current Red Hat Linux distributions is BIND, or the Berkeley Internet Name Daemon. The latest release of BIND is Version 9.2, and can be obtained from the Internet Software Consortium at `www.isc.org`.

The RPM version of BIND is also included with the Red Hat installation CD-ROMs. A very convenient and easy way to install the latest version of BIND is to look for the distribution specific package. Check the Web site for your distribution to locate the RPM for BIND. On my system, I installed the RPM using the Kpackage manager as shown in Figure 12-3. The RPM file can also be installed at the command line by using the `rpm` command.

Refer to Chapter 23 for instructions on installing and upgrading packages.

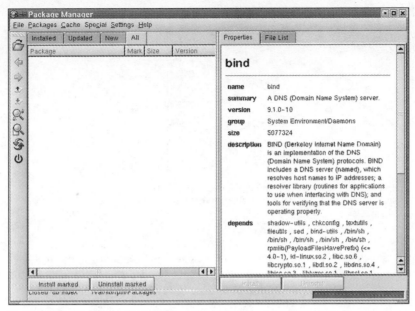

Figure 12-3: Installing the latest version of BIND using the Kpackage manager

Installing the package installs all the files necessary to set up DNS. The installation creates a directory /var/named and places two files, /var/named/named.ca and /var/named/named.local here. These files are used for localhost lookups. Two files are created in the /etc directory: /etc/named.conf and /etc/named.boot. Four files are created in /usr/sbin; these files are named, named-boot, named-xfer, and rndc. The file /usr/sbin/named is the name server daemon; named-boot is a Perl script that converts named.boot files to named.conf files; named-xfer is a transfer program for external zone files; and rndc is the name server daemon control program. The rndc program is a shell script that interacts with the named daemon to provide status information, and can also be used to start, stop, or restart the named daemon.

Understanding Types of Domain Servers

A top-level domain server, one that provides information about the domains shown in Table 12-1, is typically referred to as a Root Name Server. A search for www. muhlenberg.edu looks to the root name server for .edu for information. The root name server then directs the search to a lower-level domain name server until the information is found. You can see an example of this by using the nslookup command to search for the root name server for .edu, as shown in Figure 12-4.

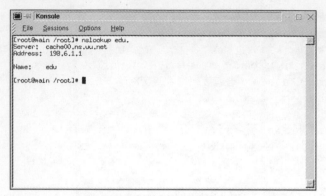

Figure 12-4: A search for the top-level root name servers for .edu

The listing shows the root name server that provides information for the .edu domain. You can continue the search for the second-level domain by adding the name of the domain you are looking for as shown in Figure 12-5.

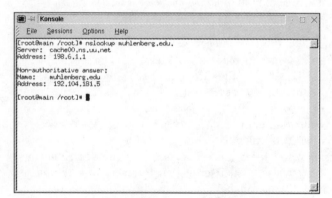

Figure 12-5: A search for the second-level domain shows the authoritative name server.

After you have found the domain you are looking for, information about that domain is provided by its local domain name servers. The three types of local domain name servers are master, slave, and caching servers. In the listing, two servers are shown; one is a master and the other is a slave.

The master contains all the information about the domain and supplies this information when requested. A master server is listed as an authoritative server when it contains the information you are seeking and it can provide that information.

The slave is intended as a backup in case the master server goes down or is not available. This server contains the same information as the master and provides it when requested if the master server cannot be contacted.

A caching server does not provide information to outside sources; it is used to provide domain information to other servers and workstations on the local network. The caching server remembers the domains that have been accessed. Use of a caching server speeds up searches since the domain information is already stored in memory, and the server knows exactly where to go rather than having to send out a request for domain information.

Where does the information that the master and slave servers provide come from? The server(s) have been configured to provide it when asked. In the next section, you learn how to configure a server to provide domain name information.

Examining Server Configuration Files

Before you begin to configure your servers, you need to take a closer look at the files you need to configure. You need five files to set up the named server. Three files are required regardless of the configuration as a master, slave, or caching-only server, and two files are used on the master server.

The three required files are

- ◆ `named.conf` — found in the /etc directory, this file contains global properties and sources of configuration files.

- ◆ `named.ca` — found in /var/named, this file contains the names and addresses of root servers.

- ◆ `named.local` — found in /var/named, this file provides information for resolving the loopback address for the localhost.

The two files required for the master domain server are

- ◆ `zone` — this file contains the names and addresses of servers and workstations in the local domain and maps names to IP addresses

- ◆ `reverse zone` — this file provides information to map IP addresses to names

You begin with the /etc/named.conf file which is shown in Figure 12-6.

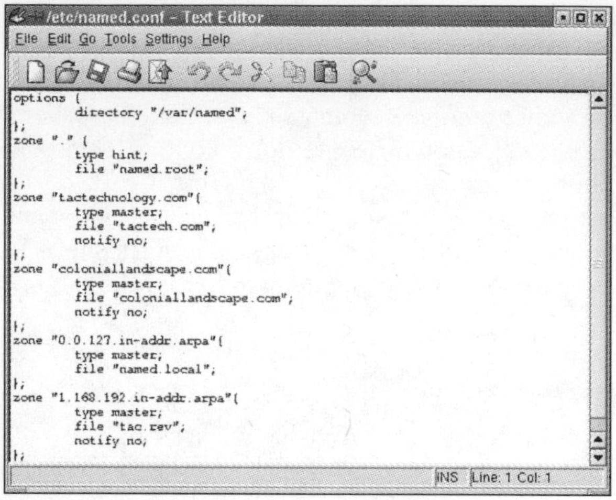

Figure 12-6: The /etc/named.conf file from the tactechnology.com domain

The named.conf file

Look at this file in more detail beginning with the lines starting with //. These are comment lines and anything following them is ignored.

Commands are passed to the file in the form of statements. Several of these statements are shown in the sample file, but you actually can use seven configuration statements. These are listed here with a brief explanation of their function.

- **options** – lists global configurations and defaults

- **include** – gets information from another file and includes it

- **acl** – specifies IP addresses used in an access control list

- **logging** – specifies log file locations and contents

- **server** – specifies properties of remote servers

- **zone** – specifies information about zones

- **key** – specifies security keys used for authentication

Information about the statement is contained within curly braces and terminated by a semicolon: {*information about server*};.

Options

The options statement is typically the first section of named.conf, and it contains information about the location of the files used by named. You can use only one options statement, but you can have more than one value for that statement. In the sample file shown in Figure 12-6, the `options` statement shows the path to where additional configuration files used by `named` are located. By specifying the directory where other files are located, it is not necessary to list the entire path to the file, just the name of the file for any files shown in the remainder of `named.conf`. Options statements use the following syntax.

```
options {
      value "property";
}
```

The list of values that can be used in the `options` statement is quite long. These values are shown, listed alphabetically, in Table 12-2.

TABLE 12-2 OPTIONS VALUES AND THEIR MEANINGS

Value	Meaning
allow-query	Accepts queries only from hosts in the address list (by default queries are accepted from any host).
	Usage: allow-query {"address-list"};.
allow-transfer	Zone transfers are accepted only by hosts in the address list (by default transfers are allowed to all hosts).
	Usage: allow-transfer {"address list"};.
auth-nxdomain	The server responds as an authoritative server (defaults to yes).
	Usage: auth-nxdomain "yes or no"; (choose one).
check-names	Host names are checked for compliance with the RFC.
	Usage: check-names "master or slave or response warn or fail or ignore"; (choose one from each group).
cleaning-interval	Specifies the time period before expired resource records are removed by the server (defaults to 60 minutes).
	Usage: cleaning-interval "number"; (specify number in minutes).
coresize	Specifies largest size for core dump files.
	Usage: coresize "size"; (specify size in bytes).
datasize	Limits server memory usage.
	Usage: datasize "size"; (specify size in bytes).

Continued

TABLE 12-2 **OPTIONS VALUES AND THEIR MEANINGS** *(Continued)*

Value	Meaning
deallocate-on-exit	Detects memory leaks (default is no).
	Usage: deallocate-on-exit "yes or no"; (choose one).
directory	Path of the directory where server configuration files are located.
	Usage: directory "path to directory"; (specify path).
dump-file	If named receives a SIGINT signal, it dumps the database to the file specified here (defaults to named_dump.db).
fake-iquery	If set to yes, the server sends a fake reply to inverse queries rather than an error (default is no).
	Usage: fake-iquery " yes or no"; (choose one).
fetch-glue	If set to yes, the server obtains the glue records for a response (default is yes).
	Usage: fetch-glue "yes or no"; (choose one).
files	Limits number of concurrently open files (default is unlimited).
	Usage: files "number"; (specify number).
forward	If set to first, the servers listed in the forwarders option are queried first, and then the server tries to find the answer itself. If set to only, just the servers in the forwarders list are queried.
	Usage: forward "first or only"; (choose one).
forwarders	Shows IP addresses of servers to forward queries (default is none).
	Usage: forwarders "IP addresses of servers"; (specify IP addresses).
host-statistics	If set to yes the server keeps statistics on hosts (default is no).
	Usage: host-statistics "yes or no"; (choose one).
interface-interval	Specifies interval for searching the network for new or removed interfaces (default is 60 minutes).
	Usage: interface-interval "time"; (specify time in minutes).
listen-on	Specifies port and interfaces on which server listens for queries (default is port 53).
	Usage: listen-on "port {address list}"; (specify port number and address list).

Value	Meaning
max-transfer-time-in	Specifies time server waits for completion of inbound transfer (default is 120 minutes).
	Usage: max-transfer-time-in "time"; (specify time in minutes).
memstatistics-file	When deallocate-on-exit is set, specifies the file where memory statistics are written (defaults to `named.memstats`).
	Usage: memstatistics-file "path to file"; (specify path and file name).
multiple-cnames	When set to yes, enables multiple CNAME usage (default is no).
	Usage: multiple-cnames "yes or no"; (choose one).
named-xfer	Specifies path to the named-xfer program.
	Usage: named-xfer "path to file"; (specify path).
notify	When zone files are updated, this option, when set to yes, sends DNS NOTIFY messages (default is yes).
	Usage: notify "yes or no"; (choose one).
pid-file	Name of file holding process ID.
	Usage: pid-file "path to file"; (specify path and file name).
query-source	Specifies port and IP address used to query other servers.
	Usage: query-source "address port";(specify IP address and port).
recursion	The server recursively searches for query answers (default is yes).
	Usage: recursion " yes or no"; (choose one).
stacksize	The amount of stack memory the server can use.
	Usage: stacksize "number"; (specify the amount of memory).
statistics-interval	The time interval for logging statistics (default is 60 minutes).
	Usage: statistics-interval "time"; (specify the time in minutes).
topology	Sets server preference for remote servers.
	Usage: topology {"address list"};.
transfer-format	When set to one-answer, only one resource record per message is sent. When set to many-answers, as many records as possible are transmitted in each message. (default is one).
	Usage: transfer-format "one-answer many-answers"; (choose one).

Continued

TABLE **12-2** OPTIONS VALUES AND THEIR MEANINGS *(Continued)*

Value	Meaning
transfers-in	Maximum concurrent inbound zone transfers (default is 10).
	Usage: transfers-in "number"; (specify the number).
transfers-out	Maximum concurrent outbound transfers.
	Usage: transfers-out "number"; (specify the number).
transfers-per-ns	Limits inbound transfers from a single server (default is two).
	Usage: transfers-per-ns "number"; (specify the number).

INCLUDE

The include statement lists the path and name of any files that you want to be included with the `named.conf` file. Use the same syntax as used in the options statement to specify the path.

ACL

This option lets you specify a list of IP addresses in an access control list. Only hosts on this list have access to the server.

LOGGING

The logging statement is where you specify your server's logging options. The logging statement contains two additional items, the channel and the category.

The channel is where you specify the location of the logged information. Logged information can be written to a file, sent to the syslog, or thrown away by specifying the appropriate command. Choosing to send the information to a file gives you several additional choices on how to handle the information. You can set the number of versions to keep, the size of the files, and whether the severity of the information and the time and category are included with the other information in the file.

The syntax for the logging statement is similar to the syntax for the option statement. The following commands send the information to a file. Items in italics indicate information you need to enter.

```
logging {
        channel channel_name {
        (file   path to file
        versions specify number or unlimited
        size specify size in bytes }If you want to send the
information to the syslog, the syntax is
```

```
logging {
        channel channel_name {
        syslog (choose where to send from following choices)
(kern,user,mail,daemon,auth,syslog,lpr,news,uucp,cron,\
        authpriv,ftp,local0 thru local7)
```

To discard the information, choose null as the destination.

```
logging {
        channel channel_name {
        null;)
```

Next you can set the severity level for the information written to the file or syslog. This section follows the sections shown previously for file or syslog. You also indicate here if you want the time, category, and severity included. If you are discarding the information, you don't need to set these parameters.

```
severity choose from critical,error,warning,notice,info,debug\
level,dynamic
print-time choose yes or no
print-severity choose yes or no
print-category choose yes or no
};
```

The category is where you specify the type of information to log. This value follows the severity and print parameters and takes the following syntax:

```
category category name {
channel name; channel name;
};
```

You can choose from over 20 categories. These are shown, alphabetically, in Table 12-3.

TABLE **12-3** LOGGING CATEGORIES

Category	Type of Information Logged
cname	Information about CNAME references
config	Information about configuration files
db	Information about databases

Continued

TABLE 12–3 LOGGING CATEGORIES *(Continued)*

Category	Type of Information Logged
default	The default if nothing is selected
eventlib	Information about event system debugging
insist	Details about failures from internal consistency checking
lame-servers	Information about lame servers
load	Information about zone loading
maintenance	Information about maintenance
ncache	Information about negative caching
notify	Information about tracing the NOTIFY protocol
os	Information about operating system problems
packet	Dumps of all sent and received packets
panic	Information about faults that shut down the server
parser	Information about processing configuration commands
queries	Information about all received DNS queries
response-checks	Information about response-checking results
security	Information about security status of server
statistics	Information about server statistics
update	Information about dynamic updates
xfer-in	Information about inbound zone transfers
xfer-out	Information about outbound zone transfers

Using the categories from the logging statement, you can obtain a large quantity of information about your server. This information can be useful if you are having problems with your DNS. You can enable logging for the area that you think is causing your problem and then read the appropriate log to find any messages that might indicate an error with your configuration.

SERVER
In the server statement you can set the properties of a remote server. You can specify whether to send queries to the remote server from the local server, and you

can set the method used for transferring information. The syntax for this statement is the same as for other statements. The valid values are:

- `bogus` — Specify yes or no (No is the default and indicates that queries are sent to the remote server.) Yes means that the remote server is not queried.

- `transfer` — Specify the number of transfers you want to allow.

- `transfer-format` — Specify whether you want one-answer or many-answers.

- `keys` — Specify key ID (currently not implemented).

ZONES

The remainder of the listings in `/etc/named.conf` shown in Figure 12-6 are zone statements. These zone statements refer to files that are called zone files. Additional options for zone statements exist, of course. Each zone statement begins with the word `zone` followed by the domain name and the data class. The four data classes are `in`, `hs`, `hesiod`, and `chaos`. If no type is specified, the default is `in`, for Internet.

Next follows the type option which specifies whether the server is a master, a slave/stub, or is the hints file. A stub server loads only NS records, not the entire domain. The hints file is used to initialize the root cache and contains a list of root servers.

Next is the name of the zone file for the specified zone. This is a pointer to the file containing the data about the zone. You look at a zone file in detail a little later in this chapter.

The six other options for the zone statements are listed here, along with an explanation of their function.

- **allow-query** — Accepts queries only from hosts in the address list (by default queries are accepted from any host).

- **allow-transfer** — Zone transfers are accepted only by hosts in the address list (by default transfers are allowed to all hosts).

- **allow-update** — Hosts in the address list are allowed to update the database.

- **also-notify** — Servers in the address list are sent a notify message when the zone is updated.

- **check-names** — Host names are checked for compliance with the RFC.

- **max-transfer-time-in** — Specifies the time the slave waits for a zone transfer.

- **notify** — When zone files are updated, this option, when set to yes, sends DNS NOTIFY messages (default is yes).

These options are the same as those shown in the options statement section and have the same function here. When listed in the options section, they apply to all zones, but if listed with a specific zone, they apply only to that zone. Settings listed in a specific zone section override those globally set in the options statement.

The named.ca file

The first zone file is known as the cache file, and it references a file called named.ca, which contains information about the world's root name servers. This information changes and needs to be updated periodically. Figure 12-7 shows the contents of this file.

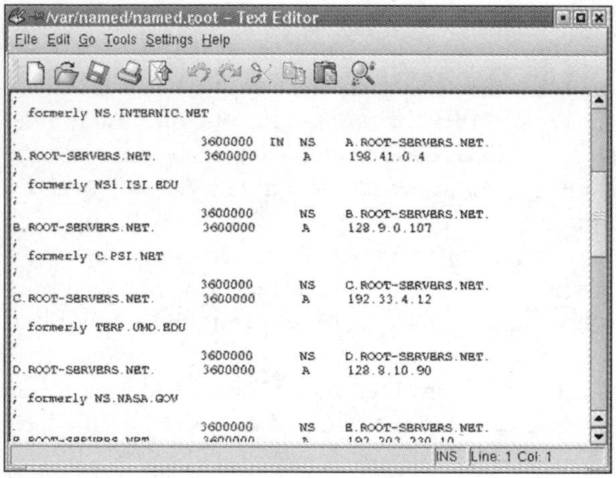

Figure 12-7: The named.ca file contains a listing of worldwide root name servers.

The named.local file

The next zone file contains information about the localhost. The file referenced here is named.local and contains information about the local domain. Figure 12-8 shows the contents of this file.

The next zone file provides name lookup information about the domain tactechnology.com, and the final zone provides reverse lookup. Reverse lookup enables you to enter the IP number and obtain the name. Next, you look at these files more closely.

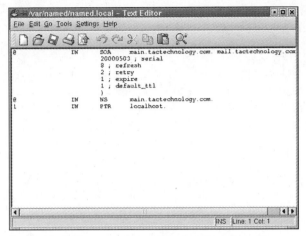

Figure 12-8: The named.local file contains information about the internal network 127.0.0.1.

Zone files

Zone files contain resource records (RR) about IP addresses. A typical zone file is shown in Figure 12-9.

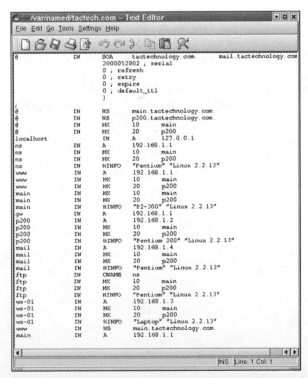

Figure 12-9: The zone file for the tactechnology.com domain

A zone file can contain many types of RRs, which are listed in the order in which they generally appear in the zone files, and explained next.

SOA — START OF AUTHORITY

The start of authority (SOA) is the first line in the zone file. The SOA identifies the name server as the authoritative source for information about this domain. Each zone file has only one SOA, and it contains the following data:

```
@  IN  SOA  main.tactechnology.com.     mail.tactechnology.com. (/
   2000052101 ; Serial
   8h         ;Refresh
   2h         ;Retry
   1w         ;Expire
   1d)        ;Minimum TTL
```

The first character in the SOA line is a special symbol that means "to look at this domain." IN means Internet. SOA means Start of authority.

The authoritative server for this domain is main.tactechnology.com., and mail.tactechnology.com. is the e-mail address of the administrator. Note the trailing period after the domain names. If these are not included, the domain name is appended to the entry.

The opening parenthesis enables the first line to be extended so that anything between the opening and closing parenthesis is considered one line.

The information within the parenthesis is passed to other name servers, secondary masters, that use this information to update their records. The line containing 2000052101 ; Serial is the serial number of the file. Secondary servers compare this number with their stored information. If the numbers are the same, the information has not changed and it is not necessary to download this file. If the serial numbers are different, the file is downloaded to update the information in the secondary server. The serial number can be any number desired as long as it can be incremented to indicate a revision to the file. The semicolon indicates that what follows to the end of the line is a comment.

Refresh is the amount of time the server should wait before refreshing its data.

Retry is the amount of time the server should wait before attempting to contact the primary server if the previous attempt failed.

Expire means that if the secondary master is unable to contact a primary master during the specified period, the data expires and should be purged.

TTL specifies the Time to Live for the data. This parameter is intended for caching name servers and tells them how long to hold the data in their cache.

All of the information contained by the SOA may be placed on one line, but it is usually written as shown previously. The order of the items is significant in the SOA header.

NS — NAME SERVERS IN THIS DOMAIN
Shows the names of the name servers.

A — THE IP ADDRESS FOR THE NAME
Shows the IP address for the name servers.

PTR — POINTER FOR ADDRESS NAME MAPPING
Used to point to the name servers.

CNAME — CANONICAL NAME
Shows the real name of the host.

MX RECORD — MAIL EXCHANGE RECORD
The MX record specifies the mail servers for the domain. In the tactech.com zone file, two MX addresses are listed, one followed by the number 10 and the other by the number 20. Any mail sent to tactechnology.com goes to main.tactechnology.com because it has a lower number. Priority is determined by the address with the lowest number receiving the highest priority. So, main is the primary mail server and p200 is the secondary mail server. If main is unable to receive mail, mail goes to p200. P200 tries to send mail to main since it is its primary mail server also. When main is again able to receive mail, it receives all the mail that p200 has received.

TXT — TEXT INFORMATION
Enables entry of descriptive information.

WKS — WELL-KNOWN SERVICE
Enables entry of descriptive information.

HINFO — HOST INFORMATION
Usually shows type of hardware and software.

The reverse zone file

The last zone file shown in the `named.conf` file in Figure 12-9 is called `tac.rev`. This file is used to provide information for reverse lookups. In the previous example you searched for tactechnology.com by using the domain name. This method is called forward address resolution since it uses a name to find an IP number and is the most common use of name resolution.

You can also find a name from an IP number, and this is called reverse address resolution. All you need to do is enter the IP address, and the server returns the domain name. Figure 12-10 shows the reverse lookup zone file for tactechnology.com.

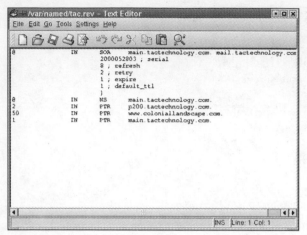

Figure 12-10: The reverse lookup zone file for
tactechnology.com

Configuring a Caching Server

Now you know which files need to be configured and you know the information that needs to be placed in them. You are ready to set up your own domain name servers. In this section you set up a caching server for the domain tactechnology.com. As stated earlier, three files are used in all three types of server configurations. In a caching-only server, these three files make up the entire configuration.

Begin by verifying the zone information in /etc/named.conf. When you installed the BIND package, the /etc/named.conf file was created and it contained zone information for your localhost, but you need to check it to be sure. You are looking for two zone lines: one indicated by a ".", referencing the file named.ca, and one shown as " 0.0.127.in.addr.arpa", referencing named.local. See Figure 12-11.

Next, you need to check the configuration of the /var/named/named.local file. This file contains the domain information for the localhost, and is typically created when BIND is installed. You usually don't have to make any changes to /var/named/named.local. This domain is a reverse domain in that it is used to map the loopback address 127.0.0.1 to the localhost name. Figure 12-12 shows the named.local file.

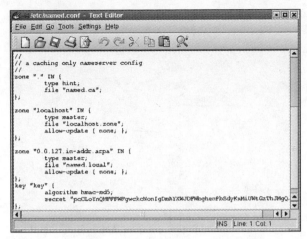

Figure 12-11: The named.conf file generated during
BIND installation

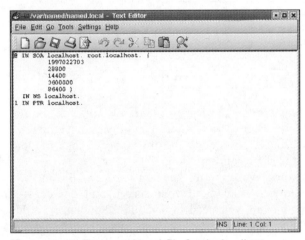

Figure 12-12: The named.local file for the localhost

You need to check the /etc/nsswitch file to be sure it contains the following
line.

```
hosts:   files   nisplus   dns
```

You need to check the /etc/resolv.conf file to make sure that the IP address
(127.0.0.1) of your localhost is listed as a name server.

Finally, you need to check that your /etc/host.conf contains the word *bind*.

After you have completed all of the previous steps, it is time to start the named
daemon and check your work.

Type **rndc start** at a command prompt, wait for the prompt to return, and then type **dig**. If you see a screen like that shown in Figure 12-13, you have successfully configured a caching server.

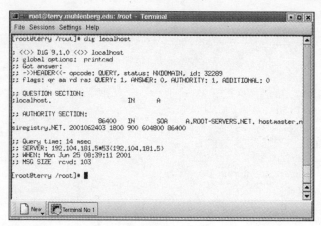

Figure 12-13: The dig command can be used to find name servers, in this case your localhost.

Configuring a Slave Server

Next you set up a slave server for your domain. The procedure is similar to, and not much more difficult than, what you have already done. You already have three of the files in place and only need to slightly modify the /etc/named.conf file and add two more files to complete the slave configuration.

On the server you want to be the slave, go to the /etc/named.conf file and add two more zones, one for the forward lookup of your server, and one for the reverse lookup. For the forward lookup, you need to add the following. (For this example, the master server is called main.tactechnology.com, and the slave is p200. tactechnology.com. Be sure to use your own domain name and IP address instead of the examples shown.)

```
zone "tactechnology.com" {
    notify no;
    type slave;
    file "tactech.com";
    masters { 192.168.1.1; };
};
```

For the reverse lookup you add this section:

```
zone "1.168.192.in-addr.arpa" {
    notify no;
```

```
    type slave;
    file "tac.rev";
    masters { 192.168.1.1; };
};
```

After modifying the /etc/named.conf file it should look like Figure 12-14. Configuration of the slave server is now complete and you can move on to configuring the master server.

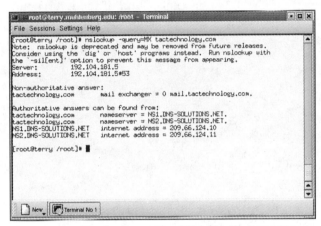

Figure 12-14: The /etc/named.conf file with the forward and reverse lookup zones added

Configuring a Master Server

The /etc/named.conf file on the master server also needs to be modified. Assuming that you already set up this server as a caching-only server, you just need to add the following lines to /etc/named.conf. (This example uses the names you defined earlier; be sure to use your own names and IP addresses.)

```
zone "tactechnology.com" {
    notify no;
    type master;
    file "tactech.com";
};
```

For the reverse lookup you add this section:

```
zone "1.168.192.in-addr.arpa" {
    notify no;
    type master;
```

```
            file "tac.rev";
    };
```

Notice that you used the same names for the files on the master server as the slave server. This is because these files are downloaded by the slave in a zone file transfer and stored on the slave in the files shown by the file option. You did not create the files on the slave but created them on the master server.

You now need to create the zone files that are referenced by the /etc/named.conf file. First you create the file /var/named/tactech.com by beginning with the Start of Authority section (SOA). For an explanation of the information contained in zone files, refer to the zone file section earlier in this chapter.

```
@   IN  SOA   main.tactechnology.com.mail.tactechnology.com. ( /
              200005203     ; Serial/
                    8h; Refresh/
                    2h; Retry/
                    1w; Expire/
                    1d); Minimum TTL/
```

Next you add name server and mail exchange information.

```
NS   main.tactechnology.com./
NS   terry.tactechnology.com./
MX   10 main;Primary Mail Exchanger/
MX   20 p200;Secondary Mail Exchanger/
```

Finally, you add information about your localhost, mail, FTP and Web server. You can also add information about every workstation on your network. Figure 12-15 shows the complete zone file for tactechnology.com.

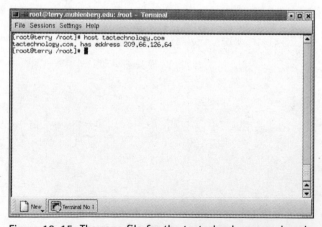

Figure 12-15: The zone file for the tactechnology.com domain

Next you set up the reverse lookup zone file which is called `tac.rev`. Again, you need to start with the SOA header as shown:

```
@  IN  SOA  main.tactechnology.com.  mail.tactechnology.com.(
           200005203;Serial
           8h          ; Refresh
      2h          ; Retry
        1w          ; Expire
      1d)        ; Minimum TTL
```

Next you add the information about your name servers and their IP addresses.

```
          NS       main.tactechnology.com.
1         PTR      main.tactechnology.com.
2         PTR      p200.tactechnology.com.
```

After you finish creating this file, it should look like Figure 12-16.

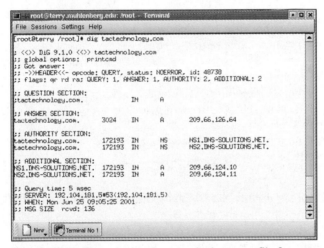

Figure 12-16: The completed reverse lookup zone file for tactechnology.com

If you have done everything as explained here, your name server should be working. You need to check your work again. But before you do, look at some of the tools available to you for checking name server information.

Using DNS Tools

The three very useful tools available for troubleshooting DNS problems that are included with BIND are

- nslookup

- host

- dig

Earlier when you set up a caching name server, you checked your work using nslookup. Nslookup is one of several programs that can be used to obtain information about your name servers. This information helps you to fix problems that may have occurred. Notice that when you start nslookup, you see a message about it being deprecated and may not be available in future releases; however, it is still available and is quite useful.

nslookup, as its name implies, is a program that can be used either interactively, or noninteractively, to look up name servers. Entering `nslookup` at a command prompt starts the search for a name server by looking in the `/etc/resolv.conf` file. If you are running a name server on your system, your localhost (127.0.0.1) is searched, as this is the first listing for a name server in `/etc/resolv.conf`. You can also tell nslookup to search for a specific server by entering a hyphen and the name of the desired server after the command. After nslookup starts, the DNS server used for searches is shown and a prompt is presented for entering commands.

The most common commands available for use with nslookup are

- `ls` — used to list information about the domain in question

- `set` — used to change search information for lookups

The set command also has many options, but the most commonly used option is to set the query type. The query type may be changed to any of the RR types you saw earlier in this chapter, plus a few other types. For example, if you want to see the mail servers on the tactechnology.com domain you could type the command as illustrated in Figure 12-17.

Another utility that is useful for obtaining information about a name server is host. Host enables you to find an IP address for the specified domain name. All that is required is the domain name of the remote host as shown in the following:

```
host tactechnology.com
```

You can also search for resource record types by using the `-t` option and the type of resource record you want to search. A sample output from host is shown in Figure 12-18.

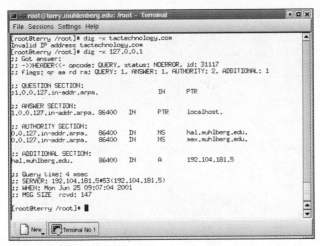

```
root@terry.muhlenberg.edu: /root - Terminal
File  Sessions  Settings  Help
[root@terry /root]# dig -x tactechnology.com
Invalid IP address tactechnology.com
[root@terry /root]# dig -x 127.0.0.1
;; Got answer:
;; ->>HEADER<<- opcode: QUERY, status: NOERROR, id: 31117
;; flags: qr aa rd ra; QUERY: 1, ANSWER: 1, AUTHORITY: 2, ADDITIONAL: 1

;; QUESTION SECTION:
;1.0.0.127.in-addr.arpa.             IN      PTR

;; ANSWER SECTION:
1.0.0.127.in-addr.arpa. 86400   IN      PTR     localhost.

;; AUTHORITY SECTION:
0.0.127.in-addr.arpa.   86400   IN      NS      hal.muhlberg.edu.
0.0.127.in-addr.arpa.   86400   IN      NS      max.muhlberg.edu.

;; ADDITIONAL SECTION:
hal.muhlberg.edu.       86400   IN      A       192.104.181.5

;; Query time: 4 msec
;; SERVER: 192.104.181.5#53(192.104.181.5)
;; WHEN: Mon Jun 25 09:07:04 2001
;; MSG SIZE  rcvd: 147

[root@terry /root]#
```

Figure 12-17: Using nslookup, you can choose the type of information you wish to query.

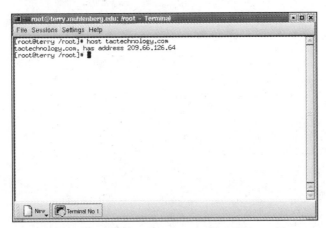

```
root@terry.muhlenberg.edu: /root - Terminal
File  Sessions  Settings  Help
[root@terry /root]# host tactechnology.com
tactechnology.com. has address 209.66.126.64
[root@terry /root]#
```

Figure 12-18: Host is an easy-to-use utility that provides a good amount of information.

The last utility you look at is dig. Dig can be used for debugging and obtaining other useful information. The basic syntax is:

```
dig (@server) domain name (type)
```

Items in parenthesis are optional. Figure 12-19 shows the output of a dig request to tactechnology.com.

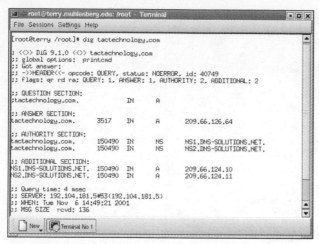

Figure 12-19: The dig utility can be used to obtain a large amount of domain information.

Dig can also be used to do reverse lookups by using the -x switch and specifying the IP address:

```
dig -x 127.0.0.1
```

This command returns the domain name of the localhost as seen in Figure 12-20.

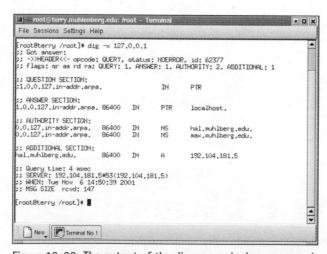

Figure 12-20: The output of the dig reverse lookup command

It's time to get back to checking the results of your efforts to set up a domain name server.

You made some changes to the `/etc/named.conf` file, so before you can check what you did, you need to restart the `named` daemon. The `named` daemon must be restarted whenever you make changes to `/etc/named.conf`. To restart `named`, you just need to type:

```
rndc restart
```

Now you can run nslookup to see if you can find your name server. After nslookup starts, it returns the name of your localhost. Now you need to look for your name server by using the `set` command to change the query type to look for name servers. Figure 12-21 shows the entire process of running nslookup, changing the query type, and the results of the query.

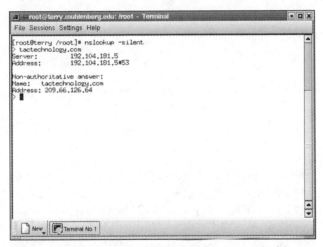

Figure 12-21: The results of the nslookup command with query type set to name server

The last thing you need to check is the reverse lookup. Start nslookup in the default mode by typing **nslookup** at the command prompt. Then you can enter the IP address of the server, which is 192.168.1.1. The result of this query is shown in Figure 12-22.

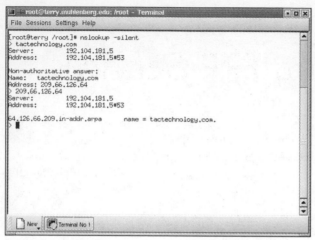

Figure 12-22: The reverse lookup of your IP address returns the name of your server.

That's it, you have successfully set up a domain name server on your system.

Summary

This chapter has provided a brief but concise overview of the Domain Name System using a small, simple network as an example. You looked at name address resolution and found out how names that are easy for people to remember are converted to numbers that computers can understand. You obtained the BIND software package and installed it on your system and located the files that had to be configured for BIND to work. After configuring the files, you set up a caching name server and tested its operation. You then configured a primary master name server, looked at some of the diagnostic utilities available for the BIND package, and used them to test your name server.

Chapter 13

Configuring FTP Services

IN TODAY'S PECKING ORDER OF INTERNET SERVICES, FTP, the File Transfer Protocol, arguably places third behind e-mail's enormous popularity and the Web's visual appeal. Nevertheless, FTP is a core Internet service, one that almost every Internet user has used at one time or another. This chapter shows you how to configure and maintain WU-FTPD, the FTP server package that comes with Red Hat Linux.

FTP itself is relatively straightforward and uncomplicated to install, configure, maintain, and monitor. The few difficulties most administrators encounter are the result of FTP's interaction with firewalls, the TCP Wrappers package, and other measures intended to increase the overall security of a Red Hat Linux system. This chapter steps through the entire process of installing, configuring, maintaining, and monitoring an FTP server. It also outlines the security issues involved in running an FTP server and suggests measures you can take to minimize security risks.

What FTP Software is Available?

The question "What FTP software is available?" really asks two different questions. The first is, "What FTP software comes with Red Hat Linux?" The second is, "What FTP software is available for me to use?" This chapter answers the first question in considerable detail but only barely answers the second one because the range of FTP server and client software available, but not shipped with, Red Hat Linux is large. Moreover, the term "FTP software" is ambiguous. It can refer to server daemons, such as the WU-FTPD server you study in this chapter; to client programs, such as the traditional `ftp` command line client included with Red Hat Linux; or to FTP "helper" programs, such as the ftpcopy package, a mirroring utility also included with Red Hat Linux. Although this chapter is devoted to configuring WU-FTPD, it does briefly describe two popular alternative FTP server programs you can use with Red Hat Linux.

Red Hat Linux's choice: WU-FTPD

The only FTP server available in any of the Red Hat Linux installation profiles is WU-FTPD, the Washington University FTP daemon, maintained by the WU-FTPD Development Group. To the standard FTP services defined in RFC 959, the core RFC (Request For Comment) that defines the FTP protocol, WU-FTPD adds the security and feature enhancements listed here:

◆ Logging all incoming and outgoing file transfers

◆ Logging all commands executed by users logged in to the server

◆ Compressing downloaded files and directories on the fly

◆ Organizing users into classes and setting limits on a per class basis

◆ Controlling uploads on a per directory basis

◆ Displaying systemwide or per directory messages, as when users log in and as logged in users navigate the FTP file system

◆ Supporting virtual hosts

In order to enable anonymous FTP support, you also need to install the anonftp RPM, which creates the necessary directory and file structure enabling anonymous FTP.

The section titled "Installing the anonftp package" later in this chapter discusses the anonftp RPM in more detail and explains how to install it.

A complete Red Hat Linux installation also installs the tftp-server package, a server implementing the Trivial File Transfer Protocol (TFTP). However, TFTP is used almost exclusively for booting diskless workstations, such as X terminals and slave nodes in clusters, or transferring files to other diskless devices, such as network routers and bridges, so it will not be mentioned again in this chapter.

Alternative FTP servers

Although Red Hat Linux uses WU-FTPD, two other popular FTP servers, ProFTPD and NcFTPd, deserve mention because they are widely used throughout the Unix and Linux community.

ProFTPD (http://www.proftpd.org/) is a free FTP server licensed under the GPL (the General Public License) and roughly modeled after the Apache Web server and designed to be more configurable and more secure than WU-FTPD. ProFTPD was written from scratch, unlike other Linux and Unix FTP servers, including WU-FTPD, which have evolved from the original BSD ftpd server. Key features that distinguish ProFTPD from WU-FTPD include:

◆ Per directory access configuration using .ftpaccess files, much like Apache's .htaccess file

◆ An anonymous FTP root directory unencumbered by required directory structures and system binaries

◆ Support for hidden files and directories

◆ Complete independence from external programs – ProFTPD is self-contained, reducing the likelihood of exploits that take advantage of external programs

◆ Runs as an unprivileged user in stand-alone mode, decreasing exposure to security attacks that attempt to exploit its root privileges

NcFTPd (http://www.ncftp.com/) is a commercial FTP server, also written from scratch, optimized for anonymous FTP service and high performance. Its primary architectural features are its self-described "no-forks" design – not spawning child processes to handle incoming connections and individual directory listings – and its independence from inetd and xinetd. It runs as a stand-alone server. It is *not* free software, but its features, security, and performance make it a popular FTP server.

Installing WU-FTPD

Depending on the type of installation you selected when you installed Red Hat Linux, anaconda, the Red Hat installation program may or may not have installed WU-FTPD. To find out, execute the command rpm -q wu-ftpd. If the output resembles the following, WU-FTPD is installed:

```
wu-ftpd-2.6.1-16
```

If WU-FTPD is installed, you can skip ahead to the section titled "Installing the anonftp package." Or, you might consider customizing WU-FTPD for your system by following the instructions in "Installing and building the source RPM" later in this section. Better still, you can install WU-FTPD's most recent version, which includes the latest security patches and bug fixes, by downloading, compiling, and installing it from the source distribution, as described in the section titled "Installing and building the source distribution" later in this section.

Chapter 23 provides detailed information and step-by-step instructions for installing RPMs, compiling source RPMs, and building and installing programs from the original source code.

If, on the other hand, you see the message package wu-ftpd is not installed, you must at least install the binary RPM before continuing with this chapter.

Installing the binary RPM

To install the WU-FTPD binary RPM from the Red Hat installation CD-ROMs, follow these steps:

1. Log in as the root user or use su to become root.

2. Mount the Red Hat Linux installation CD-ROM (disk 1).

3. Type the following command to install WU-FTPD (replace /mnt/cdrom with the mount point of your CD-ROM drive if it is different):

   ```
   # rpm -ivh /mnt/cdrom/RedHat/RPMS/wu-ftpd*rpm
   ```

4. Continue with the section titled "Installing the anonftp package."

Installing and building the source RPM

If you choose to install and build the source RPM, follow these steps:

1. Log in as the root user or use su to become root.

2. Mount the Red Hat Linux installation CD-ROM (disk 2).

3. Type the following command to install WU-FTPD (replace /mnt/cdrom with the mount point of your CD-ROM drive if it is different):

   ```
   # rpm --rebuild /mnt/cdrom/SRPMS/wu-ftpd*src.rpm
   # rpm -ivh /usr/src/redhat/RPMS/i386/wu-ftpd*rpm
   ```

4. Continue with the section titled "Installing the anonftp package."

Installing and building the source distribution

Installing and building any software package from the raw source code is the ultimate step in system customization because you can exercise almost complete control over the configuration and build process. Because Chapter 23 discusses building from source in detail, this section simply shows you the commands to execute to perform the build and installation. It does cover configuring the software in detail, however.

You can download the source code distribution from `ftp://ftp.wu-ftpd.org/pub/wu-ftpd`. After you have downloaded the source tarball or copied the tarball from this chapter's source code directory on the accompanying CD-ROM, the process consists of unpacking the source code, configuring it for your needs, building it, and installing it. The following steps walk you through the process (you must be the root user):

1. Unpack the archive using the following commands:

```
# cd /usr/local/src
# tar xzf /tmp/wu-ftpd*tar.gz
# cd wu-ftpd
```

2. Configure the software for your system using the following command:

```
# ./configure --prefix=/usr/local --enable-quota --enable-pam
--disable-newlines --enable-restart-logging
```

Even though this command appears as two lines in the text, it should be typed as a single line (which will probably wrap to the next line as you type it). `--prefix=/usr/local` makes `/usr/local` the base directory for this version: all the binaries and support files install in subdirectories of `/usr/local`. `--enable-quota` enables quota support, which enforces disk usage limitations when users upload files. `--enable-pam` enables support for PAM, pluggable authentication modules, which enhance system security. `--disable-newlines` suppresses `ftpd`'s output of unnecessary blank lines. `--enable-restart-logging` enables `ftpd` to log client `reget` commands more accurately.

Chapter 21 provides more information about disk quotas. Chapter 25 explains Pluggable Authentication Modules in detail.

3. Start compiling the software by typing the following command:

```
# make
```

4. After the build completes, install the software with the following command:

```
# make install
```

Once the installation finishes, continue with the next section.

Installing the anonftp package

As stated previously, the anonftp package creates a safe environment for anonymous FTP. In particular, it creates a chroot environment for anonymous FTP in /var/ftp and copies key files into the /var/ftp/lib, /var/ftp/bin, and /var/ftp/etc subdirectories. A *chroot* (change root) directory is a directory "jail" of sorts that severely restricts the user's view of the system. After a remote user logs in to the FTP server as the user anonymous or ftp, the FTP daemon, ftpd, places the user in a special directory, /var/ftp, that is changed to the user's root (/) directory. /var/ftp (the user's /) and its subdirectories constitute the user's entire view of the system because the user cannot cd out of the directory and, as a result, cannot see the layout of the real file system. However, because of these restrictions, certain binaries, libraries, and configuration files have to be copied into the chroot jail in order for the user to execute certain commands. This copying is what the anonftp package does.

 The file name of the FTP server daemon binary is /usr/sbin/in.ftpd. For the sake of convenience, I refer to it as ftpd throughout the chapter.

If the command rpm -q anonftp returns the message package anonftp is not installed, install it using the following steps:

1. Log in as the root user or use su to become root.

2. Mount the Red Hat installation CD-ROM (disk 1).

3. Type the following command to install the anonftp RPM (replace /mnt/cdrom with the mount point of your CD-ROM drive if it is different):

```
# rpm -ivh /mnt/cdrom/RedHat/RPMS/anonftp*rpm
```

 If you build and install WU-FTPD from source, RPM may fail, complaining about unmet dependencies. If so, retry the command by adding --nodeps to the argument list. That is,

```
# rpm --nodeps -ivh /mnt/cdrom/RedHat/RPMS/anonftp*rpm
```

Configuring the Server

Installing the WU-FTPD and anonftp packages creates a basic functioning FTP server that works for users with their own login accounts on the system and for anonymous FTP, using either the anonymous or ftp login names. However, the stock configuration is only a start, a base that you should customize to enhance security and to fit your needs. In this section, you learn how to fine-tune the default FTP server configuration.

 The ftp user name is a synonym for the user name anonymous.

The first step in FTP server configuration is to become familiar with the configuration files that control the server's behavior. Table 13-1 lists and briefly describes WU-FTPD's configuration files.

TABLE 13-1 WU–FTPD CONFIGURATION FILES

File Name	Description
/etc/ftpaccess	Controls the operation of FTP daemon, ftpd
/etc/ftpconversions	Controls the dynamic file conversions the FTP daemon performs
/etc/ftpgroups	Lists the group names and passwords for FTP private groups
/etc/ftphosts	Lists specific hosts permitted or denied FTP access
/etc/ftpusers	Lists user names not permitted to log in using FTP

Of the five files listed in Table 13-1, the ones this chapter discusses are /etc/ftpaccess, /etc/ftphosts, and /etc/ftpusers. Private FTP groups, defined in /etc/ftpgroups, are rarely necessary. By default, Red Hat Linux does not create private FTP groups, although the /etc/ftpgroups is installed. The default file conversions listed in /etc/ftpconversions should suffice for most situations.

What Are FTP File Conversions?

FTP *file conversions* enable FTP users to retrieve a file that is stored in one format using another format, provided the FTP server has been configured to convert between the two formats. For example, suppose an anonymous FTP user wants to download the file vmstat.log, a plain text file, from your FTP server, but wants to reduce the download time by converting it to a file compressed with gzip. To do so, the user enters get vmstat.log.gz (or any other destination file name that ends in .gz) at the ftp> prompt. In response, the FTP server compresses the file using gzip and then transmits the compressed file. After the download completes, the user has a file named vmstat.log.gz. The following listing illustrates the process and its results:

```
ftp> ls
-rw-r--r--    1 root     50           5593 Jul 11 19:53 herfile.Z
-rw-r--r--    1 root     50           2683 Jul 11 19:54 themfiles.tar.bz2
-rw-r--r--    1 root     50          33760 Jul 11 20:11 vmstat.log
ftp> get vmstat.log.gz
local: vmstat.log.gz remote: vmstat.log.gz
150 Opening BINARY mode data connection for /bin/gzip.
2031 bytes received in 0.22 seconds (9.1 Kbytes/s)
ftp>!ls -l vmstat.log.gz

-rw-rw-r--    1 kwall    kwall        2031 Jul 11 14:14 vmstat.log.gz
```

Note that the FTP server passes the file through /bin/gzip before sending it. The last command shows that the received file has indeed been compressed. The FTP server can perform a number of other conversions, including switching between compression formats and even uncompressing a file before sending it. These conversions are defined in the file /etc/ftpconversions.

Configuring user and host access

The /etc/ftpusers file is the simplest to understand. It contains a list of user or account names, one per line, that are not allowed to log in using FTP. This file is used to increase security. For example, if a cracker somehow obtains the root password but (stupidly) tries to log in as root using FTP, the login attempt will fail. Note that the file name is counterintuitive: user accounts listed in this file are *not* permitted to log in to the system using FTP. In general, /etc/ftpusers is used to prevent privileged user accounts, such as root, from using FTP to obtain access to the system. Listing 13-1 shows a typical Red Hat Linux /etc/ftpusers file.

Listing 13-1: A Standard /etc/ftpusers File

```
root
bin
```

```
daemon
adm
lp
sync
shutdown
halt
mail
news
uucp
operator
games
nobody
```

So, to prevent the user bubba from using FTP to log in, or, rather, to prevent user bubba from logging in to the system via FTP, append bubba to the end of /etc/ftpusers. In most cases, the default entries shown in Listing 13-1 should be sufficient, but if you install a software package, such as a database package, that requires one or more special user accounts, consider adding such special accounts to /etc/ftpusers in order to maintain strict limits on how the FTP server can be accessed.

The /etc/ftphosts file serves a purpose similar to /etc/ftpusers, limiting FTP access, but it is more flexible. /etc/ftphosts defines access rules, one per line, that permit or deny access to the FTP server based on the host from which the login originates. Each access rule consists of one of the keywords allow or deny, a user name, and one or more IP addresses. The general format for access rules is

```
allow username ipaddr [...]
deny username ipaddr [...]
```

username identifies the user name to which the rule applies, and ipaddr indicates the IP address to which the rule applies. Lines beginning with # are comments and ignored. An allow rule permits connections only from the host whose IP address matches ipaddr to log in to the FTP server as username. A deny rule prevents an FTP login using username from any connection whose host IP address matches ipaddr. As you might expect, if username is anonymous or ftp, the corresponding rule applies to the anonymous FTP user. Multiple IP addresses can be specified by separating each address with whitespace.

For example, the rule allow bubba 192.168.0.1 permits the user named bubba to log in to the FTP server if the connection originates from the IP address 192.168.0.1. Conversely, the rule deny kwall 127.0.0.1 prevents the user named kwall from logging in if the source connection is 127.0.0.1.

One feature of access rule specification in /etc/ftphosts needs to be noted. You can specify a range of IP addresses using CIDR (Classless InterDomain Routing) notation or by appending a colon followed by a netmask to ipaddr. For example, to allow bubba to log in from any IP address in the subnet 166.70.186.8, you can specify *ipaddr* as 166.70.186.8:255.255.255.248 or 166.70.186.8/29. So, the complete rule would be one of the following:

```
allow bubba 166.70.186.8:255.255.255.248
allow bubba 166.70.186.8/29
```

Configuring ftpd

By far the most important (and longest) ftpd configuration file is /etc/ftpaccess. The configuration directives in this file enable you to exercise finely grained control over ftpd's behavior. To organize the discussion of /etc/ftpaccess, its configuration directives are divided into groups of related functionality. These groups include access control and permissions, messages, logging, and WU-FTPD features. This chapter does not cover all of the supported options and directives, though, so refer to the /etc/ftpaccess man page (man 5 ftpaccess) for further information.

CONFIGURING WU-FTPD ACCESS CONTROL AND PERMISSIONS

The first group of configuration statements, listed in Table 13-2, control overall access to the FTP server and establish limits on what can be done, and how, once users have logged in to the FTP server.

TABLE 13-2 WU-FTPD ACCESS CONTROL DIRECTIVES

Directive	Description
allow-gid [%]*gid*	Permits the group with GID *gid* to access the FTP server; *gid* may be a single group name, a single numeric GID, or a range of GIDs (numeric values must be prefixed with %)
allow-uid [%]*uid*	Permits the user with UID *uid* to access the FTP server; *uid* may be a single user name, a single numeric UID, or a range of UIDs (numeric values must be prefixed with %)
anonymous-root *rootdir* [*class*]	Identifies *rootdir* as the chrooted directory for anonymous FTP for *class* (all classes if *class* is omitted)
chmod yes|no *type*	Enables or disables users of *type* (one or more of real, guest, anonymous, or class=*class*) to change file modes (the default is yes for all users except anonymous)

Directive	Description
class *class type addr*	Defines a class of *type* users named *class* with source addresses *addr*; *type* is one or more of real, guest, or anonymous; *addr* may be a single IP or a range of addresses specified with address:netmask or address/netmask notation
defaultserver allow *username*	Enables access to anonymous FTP for one or more *username*s
defaultserver deny *username*	Disables access to anonymous FTP for one or more *username*s
defaultserver private	Disables access to anonymous FTP
delete yes|no *type*	Enables or disables users of *type* (one or more of real, guest, anonymous, or class=*class*) to delete files (the default is yes for all users except anonymous)
deny *addr file*	Denies access to the FTP server to connections from *addr* and display the message in *file*; *addr* may be a single IP, a range of addresses specified with address:netmask or address/netmask notation, or !nameserved to indicate sites lacking a working nameserver
deny-gid [%]*gid*	Denies the group with GID *gid* to access the FTP server; *gid* may be a single group name, a single numeric GID, or a range of GIDs (numeric values must be prefixed with %)
deny-uid [%]*uid*	Denies the user with UID *uid* to access the FTP server; *uid* may be a single user name, a single numeric UID, or a range of UIDs (numeric values must be prefixed with %)
dns refuse_mismatch *file* [override]	Displays the contents of *file* and denies access (unless override is specified) to the FTP server if forward and reverse DNS lookups do not match
dns refuse_no_reverse *file* [override]	Displays the contents of *file* and denies access (unless override is specified) to the FTP server if the connection fails a reverse DNS lookup

Continued

TABLE 13-2 WU–FTPD ACCESS CONTROL DIRECTIVES *(Continued)*

Directive	Description
`limit` *class* `n` *times* *file*	Limits the number of connections from *class* users to *n* during the times *times*, displaying the message in *file* if the limit has been exceeded
`loginfails` *n*	Permits *n* failed login attempts before closing the connection (default is 5)
`overwrite yes|no` *type*	Enables or disables users of *type* (one or more of `real, guest, anonymous,` or `class=`*class*) to overwrite files (the default is `yes` for all users except `anonymous`)
`passwd-check none| trivial|rfc822 (enforce|warn)`	Specifies the type of password checking used with anonymous FTP and whether the policy is strictly enforced (`enforce`) or if only a warning is issued (`warn`); `none` disables password checking, `trivial` requires an @ in the password, and `rfc822` forces an RFC822-compliant address
`rename yes|no` *type*	Enables or disables users of *type* (one or more of `real, guest, anonymous,` or class=*class*) to rename files (the default is `yes` for all users except `anonymous`)
`timeout accept` *secs*	Server times out after waiting *secs* seconds (default is 120) to establish an incoming connection
`timeout connect` *secs*	Server times out after waiting *secs* seconds (default is 120) to establish an outgoing connection
`timeout data` *secs*	Server times out after waiting *secs* seconds (default is 1200) seconds for activity on the data connection
`timeout idle` *secs*	Server times out after waiting *secs* seconds (default is 900) for another command
`timeout RFC931` *secs*	Server times out after waiting *secs* seconds (default is 10) to complete user identification using the RFC931 IDENT protocol
`umask yes|no` *type*	Enables or disables users of *type* (one or more of `real, guest, anonymous,` or class=*class*) to execute the `umask` command (the default is `yes` for all users except `anonymous`)

As stated earlier, the stock FTP configuration created when you install the WU-FTPD and anonftp packages is only a starting point that can and *should* be improved before opening your server up to the world. Consider, for example, Listing 13-2, an excerpt from the standard Red Hat Linux /etc/ftpaccess file (with comments removed) showing the access control directives it uses. After analyzing the existing access control configuration, I suggest some additional directives to add to the stock configuration.

Listing 13-2: Access Control in the Standard /etc/ftpaccess File

```
deny-uid %-99 %65534-
deny-gid %-99 %65534-
allow-uid ftp
allow-gid ftp
class all real,guest,anonymous *
loginfails 5
chmod no guest,anonymous
delete no anonymous
overwrite no anonymous
rename no anonymous
passwd-check rfc822 warn
```

The first two statements prevent any system user or group account (%-99) and any account with a UID or GID greater than or equal to 65534 (%65534-) from logging in to the FTP server. Note the use of % to prefix the numeric values and how a range of values is denoted. Using the deny-uid and deny-gid directives in /etc/ftpaccess has the same effect as placing account names in /etc/ftpusers, and is actually more flexible that /etc/ftpusers. In fact, using /etc/ftpusers is deprecated, although still supported, so it is best to use /etc/ftpaccess.

After denying access to system accounts, the ftp user and group account is specifically enabled using allow-uid and allow-gid. This method illustrates a solid general approach to controlling FTP access: disable access across the board using deny-uid and deny-gid, then selectively enable access using allow-uid and allow-gid. A key caveat, however, is that you *cannot* use the deny-uid and deny-gid directives to disable anonymous FTP access. Instead, you have to use the defaultserver private directive (see Table 13-2).

The loginfails directive allows five failed login attempts (mistyped passwords) before disconnecting the user. The next four directives deny the anonymous FTP user permission to change file modes, delete files, overwrite files, or rename files. The chmod directive also prevents a guest account from using chmod. Although the default for the anonymous user is no, specifically including this information in /etc/ftpaccess makes ftpd's configuration clearer, especially to newer administrators who might not be familiar with the default values. The final directive, passwd-check rfc822 warn, requires the anonymous FTP user to use a standard e-mail address as the password. If it does not match, ftpd displays a warning message before permitting the login.

To improve access control, first change `passwd-check` to `passwd-check rfc822 enforce`. It might seem harsh to disconnect someone due to a typing mistake, and it might also seem foolish to enforce compliance because `passwd-check` validates only the form, not the content, of the supplied e-mail address, but it sets a tone from the very start that lets users know you take security seriously.

You can improve the FTP server's access control by adding the directives in the following list to `/etc/ftpaccess`:

◆ `deny !nameserved no-dns.msg`

◆ `dns refuse_mismatch dns-mismatch.msg`

◆ `dns refuse_no_reverse dns-no-reverse.msg`

◆ `limit all 10 Any too-many-users.msg`

◆ `umask no anonymous`

The first three directives deny access to connections without a valid nameserver, for which forward and reverse lookups do not match, and for which a reverse lookup fails. The primary concern is to take steps to strengthen the audit trail and to prevent connections that deliberately hide information. Of course, accidentally misconfigured systems also fail to connect, so the message files can make this clear and recommend fixing the problem. Obviously, the names of all the message files are up to you. The `limit` directive uses the `all` class (which consists, in this case, of all FTP users) to set an upper limit of ten simultaneous FTP sessions. You can modify this number of course, but the point is to set some kind of connection limit so that your system does not become bogged down due to excessive network traffic or download activity. The time specification `Any` enforces the limit at all times every day. Finally, the `umask` directive further limits the activity of the anonymous FTP account. Its absence from the default configuration is probably a simple oversight.

CONFIGURING WU-FTPD MESSAGES

You can use WU-FTPD's messaging configuration to create a friendlier FTP server and also to limit or completely disable the display of system information that crackers can use to attack your system. Table 13-3 lists most of the message-related directives permitted in `/etc/ftpaccess`.

TABLE 13-3 WU-FTPD MESSAGE CONFIGURATION DIRECTIVES

Directive*	Description
banner path	Displays the contents of the file path before clients log in; path must be defined relative to the real file system, not the root of the anonymous FTP directory

Directive[*]	Description
email *emailaddr*	Specifies *emailaddr* as the FTP maintainer's e-mail address
greeting full|brief|terse	Specifies the amount of information about the system shown before users log in (the default is full)
greeting text *message*	Specifies *message* as the greeting text shown before users log in
hostname *some.host.name*	Specifies *some.host.name* as the displayed hostname (default value is the local host's name)
message *path when* [*class*]	Displays the contents of the file *path* after users in *class* (all users if *class* is omitted) log in or when they change directories; *when* is either LOGIN or CWD=*dir*, where *dir* indicates the new directory that triggers the message
readme *path when* [*class*]	Tells users in *class* (all users if *class* is omitted) that the file *path* exists and when it was last modified after users log in or when they change directories; *when* is either LOGIN or CWD=*dir*, where *dir* indicates the new directory that triggers the message
shutdown *path*	Identifies *path* as the file to check for server shutdown information; use ftpshut to create *path*
signoff full|brief|terse	Specifies the amount of information displayed before users log out (the default is full)
signoff text *message*	Specifies *message* as the log-out message
stat full|brief|terse	Specifies the amount of server status information displayed in response to the STAT command (the default is full)
stat text|brieftext *message*	Specifies *message* as the information displayed in response to the STAT command;

[*] *For the message and readme directives, path must be specified relative to the anonymous FTP root directory if the anonymous user triggers the notification.*

As with the access control directives you looked at a moment ago, the standard Red Hat Linux message directives provide a basic configuration on which to build. The directives Red Hat Linux uses are shown in Listing 13-3. Again, after analyzing the existing file, I suggest some changes and additions to enhance the FTP server's friendliness and security.

Listing 13-3: Message Configuration in the Standard /etc/ftpaccess File

```
email root@localhost
readme README* login
readme README* cwd=*
message /welcome.msg login
message .message cwd=*
shutdown /etc/shutmsg
```

The email directive sets the e-mail address of the FTP administrator. The two readme directives cause ftpd to display the names and last modification dates of any file beginning with README*, if they exist, after users log in and each time they change to a new directory (but only the first time). The specified files must be located relative to the base directory of the anonymous FTP directory tree (/var/ftp in Red Hat Linux) in order for anonymous FTP users to see them. So, for example, given the directive readme README.NOW login, README.NOW must be located in /var/ftp.

The first message directive displays the contents of welcome.msg after a user logs in, while the second one shows the contents of the file .message in each directory a user enters (again only the first time). One good use for the .message files is to show users a listing of the directory contents, while the welcome message at login (/welcome.msg) is often used to tell users a little bit about the FTP server and to state acceptable usage policies. The shutdown directive, finally, names /etc/shutmsg as the file containing shutdown information.

The section titled "Maintaining the Server" discusses the shutdown directive in more detail.

To improve the server's security, add the following directives to /etc/ ftpaccess:

◆ greeting terse

◆ signoff terse

◆ stat terse

The theory motivating these additions is to prevent displaying any information about the server that crackers might be able to use to compromise it. greeting terse displays FTP server ready when users login, whereas the default is to display the complete hostname and the version number of the FTP daemon. `signoff terse` displays `Goodbye` when the user disconnects (the default is to list file transfer statistics and the system's hostname). By default, the `stat` directive supplies the system hostname, `ftpd`'s version number, transfer statistics, and quota information. `stat terse`, on the other hand, simply displays the connection status. Alternatively, you can supply your own `greeting`, `signoff`, and `stat` messages using the `greeting text` *message*, `signoff text` *message*, and `stat text` *message* directives, respectively (see Table 13-3).

CONFIGURING WU-FTPD LOGGING

The group of directives in Table 13-4 define `ftpd`'s logging policies. Although most administrators use logging as a usage troubleshooting tool, and rightfully so, properly configured logs also serve as an invaluable resource for monitoring system performance and security and for performing security audits.

TABLE 13-4 WU-FTPD LOGGING CONFIGURATION DIRECTIVES

Directive	Description
`log commands [type]`	Logs user commands for *type* users, or all users if *type* is omitted
`log security [type]`	Logs security violations for *type* users, or all users if *type* is omitted
`log syslog`	Logs file transfers to the system log (the default is to use the transfer log, `/var/log/xferlog`)
`log transfers [type [direction]]`	Logs file transfers for *type* users (all users if *type* is omitted) in *direction* (both directions if *direction* is omitted); *direction* is one or both of `inbound` or `outbound`
`log syslog+xferlog`	Logs file transfers to the system log and the transfer log
`logfile path`	Specifies the full path name *path* as the server transfer log file (`/var/log/xferlog` is the default)

The default Red Hat Linux `ftpd` logging configuration is inadequate, logging only the incoming and outgoing transfers (uploads and downloads) of all users. The relevant directive in `/etc/ftpaccess` is:

```
log transfers anonymous,guest,real inbound,outbound
```

To enhance the audit trail and improve your ability to monitor both usage and security issues, add the following directives to /etc/ftpaccess:

◆ log commands anonymous,guest,real

◆ log security anonymous,guest,real

◆ log syslog+xferlog

◆ logfile /var/log/xferlog

The first directive logs all commands executed by all users permitted access to the FTP server. The second one logs all violations of security rules. log syslog+xferlog causes all transfer information to be recorded in both the system log and the transfer log. The rationale for duplicating this information is to take advantage of one of syslogd's features (syslogd is the system logging daemon, unrelated to ftpd): remote logging. syslogd can be configured to maintain the system log on a remote host. Should the FTP server be compromised or the transfer log damaged or tampered with, the transfer information survives in the system log. Furthermore, if the system log is located on another system, it is much less likely that it will be damaged or lost. The last directive specifically defines the name and path of the transfer log (which uses the default value, /var/log/xferlog).

CONFIGURING WU-FTPD FEATURES

The last group of ftpd configuration directives, shown in Table 13-5, enable and disable various features of the server.

TABLE 13-5 WU-FTPD FEATURE CONFIGURATION DIRECTIVES

Directive	Description
alias *string dir*	Defines *string* as an alias for *dir* (valid only for the cd command)
compress [yes|no] [*class*]	Enables or disables on the fly file compression (the default is yes) for all user classes or for one or more classes specified in *class*
incmail *emailaddr*	Defines *emailaddr* as one or more e-mail addresses to which to send notifications of file uploads (the default is to send no notification)
lslong *command* [*options*]	Defines the command *command* (and *options*, if specified) that generates listings in response to the LIST (ls) command issued by the anonymous FTP user

Directive	Description
lsplain *command* [*options*]	Defines the command *command* (and *options*, if specified) that generates listings in response to the NLST (nlist) command
lsshort *command* [*options*]	Defines the command *command* (and *options*, if specified) that generates listings in response to the LIST (ls) command issued by all users except the anonymous FTP user
mailfrom *emailaddr*	Defines the name of the sender used to e-mail notifications of anonymous FTP file uploads (the default is wu-ftpd)
mailserver *hostname*	Specifies *hostname* as one or more mail servers used to deliver all e-mail notifications of file uploads (the default is localhost)
tar [yes|no] [*class*]	Enables or disables on the fly tar usage (the default is yes) for all user classes or for one or more classes specified in *class*

The relevant directives in Red Hat Linux's default configuration are:

```
compress yes all
tar yes all
```

These statements permit all users to use on the fly compression and tar capabilities. The actual command used for these functions are defined in /etc/ftpconversions. If you intend to permit uploads, especially for the anonymous FTP account, add the following directives to /etc/ftpaccess:

◆ incmail root@localhost

◆ mailfrom anonupload

◆ mailserver *primary.mail.server backup.mail.server*

The incmail directive sends notifications of file uploads to root@localhost. You might want to use a different address. The mailfrom statement specifies the name that will be used when ftpd sends e-mail notifications about uploads from the anonymous FTP user. Using a distinct name, such as anonupload, makes it easy to filter and select such messages. The last directive identifies the mail servers to use for sending upload notifications. The default server is localhost, but using `mailserver` enables you to list one or more alternative mail servers to use if mail service on the server is not functioning. `ftpd` tries each listed server in order until a message is accepted.

The enhanced /etc/ftpaccess file

Listing 13-4 shows an `/etc/ftpaccess` file, judiciously commented, after applying the changes and additions discussed in this section. It is available on the accompanying CD-ROM in this chapter's source code directory as `ftpaccess.better`.

Listing 13-4: A Better `ftpd` **Configuration File**

```
# Deny system and special accounts
deny-uid %-99 %65534-
deny-gid %-99 %65534-

# Permit access to the ftp user
allow-uid ftp
allow-gid ftp

# Define a class named all for convenience
class all real,guest,anonymous *

# Only 5 attempts to login
loginfails 5

# Don't let anonymous do anything dangerous
chmod no guest,anonymous
delete no anonymous
overwrite no anonymous
rename no anonymous
umask no anonymous

# Force anonymous to provide a password that
# at least looks like a valid email address
passwd-check rfc822 enforce

# Connections from remote hosts must be running
# a properly configured name server
deny !nameserved no-dns.msg
dns refuse_mismatch dns-mismatch.msg
dns refuse_no_reverse dns-no-reverse.msg

# Don't let the system get bogged down
limit all 10 Any too-many-users.msg
```

```
# The FTP administrator's email address
email root@localhost

# What messages do users see and when do
# they see them?
readme README* login
readme README* cwd=*
message /welcome.msg login
message .message cwd=*
shutdown /etc/shutmsg

# Severely restrict the display of system
# information to script kiddies and other vermin
greeting terse
signoff terse
stat terse

# Log information to the transfer log and to the
# system log about file transfers
logfile /var/log/xferlog
log syslog+xferlog
log transfers anonymous,guest,real inbound,outbound

# Log commands and security issues in the system log
log commands anonymous,guest,real
log security anonymous,guest,real

# Let users compress and tar files on the fly
compress yes all
tar yes all

# Notify someone about all file uploads, especially
# from the anonymous FTP user.
# Uncomment these if you permit file uploads on the
# server. Change the names of the mail servers, too.
#incmail root@localhost
#mailfrom anonupload
#mailserver primary.mail.server backup.mail.server
```

Administering WU-FTPD with KWuFTPd

For those who prefer graphical administration tools, Red Hat Linux installs
KWuFTPd, a KDE-based tool that offers an attractive, reasonably complete interface
for configuring WU-FTPD. If you installed KDE when you installed Red Hat Linux,

you can use KWuFTPd. This section shows you how to use KWuFTPd to make the changes and additions to /etc/ftpaccess suggested in the previous sections.

TIP Before you begin using KWuFTPd, make backup copies of WU-FTPD's configuration files (ftpaccess, ftpconversion, ftpgroups, ftphosts, and ftpusers, all in /etc). This step not only preserves a known good configuration, it also enables you to study the changes KWuFTPd makes to these files by comparing the two sets of files.

To start KWuFTPd from the GNOME desktop, select Menu→KDE menus→ System→FTPD Editor. If you are using the KDE desktop, click Menu→System→ FTPD Editor. You can also type kwuftpd in a terminal window. Figure 13-1 shows the initial screen.

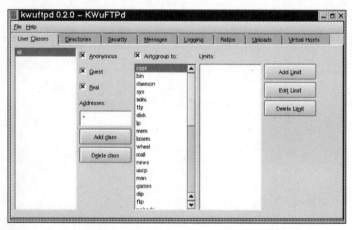

Figure 13-1: KWuFTPd groups related configuration items on tabbed windows.

Each tab in the interface contains a group of related configuration items, making configuration somewhat easier. The User Classes tab, for example, manipulates the class and limit directives in /etc/ftpaccess. You can see in Figure 13-1 that KWuFTPd parsed the existing /etc/ftpaccess file and loaded the definition for existing class, all.

You can use the User Classes tab to add the limit directive, limit all 10 Any too-many-users.msg directive. To do so, click the Add Limit button, edit the dialog box as shown in Figure 13-2, and then click the OK button to return to the User Classes tab.

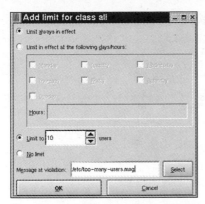

Figure 13-2: Limit the number of logged-in
users with the Add Limit dialog box.

Figure 13-3 shows the Directories tab, which implements the `anonymous-root`
and `guest-root` directives.

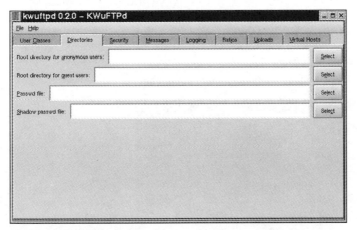

Figure 13-3: Set the chroot directory for the anonymous user on
the Directories tab.

Red Hat Linux uses the default value for `anonymous-root`, so the chroot directory for the anonymous users is the home directory specified in `/etc/passwd` for
the user named `ftp`, `/var/ftp`. The default Red Hat configuration disables guest
access, so this field is empty, too. None of the suggested modifications affect this
tab, so you can move on to Security tab, shown in Figure 13-4.

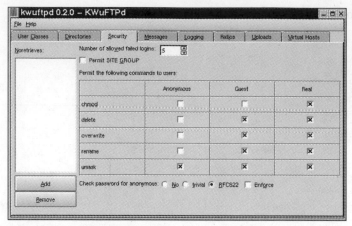

Figure 13-4: Use the Security tab to limit users' privileges on the FTP server.

The configuration directives manipulated on this tab include, among others, chmod, delete, overwrite, rename, umask, loginfails, and passwd-check. The two changes to make here involve the umask and passwd-check directives. First, remove the check next to umask under the Anonymous column, and then check the Enforce box at the end of the Check password for anonymous line. Finally, click the Messages tab, shown in Figure 13-5.

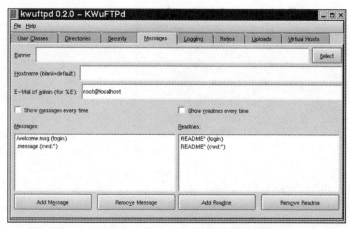

Figure 13-5: Use the Messages tab to define the messages WU-FTPD displays.

The fields on the Messages tab implement the message-related directives, in particular, email, readme, message, banner, and hostname. None of the suggested modifications involve these fields, so click the Logging tab, shown in Figure 13-6.

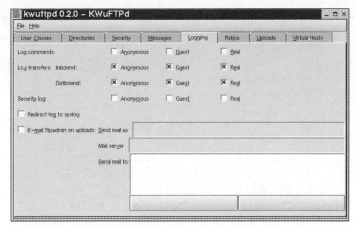

Figure 13-6: Modify the FTP server's logging behavior using the Logging tab.

The Logging tab implements all of the log directives listed in Table 13-4 plus the upload-related directives `incmail`, `mailfrom`, and `mailserver`. Figure 13-7 shows the Logging tab's appearance after modifying it to reflect the changes recommended to improve logging and upload notifications.

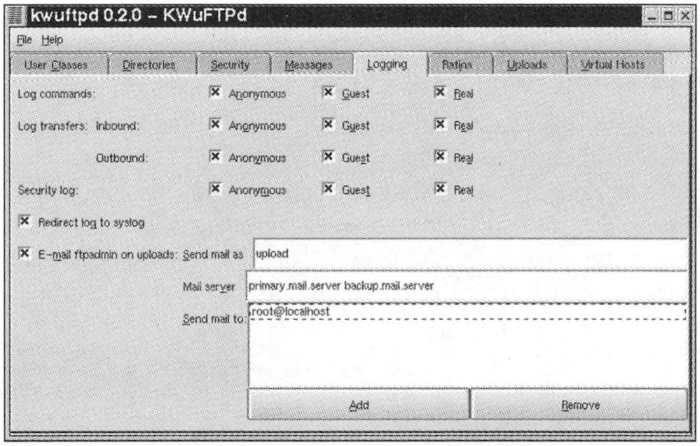

Figure 13-7: Use the Logging tab to enhance the FTP server's logging information.

This chapter did not deal with upload/download ratios, uploads, or virtual hosts, so feel free to explore the corresponding KWuFTPd's corresponding tabs — Ratios, Uploads, and Virtual Hosts — at your leisure. To save the changes, select File → Save other file to create a new file you can review before overwriting the current configuration. For reasons discussed in the next paragraph, *do not* select File → Save

/etc/ftpaccess, because doing so creates significant security problems with your FTP server.

You may have noticed that the preceding figures and text omitted a number of important `ftpd` configuration directives: `deny-uid`, `deny-gid`, `allow-uid`, `allow-gid`, `deny`, `dns`, `shutdown`, `greeting`, `signoff`, `stat`, `compress`, and `tar`. Why the omissions? KWuFTPd's interface does not include support for these directives, which provide some of WU-FTPD's most important security features.

To elaborate, if `/etc/ftpusers` does not exist, the absence of `deny-uid` and `deny-gid` enables system accounts, such as root, to log in to the server using FTP. Lacking support for the `deny` and `dns` directives, KWuFTPd inhibits your ability to deny access to incoming connections that deliberately mask their DNS information. Because KWuFTPd does not support the `greeting`, `signoff`, and `stat` directives, your FTP server provides crackers information they can use to attack, and possibly compromise, your system. As it happens, the `shutdown`, `compress`, and `tar` directives function acceptably based on WU-FTPD's default settings, but you cannot use KWuFTPd if you wish to deviate from those defaults.

If you use KWuFTPd to configure your FTP server, its incomplete support of WU-FTPD's configuration system opens major security holes. Make sure to edit the ftpaccess file KWuFTPd creates to add the missing directives.

Maintaining the Server

WU-FTPD includes a number of commands for monitoring and administering the server, including `ftpwho`, `ftpcount`, `ckconfig`, `xferstats`, `ftpshut`, and `ftprestart`. `ftpwho` and `ftpcount` provide a snapshot of users currently logged in to the FTP server and how many users in each class, as defined using the `class` directive in `/etc/ftpaccess`, are logged in. Neither command accepts any options (except `-V`, which displays version information), so they are very simple to use. The output from `ftpwho` should resemble the following, depending on usage of the FTP server:

```
# ftpwho
3959 ?    SN    0:00 ftpd: h1.none.com: anonymous/bubba@none.com
3958 ?    SN    0:00 ftpd: localhost: kwall: IDLE
3956 ?    RN    0:00 ftpd: h2.none.com: anonymous/kwall@: LIST
  -   3 users ( 10 maximum)
```

Each line of output shows the PID of the `ftpd` instance serving the login, the terminal, if any, on which `ftpd` (*not* the login session) is running, the status of the `ftpd` process, the CPU time the `ftpd` instance has consumed, and the host name of the originating connection. The last field shows the user name and connection status if the login is a real user, or the word anonymous and the given password of the anonymous FTP user.

In the example shown, ftpwho shows three connected users. The first line shows an anonymous login from h1.none.com using the password (e-mail address) bubba@none.com. The third line also shows an anonymous login, but instead of the complete password, it shows the command (LIST) that the server is currently running in that session. The second line shows that the user kwall has logged in to the FTP server from the server's own host (localhost) and that the connection is currently idle.

The ftpcount command shown in the following example merely displays a breakdown of current FTP server usage by class:

```
# ftpcount
Service class all                          -   3 users ( 10 maximum)
```

You can obtain the same total count using ftpwho, so, unless you need the per class counts, stick with ftpwho.

The ckconfig performs a simple sanity check on ftpd's configuration files, making sure they all exist in the path(s) defined at compile time. Unfortunately, however, it verifies only the existence of the files, not their content, and displays sometimes spurious error messages. For example, here is ckconfig's output after building and installing the latest WU-FTPD release:

```
# /usr/local/sbin/ckconfig
Checking _PATH_FTPUSERS :: /etc/ftpusers
I can't find it... look in doc/examples for an example.

Checking _PATH_FTPSERVERS :: /etc/ftpservers
I can't find it... look in doc/examples for an example.

Checking _PATH_FTPACCESS :: /etc/ftpaccess
ok.

Checking _PATH_PIDNAMES :: /var/run/ftp.pids-%s
ok.

Checking _PATH_CVT :: /etc/ftpconversions
ok.

Checking _PATH_XFERLOG :: /var/log/xferlog
ok.

Checking _PATH_PRIVATE :: /etc/ftpgroups
ok.
```

```
Checking _PATH_FTPHOSTS :: /etc/ftphosts
ok.
```

As the output shows, ckconfig complained that it could not find /etc/ftpusers and /etc/ftpservers. These two error messages are red herrings, though. In the first place, /etc/ftpuser's absence is acceptable because, as you learned in the previous section, it has been deprecated in favor of the deny-uid, deny-gid, allow-uid, and allow-gid directives in /etc/ftpaccess. The missing /etc/ftpservers file is an issue only if the FTP server must support virtual FTP servers, a requirement typically limited to ISPs.

 A *virtual FTP server* is an FTP server configured to support two or more distinct domain names in such a way that end users have no idea that each domain's FTP server is actually a single FTP server running on a single system.

The xferstats program is Perl script that slices and dices ftpd's transfer log and then displays a very nicely formatted report summarizing file transfers over a given period of time. Its complete syntax is:

```
xferstats [-adhr] [-f file] [-D domain] [-l depth] [-s section]
```

Invoked with no options, xferstats displays a report for the entire period of time covered in the transfer log, for the anonymous user. The report includes summary information on daily transfer volumes, total transfers by directory (xferstats peculiarly calls directories *archive sections*), and hourly transfer statistics. -f file tells xferstats to read the transfer log in file rather than read from the default log, /var/log/xferlog. -D domain limits the resulting report to the domain specified by domain. -s section specifies a section named section on which to report. -l depth, defines how deeply into the directory tree (sections) xferstats should recurse as it compiles and displays the report (the default level of detail is three subdirectories). -a, the default, includes transfer statistics for the anonymous FTP account, and -r includes statistics for real user accounts. -h, also a default, adds hourly statistics to the report. Use -d if you want to see transfers by domain name.

Listing 13-5 shows the output from a bare xferstats command, which is equivalent to xferstats -a -h.

Listing 13-5: An xferstats Report for the Anonymous FTP Account.

```
# xferstats
TOTALS FOR SUMMARY PERIOD Tue Nov 27 2001 TO Wed Nov 28 2001
```

```
Files Transmitted During Summary Period            8
Bytes Transmitted During Summary Period     23751600
Systems Using Archives                             2


Average Files Transmitted Daily                    8
Average Bytes Transmitted Daily             23751600
```

```
Daily Transmission Statistics


                  Number Of    Number of    Average    Percent Of   Percent Of
      Date        Files Sent   Bytes Sent   Xmit Rate  Files Sent   Bytes Sent
---------------   ----------   ----------   ---------- ----------   ----------

Wed Nov 28 2001            8     23751600   2968.9 KB/   100.00       100.00
```

```
Total Transfers from each Archive Section (By bytes)


                                                ---- Percent  Of ----
      Archive Section       Files Sent Bytes Sent  Files Sent Bytes Sent
-------------------------   ---------- ----------  ---------- ----------

/var/ftp/pub                        8   23751600    100.00     100.00
```

```
Hourly Transmission Statistics


                  Number Of    Number of    Average    Percent Of   Percent Of
      Time        Files Sent   Bytes Sent   Xmit Rate  Files Sent   Bytes Sent
---------------   ----------   ----------   ---------- ----------   ----------

14                        8     23751600   2968.9 KB/   100.00       100.00
```

After the summary transfer data at the top of the report, such as the total number of files transferred and the number of unique connections to the FTP server, the report is broken into three sections for daily download statistics, downloads per directory, and downloads distributed by hour. Keep in mind that these statistics are for the anonymous FTP user only. To see the report for other users, use the -r option. In order to create a report for all users, combine the -r and -a options (that is, execute the command xferstats -ar).

The last two commands you look at in this section are ftpshut and ftprestart. ftpshut performs an orderly shutdown of the FTP server, and ftprestart, as the name suggests, restarts it. An *orderly shutdown* means providing advance notification of a pending server halt and preventing new users from logging in as the scheduled shutdown time approaches. ftpshut satisfies all these requirements, as its syntax, shown next, makes clear.

```
ftpshut [-l min] [-d min] time [message]
```

message defines the shutdown notification message users see when they log in to the server. -l *min* disables new logins to the FTP server *min* minutes (the default is 10 minutes) before the scheduled shutdown. -d *min* disconnects currently logged in users *min* minutes (the default is 5 minutes). *time* specifies the time when the FTP server will close. It can be the word now, *+mins*, or *HHMM*. now results in an immediate shutdown, *+min* sets the shutdown time *min* minutes in the future, and *HHMM* sets the shutdown time to the 24-hour time *HHMM*. For example, if *time* is +30, the server will close 30 minutes from now. If *time* is 1930, the server will shut down at 19:30, or 7:30 p.m.

Do you recall the shutdown directive in /etc/ftpaccess? It defines the full path to the shutdown message file, which is /etc/shutmsg by default on Red Hat Linux systems. When you execute ftpshut, it creates (or overwrites, if it already exists) the shutdown file, storing in it the time values and message passed to ftpshut. ftpd monitors this file to check for a scheduled shutdown. For example, after executing the command ftpshut 1040 "The FTP server will be shut down at 10:40 a.m. for disk maintenance," /etc/shutmsg looks like the following:

```
2001 07 01 10 40 0010 0005
The FTP server will be shut down at 10:40 a.m. for disk maintenance
```

After the shutdown completes and ftpd restarts, it refuses all login attempts until /etc/shutmsg is deleted. The following sequence illustrates what happens when anyone tries to log in to the FTP server while /etc/shutmsg exists:

```
$ ftp ftpbeast.none.com
Connected to ftpbeast.none.com.
500 ftpbeast.none.com FTP server shut down -- please try again later.
```

How do you delete /etc/shutmsg? That's the role of ftprestart, although, of course, you could also remove it manually with the rm command. As the root user, simply type the command **ftprestart** and press Enter:

```
# ftprestart
ftprestart: /var/ftp/etc/shutmsg removed.
ftprestart: /etc/shutmsg removed.
```

At this point, access to the FTP server has been reenabled.

Strengthening FTP Security

FTP is insecure. While some FTP server daemons have better security records (or at least better *public* security records) than others, the protocol itself, the underlying design, is inherently flawed, resulting in significant exposure to security attacks. This final section of the chapter highlights (or reiterates) potential FTP security problems and offers suggestions for eliminating or reducing the risk.

Understanding and mitigating the risks

The FTP protocol's primary shortcoming is that the server and the client exchange authentication information as clear, unencrypted text. Indeed, *all* communication between an FTP server and FTP clients takes place using unencrypted text, which is easily captured and displayed using a packet sniffer such as tcpdump. So, allowing real users to access a host using FTP exposes their login passwords to ne'er-do-wells. Because FTP transmits authentication information as clear text, system accounts, such as root, are routinely denied access to a system via FTP. So, the first suggestion to reduce FTP security risks is to deny real users FTP access to the server; that is, permit only anonymous FTP.

One of the biggest criticisms of WU-FTPD is its poor security record. Every few months, it seems, a new exploit, or potential exploit, is discovered in it. Unless you are prepared to audit the code yourself to identify possible security problems and then to write and apply patches that address those flaws, the only way to reduce the risk of running WU-FTPD is to use a different server package that has a better security record. That said, the suggested modifications and additions to the /etc/ftpaccess configuration file *will* result in tighter security on the server. On a related note, bear in mind that WU-FTPD's ftpd daemon runs as a system account, that is, using a privileged user ID, so it is frequently a source of attacks designed to exploit its root privileges.

Perhaps you should not run an FTP server at all. Each service your system provides represents another potential point of attack and compromise. If you do run an FTP server exposed to the Internet and if resources permit, run it on a dedicated machine on which no other services (Web, e-mail, and so forth) are running and which has limited access to and from the internal network. In fact, some sites place the FTP server outside their firewall, hiding the internal network from the Internet. Providing a dedicated host limits the number of attack and compromise opportunities, and permits you to close all ports and disable all programs not related to FTP services. If the FTP server is compromised, limiting access to and from the internal network prevents the cracker from sniffing packets containing passwords or other sensitive information that might increase the ability to compromise the internal network and also gives crackers fewer access paths into the internal network. All of these benefits are considerably enhanced if the FTP server is placed outside of the firewall. Administration becomes a bit more difficult, but the added difficulty is a small price to pay for increasing and maintaining the security of your network.

Reconfiguring the system log

In addition to WU-FTPD's internal logging capabilities described in the section titled "Configuring WU-FTPD logging," you can modify the system logger, syslogd, to provide more information, a modification that will facilitate timely identification of security problems related to the FTP server. The process has three steps:

1. Modify the system logger. As root, edit the file /etc/syslog.conf and add the following line:

```
ftp.*                              /var/log/ftp.log
```

You can use spaces or tabs to separate the fields. This entry redirects all messages ftpd sends to the system logger (you must use the log syslog+xferlog directive in /etc/ftpaccess for this method to work) to /var/log/ftp.log. To reduce duplication and clutter in the main system log, /var/log/messages, you might want to modify the line in /etc/syslog.conf that reads:

```
*.info;mail.none;news.none;authpriv.none;cron.none
/var/log/messages
```

so that it reads:

```
*.info;mail.none;news.none;authpriv.none;cron.none;ftp.none
/var/log/messages
```

Adding ftp.none at the end of the first field prevents the system logger from writing any log messages ftpd creates to /var/log/messages. These entries appear on two lines in the text, but appear as a single line in the configuration file.

2. Restart the system logger. Execute the command /etc/rc.d/init.d/ syslog restart. If the output you see resembles the following, the changes are in place:

```
Shutting down kernel logger:                    [  OK  ]
Shutting down system logger:                    [  OK  ]
Starting system logger:                         [  OK  ]
Starting kernel logger:                         [  OK  ]
```

3. Modify the log rotation scheme to include the new FTP log file by adding the following lines to the end of /etc/logrotate.d/syslog:

```
/var/log/ftp.log {
    postrotate
        /bin/kill -HUP `cat /var/run/syslogd.pid 2>/dev/null`
2>/dev/null || true
    endscript
}
```

This entry enables the logrotate program to rotate the new log file in the same manner as other syslogd-related files.

4. Run the following script, monftp.sh, using cron:

```
# monftp.sh
# Mail the current day's FTP log to root
```

```
LOGDATE=$(date +'%b %e')
LOGFILE="/var/log/ftp.log"
SUBJECT="FTP Log for $LOGDATE"

grep ^"$LOGDATE" $LOGFILE | mail -s "$SUBJECT" root
```

monftp.sh uses grep to extract the current day's entries from
/var/log/ftp.log and pipes the output to the mail program, which
sends it to root. A suggested crontab entry for monftp.sh is

```
23 59 * * * /path/to/monftp.sh
```

This entry executes monftp.sh each day at 23:59 (1 minute before midnight). /path/to/monftp.sh must contain the complete path specification
in order for cron to find the script.

Listing 13-6 illustrates what the contents of /var/log/ftp.log look like, if you
use the suggested /etc/ftpaccess configuration file shown earlier. Essentially, it is an
almost complete transcript of an FTP session, from the daemon's perspective. Each
log entry begins with date, time, hostname, program name (ftpd) and the PID of
the process making the entry, followed by a colon, a space, and the message.

 The monftp.sh script is available in the source code directory for this
chapter on the CD-ROM accompanying this book.

Listing 13-6: Sample /var/log/ftp.log File

```
Jul 14 13:43:52 h1 ftpd[1577]: USER kwall
Jul 14 13:44:00 h1 ftpd[1577]: PASS secretword
Jul 14 13:44:00 h1 ftpd[1577]: FTP LOGIN FROM h2.none.com
[192.168.0.2], kwall
Jul 14 13:44:05 h1 ftpd[1577]: PORT
Jul 14 13:44:05 h1 ftpd[1577]: NLST
Jul 14 13:44:11 h1 ftpd[1577]: QUIT
Jul 14 13:44:11 h1 ftpd[1577]: FTP session closed
Jul 14 13:44:16 h1 ftpd[1578]: USER ftp
Jul 14 13:44:22 h1 ftpd[1578]: PASS kwall@none.com
Jul 14 13:44:22 h1 ftpd[1578]: ANONYMOUS FTP LOGIN FROM h2.none.com
[192.168.0.2], kwall@none.com
Jul 14 13:44:34 h1 ftpd[1578]: CWD pub
Jul 14 13:44:35 h1 ftpd[1578]: PORT
Jul 14 13:44:35 h1 ftpd[1578]: NLST
```

Continued

Listing 13-6 *(Continued)*

```
Jul 14 13:45:42 h1 ftpd[1578]: TYPE Image
Jul 14 13:45:48 h1 ftpd[1578]: PORT
Jul 14 13:45:48 h1 ftpd[1578]: STOR badfile
Jul 14 13:45:48 h1 ftpd[1578]: anonymous(kwall@none.com) of
h2.none.com [192.168.0.2] tried to upload /var/ftp/pub/badfile
(upload denied)
Jul 14 13:45:53 h1 ftpd[1578]: QUIT
Jul 14 13:45:53 h1 ftpd[1578]: FTP session closed
Jul 14 13:46:50 h1 ftpd[1579]: FTP LOGIN REFUSED (username in
denied-uid) FROM h2.none.com [192.168.0.2], root
Jul 14 13:47:07 h1 ftpd[1579]: FTP session closed
```

Each message indicates the FTP command (CWD, PORT, STOR) or other action executed, the arguments to that command, or error messages. Note, however, that the PASS command (such as PASS secretword) stores the passwords of real users in clear text. For this reason, /var/log/ftp.log must be readable by the root user only (which is the default). As you can see, using the system logger as described here gives you detailed information about the FTP server's activity.

Monitoring the server

In addition to the detailed logging described in the previous section, you should also use the ftpcount or ftpwho commands, described in the section "Maintaining the Server," to find out who is logged in and what they are doing. Of the two, ftpwho provides better information and is easily scripted.

Take advantage of the report the xferstats command creates. Although it provides only summary information, if you review it regularly, it is easy to identify file transfer statistics that deviate from your server's normal usage patterns. When such a deviation occurs, you can drill down into the detailed log information provided in /var/log/ftp.log to identify exactly what the deviation is and whether or not it represents a security issue.

Finally, you should carefully review file uploads (if you allow them) by using the upload notifications created using the incmail, mailfrom, and mailserver directives in /etc/ftpaccess. Security attacks, particularly attempts to compromise the root account, called *rooting* the box, often begin with such an upload.

Summary

This chapter discussed providing FTP services on your Red Hat Linux system. You read how to install WU-FTPD and how to enable anonymous FTP service by installing the anonftp package. You also learned how to configure the ftpd daemon and how to enhance Red Hat Linux's default configuration to strengthen security and improve the ability to monitor FTP server activity. The final section explained some FTP security risks and suggested several ways to reduce those risks.

Chapter 14

Configuring Mail Services

IN THIS CHAPTER

♦ E-mail explained

♦ Introducing SMTP

♦ Configuring Sendmail

♦ Configuring the e-mail client

♦ Using elm

♦ Maintaining e-mail security

♦ Configuring the NNTP server

USING ELECTRONIC MAIL, you can send messages to and receive messages from other computer users anywhere in the world. E-mail, as it is more commonly known, is a very powerful and useful tool. In this chapter you learn how e-mail works and then configure your systems to put e-mail to work for you.

E-Mail Explained

An e-mail message, just like a letter sent through regular mail, begins with a sender and ends with a receiver. In between these two people are many postal workers who ensure that the letter is properly handled. Even though the sender and receiver never see these workers, their functions are essential in moving the mail. E-mail works in a similar fashion, and although there are not many people between the sender and receiver, programs perform the same function. These programs use network protocols to do the job of ensuring that the message goes from sender to receiver. In this chapter you configure e-mail to run across TCP/IP protocols.

 Chapter 6 explains the TCP/IP protocol suite.

Before configuring an e-mail client or server, you need to understand how e-mail works and the programs to use or make available to your users. Several key components are essential for e-mail to work properly, and as a system administrator it is your responsibility to configure the following items. These items are explained in more detail later in this chapter.

◆ Programs:

- A Mail User Agent (MUA) for users to be able to read and write e-mail

- A Mail Transfer Agent (MTA) to deliver the e-mail messages between computers across a network

- A Local Delivery Agent (LDA) to deliver messages to users' mailbox files

- An mail notification program to tell users that they have new mail

◆ The TCP/IP protocols for storing e-mail messages and transferring e-mail between MTAs

◆ Other communication and mail storage components:

- Ports

- Mail queues

- Mailbox files

In the next sections of this chapter you track an e-mail message through the process from sending to delivery to learn how all the various components work to accomplish their jobs. After learning how the components work, you configure these components to build a fully functioning e-mail system for your server and clients.

Mail User Agent (MUA)

To be able to send mail, you, or your users, need a program called a Mail User Agent (MUA). The MUA, also called a mail client, enables users to write and read mail messages. Two types of MUAs are available: a graphical user interface (GUI), such as Netscape Messenger, and a command-line interface, such as Pine.

Whether your MUA is a GUI or command-line interface, after the message is composed, the MUA sends it to the mail transfer agent (MTA). The MTA is the program that sends the message out across the network and does its work without any intervention by the user. In fact, most users are unaware of the MTA, they just see their mail client.

Mail Transfer Agent (MTA)

Now that the MTA has received the message from the MUA, it can do its job. The MTA installed by default on your Red Hat system is called Sendmail. The MTA reads the information in the To section of the e-mail message and determines the IP address of the recipient's mail server. Then the MTA tries to open a connection to the recipient's server through a communication port, typically port 25. If the MTA on the sending machine can establish a connection, it sends the message to the MTA on the recipient's server using the Simple Message Transfer Protocol (SMTP).

The MTA on the receiving server adds header information to the message. The header contains information that is used for tracking the message and ensuring that it is delivered. Next the receiving MTA passes the message to another program to inform the receiver that new mail has arrived.

Local Delivery Agent (LDA)

After the LDA receives the message from the MTA, it places the message in the receiver's mailbox file that is identified by the username. On your Red Hat system this is a program called procmail. The location of the user's mailbox file is `/usr/spool/mail/<user's name>`.

The final step in the process happens when the user who is the intended receiver of the message reads the message. The user does this using the MUA on his or her PC.

An optional program is a mail notifier that periodically checks your mailbox file for new mail. If you have such a program installed, it notifies you of the new mail.

The Red Hat Linux shell has a built-in mail notifier that looks at your mailbox file once a minute. If new mail has arrived, the shell displays a message just before it displays the next system prompt. It won't interrupt a program you're running. You can adjust how frequently the mail notifier checks and even which mailbox files to watch.

If you are using a GUI, there are mail notifiers available that play sounds or display pictures to let you know that new mail has arrived.

Introducing SMTP

In the section describing the MTA, you learned that messages are sent between MTAs using SMTP. This section explains SMTP and two other protocols used to send mail, Post Office Protocol (POP3) and Internet Message Access Protocol (IMAP4). *SMTP* is the TCP/IP protocol for transferring e-mail messages between computers on a network. SMTP specifies message movement between MTAs, by the path the message takes. Messages may go directly from the sending to the receiving MTA or through other MTAs on other network computers. These other computers briefly store the message before they forward it to another MTA, if it is local to the MTA, or to a gateway that sends it to an MTA on another network.

The SMTP protocol can transfer only ASCII text. It can't handle fonts, colors, graphics, or attachments. If you want to be able to send these items, you need to add another protocol to SMTP.

The protocol you need is called Multipurpose Internet Mail Extensions, or MIME. MIME enables you to add colors, sounds, and graphics to your messages while still enabling them to be delivered by SMTP. In order for MIME to work, you must have a MIME-compliant MUA.

Understanding POP3

POP3 is the Post Office Protocol version 3. This protocol runs on a server that is connected to a network and continuously sends and receives mail. The POP3 server stores any messages it receives. POP3 was developed to solve the problem of what happens to messages when the recipient is not connected to the network.

Without POP3, the message could not be sent to the recipient if the recipient were offline. But with POP3, when you want to check your e-mail, you connect to the POP3 server to retrieve your messages that were stored by the server. After you retrieve your messages, you can use the MUA on your PC to read them. Of course, your MUA has to understand the POP3 to be able to communicate with the POP3 server.

The messages you retrieve to your PC are then typically removed from the server. This means that they are no longer available to you if you want to retrieve them to another PC.

Understanding IMAP4

The Internet Message Access Protocol version 4 (IMAP4) provides sophisticated client/server functionality for handling e-mail. IMAP4 has more features than POP3. IMAP4 enables you to store your e-mail on a networked mail server, just as POP3 does. The difference is that POP3 requires you to download your e-mail before your MUA reads it, whereas IMAP4 enables your e-mail to reside permanently on a remote server, from which you can access your mail. And you can do so from your office, your home, or anywhere else. Your MUA must understand IMAP4 to retrieve messages from an IMAP4 server.

POP3 and IMAP4 don't interoperate. While there are e-mail clients and servers that speak both protocols, you can't use a POP3 client to communicate with an IMAP4 server or an IMAP4 client to communicate with a POP3 server. When you configure an e-mail server, you must decide whether your users need POP3 or IMAP4 functionality (or both). IMAP4 servers usually require much more disk space than POP3 servers because the e-mail remains on the mail server unless the users or system administrator deletes it.

When E-mail Problems Happen

E-mail is very rarely lost in transport. This is quite an accomplishment when you consider the volume of e-mail sent each day. On occasion, e-mail messages get garbled or misrouted, just as a post office sometimes does with snail mail. E-mail can become garbled or lost due to lightning storms and other causes that disrupt power supplies. Any network that is using unshielded 10Base-T cable is more susceptible to e-mail interruptions because the cabling is not protected against atmospheric power disturbances such as lightning. Luckily, this issue is becoming less important as cabling standards improve. However, it is always a good idea to install a surge protector on your system to protect yourself from damage caused by fluctuations in the power supply.

Most e-mail problems are the result of user or system administrator error. For example, the user may type an incorrect e-mail address. Misconfiguring an e-mail server causes e-mail problems. Make sure that mailboxes sit in the right directory for your distribution. If you add file system quotas to mailboxes, be aware that at some point, users may not be able to receive new messages until they (or you) clean up the mail files.

Configuring Sendmail

A number of mail transport agents are available for Red Hat Linux, including Qmail, smail, and Sendmail. The most widely used MTA is Sendmail, which is the default MTA for Red Hat Linux.

Checking that Sendmail is installed and running

Before you start to configure Sendmail, be sure that it's installed on your computer. It probably is, because the Red Hat Linux installation program installs Sendmail. But just to be sure, check it out. The following example shows how to check, using the `rpm -q` command. The output shows not only that Sendmail is installed, but which version of Sendmail is installed.

```
root@main# rpm -q sendmail
sendmail-8.11.0-8
```

Next, make sure that Sendmail starts when your computers boot. You have several ways to check whether Sendmail is running. Pick your favorite. The next example uses `ps` to look for Sendmail. Notice that the terminal field is a "?" and that Sendmail is listening on port 25.

```
root@main# ps -auwx | grep sendmail
```

```
root  8977  0.0  0.3  1488  472  ?  S  12:16   0:00 sendmail:
accepting connections on port 25
You can also use telnet to check whether sendmail is running. You
telnet to yourself (localhost) and tell telnet specifically to use
port 25.
```

Configuring Sendmail

Many system administrators think that Sendmail is difficult to configure. If you look at its configuration file, /etc/sendmail.cf, this might seem to be the case. However, Red Hat Linux provides you with a default Sendmail configuration file that works for most sites. Your default Sendmail configuration file accepts mail deliveries to your computer, sends mail deliveries from your computer, and enables your computer to be used as a relay host.

If you need to edit the configuration file at all, you may need to make only a couple of minor changes. Here are the key lines a Red Hat Linux system administrator might want to edit in /etc/sendmail.cf. These are *not* in the order you find them in the file. In the following example, the tactechnology.com domain is set up to be a relay host.

```
# Copyright (c) 1998-2000 Sendmail, Inc. and its suppliers.
#       All rights reserved.
# Copyright (c) 1983, 1995 Eric P. Allman. All rights reserved.
# Copyright (c) 1988, 1993
#The Regents of the University of California. All rights #reserved.
#
# By using this file, you agree to the terms and conditions
# set forth in the LICENSE file which can be found at the top
# level of the sendmail distribution.
########################################################################
#####                SENDMAIL CONFIGURATION FILE
#####
########################################################################
               | File edited here |
==========
# "Smart" relay host (may be null)
DS

CHANGE THE LINE TO DEFINE THE NAME OF THE MAIL RELAY HOST (GATEWAY
COMPUTER THAT HAS THE RESPONSIBILITY FOR SENDING/RECEIVING INTERNET
MAIL).  NOTE -- NO SPACES!

DSmailrelay.tactechnology.com
==========
```

```
# my official domain name
# ... define this only if sendmail cannot automatically         #
            determine your domain
#Dj$w.Foo.COM
```

Fortunately, you do not have to be a Sendmail expert in order to perform most configuration chores. In most cases, all you need is one of the predefined configuration files in /usr/lib/sendmail.cf. The basic process is to modify one of the predefined configuration files for you own needs, regenerate /etc/sendmail.cf using the m4 macro processor, as explained in a moment, and then test your configuration. This method enables you to make incremental changes, minimizing the risk of major problems. Red Hat Linux comes with a generic Sendmail configuration file (/etc/sendmail.cf).

The m4 Macro Processor

What is a macro? A *macro* is a symbolic name for a long string of characters, much like a keyboard macro is a shorthand way to type a long series of keystrokes. Sendmail gets its rules from the entries in a Sendmail macro file. The location of the generic Sendmail macro file for Red Hat is /usr/lib/sendmail-cf/cf/generic-linux.mc.

The rules in the Sendmail macro file generate the default Sendmail configuration file, sendmail.cf. The m4 is a macro processor that reads the macro file and generates the configuration file. Unless you want Sendmail to use your own customized rules in a complex configuration, you can leave the macro file and macro processor alone. For more information on changing Sendmail's rules in the macro file, see the MailadminHOWTO on the CD-ROM accompanying this book.

An example of a macro in / is the OSTYPE macro that names the operating system. Remember that Sendmail runs on many different operating systems, not just UNIX and Linux. On a Linux system, if you look at Sendmail's macro file, you see the following line, which tells Sendmail which operating system it's running on so that Sendmail runs properly:

```
OSTYPE(`linux')
```

On Linux, the OSTYPE macro comes predefined so that you don't need to worry about it.

If you really want complete, technical information about the macro file and how it works, read the /usr/lib/sendmail-cf/README file.

Understanding and managing the mail queue

Sometimes e-mail messages can't go out immediately, and the reasons are varied. Perhaps your network is down. Maybe your intranet's connection to the Internet is sporadic. Maybe the recipient's computer is unavailable. Whatever the reason, users can continue to compose e-mail with their MUAs. When they send the mail,

Sendmail puts the message into the mail queue and keeps trying to send the message at intervals defined for the Sendmail daemon. You can find out what these intervals are by checking the initialization script that starts Sendmail. The following brief excerpt is from the file /etc/rc.d/rc2.d/S80sendmail. The first line defines the interval to retry as one hour (1h). You can specify the interval in h (hours), m (minutes), or s (seconds). This Red Hat version defines the variable QUEUE and sets it to 1h. Some distributions hard-code the interval right into the Sendmail command (sendmail -q1h). The last two lines of the excerpt show the Sendmail startup command. The -q$QUEUE in the last line sets the retry time to one hour. The -bd option in the next-to-last line of the excerpt starts Sendmail as a daemon.

```
QUEUE=1h
fi

# Check that networking is up.
[ ${NETWORKING} = "no" ] && exit 0

[ -f /usr/sbin/sendmail ] || exit 0

RETVAL=0

start() {
        # Start daemons.

    echo -n "Starting sendmail: "
    /usr/bin/newaliases > /dev/null 2>&1
    for i in virtusertable access domaintable mailertable ; do
            if [ -f /etc/mail/$i ] ; then
                makemap hash /etc/mail/$i < /etc/mail/$i
            fi
        done
daemon /usr/sbin/sendmail $([ "$DAEMON" = yes ] && echo -bd) \
                          $([ -n "$QUEUE" ] && echo -q$QUEUE)
```

Configuring POP3

The steps involved in setting up POP3 include:

1. Installing the package that contains the POP3 daemon

2. Editing the file /etc/inetd.conf to make POP3 services available

3. Restarting the inetd daemon to make the changes in step 2 take effect

4. Checking that the POP3 daemon is accepting connections

Your Linux operating system installation procedure may have already set up POP3 for you. Before you start setting up POP3, therefore, you should use your favorite package manager to query whether POP3 is already installed.

Red Hat bundles IMAP4 and POP3 software together. When you query the RPM database for POP3, you need to look for it under the IMAP name:

```
root@main# rpm -q imap
```

Chapter 23 describes how to use various package managers to query and install packages.

Configuring IMAP4

To configure IMAP4, you follow the same basic steps as with POP3:

1. Installing the package that contains the IMAP4 daemon.

2. Editing the file /etc/inetd.conf to make IMAP4 services available. This step is usually done when you install Linux.

3. Restarting the inetd daemon to make the changes in step 2 take effect.

4. Checking that the IMAP4 daemon is accepting connections. You can telnet to your own computer on port 143, as shown next, to see whether IMAP4 is accepting connections:

```
terry@main# telnet localhost 143
Trying 127.0.0.1...
telnet:Connected to localhost.
Esc character is '^'.
* OK localhost IMAP4rev1 v11.240 server ready
```

Your Red Hat Linux operating system installation procedure may have already set up IMAP4 for you. Before you start setting up IMAP4, therefore, you should use RPM to query whether it is already installed.

Setting up aliases to make life easier

Mail aliases are useful for creating distribution lists and for making access to users more convenient. For example, if people have trouble spelling someone's name, you can create an alias with alternate spellings, so if someone misspells the name, the mail still reaches the intended recipient. You can also alias a nonexistent user to a real user. For example, you could set up an alias, bozo, which redirects all mail intended for bozo to user Wilson. The aliases file is usually /etc/aliases. The following example contains entries for

◆ System aliases for mailer-daemon and postmaster, which are required.

◆ Redirections for pseudo accounts such as lp, shutdown, and daemon. Most of these are all aliased to root by default, but you can change them.

◆ User aliases, such as bozo.

◆ Distribution lists, such as TCPAuthors.

```
# Basic system aliases -- these MUST be present.
mailer-daemon:  postmaster
postmaster:     root
# General redirections for pseudo accounts.
daemon:         root
lp:             root
sync:           root
shutdown:       root
usenet:         news
ftpadm:         ftp
ftpadmin:       ftp
ftp-adm:        ftp
ftp-admin:      ftp

# trap decode to catch security attacks
decode:         root

# Person who should get root's mail
root:           terry

#Users
wilson:         bozo


#Distribution lists
terry,wilson:                   clowns
```

To create an entry in the aliases file, use your favorite editor. Each entry consists of the username, a colon, space(s) or tab(s), and the alias. After you save the file, you must run the newaliases command to make the changes take effect. This step is necessary because Sendmail looks at the binary file /etc/mail/aliases.db to read alias information. The newaliases command reads your aliases text file and updates the binary file.

Using other files and commands with Sendmail

Glancing through your Sendmail configuration file shows that Sendmail uses several files. The following list describes some of them. Your system may not use all of these files.

/usr/sbin/sendmail (also /usr/lib/sendmail, depending on your distribution) — The sendmail daemon executable image

mailq or sendmail -bp — Shows the contents of the mail queue:

```
root@main# mailq
/var/spool/mqueue is empty
root@main# sendmail -bp
/var/spool/mqueue is empty
```

/var/spool/mqueue — The file that holds the mail queue

/var/spool/mail — The file that holds a user's mail (the mailbox file), for example:

```
root@main# ls /var/spool/mail/*
-rw-rw----   1 terry   mail        0  Jun 21 23:53 /var/spool/mail/terry
-rw-rw----   1 wilson  mail      554  Mar 14 21:48 /var/spool/mail/wilson
-rw-------   1 root    root     6416  Jan 26 04:02 /var/spool/mail/root
```

For security, be sure that all mailbox files are readable and writable only by their owners.

/etc/mail/access — List of addresses not permitted to send mail to your system

/etc/mail/relay-domains — List of hosts that are permitted to relay e-mail through your system

/etc/mail/local-host-names — Other names for your system

/etc/mail/virtusertable — Maps e-mail addresses to usernames on the system

Configuring the E-Mail Client

You need to configure an e-mail client (MUA) before you and your users can receive and send e-mail. The MUA(s) you decide to configure depend on user preferences and which user interfaces are available on your computer. If your Red Hat Linux system has no GUI, you must choose a text-based e-mail client. The next sections show you how to configure one GUI MUA (Netscape Messenger) and three of the most popular text-based MUAs (mail, elm, and Pine). Although the steps vary for other clients, the basic concepts are the same for configuring all MUAs.

Configuring Netscape Messenger

Most Linux users are familiar with Netscape Navigator, the browser that comes with Red Hat Linux. Navigator is just one program in the Netscape Communicator suite. Another program in the Communicator suite is the Netscape Messenger e-mail client program. Since most major distributions include Netscape Communicator, you probably already have the package installed on your system. As usual with configuring software, you should use your favorite package manager query to be sure you have Messenger. The following example uses rpm (piped through grep to search for all packages that include "netscape" in their name) to query all installed packages to determine whether the Netscape package is installed.

```
root@main# rpm -qa | grep netscape
netscape-communicator-4.75-2
netscape-common-4.75-2
netscape-navigator-4.75-2
```

Chapter 23 describes how to install new software packages.

You can easily find Netscape Communicator and its tools on the Web. See a list of Communicator packages for various distributions at http://rpmfind.net/linux/rpm2html/search.php?query=netscape.

Netscape Messenger has several advantages: it's easy to configure, it's easy to use, and it integrates well with Netscape Navigator. The major disadvantage of Messenger is that it runs somewhat slowly.

TIP You can open the Messenger window from within the Navigator browser by pressing the keys ALT+2.

Setting up Netscape Messenger consists of three main parts:

1. Filling out forms.

   a. The Identity form tells Messenger who you are.

   b. The Mail Server form tells Messenger which e-mail server to retrieve your mail from.

2. Configuring the Incoming Mail Server.

3. Configuring the Outgoing Mail Server.

Filling Out the Messenger Forms

To fill out the Messenger forms, follow these steps:

1. To display the Identity and Mail Server forms, start Messenger, and then select Preferences from the Edit menu. Expand the Mail and Newsgroups item by clicking its arrow as shown in Figure 14-1.

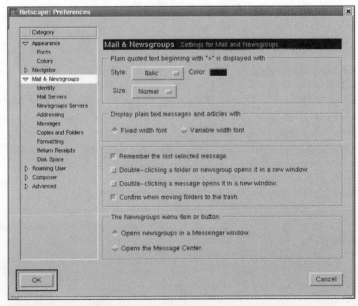

Figure 14-1: Expand Mail and Newsgroups to see the Identity and Mail Servers choices.

2. Select Identity from the menu to display the Identity dialog box. Add your name and e-mail address in the dialog box as shown in Figure 14-2.

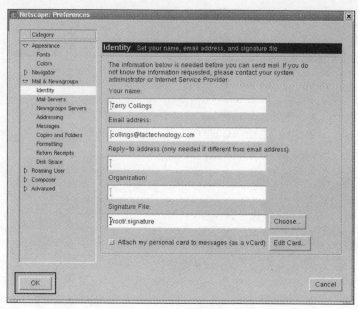

Figure 14-2 Add your name and e-mail address to create your e-mail identity.

3. Next you need to let Messenger know which of your ISP's servers deliver your e-mail. If you're a user, ask your system administrator for this information. If you're the system administrator, you already set this up when you selected an ISP. Click Mail Servers. A list of mail servers that Messenger can fetch mail from appears in the top part of the dialog box. Select a server to deliver your incoming mail and click the Edit button to fill in your username and local mail directory. When you're done filling in the form, click Add. In Figure 14-3, the Mail Servers box shows that both the POP3 server and the SMTP server reside at the ISP.

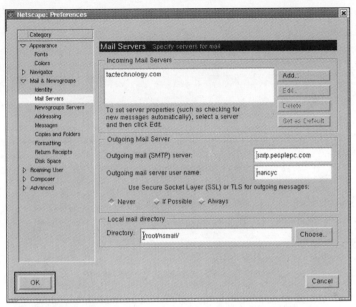

Figure 14-3: Setting up your incoming and outgoing mail servers

4. When you click the Add button next to a server on the list, a form appears for you to fill in. You need to choose a server type from POP3 and IMAP4. You must specify your username and password and some protocol-related parameters.

5. If you are using an MTA such as Sendmail (described earlier in this chapter), you need to select the `movemail` option. The mta and fetchmail programs coopcrate to retrieve your mail messages and insert them into a mail folder, usually a subdirectory (named after your account) under `/var/spool/mail`. Be sure to tell Messenger the name of the subdirectory where movemail can find your e-mail.

The way you set up the Outgoing Mail Server depends on whether you run your own MTA and SMTP server or whether the SMTP server belongs to your ISP. If you have your own SMTP server and MTA, you choose the hostname of the computer where your SMTP server runs.

If you want outgoing mail to go directly to your ISP, you type the hostname of your ISP's SMTP server. Some ISPs require that you enter your account name again.

Using Netscape Messenger

Once Messenger is configured, you can run it separately or inside the Navigator window. The Messenger window contains three parts as seen in Figure 14-4.

◆ A list of your folders

◆ A list of e-mail messages in the currently selected folder

◆ The e-mail message you are currently reading

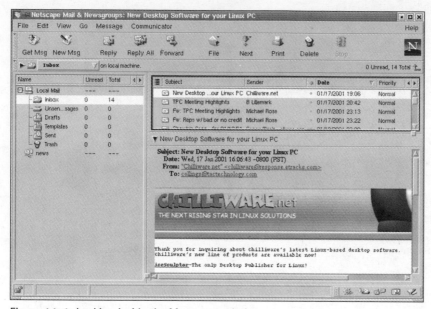

Figure 14-4: Looking inside the Messenger window

Within Messenger, you have three choices for retrieving your messages:

◆ From the File menu, select File → Get New Messages.

◆ Click Get Msg on the toolbar.

◆ Press Alt+2.

Reading messages, storing them in folders, and deleting them is easy, but when in doubt, use the Help menu in the far right corner of the window.

If your mail resides on a POP3 or IMAP4 server, Messenger asks for your password before retrieving your messages to your inbox folder.

You have three choices for composing messages:

◆ From the Message menu, select Message → New Message.

◆ Click New Msg on the toolbar.

◆ Press Alt+M.

Messenger displays a form where you enter the message and the e-mail addresses of the recipients. Figure 14-5 shows the Compose window with a message in progress.

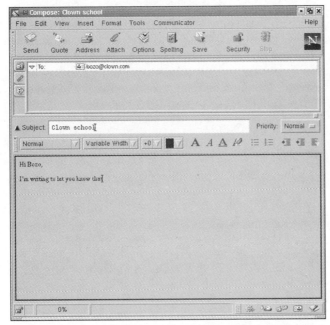

Figure 14–5: Composing an e-mail message using Netscape Mail

When you're finished composing your message, you can either send it immediately or select Send Later from the File menu (the Alt+Shift+Enter key combination). If you want to send your message immediately, select Send Now from the File menu or press the Alt+Enter key combination. You must be connected to the network to be able to send messages immediately.

If you select Send Later, Messenger stores your mail message in the Unsent folder. The messages remain there until you connect to your ISP and select Send Unsent Messages from the File menu.

Sending e-mail from the command line

If you are not using a GUI-style desktop like GNOME or KDE, you are using one of the older text-based or console e-mail clients. Text-based e-mail clients perform an interesting balancing act between efficiency and user-friendliness. Older e-mail clients, such as mail and elm, were designed when computers ran more slowly. Their lack of a graphical interface let them send and retrieve e-mail quickly.

Friendlier programs like Pine are more popular these days as the cost of processor cycles has dramatically decreased. This section covers mail, elm, and Pine, the three most popular text-based programs.

Reading mail with Mail

Mail is the oldest, most primitive e-mail client. It has the advantage of being installed on every Linux system. It is also the most lightweight e-mail program, making it ideal for running on very old computers. It also doesn't require a GUI system such as the X Window System. In fact, mail works very well in shell scripts.

Sending e-mail using the mail program is simple.

1. At the command line, enter the command `mail`, followed by the recipient's e-mail address:

   `mail <destination@recipient.com>`

2. Press Enter. Mail responds with the `Subject:` prompt.

3. Type in the subject of your e-mail and press Enter a second time.

4. Now compose your message, just as you would a regular letter.

5. After you finish your message, press Enter.

6. Type a period on a line by itself, and then press Enter a second time. This step lets mail know that you are done composing the message. Mail displays the letters EOT (End Of Text) and sends your message on its way.

The screen should resemble the following listing (of course, the message you type would be different):

```
$ mail localhost
Subject: Type the Subject Here

Dear User,

I'm showing you how to use the mail e-mail
client. When you finish the message, press
Enter, and then type a period on a line by itself
to indicate the end of the message.

.

EOT
```

On newer versions of the mail program, after typing a period and pressing Enter, you get a CC : prompt. CC stands for *carbon copy,* and you can use this field to enter additional e-mail addresses.

To retrieve mail using the mail program, perform the following steps:

1. Type mail on the command line without any arguments. Mail lists information about itself, the location of your stored e-mails, and the e-mails you have received. It also gives you an ampersand (&) prompt, where you can enter commands to read, save, or delete mail.

2. Type any command you want to use at the ampersand sign prompt and press Enter.

Typing ? causes mail to display a short help screen listing the keystrokes it understands. They are listed in Table 14-1.

TABLE 14-1 COMMAND OPTIONS FOR THE MAIL PROGRAM

Command	Action
+	Move to the next e-mail.
-	Move back to the previous e-mail.
?	Show a list of mail commands.
R	Reply to sender.
d	Delete an e-mail.
h	Show the list of e-mails.
n	Go to the next e-mail and list it.
q	Quit, and save e-mail.
r	Reply to the sender and all the e-mail's original recipients.
t	List the current message.
x	Quit, and don't save e-mails.

Using Elm

The elm mail client is slower than mail but has many more features. It was the first mail program to incorporate e-mail aliases. It also mimics the vi editor, so many people find it familiar and easy to use. To send or receive e-mail using elm, type elm at the command prompt. Elm brings up its own list of commands, which are listed in Table 14-2. Figure 14-6 shows the main elm screen.

TABLE 14-2 ELM COMMANDS

Command	Action
D	Delete mail.
U	Undelete mail.
M	Mail a message.
R	Reply to an e-mail.
F	Forward e-mail.
Q	Quit elm.

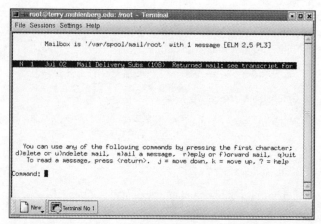

Figure 14-6: Elm is a simple but powerful text-based e-mail client.

Creating mail aliases in elm

One of elm's biggest advantages over mail is that it enables you to easily create mail aliases. Rather than typing out a long e-mail address (which in this day of ever lengthening domain names can be quite a chore), you can create an e-mail alias to save yourself a few keystrokes. To create a new alias, do the following:

1. Type `elm` to start the elm mail program.

2. Type `a` to bring up the aliases menu.

3. Type `n` to create the new alias. Elm leads you through the process of creating a new alias by asking for the person's first and last name, e-mail address, and, finally, what you want the alias to be.

4. Type `r` to exit the alias menu and return to the main elm screen.

Figure 14-7 shows elm's alias creation screen.

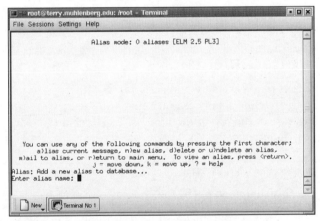

Figure 14-7: Elm makes creating aliases a simple, straightforward process.

Using Pine

The University of Washington developed Pine in order to provide its employees an e-mail client that was simpler and easier to use than elm. Indeed, the name Pine was originally an acronym for *pine is not elm*. To start Pine, type `pine` at the command line. Figure 14-8 shows Pine's main screen.

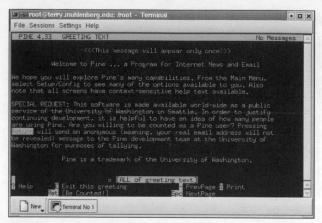

Figure 14-8: Pine's main screen is the gateway to all of its functionality.

At the bottom of the Pine screen, you see the list of commands available. If you do not see the command you want to execute, use the o command, which shows other commands you can use on the current screen.

Working with Pine attachments

One of Pine's biggest contributions to the e-mail world is that it was the first e-mail client to handle attachments reliably. Pine simply requires that you identify the file you want to attach, and it takes care of the rest of the process. To attach a file to an e-mail composed in Pine, do the following.

1. Type pine to start the Pine mail program.

2. Type c (for compose) — this command opens the composition screen.

3. Use the down-arrow key to move your cursor to the third line from the top of the screen, which is labeled Attchmnt.

4. Press Ctrl+J. Pine asks you for the name of a file to attach.

5. Enter the name of the file you want to attach. Figure 14-9 illustrates Pine's prompting for the name of a file attachment.

6. Pine prompts you for a comment. You don't have to enter one.

7. Press Enter, and your e-mail (plus the attachment) is on its way.

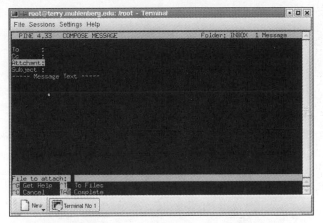

Figure 14-9: Pine prompts you for the attachment name.

Maintaining E-Mail Security

Do you think you have nothing to hide? Maybe you don't, but e-mail security is always a privacy issue even if you aren't mailing credit card numbers or corporate secrets. Using S/MIME for security is only a first step in protecting your users and yourself.

Protecting against eavesdropping

Your mail message goes through more computers than just yours and your recipient's because of store and forward techniques. All a cracker has to do to snoop through your mail is use a packet sniffer program to intercept passing mail messages. A *packet sniffer* is intended to be a tool that a network administrator uses to record and analyze network traffic, but the bad guys use them too. Dozens of free packet sniffing programs are available on the Internet.

Using encryption

Cryptography isn't just for secret agents. Many e-mail products enable your messages to be encrypted (coded in a secret pattern) so that only you and your recipient can read them. Lotus Notes provides e-mail encryption, for example.

Using a firewall

If you receive mail from people outside your network, you should set up a firewall to protect your network. The *firewall* is a computer that prevents unauthorized data from reaching your network. For example, if you don't want anything from ispy.com to penetrate your net, put your net behind a firewall. The firewall blocks out all ispy.com messages. If you work on one computer dialed in to an ISP, you can still install a firewall. Several vendors provide personal firewalls, and some of them are free if you don't want a lot of bells and whistles.

Don't get bombed, spammed, or spoofed

Bombing happens when someone continually sends the same message to an e-mail address either accidentally or maliciously. If you reside in the U.S. and you receive 200 or more copies of the same message from the same person, you can report the bomber to the FBI. The U.S. Federal Bureau of Investigation has a National Computer Crimes Squad in Washington, DC, telephone +1-202-325-9164.

Spamming is a variation of bombing. A spammer sends junk mail to many users (hundreds and even thousands). You easily can be an accidental spammer. If you choose your e-mail's "Reply All" function, and you send a reply to a worldwide distribution list, you are a spammer.

Spoofing happens when someone sends you e-mail from a fake address. If spoofing doesn't seem like it could be major problem for you, consider this: you get e-mail from a system administrator telling you to use a specific password for security reasons. Many people comply because the system administrator knows best. Imagine the consequences if a spoofer sends this e-mail faking the system administrator's e-mail address to all the users on a computer. All of a sudden, the spoofer knows everyone's passwords and has access to private and possibly sensitive or secret data. Spoofing is possible because plain SMTP does not have authentication capabilities. Without authentication features, SMTP can't be sure that incoming mail is really from the address it says it is. If your mail server enables connections to the SMTP port, anyone with a little knowledge of the internal workings of SMTP can connect to that port and send you e-mail from a spoofed address. Besides connecting to the SMTP port of a site, a user can send spoofed e-mail by modifying their Web browser interfaces.

 You can protect your data and configure your mail system to make mail fraud more difficult. If someone invades your mail system, you should report the intrusion to the Computer Emergency Response Team (CERT). You can find the reporting form on the Internet at `ftp://info.cert.org/pub/incident_reporting_form`.

Be careful with SMTP

Use dedicated mail servers. First of all, keep the number of computers vulnerable to SMTP-based attacks to a minimum. Have only one or a few centralized e-mail servers, depending on the size of your organization.

Allow only SMTP connections that come from outside your firewall to go to those few central e-mail servers. This policy protects the other computers on your network. If your site gets spammed, you have to clean up the central e-mail servers, but the rest of your networked computers are okay.

If you use packet filtering, you need only configure your e-mail servers. Packet filtering analyzes packets based on the source and destination addresses. The analysis decides whether to accept the packets and pass them through to your networks or to reject them as being unsafe. Firewalls often use packet filtering techniques. The latest stable kernel, 2.4, has built-in packet filtering capabilities.

Using Newsgroups

"News" is a bit of a misnomer in the technology world, having really nothing to do with journalism. Newsgroups are public electronic discussion groups, called forums. A newsgroup may reside on a single computer with no network access or on any kind of network. Usenet is a TCP/IP service for the world's largest collection of newsgroups. Each newsgroup is an electronic conversation group about a particular topic. When computer users talk about "news," they usually mean Usenet news. At last count, there were nearly 50,000 newsgroups dedicated to pursuits as varied as culinary arts and skydiving. To get news on any of these topics, you first need access to a News server. Usually, your ISP provides this access, but if you want to run your own news server, you need to set up your news transport software, the NNTP server.

Why would you want to run your own news server? If you manage a large intranet, it performs better, and it's more convenient for you if you run your own news server on the intranet. Your news server must connect to the Internet if users want to participate in newsgroups outside of your intranet. Then users connect to your intranet's news server rather than each user having a separate connection to an ISP. Another benefit of running your own news server is that you can create private newsgroups as forums for business, organizational, and technical topics. These private newsgroups are available only inside your intranet.

Configuring the NNTP server

NNTP, which stands for Network News Transport Protocol, is built into all current news handling software for Linux today. NNTP's success comes from the fact that it was one of the first news programs that used the TCP/IP-style protocol in its connection between a news client and a news server.

The NNTP server can run as either a program managed by the all-important Internet daemon (inetd), which controls all Internet connections on a Linux box, or as a stand-alone server program that starts at boot time. If you decide to run NNTP at boot time, you need to edit the /etc/rc.inet2 file.

If you want to start it from the Internet daemon, complete the following steps:

1. Log in as the root administrative account.

2. Open the file /etc/inetd.conf.

3. Look for the following line in the file:

```
#nntp  stream tcp nowait    news   /usr/etc/in.nntpd   nntpd
```

4. Delete the hash mark in front of the line, save, and then quit. A hash mark in Linux tells the machine to ignore the line. Removing the mark is the equivalent of turning a switch to On, since Linux ignores it.

 TIP If you can't find the line to uncomment, type the line in yourself. Be sure to omit the hash mark.

5. Open the file /etc/services.

6. Look for the following line:

```
#nntp    119/tcp    readnews    untp  # Network News Transfer
    Protocol
```

7. Again, uncomment this line or type it in.

8. Next, create a directory for your news to be stored (spooled). You should create this in the /tmp directory so that it is removed upon a reboot of the system. Do this by typing the following at the command prompt and pressing Enter:

```
mkdir /var/spool/news/tmp
```

9. Finally, use the chown command to change the ownership of the file to the news system account:

```
chown news.news /var/spool/news/tmp
```

Reading newsgroups in Pine

The Pine program enables you to read the Internet's newsgroups. While use of Pine as a newsreader has declined in recent years as Netscape has become more popular, Pine is still a good method, particularly if you're running an older, slower machine that could benefit from the relative quickness of a nongraphical newsreader.

To get your Pine mail reader to handle newsgroups, you need to create the .newsrc file that Pine reads to determine which newsgroups you want to read. To do so, complete the following steps:

1. Using vi, create a file called .newsrc.

2. Type in the list of newsgroups you'd like to read about. For example, your list might include:

```
misc.games
alt.automobiles_used
comp.linux.caldera
```

3. Save and quit the file.

4. Next, complete the process by configuring the Pine mail program to han-dle NNTP-based news. Start Pine at the command line by typing **pine**.

5. Type **S** for Setup.

6. Type **C** to get to the configuration screen.

7. Use the down arrow key to highlight `nntp-server`.

8. Type **C** to change the configuration.

9. Type in the name of your ISP's news server, and then press Enter.

10. Type **Q** to exit Pine.

11. When Pine asks you if you want to save the changes, type **Y** for yes.

From now on, when you start Pine and look at your mail folders, you also have the option to look at your listed newsgroups.

Configuring Netscape for news

Today, the most popular option is to configure Netscape to handle your news as well as electronic mail for you. Netscape news is a lot more user-friendly for many people because it looks like Outlook, Internet Explorer, or Eudora.

 You must be running a GUI to use Netscape.

To configure Netscape to handle news, perform the following steps:

1. Start Netscape Communicator.

2. Choose the Edit pull-down menu at the top of the screen.

3. Select Preferences by clicking it.

4. The Preferences screen appears. You see a list of Categories on the left-hand side of the Preference screen as shown in Figure 14-10.

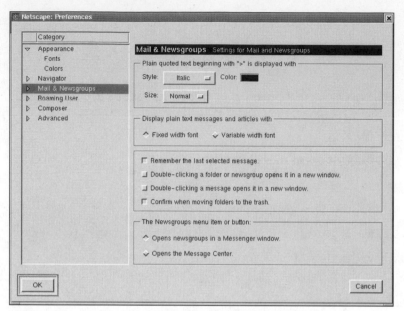

Figure 14-10: Choosing the category from the Preferences screen

5. Midway down the list of choices is Mail & Newsgroups. Click the arrow immediately to the left of this setting. The arrow flips down, and you get a menu of different categories under the Mail & Newsgroups listing.

6. Click Newsgroups Servers. The screen to the right lists the settings. The default, News, is the only one listed, since you haven't set anything yet. See Figure 14-11.

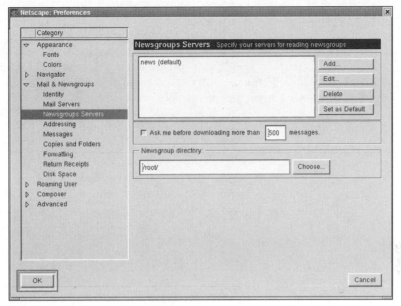

Figure 14-11: The Newsgroups Servers screen

7. If you don't want to use the default or your ISP instructs you not to, click the Add button.

8. A new screen appears where you can type the server's name in the blank text field as shown in Figure 14-12.

Figure 14-12: Adding a news server

9. Click OK when finished.

10. You are returned to the Preferences screen. If you want to exit the Preferences screen and return to Netscape, click the close button, marked with an X in the upper right corner.

Summary

This chapter explained the steps a message takes through MUAs, MTAs (Sendmail), TCP/IP protocols, LDAs, mail notification programs, mail queues, and mailboxes. Along the way you learned how to configure both the client and server sides of an e-mail system. You also learned how to set up a news server so that users can read and participate in Usenet discussions and forums.

Chapter 15

Configuring a Web Server

IN THIS CHAPTER

- ◆ Introducing Apache

- ◆ Installing and configuring Apache

- ◆ Using CGI, SSI, and SSL

- ◆ Monitoring the server

- ◆ Improving performance

- ◆ Maintaining server security

SIMPLY STATED, the Apache Web server is the most popular Web server in the world. Similarly, creating a low-cost and stable Web server is one of the most common reasons individuals and organizations use Linux. Indeed, some surveys indicate 30 percent of all Web servers run a combination of Linux and Apache. In this chapter, you learn how to install, configure, and maintain the Apache Web server on your Red Hat Linux System.

Introducing Apache

Before proceeding to the meat of this chapter, this section highlights the history of the Apache Web server, describes its key features, and provides pointers to additional Apache resources that you may find useful.

A short history of Apache

The Apache Web server began life as the NCSA (National Center for Supercomputing Applications) HTTP server (called *httpd* throughout the rest of this chapter). NCSA's server was the most popular of the early HTTP servers and its source code was in the public domain. After NCSA's active development of their httpd effectively stopped (late 1994 and early 1995), a small group of Web administrators who had modified the source code to address site-specific needs or to patch various bugs gathered together to coordinate their activities and merge their code changes into a single code tree.

In April 1995, this loosely organized group of Web masters, the original Apache Group, released the first official version of Apache intended for public consumption, Apache 0.6.2. Despite its known warts, the Apache server was instantly popular. However, even as the development team continued to stabilize the existing code base, add new features, and generate documentation, other members undertook a fundamental redesign that rather quickly (August 1995) resulted in Apache 0.8.8. This first (beta) release based on the redesigned architecture still bears a strong resemblance to the Apache available today. Another round of code base stabilization, bug fixes, feature enhancements, and documentation updates concluded on November 30, 1995. The next day, December 1, 1995, the Apache Group released Apache 1.0, the version that cemented Apache's status as the Internet's #1 HTTP server.

Although the actual numbers fluctuate, and overall growth of Apache's usage (and of the Web servers in general) has begun to flatten out, periodic Internet-wide surveys conducted by Netcraft (http://www.netcraft.com/survey/) consistently demonstrate that, seven years after its first releases, Apache continues to be the most widely used Web server, surpassing all other Web servers — *combined*.

For more information about Apache's history, read "About Apache" at http://httpd.apache.org/ABOUT_APACHE.html.

Whence the Name "Apache"?

Here is the answer to *the* most frequently asked question about Apache, taken directly from the Apache FAQ (http://httpd.apache.org/docs/misc/FAQ.html#name):

3. Why the name "Apache"?

    A cute name which stuck. Apache is "A PAtCHy server." It was based on some existing code and a series of "patch files."

    For many developers it is also a reverent connotation to the Native American Indian tribe of Apache, well-known for their superior skills in warfare strategy and inexhaustible endurance. Online information about the Apache Nation is tough to locate; we suggest searching Google, Northernlight, or AllTheWeb.

In addition, http://www.indian.org/welker/apache.htm is an excellent resource for Native American information.

Apache features

The complete list of Apache's features easily runs to three or four pages, far too many and far too tedious to recite here. In fact, many of its "features" are downright mundane because it performs the same function as any other Web server: sending some sort of data down the wire in response to a properly formatted request from a Web client. In another sense, these features, more properly called "functionality," are unremarkable because Apache is a standards-driven program providing mandated functionality. That is, many of its capabilities are the result of its full compliance with version 1.1 of the HTTP protocol. Apache implements all the required functionality described in RFC2616, the document that defines the current Web server protocol, HTTP/1.1 (Hyper Text Transfer Protocol version 1.1). Of course, the manner in which Apache implements mandated features is anything but mundane.

Apache's true standout features are its speed, configurability, stability, and rich feature set. Most benchmark studies have shown Apache to be faster than many other Web servers, including commercial servers. Apache is also both easy to configure and easy to reconfigure. Its configuration information resides in plain text files and uses simple English-language directives. Reconfiguring a running server is a simple matter of changing the appropriate configuration directive and restarting the server.

Few seriously question Apache's stability, even among its competitors. Sites receiving millions of hits each day report no problems. Moreover, while no software product of any complexity can be considered bug-free, Apache is beset with fewer (known) bugs than other Web servers, particularly closed source servers. Many factors contribute to Apache's stability, but the two most important are eyeballs and axle grease.

I hear you saying to yourself, "Huh? Eyeballs and axle grease? What *is* he talking about?" Read on for the answer:

◆ More eyeballs means fewer bugs. Apache's source code is freely available, so hundreds of developers have looked at it, found bugs, fixed them, and submitted their fixes for inclusion in the code base. Similarly, Apache's enormous user base means that virtually every segment of its code has been tested in real-world environments, uncovering most major bugs and many minor ones.

◆ The squeaky wheel gets the grease. Combine Apache's widespread usage with Web site administrators who quickly complain about server bugs and insist on the absolutely vital requirement to maintain a secure Web server, and you can easily understand why the Apache team consistently and frequently releases patches for confirmed bugs and security holes, often within just a few hours of their discovery.

The balance of Apache's features are the result of developer and user input. Apache is an open source software project (indeed, Apache is the poster child for the successful open source software project), so anyone can contribute code for inclusion in the server, although whether or not such code is accepted is up to members of the core Apache team. User feedback drives Apache's development and defines its feature set. A very short list of such features includes, in no particular order:

◆ Apache is easily extensible using Dynamic Shared Objects (DSOs), more commonly known as *modules*. Modules extend Apache's capabilities and new features without requiring recompilation because they can be loaded and unloaded at runtime, just as shared libraries are dynamically loaded and unloaded.

◆ Apache uses a binary database format for authenticating users' requests for password-protected Web pages. This format enables Apache to support very large numbers of users without becoming bogged down executing authentication requests.

◆ Apache supports virtual hosts, also known as *multi-homed servers*, which enables a single machine to provide Web services for multiple domains or IP addresses (or hostnames).

◆ Apache enables administrators to define multiple directory index files, the default page to display when a Web client requests a directory URL. So, for example, the server can return `index.html`, `index.htm`, `index.php`, or execute a script named `index.cgi` when a client requests a directory URL, depending on what Apache finds in the requested directory.

◆ Another boon for Web server administrators is Apache's rich support for server logging. You can define custom log file formats and control the level of detail contained in each log entry. Apache can send log file output to named pipes (FIFOs) on systems that support named pipes, primarily Linux, Unix, and similarly designed operating systems. This feature enables any arbitrary log manipulation that can be accomplished using a named pipe. In fact, Apache can be configured to generate a unique identifier that distinguishes one hit from every other hit, although there are some restrictions that apply.

◆ Within limits, Apache automatically adjusts to the capabilities of connected Web clients, a process called *content negotiation*. If a Web client is broken in a way that Apache can determine, incompletely or improperly implements HTTP standards, or does not support a given HTML specification (or, at least, the specification Apache supports), it sends Web pages modified to give the best representation of the requested information based on what the client can process.

You learn more about these and many other Apache features as you read the chapter.

Finding more information about Apache

Considering Apache's popularity, there is no shortage of information about it on the Internet. This section lists a small subset of such resources, accessible in many cases directly from Apache's home pages.

WEB PAGES

The following Web sites are the first places you should visit if you need more information about Apache and the Apache project.

◆ The Apache Software Foundation

    http://www.apache.org/

◆ The Apache Project Home Page

    http://httpd.apache.org/

◆ The Apache Module Registry

    http://modules.apache.org/

◆ *Apache Week*

    http://www.apacheweek.com/

MAILING LISTS AND NEWSGROUPS

Much of the ongoing support and development of Apache takes place, or at least is discussed, in Usenet newsgroups and on mailing lists. The following links will get you connected to the primary Apache-related mailing lists and newsgroups.

◆ News and announcements

    http://httpd.apache.org/lists.html#http-announce

◆ Usage and general support

    http://httpd.apache.org/lists.html#http-users

    news://comp.infosystems.www.servers.unix/

◆ Development

    http://httpd.apache.org/lists.html#http-dev/

The mailing lists are archived and searchable at the following Web sites:

◆ ApacheLabs

    http://www.apachelabs.org/

◆ AIMS

    http://marc.theaimsgroup.com/

◆ GeoCrawler

`http://www.geocrawler.com/`

How Web Servers Work

To understand Apache, its configuration, and how to fine-tune it for your own environment, you should understand how Web servers work in general. Otherwise, lacking this context, Apache's behavior and configuration might seem arbitrary. Figure 15-1 shows the general process that takes place when a Web browser requests a page and the Apache Web server responds.

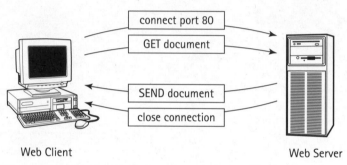

Figure 15-1: Apache transmits a document according to a client's request.

The Web client (a browser in this case) first performs a DNS lookup on the server name specified in the URL, obtains the IP address of the server, and then connects to port 80 at that IP address (or another port if the server is not using the default HTTP port). When the connection is established, the client sends an HTTP GET request for the document in the URL, which could be, among other possibilities, a specific HTML document, an image, a script, or a directory listing.

After the server receives the request, it translates the document URL into a file-name on the local system. For example, the document URL `http://localhost/`
`~kwall/news.html` might become `/home/kwall/public_html/news.html`. Next, Apache evaluates whether or not the requested document is subject to some sort of access control and requests a user name and password from the client or rejects the request outright, depending on the type of access control in place. If the requested URL specifies a directory (that is, the URL ends in /) rather than a specified document, Apache looks for the directory index page, `index.html` by default, and returns that document to the client. If the directory index page does not exist, Apache might send a directory listing in HTML format back to the client or send an error message, depending on how the server is configured. The document can also be a specially written script, a CGI (Common Gateway Interface) script. In this case, Apache executes the script, if permitted to do so, and sends the results back to the

client. Finally, after Apache has transmitted the requested document and the client receives it, the client closes the connection and Apache writes an entry in one or more log files describing the request in varying levels of detail.

Depending on how the page is written and what it contains, additional processing takes place during the transfer. For example, embedded scripts or Java applets are transferred to and execute on the client side of the connection; server-side includes (discussed in the section titled "Configuring Apache for SSI"), however, are processed on the server side, as are CGI scripts, database access, and so forth.

Installing Apache

Depending on the installation profile you chose when you installed Red Hat Linux, anaconda may or may not have installed Apache. To find out, execute the command rpm -q apache. If the output resembles the following (the version numbers may be slightly different by the time you read this book), Apache is installed:

```
apache-1.3.20-16
```

If Apache is installed, you can skip ahead to the section titled "Additional packages to install." You might consider customizing Apache for your system by compiling it yourself using the instructions in "Installing and building the source RPMs" later in this section. Another alternative is downloading, compiling, and installing Apache's source distribution, as described in "Installing and building the source distribution" later in the chapter.

Chapter 23 provides detailed information and step-by-step instructions for installing RPMs and compiling source RPMs. It also explains how to build and install programs from the original source code.

If, on the other hand, you see the message package apache is not installed, you must at least install the binary RPM before continuing with this chapter.

Installing the binary RPMs

To install the Apache binary RPMs from the Red Hat installation CD-ROM, follow these steps:

1. Log in as the root user or use su to become root.

2. Mount the Red Hat Linux installation CD-ROM (disk 1).

3. Type the following command to install Apache and its supporting packages (replace /mnt/cdrom with the mount point of your CD-ROM drive if it is different):

```
# rpm -ivh /mnt/cdrom/RedHat/RPMS/apache*rpm
```

4. Continue with the section titled "Additional packages to install."

Installing and building the source RPMs

If you choose to install and build the source RPMs, follow these steps:

1. Log in as the root user or use su to become root.

2. Mount the Red Hat Linux installation CD-ROM (disk 2).

3. Type the following command to install Apache's source RPMs (replace /mnt/cdrom with the mount point of your CD-ROM drive if it is different):

```
# rpm --rebuild /mnt/cdrom/SRPMS/apache*src.rpm
# rpm -ivh /usr/src/redhat/RPMS/i386/apache*rpm
```

4. Continue with the section titled "Additional packages to install."

Installing and building the source distribution

Installing and building Apache's source distribution enables you to select configuration defaults and compiled-in features that suit *your* needs, not someone else's. This section guides you through building Apache from scratch. To save download time, this chapter's source code directory includes the latest released version of the Apache Web server available at the time this book went to press. You might want to check Apache's home page (http://httpd.apache.org/) for updates, patches, or even a newer release, but the build process described here remains substantially unchanged.

1. Copy the tarball from the CD-ROM to /tmp.

2. Become the root user using su and then cd to /usr/local/src:

```
# cd /usr/local/src
```

3. Unpack the archive:

```
# gzip -cd < /tmp/apache_1.3.22.tar.gz | tar xf -
```

4. cd into the base directory of the source code tree:

```
# cd apache_1.3.22
```

5. Read the release documentation to familiarize yourself with changes, updates, new features, and known problems. At a bare minimum, read the files INSTALL, README, and README.configure.

6. If you are impatient, you can build and install Apache using its standard configuration, which installs the finished product into `/usr/local/apache`, by executing the following sequence of commands:

```
# ./configure
# make
# make install
```

The following is from `http://www.php.net/manual/en/install.unix.php`:

```
1.   gunzip apache_1.3.x.tar.gz
2.   tar xvf apache_1.3.x.tar
3.   gunzip php-x.x.x.tar.gz
4.   tar xvf php-x.x.x.tar
5.   cd apache_1.3.x
6.   ./configure --prefix=/www
7.   cd ../php-x.x.x
8.   ./configure --with-mysql --with-apache=../apache_1.3.x --
enable-track-vars
9.   make
10.  make install
11.  cd ../apache_1.3.x
12.  ./configure --activate-module=src/modules/php4/libphp4.a
13.  make
14.  make install
15.  cd ../php-x.x.x
16.  cp php.ini-dist /usr/local/lib/php.ini
17.  Edit your httpd.conf or srm.conf file and add:
        AddType application/x-httpd-php .php
18.  Use your normal procedure for restarting the Apache
server. (You must stop and restart the server, not just cause
the server to reload by use a HUP or USR1 signal.)
```

Apache does not use the GNU Autoconf package to configure the source tree before building, despite using a script named `configure` to perform the configuration. Instead, it uses APACI, the Apache Autoconf Interface. APACI is an Autoconf-*style* interface for source code configuration.

For the time being, you can disregard the following error messages, if you receive them, displayed near the end of the build process (the addresses, shown in bold face, may be different on your system):

```
htpasswd.o: In function `main':
```

```
htpasswd.o(.text+0xa9a): the use of `tmpnam' is dangerous,
better use `mkstemp'
htdigest.o: In function `main':
htdigest.o(.text+0x462): the use of `tmpnam' is dangerous,
better use `mkstemp'
```

The linker generates these messages during the final link stage to remind programmers that the tmpnam call, part of the standard C I/O library, has known security problems and should be replaced with the safer mkstemp call.

7. If you are somewhat more patient, use the following command line to configure, build, and install Apache:

```
# OPTIM="-O2" CFLAGS="-march=CPU -mcpu=CPU" \
./configure \
--prefix=/usr/local/apache \
--enable-module=all \
--enable-shared=max
# make
# make install
```

OPTIM="-O2" is the optimization level passed to GCC. The CFLAGS argument uses CPU to generate code in the Apache binaries that takes advantage of your CPU's features. CPU can be one of i386, i486, i586 or pentium (for Pentium CPUs), i686 or pentiumpro (for Pentium Pro or better CPUs) or k6 for AMD's K6 CPU. --prefix=/usr/local/apache defines /usr/local/apache as Apache's base installation directory. --enable-module=all compiles and activates all of the modules shipped in the standard Apache distribution. The --enable-shared=max statement, finally, enables the modules built with --enable-module=all to be built as shared objects that Apache can load and unload at runtime on an as-needed basis.

8. Regardless of the method you used to build Apache, make sure a previous installation of it is not running. If you had previously installed Red Hat's Apache binary, execute the following command:

```
# /etc/rc.d/init.d/httpd stop
```

If ps -ax still shows running httpd processes, use the following command to kill them:

```
# pkill httpd
```

9. Start the new Apache installation as follows:

```
# /usr/local/apache/bin/apachectl start
```

10. Finally, test the Web server by browsing its default home page. From any network accessible system, try http://your.host.name/ or http://web.server.ip.addr/ (replace your.host.name with your system's

hostname or *web.server.ip.addr* with your system's IP address). If these options do not work, there is most likely some sort of network configuration problem. So, from the system in question, try `http://localhost/` or `http://127.0.0.1/`. If any of these methods work, you should see a page resembling Figure 15-2.

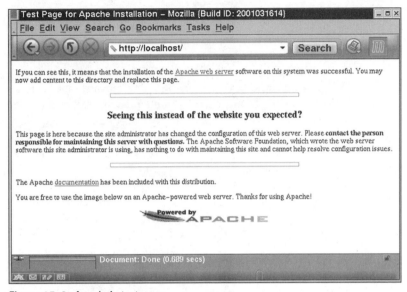

Figure 15–2: Apache's test page

11. If you do not want to continue running the newly installed server, shut it down with the following command:

`# /usr/local/apache/bin/apachectl stop`

12. Continue with the next section, "Additional packages to install."

Additional packages to install

The section titled "Creating a Secure Server with SSL" explains how to enable, configure, and use mod_ssl, a module giving Apache strong cryptography using the Secure Sockets Layer (SSL) and Transport Layer Security (TLS). Naturally, mod_ssl needs to be installed. If you built and installed Apache using the source RPMs as described earlier, mod_ssl is already installed. Otherwise, use the following procedure to install it:

1. Log in as the root user or use su to become root.

2. Mount the Red Hat Linux installation CD-ROM (disk 1).

3. Type the following command to install Apache and its supporting pack-ages (replace `/mnt/cdrom` with the mount point of your CD-ROM drive if it is different):

```
# rpm -ivh /mnt/cdrom/RedHat/RPMS/mod_ssl*rpm
```

Configuring Apache

This section shows you how to configure Apache. Configuring Apache, especially for new or inexperienced administrators, seems a daunting task at first glance. The terminology is confusing, the concepts unfamiliar, and the configuration file intimidating. This section could have been subtitled "Demystifying Apache configuration" because it defines the terms, explains the concepts, and removes, or at least reduces, the intimidation. If you read carefully, by the time you reach the end of the section, you will see that Apache is easy to configure, in large part because its developers and maintainers have taken the trouble to define sensible defaults for most configuration items, and to create, with the help of a dedicated user community, a pleasantly complete documentation set.

Using the default Red Hat configuration as a base, you learn about groups of related Apache configuration directives and analyze the corresponding entries in Red Hat Linux's default Apache configuration. Finally, after evaluating a variety of changes and additions to the default configuration, you learn how to use Red Hat's new Apache configuration tool, `apacheconf` to maintain the Web server configuration.

Apache's startup process

When Apache starts, either during system boot or when invoked after boot using the init script `/etc/rc.d/init.d/httpd` or the Apache-provided script `apachectl`, it reads and processes three files, in order: `/etc/httpd/conf/httpd.conf`, `/etc/httpd/conf/srm.conf`, and `/etc/httpd/access.conf`. The default location for each of these files is compiled into Apache but can be overridden using the `-f` option discussed later in the chapter. Apache also reads `/etc/mime.types`, which configures the MIME subsystem by mapping file name extensions to content types.

Using a single file simplifies maintaining the configuration file. `httpd.conf` is the primary configuration file. However, for backward compatibility with the original NCSA server conf and early versions of Apache, `srm.conf` and `access.conf` are also supported, but their use is deprecated. All configuration directives can and should be placed in `httpd.conf` or included from other files specified using the `Include` directive.

 A more complete and far more amusing explanation of the reason for three configuration files is available on the Web at Apache's home page, `http://httpd.apache.org/info/three-config-files.html`.

After processing these configuration files, Apache performs some other sanity checks and opens its log files. Next, this initial Apache process, often called the *master server*, which is owned by root in most cases, launches one or more child processes, as defined by the process creation directives discussed shortly, that are owned by a less privileged user and group (apache, on Red Hat Linux). These child processes do the actual work of listening for requests on the HTTP port (80, by default) and answering them.

Apache is highly configurable, a fact reflected in its configuration language, which contains, at the time this book was written, 210 distinct directives. Some directives are operating system specific, some provide backward-compatibility for deprecated features, and some are or should be used in only very specific situations. To keep the discussion manageable and to hold your attention, the configuration directives discussed in this chapter are limited to those that affect basic server configuration, those that reflect Red Hat Linux configuration options, and those that permit you to implement common configuration customizations.

The following sections follow the basic layout of the primary Apache configuration file, /etc/httpd/conf/httpd.conf, which is organized into three sections. The first section configures Apache's global characteristics, the second section configures the primary or default server (the Web server that responds to all requests not handled by virtual hosts), and the third section configures virtual hosts.

Configuring global Apache behavior

The first group of configuration directives you examine, shown in Table 15-1, control the behavior of the server process as a whole. The default values set by the Apache Project or by Red Hat appear in bold face with those directives that have default values.

TABLE 15-1 GLOBAL CONFIGURATION DIRECTIVES

Directive	Description
ServerType **standalone**	Controls whether or not Apache runs as a stand-alone process or runs from inetd (xinetd on Red Hat Linux)
ServerRoot **/etc/httpd**	Defines the top level directory for Apache's configuration files and log files (including error logs)
PidFile **/var/run/httpd.pid**	Defines the file containing the PID of the master server process

Continued

TABLE 15-1 GLOBAL CONFIGURATION DIRECTIVES *(Continued)*

Directive	Description
Timeout 300	Defines the maximum time in seconds Apache waits for packet send and receive operations to complete
KeepAlive On	Permits multiple requests on the same connection, speeding up delivery of HTML documents
MaxKeepAliveRequests 100	Sets the number of requests permitted per connection
KeepAliveTimeout 15	Sets the number of seconds permitted to elapse between requests from the same client on the same connection when KeepAlive is On
MinSpareServers 5	Defines the minimum number of spare (idle) child servers permitted
MaxSpareServers 20	Defines the maximum number of spare (idle) child servers the master server spawns
StartServers 8	Defines the number of child servers created when Apache starts
MaxClients 150	Sets the maximum number of simultaneous connections (child servers) supported
MaxRequestsPerChild 100	Sets the maximum number of requests each child server fills before terminating
Listen *[ipaddress:]*80	Determines the combination of IP address and port on which Apache listens for connections; multiple Listen directives may be used
LoadModule *modname filename*	Links the module or library *filename* into the server and adds it to the list of active modules using the name *modname*
ClearModuleList	Clears Apache's built-in list of active modules, which must then be rebuilt using the AddModule directive
AddModule *module*.c	Activates the built-in but inactive module *module*.c

Some of the items in Table 15-1 bear additional discussion. When specifying the names of log files or additional configuration files, these names are appended to ServerRoot unless they begin with /. That is, if ServerRoot is /etc/httpd and a log file is specified as logs/mylog.log, the complete name is taken as /etc/httpd/logs/mylog.log, whereas /logs/mylog.log is interpreted as an absolute path name.

Specifying KeepAlive On results in significant performance improvements because it eliminates the overhead involved in initiating new HTTP connections between clients and the Web server. The MinSpareServers and MaxSpareServers directives enable Apache to self-regulate, adding and deleting child processes as Web server usage fluctuates. When more than MaxClients attempt to connect, each connection request is put onto a queue (in particular, a FIFO or *first-in-first-out* queue) and serviced in the order received as current connections close. For users, too long a wait, however, causes them either to send another request or to disconnect. Busy Web sites may need to adjust this value to accommodate heavy traffic.

For most sites, the default values for the configuration directives in Table 15-1 should be sufficient. In particular, do not modify the order in which modules are loaded and activated using the LoadModule and AddModule directives unless you know what you are doing. Some modules depend on other modules in order to function properly. Apache does not start if problems occur loading modules.

Listing 15-1 shows the corresponding entries from Red Hat's default Apache configuration, except for the LoadModule, AddModule, and ClearModuleList directives. Comments have been removed to save space and simplify the presentation.

Listing 15-1: Red Hat Linux's Global Configuration Directives

```
ServerType standalone
ServerRoot "/etc/httpd"
LockFile /var/lock/httpd.lock
PidFile /var/run/httpd.pid
ScoreBoardFile /var/run/httpd.scoreboard
Timeout 300
KeepAlive On
MaxKeepAliveRequests 100
KeepAliveTimeout 15
MinSpareServers 5
MaxSpareServers 20
StartServers 8
MaxClients 150
MaxRequestsPerChild 100
Listen 80
```

Nothing in Listing 15-1 *necessarily* needs to be changed. You might consider reducing the MaxSpareServers value to 10 and the StartServers value to 5, the default values given these directives by the Apache Group. Then, as you develop a usage profile for your Web server, adjust them if necessary.

Configuring the default server

As noted a moment ago, the *default* or *primary* server refers to the Web server that responds to all HTTP requests not handled by virtual hosts, also known as *virtual servers*. Without going into detail yet, a *virtual server* or *virtual host* is a Web server that runs on the same machine as the default server but that is distinguished from the main server by a different host name or IP address. Nonetheless, configuration directives defined for the primary server also apply to virtual servers unless specifically overridden. Conversely, directives used to configure the default server can also be used to configure virtual servers.

 The next section, "Configuring virtual servers," discusses configuration directives specific to virtual servers and discusses virtual servers in general.

Table 15-2 lists directives used to configure the default server. Again, the default values for each configuration directive, whether assigned by the Apache Group or by Red Hat, are shown in bold face.

TABLE 15-2 DEFAULT SERVER CONFIGURATION DIRECTIVES

Directive	Description
Port 80	Defines the port on which the primary server listens for connections if no BindAddress or Listen directive specifies a port number with :port; has no effect otherwise
User [#]apache	Specifies the user name or, if prefixed with #, the UID under which the child servers execute
Group [#]apache	Specifies the group name or, if prefixed with #, the GID under which the child servers execute
ServerAdmin root@localhost	Defines the e-mail address included in error messages displayed to client connections
ServerName	Specifies an alternative name for the server, such as www.mydomain.com, that is different than the host's actual name (webbeast.mydomain.com)

Directive	Description
DocumentRoot "/var/www/html"	Sets the base directory from which all requested documents will be served; document URLs (file names) are interpreted relative to DocumentRoot; see also UserDir
UserDir public_html	Defines the subdirectory in a user's home directory that is used when clients request documents belonging to a specific user
DirectoryIndex filename	Specifies one or more filenames that serve as a directory index when a request does not specify a particular file or document
AccessFileName .htaccess	Lists one or more file names in the complete path to the requested document that define and control access to documents in each directory or subdirectory at the same level as or below the topmost directory where the file(s) specified by AccessFileName (if any) is found
UseCanonicalName On	Controls how Apache constructs a self-referential URL; if set to On, use ServerName and Port; if set to Off, use the host name and port supplied by the client (if any) or the canonical name otherwise
TypesConfig /etc/mime.types	Sets the file name of the MIME types configuration file (relative to ServerRoot if the file name does not begin with /), which maps file name extensions to content types (see also AddType)
DefaultType text/plain	Defines the default MIME type when a requested document's MIME type cannot be determined using the TypesConfig or AddType directives
HostnameLookups Off	Controls whether or not Apache performs DNS lookups on connecting hosts in order to log host names
ErrorLog /var/log/httpd/ error_log	Defines the name of Apache's error log, relative to ServerRoot if the file name does not begin with /
LogLevel warn	Sets the amount and detail of information Apache records in its error log

Continued

TABLE 15-2 DEFAULT SERVER CONFIGURATION DIRECTIVES *(Continued)*

Directive	Description
LogFormat *formatstr*	Defines the format in *formatstr* Apache uses for messages it logs in the access log (see also TransferLog and CustomLog)
CustomLog /var/log/httpd/ access_log combined	Defines the name of Apache's access log and the log format used when logging requests to the server
ServerSignature On	Directs Apache to append the ServerName and version number as a footer to generated documents, such as error message, FTP file listings, and so forth
Alias *urlpath dirpath*	Links the directory *urlpath*, specified relative to DocumentRoot, to the file system directory *dirpath*, which is outside the server's file system
ScriptAlias *urlpath dirpath*	Functions exactly like the Alias directive and also indicates that *dirpath* contains executable CGI scripts
IndexOptions FancyIndexing	Specifies the behavior of Apache's directory indexing feature
AddIconByEncoding *icon mimeencoding*	Sets *icon* as the icon to display next to files with the MIME encoding of *mimeencoding*; used with the FancyIndexing directive
AddIconByType *icon mimetype*	Sets *icon* as the icon to display next to files with the MIME type of *mimetype*; used with the FancyIndexing directive
AddIcon *icon name*	Sets *icon* as the icon to display next to files ending with *name*; used with the FancyIndexing directive
DefaultIcon /icons/ unknown.gif	Sets the default icon displayed next to files whose MIME or content type cannot be determined; used with the FancyIndexing directive
AddDescription *str file*	Adds the string *str* as the description for one or more files named *file*; used with the FancyIndexing directive
ReadmeName README.html	Defines README.html as the file whose contents will be appended to the end of a directory listing

Directive	Description
HeaderName **HEADER.html**	Defines **HEADER.html** as the file whose contents will be inserted at the top of a directory listing
AddEncoding *mimeencoding name*	Adds the MIME encoding specified by *mimeencoding* for files ending with *name*, overriding previous encodings for *name*
AddLanguage *mimelang name*	Maps the file name extension specified by *name* to the MIME language *mimelang*, overriding existing mappings for *name*
AddType *mimetype name*	Adds the specified *mimetype* for files ending in *name* to the list of MIME types read from the TypeConfig file

To facilitate further discussion of the directives in Table 15-2, Listing 15-2 shows the corresponding entries from Red Hat's default Apache configuration. I removed comments from the configuration file to shorten the listing and simplify the discussion.

Listing 15-2: Red Hat Linux's Default Server Configuration Directives

```
Port 80
User apache
Group apache
ServerAdmin root@localhost
DocumentRoot "/var/www/html"
<Directory />
    Options FollowSymLinks
    AllowOverride None
</Directory>
<Directory "/var/www/html">
    Options Indexes Includes FollowSymLinks
    AllowOverride None
    Order allow,deny
    Allow from all
</Directory>
UserDir public_html
DirectoryIndex index.html index.htm index.shtml index.php index.php4 index.php3
index.cgi
AccessFileName .htaccess
```

Continued

Listing 15-2 *(Continued)*

```
<Files ~ "^\.ht">
    Order allow,deny
    Deny from all
</Files>
UseCanonicalName On
TypesConfig /etc/mime.types
DefaultType text/plain
<IfModule mod_mime_magic.c>
    MIMEMagicFile conf/magic
</IfModule>
HostnameLookups Off
ErrorLog /var/log/httpd/error_log
LogLevel warn
LogFormat "%h %l %u %t \"%r\" %>s %b \"%{Referer}i\" \"%{User-Agent}i\"" combine
d
LogFormat "%h %l %u %t \"%r\" %>s %b" common
LogFormat "%{Referer}i -> %U" referer
LogFormat "%{User-agent}i" agent
CustomLog /var/log/httpd/access_log combined
ServerSignature On
Alias /icons/ "/var/www/icons/"
<Directory "/var/www/icons">
    Options Indexes MultiViews
    AllowOverride None
    Order allow,deny
    Allow from all
</Directory>
ScriptAlias /cgi-bin/ "/var/www/cgi-bin/"
<Directory "/var/www/cgi-bin">
    AllowOverride None
    Options ExecCGI
    Order allow,deny
    Allow from all
</Directory>
IndexOptions FancyIndexing
AddIconByEncoding (CMP,/icons/compressed.gif) x-compress x-gzip
AddIconByType (TXT,/icons/text.gif) text/*
AddIconByType (IMG,/icons/image2.gif) image/*
AddIconByType (SND,/icons/sound2.gif) audio/*
AddIconByType (VID,/icons/movie.gif) video/*
AddIcon /icons/binary.gif .bin .exe
AddIcon /icons/binhex.gif .hqx
AddIcon /icons/tar.gif .tar
AddIcon /icons/world2.gif .wrl .wrl.gz .vrml .vrm .iv
```

```
AddIcon /icons/compressed.gif .Z .z .tgz .gz .zip
AddIcon /icons/a.gif .ps .ai .eps
AddIcon /icons/layout.gif .html .shtml .htm .pdf
AddIcon /icons/text.gif .txt
AddIcon /icons/c.gif .c
AddIcon /icons/p.gif .pl .py
AddIcon /icons/f.gif .for
AddIcon /icons/dvi.gif .dvi
AddIcon /icons/uuencoded.gif .uu
AddIcon /icons/script.gif .conf .sh .shar .csh .ksh .tcl
AddIcon /icons/tex.gif .tex
AddIcon /icons/bomb.gif core
AddIcon /icons/back.gif ..
AddIcon /icons/hand.right.gif README
AddIcon /icons/folder.gif ^^DIRECTORY^^
AddIcon /icons/blank.gif ^^BLANKICON^^
DefaultIcon /icons/unknown.gif
ReadmeName README.html
HeaderName HEADER.html
IndexIgnore .??* *~ *# HEADER* README* RCS CVS *,v *,t
AddEncoding x-compress Z
AddEncoding x-gzip gz tgz
AddLanguage en .en
AddLanguage fr .fr
AddLanguage de .de
AddLanguage da .da
AddLanguage el .el
AddLanguage it .it
LanguagePriority en fr de
<IfModule mod_php4.c>
  AddType application/x-httpd-php .php4 .php3 .phtml .php
  AddType application/x-httpd-php-source .phps
</IfModule>
<IfModule mod_php3.c>
  AddType application/x-httpd-php3 .php3
  AddType application/x-httpd-php3-source .phps
</IfModule>
<IfModule mod_php.c>
  AddType application/x-httpd-php .phtml
</IfModule>
AddType application/x-tar .tgz
AddType text/html .shtml
AddHandler server-parsed .shtml
AddHandler imap-file map
```

Continued

Listing 15-2 *(Continued)*

```
BrowserMatch "Mozilla/2" nokeepalive
BrowserMatch "MSIE 4\.0b2;" nokeepalive downgrade-1.0 force-response-1.0
BrowserMatch "RealPlayer 4\.0" force-response-1.0
BrowserMatch "Java/1\.0" force-response-1.0
BrowserMatch "JDK/1\.0" force-response-1.0
<IfModule mod_perl.c>
  Alias /perl/ /var/www/perl/
  <Location /perl>
    SetHandler perl-script
    PerlHandler Apache::Registry
    Options +ExecCGI
  </Location>
</IfModule>
Alias /doc/ /usr/share/doc/
<Location /doc>
  order deny,allow
  deny from all
  allow from localhost .localdomain
  Options Indexes FollowSymLinks
</Location>
```

Because the default configuration file does not use `BindAddress` or `Listen` directives, the `Port 80` directive indicates that the server listens on port 80 for incoming requests. Because 80 is the default port, this does not need to be specified, but it does make the configuration slightly more transparent. When using a port below 1024, one of the privileged ports, the master server *must* be started by root. If you wish, you can configure Apache to listen on an unprivileged port (for example, with a `Port 8080` directive), in which case, the master server does not have to be run by the root user and group.

The `User` and `Group` directives indicate that the child servers are owned by the user and group apache, which are safer because they do not have the same privileges as the root user. In order to run the child servers under less privileged users in this fashion, the master server *must* be started by the root user. Why? Only processes running with root permissions can change their UID and GID at runtime in order to maintain the Linux security model.

The `ServerName` directive defines the name returned to clients if it is different from the host server's actual name. For example, if the server's DNS name is webbeast.mydomain.com, you can specify `ServerName www.mydomain.com` in order for the server to respond to requests sent to http://www.mydomain.com/.

The `DocumentRoot /var/www/html` directive sets the server's base document directory to /var/www/html, meaning that all URLs are served relative to this directory. For example, if the server is named www.mydomain.com, then given a client request for the URL http://www.mydomain.com/index.html, the server would return the file /var/www/html/index.html to the client.

Each `<Directory >`</`Directory`> block configures access information for the named directory (or directories) and its subdirectories. The first block sets the default permissions for all directories:

```
<Directory />
    Options FollowSymLinks
    AllowOverride None
</Directory>
```

In this case the applicable directory is the server's root directory, /. Other `<Directory>`</`Directory`> blocks apply to /var/www/html, /var/www/icons, and /var/www/cgi-bin.

The `Options` directive specifies the server features that apply to the named directory. Values for the `Options` directive can be a space-delimited list of one or more of the following:

◆ `All` — Enables all options except `MultiViews`. `All` is the default `Option`.

◆ `ExecCGI` — Enables execution of CGI scripts.

◆ `FollowSymLinks` — Enables the server to follow symbolic links in this directory.

◆ `Includes` — Enables SSI (server-side includes).

◆ `IncludesNOEXEC` — Enables SSI but disables the SSI #exec command and the use of #include for CGI scripts.

◆ `Indexes` — Instructs the server to return a formatted listing of a directory for which no directory index, such as index.html, exists.

◆ `MultiViews` — Enables MultiView searches. If the server receives a request for a resource that does not exist, for example, /docs/resource, then the server scans the directory for all files named resource.*, if any, assigns them the same media types and content encodings they would have had if the client had asked for one of them by name, chooses the best match to the client's requirements, and returns that document.

◆ `None` — Disables all special directory features in this directory and its subdirectories.

◆ `SymLinksIfOwnerMatch` — Instructs the server to follow only those symbolic links for which the target file or directory has the same UID as the link.

Options preceded by a + are added to `Options` currently in force, and those preceded by a - are removed from `Options` currently in force. If multiple `Options` could apply to a directory, then the most specific one is applied. However, if *all* of the options in an `Options` directive are prefixed with + or -, the options are merged.

What is Content Negotiation?

Content negotiation refers to the technique Web clients and servers use to select how to present a resource, such as a document, that is available in several different formats. For example, suppose a Web page is available in different languages. One way to select the proper language is to give the user an index page from which she chooses the desired language. Content negotiation enables the server to choose the preferred language automatically based on information a Web browser sends indicating what representations it prefers. For example, a browser could indicate that it would like to see information in French, if possible, or else in English if French is not available. Browsers indicate their preferences by transmitting specific data in each HTTP request's header. To request only French representations, the browser would send

```
Accept-Language: fr
```

The next request shows a request that accepts both French and English, but prefers French:

```
Accept-Language: fr; q=1.0, en; q=0.5
```

Note that these preferences apply only when there is a choice of representations and when the choices vary by language.

So, the only option enabled for all of the directories under the server root (/) is the `FollowSymLinks` option. From this point forward, any divergence from this default must be specified, as in following the directory block:

```
<Directory "/var/www/html">
    Options Indexes Includes FollowSymLinks
    AllowOverride None
    Order allow,deny
    Allow from all
</Directory>
```

The `AllowOverride` directive tells the server which directives declared in access files specified by the `AccessFileName` directive (`AccessFileName .htaccess`, in this case) it should honor. If set to `None`, the server ignores the access files. If set to `All`, any directive valid in the current context is enabled. For the server's root directory and its subdirectories, therefore, the server ignores access files unless `AllowOverride All` is specifically set for a given directory under the server root.

The `Order` directive controls the default access policy for various resources` such as files and directories, and the order in which the server evaluates `Allow` and `Deny` directives for those resources. `Order` can be one of the following:

◆ Order Deny,Allow — Evaluate Deny directives before Allow directives
and enable access by default. Clients not matching a Deny directive *or*
matching an Allow directive is allowed access.

◆ Order Allow,Deny — Evaluate Allow directives before Deny directives
and deny access by default. Clients not matching an Allow directive *or*
matching a Deny directive is denied access.

◆ Order Mutual-failure — Only clients appearing in the Allow list *and*
not appearing in the Deny list are permitted to access the server. This
ordering has the same effect as Order Allow,Deny. Apache's documentation states that Mutual-failure should be used instead of Order
Allow,Deny.

For the server root directory, for example, all clients are permitted to access it, and
Allow directives are evaluated before Deny directives. However, the
<Files></Files> block specifies that access to all files beginning with .ht is denied
to all clients, preventing clients from viewing their contents, an important measure
considering that access files can contain security-sensitive information (a Files
directive has the same effect for files that a Directory directive has for directories).

All directives inside an <IfModules></IfModule> block are evaluated only if
the indicated module is loaded. The default configuration file has a number of such
blocks. For example, consider the following IfModule directive:

```
<IfModule mod_mime_magic.c>
    MIMEMagicFile conf/magic
</IfModule>
```

If the mod_mime_magic module is loaded, the MIMEMagicFile directive causes
Apache to read the contents of the configuration file named magic (/etc/httpd/
conf/magic in this case), which is a file that gives Apache the ability to determine
file types by reading the first few bytes of a file (mod_mime_magic works much like
the Linux file command works and is, in fact, based on an older version of the file
command). The MIMEMagicFile directive complements and extends the MIME typing
provided by the TypesConfig /etc/mime.types directive.

The logging directives control the level and format of Apache's log output. The
directive ErrorLog /var/log/httpd/error_log specifies the error log Apache uses.
The four LogFormat directives define log formats named combined, common,
referer, and agent (yes, referer *is* misspelled). These named formats can then be
used in other log-related directives to identify the output format. For example, the
CustomLog directive CustomLog /var/log/httpd/access_log combined uses the
combined format defined previously to log entries. The CustomLog directive indicates
the file used to log all requests sent to the server. Entries look like the following:

```
127.0.0.1 - - [21/Aug/2001:01:57:17 -0600] "GET /ssitest.html HTTP/1.1"
200 203 "-" "Mozilla/5.0 (X11; U; Linux 2.4.2-2 i686; en-US; 0.7)
Gecko/20010316"
```

```
127.0.0.1 - - [21/Aug/2001:01:57:32 -0600] "GET /ssitest.shtml HTTP/1.1"
404 296 "-" "Mozilla/5.0 (X11; U; Linux 2.4.2-2 i686; en-US; 0.7)
Gecko/20010316"
127.0.0.1 - - [21/Aug/2001:01:58:14 -0600] "GET /ssitest.shtml HTTP/1.1"
200 215 "-" "Mozilla/5.0 (X11; U; Linux 2.4.2-2 i686; en-US; 0.7)
Gecko/20010316"
```

These log entries from the access log record the requests the server processed when testing the `ssitest.html` Web page and when I loaded it to take the screenshot in Figure 15-3.

The long series of `AddIconByEncoding`, `AddIconByType`, and `AddIcon` directives define the various icons displayed next to files with a given icon. The directive `AddIcon /icons/tar.gif .tar`, for example, indicates that files ending with `.tar` should have the image `/icons/tar.gif` displayed next to them. Note that the directory `/icons/` was aliased to `/var/www/icons/` using the `Alias` directive `Alias /icons/ "/var/www/icons/"` earlier in the `httpd.conf` file, so the file system path to tar.gif is expanded to `/var/www/icons/tar.gif`. As a fallback measure, the directive `DefaultIcon /icons/unknown.gif` defines the default icon Apache displays if it cannot determine the file type of a given file based on the definitions given by the `TypesConfig` and `MIMEModMagic` directives and additional types appended to the MIME type listing using `AddType` directives.

The `AddLanguage` directives map file names to language encodings. So, for example, files ending with `.en` are treated as English documents, and files ending with `.en.gz` or `.en.tgz` are treated as `gzip` compressed English documents. The `LanguagePriority` directive, similarly, determines which file the server returns if the browser does not indicate a preference. For example, if the files `index.en.html` and `index.fr.html` both exist and a client does not specify a preferred content language, the server returns `index.en.html`.

The `BrowserMatch` directives set environment variables that can be used in CGI scripts and SSI based on the information in the User-Agent HTTP request header field. The first argument is the text to match from the request header. The second and subsequent arguments name the variables to set, and, optionally, the values to which they should be set. The variable assignments can take one of the following forms:

◆ *varname* — Sets *varname* to *1*

◆ *!varname* — Removes (unsets) *varname* if it was already set

◆ *varname=value* — Assigns *value* to *varname*

If a string matches multiple `BrowserMatch` strings, they merge. Entries are processed in the order in which they appear, and later entries can override earlier ones.

Configuring virtual servers

Table 15-3 shows the Apache configuration directives that control the configuration and behavior of virtual servers.

TABLE 15-3 VIRTUAL SERVER CONFIGURATION DIRECTIVES

Directive	Description

`<Virtual Host  ipaddr[:port]>`
`  directives`
`</VirtualHost>`
	Defines a virtual host whose IP address is *addr* (listening on *port*, if specified); *directives* are one or more of the directives listed previously and override the directives listed for the default server

`NameVirtualHost ipaddr[:port]`	Defines the IP address *addr* (listening on *port*, if specified) for a name-based virtual host
`ServerName fqdn`	Sets the name of the virtual server to the FQDN *fqdn*
`ServerAlias altname`	Enables the virtual server to respond to one or more alternate host names *altname* when used with name-based virtual hosts

---

Virtual servers are primarily used to support multiple domains on a single system, but they can also be used to enable multiple workgroups or departments on the same network to maintain independent Web pages without burdening you with too much additional administrative responsibility or requiring dedicated departmental Web servers. A typical virtual server definition might resemble the following:

```
...
Port 80
ServerName webbeast.domain.com
NameVirtualHost 192.168.0.1
<VirtualHost 192.168.0.1>
    DocumentRoot /var/www/thisdomain
    ServerName www.domain.com
</VirtualHost>
<VirtualHOst 192.168.0.1>
    DocumentRoot /var/www/thatdomain
    ServerName www.that.domain.com
</VirtualHost>
```

This example assumes that DNS lists www.domain.com and www.that.domain.com as aliases (that is, CNAME resource records) for the IP address 192.168.0.1, meaning that lookups for those two names and for webbeast.domain.com resolve to 192.168.0.1. The NameVirtualHost directive defines the server's IP address, 192.168.0.1, and ServerName identifies the machine running the server, webbeast.domain.com. A request to www.this.domain.com is served from the /var/www/thatdomain document root directory, but requests to www.domain.com are served from /var/www/thisdomain. The main or default server serves only requests sent to localhost (127.0.0.1) because requests to all other IP addresses about which Apache knows are served by the www.domain.com except those specifically sent to www.that.domain.com.

Configuring Apache for SSI

SSI, or server-side includes, are specially-formatted statements placed in HTML documents and evaluated by the server before the server sends the document to a client. SSI lets you add dynamically generated content to an existing HTML page without needing to generate the entire page using CGI or another dynamic page generation technique. SSI is best used to add small amounts of dynamically generated content to otherwise static documents. SSI is a great way to add small pieces of information, such as the current time, to a Web page.

Enabling SSI

The default Red Hat Linux Apache configuration enables SSI for the document root (/var/www/html):

```
<Directory "/var/www/html">
    Options Indexes Includes FollowSymLinks
    AllowOverride None
    Order allow,deny
    Allow from all
</Directory>
```

The Options Include directive instructs Apache to process files it serves for SSI directives. The next step is to tell Apache which files to parse for SSI directives. Red Hat Linux uses Apache's AddType and AddHandler directives to identify SSI files:

```
AddType text/html .shtml
AddHandler server-parsed .shtml
```

The first line adds the file extension .shtml to the text/html MIME type. The AddHandler directive tells Apache that files with an .shtml extension should be processed using mod_include, the module that provides Apache's SSI support (the default Red Hat httpd.conf file should contain these directives).

TIP   If, for some reason, you have to add the `AddType text/html .shtml` and
`AddHandler server-parsed .shtml` directives to the `httpd.conf`
file, the server must be restarted to make them take effect. You can use one
of the following commands to force Apache to reread its configuration file:

```
/etc/rc.d/init.d/httpd restart
/etc/rc.d/init.d/httpd reload
```

The first command stops and restarts the server. The second one sends
Apache the SIGHUP signal, which causes it to reread `httpd.conf`. The
effect is the same regardless of which command you use.

Testing the configuration

To test the configuration, create the Web page shown in Listing 15-3, naming it
`ssitest.shtml` and placing it in Apache's document root directory (the directory
specified by the `DocumentRoot` directive):

Listing 15-3: SSI Test Document

```
<html>
<head>
 SSI Test Page
</head>

<body>
 <center>
  SSI Test Page Output
  <hr>
  <p>
   This file was last modified on:
  <p>
  <!--#echo var="LAST_MODIFIED" -->
  <p>
  <hr>
 </center>
</body>
</html>
```

SSI directives look like HTML comments. Their general form is:

```
<!--#element attribute=value ... -->
```

Because SSI directives look like comments, if SSI is improperly configured on
the server, the browser ignores the contents. Otherwise, the server creates properly

formatted HTML output that Web browsers render properly. In Listing 15-3, the SSI directive is `<!--#echo var="LAST_MODIFIED" -->`. It uses a built-in variable, `LAST_MODIFIED`, which contains the date the current file was last modified. Finally, open the document in your Web browser, using the URL `http://localhost/ssitest.shtml` if accessing the server locally or `http://your.server.name/ssitest.shtml` if accessing the server remotely (replace `your.server.name` with the name of your Web server). Figure 15-3 shows how the page appears in the Mozilla Web browser.

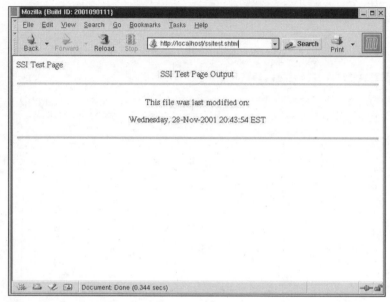

Figure 15-3: ssitest.html as seen in Mozilla

As you can see in Figure 15-3, the HTML shows that the file in question (`ssitest.shtml`) was last modified on November 28 at 8:43 p.m. After confirming that SSI is properly configured using the test page, your configuration is complete.

CGI Scripts

CGI, the Common Gateway Interface, is a protocol that defines a standard method enabling Apache (well, *any* Web server) to communicate with external programs. These programs are known as *CGI scripts* or *CGI programs*. CGI scripts are commonly used to create or update Web pages or parts of Web pages dynamically, much like SSI, but CGI scripts are more flexible than SSI and provide additional functionality that SSI cannot. For example, CGI scripts can be used for user authentication, to create a user interface on a Web page, and, within limits, in any situation in which a Web-based interface is used to execute programs and display the results in a near real-time environment. This section briefly explains Apache configuration directives and procedures that enable CGI.

As you might suspect by this point, your first task is to ensure that Apache's configuration permits CGI script execution. The `ScriptAlias` directive associates a directory name with a file system path, which means that Apache treats every file in that directory as a script. If not present, add the following directive to `httpd.conf`:

```
ScriptAlias /cgi-bin/ "/var/www/cgi-bin"
```

This directive tells Apache that any URL beginning with `/cgi-bin/` should be served from `/var/www/cgi-bin`. Thus, given a URL of `http://localhost/cgi-bin/cgiscript.pl` or `http://your.server.name/cgi-bin/cgiscript.pl`, Apache reads and executes the script `/var/www/cgi-bin/cgiscript.pl`. If necessary, modify the configuration file to include the `ScriptAlias` directive shown, and restart Apache as explained previously. Then use the script in Listing 15-4 to test the configuration.

Listing 15-4: A CGI Test Script

```perl
#!/usr/bin/perl
print "Content-type: text/html\r\n\r\n";
$now_string = gmtime;
print "Current time is $now_string";
```

Save this script as `cgitest.pl`, make it executable (`chmod a+x cgitest.pl`), and then put it in `/var/www/cgi-bin`. Finally, open the URL `http://localhost/cgi-bin/cgitest.pl` if accessing the server locally or `http://your.server.name/cgi-bin/cgitest.pl` if accessing the server remotely (replace *your.server.name* with the name of your Web server). Figure 15-4 shows sample output from the CGI test script.

If you see similar output, your server's CGI configuration works. If you enable CGI execution for other directories, make sure to test those configuration options as well before putting the server into production.

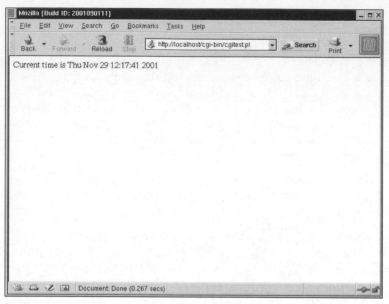

Figure 15-4: The CGI test script viewed in Mozilla

Creating a Secure Server with SSL

A secure Web server consists of two components: the SecureSockets Layer (SSL) protocol and, usually, a digital certificate from a Certificate Authority (CA). SSL provides encrypted communications and handles authentication needs between a Web browser and your Web server. A CA provides a generally accepted digital certificate and provides an additional level of authentication for your Web server because the CA guarantees that your Web server is, in fact, *your* Web server and not someone else's. To create a secure Web server, you must have at least the following four packages installed:

◆ *apache* – Provides the Apache Web server.

◆ *mod_ssl* – Installs the mod_ssl Apache loadable module, which provides strong encryption for Apache and gives Apache the ability to use SSL and its companion protocol, Transport Layer Security (TLS).

◆ *openssl* – Implements the SSL and TLS protocols and a general purpose encryption library.

◆ *mm* – Enables multiple instances of Apache to share state information.

Obtaining a Digital Certifcate from a Certificate Authority

Obtaining a digital certificate from a CA is an uncomplicated but potentially time-consuming process. Briefly, here are the steps to take to obtain a CA-issued digital certification:

1. Create a private and public key pair to use for encrypting communication with your Web server.

2. Using the newly created public key, create a certificate request containing information about your server and the company with which the server is associated.

3. Send the certificate request, accompanied by documents verifying your identity, to the CA of your choosing. To see a list of reputable, generally accepted CAs, click the Security button on your browser's toolbar, then click Signers to view a list of CAs from whom your browser (and, by extension, most popular browsers) accepts certificates.

4. After the CA satisfies itself that your supporting documents confirm your identify, they issue you a digital certificate.

5. Install the certificate on your Web server, and it can process secure transactions.

A secure Web server uses a digital certificate to identify itself to Web browsers. This chapter shows you how to generate your own certificate, known as a *self-signed certificate.* You can also obtain a certificate from Certificate Authority or CA. A certificate from a reputable CA guarantees to people using your Web site that your site is associated with your company or organization. Self-signed certificates should not be used in most production environments because self-signed certificates are not automatically accepted by a Web browser. Rather, the browser asks the user if they wish to accept the certificate before creating a secured connection. After you create a self-signed certificate (or obtain a signed certificate from a CA), you need to install it so Apache can use it to create SSL-encrypted communication sessions.

Generating the encryption key

If you installed Apache during the initial Red Hat Linux installation or afterward using the RPM, a temporary key and a test certificate were automatically generated for you in order to enable Apache's default configuration to work properly. However, to use the secure server, your must generate your own key and create or obtain a certificate that properly identifies your server. The first step is to generate a key using the following procedure:

1. Remove the temporary key and certificate files generated during the installation:

```
# cd /etc/httpd/conf
# rm ssl.key/server.key
# rm ssl.crt/server.crt
```

2. Create your own key file:

```
# /usr/bin/openssl genrsa 1024 > ssl.key/server.key
```

You should see output that resembles the following:

```
Generating RSA private key, 1024 bit long modulus
.................++++++
.......++++++
e is 65537 (0x10001)
Enter PEM pass phrase:
```

3. Type a password or pass phrase and press Enter.

4. When prompted, retype the password or pass phrase to verify that it is correct:

```
Verifying password - Enter PEM pass phrase:
```

5. Execute the following command to ensure that permissions are correctly set on the key file:

```
# chmod go-rwx /etc/httpd/conf/ssl.key/server.key
```

 Make a backup copy of server.key and keep the backup copy in a safe, secure place. If you lose server.key *after* using it to create your digital certificate request, the certificate will no longer work and the CA will not be able to help you — you must request and pay for a new certificate.

Generating a self-signed certificate

After creating your encryption key, use the following command to create a self-signed certificate:

1. Execute the following commands:

```
# cd /etc/httpd/conf
# make testcert
```

You should see output resembling the following:

```
umask 77 ; \
/usr/bin/openssl req -new -key
/etc/httpd/conf/ssl.key/server.key -x509 -days 365 -out
/etc/httpd/conf/ssl.crt/server.crt
Using configuration from /usr/share/ssl/openssl.cnf
Enter PEM pass phrase:
```

2. Enter the password you created in the previous section to confirm your identity.

3. After your password is accepted, the certificate generation process prompts you for additional information. Respond to the prompts, which should resemble the following (the output shown is wrapped because of layout constraints). The responses you enter are shown in bold face:

```
You are about to be asked to enter information that will be
incorporated into your certificate request.
What you are about to enter is what is called a Distinguished
Name or a DN.
There are quite a few fields but you can leave some blank
For some fields there will be a default value,
If you enter '.', the field will be left blank.
-----
Country Name (2 letter code) [AU]:US
State or Province Name (full name) [Some-State]:Indiana
Locality Name (eg, city) []:Indianapolis
Organization Name (eg, company) [Internet Widgits Pty
Ltd]:KurtWerks
Organizational Unit Name (eg, section) []:
Common Name (eg, your name or your server's hostname)
[]:localhost.localdomain
Email Address []:kwall@kurtwerks.com
```

4. Restart the server after generating the certificate using the following command:

```
# /etc/rc.d/init.d/httpd restart
```

Testing the self-signed certificate

After generating the key and certificate as explained in the previous two sections, you should have a file named /etc/httpd/conf/ssl.key/server.key, which contains your key, and a file named /etc/httpd/conf/ssl.crt/server.crt, which contains your certificate. To test the new certification, point your Web browser at your server's home page using the URL https://your.web.server/.

The s after http in the URL is *required*. The https prefix is used for secure HTTP transactions. The unsecured server can still be accessed using the more familiar http prefix in the URL.

If you are not using a certificate from a CA, follow the instructions provided by your browser to accept the certificate. You can accept the defaults by clicking Next until the dialogs are finished. Once the browser accepts the certificate, you will see your default home page. Unlike the unsecured Apache server, which uses port 80, the secure server uses port 443. The default Red Hat configuration for the secured server listens to both ports, so no further configuration is necessary.

Summary

This chapter introduced you to Apache Web server configuration. You received an overview of the Apache project and a short history of the Apache server. After you found out how to download, build, and install Apache, you learned in detail how to configure Apache for your Red Hat Linux system. In the last three sections you saw how to use server-side includes and CGI scripts and how to configure a secure Apache server using SSL.

Part IV

Red Hat Linux System Maintenance

IN THIS PART:

This part provides a detailed discussion of the tasks required to maintain your system and ensure that it runs optimally. Chapters in this part deal with using the Red Hat Network, upgrading and customizing the kernel, configuring the system on the command line, and using scripts to automate tasks. This part also discusses performance monitoring, administering users and groups, backing up and restoring the file system, and installing software packages.

Chapter 16

Using the Red Hat Network

THE RED HAT NETWORK is a program that is installed by default when you install the Red Hat operating system Version 7 or greater. The package is also available for Version 6.2 and can be downloaded from the Red Hat Web site. The Red Hat Network software is used to register a profile with Red Hat that contains information about the software packages installed on your system. Whenever a package update is available, for whatever reason, you receive an e-mail notification from Red Hat.

This might not sound like much at first, but think about the many steps involved in keeping your system up-to-date with the latest versions of the hundreds of packages that are installed on your system. The Red Hat Network practically eliminates the need for you to search for these packages because you receive this information by e-mail. As a registered Red Hat Network user, you can also search for updates by using the Update Agent. With the introduction of the Red Hat Network, you can now easily keep your system running reliably and securely. A few steps are involved in setting up the Red Hat Network, but they are well worth the effort. In this chapter you learn how to register your system with Red Hat, configure the Update Agent, and then connect to look for updated files. The first step is registering, and this procedure is covered in the next section.

Registering Your System

Before you can begin using the Red Hat Network, you must first register your system with Red Hat by using the Red Hat Network registration client. You should first check that the necessary software is installed on your system by issuing the following command.

```
rpm -q rhn_register
```

If the registration client is installed, you should see the name of the package and its version number, similar to the following:

```
rhn_register-1.3.1-1
```

If the package is not installed, you see

```
package rhn_register is not installed
```

 You may also register for the Red Hat Network at the Red Hat Web site by using your Web browser to go to `http://ww.redhat.com/network` and filling in the online registration form.

In addition to the rhn_register package needed for registration, you also need the Update Agent package, up2date, to be able to obtain the updates from Red Hat. If you are planning to register and run the Update Agent graphically using GNOME or KDE, two additional packages are required — rhn_register-gnome and up2date-gnome. In my opinion it is much easier to use the graphical interface to update the system, and I highly recommend it. If the packages are not installed, you can find them on CD 1 of Red Hat Version 7 or greater, or you can download them from the Red Hat FTP site. If you are downloading the packages, be sure that you obtain the latest version. After downloading the necessary packages, you can install them using the `rpm -i` command.

After you are sure that the necessary packages are installed, you can begin to register your system with the Red Hat Network. You must be logged in as root to perform the registration and you must have a connection to the Internet to be able to log on to the Red Hat Web site. If you are not connected to the Internet, you receive an error message and the program closes when you click OK.

Start the registration client by following the appropriate step for your system.

◆ From the command line type **rhn_register**.

◆ From the KDE desktop, click the K on the Panel Main Menu → System → Red Hat Network.

◆ From the GNOME desktop, click the Main Menu Icon → Programs → System → Red Hat Network.

You now see the Red Hat Network welcome screen that provides a description and lists the benefits of the Red Hat Network. If you choose not to use the Red Hat Network, you can click Cancel to end the process. Otherwise, click Next to continue to the Red Hat Privacy Statement screens, and then click Next to go to the User Account screen shown in Figure 16-1.

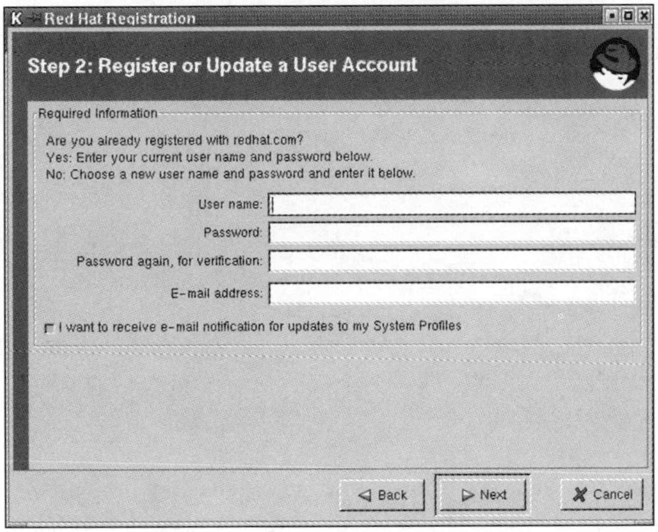

Figure 16-1: The Red Hat Network User Account screen is where you enter your personal information.

On this screen you must fill in the user name and password that you want to use to access the Red Hat Network. The user name must be at least four characters and can not contain any spaces, tabs, line feeds, or reserved characters such as ', &, +, or %. You also enter your e-mail address here and can indicate that you want to receive e-mail notification of updates by checking the box. When you have entered the appropriate information, click Next to continue to another screen that enables you to enter additional information about yourself. All information on this page is optional, so you can fill in the information if you choose. Whether you enter additional information on this page or not, click Next to continue.

You now register a system profile for the hardware in your system. You do this by giving your system a profile name and, optionally, a service ID number. Figure 16-2 shows the System Profile – Hardware registration form.

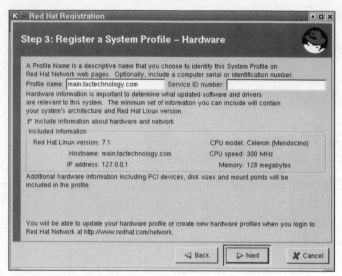

Figure 16-2: The System Profile – Hardware registration screen lists information about your system architecture and Red Hat version number.

On this screen, the default Profile name is the hostname of the computer, but you may change this to whatever name you like. You may also enter a Service ID number that helps you to identify the computer. The Service ID number is not a requirement. The check box for including information about your hardware and network is checked by default. Information about your computer's architecture and Red Hat version number are automatically filled in by the registration client from probing your system. If you don't want this information in your system profile, click the box to disable this feature. When you are finished, click Next to continue.

The registration client now probes your system to determine which packages are installed on your system. When the probing is finished, a list similar to that shown in Figure 16-3 is displayed showing all the packages on your system, and by default they are selected to be included with your system profile.

If you do not want a package included, click the box next to the package name to remove it from the list. After making your selections, click Next to continue. Your system profile now is sent to the Red Hat Network. After the registration process is finished, you receive a confirmation message stating that you have successfully registered your system profile on the Red Hat Network. Now you are ready to configure the Update Agent.

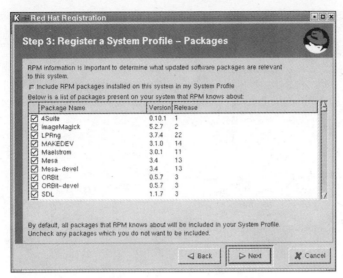

Figure 16-3: The Packages registration screen shows the packages installed on your system.

Configuring the Red Hat Update Agent

Before you can use the Red Hat Update Agent, you need to configure it. Start the Update Agent Configuration tool as follows.

◆ From the command line type **up2date-config**.

◆ From the KDE desktop, click the K on the Panel → System → Update Agent Configuration.

◆ From the GNOME desktop, click the Main Menu Icon → Programs → System → Update Agent Configuration.

The Red Hat Network Configuration dialog box, as shown in Figure 16-4, now opens.

This dialog box has three tabs labeled General, Retrieval/Installation, and Package Exceptions. The General tab is the tab shown by default when the dialog box opens. If you need to use a proxy server to connect to the Web, you can enter this information here by first clicking the box labeled Enable HTTP Proxy, and then entering the name of your server in the field next to the check box. If you need to use authentication, you can enable it by clicking the Use Authentication check box and filling in the fields with the Username and Password.

The next tab is the Retrieval/Installation settings tab shown in Figure 16-5.

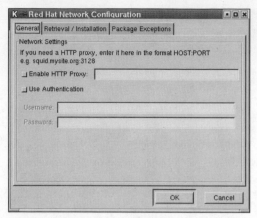

Figure 16-4: The Red Hat Network Configuration dialog box enables you to change the configuration of the Update Agent.

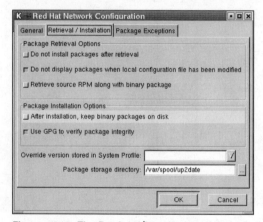

Figure 16-5: The Retrieval/Installation dialog box options control package retrieval and installation.

In this dialog box you can choose options that affect how the packages are retrieved and subsequently installed. The package retrieval options are

◆ Do not install packages after retrieval – By default, packages are automatically installed after they are retrieved. If you enable this option, packages are retrieved to the specified directory but not installed.

◆ Do not display packages when local configuration file has been modified – If you have manually modified configuration files for packages on your system, these packages are not displayed by default. If you disable this option, the packages are displayed.

◆ Retrieve source RPM along with binary package – By default the source RPM is not downloaded with the binary version of the package. By enabling this option, you also retrieve the source of the RPM.

The package installation options are

◆ After installation, keep binary packages on disk – By default, the packages are removed from the local disk after they are installed. Enabling this option leaves a copy of the package in the specified directory.

◆ Use GPG to verify package integrity – By default, for security purposes, the packages are verified to ensure they contain the Red Hat GPG signature. If you disable this option, the security check is not performed.

The last two options in this dialog box are

◆ Override version stored in System Profile – By filling in the field you can override the version stored in your System Profile with the version in the field.

◆ Package storage directory – Here you can specify the storage location of the packages on your system.

The last tab is the Package exceptions tab. Choosing this tab opens the Package Exception dialog box shown in Figure 16-6.

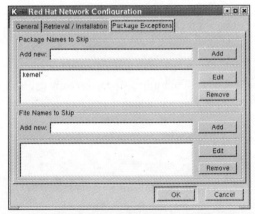

Figure 16-6: The Package Exceptions dialog box lets you choose to exclude packages.

In this dialog box, you can choose to exclude packages by either the name of the package or the name of the file. To exclude a package by package name, type the name of the package in the Add new field in the Package Names to Skip section, and then click the Add button. To exclude a package by file name, type the name of the file in the Add new field in the File Names to Skip section, and then click the Add button.

After you have made any changes to the three tabbed dialog boxes, click OK. Your configuration changes are saved and you can now use the Update Agent.

Using the Red Hat Update Agent

The Update Agent is a valuable tool for you, as it helps you to keep your system running the most current versions of the packages installed on your system. Be sure you are logged in as root before running the Red Hat Update Agent.

 The Red Hat Network is free for one system only. If you are installing the Red Hat Network on more than one system, you receive a message for each additional system telling you to go to the Red Hat Network site and enable the software for your system. You have to purchase additional licenses for each additional system.

The Update Agent can be started as follows:

- ◆ From the command line type **up2date**.
- ◆ From the KDE desktop, click the K on the Panel → System → Update Agent.
- ◆ From the GNOME desktop, click the Main Menu Icon → Programs → System → Update Agent.

If you are running the Update Agent from the command line, you can use the options listed in Table 16-1 (obtained from Red Hat).

TABLE 16-1 COMMAND LINE OPTIONS

Argument	Description
--configure	Graphically configure Red Hat Update Agent options through the Red Hat Update Agent Configuration Tool.
-d, --download	Download packages only, do not install them. This argument overrides the configuration option Do not install packages after retrieval.

Argument	Description
-f, --force	Force package installation. This option overrides the file, package, and configuration skip lists.
-i, --install	Install packages after they are downloaded. This argument overrides the configuration option Do not install packages after retrieval.
-k, --packagedir	Specify a colon separated path of directories to look for packages before trying to download them.
-l, --list	List packages available for retrieval/installation.
--nosig	Do not use GPG to check package signatures.
--tmpdir=directory	Override the configured package directory. The default location is /var/spool/up2date.
--justdb	Only add packages to the database and do not install them.
--dbpath	Specify a path where an alternate RPM database to use is found.

When the Update Agent starts, you are prompted to install the Red Hat GPG key that is used to verify the Red Hat security signature on the downloaded packages. Click Yes to install the key. You now see the Red Hat Update Agent Welcome screen as shown in Figure 16-7.

 If you are running the Update Agent from the command line and do not have X installed, you have to install the GPG key manually. Go to the Red Hat Web site address http://www.redhat.com/about/contact. Click the link Public Encryption key, and then click download. From the command line, issue the following command to install the key:

gpg -import redhat.asc

You should receive a message indicating that the key was installed.

To begin updating your system, click Next and the Update Agent connects to the Red Hat Network to obtain a list of updates for your system. If your system is already current, you see a dialog box telling you that no additional packages are needed. If your system is in need of updating, you see a list of packages that can be retrieved, similar to that shown in Figure 16-8.

Figure 16-7: The Red Hat Update Agent Welcome screen

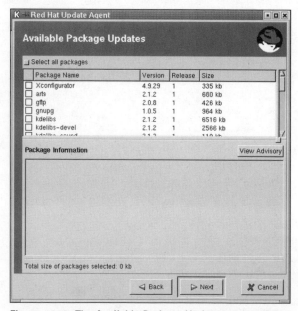

Figure 16-8: The Available Package Updates screen lists updated packages you can download.

You must choose the packages you want to download by clicking the box to the left of the package name. To select all packages, click the button to the left of Select all packages. After you've finished selecting packages, click Next. You see the status of the download as each package is retrieved and an All Finished when all packages have been retrieved. If you didn't change the default setting in the Update Configuration Retrieval/Installation settings to automatically install packages, the packages that were retrieved are immediately installed after download. You see a progress indicator as they are being installed followed by an All Finished message. The All Finished screen lists the packages that have been updated. Click Finish to end the Update Agent session.

As long as you install the latest packages automatically, your system always synchronizes with System Profile stored on the Red Hat Network. If you download and install the packages yourself, you must update the RPM package list in your System Profile manually by running the command:

```
up2date -p
```

Using the Red Hat Network via the Internet

You can access the Red Hat Network using any Web browser. In fact if you have multiple machines, you can manage them at the same time. All you need to do is go to the Red Hat Web site at `http://www.redhat.com/network` and log in (see Figure 16-9).

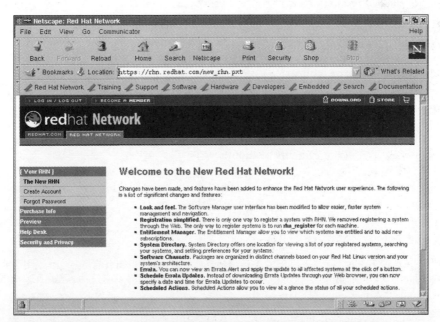

Figure 16-9: Logging in to the Red Hat Network from the Red Hat Web site

You use the same user name and password that you used when you registered your System Profile earlier in this chapter. After logging in, your main page, as shown in Figure 16-10, displays.

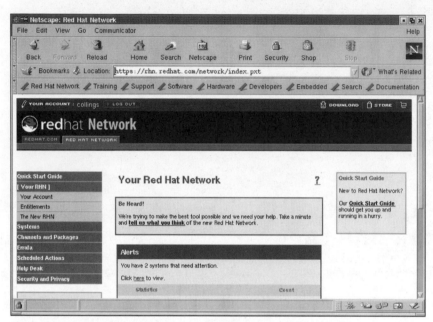

Figure 16-10: The Red Hat Network Main page for your System Profile

Red Hat Network Main page tab

The Main page shown in Figure 16-10 may not look exactly like your page. The information shown here is dependent on the preferences you may have chosen. Beginning at the top of the page is the navigation bar for choosing other pages presenting different information. Moving down the page is the Software Manager section which shows the status, either on or off, of e-mail notification, security alerts, bug fixes, and enhancements available.

Total System Profiles is the number of profiles registered with the Red Hat Network. The last item on the page is the Latest Errata Alerts section, which lists the type of advisory and the package to which it relates.

Your Network page tab

Returning to the Navigation Bar, click Your Network to see the status of your entire network. Each system that is registered with the Red Hat Network is shown here. See Figure 16-11 for a sample view of this page.

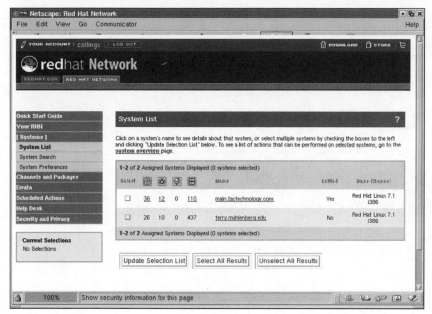

Figure 16-11: The Your Network page of the Red Hat Network shows all of the systems you have registered.

The three tabs on this page are Systems Overview, Errata Alerts, and Assign Service Levels.

SYSTEMS OVERVIEW

On the Systems Overview tab, in addition to showing each system on your network, any alerts for each system are shown to the left of the system name with different icons representing different types of alerts.

Clicking an individual system name shows detailed information about that system as well as additional tabs for Errata Alerts, Package Profile, and Hardware Profile. The detailed information is the system architecture and the operating system and version number.

To add a new system, click the Add System Profile link in the far right column of the first empty row. After entering the system, you need to click the upgrade link in the Service Level column or click the Assign Service Levels tab to upgrade or downgrade a system or purchase additional licenses.

ASSIGN SERVICE LEVELS

Figure 16-12 shows the Assign Service Levels page.

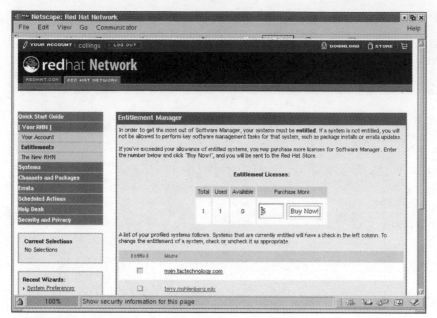

Figure 16-12: You can purchase additional licenses on the Assign Service Levels page.

On the left side of this screen are the systems for which service has not been registered, shown in a box titled, as you might expect, no service. On the right side are the systems for which service has been registered, titled Software Manager. You can select a system from either box and upgrade or downgrade it as appropriate. But you can have only one free system, so if you want to register additional systems and create System Profiles, you need to purchase additional licenses. And you can do so on this page.

ERRATA ALERTS

The Errata Alerts tab shows alerts for the currently selected system in five columns. The first column, status, indicates whether you have read the file. The second column shows the date of the alert. The third column describes the type of alert, the fourth column is a link to more detailed information about the alert, and the last column shows how many of your systems are affected by the alert. Clicking the Errata Report link for an alert takes you to another page that enables you to download the update or add it to a list of files you wish to download.

If you have configured your retrieval/installation settings to automatically download and install updated packages, it is not necessary to manually download them.

Search Errata Alerts tab

Returning to the Main page, click the Search Errata Alerts tab on the navigation bar. This page enables you to search for all available errata by location, type, or date. This feature may be useful for finding information about earlier operating system releases or specific types of alerts.

Preferences tab

The Preferences tab is where you can change many of the "look and feel" options of the Red Hat Network. Figure 16-13 shows the Preferences page and the many items that can be modified.

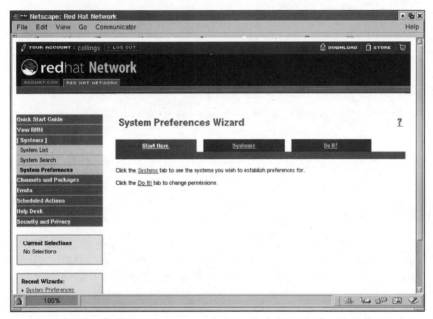

Figure 16-13: The Preferences page is the place to change the functionality and appearance of the Red Hat Network.

The Errata Alerts and RPM Updates tab lets you choose the information you want displayed and its location. You can choose for which systems you want updates displayed, and you can choose the category of RPMs you want.

The General tab is where you set the date and time display, the timeout value for account inactivity, and the security level for your connection.

The Customize Main Page tab controls the information displayed on your Main page after you log in to the Red Hat Network. Here you can choose your favorite guides and forums that can help you obtain information on various topics with a single mouse click.

Finally, the User Info tab is where you go to change your password or contact information. The password was created when you registered your account. The contact information was sent to the Red Hat Network when you registered your system if you filled out the optional personal information form.

After making any changes, be sure to click the Update Account button at the bottom of each page. If you make any changes but do not click the Update Account button, the changes are not registered.

Help Desk tab

This tab takes you to online help. Selections from this tab deal with security and privacy and terms and conditions. You will also find a FAQ section and a link to contact Red Hat Customer Service. Here also is information for using the Red Hat Network with Red Hat Linux Version 6.2.

You should not routinely install the latest update of a software package without considering the implications of such an action. You should research the update and decide whether installing the updated package would benefit your system. In many cases, updating one package can affect the operation of other programs running on your system, perhaps even making them unrunnable.

Summary

In this chapter you learned about the Red Hat Network, which is used for updating your system. The Red Hat Network continuously monitors your system based on the profile you registered. Whenever an updated version of a package is available, the Red Hat Network notifies you of the type of update via e-mail so you can take immediate action. Using the Red Hat Network ensures that you are running the latest and most secure versions of the packages installed on your system. This means that you work more efficiently and your system is more secure and productive.

Chapter 17

Upgrading and Customizing the Kernel

BECAUSE THE LINUX KERNEL is available in source code form, you can customize it to fit precisely your needs. This chapter shows you how to rebuild the Red Hat Linux kernel. In particular, it covers whether and when to upgrade the kernel, where to obtain the source code, how to download and install it, how to configure the source code specifically for your system, how to compile it, how to install a new kernel, and how to configure your system to boot the new kernel while retaining the ability to boot a known good kernel should something go awry.

Should You Upgrade to a New Kernel?

As you know, the kernel is the core of the operating system, and runs the CPU, manages system memory, controls access to disk drives, and contains device drivers that enable you to interact with the system and use the hardware and peripherals attached to the computer. As perverse as it might seem at first glance, the ability to update and customize the Linux kernel is one of the things that many like best about Linux. Naturally, this feature appeals most to incurable tweakers and tinkers, but it also appeals to system administrators who are responsible for wringing the most performance and benefit out of their existing hardware and software. In some cases, rebuilding the kernel is required in order to support new hardware that is not supported, or that is poorly supported, by your system's existing kernel.

419

Should you upgrade to a new kernel? Strictly speaking, no. That is, it is rarely *necessary* to do so. The kernel provided with Red Hat Linux supports the vast majority of existing PC hardware. Moreover, practically all of the functionality that most users need (both in hobbyist and home environments and in business and professional settings) is already available in the current kernel (version 2.4.9 at the time this paragraph was written). Finally, many users, especially those coming from a predominantly Windows environment, are conditioned to downloading and installing the latest and greatest version of application X, whether or not they need the features and bug fixes it provides. The fact is that most users do not need to do this because they use perhaps 20 percent of the feature sets of existing software. Adding still more unused features contributes to software bloat and, potentially, to system instability.

In some cases, however, it *is* necessary to rebuild the kernel, usually to provide better support for the odd hardware device, to add support for new hardware you have added to an existing system, to add a driver for a device not supported by the existing kernel, to fix the occasional bug, or to close a security hole.

These caveats notwithstanding, it is almost always *desirable* to create a custom kernel. The stock Red Hat Linux kernel is configured and compiled to support the widest possible array of hardware. Although there is nothing wrong with that, you can usually achieve better performance with a smaller kernel that you have configured to fit precisely the hardware you have and to fit into the software environment.

So much for the practical reasons for and against upgrading to a new kernel. A significant portion of the Linux community, particularly home users, hobbyists, and developers, constantly upgrade and rebuild their kernels simply because they can or for the sheer satisfaction of the undertaking. "Because I can," "because it's there," or "because I want to" are not therefore less valid because they are not immediately practical. For many, including the authors of this book, Linux is a hobby, just as is stamp collecting or flying model airplanes — few people question the value of these more traditional hobbies or ask why people pursue them, so why should this newer hobby be considered any different?

Chances are, however, that if you are reading this book, the previous paragraph amounts to preaching to the choir. If not, the following list summarizes the most common reasons you might want or need to upgrade or customize the kernel on your Red Hat Linux system:

◆ You can recompile the kernel to support your specific CPU, especially features that improve performance. The default Red Hat Linux installation installs a kernel configured to run on the widest possible variety of Intel CPUs. As a result, it does not take advantage of all the features and improvements available in the newest CPUs.

◆ Similarly, the default kernel often includes system features that you do not need or does not include features that you do need or want. Customizing and recompiling the kernel enables you to remove unnecessary or unwanted features and to add needful and desired features.

◆ The default kernel supports an enormous variety of the most common hardware, but no single system needs all of that support. You might want to create a new kernel that includes support for only the hardware actually installed on your system.

◆ If you have a system with hardware not supported when you installed Red Hat Linux or for which only experimental support was available, you can rebuild the kernel to include that support once it becomes available or to improve existing support.

Upgrading versus customizing

As used in this chapter, *upgrading the kernel* and *customizing the kernel* refer to two different procedures, although both require recompiling and installing the kernel. *Customizing the kernel* refers to reconfiguring an existing kernel source code tree, recompiling it, installing the new kernel, and booting it. *Upgrading the kernel* means obtaining an updated version of the kernel source code, either the complete source tree (now over 21MB) or one or more patches (described later in the section titled "Patching the kernel"), followed by reconfiguring, recompiling, installing, and booting the new kernel. To put it another way, upgrading the kernel means obtaining new source code and customizing it. The end result of both upgrading and customizing the kernel is the same: a new kernel configured to your liking.

Checking your current kernel version

Before building a new kernel, in particular upgrading the kernel, you need to know which version you are running. You have several ways to check the current version. The canonical method that works on any running Linux system is to use the `uname` command, which displays a single line of output containing a variety of system information, depending on the command line option used. Its syntax is:

```
uname [-amnrspv]
```

Invoked with no options, `uname` prints `Linux`. To obtain the kernel version that is currently running, use the `-r` option, which prints the operating system release level. For example:

```
$ uname -r
2.4.6-3.1
```

The first three numbers are the kernel version, so the system in question is running kernel version 2.4.6. The last two numbers, 3.1, are Red Hat specific, indicating that the running kernel is the third build of the RPM for version 2.4.6 of the kernel. The kernel build instructions provided later in the chapter build a kernel from pristine source code downloaded from one of the dozens of kernel archive sites. The downloaded kernel source does not include the last two Red Hat–specific kernel version numbers.

Table 17-1 lists the meanings of uname's other options.

TABLE 17-1 uname COMMAND LINE OPTIONS

Option	Description
-a	Displays all information
-m	Displays the hardware (CPU) type
-n	Displays the system's host name
-s	Displays the operating system name (equivalent to uname)
-p	Displays the system's processor type
-v	Prints the Linux version, that is, when it was compiled

The -v option consists of a sequence number followed by a date and time stamp, useful information if you build several kernels in a single day:

```
$ uname -v
#1 Tue Jul 24 14:54:56 EDT 2001
```

Another way to check which version of the kernel you are running is to query the RPM database. You can use either of the following commands. The first command shows only the version of the kernel binary that is installed.

```
$ rpm -q kernel
kernel-2.4.6-3.1
```

The next command shows all the kernel related RPMs installed.

```
$ rpm -qa | egrep kernel
kernel-headers-2.4.6-3.1
kernel-doc-2.4.6-3.1
kernel-source-2.4.6-3.1
kernel-2.4.6-3.1
kernel-pcmcia-cs-3.1.27-5
```

Using RPM to install, upgrade, and query RPM packages is covered in detail in Chapter 23. The next section of this chapter, "Building a New Kernel," shows the bare bones command to install the kernel related RPMs if they are not installed.

The second command queries the entire RPM database and uses the egrep command to show only the output lines that contain the word "kernel." If you are considering rebuilding your kernel, the second command is probably more useful to you because it lets you know which kernel related packages you have installed. The following list briefly describes each package.

- **kernel-headers:** Contains the C header files for the Linux kernel. The header files define structures and constants that are needed for building most standard programs, and are also needed for rebuilding the kernel.

- **kernel-doc:** Contains documentation files from the kernel source. Various portions of the Linux kernel and the device drivers shipped with it are documented in these files. Install this package if you need a reference to the options that can be passed to Linux kernel modules at load time.

- **kernel-source:** Contains the source code files for the Linux kernel.

- **kernel:** Contains the Linux kernel, the core of the Red Hat Linux operating system.

- **kernel-pcmcia-cs:** Contains a set of loadable kernel modules that implement PCMCIA (also known as *CardBus*) support for laptop computers.

Building a New Kernel

Rebuilding the kernel involves the following steps:

1. Downloading and installing the kernel source code

2. Configuring the kernel

3. Building the kernel

4. Building and installing kernel modules (if any)

5. Installing the kernel and setting up the GRUB boot loader

The rest of this chapter describes these steps in greater detail. If you choose not to upgrade to the latest kernel version and simply want to customize your current kernel, you can skip ahead to the section titled "Customizing the kernel" and continue reading from there. The sections, "Obtaining the latest kernel version" and

"Patching the kernel," assume that you want to download and install the most current version of the kernel source code.

Obtaining the latest kernel version

After you have determined the version of the kernel you are currently running, the next step is to obtain the latest version of the kernel source code. For simplicity's sake, the discussion assumes you want to use the stable kernel version. At any given time, there are almost always two versions of the Linux kernel available, the stable or production version and the unstable or development version. You can differentiate between the versions by looking at the kernel version numbers.

The kernel version numbering system is easy to understand. Kernel versions are numbered using the format *major.minor.patch*, where *major* is the major version number, *minor* is the minor version number, and *patch* is the patch level. The *major version number*, currently 2, changes very infrequently and represents substantial or fundamental changes between kernel releases. The *minor version number*, 4 in the examples shown in the previous section, changes much more often as new features are added to the kernel, such as new file systems, as major subsystems undergo significant remodeling, as significant bugs are fixed, or as security patches are incorporated into the source code. The *patch level* (6 in the previous examples), finally, represents minor changes, such as corrected typos, updates to README files, and the like – little of the functionality changes.

The minor version number is the key to distinguishing between the stable and development kernels. An even-numbered minor version denotes a stable kernel and an odd-numbered minor version signifies a development kernel. Currently, for example, the stable kernel version is 2.4; the development or unstable kernel, which is not yet under development because efforts are focused on stabilizing the newly-released 2.4 series kernels, will probably be numbered 2.5. To be precise, at the time this paragraph was written, the stable kernel version was 2.4.9 (major version 2, minor version 4, patch level 9), while the development branch will be 2.5 when Linux starts accepting new features for possible inclusion in the next release of the production kernel, which will be numbered either 2.6 or 3.0.

Unless you like living on the edge or are actively involved in kernel development, stick with the production or stable kernel releases. Development kernels are, by definition, unstable and might crash, if they compile at all. If you do decide to play with the unstable kernel versions, use them on a system you do not mind trashing or reinstalling because you might have to do precisely that. Under *no* circumstances should you run a development series kernel on a mission-critical system or one containing valuable data.

INSTALLING THE KERNEL SOURCE CODE FROM RPMS

If you want simply to play with the kernel, it is easiest to load the source code from the kernel RPMs on the Red Hat Linux CD-ROMs. The complete source code distribution runs to more than 22MB, so unless you have broadband access to the Internet, it is also *faster* to use the Red Hat RPMs. If the RPM command shown in the previous section did not produce output resembling the examples, you need to install the kernel RPMs. To do so, follow these steps:

1. Log in as `root` and insert the Red Hat Linux CD-ROM (disk 1) into the CD-ROM drive.

2. Use the `mount` command to mount the CD-ROM drive on a directory in the file system:

   ```
   # mount /mnt/cdrom
   ```

3. Install the `kernel-headers` RPM using the following command:

   ```
   # rpm -ivh /mnt/cdrom/RedHat/RPMS/kernel-headers*
   Preparing...
   ########################################### [100%]
      1:kernel-headers
   ########################################### [100%]
   ```

   Note that the output shown in the text wraps to another line, due to the book's page layout.

4. Unmount the first CD-ROM:

   ```
   # umount /mnt/cdrom
   ```

5. Place the second installation CD-ROM (disk 2) in the drive and mount it as shown in Step 2.

6. To install the kernel source files and documentation, use the following command:

   ```
   # rpm -ivh /mnt/cdrom/RedHat/RPMS/kernel-{doc,source}*
   Preparing...
   ########################################### [100%]
      1:kernel-doc
   ########################################### [ 50%]
      2:kernel-source
   ########################################### [100%]
   ```

   The output shown in the text wraps to another line, due to the book's page layout.

   The installation might appear to proceed slowly, especially with the kernel source code RPM, because it is over 23MB. After RPM finishes installing the kernel source package, the necessary source files appear in the `/usr/src/linux-2.4` directory.

After installing the source code from the RPMs, you can skip ahead to the section titled "Customizing the kernel."

INSTALLING THE KERNEL SOURCE CODE FROM THE INTERNET

The method the authors of this book prefer for upgrading and customizing the kernel is to work with the pristine source code as distributed from the various kernel archive sites scattered around the Internet. Why? Each major Linux vendor, including Red Hat, applies patches to the kernel source code that support the hardware of their strategic partners. There is nothing wrong with this practice because Linux is open source software, but it *does* have the unfortunate side effect of causing the source code distributed by Red Hat to diverge from the source code Linux maintains. As a result, applying patches becomes a hit-or-miss affair (see the section titled "Patching the kernel" to learn how and why to use kernel patches to upgrade the source code).

The primary site for the kernel source code is `http://www.kernel.org/` (see Figure 17-1).

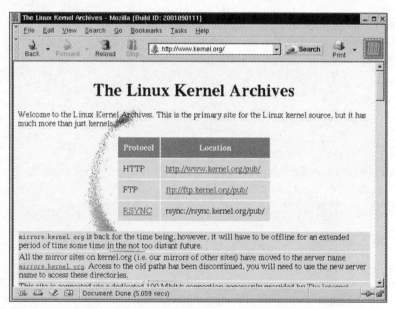

Figure 17-1: The Linux Kernel Archives home page

However, because kernel.org is heavily loaded, especially after a new release, you are better off using one of its many mirrors throughout the world. Often, you can find one close to you — most countries have at least one mirror and some, like the United States and the United Kingdom, have many. In fact, the Linux Kernel Archives Mirror System, described following Figure 17-2, currently consists of

112 sites in 46 countries or territories, and another 195 countries or territories are supported from remote sites. To locate a mirror near you, point your Web browser at `http://www.kernel.org/mirrors/`, scroll down the alphabetically-ordered list of countries, and click your country name to view a list of mirror sites in your country. Figure 17-2, for example, shows part of the list of HTTP mirror sites in the United States:

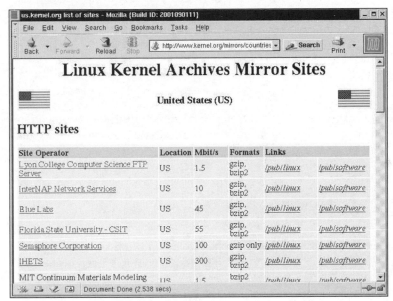

Figure 17-2: Linux Kernel Archives mirror sites in the United States

The kernel's archive mirror system is set up so that for each two-letter country code you can simply use the host names `http://www.`*country*`.kernel.org/` or `ftp.`*country*`.kernel.org` to reach a mirror supporting that specific country. For example, in the United States, you would use the URL `http://www.us.kernel.org/` in your Web browser. Each mirror has a full archive of `/pub/linux`, the top-level kernel source directory, but it may not carry the source code in both gzip and bzip2 compression formats — the bzip2 format takes less time to download than gzip format.

After locating an archive that is near you, in network terms, download the desired file. The instructions that follow assume you use the standard FTP client in a terminal window, such as an xterm.

1. Change directories to a directory to which you have write permission, for example, your home directory:

   ```
   $ cd ~
   ```

2. Open an FTP session to the archive site you selected and log in as the anonymous user using your e-mail address as the password:

```
# ftp ftp.us.kernel.org
220 ProFTPD 1.2.0pre10 Server (Global NAPs)
[kernel.gnaps.com]
Name (ftp.us.kernel.org:root): anonymous
331 Anonymous login ok, send your complete e-mail address as
password.
Password:
230 Anonymous access granted, restrictions apply.
Remote system type is UNIX.
Using binary mode to transfer files.
ftp>
```

3. Change directories to the kernel source code directory. The exact location of this directory varies from mirror to mirror, so you may have to use the ls command to locate it.

```
ftp> cd /pub/linux/kernel
```

4. Change directories to the v2.4 directory:

```
ftp> cd v2.4
```

5. Execute the following command to see a listing of the full source code trees for the 2.4 kernel series (the listing is truncated to preserve space):

```
ftp> ls linux-2.4*
...
-rw-r--r--   1 kernel    kernel    22192379 Aug 11 04:13 linux-2.4.8.tar.bz2
-rw-r--r--   1 kernel    kernel         248 Aug 11 04:13 linux-2.4.8.tar.bz2.sign
-rw-r--r--   1 kernel    kernel    27402470 Aug 11 04:13 linux-2.4.8.tar.gz
-rw-r--r--   1 kernel    kernel         248 Aug 11 04:13 linux-2.4.8.tar.gz.sign
-rw-r--r--   1 root      kernel    22232256 Aug 16 18:32 linux-2.4.9.tar.bz2
-rw-r--r--   1 root      kernel         248 Aug 16 18:32 linux-
2.4.9.tar.bz2.sign
-rw-r--r--   1 root      kernel    27474071 Aug 16 18:32 linux-2.4.9.tar.gz
-rw-r--r--   1 root      kernel         248 Aug 16 18:32 linux-
2.4.9.tar.gz.sign
```

6. Identify the file to download. In this case, I download the 2.4.8 archive file in bzip2 format, that is, linux-2.4.8.tar.bz2.

7. Make sure you are in binary download format:

```
ftp> binary
```

8. Use the following commands to download the archive file and its MD5 checksum file (`linux-2.4.8.tar.bz2.sign`):

```
ftp> get linux-2.4.8.tar.bz2
ftp> get linux-2.4.8.tar.bz2.sign
```

9. Close the FTP session:

```
ftp> bye
```

After you have the archive file, verify the file's integrity and unpack it as described in the next section.

VERIFYING AND UNPACKING THE ARCHIVE

Before you unpack the archive, you should check its signature to make sure that it has not been tampered with. Files placed in the Linux Kernel Archives are OpenPGP-signed, and you can use that digital signature to prove that a file, especially one obtained from a mirror site or any other location, really originated at the Linux Kernel Archives. The current Linux Kernel Archives OpenPGP key is always available from `http://www.kernel.org/signature.html`.

 The OpenPGP signature does *not* guarantee that the Linux Kernel Archives master site itself has not been compromised, only that the file you obtained has not somehow been altered.

The first step is to import the Linux Kernel Archive key. With an active Internet connection, execute the following command:

```
$ gpg --keyserver wwwkeys.pgp.net --recv-keys 0x517D0F0E
gpg: requesting key 517D0F0E from wwwkeys.pgp.net ...
gpg: key 517D0F0E: public key imported
gpg: Total number processed: 1
gpg:               imported: 1
```

This step adds the Linux Kernel Archive key to root's public key ring. Next, change directories to the directory in which you downloaded the source files and execute the following commands, again as the root user, to verify the file signature:

```
$ gpg --verify linux-2.4.8.tar.bz2.sign linux-2.4.8.tar.bz2
gpg: Signature made Fri 10 Aug 2001 10:21:01 PM MDT using DSA key ID
517D0F0E
gpg: Good signature from "Linux Kernel Archives Verification Key
<ftpadmin@kernel.org>"
```

As long as you see the two lines of output shown in the example (beginning with gpg:), the file is authentic. Replace the file names used in the preceding command with file names that reflect the files you downloaded. Because you probably have not added a trusted path to the archive verification key, this command probably also generates the following error message, which you can safely disregard:

```
Could not find a valid trust path to the key.  Let's see whether we
can assign some missing owner trust values.

No path leading to one of our keys found.

gpg: WARNING: This key is not certified with a trusted signature!
gpg:          There is no indication that the signature belongs to the owner.
gpg: Fingerprint: C75D C40A 11D7 AF88 9981  ED5B C86B A06A 517D 0F0E
```

Now you are ready to unpack the archive. If you downloaded a bzip2 format archive file, execute the following command:

```
$ bunzip2 -c linux-2.4.8.tar.bz2 | tar -xf -
```

This command uncompresses the archive file using bunzip2 and pipes the output to the tar command, which extracts the archive. The operation might take some time to complete because bzip2 compression and decompression takes longer than the more familiar and faster gzip compression. If you downloaded the gzip formatted archive, the proper command to use is:

```
$ gunzip -c linux-2.4.8.tar.gz | tar -xf -
```

The end result of either command is a new directory named linux in the directory in which you decompressed and extracted the archive that contains version 2.4.8 of the Linux kernel source code.

Patching the kernel

If you have already downloaded the main source code tree, you can save both bandwidth and time by downloading and applying patches. Patches contain only changes to the underlying files from one kernel version to the next. For example, if you downloaded the 2.4.8 kernel source code tree, you do not need to download the 2.4.9 source code, only the patch, which is named, in this case, patch-2.4.9.tar.bz2. If, alternatively, you have the source code for version 2.4.5, you need to download four patches (patch-2.4.9.tar.bz2, patch-2.4.9.tar.bz2, patch-2.4.9.tar.bz2, patch-2.4.9.tar.bz2) and apply them in sequential order. The following procedure illustrates the process:

1. Change directories to a directory to which you have write permission, for example, your home directory:

```
$ cd ~
```

2. Open an FTP session to the archive site you selected and log in as the anonymous user using your e-mail address as the password:

```
# ftp ftp.us.kernel.org
220 ProFTPD 1.2.0pre10 Server (Global NAPs)
[kernel.gnaps.com]
Name (ftp.us.kernel.org:root): anonymous
331 Anonymous login ok, send your complete e-mail address as
password.
Password:
230 Anonymous access granted, restrictions apply.
Remote system type is UNIX.
Using binary mode to transfer files.
ftp>
```

3. Change directories to the kernel source code directory. The exact location of this directory varies from mirror to mirror, so you may have to use the ls command to locate it.

```
ftp> cd /pub/linux/kernel
```

4. Change directories to the v2.4 directory:

```
ftp> cd v2.4
```

5. Execute the following command to see a listing of the full source code trees for the 2.4 kernel series (the listing is truncated to preserve space):

```
ftp> ls patch-2.4*
...
-rw-r--r--   1 root      kernel       785040 Aug 11 04:13
patch-2.4.8.bz2
-rw-r--r--   1 root      kernel          248 Aug 11 04:13
patch-2.4.8.bz2.sign
-rw-r--r--   1 root      kernel      1008692 Aug 11 04:13
patch-2.4.8.gz
-rw-r--r--   1 root      kernel          248 Aug 11 04:13
patch-2.4.8.gz.sign
-rw-r--r--   1 root      kernel       607194 Aug 16 18:32
patch-2.4.9.bz2
-rw-r--r--   1 root      kernel          248 Aug 16 18:32
patch-2.4.9.bz2.sign
-rw-r--r--   1 root      kernel       722077 Aug 16 18:32
patch-2.4.9.gz
-rw-r--r--   1 root      kernel          248 Aug 16 18:32
patch-2.4.9.gz.sign
```

6. Identify the file or files to download. In this case, I download the 2.4.p patch file in bzip2 format, that is, `patch-2.4.9.tar.bz2`.

7. Make sure you are in binary download format:

```
ftp> binary
```

8. Use the following commands to download the archive file and its MD5 checksum file (`patch-2.4.8.tar.bz2.sign`):

```
ftp> get patch-2.4.9.bz2
ftp> get patch-2.4.9.bz2.sign
```

9. Close the FTP session:

```
ftp> bye
```

10. Use the procedure described earlier to verify the downloaded file, substituting the appropriate file names.

The next step is to apply the patch. To do so, change directories to the directory in which you unpacked the kernel source code. So, for example, if you unpacked the kernel source code in your home directory, change to that directory. Next, execute the following command for each patch file, in sequential order:

```
$ bunzip2 -c patch-2.4.NN.bz2 | patch -p0
```

Replace *NN* with the patch number of each patch you want to apply. In terms of the example used in this chapter, because I downloaded the full 2.4.8 source code tree, I need only apply the patch to version 2.4.9. So, the command to execute is

```
$ bunzip2 -c patch-2.4.9.bz2 | patch -p0
patching file linux/CREDITS
patching file linux/Documentation/Configure.help
patching file linux/Documentation/DMA-mapping.txt
patching file linux/Documentation/SubmittingDrivers
...
patching file linux/net/unix/af_unix.c
patching file linux/net/wanrouter/wanmain.c
patching file linux/net/wanrouter/wanproc.c
patching file linux/net/x25/af_x25.c
```

The exact list of file names varies from patch to patch, and some patches change more files than others. The end result, however, is a kernel source tree updated to the latest version.

Finally, execute the following two commands to ensure you are working with a pristine source tree:

```
$ cd linux
$ make mrproper
make[1]: Entering directory `/home/kwall/linux/arch/i386/boot'
rm -f tools/build
rm -f setup bootsect zImage compressed/vmlinux.out
rm -f bsetup bbootsect bzImage compressed/bvmlinux.out
make[2]: Entering directory
`/home/kwall/linux/arch/i386/boot/compressed'
rm -f vmlinux bvmlinux _tmp_*
make[2]: Leaving directory
`/home/kwall/linux/arch/i386/boot/compressed'
...
rm -f .depend
rm -f /home/kwall/linux/scripts/mkdep-docbook
make[1]: Leaving directory `/home/kwall/linux/Documentation/DocBook'
```

The `make mrproper` command removes any detritus remaining from previous kernel compiles — if you are starting from scratch, you can skip this step, but it does no harm to include it, either. At this point, you are ready, at length, to configure the kernel.

Customizing the kernel

Customizing the kernel involves two steps, choosing between building a modular or monolithic kernel, and then performing the actual kernel configuration. When configuring the kernel, you have two options for the device drivers needed to support various hardware devices in Linux:

♦ *Build device support directly into the kernel.* You can build the drivers for all hardware on your system into the kernel. As you can imagine, the size of the kernel grows as device driver code is incorporated into the kernel. A kernel that includes all necessary device driver support is called a *monolithic kernel.*

♦ *Use modules to provide device support.* You can create the necessary device drivers in the form of modules. A *module* is a block of code that the kernel loads and unloads on an as-needed basis while it is running. Modules enable you to add support for a device without having to rebuild the kernel for each new device you add to your system. Modules do not have to be device drivers; you can use them to add any sort of new functionality to the kernel. A kernel that uses modules is called a *modular kernel.*

As it happens, you do not have to choose between fully monolithic or fully modular kernel. Creating a *hybrid* kernel is a common practice, one that links some support directly into the kernel while building other, infrequently used device drivers in the form of modules. For a company such as Red Hat, it makes sense to distribute a modular kernel. Red Hat provides a generic kernel along with a large number of modules to support many different types of hardware. The installation program configures the system to load only those modules needed to support the hardware installed in a user's system. The example shown in this chapter builds a hybrid kernel.

After choosing between a modular or monolithic kernel, you begin the configuration process proper. You can use one of three options for the configuration interface: an X Window System-based configuration tool, a text based GUI, or an interactive, command-line based tool. The end result is the same, so choose the interface with which you feel most comfortable. The example configuration that follows concentrates on the X-based configuration, but the overall process is the same for all three methods. Regardless of which method you choose, you must be in the linux directory created when you unpacked the source code archive before beginning:

```
$ cd ~/linux
```

CONFIGURING THE KERNEL USING MAKE XCONFIG

Type make xconfig to use an X Window System-based configuration program to configure the kernel. After a short pause, during which the GUI tool builds itself, you see a dialog box resembling Figure 17-3.

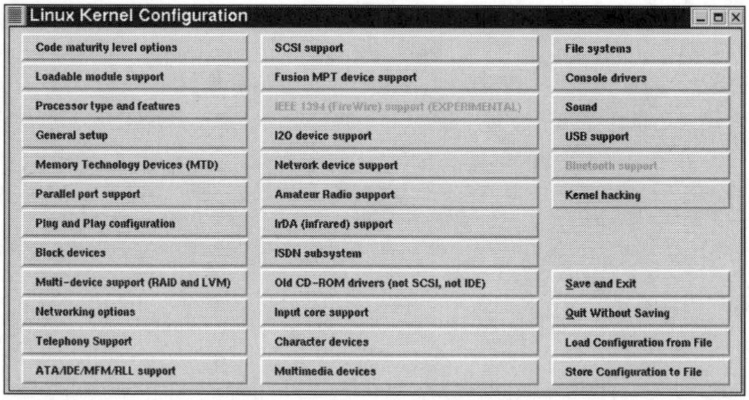

Figure 17-3: The Linux Kernel Configuration dialog box

To configure the kernel, click each button in the main dialog box and select the configuration options that suit your needs or liking. You will find it easiest to start with the Code maturity level options (see Figure 17-4).

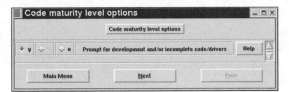

Figure 17-4: The Code maturity level options dialog box

Some of the various things that Linux supports (such as network drivers, new hardware devices, network protocols, and so on) have not been adequately tested. Clicking Y in the Code maturity level options dialog box enables you to select and configure such options during the configuration process. Clicking N disables these features, and you will not be prompted for them. This option also makes obsolete drivers available, that is, old drivers that have been replaced by something else or that are scheduled to be removed in a future kernel release. You should probably click N here unless you enjoy living on the edge or running the risk of crashing your system.

As you configure the kernel, you have to select how to include support for specific devices. For many configuration options, you must choose one of the following:

◆ Click *y* to build support for a given option into the kernel or to accept a configuration option.

◆ Click *m* to use a module for the indicated device or option (not available for all configuration items).

◆ Click *n* to skip the support for that specific device or to disable that item.

For example, in the Code maturity level options dialog box, click the radio button next to *y* if you want to enable configuration dialog boxes for experimental features or incomplete device drivers. Click the *n* radio button if you do not want to see such dialog boxes. Note that in this case, if you select *y* and then click the Main Menu button to return to the main configuration dialog box, buttons that were previously greyed out, such as the IEEE 1394 (FireWire) support (EXPERIMENTAL) and the Bluetooth support buttons, are now available. If a device does not have a modular device driver, you do not see the *m* option.

The kernel configuration discussed in this chapter does not illustrate configuring experimental kernel options.

For almost every configuration option in a given configuration dialog box, you can click the Help button to get detailed or additional information about the option in question. Figure 17-5 shows the configuration help for the sole option in the Code maturity level options dialog box. When you are done reading the help text, click the OK button to close the help screen.

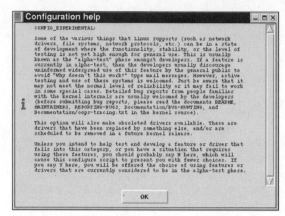

Figure 17-5: A Configuration help dialog box

After you have completed selecting the configuration options in a dialog box, click the Next button to proceed to the next dialog box. All dialog boxes except the first one enable you to click the Prev button to return to the previous dialog box, and all dialog boxes have a Main Menu button that returns you to the main Linux Kernel Configuration dialog.

The next few pages illustrate most of the main configuration dialogs and describe their purpose and the effect the options have on the compiled kernel. Due to space restrictions, all of the possible dialog boxes are not covered, nor are all of the possible configuration options. If you need additional information, use the Help button in the configuration dialogs.

Figure 17-6 shows the Loadable module support dialog box. As explained earlier in the chapter, kernel modules are small pieces of compiled code which can be inserted in or removed from a running kernel to add and remove support for infrequently used hardware devices and to enable and disable support for other types of functionality. If you want to use modules, click *y* for all three options. If you are unsure, you should still click *y* for all three options. Later in the configuration process, you need to identify which drivers and kernel functionality to build as modules, which to include in the kernel, and which to disregard completely.

If you click *y* for the third item, Kernel module loader, the kernel is able to load modules without requiring your intervention. Be sure to read the file `Documentation/kmod.txt` to learn how to configure `kmod`, the kernel module autoloader. Click Next to continue with the configuration.

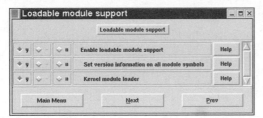

Figure 17-6: The Loadable module support dialog box

In the next dialog box, shown in Figure 17-7, you can customize the kernel for your particular CPU. Proceed cautiously here because you can easily create a kernel that doesn't boot. This information is used to configure the build process to optimize code generation to take advantage of specific CPU features. In order to compile a kernel that can run on Intel x86 CPUs, click the 386 option.

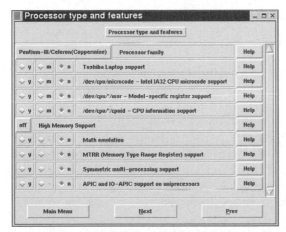

Figure 17-7: The Processor type and features dialog box

Here are the settings, taken from the help text, recommended for the best speed on a given CPU:

◆ 386 for the AMD/Cyrix/Intel 386DX/DXL/SL/SLC/SX, Cyrix/TI86DLC/ DLC2, UMC 486SX-S and NexGen Nx586

◆ 486 for the AMD/Cyrix/IBM/Intel 486DX/DX2/DX4 or SL/SLC/SLC2/ SLC3/SX/SX2 and UMC U5D or U5S

◆ 586/K5/5x86/6x86/6x86MX for generic Pentium CPUs

◆ Pentium-Classic for the original Intel Pentium processors

- `Pentium-MMX` for the Intel Pentium MMX

- `Pentium-Pro/Celeron/Pentium-II` for the Intel Pentium Pro/Celeron/ Pentium II

- `Pentium-III/Celeron(Coppermine)` for the Intel Pentium III and Celerons based on the Coppermine core

- `Pentium-4` for the Intel Pentium 4

- `K6/K6-II/K6-III` for the AMD K6, K6-II and K6-III (also known as K6-3D)

- `Athlon/Duron/K7` for the AMD K7 family (Athlon/Duron/Thunderbird)

- `Crusoe` for the Transmeta Crusoe series

- `Winchip-C6` for original IDT Winchip

- `Winchip-2` for IDT Winchip 2

- `Winchip-2A/Winchip-3` for IDT Winchips with 3dNow! capabilities

- `CyrixIII/C3` for VIA Cyrix III or VIA C3

Unless you have more than 1GB of physical RAM installed in your system, leave High Memory Support set to *off*. Similarly, if you do not have multiple CPUs, select *n* for Symmetric multiprocessing support. You can safely leave the other options at their default values as shown in Figure 17-7. Click Next to continue.

You can use the General setup dialog box, shown in Figure 17-8, to enable and disable a variety of miscellaneous kernel features. Again, the default values are reasonable for most systems. However, if you are not configuring a kernel for a laptop, click the PCMCIA/CardBus support button, click *n* for PCMCIA/CardBus support on the PCMCIA/CardBus support dialog box, and then click OK to save the change. Click Next to continue.

If you do not use flash memory chips or similar devices, click the Next button in the appropriate dialog boxes to skip each of the following configuration dialogs:

- Memory Technology Devices (MTD)

- RAM/ROM/Flash chip drivers

- Mapping drivers for chip access

- Self-contained MTD device drivers

- NAND Flash Device Drivers

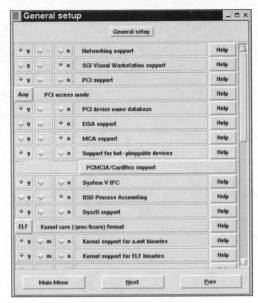

Figure 17-8: The General setup dialog box

Eventually, you see the Parallel port support configuration dialog box, shown in Figure 17-9. You should click *y* or *m* for both the Parallel port support and PC-style hardware options if you want to use a printer, ZIP drive, or other device attached to your system's parallel port. Click Next to continue.

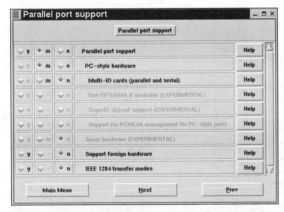

Figure 17-9: The Parallel port support dialog box

Figure 17-10 shows the Plug and Play configuration dialog box. Most modern PCs and PC BIOSes support the Plug and Play protocol, so click *y* or *m* for the Plug and Play support, and if you have any legacy ISA bus devices, click *y* or *m* for the ISA Plug and Play option. If you do not have ISA devices in your system, leave this option disabled (click *n*) and then click Next to continue.

Figure 17-10: The Plug and Play configuration dialog box

The Block devices dialog box (see Figure 17-11) enables you to configure support for block devices such as disk drives, drives attached to the parallel port, a few RAID controllers (such as the Compaq SMART2 and Mylex RAID cards), and RAM disks, which are important if you need initrd (Initial RAM Disk) support, such as for booting from a SCSI disk. A *block device* is so-named because I/O to such a device occurs in groups, or blocks, of bytes, rather than one byte at a time as occurs with character devices, which read and write one character at a time.

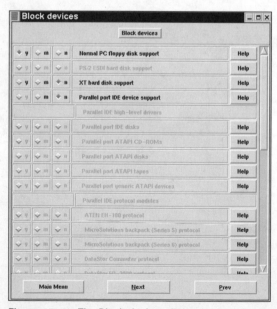

Figure 17-11: The Block devices dialog box

At a bare minimum, click *y* or *m* for Normal PC floppy disk support (unless, for some reason, your system does not have a standard 3.5-inch floppy drive). If you have one of the parallel port IDE devices, click *m* for Parallel port IDE device support, and then click *m* next to the device you want to use. Be sure, in this case, to read the help text and note any conditions, qualifications, or caveats related to driver support for the selected device. Scroll down to the bottom of the dialog box and click *y* for RAM disk support, followed by *y* for Initial RAM disk (initrd) support if you know that you need an initial RAM disk (initrd) in order to boot — the easiest way to make this determination is to execute the command `ls -l /boot`. If you see a file name that begins with `initrd`, such as `initrd-2.4.2.img`, then you need initrd and RAM disk support. Click Next to continue.

Figure 17-12 shows the configuration dialog for enabling kernel support for software RAID (Redundant Array of Independent Disks) and for LVM (Logical Volume Management). Software RAID enables you to combine multiple hard disk partitions to create a single logical block device. It is called Software RAID because the kernel, rather than special hardware, implements the RAID functionality. LVM combines multiple devices in a volume group. A *volume group* is roughly analogous to a virtual disk. You can resize volume groups after creating them as your disk space capacity requirements change. For more information, read `Documentation/LVM-HOWTO`. Most people do not need this support, which is disabled by default.

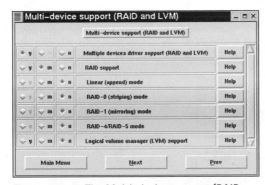

Figure 17-12: The Multi-device support (RAID and LVM) dialog box

The Networking options dialog box (see Figure 17-13) enables you to configure a wide array of networking options for your system. If you want to use programs like tcpdump, a packet sniffer that facilitates troubleshooting opaque network problems, click *y* or *m* for the Packet socket option. If you connect this system to the Internet and want to use a packet filter (firewall), click *y* to enable Network packet filtering, which enables you to use the Netfilter firewall feature, which replaces ipchains (the 2.2 kernel packet filter). Netfilter also enables you to use your Red Hat Linux system for IP masquerading. *IP masquerading*, also known as *NAT* or Network Address Translation, enables you to route all Internet traffic through a single system without requiring all systems to have valid Internet addresses (IPs) and without making the systems on the internal network visible to the Internet. Make sure, too that the following three options are enabled, because they provide standard networking functionality:

- ◆ Unix domain sockets
- ◆ TCP/IP networking
- ◆ IP: multicasting

Scrolling down in the Networking options dialog box, click *y* for IP: TCP syn-cookie support, which enables legitimate users to continue to use systems that are experiencing a SYN flood, a type of denial of service attack. If you do enable this option, you also need to enable `sysctl` and `/proc` file system support later in the configuration process (which you should do anyway) and add the following command to `/etc/rc.d/rc.local` or another initialization script:

```
echo 1 > /proc/sys/net/ipv4/tcp_syncookies
```

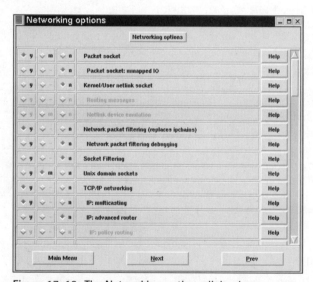

Figure 17-13: The Networking options dialog box

 Chapter 26 explains how to use both ipchains and iptables to create and maintain firewalls.

If you need support for IPX or the Appletalk protocols, enable those options as well, and then click Next to view the IP: Netfilter Configuration dialog box. If you intend to use IP masquerading, click *m* or *y* to enable the Connection tracking and IP tables support options. If you are building a modular kernel, click *m* for the following options:

◆ Packet filtering

◆ REJECT target support

◆ Full NAT

◆ MASQUERADE target support

◆ REDIRECT target support

◆ Packet mangling

◆ LOG target support

◆ ipchains (2.2-style) support

Click Next to bypass the IPv6: Netfilter Configuration and QoS and/or fair queuing dialog boxes.

When you get to the ATA/IDE/MFM/RLL dialog box, you should almost certainly click *y* here unless you have a *SCSI only* system, and then click Next to display the IDE, ATA and ATAPI Block devices dialog box, shown in Figure 17-14. Click *y* or *m* for Enhanced IDE/MFM/RLL disk/cdrom/tape/floppy support if you have any IDE devices that you want to use — if you want to boot from such a device, like an IDE disk drive, click *y* to build support into the kernel. You might want to enable PCMCIA IDE support if your laptop uses PCMCIA devices. Scrolling down, you can disable and enable support for specific devices such as IDE CD-ROM and floppy drives, for bug fixes and workarounds for specific IDE chipsets that have known problems, such as the CMD640 or RZ1000 chipsets, and for a large number of specific chipsets and controllers. If you do not need such support, click *n*. The other values are fine at their defaults, so click Next to continue.

Figure 17-15 shows the SCSI support dialog box. This dialog box has a number of subdialogs that permit you to configure the low-level drivers pertaining to specific SCSI devices and controllers (see Figure 17-16), so take some time to review the information carefully, resorting to the help text if necessary. In particular, older SCSI controllers often need to have their I/O addresses and IRQ numbers specified in the kernel configuration dialog. Drivers for new controllers usually can auto-detect the I/O addresses and IRQ numbers.

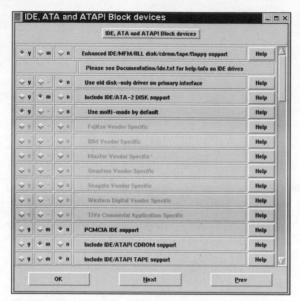

Figure 17-14: The IDE, ATA and ATAPI Block devices dialog box

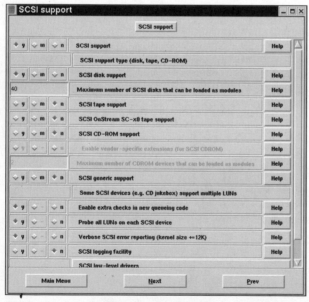

Figure 17-15: The SCSI support dialog box

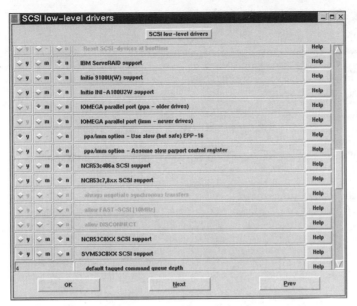

Figure 17-16: The SCSI low-level drivers dialog box

Note that if you want to use an Iomega Zip drive that attaches to a parallel port, you should click *y* or *m* for SCSI support and SCSI disk support, and then enable support for either IOMEGA parallel port (ppa – older drives) or IOMEGA parallel port (imm – newer drives) depending on the type of Zip drive. Briefly, if your Zip drive came with a cable labeled "AutoDetect," click *n* to disable the ppa module and *m* to use the imm module). The good news is that both the ppa and imm drivers enable you to use both the Zip drive and a printer while running Red Hat Linux, just as you can with Windows.

Additional information on configuring and using Zip drives under Red Hat Linux is available in the README file for the ppa module, which is part of the kernel source code distribution (see *kerneldir*/drivers/scsi/README.ppa, where *kerneldir* is the top-level directory of the kernel source tree) and also The Linux 2.4 SCSI subsystem HOWTO, which is available online at http://www.linuxdoc.org/HOWTO/SCSI-2.4-HOWTO/index.html.

Figure 17-17 shows the Network device support dialog box, which enables you to configure NICs and other networking-related hardware.

Figure 17-17: The Network device support dialog box

If you have a network card of any sort, click *y* for Network device support. The Dummy net driver support is not strictly required, but it does enable you to assign a configurable IP address to otherwise inactive PPP addresses, which can make programs requiring an Internet connection work properly. Because it does not increase the size of the kernel, click *m* or *y*. Enable FDDI support if you need support for fiber optic networking. PLIP (parallel port) support builds a module that enables you to create a network connection using the parallel port, but most people do not need this. If you are building a kernel on a system that connects to the Internet using a PPP (point-to-point protocol) connection, click *m* or *y* for PPP support and click *m* for the following options:

◆ PPP support for async serial ports

◆ PPP support for sync tty ports

◆ PPP Deflate compression

◆ PPP BSD-Compress compression

Leave SLIP (serial line) support disabled unless you use SLIP instead of PPP. Enable Fibre Channel driver support only if you need it. The dialog boxes for specific classes of network devices, such as ARCnet, Ethernet (10 or 100Mbit), Ethernet (1000Mbit), Token Ring devices, PCMCIA network device support, and so on, enable you to configure support for these devices if you need it. Although you can probably skip or ignore the dialog boxes for devices you do not use, it does not hurt anything to look at each one and make sure that support *is* in fact disabled for unnecessary devices. Each dialog box has an option at the top for disabling that category of device. Figure 17-18, for example, shows the ARCnet devices dialog box — notice that all ARCnet support is disabled (the configuration items are greyed out) because *n* is clicked for ARCnet support. Each class of devices can be similarly disabled. Use the Next button in each dialog to proceed sequentially through each class of devices.

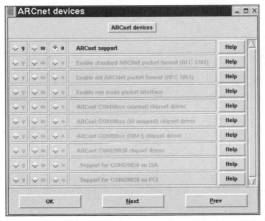

Figure 17-18: The ARCnet devices configuration dialog box

Figure 17-19 shows the configuration dialog box for 10 or 100MB Ethernet devices. Devices are organized by manufacturer, and then by make or model (and, in some cases, submodels). For instance, the system used for this chapter's example (see Figure 17-19) has a 3COM 3c590 Boomerang NIC, so support for 3COM cards in general is enabled, which activates the options for 3COM cards, and support for this particular card is being built as a module.

 You also may need specifically to disable PCMCIA network device support — for some reason, the kernel configuration enables this support on some systems, even if they do not have PCMCIA devices.

Before exiting the Ethernet (10 or 100Mbit) dialog box, make sure to scroll down to the EISA, VLB, PCI, and on board controllers option and click *n* (unless, of course, you have such a device, in which case, you should configure it).

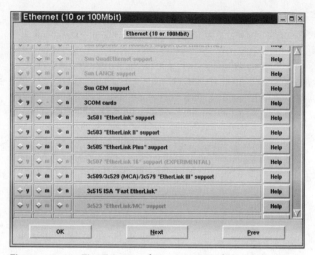

Figure 17-19: The Ethernet (10 or 100Mbit) dialog box

If you need support for proprietary CD-ROM interfaces, such as the old Panasonic or Sound Blaster CD-ROMs, configure them appropriately using the Old CD-ROM drivers dialog box, shown in Figure 17-20. *Do not use this box to configure SCSI or IDE CD-ROM drives!* You need this support only if you have one of the drives listed in the dialog box. Click the Next button to continue.

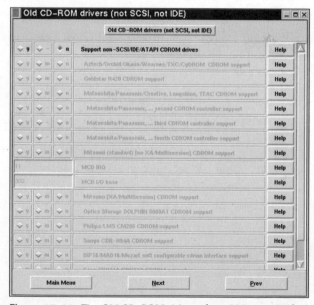

Figure 17-20: The Old CD-ROM drivers (not SCSI, not IDE) dialog box

If you need support for USB (Universal Serial Bus) input devices, such as mice, keyboards, or joysticks, click *m* or *y* for the Input core support option when you see the Input core support dialog box (see Figure 17-21), and then click *m* for the device you want to use. If you need support for a USB digitizer or graphic tablet, click *m* for Mouse support and then provide the horizontal and vertical screen resolution values in the corresponding check boxes. Click the Next button to continue.

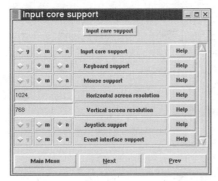

Figure 17-21: The Input core support dialog box

Figure 17-22 shows part of the configuration dialog box for character devices, which includes serial ports, keyboards (strictly speaking, TTYs), printers, mice, joysticks, tape drives, special purpose chips and devices such as watchdog cards and clock chips, and a selection of video adapters. You can also configure such devices that are provided by PCMCIA cards. Only the top of the dialog is shown because it is rather long — character devices are the primary means of interacting with a Linux system, so the array of supported devices is mind-numbingly long.

At a bare minimum, make sure that the first three configuration options are enabled:

◆ Virtual terminal

◆ Support for console on virtual terminal

◆ Standard/generic (8250/16550 and compatible UARTs) serial support

If you have a special serial card, such as a multiport serial device, click *y* for Non-standard serial port support to enable the configuration of those devices, and then select your devices from the long list of support hardware and configure it appropriately. The defaults for Unix98 PTY support should be sufficient. If you intend to use a printer attached to this system, click *m* or *y* for Parallel printer support. Support for special-purpose devices, such as the enhanced real-time clock or the hardware random number generator, is optional. Read the help text if you want to experiment with these features.

Continuing further down the character devices dialog box, the next set of options, for motherboard and graphics chipsets, is also optional. AGP (Accelerated Graphics Support) GART (Graphics Aperture Relocation Tables) support enables XFree86 to use AGP graphics acceleration for 3D display, a nice feature if your video hardware supports it. If you enable this support and have one of the support graphics chipsets, enable support for the graphics chipset and edit your XFRee86 configuration file to load the GLX module. You must also have a supported graphics chipset if you want to enable the Direct Rendering Manager, which provides kernel support for XFree86 4.1's DRI (Direct Rendering Infrastructure), which permits direct access to video hardware and results in significant performance increases for OpenGL 3D graphics. When you have completed configuring the primary character device support options, click the Next button to continue.

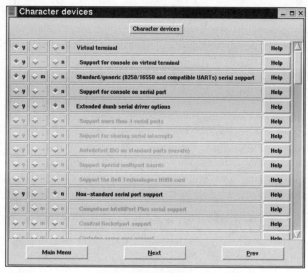

Figure 17-22: The Character devices dialog box

The next series of dialog boxes enable you to configure character devices subsets. Unless you know you need I2C support, skip the dialog by clicking Next. If you use a mouse (most users do), especially PS/2 mouse support, enable this support by clicking *y* or *m* in the Mice dialog box, and then click Next. Similarly, configure joystick support and support for various watchdog cards if you need it. The Ftape configuration dialog box enables you to configure support for a wide variety of floppy tape devices. Click Next to proceed. Finally, if you need to support PCMCIA character devices, use the PCMCIA character devices configuration to configure support for PCMCIA serial devices, and then click Next to continue.

Figure 17-23 shows the first of the series of Multimedia devices configuration dialog boxes. As usual, only enable support and configure devices you have or use, clicking Next to skip unnecessary devices.

Figure 17-23: The Multimedia devices dialog box

The primary File systems configuration dialog box, shown in Figure 17-24, enables you to configure support for the file systems you expect to use or access from your system. New in Red Hat Linux is support for the ext3 file system, which includes journaling and other high-end features. Read Chapter 4 to find out how to work with the ext3 file system and take advantage of its features and benefits, and how to avoid potential problems and known pitfalls.

If you intend to use file system quotas, as described in Chapter 21, click *y* to enable Quota support. Click *m* or *y* for Kernel automounter version 4 support (also supports v3) if you want to mount and unmount file systems on the fly. Similarly, if you need to access various DOS or Windows file systems, click *m* or *y* for DOS FAT fs support and for MS-DOS and VFAT file systems. As a general rule, build non-Linux file system support as modules to minimize the size of the kernel. Other file systems you may want to enable include

◆ Virtual memory file system support — enables the kernel to utilize swap disks and swap files

◆ ISO 9660 CD-ROMs — enables kernel support for the standard CD-ROM file system

◆ Microsoft's Joliet extensions — enables the kernel to support Microsoft Windows long file name extensions for CD-ROMs

◆ /proc file systems support — enables applications to utilize the proc interface to kernel tuning and information

◆ /dev/pts for Unix98 PTYs — enables kernel support for the standard Unix-style terminal interface

◆ ext2 — enables kernels support of the ext2 file system, the current native Linux file system

◆ ext3 — enables the kernel to support the ext3 file system, a journaling version of the ext2 file system

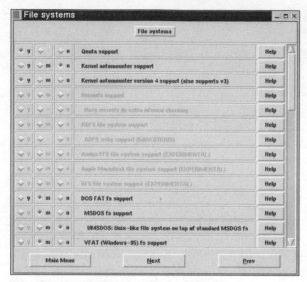

Figure 17-24: The File systems dialog box

Click Next to continue, which brings up the Network File Systems configuration dialog box, shown in Figure 17-25. I recommend enabling support for NFS (Network File System) version 3, which has considerable improvements and better kernel support for NFS, so click *y* for Provide NFSv3 client support and Provide NFSv3 server support.

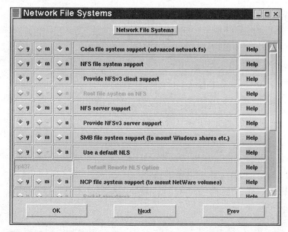

Figure 17-25: The Network File Systems dialog box

Chapter 7 discusses NFS server and client configuration in detail. Chapter 9 explains how to use Samba to access Windows file systems.

If you want to use Samba to access Windows file systems, click *m* or *y* for SMB file system support (to mount Windows shares, and so forth). Similarly, click *m* or *y* for NCP file system support if you need to mount Netware file systems, and then select the specific options for Netware file systems as fits your situation. When you are done, click Next to continue.

In addition to support for foreign (non-Linux) file systems, you will find it advantageous to configure the kernel to provide support for foreign partition types. After clicking *y* for Advanced partition selection on the Partition Types dialog, select the specific partition types you want to use by clicking *y* next to the appropriate partition types listed in the dialog box. When you have finished, click Next to continue, which brings up the Native Language Support configuration dialog box. Here, click *m* or *y* to load the code page for your particular locale or language, and then click Next to continue, which opens the Console drivers dialog box, shown in Figure 17-26.

Click *y* to enable both VGA text console and Video mode selection support. The latter option enables you to use the `vga=` kernel option to select the high resolution text modes your video adapter most likely supports. The file `Documentation/svga.txt` in the kernel source code tree explains how to use this feature in greater detail. Click Next to continue the configuration process.

Figure 17-26: The Console drivers dialog box

Use the Sound dialog box (see Figure 17-27) to configure support for your sound card, if any. Because the kernel now supports an amazingly wide array of sound cards, it simply is not possible to describe each option in this space. Locate the device or chipset for which you need support, enable it, and be sure to read and understand the help text and any supporting documentation to ensure that you can take full advantage of your sound card. If the list does not include a driver for your particular card, you might be able to use the OSS (Open Sound System) modules to run your sound card. To do so, click *m* or *y* for OSS sound modules (scroll down the dialog box to find this option), and then click *m* or *y* to build the module or modules for your card. Click Next to continue.

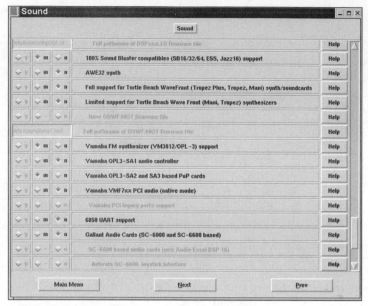

Figure 17-27: The Sound dialog box

Figure 17-28 shows the USB support dialog box. Select the devices you need to support, and then click Next to continue.

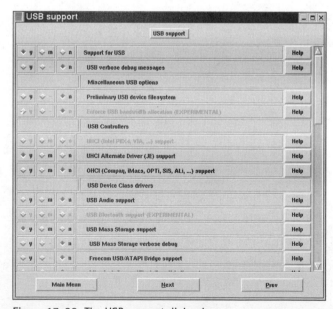

Figure 17-28: The USB support dialog box

Figure 17-29 shows the final configuration option, the Kernel hacking dialog box. Unless you will be hacking the kernel, leave this option set to *n*.

Figure 17-29: The Kernel hacking dialog box

Click Main Menu to return to the primary Linux Kernel Configuration dialog box (see Figure 17-3). At this point, you are ready to save the configuration and proceed with compiling the kernel. To do so, use the following procedure, which includes a precautionary step, saving a backup copy of the configuration options you have just spent some time selecting:

1. Click Store Configuration to File to save a backup copy of the configuration file to a file *outside* of the kernel source code tree. In Figure 17-30, for example, the file is being saved to /home/kwall/config-2.4.9.

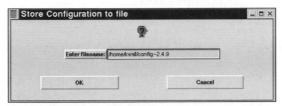

Figure 17-30: Saving the kernel configuration to a backup file

2. Click Save and Exit to save the configuration file where the build process can find it.

3. After reading the Kernel build instructions dialog box (see Figure 17-31), click OK to close it and exit the kernel configuration.

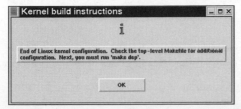

Figure 17-31: The Kernel build instructions dialog box

4. Unless you are interested in using other kernel configuration interfaces, continue with the section titled "Compiling and Installing the New Kernel."

CONFIGURING THE KERNEL USING MAKE MENUCONFIG

Type make menuconfig to configure the kernel configuration using a text mode menu interface. The configuration options are the same as those provided by the make xconfig X interface, but the interface itself is slightly different. The initial screen resembles Figure 17-32.

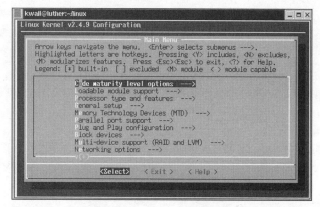

Figure 17-32: The initial text mode kernel configuration menu

The following list shows the keystrokes you can use:

◆ Use the arrow keys to move the blue highlight cursor up and down the menu.

◆ Highlighted letters are hotkeys.

◆ To select an item, press Enter.

◆ Submenus are indicated by --->.

◆ To enable a configuration option, press *y* or *.

◆ To disable a configuration option, press *n*.

◆ Configuration items preceded by angle brackets (<>) can be built as modules.

◆ Press *m* to build options as modules.

◆ Press ? or use the Help button to view the help text for a given option.

◆ Press the Tab key to move the cursor from the menu to the buttons at the bottom and to move between the buttons.

For example, use the arrow key to move the cursor down to the `Networking options --->` selection. Then press Enter to open the submenu, which is shown in Figure 17-33.

Figure 17-33: The Networking options configuration menu

The `TCP syncookie support (disabled per default)` option has an * next to it, meaning it has been enabled. The other options have not been included or enabled. The `IP: tunneling` and `IP: GRE tunnels over IP` options have (empty) <>, meaning that they can be built as modules by pressing *m* or built into the kernel by typing *y* or * (see Figure 17-34). Many of the so-called submenus have submenus of their own. In Figure 17-33, for example, the `IP: Netfilter Configuration --->` option indicates the existence of a subsubmenu, as it were. Pressing Enter results in Figure 17-34, the IP: Netfilter Configuration menu. Note that all of the options on this menu are being built as modules, as indicated by the M in the angle brackets next to each option.

Figure 17-34: The IP: Netfilter Configuration submenu

When you have completed the configuration process, use the Exit button to exit the configuration menus — you may have to press it several times. Before it exits, the configuration tool gives you the option to save the changes, as shown in Figure 17-35. Highlight the Yes button and press Enter to save the new configuration (or No to abandon it) and exit the utility. At this point, you are ready to build and install the kernel as explained in the section titled "Compiling and Installing the New Kernel."

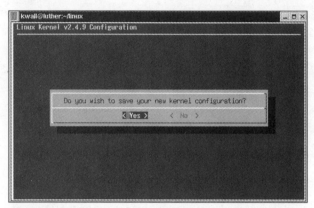

Figure 17-35: Save the kernel configuration before exiting the configuration tool.

CONFIGURING THE KERNEL USING MAKE CONFIG

Type make config to use a text-based program that prompts you for each configuration option one by one. When you use this option, you undergo a long question-and-answer process to specify the configuration process. As with the other kernel configuration methods, you have to select how to include support for specific devices and features. For most configuration options, you must type one of the following choices:

- ◆ y to build support into the kernel
- ◆ m to use a module
- ◆ n to skip the support for that specific device
- ◆ ? to get help on that kernel configuration option

If a device does not have a modular device driver, you do not see the m option. For some configuration options, you may have to type a specific answer. For example, when responding to the processor type, you type Pentium to indicate that you have a Pentium PC. When you complete the configuration process, use the instructions in the next section to compile and install the kernel.

Compiling and installing the new kernel

Regardless of the configuration interface you used, the next step is to follow the instructions shown in Figure 17-31, namely, execute `make dep` to remake the kernel's dependencies properly, and then to build the kernel, the modules, and to install the kernel and modules. Here are the steps to follow:

1. In the top-level directory of the kernel source tree ($HOME/linux in this example), execute the following commands:

   ```
   $ make dep
   $ make bzImage
   ```

TIP When I build the kernel, I prefer to see only the error messages in order to make it easier to track down build errors, so I redirect stdout to a file and use `tee` to copy stderr to a file while displaying on the screen, too. For example, to build the kernel image, the command I use is:

```
make bzImage > bzImage.log 2>| tee bzImage.err
```

If you want to save stdout and stderr to the same file, which places errors in the context of standard kernel compilation output, use the following command line:

```
make bzImage > bzimage.log 2>&1
```

2. If you opted to build a modular or hybrid kernel as described earlier, execute the following command in order to build the modules:

   ```
   $ make modules
   ```

   Assuming nothing has gone awry, the kernel built successfully and you are ready to install the new kernel and, if necessary, the modules.

3. The next few commands require root privileges, so use `su` to become the root user:

   ```
   $ su
   Password:
   #
   ```

4. Make a backup copy of your existing kernel in case the new kernel does not boot properly.

5. Copy the new kernel into place:

   ```
   # cp linux/arch/i386/boot/bzImage /boot/vmlinuz-2.4.9
   ```

6. If you opted to build a modular or hybrid kernel, install the modules:

```
# make modules_install
```

7. If you need an initial RAM disk (usually because your boot device is a SCSI disk), create it using `mkinitrd`:

```
# mkinitrd -v /boot/initrd-2.4.9.img 2.4.9
```

The next step is to configure your bootloader, GRUB, to boot the new kernel, as described in the next section.

Configuring GRUB

GRUB, the Grand Unified Bootloader, is the default bootloader in Red Hat Linux 7.2. The following listing shows a typical GRUB configuration file (usually `/boot/grub/grub.conf`):

```
default=0
timeout=10
splashimage=(hd0,0)/grub/splash.xpm.gz
title Red Hat Linux (2.4.7-2)
        root (hd0,0)
        kernel /vmlinuz-2.4.7-2 ro root=/dev/sda2
        initrd /initrd-2.4.7-2.img
```

To activate the new kernel, add the following lines below the existing entries:

```
title Test Kernel (2.4.9)
        root (hd0,0)
        kernel /vmlinuz-2.4.9 ro root=/dev/sda2
        initrd /initrd-2.4.9.img
```

Of course, modify the root device (`/dev/sda2` in this example) to reflect your system. This single change is all you need to do to make GRUB aware of the new kernel — GRUB reads this file at boot time and uses it to build a menu of options.

Booting the custom kernel

After you have updated GRUB's menu file, reboot, select the new kernel from GRUB's menu, press Enter, and, if everything has gone well, your Red Hat Linux system should boot your shiny new kernel. To make sure you've booted the proper kernel, execute the `uname` command. For example:

```
$ uname -a
Linux luther 2.4.9 #1 Thu Sep 6 13:09:57 MDT 2001 i686 unknown
```

The output indicates that the kernel was built 6 September 2001 and that the version number is 2.4.9, which is to say, the system in question is running the kernel configured and compiled in this chapter.

Summary

In this chapter you learned how to configure, build, and install a new Linux kernel. After reading about the difference between upgrading and customizing the kernel, you learned how to obtain and install the kernel source code, how to configure the kernel using several configuration interfaces, and how to install and boot your newly compiled custom kernel. Finally, you found out how to configure GRUB to boot the new kernel while retaining the ability to fall back to a known good kernel if the new one does not load properly.

Chapter 18

Configuring the System on the Command Line

IN THIS CHAPTER

◆ Administering your system from the command line

◆ Administering users and groups

◆ Managing the file system

◆ Administering processes

◆ Tracking and controlling system resources

◆ Maintaining the date and time

◆ Creating and restoring backups

THIS CHAPTER EXPLAINS how to use command line programs to perform system and network administration tasks. Using GUI tools for system administration is convenient when such tools are available, but they are not always available and often fail to offer a complete interface to subsystem administration. In fact, many GUI administration tools are little more than graphical wrappers around the command line programs you learn to use in this chapter.

Administering a System at the Command Line

Why should you learn how to administer your Red Hat Linux system from the command line? First, although the range of GUI system and network administration tools available for Red Hat Linux systems continues to grow in both number and sophistication, not all administrative tasks have a matching GUI tool, and the available tools are often incomplete, out-of-date, or as unintuitive and awkward to use as the command line programs they attempt to replace.

Secondly, GUI tools are not always available. Linux systems installed strictly as server machines, rather than desktop or end user workstations, rarely run the X Window System, much less have it installed. They are not only *headless*, that is, lack an attached monitor, they usually lack an attached keyboard or mouse. Running the X Window System on a server uses CPU cycles, RAM, disk space, process table entries, and file descriptors, better used to provide another service. Moreover, underpowered systems may lack the horsepower to run the X Window System, and thus GUI tools.

Another shortcoming of graphical tools is, ironically, the very user friendliness that makes them so popular. That is, graphical administration tools *require* user interaction – they do not readily, if at all, lend themselves to automated, unattended execution. They are rarely scriptable or support the capability of making bulk changes, such as adding 25 user accounts in a single operation. On the other hand, you rarely find a command line tool that *cannot* be scripted in order to facilitate bulk system changes or that *cannot* be automated using cron or another scheduling utility. In a small environment with few users, workstations, and servers, the inability to script GUI configuration and administration tools may not be an issue. However, system administration becomes a challenge even at the top end of the so-called "small business" sector, say 25 users and workstations, 2 or 3 servers, and half a dozen printers. Administrators, and there are usually several, at large installations with multiple servers, dozens or hundreds of users and workstations, plus all of the associated administrative overhead, *must* be able to make bulk changes and perform system maintenance and administration unattended and automatically. To do otherwise is simply impractical.

 Chapter 19 shows you how to write Bash shell scripts and use scripts to automate system administration tasks.

Finally, graphical administration tools, by their very nature, encourage uninformed or ill-informed system administration habits. GUI tools deliberately hide complex, often unintuitive configuration files and commands behind an attractive, convenient interface. Hiding the complexity does not make it disappear, though. In fact, it may make it worse because you never learn how a service really works, how to troubleshoot a misbehaving daemon, or how to customize a program using a command line program or option the GUI tool does not support. In some cases, thankfully less common, GUI tools interfere with system administration tasks because, for example, the modifications they make to a configuration file overwrite your own changes.

Should you use graphical system administration tools? Absolutely. They are helpful, convenient, and timesaving additions to every system administrator's toolbox. Not every problem is a nail, so you need more tools than a hammer. That is, GUI tools are only *one* of many tools at your disposal. You do yourself, your employer, your colleagues, and your users a valuable service if you take the time to understand the details of system administration. Think of it this way: if the graphical utility for configuring a mission-critical service stops working for some reason, do you *really* want to tell your boss you do not know how to fix it? You need to know how to use the perfectly serviceable command line utility.

The following seven sections discuss user and group administration, file system management, working with processes, network maintenance, monitoring and controlling system performance, configuring the system logs, keeping the system's date and time accurate, and creating and restoring backups. Because many commands can be used by both normal users and the root user, discussion focuses on usage and options pertinent to administrative needs.

Administering Users and Groups

The commands covered in this section concern user and group management. Commands used for working with users and groups fall into three broadly defined categories: creating, modifying, and deleting user accounts, creating, modifying, and deleting group accounts, and displaying current and historical login and usage information.

 Chapter 21 discusses user and group management in detail. Please refer to that chapter for examples of using the commands discussed in this section.

Working with user accounts

One of the most common administrative tasks is working with user and group accounts. The commands you use most often are

- ◆ useradd — Creates user login accounts
- ◆ userdel — Deletes user login accounts
- ◆ usermod — Modifies user login accounts
- ◆ passwd — Sets or changes account passwords
- ◆ chsh — Sets or changes a user's default shell
- ◆ chage — Modifies password expiration information

The useradd command creates new user accounts and, when invoked with the -D option, modifies the default values applied to new accounts. As a result, it can be invoked in two ways. The syntax of the first form is

```
useradd [-c comment] [-d home_dir] [-e expire_date]
        [-f inactive_time] [-g initial_group]
```

```
[-G group[,...]] [-m [-k skeleton_dir] | -M]
[-p passwd] [-s shell] [-u uid [-o]]
[-n] [-r] username
```

The first form creates a new user account named *username*. Optional values not specified using options are assigned default values drawn from /etc/login.defs and /etc/default/useradd. Table 18-1 lists the options useradd accepts.

TABLE **18-1 useradd OPTIONS AND ARGUMENTS**

Option	Description
-c *comment*	Uses *comment* for the name field
-d *home_dir*	Names the new user's home directory *home_dir*
-e *expire_date*	Sets the account's expiration date to *expire_date*
-f *inactive_time*	Disables the account *inactive_time* days after the password expires
-g *initial_group*	Sets the user's primary group membership, or *login group*, to *initial_group*
-G [*group*[,...]]	Makes the user a member of each supplemental group *group*
-m	Creates the home directory if it does not exist and copies the files and directory structure in /etc/skel to the new directory
-k *skeleton_dir*	Copies the files and directory structure in *skeleton_dir*, not /etc/skel, to the new home directory; must be specified with -m
-M	Disables creation of the home directory; cannot specify -m and -M
-p *passwd*	Sets the account password to the encrypted password *passwd*
-s *shell*	Sets the user's default shell to *shell*
-u *uid*	Sets the user's UID (User ID) to *uid*, which must be a unique number
-o	Allows the UID specified with -u *uid* not to be unique; must be specified with -u

Option	Description
-n	Disables use of Red Hat Linux's user private groups
-r	Creates a system account (an account with a UID less than 100) but does not create a home directory
username	Sets the login name to *username*

TIP The adduser program is a symbolic link to useradd.

The second way to invoke useradd uses the -D option. Invoked with only -D, *useradd* displays its current default settings. Using -D with any of the options listed in Table 18-2 modifies the default value for the corresponding field. Here is the syntax for the second form:

```
useradd -D [-g default_group] [-b default_home_dir]
        [-f default_inactive_time] [-e default_expire_date]
        [-s default_shell]
```

useradd's default values are stored in /etc/default/useradd.

TABLE 18-2 OPTIONS FOR CHANGING useradd DEFAULTS

Option	Description
-g *default_group*	Sets the default group to *default_group*
-b *default_home_dir*	Sets the default home directory to *default_home_dir*
-f *default_inactive_time*	Sets the default account disable time to *default_inactive_time* days
-e *default_expire_date*	Sets the default account expiration date to *default_expire_date*
-s *default_shell*	Sets the default login shell to *default_shell*

The userdel command deletes a user account and, optionally, related files. Its syntax is

```
userdel [-r] username
```

username identifies the user account to delete. Using -r deletes the corresponding home directory and mail spool. Without -r, userdel removes only the account references in the user and group database files. You cannot delete the account of a logged in user, so userdel fails if *username* is logged in.

The usermod command modifies an existing user account. Its syntax is

```
usermod [-c comment] [-d home_dir [-m]] [-e expire_date]
        [-f inactive] [-g initial_group]
        [-G group[,...]] [-l new_username] [-p passwd]
        [-s shell] [-u uid [-o]] [-L|-U] username
```

usermod accepts the options and arguments listed in Table 18-1 for useradd and adds three new ones, -l *new_username*, -L and -U. -l *new_username* changes the account name from *username* to *new_username*. -L disables (locks) *username*'s account by placing a ! in front of the user's encrypted password in /etc/shadow. -U enables (unlocks) the account by removing the !. At least one option must be specified, but -p, -U, and -L may not be used together in any combination. If *username* is logged in, usermod fails because you cannot change the login name of a logged in user.

The passwd command, generally regarded as "the password changing utility," actually has more capabilities than merely changing passwords. In general, it updates all of a user's authentication tokens, of which the login password is only one. Its syntax is:

```
passwd [-dkluf] [-S] username
```

-d removes the password for *username*, disabling the account. -k causes passwd to update only expired authentication tokens (passwords, in this case). -l or -u lock or unlock, respectively, *username*'s password by placing and removing a ! in front of *username*'s password in /etc/shadow. The -S option, finally, displays a short status message about *username*, indicating whether the account is locked or unlocked, the kind of encryption used, and so forth.

The chsh command changes a user's login shell. Its syntax is

```
chsh [-s shell ] [-l] [username]
```

-s *shell* sets *username*'s login shell to *shell*. Unless configured otherwise, *shell* can be the full pathname of any executable file on the system. One common way to take advantage of this feature is to disable an account by setting shell to /bin/false or another command that does not give the user a login prompt. Using the -l option displays the shells listed in /etc/shells.

The `chage` command changes the expiration policy for a user's password. Its syntax is

```
chage [-l] [-m mindays] [-M maxdays] [-d lastday] [-I inactive]
      [-E expiredate] [-W warndays] username
```

Table 18-3 lists the valid options that `chage` accepts.

TABLE 18-3 OPTIONS FOR THE `chage` COMMAND

Option	Description
username	Specifies *username* as the account name to query or modify
-l	Displays expiration information for *username*
-m *mindays*	Sets *mindays* days as the minimum amount of time permitted between password changes
-M *maxdays*	Sets *maxdays* days as the maximum number of days a password is valid
-d *lastday*	Sets *lastday* as the date on which the password was last changed, expressed as the number of days elapsed since 1 January 1970. *lastday* can be set using a more convenient date format, such as June 21, 2001 or 2001-0621
-I *inactive*	Sets *inactive* days as the number of days *username*'s account may be inactive *after* the password has expired before the account is locked
-E *expiredate*	Sets *expiredate* as the date on which *username*'s account expires
-W *warndays*	Sets *warndays* as the number of days before the password expires that a warning message is issued

---

If no options are used, `chage` goes into interactive mode, prompting the user for each item of information.

Working with group accounts

The commands for working with group accounts are

◆ `groupadd` – Creates a group account

♦ groupdel — Deletes a group account

♦ groupmod — Modifies a group account

In large part, the group account administration commands parallel the interface of user administration commands with similar names, except that the group commands have fewer command line options.

To create a new group, call groupadd, passing it at least the name of the new group. Its syntax is:

```
groupadd [-g gid [-o]] [-rf] group
```

group is the name of the group to create. -g *gid* sets the GID of the new group to *gid*, which must be unique. If -o is specified with -g, *gid* does *not* have to be unique. The -r option creates a system group account, one with a GID below 100. If the group named *group* already exists, groupadd refuses to create the account and exits with an error. The (poorly chosen) -f option suppresses this error message (the duplicate group is not created).

To delete a group, use the command groupdel *group*, where *group* is the name of the group you want to delete. You cannot delete a user's primary group, however, which poses a problem in isolated cases because Red Hat Linux uses a user private groups permissions scheme.

Chapter 21 describes Red Hat Linux's user private group convention in detail.

groupmod changes a group's GID or its name. Its syntax is:

```
groupmod [-g gid [-o]] [-n new_group_name ] group
```

group indicates the group to modify, -g *gid* sets the group's GID to *gid*, and -n *group_name* renames *group* to *new_group_name*. -o permits *gid* to be nonunique.

Modifying multiple accounts simultaneously

As remarked at the beginning of the chapter, one of the advantages of command line tools is that they can be used to perform bulk or mass changes. Two commands, chpasswd and newusers, make multiple changes to the user password database in a single operation.

The newusers command creates new user accounts and updates existing ones in a batch operation. It takes a single argument, the name of a file listing the accounts to create or modify, one per line. Each line has the same format as the entries in /etc/passwd:

username:*password*:*uid*:*gid*:*gecos*:*homedir*:*shell*

If *username* already exists, newusers ignores *uid*. *password* must be plain text (newusers encrypts it at run time). Similarly, for new and existing users, *newusers* creates *homedir* if it does not exist.

The chpasswd command updates existing user passwords *en masse*. It reads a file consisting of colon-separated *username:password* pairs. *password* must be plain text, which will be encrypted at run time, unless chpasswd is invoked with the -e option, in which case *password* must already be encrypted using a crypt(3)-compatible encryption algorithm.

Type man 3 crypt to learn more about how the password is encrypted.

Viewing login and process information

To view current and past login information and to determine what processes users are running, you can use one of the following commands:

◆ last — Displays historical login information

◆ who — Displays information about currently logged in users

◆ w — Displays a user's currently running process

last prints the username, tty, date, time, elapsed time, and the hostname or IP address of the remote host, if applicable, from which the login originated of all user logins, starting with the most recent login. Its syntax is

last [-R | [-ai]] [-*num* |-n *num*] [*username*] [*tty*]

By default, last lists all the entries in /var/log/wtmp, so you can use -*num* and -n *num* to specify the number of output lines to display. Ordinarily, last displays the hostname in the third column, but using -a places the hostname in the right-most column, -i shows the hostname's IP address, and -R completely suppresses display of the hostname. To view the login activity of a specific user, use the *username* argument. *tty* enables you to view logins per TTY. Multiple *username*s and *tty*s can be listed.

The who command displays information about currently logged in users. Its default output includes the username, login TTY, and the date and time each user logged in. who's syntax is:

```
who [-Hil] | [-q]
```

Using the -H option adds column headings to who's output. Specifying -i adds each user's idle time to the display. Use -l to force who to show complete FQDNs (Fully Qualified Domain Names). To obtain the total number of logged in users, use the -q option by itself.

The w command is very similar to who, except that it also displays the command line of each user's currently running process and a summary of each user's CPU usage. w's syntax is:

```
w [-husf] [username]
```

By default, w prints header information when it starts; -h disables the header. -s generates a short output format that omits the login time and the CPU usage. -f disables displaying the host from which users are logged in. Specifying *username* lists only *username*'s login session and process information.

Managing the File System

A significant portion of administrative time and effort involves file system maintenance. These tasks include modifying existing file systems, creating new ones, fixing broken ones, monitoring all of them, and ensuring that users do not monopolize any of them. The file system maintenance commands this section covers have been divided into three categories: commands for creating and maintaining file systems, commands for working with files and directories, and commands for managing disk space usage.

File system management is important enough that this book devotes an entire chapter to it — Chapter 4.

Creating and maintaining file systems

Unless you have an extremely active system, creating and formatting a file system is an infrequent necessity. Actively *maintaining* a file system, however, is an ongoing process. The commands for creating, formatting, and checking the integrity of Red Hat Linux file systems discussed in this section are

- ◆ `fdisk` — Creates, deletes, and modifies hard disk partitions

- ◆ `me2kfs` — Creates a file system on a device

- ◆ `e2fsck` — Checks, and optionally repairs, a Linux file system

- ◆ `symlinks` — Validates, and optionally repairs, symbolic links

- ◆ `mount` — Mounts a file system

- ◆ `umount` — Unmounts a file system

- ◆ `mkswap` — Creates a swap partition or file

- ◆ `swapoff` — Disables a swap partition or file

- ◆ `swapon` — Enables a swap partition or file

The `fdisk` program prepares hard disks to hold Linux file systems. It is an interactive program and accepts few command line options. You can invoke it using one of the following forms:

```
fdisk -s partition
fdisk [-lu] device
```

The first form uses the `-s` option to display the size in (blocks) of the disk partition specified by *partition* and then exits. The second form operates on the disk specified by device. The `-l` option, lists the disk geometry of *device*, followed by a columnar list of each partition on *device* that shows each partition's boot status, starting and ending cylinders, total size (in 512 byte blocks), and the partition type. If `device` is omitted, `fdisk` lists the same information based on the contents of the file `/proc/partitions`. The `-u` option instructs `fdisk` to show disk and partition sizes in terms sectors instead of cylinders. Omitting `-l` (second form) starts an interactive `fdisk` session on *device*.

`mke2fs` creates a Linux ext2 file system on a disk. Its syntax is

```
mke2fs [-c | -l list] [-b size] [-i bytes-per-inode] [-n]
       [-m reserve] [-q] [-v] [-L label] [-S] device
```

device indicates the disk partition or other device on which to create the file system. Specifying `-n` results in a test run; `mke2fs` goes through the entire creation process but does not actually create the file system. Use `-q` to suppress output, for example, when `mke2fs` is used in a script. Conversely, use `-v` to generate verbose output.

To check the disk for bad blocks while creating the file system, specify `-c`, or use `-l` *list* to read a list of known bad blocks from the file named *list*. By default, `mke2fs` calculates file system block sizes based on the size of the underlying partition, but you can specify `-b` *size* to force a block size of 1024, 2048, or 4096 bytes. Similarly, to override the default inode size, use `-i` *bytes-per-inode* (*bytes-per-inode* should be no smaller than the block size defined with -b *size*). -m *reserve* instructs mke2fs to make *reserve* percent of the file system for the root user. If -m *reserve* is omitted, the default reserve space is 5%. -L *label* sets the file system's volume label, or name, to *label*.

Normally, mke2fs refuses to run if *device* is not a block device (a disk of some sort) or if it is mounted; -F overrides this default. -S, finally, causes mke2fs to write only the superblocks and the group descriptors and to ignore the block and inode information. In essence, it attempts to rebuild the high level file system structure without affecting the file system contents. It should be used only as a final attempt to salvage a badly corrupted file system, and may not work. The manual page recommends running e2fsck immediately after using -S.

e2fsck checks a file system for possible corruption and repairs any damage found. Its syntax is:

```
e2fsck [-pcnyfvt] [-b sblock] [-B size] [-l list] device
```

device is the partition (/dev/hda1, for example) to test. -b *sblock* tells e2fsck to use the backup superblock located on block number *sblock*. -B *size* specifies block sizes of *size* bytes. -l *list* instructs e2fsck to add the block numbers listed in the file name *list* to the list of known bad blocks. Using -c causes e2fsck to identify bad blocks on the disk. Ordinarily, e2fsck asks for confirmation before repairing file system errors; specifying -p disables any confirmation prompts, -n automatically answers "No" to all questions and sets the file system read-only, and -y automatically answers "Yes" to all questions. e2fsck's default behavior is not to check a file system that is marked clean, but using -f forces it to do so. -v enables verbose output. -t generates a timing report at the end of e2fsck's operation.

The symlinks command scans directories for symbolic links, displays them on the screen, and repairs broken or otherwise malformed symbolic links. Its syntax is:

```
symlinks [-cdrstv] dirlist
```

dirlist is a list of one or more directories to scan for symbolic links. -r causes symlinks to recurse through subdirectories. -d deletes dangling links, symbolic links whose target no longer exists. -c converts *absolute links*, links defined as an absolute path from /, to *relative links*, links defined relative to the directory in which the link is located. -c also removes superfluous / and . elements in link definitions. -s identifies links with extra ../ in their definition and, if -c is also specified, repairs them. To see what symlinks would do without actually changing the file system, specify -t. By default, symlinks does not show relative links; -v overrides this default.

To make an existing file system available, it has to be mounted using the mount command. mount's syntax is:

```
mount -a [-fFnrsvw] [-t fstype]
mount [-fnrsvw] [-o fsoptions] device | dir
mount [-fnrsvw] [-t fstype] [-o fsoptions] device dir
```

The first two forms use the information in /etc/fstab when mounting file systems. Invoked with no options, mount lists all mounted file systems, and specifying only -t *fstype* lists all mounted file systems of type *fstype*. *fstype* will be one of devpts, ext2, iso9660, or vfat, but many other file system types are supported — the complete list of valid types is available in mount's manual page.

The -a option mounts all the file systems listed in /etc/fstab (subject to restriction using the -t option as explained in the previous paragraph) that are configured using the auto mount option (see Table 18-5). The second form is most commonly used to override the mount options, using -o *fsoptions*, listed in /etc/fstab. Note that you only have to specify *device*, the device containing the file system, or *dir*, where in the directory hierarchy the file system should be attached.

Use the third form to mount file systems not listed in /etc/fstab or to override information it contains. The third form is also the most widely used. In general, it attaches the file system on *device* to the system's directory hierarchy at the mount point *dir*, using a file system type of *fstype* and the file system options *fsoptions*. Table 18-4 lists mount's global options. *fsoptions* is a comma-delimited list of one or more of the options listed in Table 18-5.

Because Linux supports so many file systems, this chapter discusses only a few of the many file systems and file system options. mount's manual page contains a complete list of the file systems and their corresponding mount options that Linux currently supports.

TABLE 18-4 GLOBAL OPTIONS FOR THE mount COMMAND

Option	Description
-a	Mounts all file systems, subject to restrictions specified using -t
-F	Mounts all file systems (used only with -a) in parallel by creating new processes for each file system to mount
-f	Fakes the mount operation, doing everything but actually mounting the file system
-h	Displays a short usage message
-n	Mounts the file system without creating an entry in the mount table (/etc/mtab)

Continued

TABLE 18-4 GLOBAL OPTIONS FOR THE mount COMMAND *(Continued)*

Option	Description
-o *fsoptions*	Mounts the file system using the file system-specific options *fsoptions*
-r	Mounts the file system in read-only mode
-s	Ignores options specified with -o that are invalid for the given file system type (the default is to abort the mount operation)
-t *fstype*	Restricts mount's operation to file system types of type *fstype* (first and second forms) or specifies the file system type of the file system being mounted (third form)
-v	Prints informational messages while executing (verbose mode)
-w	Mounts the file system in read-write mode

TABLE 18-5 COMMON FILE SYSTEM OPTIONS FOR THE mount COMMAND

Option	Type*	Description
async	1	Enables asynchronous system I/O on the file system
auto	1	Enables mounting using the -a option
defaults	1	Enables the default options (rw, suid, dev, exec, auto, nouser, async) for the file system
dev	1	Enables I/O for device files on the file system
exec	1	Enables execution of binaries on the file system
gid=*gid*	2, 3	Assigns the GID *gid* to all files on the file system
mode=*mode*	3	Sets the permissions of all files to *mode*
noauto	1	Disables mounting using the -a option
nodev	1	Disables I/O for device files on the file system
noexec	1	Disables execution of binaries on the file system
nosuid	1	Disables set-UID and set-GID bits on the file system
nouser	1	Permits only root user to mount the file system

Option	Type*	Description
ro	1	Mounts the file system in read-only mode
remount	1	Attempts to remount a mounted file system
rw	1	Mounts the file system in read-write mode
suid	1	Enables set-UID and set-GID bits on the file system
sync	1	Enables synchronous file system I/O on the file system
user	1	Permits nonroot users to mount the file system
uid=*uid*	2, 3	Assigns the UID *uid* to all files on the file system

1=All file systems, 2=devpts, 3=iso9660

To unmount a file system, use the command umount. Its syntax is much simpler, thankfully, than mount's:

```
umount -a [-nrv] [-t fstype]
umount [-nrv] device | dir
```

All of umount's options and arguments have the same meaning as they do for mount, except for -r. Of course, the options must be understood in the context of unmounting a file system. If -r is specified and unmounting a file system fails for some reason, umount attempts to mount it in read-only mode.

To create and manipulate swap space, use the mkswap, swapon, and swapoff commands. mkswap initializes a swap area on a device (the usual method) or a file. swapon enables the swap area for use, and swapoff disables the swap space. mkswap's syntax is:

```
mkswap [-c] device [size]
```

device identifies the partition or file on which to create the swap area and *size* specifies the size, in blocks, of the swap area to create. *size* is necessary only if you want a swap area smaller than the available space. If *device* is a file, it must already exist and be sized appropriately. -c performs a check for bad blocks and displays a list of any bad blocks found.

TIP To create a swap file before using mkswap, use the following command:

```
dd if=/dev/zero of=/some/swap/file bs=1024 count=size
```

Replace */some/swap/file* with the file you want, and *size* with the size of the swap area, in blocks, you want to create.

To enable the kernel to use swap devices and files, use the swapon command. Its syntax takes three forms:

```
swapon -s
swapon -a [-ev]
swapon [-p priority] [-v] device
```

The first form displays a summary of swap space usage for each active swap device. The second form, normally used in system startup scripts, uses -a to activate all swap devices listed in /etc/fstab. If -e is also specified, swapon ignores devices listed in /etc/fstab that do not exist. The third form activates the swap area on device, and, if -p priority is also specified, gives device a higher priority in the swap system than other swap areas. priority can be any value between 0 and 32,767 (specified as 32767), where higher values represent higher priorities. -v prints short status messages.

To deactivate a swap area, use the swapoff command. Its syntax is simple:

```
swapoff -a | device
```

Use -a to deactivate all active swap areas, or use device to deactivate a specific swap area. Multiple swap areas may be specified using whitespace between device identifiers.

Working with files and directories

This section reviews the basic call syntax of the following commands:

◆ chmod — Modifies file and directory permission settings

◆ chown — Modifies file and directory user ownership

◆ chgrp — Modifies file and directory group ownership

◆ lsattr — Lists special file attributes on ext2 files

◆ chattr — Modifies special file attributes on ext2 files

◆ stat — Shows detailed file information

◆ fuser — Displays a list of process IDs using a file

◆ lsof — Identifies files opened by a process

Here are the syntax summaries for chmod, chown, and chgrp:

```
chmod [-cfRv] symbolic-mode file
chmod [-cfRv] octal-mode file
chown [-cfhRv] owner[:[group]] file
chown [-cfhRv] :group file
chgrp [-cfhRv] group file
```

chmod, chown, and chgrp accept the common options -c, -v, -f, -R, and *file*. *file* is the file or directory to modify and multiple *file* arguments can be specified. -R invokes recursive operation on the subdirectories and of *file*; -v generates a diagnostic for each file or directory examined; while -c generates a diagnostic message only when it changes a file. -f cancels all but fatal error messages.

chmod has two forms because it understands both symbolic and octal notation for file permissions. For both forms, *file* is one or more files on which permissions are being changed. *symbolic-mode* uses the symbolic permissions notation, while *octal-mode* expresses the permissions being set using the standard octal notation.

 For a quick refresher on using octal and symbolic permissions notation, refer to the chmod manual page.

With the chown and chgrp commands, *group* is the new group being assigned to *file*. For the chown command, *owner* identifies the new user being assigned as *file*'s owner. The colon (:) enables chmod to change *file*'s group ownership. The format *owner:group* changes *file*'s user and group owners to *owner* and *group*, respectively. The format *owner:* changes only *file*'s owner and is equivalent to chown *owner file*. The format *:group* leaves the owner untouched but changes *file*'s group owner to *group* (equivalent to chgrp *group file*).

The lsattr and chattr commands are Linux-specific, providing an interface to special file attributes available only on the ext2 file system. lsattr lists these attributes, and chattr sets or changes them. lsattr's syntax is

lsattr [-adRVv] *file*

file is the file or directory whose attributes you want to display; multiple whitespace separated *file* arguments may be specified. -a causes the attributes of all files, such as hidden files, to be listed. -d lists the attributes on directories, rather than listing the contents of the directories, and -R causes lsattr to recurse through subdirectories if *file* names a subdirectory.

chattr's syntax is

chattr [-RV] [-v *version*] +|-|=*mode file*

file is the file or directory whose attributes you want to display; multiple whitespace separated *file* arguments may be specified. -R causes lsattr to recurse through subdirectories if *file* names a subdirectory. -v *version* sets a version or generation number for *file*. +*mode* adds *mode* to *file*'s attributes; -*mode* removes *mode* from *file*'s attributes; =*mode* sets *file*'s attributes to *mode*, removing all other special attributes. *mode* can be one or more of the following:

A — Do not change *file*'s atime (last access time)

S — Update *file* synchronously

a — *file* is append-only

c — Kernel automatically compresses/decompresses *file*

d — *file* cannot be dumped with the dump command

I — *file* is immutable (cannot be changed)

s — *file* will be deleted securely using a special secure deletion algorithm

u — *file* cannot be deleted

The stat command displays detailed file or file system status information. Its syntax is

```
stat [-l] [-f] [-t] file
```

file specifies the file or directory about which you want information. Use multiple whitespace delimited *file* arguments to specify multiple files. If -l is used and *file* is a link, stat operates on the link's target (the file that is linked) rather than the link itself. Using -f causes stat to display information about *file*'s file system, not *file*. Specifying -t results in a shorter (terse) output format suitable for use in scripts.

Often, an administrator needs to identify the user or process that is using a file or socket. fuser provides this functionality. Its syntax is

```
fuser [-a | -s] [-n namespace] [-signal] [-kimuv] name
```

name specifies the file, file system, or socket to query. By default, fuser assumes that *name* is a file name. To query TCP or UDP sockets, use -n *namespace*, where *namespace* is udp for UDP sockets and tcp for TCP sockets (file is the default *namespace*). -a results in a report for all *name*s specified on the command line, even if they are not being accessed by any process. -s, on the other hand, causes fuser to run silently (do not use -s with -a, -u, or -v). -k kills processes using *name* with the signal SIGKILL; use -*signal* to specify an alternate signal to send. Use -i (interactive) to be prompted for confirmation before killing a process. Only use -i with -k. -m indicates that *name* specifies a file system or block device, so fuser lists all processes using files on that file system or block device. -u adds the user name of a process's owner to its output when listing processes. -v, finally, generates a verbose, ps-like listing of processes using the specified *name*.

lsof performs the reverse function from fuser, showing the files open by a given process or group of processes. A simplified version of its syntax is

```
lsof [-LlNRst] [-c c] [+f | -f] [+r | -r [t]] [-S [t]] [file]
```

file specifies the file or file systems (multiple *file* arguments are permitted) to scan. Specifying -c *c* selects processes executing a command that begins with the letter *c*. -f causes *file* to be interpreted as a file or pathname, +f as a file system name. -L suppresses displaying the count of files linked to *file*. -l displays UIDs rather than converting them to login names. Specifying -N includes a list of NFS files in lsof's output. +r causes lsof to repeat the display every 15 seconds (or *t* seconds if *t* is specified) until none of the selected files remain open; -r repeats the display indefinitely. -R lists the parent process ID of displayed processes. -S enables lsof to time out after 15 seconds, or after *t* seconds if *t* is specified.

Managing disk space usage

Monitoring and controlling disk space usage is another important part of a system administrator's tasks. The commands covered in this section for managing disk space usage include the following:

- ◆ df — Shows available (free) disk space on mounted file systems
- ◆ du — Shows disk space usage for files, directories, and file systems
- ◆ edquota — Modifies user disk space quota limits
- ◆ quota — Displays current disk usage and disk usage limits
- ◆ quotaoff — Disables disk quotas on file systems
- ◆ quotaon — Enables disk quotas on file systems
- ◆ quotactl — Manages the quota system
- ◆ quotastats — Prints statistics about the quota system
- ◆ repquota — Displays a report summarizing disk quota usage
- ◆ setquota — Sets disk quotas
- ◆ quotacheck — Compares disk usage to limits set using the quota system

Implementing and using the quota subsystem is discussed in detail in Chapter 21. Please refer to that chapter for examples and illustrations of the quota commands introduced in this section.

The df and du commands perform complementary functions, listing detail and summary information about the amount of disk space free and used, respectively. df's syntax is

```
df [-ahklTmx] [-t type] [--sync|--nosync] [name]
```

name, which can contain multiple whitespace delimited values) is the name of a file whose file system should be checked, or the file system itself (the default is all mounted file systems). -a includes empty file systems in the display, which would ordinarily be omitted. -h uses more familiar display units, such as GB, MB, or KB, rather than default, blocks. -k causes df to use block sizes of 1024 bytes, and -m block sizes of 1,048,576 bytes. -l limits df's report to local file systems, ignoring, for example, NFS mounted file systems. -x limits df's report to the current file system or the file system to which *name* refers. -t type limits the report to file systems of *type*, and --nosync prevents df from syncing file systems before generating its report (the default is to sync the disks to obtain the most accurate report).

du displays information about the disk space used. Its syntax is

```
du [-abcDhklmSsx] [-X file] [--exclude=path] [--max-depth=n] [name]
```

name, which can contain multiple whitespace delimited values) is the name of a file whose file system should be checked, or the file system itself (the default is all mounted file systems). -a displays counts for all files, not just directories. -b prints all sizes in bytes. -c displays a grand total for *names*. -h uses more familiar display units, such as GB, MB, or KB, rather than default, blocks. -k causes df to use block sizes of 1024 bytes, and -m block sizes of 1,048,576 bytes. -l limits df's report to local file systems, ignoring, for example, NFS mounted file systems. If a file or directory in *name* includes a symbolic link, -L causes it to be dereferenced to obtain the target's disk usage, rather than the link's usage. -S ignores subdirectories, which are recursed by default. -s results in a summary total for each *name* rather than a detailed report for each file in *name*. -x limits du's report to the current file system or the file system to which *name* refers. -X file causes du to ignore any file matching a pattern contained in file. Similarly, use --exclude=*pattern* to specify a single pattern to ignore. --max-depth=*n*, finally, limits the displayed report to directories (or files, if --all specified) within *n* levels of a path specified by *name* (all directories and files are evaluated, but the granularity of the report is limited to *n* levels).

As you learn in Chapter 21, the quota package is valuable for establishing and enforcing disk space usage policies. The discussion here summarizes its syntax.

edquota edits established quotas for users and groups. Its syntax is

```
edquota [-p model] [-ug] name
edquota [-ug] -t
```

The first form edits the quota for the user named *name* (equivalent to -u name), or, if -g is specified, the group named *name*. Using -p model applies the quotas established for the prototype user or group *model* to the user or group *name*. The second form uses the -t option to edit the soft time limits for each file system on which quotas are enforced. Add -u or -g to restrict the edits to users or groups.

repquota displays a report summarizing the quota policy in place and actual quota usage for a given file system. Its syntax is

```
repquota [-vugs] -a | filesystem
```

-a displays a report for all mounted file systems (the default). *filesystem* limits the report to the specified file system (multiple file systems may be specified using whitespace to separate the names). -v forces a verbose report that includes file systems on which there is no usage. Use -u to restrict the report to users, or -g to limit it to groups. -s includes summary statistics in the report.

setquota sets disk quotas and the time limits permitted for exceeding the soft quotas. It is ideally suited for use in scripts. Its syntax is

```
setquota [-u | -g] filesys softb hardb softi hardi name
setquota [-u | -g] filesys -p model name
setquota -t  [-u | -g] filesys timeb timei
```

 The manual page for setquota mistakenly uses -p instead of -t for the third form.

In all forms of the command, -g interprets *name* as a group name rather than a user name, which is the default (equivalent to specifying -u), *filesys* as the file system to which the quota should be applied, and *name* as the user or group name to which the quotas or limits apply. In the first form, *softb* and *softi* represent the soft limits for numbers of blocks and inodes, respectively, used. *hardb* and *hardi* represent the hard (absolute) usage limits in terms of numbers of blocks and inodes, respectively. The second form duplicates the limits set for the user or group *model* for the user or group *name*. The third form sets *timeb* and *timei*, in numbers of seconds, during which the soft limits on block and inode usage, respectively, may be exceeded on *filesys*.

quota prints current disk usage and limits. Its syntax is

```
quota -q [-gv]
quota [-v | -q] user
quota [-gv] group
```

The first form, intended for use by users, prints a short usage report identifying file systems where usage exceeds the quota. If -g is also specified, quotas for groups of which the user is a member are also displayed. -v includes in the report file systems on which no space is used or for which no quota has been set. The second form enables root to see the quota usage report for the specified *user* (-v and -q function as described). The third form displays the report for the specified *group*, subject to modification by -v and -q.

To enable and disable quotas, use the `quotaon` command. Its syntax is

```
quotaon [-e | -d] [-vug] -a | filesys
```

filesys identifies the file system on which to enable or disable quotas (do not use with `-a`). Use `-a` to affect all mounted file systems to which quotas have been applied. `-e` enables quotas (the default); `-d` disables quotas. `-v` displays a short message for each file system as quotas are enabled or disabled. `-u` affects only user quotas; `-g` affects only group quotas.

 The `quotaoff` command, not covered here, makes `-d` the default behavior and, in fact, is merely a symbolic link to `quotaon`.

Administering Processes

Administering processes includes identifying, monitoring, controlling, modifying, and obtaining a variety of information about them. The `ps`, `top`, and `kill` commands are the most familiar commands used for working with processes, but there are others that are more focused and, especially in the case of the `ps` command, probably easier to use. This section looks at three categories of commands:

- Commands used to obtain process information
- Commands used to send signals, usually the kill signal (`SIGKILL`), to processes
- Commands used to modify running processes

Obtaining process information

Process information is easy to obtain, if you know how to get it. The commands discussed in this section include the following:

- `ps` — Displays process status
- `pgrep` — Lists the PIDs of processes matching a given pattern
- `pidof` — Displays the PID of the process running a specified program
- `pstree` — Displays processes in a hierarchical format
- `top` — Displays process information and status on an ongoing basis
- `tload` — Displays a text mode load average graph

Tables 18-6 through 18-9 borrow the layout of ps's syntax description from its manual page and organize each group of options into tables based on the options' purpose. However, the following tables omit all GNU long options (those preceded with --) and options related to defining custom output formats. ps supports both Unix98 options, which are preceded by a hyphen (-) , and BSD options, which lack the initial -. Where the functionality is identical or very similar, the BSD options have been omitted. In some cases, apparently identical Unix98 and BSD are listed because the BSD option shows different output from the similarly invoked Unix98 option.

TABLE 18-6 BASIC PROCESS SELECTION

Option	Description
-N	Negates the selection criteria specified with other options
-a	Selects all processes with a TTY except session leaders
-d	Selects all except session leaders
-e	Selects all processes
T	Selects all processes on the invoking terminal
r	Selects only running processes
x	Selects processes without controlling TTYs

TABLE 18-7 PROCESS SELECTION BY CATEGORY

Option	Description
-C command	Selects by command name matching pattern command
-G rgid|name	Selects by RGID (Real Group ID) rgid or group name
-U ruid|name	Selects by RUID (Real User ID) ruid or user name
-p pid	Selects by PID pid
-u euid|name	Selects by EUID (Effective User ID) euid or user name
p pid	Selects by PID pid and displays command line
U name	Selects processes for user name and displays command line

TABLE 18-8 STANDARD OUTPUT FORMATS

Option	Description
-f	Displays full listing
-j	Displays output in jobs format
-l	Displays output in long format
j	Displays output in job control format
l	Display long output format
s	Displays output in signal format
v	Displays output in virtual memory format

TABLE 18-9 MODIFYING OUTPUT FORMAT

Option	Description
-H	Show process hierarchy (forest)
-w	Wide output
C	Use raw CPU time for %CPU instead of decaying average
S	Include some dead child process data (as a sum with the parent)
c	True command name
e	Show environment after the command
f	ASCII-art process hierarchy (forest)
h	Do not print header lines (repeat header lines in BSD personality)
w	Wide output

If ps's plethora of options and arguments seems daunting, the pgrep command provides relief because it provides a simpler interface, enabling you to select processes using simple pattern matching. It lists the PIDs (Process IDs) of processes matching the specified pattern. You can then use those PIDs with ps's p or -p options to obtain more information, if you wish. pgrep's syntax is

```
pgrep [-flnvx] [-P ppid] [-u euid] [-U uid] [-G gid] [pattern]
```

If you specify multiple criteria, the selected processes match *all* criteria, so keep the selection criteria as simple as possible. *pattern* contains the expression to match against process names or command lines. -f matches *pattern* against the process name (the default if -f is not specified) or the full command line. -l causes pgrep to list both the PID and the process name. If multiple processes match *pattern* and other criteria, -n limits the output to the most recently started process. -v reverses the matching, showing all processes not matching the specified criteria. -x forces an exact match of *pattern*. -P *ppid* restricts the output to matches with a parent PID of *ppid*. Similarly, -u *euid*, -U *uid*, and -G *gid*, limit the output to processes whose EUIDs, UIDs, and/or GIDs, respectively, match *euid*, *uid*, and/or *gid*, respectively. Multiple *ppid*s, *euid*s, *uid*s, and *gid*s may be specified by separating each with commas.

pidof enables you to locate the PID of a process by name. Its syntax is

pidof [-s] [-x] [-o *pid*] *program*

program is the base name of the program whose PID(s) you want to find. You can specify multiple *program*s by separating their names with whitespace. -s returns only the first PID located, additional PIDs are ignored. -x causes pidof to return the PID(s) of shell scripts running *program*. -o *pid* lists one or more PIDs that pidof should ignore (omit).

pstree displays all running processes as a tree, making clear the parent/child relationships between processes. Its syntax is

pstree [-a] [-c] [-H *pid*] [-n] [-p] [-G] [*basepid* | *baseuser*]

Called with no arguments, pstree shows all processes, with init as the root. Specifying *basepid* or *baseuser* begins the display from the PID specified by the PID *basepid* or the user name *baseuser*, respectively. -a includes the command line for each process. -c expands identically named child processes (such as the mingetty instance spawned for each terminal). -H *pid* highlights the PID *pid* and its ancestor (parent) processes. If *pid* does not exist, pstree exits with an error. -n sorts the output by PID (the default is by ancestry). -p causes each process's PID to display and implies -c. -G, finally, draws the tree using the VT100 drawing characters rather than the default ASCII characters |, +, -, and `.

top displays real time CPU and memory usage and current system uptime information. Although it is an interactive command, top is a vital tool in every system administrator's toolbox, so its command line interface (not its interactive use) is covered here.

top [-bcisqS] [-d *delay*] [-p *pid*] [-n *iter*]

-d *delay* specifies the number of seconds between screen updates (default is 5), and -q specifies constant updates, which run at the highest priority if used by the root user. -p *pid* identifies up to twenty PIDs in whitespace delimited *pid*s to monitor. top continues to run unless -n *iter* is specified, *iter* defining the number of iterations top refreshes its display before exiting (0 is interpreted as 1). -S enables cumulative mode, in which each process's CPU time is shown as a sum and includes the CPU time of any dead child processes. Of course, for a child process's time to count, it must have died. -s runs top in secure mode and disables potentially dangerous commands in the interactive interface, such as k, which can kill processes. -i instructs top to omit idle or zombie processes from its display. -b, finally, runs top in batch mode and runs until specifically killed or until the number of iterations specified with -n have elapsed (all other command line input ignored).

tload displays a real-time text mode graph of the system's *load average*, which is the number of processes waiting to run during the last minute, the last five minutes, and the last fifteen minutes. Its syntax is:

```
tload [-s scale] [ -d delay ] [tty]
```

tload displays its graph to the current terminal, unless *tty* is specified, when it then becomes tload's output target. -d *delay* sets the delay between graph updates to *delay* seconds (if *delay* is 0, the graph never updates). -s *scale* sets the vertical height of the graph in *scale* characters. Thus, the smaller the value of *scale*, the larger the scale.

Terminating processes

"Signaling processes" might be a better title for this section, because the commands it discusses (see the following list), can be used to send any signal, not just one of the kill signals, to a running process. Kill signals are the most common, of course, but the complete list of *possible* signals is significantly longer. The commands this section covers include

- ◆ kill — Sends a signal to a process
- ◆ pkill — Kills or sends another signal to a process matching a given pattern
- ◆ killall — Kills processes by name

Most Linux users are familiar with the kill command. Note, however, that most shells, including Bash, have a built-in kill command. The shell's kill is executed before /bin/kill in most shells because they execute built-in commands, aliases, and functions, where applicable, before using a command in the PATH. The discussion here covers the kill command /bin/kill, not the shell command. kill's syntax is:

```
kill [-s signal | -p] [-a] [--] pid
kill -l
```

pid is one or more whitespace delimited tokens specifying the processes to kill. Each token can be a PID (where *pid* > 0); a process name; -1, which kills all processes with PIDs between 2 and 35,767; or -*pid*, which kills all processes in the process group whose PGID (Process Group ID) is *pid*. If you specify -a, all processes matching *pid* are killed (only root may use -a). -p lists only the PID; no processes are killed. -s *signal* indicates the signal to send; *signal* can be either a numeric or symbolic name, as shown with kill -l.

pkill, which has a comparable call interface to pgrep, sends a signal to one or more processes matching a given pattern. Its syntax is

```
pkill [-signal] [-fnvx] [-P ppid] [-u euid] [-U uid] [-G gid]
[pattern]
```

If you specify multiple criteria, the selected processes match *all* criteria, so keep the selection criteria as simple as possible. *pattern* contains the expression to match against process names or command lines. -*signal* specifies the numeric or symbolic signal to send (SIGTERM is the default). -f matches *pattern* against the process name (the default if -f is not specified) or the full command line. If multiple processes match *pattern* and other criteria, -n sends the signal to the most recently started process. -v reverses the matching, showing all processes not matching the specified criteria. -x forces an exact match of *pattern*. -P *ppid* sends the signal to processes whose parent process has a PID of *ppid*. Similarly, -u *euid*, -U *uid*, and -G *gid* sends the signal to processes whose EUIDs, UIDs, and/or GIDs, respectively, match *euid*, *uid*, and/or *gid*, respectively. Multiple *ppid*s, *euid*s, *uid*s, and *gid*s may be specified by separating each with commas.

killall kills all processes matching a name. Its syntax is

```
killall [-l] | [-giqvw] [-signal] name
```

Specifying -l lists the numeric value and symbolic names of all recognized signals, and it cannot be used with any other options or arguments. *name* lists the command whose process should be signaled. Multiple *name*s may be specified if separated by whitespace. -*signal* specifies the signal to send; SIGTERM is the default. -g kills the process group to which *name* belongs. -i runs killall in interactive mode and requests confirmation for each *name* signaled. -q suppresses error messages if no processes match *name*. -v displays a short message if the signal was sent successfully. -w instructs killall to wait for each *name* to die.

Modifying process priorities

In some cases, it is not necessary to terminate a process, but simply to modify the priority at which it runs. The following two commands accomplish this goal.

◆ nice — Starts a program with a given scheduling priority

◆ renice — Alters the scheduling priority of one or more running processes

The `nice` command enables you to start a program with a higher or lower nice number, which controls how much CPU time the kernel gives a program relative to other programs with the same priority. The `nice` command's syntax is

```
nice [-n value | -value] [prog [arg]]
```

`prog` is the program to run. `arg` lists the arguments to `prog`, and is specified using the format `prog` understands. `value` expresses the modified nice number at which to run `prog`. Valid values for `value` are -20 to 19, smaller values representing a higher priority relative to other programs.

Use the `renice` command to modify the CPU scheduling priority of a running process. Its syntax is

```
renice priority [[-p] pid] [[-g] pgrp] [[-u] user]
```

`priority` expresses the new nice number at which to run the specified process(es). `-p pid` identifies the processes to modify by PID. `-g pgrp` modifies all processes in the process group `pgrp`. `-u user` causes all processes owned by `user` to run at the new `priority`.

Part II of this book is entirely devoted to network configuration, so we have omitted discussion of network configuration commands in this chapter and cover the material in the relevant chapters of Part II.

Tracking and Controlling System Usage

Administrators must know how to monitor memory and CPU usage at a finely grained level. The commands discussed in this section make such close monitoring possible. They include:

♦ `vmstat` – Displays virtual memory usage information

♦ `sar` – Collects, saves, and reports a broad range of system usage statistics

Chapter 20 covers evaluating and improving system performance and includes many examples and illustrations of the `vmstat` and `sar` commands.

vmstat provides a detailed report covering process activity, paging, memory usage, disk I/O, and CPU usage. Its syntax is

vmstat [-n] [*delay* [*count*]]

delay specifies the number of seconds between vmstat's updates. *count* expresses the number of iterations vmstat executes. -n prints vmstat's report header once, rather than repeatedly.

For many years, the sar (an acronym for System Activity Report) command, well known and widely used in the Unix world, was not available as a native Linux command. Fortunately, it is now available (at least on Red Hat Linux systems), and it provides a wealth of information allowing system administrators a very detailed view of system activity. A slightly shortened version of its syntax is

```
sar [-b] [-B] [-c] [-r] [-R] [-t] [-u] [-v] [-w] [-y]
    [-n {DEV | EDEV | SOCK | FULL}]
    [-x {pid | SELF | SUM | ALL}]
    [-X {pid | SELF | ALL}]
    [-I {irq | SUM | ALL | XALL}]
    [-o [ofile] | -f [ifile]] [-s [hh:mm:ss]]
    [-e [hh:mm:ss]] [interval [count]]
```

interval specifies in seconds how often sar displays its statistics. If *count* is also specified, it states the number of samples to be taken. -o *ofile* names the output file in which sar should save its reports, and -f *ifile* instructs sar to display a report using the data (saved in a binary format) read from *ifile*. If -f is specified, -s and -e define the starting and ending times, respectively, in military format, sar uses to create its report. The default values for -s and -e are 08:00:00 and 18:00:00, respectively, but these can be overridden using *hh:mm:ss* arguments to either or both options.

Use -b to report disk I/O and data transfer statistics. -B produces data on the system paging activity. -c includes data on process creation. -r reports memory and swap usage statistics, and -R reports raw memory usage data. -u provides data on the CPU utilization for user, kernel, idle, and niced processes. -v reports the usage of the kernel's file-related structures. -w produces the number of CPU context switches, and -y displays the number of receive and transmit interrupts detected on each serial line (usually, a TTY device).

Depending on the argument provided, -n reports a variety of network performance and traffic statistics. The DEV keyword specifies normal traffic statistics, EDEV specifies error reports, SOCK requests a report on sockets currently in use, and FULL requests DEV, EDEV, and SOCK.

The -x option requests detailed process information for the process whose PID is *pid*. If SELF is specified, sar reports on itself, while ALL includes the sar process along with all other processes. The SUM directive, ignored if -o is specified, lists the system's total major and minor page faults. To report on child processes, use -X, which has the same restrictions as -x and does not report the summary data produced with -x's SUM directive.

The -I option reports system interrupt activity for a specific IRQ if *irq* is specified, all IRQ's if ALL is used, or total interrupts per second if SUM is asserted. The XALL directive includes APIC interrupts in the report.

Maintaining the Date and Time

In most situations, maintaining the system date and time is a secondary concern. In larger networks, however, particularly those with multiple servers, synchronizing the time across the network is considerably more important. This is especially true for file and database servers, which use finely-grained time values to govern disk writes, reads, and to maintain logs of their activity should one or more operations need to be rolled back. This section discusses key commands for showing, setting, and maintaining the date and time on a Red Hat Linux system, specifically:

- hwclock — Displays and sets the hardware clock
- date — Displays and sets the system time and date
- rdate — Displays and sets the system clock from a network time server

 Unlike most of the sections in this chapter, this section includes examples and illustrations because the material they cover is not discussed elsewhere in the book.

The hwclock command displays and sets the hardware clock. Its syntax is

```
hwclock [-a | -r | -s | -u | -w | --set --date=newdate]
```

hwclock invoked by itself or with the -r option displays the current time, converted to local time, as maintained by the computer's hardware clock (often called the RTC, or Real Time Clock). Specifying -w updates the hardware clock with the system time, while -s updates the system time based on the hardware time. The following examples first show the current system and hardware time, then updates the hardware clock to the system time using the -w option:

```
# date
Sun Jul  8 19:15:50 MDT 2001
# hwclock
Sun 08 Jul 2001 07:15:49 PM MDT  0.067607 seconds
# hwclock -w
```

```
# hwclock
Sun 08 Jul 2001 07:16:03 PM MDT  0.899255 seconds
```

Note that after syncing the hardware clock to the system clock, the hardware clock gained approximately 14 seconds (of course, some time elapsed while the commands were typed). Using `hwclock -w` or `hwclock -s` in a system initialization script (or, as you will see shortly, using `rdate` to sync the system and hardware time to an external time source), enables you to maintain accurate and consistent time on your Red Hat Linux system.

Updating the system time after the system has booted could cause unpredictable behavior. Do not use the `-s` option except early in the system initialization process.

Use the `-u` option to tell `hwclock` that the time stored in the hardware clock is maintained in UTC (Coordinated Universal Time) format, rather than in the local time (the default). The `-a` option enables you to adjust the hardware clock's time to account for systematic drift in its time. `--set`, finally, sets the hardware clock to the date and time specified by the *newdate* argument to the `--date` option. *newdate* can be any date in a format accepted by the `date` command. The next example shows how to use the `--set` argument to update the system time.

Yes, you read that correctly. The acronym almost always appears as UTC, even though it refers to Coordinated Universal Time or Universal Coordinate Time — just another one of the curious Linux/Unix idiosyncrasies.

```
# hwclock --set --date="July 8, 2001 7:24 PM"
# hwclock
Sun 08 Jul 2001 07:24:05 PM MDT  0.429153 seconds
```

As you will see in the discussion of the `date` command, you can use practically any common date and time specification to set the date using `hwclock` and `date`.

The date command displays the current time in a specified format or sets the system time to the specified value. Its syntax comes in two forms:

```
date [-d datestr] [-f datefile] [-r reffile] [+format]
date [-u] [MMDDhhmm[[CC]YY][.ss]] | -s datespec
```

The first form displays the time in the format specified by *format* subject to modification by one of the -d, -f, -r, or -u options. By default, date prints the current date and time, but specifying -d *datestr* prints the date and time in *datestr*; -f *datefile* prints the date and time of the date strings contained in the file *datefile* (one per line); and -f *reffile* prints the date and time that *reffile* was last modified. The next three examples show date's output using these first three options.

```
$ date -d "July 6, 2004 11:48 AM"
Tue Jul  6 11:48:00 MDT 2004
$ cat datefile
January 1, 2010 00:01:01
December 31, 2010 11:59:59 PM
[root@luther /root]# date -f datefile
Fri Jan  1 00:01:01 MST 2010
Fri Dec 31 23:59:59 MST 2010
$ date -r /boot/vmlinuz
Sun Apr  8 18:57:28 MDT 2001
```

Note that regardless of how the source or input date is formatted, date's output always has the same format. To modify the output format, use the +*format* argument. Specify *format* using one or more of the tokens listed in Table 18-10.

TABLE 18-10 OUTPUT FORMAT TOKENS FOR THE date COMMAND

Token	Description
%a	Prints the locale's three-letter abbreviated weekday name (Sun–Sat)
%A	Prints the locale's full weekday name (Sunday–Saturday)
%w	Prints the day of the week (0–6, 0 represents Sunday)
%d	Prints the day of the month (01–31)
%e	Prints the blank padded day of the month (1–31)
%j	Prints the day of the year (001–366)
%U	Prints the week number of the year, with Sunday as the first day of the week (00–53)
%V	Prints the week number of the year, with Monday as the first day of the week (01–52)

Token	Description
%W	Prints the week number of the year, with Monday as the first day of the week (00–53)
%b	Prints the locale's three-letter abbreviated month name (Jan–Dec)
%B	Prints the locale's full month name (January–December)
%m	Prints the two-digit month (01–12)
%y	Prints the last two digits of the year (00–99)
%Y	Prints the four-digit year (1970)
%D	Prints the date (mm/dd/yy)
%x	Prints the locale's date representation (mm/dd/yy)
%S	Prints the two-digit second (00–60)
%M	Prints the two-digit minute (00–59)
%H	Prints the two-digit hour in 24-hour format (00–23)
%I	Prints the two-digit hour in 12-hour format (01–12)
%p	Prints the locale's AM or PM
%Z	Prints the time zone (for example, MDT) or nothing if no time zone is determinable
%T	Prints the 24-hour time (hh:mm:ss)
%r	Prints the 12-hour time (hh:mm:ss AM|PM)
%X	Prints the locale's time representation (same as %H:%M:%S)
%c	Prints the locale's date and time (Sat Nov 04 12:02:33 EST 1989)
%s	Prints the seconds elapsed since 00:00:00, Jan 1, 1970
%%	Prints a literal %
%n	Prints a newline
%t	Prints a horizontal tab

Here are some examples using +format. The first example prints the 4-digit year, the Julian day, the hour in 24-hour format, the minute, and the second, separating each element with a hyphen (-). Note that characters, such as the hyphen, that are not part of a formatting token (prefixed with %) are interpreted literally as part of the output.

```
$ date +%Y-%j-%H-%M-%S
2001-189-20-44-05
```

The next example mimics date's standard output for US locales. Note that because the *format* string contains spaces, you have to use strong (') or weak quotes (") to prevent the shell from interpreting the spaces:

```
$ date +'%a %b %e %H:%M:%S %Z %Y'
Sun Jul  8 20:49:24 MDT 2001
```

The final example shows the current date and time using full names for the month and day using the standard 12-hour time format:

```
$ date +"%A, %B %d, %Y%n%-I:%M %p"
Sunday, July 08, 2001
8:59 PM
```

The example also used the %n to insert a newline and the - modifier between % and I to remove the default padding GNU date inserts into numeric fields. Again, because the *format* string used spaces, the string had to be surrounded with quotes.

Use the second form of the date command to set the system date and time. Use -u to indicate that the specified date and time are relative to Coordinated Universal Time. The string *MMDDhhmmCCYY.ss* defines the time to set. The pairs of characters, in order, mean

MM — The month

DD — The day

hh — The hour

mm — The minute

CC — The century (optional)

YY — The year (optional)

ss — The second (optional)

So, for example, to set the current system date and time to 11:59 p.m. on December 31, 2002, you would execute the command (as root):

```
# date 123123592002
Tue Dec 31 23:59:00 MST 2002
```

Fortunately, you can also use more familiar date and time specifications. In fact, GNU date can interpret most commonly used date and time formats. To use this type of syntax, use the -s option and place the date in quotes if it contains embedded whitespace. For example, the following command sets the current date and time to 5:55:55 a.m. on May 5, 1955:

```
# date -s "May 5, 1955 5:55:55 am"
Thu May  5 05:55:55 MST 1955
```

The next command just sets the time, leaving the date untouched:

```
# date -s "9:33 PM"
Thu May  5 21:33:00 MST 1955
```

The last example, finally, corrects the date, but, unfortunately, has the side effect of resetting the time:

```
# date -s "07/08/2001"
Sun Jul  8 00:00:00 MDT 2001
```

The rdate command is a simple, effective way to maintain accurate system and hardware clock time on your system. Its syntax is

```
rdate [-sp] host
```

host indicates the name of the network time server to contact. If -p is specified, rdate prints the time *host* returns and, if -s is also specified, the system time is set to the time *host* returns. rdate, like hwclock, is best used during system initialization.

 Of course, because it needs network connectivity, rdate must be executed after network has started, perhaps during one of the scripts executed when starting run level 3.

Creating and Restoring Backups

As you learn in Chapter 22, regularly backing up all or part of the file system is a vital part of maintaining a Red Hat Linux system. The commands most common used to perform this key function are:

- ◆ find — Searches for files in a directory tree
- ◆ tar — Copies files into, updates files, and extracts files from tar formatted archives

- ◆ gzip – Compresses files
- ◆ gunzip – Uncompresses files compressed with gzip

Chapter 22 is dedicated to the subject of securing data using backups.

The find command enables you quite precisely to identify the files to back up. Its syntax is somewhat complicated, so I present a simplified version of it here.

find [path] [option] [test] [action]

path defaults to the current directory. It can be specified using standard path specifications. test lists one or more criteria a file or directory should meet in order for find to do something with it. Table 18-11 lists common tests.

TABLE 18-11 TESTS FOR THE find COMMAND

Test	Description
-amin n	File was last accessed n minutes ago
-atime n	File was last accessed n*24 hours ago
-cmin n	File or one of its attributes was last changed n minutes ago
-ctime n	File or one of its attributes was last changed n*24 hours ago
-empty	File is empty
-gid n	File's GID (group ID) is n
-group name	File's group owner is named name
-links n	File has n hard links to it
-mmin n	File's contents were last changed n minutes ago
mtime n	File's contents were last changed n*24 hours ago
-name pattern	File's name matches the pattern pattern
-nouser	No user corresponds to the file's UID
-nogroup	No group corresponds to the file's GID

Test	Description
-path *pattern*	File's path matches the pattern *pattern*
-type [bcdpfls]	File is a block, character, device, named pipe, regular file, symbolic link, or a socket, respectively
-uid *n*	File's UID (user ID) is *n*
-user *name*	File's user owner is named *name*

Numeric arguments of *n* can be preceded with + to indicate greater than *n* and - to indicate less than *n*, allowing ranges of values to be specified.

action defaults to -print, which displays the file's full path. Other actions include -fprint *file*, which prints the file's full path to the file named *file*; -ls, which displays a file listing using the format of ls -dils; -fls *file*, which prints the output of the -ls action to the file named *file*; and -exec *command*, which enables you to run the command *command* on each file located.

option can be used to modify the find's behavior globally or to modify certain of its tests. For example, -follow causes find to dereference symbolic links, so that the -type test tests the *target* of a symbolic link, not the link itself. -daystart causes -atime, -ctime, and -mtime to measure time from the beginning of the current day instead of 24 hours ago. The -maxdepth *levels* option limits find's directory recursion to no more than *levels* below its command line argument. -depth processes a directory's subdirectories before the directory itself.

The tar command can be used to create, update, and restore backups. Again, its command line syntax is rather complex, so the discussion here is simplified and covers typical usage.

```
tar [-crtux] [-f archive] [-vmpvOW] [-jzZ] file
```

file indicates one or more files on which tar operates. That is, *file* is added to or extracted from an archive. Multiple *file*s can be specified, and *file* can also be a path or a file specification using wildcards and regular expressions.

The first group of options define tar's primary operation: -c creates an archive with *file*, -r appends *file* to an archive, -t lists an archive, -u updates an archive if *file* is newer than the version already in the archive, and -x extracts *file* from an archive (if *file* is omitted, tar extracts the entire archive). -f *archive* identifies *archive* as the file or device to use for the archive. If this option is omitted when extracting an archive, tar reads from stdin.

The next group of options modifies how tar works. -v results in a verbose listing as tar operates. -p causes tar to extract files using the same permissions as those stored in the archive, while -m does not extract the file modification times from the archive. -O causes tar to extract an archive to stdout. -W verifies the archived files after the archive is written.

The final group of options control tar's handling of file compression. If -j is specified, tar compresses or decompresses the file using bzip2 or bunzip2. Use -z to use gzip and gunzip, and -Z to use compress and uncompress.

Here are three examples to make the discussion clear.

◆ tar -cf /dev/st0 /home creates an archive of all files under /home on the SCSI tape drive /dev/st0.

◆ tar -czWf $HOME/images.tar.gz $HOME/images/*png creates a gzipped archive file named images.tar.gz in the user's home directory containing all files ending in png in the directory $HOME/images. After writing the archive, tar verifies it.

◆ tar -xjvf /tmp/images.tar.bz2 extracts the entire archive stored in the file /tmp/images.tar.bz2 into the current directory, uncompressing it using bunzip2, and displaying a verbose listing as it works.

gzip and gunzip can be used to compress and decompress, respectively, files in order to conserve space. Note that gzip and gunzip are the same file. When invoked as gunzip, gzip is called with the -d option. Thus, their syntax is identical. Their syntax is:

gzip [-cdlrtv19] [file]

file names one or more files or directories to compress or decompress (you cannot decompress a directory, only a file). If file is omitted, gzip and gunzip read stdin. Specify -c to send output to stdout and preserve file. If gzip is invoked with -d, it behaves like gunzip. Use -l to list the contents of a compressed file. Specifying -q makes gzip operate quietly, suppressing warning messages. To compress subdirectories, use the -r option to invoke recursive operation. To verify that a compressed file has not been corrupted, use the -t option. -v invokes verbose operation. Specifying -1 makes gzip operate as fast as possible, sacrificing compression quality; -9, on the other hand, obtains the best possible compression at the expense, often noticeable, of speed. Values between -1 and -9 express different tradeoffs between speed and compression, the default being -6, which gives a preference to compression while still maintaining satisfactory speed.

Summary

In this chapter, you learned the basic commands that every system administrator must know how to use in a command line environment. You explored a number of commands for working with users and groups, including adding and deleting users and groups and how to modify multiple accounts simultaneously. You also learned how to obtain useful information about who is logged in and what they are doing. Managing file systems is also important, and the chapter discussed commands for creating and checking file systems, manipulating, and managing disk space usage using quotas. Process administration commands discussed included commands for identifying what processes are active, killing processes, and modifying running processes. Finally, you learned a number of commands for getting a high-level view of CPU, memory, and disk usage, managing the date and time, and creating and restoring file system backups.

Chapter 19

Using Scripts to Automate Tasks

IN THIS CHAPTER

- ◆ Understanding Bash programming
- ◆ Working with processes and job control
- ◆ Creating backups
- ◆ Automating scripts
- ◆ Writing, testing, and debugging scripts
- ◆ Selecting a scripting language

SYSTEM ADMINISTRATION DUTIES, such as adding users, creating backups, and monitoring system or network performance, are frequently performed on a repetitive or ongoing basis. As a result, such duties are prime candidates for automation because repeatedly typing the same commands is tedious, error-prone, and time-consuming.

 The discussion assumes that you are comfortable using Bash as an end user and concentrates on Bash features from a shell programmer's perspective.

This chapter teaches you to use Bash's programming language to automate standard system administration tasks. After you read an overview of the fundamentals of Bash programming, you will learn how to use some very useful shell utility programs that ease the task of shell scripting. You will also receive some guidance in selecting an alternative scripting language if you do not like Bash or find its abilities insufficient for your needs.

Understanding Bash Programming

As a programming language, Bash has all the features one would expect: wildcards, variables, operators, functions, and input and output capabilities. Although Bash's programming support is not as complete, fully featured, or powerful as traditional programming languages such as C or Python, it is nevertheless surprisingly capable and well-suited to the task. In this section you will learn about wildcards, command line expansion, variables, operators, flow control, shell functions, input and output processes, and command line arguments in scripts.

Wildcards and special characters

Wildcards are single characters that stand for or substitute for one or more values. Bash uses the familiar * and ? as wildcards. * stands for one or more characters and ? represents any single character. For example, the command ls d* executed in /bin on a Red Hat Linux system should result in the output resembling the following:

```
$ ls d*
date  dd  df  dmesg  dnsdomainname  doexec  domainname
```

The command ls d?, however, shows only the commands beginning with d followed by any single alphanumeric value:

```
$ ls d?
dd  df
```

The command ls ??, shows all files with names consisting of any two alphanumeric characters:

```
$ ls ??
cp  dd  df  ed  ex  ln  ls  mv  ps  rm  sh  su  vi
```

The * and ? characters are useful, but somewhat blunt tools. Bash also supports set operators or set wildcards. *Set operators* allow you to define a range or set of characters to use as wildcards. The notation for defining a set is [*set*], where [and] delimit the range and *set* lists the alphanumeric characters making up the range. The range can be inclusive, disjoint, discrete, or a combination of all three. An *inclusive set* includes all the characters in the set, and is defined using a hyphen, for example, [b-f]. A *disjoint set* is at least two inclusive ranges separated by a comma (,), such as [1-4,7-0]. A *discrete set* refers to a simple list of characters, such as [13579]. Table 19-1 lists some examples of the kinds of sets you can create using the [] set operator.

TABLE 19-1 EXAMPLES OF SETS

Set	Explanation
[b-f]	Denotes any characters in the set b, c, d, e, f
[1-4,7-9]	Denotes any two numbers, the first of which must be 1, 2, 3, or 4 and the second of which must be 7, 8, or 9
[aeiou]	Denotes any character that is a vowel
[b,aeiou]	Denotes any character that is either b or a vowel
[aeiou][a-z]	Denotes any vowel followed by any lowercase character between and including a and z

For the second set in Table 19-1, possible matches include 17, 38, and 49, but 57 and 94 do not match. The next few commands show a few examples of using this set notation in the /bin directory on a Red Hat Linux system.

```
$ ls [b-c]*
basename  bash2  cat    chmod   consolechars  cpio  cut
bash      bsh    chgrp  chown   cp            csh
```

The resulting set consists of any file name beginning with b or c.

```
$ ls [b-d,f]?
cp  dd  df
```

The resulting display consists of any file name beginning with b, c, d, or f followed by any single alphanumeric character.

```
$ ls [a-z][a-z][a-z]
ash  awk  bsh  cat  csh  cut  pwd  red  rpm  rvi  sed  tar
```

The resulting display consists of files whose name is made up of any combination of three lowercase characters between a and z, inclusive.

Bash also has a way to reverse the meaning of the set notation. That is, the notation [!set] refers to all characters not in the set defined by set. So, for example, an easy way to look for all file names not beginning with a consonant is to use [!aeiou]*, that is:

```
$ ls [!aeiou]*
basename    cut       gettext   mkdir     red       stty
bash        date      grep      mknod     rm        su
bash2       dd        gtar      mktemp    rmdir     sync
bsh         df        gunzip    more      rpm       tar
cat         dmesg     gzip      mount     rvi       tcsh
...
```

Bash's wildcard and set operators are a subset of its special characters, also called metacharacters. *Metacharacters* are characters to which Bash assigns a special meaning or interpretation. Table 19-2 lists all of Bash's special characters.

TABLE 19-2 BASH SPECIAL CHARACTERS

Character	Description
*	Multicharacter wildcard
?	Single-character wildcard
<	Redirect input
>	Redirect output
>>	Append output
|	Pipe
{	Start command block
}	End command block
(	Start subshell
)	End subshell
`	Command substitution
$	Variable expression
'	Strong quote
"	Weak quote
\	Interpret the next character literally
&	Execute command in background
;	Command separator
~	Home directory
#	Comment

You should already be familiar with redirecting input and output and using pipes, but you will see examples of all three operations later in the chapter. Input and output redirection should be familiar to you. Commands in a block, that is, delimited by { and } elicit different behavior from Bash than commands executed in a subshell, that is, commands delimited by (and).

You will read about subshells in the section titled "Shell functions" later in the chapter.

The commands between two ` characters cause command substitution, that is, their output or result replaces the expression itself. Consider the command ls `which tar`. Before ls executes, `which tar` will be replaced by its result (/bin/tar, in this case). So, for example the two commands

```
$ which tar
/bin/tar
$ ls -l /bin/tar
-rwxr-xr-x    2 root      root        150908 Mar  6 11:34 /bin/tar
```

produce the same result as the single command

```
$ ls -l `which tar`
-rwxr-xr-x    2 root      root        150908 Mar  6 11:34 /bin/tar
```

Command substitution is very commonly used in shell scripts, and you will see it used throughout this chapter. Another commonly used metacharacter is $, used to obtain the value of a variable, as in the command echo $PATH.

Why are ' and " called strong quote and weak quote characters, respectively? In short, because ' is stronger than ". That is, ' forces Bash to interpret *all* special characters literally, while " protects only *some* of Bash's special characters from interpretation as special characters. To illustrate, compare the effect of ' and " on the output of the command echo $PATH:

```
$ echo $PATH
/usr/local/bin:/bin:/usr/bin:/usr/X11R6/bin:/home/kwall/bin
$ echo "$PATH"
/usr/local/bin:/bin:/usr/bin:/usr/X11R6/bin:/home/kwall/bin
$ echo '$PATH'
$PATH
```

Note how using ' around the PATH variable caused it to be echoed literally, rather than producing the path listing displayed by the other two commands. You will see the implication of this difference throughout the scripts used in this chapter.

Using variables

Like any programming language, Bash has *variables*, named entities that store values. Bash supports both string or character variables and numeric (integer) variables. By convention, variables are named using upper case characters, but this is only a convention, and one not universally followed. For purposes of discussion, this section examines user-defined variables, predefined variables, and positional variables.

 If you read the Bash manual page, it might seem that my discussion of variables contradicts the manual page, which treats variables as "parameters that have names." I avoided the manual page's approach because it was potentially confusing, especially for nonprogrammers. The information I present is correct, I just don't use the same terminology as the author of the manual page.

A *user-defined* variable is just that, a variable created by the shell programmer or end user, rather than one of the many predefined variables intrinsic to Bash. To assign a value to a variable, use the following syntax:

```
varname=value
```

To obtain a variable's value, you can use one of the following two formats:

```
$varname
${varname}
```

Of the two formats, $varname is more commonly used, but ${varname} is more general. You *must* use the second form in order to distinguish variable names from trailing letters, digits, or underscore characters. Consider a variable named STRVAR with the value See Rock City!. Suppose you want to display STRVAR's value followed by an underscore character. The following command fails because Bash attempts to print the value of the variable STRVAR_, not STRVAR.

```
$ echo $STRVAR_
```

In this situation, you must use the more general form, illustrated in the following:

```
$ echo ${STRVAR}_
```

Listing 19-1 shows the code for refvar.sh, a script illustrating this distinction.

Listing 19-1: Referencing Variables

```
#!/bin/sh
# refvar.sh - Referencing a variable

STRVAR='See Rock City!'
echo '${STRVAR}_ yields: ' ${STRVAR}_
echo '$STRVAR_ yields  : ' $STRVAR_
```

The output from the script, shown in the following, makes it clear that $STRVAR_ prints nothing, but ${STRVAR}_ produces the expected output:

```
$ ./refvar.sh
${STRVAR}_ yields:  See Rock City!_
$STRVAR_ yields  :
```

All of the scripts referred to in this chapter are available in this chapter's source code directory on the CD-ROM accompanying this book.

Many of Bash's *predefined* or built-in variables are environment variables, such as BASH_VERSION or PWD. The complete list is available from the Bash man page. Table 19-3 lists commonly used Bash predefined variables:

TABLE 19-3 **BASH 2.x PREDEFINED VARIABLES**

Variable Name	Description
PPID	Stores the process ID of the Bash's parent process.
PWD	Contains the current working directory (as set by the cd command).
OLDPWD	Stores the most previous working directory (as set by the next most recent cd command).
UID	Contains the user ID of the current user as set when the shell started.
BASH_VERSION	Stores the version string of the current Bash instance.

Continued

TABLE 19-3 BASH 2.x PREDEFINED VARIABLES *(Continued)*

Variable Name	Description
RANDOM	Returns a random number between 0 and 32,767 each time it is referenced.
OPTARG	Contains the last command line argument read using the getopts built-in command.
OPTIND	Points to the array index of the next argument to be processed using the getopts built-in command.
HOSTNAME	Stores the name of the current host system.
SHELLOPTS	Contains a colon-separated string of the currently enabled shell options (as set using the set -o shell built-in command).
IFS	Stores the value of the Internal Field Separator, used to define word boundaries. The default value is a space, a tab, or a new line.
HOME	The home directory of the current user.
PS1	Defines the primary command prompt. The default value is "\s-\v\$ ".
PS2	Defines the secondary command prompt, used to indicate that additional input is required to complete a command.
HISTSIZE	The number of commands retained in Bash's command history. The default value is 500.
HISTFILE	The name of the file in which Bash stores the command history. The default value is $HOME/.bash_history.

Listing 19-2 shows the code for predef.sh that displays the names and values of a select subset of Bash's predefined variables.

Listing 19-2: Referencing Predefined Bash Variables

```
#!/bin/sh
# predef.sh - Show the values of a select predefined
#             Bash variables

echo "        PPID = $PPID"
echo "BASH_VERSION = $BASH_VERSION"
echo "      RANDOM = $RANDOM"
echo "   SHELLOPTS = $SHELLOPTS"
```

```
echo "        IFS = $IFS"
echo "   HISTSIZE = $HISTSIZE"
```

The output from this script should resemble the following:

```
$ ./predef.sh
        PPID = 663
BASH_VERSION = 2.04.21(1)-release
      RANDOM = 19869
    SHELLOPTS = braceexpand:hashall:interactive-comments
         IFS =

   HISTSIZE = 1000
```

The value of PPID and RANDOM will surely vary on your system.

Bash has another group of predefined variables, positional parameters. *Positional parameters* are variables that contain the arguments, if any, passed to a script on its command line. The parameter 0 contains the name of the script; the actual parameters begin at 1. If there are more than nine such parameters, you must use the ${} syntax, such as ${10}, to obtain their values. Positional parameters passed to a script are read-only, that is, you cannot change their values.

In addition to the numerically named positional parameters, Bash recognizes three special ones, #, @, and *. # is the number of positional parameters passed to the script, not counting 0. * contains a list of all the positional parameters passed to a script, except 0, formatted as a string. Each parameter is separated from the others by the first character of IFS, the internal field separator. @, finally, is a list of all of the positional parameters stored as separate strings delimited by weak quotes.

Bash operators

In a programming context, *operators* are tokens that perform some sort of operation or manipulation. For example, many programming languages use the plus sign, +, to indicate addition and the asterisk, *, to indicate multiplication. Bash operators behave similarly. They fall into several categories, including comparison operators, file test operators, substitution operators, and pattern matching operators. This section looks at each class of operators and shows examples of how to use them.

COMPARISON OPERATORS

Comparison operators, the simplest to use and understand, compare one variable or value to another, returning 0 if the comparison is true or 1 if the comparison is false. There are two sets of comparison operators, one for string or character data and one for numeric (integer) data. Tables 19-4 and 19-5 list Bash's string and numeric operators.

TABLE 19-4 BASH STRING COMPARISON OPERATORS

Operator	Expression	True if...
=	$str1 = str2$	$str1$ matches $str2$
==	$str1 == str2$	$str1$ matches $str2$
!=	$str1 != str2$	$str1$ does not match $str2$
<	$str1 < str2$	$str1$ is less than $str2$
>	$str1 > str2$	$str1$ is greater than $str2$
-n	$-n\ str$	str's length is nonzero
-z	$-z\ str$	str's length is zero

TABLE 19-5 BASH NUMERIC COMPARISON OPERATORS

Operator	Expression	True if...
-eq	$val1$ -eq $val2$	$val1$ equals $val2$
-ne	$val1$ -ne $val2$	$val1$ is not equal $val2$
-ge	$val1$ -ge $val2$	$val1$ is greater than or equal to $val2$
-gt	$val1$ -gt $val2$	$val1$ is greater than $val2$
-le	$val1$ -le $val2$	$val1$ is less than or equal to $val2$
-lt	$val1$ -lt $val2$	$val1$ is less than $val2$

When comparing strings, keep in mind that A–Z come before a–z in the ASCII character set, so A is "less than" a and foo is "greater than" bar.

TIP If you are not familiar with the ASCII sort order, Red Hat Linux includes a man page (man ascii) that lists the ASCII character set.

Listings 19-3 and 19-4, strcmp.sh and numcmp.sh, respectively, illustrate the use of the string and comparison operators.

Listing 19-3: Using Bash String Comparison Operators

```
#!/bin/sh
# strcmp.sh - Using Bash string comparison operators

C1="b"
C2="F"
S1="STRING"
S2="string"
S3="some darn string"

if [[ $C1 > $C2 ]]; then
        echo "$C1 is greater than $C2"
else
        echo "$C1 is less than $C2"
fi

if [[ $S1 > $S2 ]]; then
        echo "$S1 is greater than $S2"
else
        echo "$S1 is less then $S2"
fi

if [[ -n $S3 ]]; then
        echo "S3 is $S3"
else
        echo "S3 is empty"
fi

if [[ -z $S4 ]]; then
        echo "S4 is empty"
else
        echo "S4 is $S4"
fi
```

strcmp.sh's output looks like this:

```
$ ./strcmp.sh
b is greater than F
STRING is less then string
S3 is some darn string
S4 is empty
```

A few notes are in order. First, do not worry about understanding the syntax of the if...then...else construct right now. The section titled "Flow control" later in the chapter discusses it, so just accept that it works for the time being. Secondly, the [operator must be terminated with a]. Finally, as noted earlier, F precedes b in the ASCII character set, so b is greater than F lexicographically. Similarly, STRING is less than string. The last two tests use the -z and -n operators to test for empty and nonempty strings.

Listing 19-4 presents numcmp.sh, a script that illustrates how to use some of Bash's numeric comparison operators.

Listing 19-4: Using Bash Numeric Comparison Operators

```
#!/bin/sh
# numcmp.sh - Using Bash numeric comparison operators

W=7
X=10
Y=-5
Z=10

if [ $W -gt $X ]; then
        echo "W is greater than X ($W > $X)"
else
        echo "W is less than X ($W < $X)"
fi

if [ $X -lt $Y ]; then
        echo "X is less than Y ($X < $Y)"
else
        echo "X is greater then Y ($X > $Y)"
fi

if [ $X -eq $Z ]; then
        echo "X equals Z ($X = $Z)"
fi

if [ $Y -le $Z ]; then
        echo "Y is less than or equal to Z ($Y <= $Z)"
else
        echo "Y is greater than or equal to Z ($Y >= $Z)"
fi
```

numcmp.sh's output should be

```
$ ./numcmp.sh
W is less than X (7 < 10)
X is greater then Y (10 > -5)
X equals Z (10 = 10)
Y is less than or equal to Z (-5 <= 10)
```

The next section extends your ability to work with numeric values in shell scripts, showing you how to use arithmetic operators to perform basic arithmetic operations in Bash shell scripts.

ARITHMETIC OPERATORS

If Bash allows you to compare numeric values and variables, it follows that Bash allows you to perform arithmetic on numeric values and variables. In addition to the comparison operators discussed in the previous section, Bash uses the operators listed in Table 19-6 to perform arithmetic operations in shell scripts.

TABLE 19-6 BASH ARITHMETIC OPERATORS

Operator	Expression	Description
++	var++	Increments *var* after obtaining its value
++	++var	Increments *var* before obtaining its value
--	var--	Decrements *var* after obtaining its value
--	--var	Decrements *var* before obtaining its value
+	var1 + var2	Adds *var1* and *var2*
-	var1 - var2	Subtracts *var2* from *var1*
*	var1 * var2	Multiplies *var1* by *var2*
/	var1 / var2	Divides *var1* by *var2*
%	var1 % var2	Calculates the remainder of dividing *var1* by *var2*
=	var = op	Assigns result of an arithmetic operation *op* to *var*

The complete list of Bash's arithmetic operators also includes bitwise and logical functions, a conditional evaluation operator, C-style assignment operators, and a comma operator. Refer to Bash's excellent manual page for complete details.

SUBSTITUTION OPERATORS

The substitution operators, also known as *string operators*, determine whether or not a string variable is empty and manipulate the variable based on the result of that test. The string operators make it easy to assign or change the values assigned to variables that have string or character values. Table 19-7 lists each operator and briefly describes its function.

TABLE 19-7 BASH SUBSTITUTION OPERATORS

Operator	Expression	Description
:-	${var:-word}	If *var* exists and is nonempty, return its value. Otherwise, return *word*. *var* is not changed.
:=	${var:=word}	If *var* exists and is nonempty, returns its value. Otherwise, assign *word* to *var* and return the new value (*word*).
:+	${var:+word}	If *var* exists and is not empty, return *word*. Otherwise, return null.
:?	${var:?message}	If *var* exists and is nonempty, returns its value. Otherwise, display "bash2: $var:$message" and abort the current command. If executed in a script, the script name replaces bash2.
:n	${var:offset[:length]}	Returns a substring of *var* that is length characters long, beginning at *offset*. If *length* is omitted, return the entire substring beginning at *offset*.

Suppose you have a variable named DATADIR initialized to /var/data/. The shell script in Listing 19-5 shows how the first four substitution operators listed in Table 19-7 behave:

Listing 19-5: Using Bash Substitution Operators with a Set Variable

```
#!/bin/sh
# subst1.sh - Using Bash substitution operators
#             with a set variable

DATADIR="/var/data"
echo ${DATADIR:-/var/data/current}
echo ${DATADIR:=/var/data/current}
echo ${DATADIR:+/var/data/current}
echo ${DATADIR:?/var/data/current}
```

subst1.sh's output should resemble the following:

```
$ ./subst1.sh
/var/data
/var/data
/var/data/current
/var/data
```

The output is largely uninteresting because DATADIR is set. The third command, using :+, though, returns the alternate value /var/data/current because DATADIR is set. Contrast this output to that resulting from Listing 19-6, subst2.sh, which shows how each operator works if DATADIR is *not* set.

Listing 19-6: Using Bash Substitution Operators with an Empty Variable

```
#!/bin/sh
# subst2.sh - Using Bash substitution operators
#             with an empty variable

echo ${DATADIR:-/var/data/current}
echo ${DATADIR:=/var/data/current}
echo ${DATADIR:+/var/data/current}
unset DATADIR
echo ${DATADIR:?"variable not set"}
```

subst2.sh uses Bash's unset command to remove DATADIR (clear its value) because the :+ operator sets the value of DATADIR. The output from this script should be

```
$ ./subst2.sh
/var/data/current
/var/data/current
/var/data/current
./subst2.sh: DATADIR: variable not set
```

Note that the first three operators display the alternate value for DATADIR, /var/data/current. The fourth one, however, displays the error message specified in the script because DATADIR is unset (empty).

The last operator in Table 19-7 is usually called the *substring operator* because it returns a substring of its variable (the character count begins at 0, not 1). Again, consider the DATADIR variable defined as /var/data. The expression ${DATADIR:3} returns the entire substring beginning at position 3, while {DATADIR:1:5} returns the characters in positions 1–5. That is:

```
$ DATADIR=/var/data
$ echo ${DATADIR:3}
r/data
$ echo ${DATADIR:1:5}
var/d
```

In what situations can you use Bash's substitution operators? They are most useful for setting or using default values. A script that cleans directories of temporary files might use :+ to reset a variable containing a directory name to a default starting point. A script could use the :? operator to abort if an important variable is unset. The substring operator, (:), is useful in a variety of situations because it makes it easy to parse the specific pieces of information that interest you out of a string variable. The main consideration to keep in mind is that all of the substitution operators work best with data that is in a known format, has a fixed length, and whose appearance does not change, such as the output of the ls command, listings of tar archives, and any data the form of which you control. To work with freely formatted string data or variable length data, use the pattern matching operators discussed in the next section

PATTERN MATCHING OPERATORS

Before discussing the pattern matching operators, it will be helpful to define what pattern matching is. A *pattern* is a string that contains one of the wildcard characters discussed at the beginning of the chapter, *, ?, and []. *Pattern matching*, then, refers to matching all or part of a variable's string value to such a pattern, and *pattern matching operators* are the Bash operators that perform these matches. Table 19-8 lists Bash's pattern matching operators.

TABLE 19-8 BASH PATTERN MATCHING OPERATORS

Operator	Expression	Description
#	${var#pattern}	Deletes the shortest match of *pattern* from the front of *var* and returns the rest.
##	${var##pattern}	Deletes the longest match of *pattern* from the front of *var* and returns the rest.
%	${var%pattern}	Deletes the shortest match of *pattern* from the end of *var* and returns the rest.
%%	${var%%pattern}	Deletes the longest match of *pattern* from the end of *var* and returns the rest.
/	${var/pattern/str}	Replaces the longest match of *pattern* in *var* with *str*. Replaces only the first match.
//	${var//pattern/str}	Replaces the longest match of *pattern* in *var* with *str*. Replaces all matches.

The prototypical use of Bash's pattern matching operators is to manipulate file and path names. You can use #, ##, %, and %% to strip directory or file name components from path names. Listing 19-7, match.sh, shows the result of using each of these operators on the PATH environment variable.

Listing 19-7: Bash Pattern Matching Operators

```
#!/bin/sh
# match.sh - Using Bash's pattern matching operators

echo ${PATH}
echo ${PATH#/usr/kerberos/bin:}
echo ${PATH##/usr/kerberos/bin:}
echo ${PATH%$HOME/bin}
echo ${PATH%%$HOME/bin}
```

The first command shows the PATH variable's normal value to provide a point of reference. The next two commands use # and ## to delete the longest and shortest matches of the string /usr/kerberos/bin: from the front of PATH and return the rest. The last two commands use % and %% to delete the longest and shortest matches of $HOME/bin from PATH. The output will vary slightly on your system, but should resemble the following:

```
$ echo $PATH
/usr/kerberos/bin:/bin:/usr/bin:/usr/X11R6/bin:/home/kwall/bin
/bin:/usr/bin:/usr/X11R6/bin:/home/kwall/bin
/bin:/bin:/usr/bin:/usr/X11R6/bin:/home/kwall/bin
/usr/kerberos/bin:/bin:/usr/bin:/usr/X11R6/bin:
/usr/kerberos/bin:/bin:/usr/bin:/usr/X11R6/bin:
```

The last two statements, using % and %%, show how to use variables, HOME in this case, to define a pattern to match.

The / and // operators perform the familiar search and replace operation. / performs a single search and replace operation, and // results in a global search and replace. For example, the following command uses // to replace each colon (:) in the PATH environment variable with a new line:

```
$ echo -e ${PATH//:/\\n}
/usr/kerberos/bin
/usr/local/bin
/bin
/usr/bin
/usr/X11R6/bin
```

The path listing is much easier to read when displayed this way. The -e argument to echo causes it to treat the escape sequence \n as a new line rather than a literal string. Oddly, though, you also have to escape the escape sequence in order for echo to interpret it!

FILE TEST OPERATORS

Many common administrative tasks involve working with files and directories. Bash makes it easy to perform these tasks because it has a rich set of operators that perform a variety of tests. You can, for example, determine if a file exists at all or if it exists but is empty, if a file is a directory, and what the file's permissions are. Table 19-9 lists commonly used file test operators.

TABLE 19-9 BASH FILE TEST OPERATORS

Operator	Description
-d *file*	*file* exists and is a directory.
-e *file*	*file* exists.
-f *file*	*file* exists and is a regular file (not a directory or special file).
-g *file*	*file* exists and is SGID (set group ID).
-r *file*	You have read permission on *file*.
-s *file*	*file* exists and is not empty.
-u *file*	*file* exists and is SUID (set user ID).
-w *file*	You have write permission on *file*.
-x *file*	You have execute permission on *file* or, if *file* is a directory, you have search permission on it.
-O *file*	You own *file*.
-G *file*	*file*'s group ownership matches one of your group memberships.
file1 -nt *file2*	*file1* is newer than *file2*.
file1 -ot file2	file1 is older than *file2*.

The script in Listing 19-8 illustrates how to use the file test operators. It applies several file test operators to each file in the top level of a directory name provided as an argument.

Listing 19-8: File Test Operators

```
#!/bin/sh
# filetest.sh - Illustrate file test operators
# Arguments: Name of directory to scan

# Have to provide the argument
if [[ $# != 1 ]]; then
    echo "usage: filetest.sh DIR"
    exit 1
fi

# Only accept directory arguments
if [ ! -d $1 ]; then
    echo "$1 is not a directory"
    exit 1
fi

# Process each file in the directory
for FILE in $1/*
do
    # Ignore directories and special files
    if [ -f $FILE ]; then
        echo $FILE
        if [ -r $FILE ]; then
            echo -e "\tReadable by $USER"
        fi
        if [ -w $FILE ]; then
            echo -e "\tWritable by $USER"
        fi
        if [ -x $FILE ]; then
            echo -e "\t/Executable by $USER"
        fi
        if [ -O $FILE ]; then
            echo -e "\tOwned by $USER"
        fi
    fi
done
```

The first if statement ensures that the script was called with one argument, using the $# positional parameter discussed earlier in the chapter. If not, it displays a usage message and exits; otherwise, execution continues with the next if statement. The second if statement makes sure that the argument passed to filetest.sh (the $1 parameter) is a directory name. If it is not, the script exits after displaying an error message. Otherwise, processing continues with the for loop.

The section titled "Determinate loops using `for`" explains the syntax of the `for` statement.

The `for` loop processes each file in the directory. For each file, the script first tests whether or not it is a regular file using the `-f` operator. If it is not, it skips to the next file. Otherwise, `filetest.sh` tests whether or not the user executing the script has read, write, and execute permission on the file (using the `-r`, `-w`, and `-x` operators, respectively), whether or not the user owns the file (using the `-O` operator), displays the results of each test on `stdout`, and then repeats these tests for the next file. After evaluating the last file, the script exits.

The output of this script will vary, of course, but it should resemble the following:

```
$ ./filetest.sh $HOME
/home/kwall/CliffHanger_1.pps
        Readable by kwall
        Writable by kwall
        Owned by kwall
/home/kwall/important.txt.gz
        Readable by kwall
        Writable by kwall
        Owned by kwall
/home/kwall/newapt.bmp
        Readable by kwall
        Writable by kwall
        Owned by kwall
/home/kwall/Plaid2.jpg
        Readable by kwall
        Writable by kwall
        Owned by kwall
/home/kwall/vmstat.out
        Readable by kwall
        Writable by kwall
        Owned by kwall
```

Flow control

Any programming language worth the name must support *flow control*, the ability to control the order in which code executes. Flow control allows code to loop, branch, or execute conditionally. To *loop* means to execute the same block of code multiple times. To *branch* means to execute a block of code specific to the value of a condition. *Conditional execution* means to execute or not to execute code, depending on the value of some variable. Bash supports flow control, and this section explains the syntax and use of all its flow control structures, listed in Table 19-10.

TABLE 19-10 BASH FLOW CONTROL STATEMENTS

Statement	Type	Description
if	Conditional	Executes code if a condition is true or false
for	Looping	Executes code a fixed number of times
while	Looping	Executes code while a condition is true or false
until	Looping	Executes code until a condition becomes true or false
case	Branching	Executes code specific to the value of a variable
select	Branching	Executes code specific to an option selected by a user

CONDITIONAL EXECUTION USING IF

The syntax of Bash's if statement is shown in the following:

```
if condition then
        statements
[elif condition
        statements]
[else
        statements]
fi
```

condition is the control variable that determines which *statements* execute. elif is Bash's equivalent to else if in other programming languages. fi signals the end of the if structure. Be careful when creating *condition* because if checks the exit status of the *last* statement in *condition*. That is, if *condition* consists of multiple tests, only the last one (unless grouping using () is applied) affects the control flow. Most Linux programs return 0 if they complete successfully or normally and nonzero if an error occurs, so this peculiarity of Bash's if statement usually does not pose a problem.

Bash's if statement works just like the if structures in most other programming languages. If the exit status is 0 (true), then *statements* will be executed. If it is nonzero (false), the statements following an elif or else clause, if present, will be executed, after which control jumps to the first line of code following fi. The else clause executes only if all other *conditions* in elif clauses are false. The else and elif clauses are optional and you can use multiple elif clauses if you wish.

While *most* Linux programs return 0 if they complete successfully and nonzero otherwise, this is not universally true. The diff program, for example, returns 0 if it does not find differences, 1 if it does, or 2 if a problem occurred. Nonstandard exit values such as these can alter the way a shell script works, so double-check return codes in a program's or command's documentation.

Evaluating exit codes, and the order in which you evaluate them, is important because Bash allows you to use the && and || operators to combine exit codes in *condition*. && is known as a *logical AND*, which means that a condition is true if and only if the expressions on both sides of the && operator are true. So, given the condition *expression1 && expression2*, the condition is true if and only if *expression1* and *expression2* are true. If *expression1* is false (nonzero), Bash will not evaluate *expression2*. The ||, called a *logical OR*, requires only that either one or the other of the expressions on either side of the operator be true. Thus, the condition *expresison1 || expression2* is true if either *expression1* or *expression2* is true. The condition follows the general form *expression1 || expression2*.

How do these operators work? Suppose that you have to change the current working directory and copy a file before executing a certain code block. One way to accomplish this is to use nested if statements, as in the following snippet:

```
if cd $DATADIR then
    if cp datafile datafile.bak then
        #
        # Code here
        #
    fi
fi
```

Using the && operator, you can write this much more concisely, as the following code snippet illustrates:

```
if cd $DATADIR && cp datafile datafile.bak then
    #
    # Code here
    #
fi
```

Both code snippets accomplish the same thing, but the second example is shorter and, in my opinion, easier to read and understand because you do not get bogged down sorting out the nested ifs. If, for some reason, the cd command fails, Bash will not attempt the copy operation.

Several shell scripts in this chapter have used the `if` structure, so refer to the previous examples to see various ways to use `if`.

DETERMINATE LOOPS USING FOR

The `for` structure allows you to execute a section of code a fixed number of times, so the loops it creates are called *determinate*. The `for` loop is a frequently used loop tool because it operates neatly on lists of data, such as Bash's positional parameters ($1-$9) or lists of files in a directory. The general format of the for statement is shown here:

```
for value in list
do
    command
    [...]
done
```

list is a whitespace separated list of values, such as file names. *value* is a single list item; for each iteration through the loop, Bash sets *value* to the next element in *list*. *command* can be any valid Bash expression, and, naturally, you can execute multiple *command*s. *command* typically uses or manipulates *value*, but it does not have to.

The `for` statement is a Bash built-in command, so you can type `help for` at the command prompt to get a quick syntax summary.

Suppose you want to copy a number of files in the same directory, adding the extension `.bak` to the copies. DOS users accustomed to the way DOS copies multiple files are dismayed when they discover that the same approach does not work in Linux. To illustrate, the following DOS command uses the `COPY` command to copy every file with a `.dat` extension, replacing `.dat` with `.bak`:

```
C:\> copy *.dat *.bak
data1.dat
data2.dat
data3.dat
        3 file(s) copied
```

The same method does not work for Linux's `cp` command because if you specify multiple files to copy, `cp` expects the final argument to be a directory. One way around this inconvenience is to use Bash's `for` loop. The following example illustrates using `for` at the command line to emulate the DOS `COPY` command's behavior:

```
$ for FILE in *.dat
> do
>          cp -v $FILE ${FILE%.dat}.bak
> done
`data1.dat' -> `data1.bak'
`data2.dat' -> `data2.bak'
`data3.dat' -> `data3.bak'
```

The cp command's -v (verbose) option causes it to display what it is doing. Note the use of the % pattern matching operator to replace .dat with .bak for each file copied. Notice also how the Bash command prompt changes to the secondary prompt (PS2), >, indicating that Bash needs more input to complete the command. Listing 19-8 showed a slightly more complex usage of the for loop.

INDETERMINATE LOOPS USING WHILE AND UNTIL

The for loop is ideal when you know in advance, or can determine before entering the loop, how many times a given section of code must execute. If you do not know in advance or cannot determine at runtime how many times to execute a code block, you need to use one of Bash's indeterminate loop structures, while and until. while and until constructs cause continued code execution as long as or until a particular condition is met. The key here is that your code must ensure that the condition in question is eventually met, or you will get stuck in an infinite loop.

The general form of a while loop is:

```
while condition
do
    command
    [...]
done
```

In a while loop, as long as *condition* remains true, execute each *command* until *condition* becomes false. If *condition* is initially false, execution jumps to the first statement following done.

The general form of the until loop is:

```
until condition
do
    command
    [...]
done
```

until's structure and meaning is the opposite of while's because an until loop executes as long as *condition* is false; a while loop executes as long as *condition* is true.

Listing 19-9 illustrates the use of Bash's while loop. It makes 150 copies of a file named junk in the current directory.

Listing 19-9: Bash while Loops

```
#!/bin/sh
# while.sh - Illustrate using Bash while loops

declare -i CNT
CNT=1

if [ ! -r junk ]
then
    touch ./junk
fi

while [ $CNT -le 150 ]
do
    cp junk junk.$CNT
    CNT=$CNT+1
done
```

while.sh illustrates several Bash programming features. Of course, you see the while loop in action. It also uses the -e file test operator to test for the existence of the file named junk and, if it does not exist, uses the touch command to create it. The declare statement creates an integer variable, CNT, to server as the loop control variable. Each iteration of the loop increments CNT, making sure that the loop condition eventually becomes false. Do not forget to delete the files the script creates!

The following code snippet shows how to use an until loop to accomplish the same thing as the while loop in Listing 19-9.

```
until [ $CNT -gt 150 ]
do
    cp junk junk.$CNT
    CNT=$CNT+1
done
```

The logic of the condition is different, but the end result is the same. In this case, using a while loop is the appropriate way to handle the problem.

SELECTION STRUCTURES USING CASE AND SELECT

This section discusses the case and select selection structures, which allow a shell script to execute a specific section of code depending on the value of a variable or expression or in response to user input. You will learn about the case statement first and then about the select statement.

THE CASE STATEMENT The `case` structure, approximately comparable to C's `switch` keyword, is best suited for situations in which a variable or expression can have numerous values and as a replacement for long if blocks. The complete syntax for `case` is as follows:

```
case expr in
    pattern )
        commands ;;
    pattern )
        commands ;;
    ...
esac
```

The space between *pattern* and) is required, as is the space between *commands* and ;;. *expr* can be any valid Bash expression. *expr* is compared to each *pattern* until a match is found, at which point the commands associated with the first match are executed. ;;, equivalent to C's `break`, signals the end of the code block and causes control to jump to the first line of code past `esac` (case in reverse), which marks the end of the `case` structure. If no pattern matches, execution resumes at the first line of code after `esac`. Listing 19-10 shows the `case` statement at work.

Listing 19-10: Using the case Statement

```
#!/bin/sh
# case.sh - Using the case selection structure

clear
echo -n "Type a single letter, number, or punctuation character: "
read -n 1 OPT
echo

case $OPT in
    [[:upper:]] ) echo "$OPT is an upper case letter" ;;
    [[:lower:]] ) echo "$OPT is a lower case letter" ;;
    [[:digit:]] ) echo "$OPT is a digit" ;;
    [[:punct:]] ) echo "$OPT is punctuation" ;;
esac
```

After clearing the screen with the `clear` command, the script prompts for a single character of input and uses the `read` built-in to read a single character from `stdin` and store it in `OPT`. The `case` statement uses a special notation, explained shortly, to represent sets of characters. If the character typed at the prompt matches one of the four patterns ([:upper:], [:lower:], [:digit:], or [:punct:]), `case.sh` displays the appropriate message. If no match is found, the script silently exits.

In addition to illustrating the case selection structure, `case.sh` introduces two new Bash programming elements, `read` and character classes. You will learn about the `read` built-in command in the section "Processing input and output" later in the chapter. A *character class* is a symbolic name embedded between [: and :] that represents a group of characters. In fact, character classes are special cases of the [] set notation described in the section titled "Wildcards and special characters" near the beginning of the chapter. For example, the set [a-z] is equivalent to the character class [:lower:]. The most common character classes are listed in Table 19-11.

TABLE 19-11 COMMON BASH CHARACTER CLASSES

Class	Description
alnum	All alphabetic and numeric characters
alpha	All alphabetic characters
digit	All numerals
lower	All lowercase letters
punct	All punctuation symbols
upper	All uppercase letters

THE SELECT STATEMENT The select control structure makes it easy to create menus. Indeed, it seems almost to have been designed specifically for that purpose. Its syntax is

```
select value [in list]
do
     commands
done
```

The `select` statement creates a numbered menu for each *value* in *list*. Selecting the number corresponding to a *value* causes *commands* to execute. Listing 19-11, dircnt.sh, illustrates how `select` works. It counts the number of files in a user-specified directory, using the `select` statement to identify the directory to analyze.

Listing 19-11: Creating Menus with select
```
#!/bin/sh
# dircnt.sh - Using the select statement

PS3="[Number]: "
IFS=:
```

Continued

Listing 19-11 *(Continued)*

```
clear

select ITEM in $PATH Quit
do
    [ "$ITEM" = "Quit" ] && exit 0
    if [ "$ITEM" ]; then
        CNT=$(ls -Al $ITEM | wc -l)
        echo "$CNT files in $ITEM"
    else
        echo "Invalid selection"
    fi
    echo
done
```

The script first sets the PS3 environment variable, which is the prompt that select displays to request user input. Next, it sets the IFS (internal field separator) variable to : to enable select properly to parse the PATH environment variable. After clearing the screen, it enters a loop, presenting a numbered menu of options derived from the PATH variable and the literal string Quit. Then it prompts the user to make a choice, as shown in the following (the exact appearance depends on the value of the PATH variable):

```
1) /usr/kerberos/bin   4) /usr/bin          7) Quit
2) /usr/local/bin      5) /usr/X11R6/bin
3) /bin                6) /home/kwall/bin
[Number]:
```

If the user selects the numeral corresponding to the Quit option (7 in this example), dircnt.sh exits. Selecting a valid choice (1–6 in this case) stores the corresponding directory name in ITEM, which is then used in the statement CNT=$(ls -Al $ITEM | wc -l). This command counts the number of files (not including . and ..) in the directory specified by ITEM. The file count is displayed to stdout, and the menu redrawn. If the user makes an invalid selection, dircnt.sh displays an error message and then redraws the menu.

Bash has a fully capable range of flow control structures. Although they behave in ways slightly differently than their counterparts in traditional programming languages like C, C++, or Pascal, they enable you to create powerful, flexible shell scripts.

Shell functions

Shell functions offer two important advantages over aliases. First, shell functions execute faster because they are already stored in memory and do not execute in a subshell. A *subshell* is a complete Bash session (another kernel process, in fact) created each time you invoke a script. On a slow or heavily loaded system, the overhead involved in spawning new processes for subshells can result in a significant performance penalty, so shell functions sidestep this potential problem. Secondly, shell functions increase the modularity of your scripts. If you store frequently used shell functions in a separate file, you can use the source built-in to read that file into your scripts. Then, if you change a function, you have to change only one file rather than edit each file that uses the script.

Define shell functions using one of the following two forms:

```
function fname
{
    commands
}
```

   or

```
fname()
{
    commands
}
```

fname is the name of the function and *commands* are the statements and expressions that define its behavior. Both forms are widely used and there is no difference between them. Typically, you define functions at the beginning of a script, before they are used, but doing so is not required. The following example defines a function (at the command prompt) named mydate that displays the output of the date command in a custom format.

```
$ function mydate
> {
> date '+%A, %B %d, %Y'
> }
$
```

To use a function, simply invoke it using its name followed by any arguments it needs. Once a function has been defined, you can use it on the command line or in a script. For example, to use the mydate shell function just defined on the command line, type its name at the Bash prompt:

```
$ mydate
Wednesday, June 27, 2001
```

Alternatively, place the definition in a script and then execute the script. The Red Hat Linux startup scripts use precisely this strategy. The file /etc/rc.d/init.d/functions defines at least 15 shell functions used throughout the initialization scripts. Near the top of every init script in /etc/rc.d/init.d you will find these two lines:

```
# Source function library.
. /etc/rc.d/init.d/functions
```

The key command is . /etc/rc.d/init.d/functions, which allows the init script to use the functions defined in the file. In fact, studying the contents of /etc/rc.d/init.d/functions gives you great insight into using Bash functions and into the larger subject of shell programming in general.

Processing input and output

Bash sports a surprisingly rich collection of input and output features. Many of them, such as manipulating file descriptors or reading and writing to device files, are esoteric and most useful to low-level system programmers and will not be covered in this section. Rather, it covers I/O redirection, using the echo command for output, and using the read command for input.

REDIRECTING I/O

The basic I/O redirectors, > and <, redirect output from stdout and input from stdin, respectively. Most often, > is used to save the output from a command to a file. For example, the command cat /etc/passwd > out captures the output of the cat command and sends it to a file named out in the current directory. To capture stderr output to a file, put a 2 immediately in front of >. For example, if you invoke tar with no options or arguments, it displays an error message to stderr (usually the display). The following command sends the error message to /dev/null (the bit bucket):

```
$ tar 2> /dev/null
```

Of course, you can also redirect stdout to /dev/null. In fact, it is common practice in shell scripts to redirect both stdout and stderr to /dev/null. Why? In many cases, a command's output is less important than whether or not it succeeded or failed. Because most programs return an exit code indicating success (usually 0) or failure (usually any nonzero value), from a programmatic standpoint it is sufficient to use the predefined Bash variable ? to check a program's exit status. In other cases, hiding output gives a script a more polished, professional appearance and lets *you* control how your script appears to users.

 To redirect stdout and stderr to the same file, such as /dev/null, use a command of the form

mycommand > /dev/null 2>&1

Replace *mycommand* with the command and any arguments the command requires. The notation 2>&1 redirects stderr to stdout, which was previously redirected to /dev/null. A less familiar but functionally identical form and more concise version of this command is

mycommand &> /dev/null

The section titled "Redirecting Standard Output and Standard Error" in the Bash man page explains how and why this syntax works.

If you use > to redirect stdout to an existing file, you will lose the file's original contents. To avoid this circumstance, use Bash's append operator, >>, which adds data to the end of a file, thus protecting the file's original contents.

To redirect stdin, which is ordinarily the keyboard, use the input redirector, <. For example, the command cat < /etc/passwd > out redirects both input and output.

So-called here-documents, which use the << operator, are an interesting case of input redirection. The term *here-document* derives from the fact that Bash reads its input from the current source, "here," if you will, rather than from stdin or a separate file. A here-document stores the input to a command in the script. The syntax, which looks somewhat odd, is:

```
command << label
    commandinput
label
```

label demarcates the beginning and end of the command's input. *commandinput* is the input itself and *command* is the program or utility or command to execute. This syntax says that *command* should read *commandinput* until it encounters *label* on a line by itself.

A typical use of here-documents is for scripting programs that lack a convenient scripting interface. The familiar ftp client program is a fine example of this. Listing 19-12, ftp.sh, illustrates how to script the ftp client using a here-document.

Listing 19-12: Scripting ftp Using a Here-Document

```
#!/bin/sh
# ftp.sh - Scripting ftp using a here-document

USER=anonymous
PASS=kwall@kurtwerks.com

ftp -i -n << END
open localhost
```

Continued

Listing 19-12 *(Continued)*

```
user $USER $PASS
cd pub
ls
close
bye
END
```

ftp -i -n uses -i to start in noninteractive mode and -n to suppress the automatic login. The script uses END as the label to signal the end of input. Using various ftp commands, the script first opens an ftp session to localhost. Then it sends the login sequence using the USER and PASS variables defined at the beginning of the script. Once logged in, it changes to the standard public ftp directory, pub, and then executes an ls command to demonstrate that the script worked. Finally, it closes the connection and exits the program. When Bash encounters the second END label, the script exits.

The output shown in the following illustrates ftp.sh in action:

```
$ ./ftp.sh
total 0
-rw-r--r--   1 root      50             0 Jun 28 04:18 herfile
-rw-r--r--   1 root      50             0 Jun 28 04:18 hisfile
-rw-r--r--   1 root      50             0 Jun 28 04:18 myfile
-rw-r--r--   1 root      50             0 Jun 28 04:18 ourfile
-rw-r--r--   1 root      50             0 Jun 28 04:18 yourfile
```

Another typical use for here-documents is to include documentation, such as online help, in scripts.

STRING I/O

Many of the scripts that you have seen in this chapter use the echo command to display information. It supports a number of useful options. You have already seen -e, which enables the interpretation of escaped characters, such as \n (newline) and \t (tab). echo's -n option omits appending the final newline to its output. Table 19-12 lists escape sequences that echo interprets when called with the -e option.

TABLE 19-12 echo ESCAPE SEQUENCES

Sequence	Description
\a	Alert
\b	Backspace

Sequence	Description
\c	Omits the final newline appended to output
\f	Formfeed
\r	Return
\v	Vertical tab
\n	Newline
\\	A single \

To work with string input, use the read command. Its syntax is

```
read var1 var2 ...
```

Although ideal for getting input in an interactive mode from a user, read also works with files. In interactive mode, read is simple to use, as the following code fragment illustrates:

```
echo -n 'Name: '
read NAME
echo "Name is $NAME"
```

Using read to process text files is somewhat more complicated. The easiest way is to create a script and then redirect its input from the file you want to process. Listing 19-13 processes the contents of /etc/passwd.

Listing 19-13: Using read to Process a Text File

```
#!/bin/sh
# read.sh - Using read to process a text file

IFS=:
while read name pass uid gid gecos home shell
do
    echo "*********************"
    echo "name   : $name"
    echo "pass   : $pass"
    echo "uid    : $uid"
    echo "gid    : $gid"
    echo "gecos  : $gecos"
    echo "home   : $home"
    echo "shell  : $shell"
done
```

Setting IFS enables the script to parse the /etc/passwd entries properly. The while read statement reads each line of input, assigns the value of each field to the appropriate variable, and then uses the echo command to display the password information on stdout. You can execute this script with (at least) one of the following two commands:

```
$ ./read.sh < /etc/passwd
```

or

```
$ cat /etc/passwd | ./read.sh
```

The output should be identical regardless of which command you use. Table 19-13 lists useful options the read command accepts.

TABLE 19-13 USEFUL read OPTIONS

Option	Description
-n *num*	Reads *num* characters from stdin
-p *prompt*	Displays *prompt* followed by a space to solicit user input
-s	Disables echoing input read from stdin
-t *secs*	Cancels the read operation after *secs* seconds elapse without reading an input line

Using read's -p option allows user input code to be more concise. For example, the statement read -p "User Name: " NAME is identical to the following fragment:

```
echo "User Name: "
read NAME
```

Listing 19-10, case.sh, uses read -n 1 to read a single character from standard input. The -s (presumably, a mnemonic for silent), is ideal for reading a user password or other sensitive information. The following commands define a shell function, getpass, that uses all four of the options listed in Table 19-13 to read a user's password, and then invokes the function.

```
$ getpass()
> {
> read -s -p "Password: " -n 8 -t 5 PWORD
> echo -e "\nYou entered: $PWORD";
```

```
> }
$ getpass
Password: [At the prompt, type your password and press Enter.]
You entered: secret
```

-t 5 causes the read command to time out if the user does not press Enter in 5 seconds (the echo command still executes, though). -n 8 causes read to read no more than 8 characters from stdin. As you can see in the output, -s suppressed displaying what the user typed.

Working with command line arguments

Most nontrivial shell scripts need to handle arguments passed to them on the command line. In order to maintain consistency with Linux's command line environment, options should be preceded with a - (for example, foo -v). Bash's getopts built-in command makes meeting both of these requirements simple. getopts' basic syntax is quite simple:

getopts *optionstring varname*

optionstring consists of a string of letters and colons. Letters define the valid option characters; if an option requires an argument, it must be followed by a colon (:). *varname* stores the option character that is being evaluated. Listing 19-14, getopts.sh, illustrates the use of getopts and simplifies the subsequent explanation of how it works.

Listing 19-14: Using Bash's getopts Command

```
#!/bin/sh
# getopts.sh - Using Bash's getopts command to
#              process command line arguments

while getopts "xy:z:" OPT;
do
    case $OPT in
        x ) XOPT='You used -x' ;;
        y ) YOPT="You used -y with $OPTARG" ;;
        z ) ZOPT="You used -z with $OPTARG" ;;
        ? ) echo 'USAGE: getopts.sh [-x] [-y arg] [-z arg]'
            exit 1 ;;
    esac
done

echo ${XOPT:-'did not use -x'}
```

Continued

Listing 19-14 *(Continued)*

```
echo ${YOPT:-'did not use -y'}
echo ${ZOPT:-'did not use -z'}

exit 0
```

getopts processes each character in *optionstring*, picking options off one at a time and assigning them to *varname*. An option character followed by a : indicates that the option requires an argument, which getopts assigns to OPTARG, one of Bash's predefined variables. As long as options remain to be processed, getopts returns 0, but after it has processed all options and arguments, it returns 1, making getopts suitable for use in a while loop.

As you can see in Listing 19-14, the valid options are x, y, and z. Because y and z are each followed by a :, they require arguments. The case statement handles each of the valid options and also includes a default case, indicated by ?, that prints a usage message and exits the script if it is invoked with invalid options (options not listed in *optionstring*). The arguments passed with the y and z options are stored in OPTARG. The echo statements at the end of the script report the option used and, if applicable, the value of its corresponding argument.

This ends your whirlwind survey of the fundamentals of Bash programming. The next two sections, "Processes and Job Control" and "Creating Backups," present sample scripts for monitoring and managing processes and creating backups, using many of the concepts and features discussed in this section.

Using Processes and Job Control

This section presents a few Bash shell scripts that automate process monitoring and management. They use both Bash built-in commands and standard Linux commands and utilities available on any Red Hat Linux system. As is often the case in Linux, there are many ways to accomplish most administrative tasks, so consider the scripts in this section starting points rather than the only valid ways to perform a certain task.

Listing 19-15, kujob.sh, kills all processes owned by the user whose login name is passed as an argument to the script.

Listing 19-15: Killing a Selected User's Jobs

```
#!/bin/sh
# kujob.sh - Kill all processes owned by a user
# Arguments - User's login name

# Must be root
[ $UID -eq 0 ] || usage root
```

```
# Were we called properly?
getopts ":u:" OPT || usage syntax
[ "$OPT" = ":" ] && usage arg

# Does the user exist?
UNAME=$OPTARG
grep $UNAME /etc/passwd &> /dev/null || usage user

# Kill the user's processes
for SIG in TERM INT HUP QUIT KILL
do
    echo "Trying SIG$SIG"
    pkill -$SIG -u $UNAME &> /dev/null
    sleep 1
    pgrep -u $UNAME &> /dev/null || exit 0
done

# Display a short usage message
function usage
{
    ERR=$1
    case $ERR in
        "root" ) echo "Only root can run this script" ;;
        "syntax" ) echo "USAGE: kujob.sh -u UNAME" ;;
        "arg" ) echo "-u requires user name" ;;
        "user" ) echo "No such user" ;;
    esac
    exit 1
}
```

The usage function is a crude but convenient error handler. It always terminates the script after displaying the error message associated with the argument it is passed. It is convenient because it centralizes all of the script's error handling; it is crude because it makes no attempt to recover from errors.

The first block of code uses Bash's built-in UID variable to see if root, whose user ID (UID) is 0, is invoking the script. If the test returns false, meaning the user running the script is not root, kujob.sh calls usage with an argument of root. Otherwise, execution continues.

The second block of code uses getopts to process its command line arguments. The only valid option, as you can see in the option string, is -u. The first : (in front of u) turns off Bash's default error messages, allowing the script to provide its own error messages. The trailing :, as you recall, means that -u requires an argument. If an invalid option was used, kujob.sh calls usage with an argument of syntax. The following line makes sure the required login name argument was provided. getopts stores a : in the OPT variable if a required argument was omitted, so if the test returns true, it calls usage with the arg argument.

Once `kujob.sh` determines it was invoked properly, the next code block performs a sanity check: making sure the named user actually exists. The rest of the script relies on this information. After copying the user name passed to the UNAME variable, the grep command searches for that name in the /etc/passwd file. If it is present, grep returns 0 (true) and execution continues with the for statement. If the name is not present, grep returns 1 (false) and `kujob.sh` calls usage with an argument of user. Note how both stderr and stdout from the grep command are redirected to /dev/null, resulting in a more polished runtime appearance for the script.

Finally, `kujob.sh` attempts to kill all of the user's processes. The signals it uses are listed in order of increasing severity and prejudice (see the signal(7) man page for more information). If one signal fails to kill a process, the next strongest one is tried until all processes associated with the user have been killed. The sleep 1 statement gives the kernel time to complete the housekeeping associated with process termination before the script continues. After all the user's processes have been terminated, the script exits (pgrep returns 1, or false, if it finds no processes that match the specified search criteria).

In addition to terminating the user's processes, `kujob.sh` kills the user's login shell, too. Be careful when using this script.

The pkill and pgrep commands are part of the procps package, a suite of process management and monitoring tools. pkill and pgrep, in particular, provide a simpler interface to the ps command and its bewildering array of command line options. In short, the pkill statement sends the signal specified by SIG to all processes owned by the user in UNAME, specified by the -u $UNAME construct. pgrep, using the same -u option, lists the process IDs (PIDs) of all processes that match (you do not see them, however, because pgrep's stdout and stderr are redirected to /dev/null). See the pkill and pgrep man pages for further information.

The script in Listing 19-16, dskusg.sh, prints a report of disk usage for each mounted file system, sorting the output from the largest to the smallest directory.

Listing 19-16: Displaying Disk Usage Sorted by Top-Level Directory Size

```
#!/bin/sh
# dskusg.sh - Print disk usage on each file system for top level
#             directories in descending order

[ $UID -eq 0 ] || usage
for FS in $(grep  ^\/ /etc/mtab | cut -f2 -d" ")
do
    echo -e "$FS\n--------"
```

```
        du -x --max-depth=1 --exclude=/dev* $FS | sort -rg
        echo
done
function usage
{
        echo "You must be root to get an accurate report"
        exit 1
}
```

The first statement makes sure the user executing the script is the root user, printing an error message and exiting if the user is not root or root equivalent. Normal users do not have access to many directory trees on a Red Hat Linux system (such as /root and parts of /var/log, so this statement makes sure the report is accurate and, in the process, eliminates the necessity to redirect stderr to /dev/null. The script selects mounted file systems as listed in /etc/mtab, which contains the list of currently mounted file systems. It uses /etc/mtab rather than mount's output or the contents of /proc/mounts because /etc/mtab is easier to parse. For each file system, the script prints the file system name, followed by the disk usage (in blocks) of the file system itself, followed by the top level directories on each file system in descending order of disk usage, accomplished using the --maxdepth=1 argument. Using the -x option limits du to analyzing the given file system. This prevents the script from analyzing /proc, for example. --exclude=/dev* keeps the /dev special files out of the analysis. By piping the output to sort, the script can sort its output, using -g to sort based on numeric values and -r to reverse the sorting order. The output from this script might resemble the following:

```
# ./dskusg.sh
/
--------
172552  /
106636  /var
39720   /lib
10892   /etc
9252    /sbin
5376    /bin
268     /root
48      /tmp
48      /tftpboot
16      /lost+found
12      /mnt
4       /opt
4       /misc
4       /.automount
```

```
/boot
--------
3485      /boot
12        /boot/lost+found

/home
--------
297920    /home
270828    /home/kwall
27048     /home/bubba
24        /home/mysql
16        /home/lost+found

/usr
--------
2113504  /usr
853948   /usr/share
746872   /usr/lib
167220   /usr/bin
126072   /usr/X11R6
102200   /usr/src
59948    /usr/include
30428    /usr/sbin
12236    /usr/i386-glibc21-linux
6228     /usr/libexec
5512     /usr/kerberos
2612     /usr/games
120      /usr/html
80       /usr/local
16       /usr/lost+found
4        /usr/etc
4        /usr/dict
```

Listing 19-17, `vmstat.sh`, runs the `vmstat` command, redirecting its output to a file for later analysis using a spreadsheet or other analysis tool. `vmstat.sh` is intended to run as a `cron` job. The section titled "Automating Scripts" later in this chapter discusses `cron` and the `at` facility to run scripts automatically.

Listing 19-17: Collecting vmstat Statistics for Offline Analysis

```
#!/bin/sh
# vmstat.sh - Collect vmstat reports for later analysis

LOG=/var/log/vmstat.log.$$
[ $UID -eq 0 ] || LOG=$HOME/vmstat.log.$$
```

```
DELAY=${1:-60}

vmstat -n $DELAY >> $LOG
```

The first statement sets the default log file to which `vmstat`'s output will be saved. The next statement changes this default if the invoking user is not root, because normal users do not have write permission in the /var/log directory tree. The $$ operator returns the script's PID and is used in this case to distinguish one log file from another. The next statement uses one of Bash's substitution operators to set a default value for number of seconds between `vmstat`'s updates. As you recall, the `:-` operator sets `DELAY` to the value of the positional parameter 1 (referenced using $1), or assigns a default value of 60 if 1 is null or not set. Note that the script has to use the `:-` operator rather than `:=`, because the positional parameters are read only at run time and the "natural" substitution operator to use in this case, `:=`, would cause an error because it attempts to set the 1's value. Finally, the script calls `vmstat`, using `-n` to print the header only once, with a delay as specified, and redirecting the output to the file specified by `LOG`.

`vmstat.sh`'s output should resemble the following after running a few minutes:

procs			memory				swap		io		system		cpu		
r	b	w	swpd	free	buff	cache	si	so	bi	bo	in	cs	us	sy	id
0	1	0	4548	6936	47624	10528	0	0	7	3	104	12	0	0	99
0	0	0	4548	5252	47640	11920	0	0	6	1	103	13	0	0	100

In this case, the output was stored in the file /home/kwall/vmstat.log.1933. Of course, on your system, the file would have a different PID at the end.

Creating Backups

The scripts in this section automate the process of taking system backups, as discussed in Chapter 22, using the `find` and `tar` commands discussed in Chapter 18. Again, these scripts are not the last word in backup automation, just a starting point to adapt and customize to meet your own needs. Listing 19-18 shows how the first script, `fullback.sh`, performs a full system backup. The second script, `incrback.sh`, shown in Listing 19-19, performs an incremental backup of all files that have changed during the preceding 24 hours.

Listing 19-18: Performing a Full System Backup

```
#!/bin/sh
# fullback.sh - Backup the entire system except for
#               /proc, /dev, /tmp, /var/lock, /var/state, NFS mounts
```

Continued

Listing 19-18 *(Continued)*

```
BACKUPDEV=/dev/nst0
DATE=$(date +%Y%j)
FILES=/tmp/fullback.$DATE

find / ! -fstype nfs -fprint $FILES

tar -cvPW -T $FILES -f $BACKUPDEV \
    --exclude=/proc* \
    --exclude=/dev* \
    --exclude=/tmp* \
    --exclude=/var/lock* \
    --exclude=/var/state*
```

Listing 19-19: Performing an Incremental System Backup

```
#!/bin/sh
# incrback.sh - Backup files that have changed in the last 24 hours
#               except for files except for files in /proc, /dev,
#               /tmp, /var/lock, /var/state, and NFS mounts

BACKUPDEV=/dev/nst0
DATE=$(date +%Y%j)
FILES=/tmp/incrback.$DATE

find / ! -fstype nfs -a -mtime -1 -fprint $FILES

tar -cvPW -T $FILES -f $BACKUPDEV \
    --exclude=/proc* \
    --exclude=/dev* \
    --exclude=/tmp* \
    --exclude=/var/lock* \
    --exclude=/var/state*
```

Both scripts function almost identically. The first three lines of each script set some variables, making the script easier to maintain. BACKUPDEV identifies the device (which could be a file) on which to store the archive. DATE is used to add a unique identifier to the end of the FILES variable, which names a file to store the list of files to back up. fullback.sh finds all files that are not NFS mounts (! -fstype nfs) and writes their names to the file identified by FILES (-fprint $FILES), while incrback.sh uses find's -a statement, which means AND, to combine the -fstype test with the -mtime test to find only those files modified during the previous 24 hours (-mtime -1).

The tar command then creates (-c) an archive on the device named by BACKUPDEV (-f BACKUPDEV), operating verbosely (-v), retaining the leading / on each file name (-P), and reading the list of files to archive from the file named in

FILES (-T $FILES). The series of --exclude= statements prevent volatile or unimportant files in /proc, /dev, /tmp, /var/lock, and /var/state from being added to the archive. Finally, the -W option causes tar to verify the archived file copies against the originals after the archive is written.

Automating Scripts

Admittedly, scripts enable a greater degree of customization, flexibility, and convenience in performing system administration tasks, but repeatedly typing script names soon becomes just as tedious and impractical as complete command line invocations. You can use at and cron to run commands automatically and unattended, enabling you to realize the full power and benefit of the scripting administrative tasks.

Use the at command to schedule scripts you want to run later and that you want to run only once. Use the cron facility for programs and scripts that need to run on some sort of regular schedule.

Using at for one-shot jobs

The at command provides an interface to the atd daemon's scheduler. It is the atd daemon that executes the scripts. Scheduling a job with at is surprisingly simple to do: just type at followed by the time at which you want the script to run, and then press Enter. For example, the following sequence of commands schedules the /home/kwall/bin/incrback.sh script to run at 1:05 a.m. tomorrow morning.

```
$ at 1:05
warning: commands will be executed using (in order) a) $SHELL b)
login shell c) /bin/sh
at> /home/kwall/bin/incrback.sh
at> <EOT>
job 11 at 2001-07-10 01:05
$
```

The at> prompt is a small interactive shell for scheduling commands. The initial command, at 1:05, used the simplest possible format for specifying the time. Table 19-14 shows additional options for indicating time to at. Once you have the at> prompt, enter scripts and other commands just as you would at the shell prompt. To specify multiple commands, press Enter after each command, type the next one, press Enter, and so on. Press Ctrl+D after you have entered all the commands you want. at responds with the <EOT> sign and then displays a job number (11, in the example) for your commands and the date and time (July 10 at 1:05 a.m.) the job will execute.

TABLE 19-14 SPECIFYING TIME WITH THE at COMMAND

Command	When the Job Runs
at now	Executes the job immediately.
at now + 15 minutes	Executes the job 15 minutes from now.
at now + 2 hours	Executes the job 2 hours from now.
at now + 10 days	Executes the job 10 days from now.
at noon	Executes the job at noon today. If it is past noon, the job executes tomorrow at noon.
at now next hour	Executes the job 60 minutes from now.
at 15:00 tomorrow	Executes the job at 3:00 p.m. tomorrow.
at 1:05am	Executes the job at 1:05 a.m. today (if it is past 1:05 a.m., the job executes tomorrow at 1:05 a.m.
at 3:00 Aug 16, 00	At 3:00 a.m. on August 16, 2000.

To view the current list of jobs in the at queue, use the atq command. To remove a job from the queue, use the atrm command. The following commands show the current list of jobs using atq, and then removing them using atrm.

```
$ atq
10      2001-07-10 01:05 a kwall
11      2001-07-11 01:05 a kwall
$ atrm 10 11
```

The first field of atq's output shows its job number, the same one displayed when you submitted the job. The rest of the fields are, in order, date and time the job will execute, the queue (a, in this case), and the user who submitted the job. Only the root user can see all of the jobs submitted; normal users can see only their own. Removing a job from the queue is a simple matter of typing atrm followed by the job number of the job you want to remove, as shown in the example.

Using cron for regularly scheduled jobs

To run a script automatically at regular intervals, use the cron service. You schedule repeating jobs using the crontab command, either by placing the script name and scheduling information in a specially formatted file that crontab reads, or using crontab interactively. The cron daemon, crond, takes care of running the job and, as with at, e-mails its output to you.

To use cron, you need to understand the format of its job file, also called a *crontab* (which should not be confused with the crontab command, although the two are related). Each job in a crontab file is specified on a single line and each line contains at least six fields. The first five define when the job executes, and the sixth and subsequent fields name the script or program to run, along with any arguments the script or program takes. For example, this line executes the incrback.sh shell script in 1:05 a.m. each day:

```
05 01 * * * incrback.sh
```

Table 19-15 lists the meaning of the first five fields.

TABLE 19-15 Crontab FIELD VALUES

Field	Description	Valid Values
1	Minute	0–59
2	Hour	0–23
3	Day of month	0–31
4	Month	1–12 (1 is January)
		Three letter month abbreviations (Jan, Feb, Mar, Apr, May, Jun, Jul, Aug, Sep, Oct, Nov, Dec)
5	Day of week	0–7 (0 and 7 both mean Sunday, 1 is Monday)
		Three letter day abbreviations (Sun, Mon, Tue, Wed, Thu, Fri, Sat)

Entries may be single values, a comma-delimited set of values to specify multiple days, a range of values separated by a hyphen (-), or any combination of these three options. An asterisk (*) represents all possible values for that field. So, an asterisk in the hour field means a job would execute every hour of the day.

For example, to run incrback.sh at 4:55 p.m. on the 1st and 15th of January, March, June, and September, the crontab entry would look like one of the following:

```
55 16 1,15 1,3,6,9 * incrback.sh
55 16 1,15 Jan,Mar,Jun,Sep * incrback.sh
```

In this case, the * in the day of the week field is ignored because it is overridden by the other date and time specifications.

The easiest way to schedule a job with cron is to place the crontab entry in a file, and then invoke the `crontab` command with the file name as an argument. So, if one of the crontab entries shown previously was stored in a file named `kwall.crontab`, you would submit the job using the following command:

```
$ crontab kwall.crontab
```

To verify that the job is indeed scheduled, type `crontab -l` to list your crontab entries:

```
$ crontab -l
# DO NOT EDIT THIS FILE - edit the master and reinstall.
# (/tmp/crontab.2433 installed on Mon Jul  9 17:48:30 2001)
# (Cron version -- $Id: crontab.c,v 2.13 1994/01/17 03:20:37 vixie
Exp $)
55 16 1,15 1,4,6,9 * incrback.sh
```

To remove all of your cron jobs, type `crontab -r`. Once you become comfortable with the crontab format, you might find it most convenient to use crontab's interactive mode. To do so, type `crontab -e`. The interactive mode uses the `vi` editor, so use `vi` keystrokes to enter, edit, save your changes, and, of course, to exit the interactive mode.

Writing, Testing, and Debugging Scripts

Naturally, you write a script using your preferred editor. If it is a complex script, you might find it easiest to write a bit at a time, breaking the script into small functional units that are easiest to test and debug. As each small unit is completed, move on to the next one. As explained in the section "Shell functions" earlier in the chapter, if you find yourself writing the same kind of code over and over, turn that code into a shell function. Not only will it be easier to read your script, it will also be easier to write and, as you gain experience with shell programming, you will be able to reuse that function in other scripts.

Finally, as you work on the script, be sure to make liberal use of comments (prefixed with #, recall) to remind yourself of the brilliant idea you had. You may not need the comment tomorrow or next week, but six months from now when you revisit the code, that comment will be quite helpful. Do not let yourself be fooled by the rationalization that you will use a script only a few times, either. It is quite amazing how often those little throwaway, one-off scripts become an essential tool used for months and years.

When it comes to testing your script, test each section to ensure that the basic functionality works as designed. Then, especially if it performs a vital function like a system backup, test it more thoroughly. If it accepts command line arguments, see what happens if the arguments are not of the type they are supposed to be (such as character arguments where numeric values are expected). Test what happens if no arguments are supplied and what happens if too many or too few arguments are given. Be especially vigilant if the script is interactive and takes input from users, because all sorts of unanticipated input and situations are likely in such a situation. Finally, be sure to test boundary conditions, such as values that overrun or under-run normally expected values.

To help debug your scripts, Bash provides a couple of helpful options: `set -n` and `set -x`. `set -n` reads commands but does not execute them, so a syntax error in the script displays but does not otherwise execute. Similarly, the `set -x` option causes Bash to display each statement after expanding most variables and statements, so you can see what Bash is executing when something goes wrong. To use these options, place `set -n` or `set -x` at the beginning of the script, before any other shell commands. Then before exiting the script, unset the options using `set +n` and `set +x`, as appropriate.

Listing 19-20 shows a very short script, `debugme.sh`, which illustrates how `set -x` works. Although it has no errors, it should be easy to see how `set -x` makes it clearer what Bash is doing when it evaluates statements, expands variables, and so forth.

Listing 19-20: Using set -x to Debug a Shell Script

```
#!/bin/sh
# debugme.sh - Show usage of set -x

set -x
echo ARG1 was ${1:-"default value"}
set +x
```

Called with no arguments, `debugme.sh`'s output should be the following:

```
$ ./debugme.sh
+ echo ARG1 was 'default value'
ARG1 was default value
+ set +x
```

The plus sign (+) preceding a statement shows the statement or expression Bash is about to execute. The next line shows the actual output or result of the statement.

Selecting a Scripting Language

In the beginning of Chapter 18 I remarked that not all problems are nails, so you need more tools than a hammer. That quip applies to scripting languages as well as it does to system administration tools. Bash is certainly not the only language available for scripting system administration tasks. Perl is very popular and extremely capable, as is Python. In fact, both Perl and Python are full programming languages with a number of extensions and modules perfectly suited to the system administration duties discussed throughout this book. If Bash does not do what you want it to do, or if it makes it awkward to do so, consider learning Perl or Python, because they almost certainly make some tasks easier and are surely more capable than Bash.

Nevertheless, just as GUI administrative tools are not uniformly available, neither are Perl or Python (although Perl is much more likely to be installed on a given system than is Python). For that matter, Bash may not be available, either, but it is so similar to the Bourne shell, the default shell on almost every Unix system, that the programming skills you learn with Bash transfer almost completely to Bourne. The Korn shell, another contributor to Bash's features, is also widely available on most Unix systems and, increasingly, Linux systems.

The point is that you should not dispense with shell programming altogether just because Perl or the scripting language du jour is better or more popular. Savvy, experienced administrators keep a fully stocked tool belt, and basic shell programming skills should hang on every administrator's belt.

Summary

This chapter discussed shell programs, scripts, as tools to ease the burden of system administration by handling certain tasks programmatically. First, you received a thorough introduction to the basics of Bash shell programming, including wildcards, shell variables, operators, Bash's flow control structures, shell functions, input and output processes, and command line arguments. The chapter presented a number of scripts that showed many of these shell programming features in action. You reviewed scripts for working with running processes, killing processes, reporting disk usage, and creating backups. You also learned how to use at and cron to run scripts automatically, and got some final tips and hints on writing, testing, and debugging shell scripts.

Chapter 20

Performance Monitoring

IN THIS CHAPTER

- ◆ Diagnosing performance problems

- ◆ Monitoring overall performance

- ◆ Monitoring running processes

- ◆ Monitoring memory use

- ◆ Monitoring disk usage and performance

- ◆ Monitoring CPU use

- ◆ Monitoring network usage

PERFORMANCE MONITORING, like system security, is a journey, not a destination. That is, performance monitoring is best understood as a continual, ongoing process rather than a final goal obtained once and for all. After you have installed, configured, and stabilized your system, you should put in place a regular performance monitoring regimen to maintain the best possible performance and identify potential trouble spots *before* they begin to degrade performance. Over time, however, and perhaps inevitably, system performance inescapably erodes, and when it occurs, you should have a list of areas to check and some tools that enable you to differentiate quickly between real and perceived performance problems. This chapter gives you some basic tools for identifying and solving, or at least isolating, genuine performance problems.

Having a quick checklist of potential problem areas simplifies the performance troubleshooting process. When your system's performance suddenly seems to be below average, a short list of suspects should include the following:

- ◆ Running processes

- ◆ Memory usage

- ◆ Disk performance

- ◆ Network traffic

- ◆ CPU saturation

This chapter devotes a section to troubleshooting problems related to each of the items in the preceding list.

Performance monitoring tools are divided into two broad categories: high-level tools that impose a negligible performance hit and provide a correspondingly general overview of system performance and low-level tools that provide detailed views of system performance at the component level and exact a significant and noticeable performance penalty. There is room and need for both types of tools in the performance monitoring spectrum.

This chapter looks first at the process to follow when analyzing system performance. Next, it introduces some tools and techniques for taking a quick snapshot of a system's overall performance. Finally, it shows you how to drill down into each of the major subsystems and, in some cases, down to the level of individual hardware and software components to analyze their performance using some programs that provide detailed information about running processes, memory utilization, disk usage and I/O throughput, and network traffic.

Diagnosing Performance Problems

As just stated, performance monitoring is a process. So, this section describes a general approach that you can follow to track down performance problems to monitor. As you read, bear in mind that the method described here is not etched in stone, but is instead a guide you can adapt to your own preferences and the needs of the system or systems you maintain. Briefly, the general procedure is to determine the overall status of the system and then to examine specific subsystems. Sometimes the overall status might give you a hint about which subsystem to evaluate, but, more often than not, you need to look at each of the major subsystems (disk, memory, network, and CPU) until you find the real problem. Over time, as you become experienced using the diagnostic procedures outlined in the following paragraphs, you will likely adapt them to suit your needs. More than anything else, you need to develop a systematic approach for isolating and solving performance problems. One thing is certain: consistently following the approach outlined in this chapter *does* help you develop an intuitive sense of where to look when an apparent performance problem emerges.

The key word in that last sentence is *apparent*. Some perceived performance problems are not problems at all, but, rather, predictable and highly transient or temporary situations (bottlenecks). They reflect normal usage and are not worth troubling yourself over. The following anecdote illustrates the point. One of the authors of this book used to maintain an electronic data interchange (EDI) system whose key components consisted of a number of busy dial-up connections, an enormous, heavily used database, and about two dozen experienced Unix users. Every morning at 8:00 a.m., they all arrived at work, got their coffee, and logged in. By 8:05, the host running the EDI system, named `wine`, usually slowed to a glacial pace, only to recover within 10 or 15 minutes, at most.

Was this a performance problem? Yes. `wine`'s response time slowed dramatically. Neverthless, and this is the key point, wine's *business function* was not impaired. No revenue was lost, and all users were able to continue working, albeit more slowly than they preferred, so the problem was not worth the effort to solve. Twenty-five people almost simultaneously accessing the same files on a system already heavily loaded with data processing represented an entirely predictable but very short-term performance hit on the system.

On the other hand, if `wine`'s business function had been to handle 911 emergency calls, slow response time of any sort would have been utterly unacceptable and would have demanded an instant solution. The point that I make repeatedly in this chapter is that you need to be aware of the context in which a *perceived* problem occurs and take into account a system's normal usage patterns before deciding that something is a problem that needs to be fixed. Had the slow response lasted longer, impaired `wine`'s business function, or prevented people from working, it *would* have posed a significant problem. They could have taken measures to address the problem. For example, they could have used NIS for authentication, mounted their home directories from a dedicated NFS server, or adjusted processing times for the database, but these were major modifications not warranted by the situation.

Overall System Status

To get some sense of the system's overall performance status, the most common command is `uptime`. `uptime` displays a one-line report that shows how long the system has been up, how many users are logged in, and the system load averages during the last 1, 5, and 15 minutes. The *load average* represents the number of jobs waiting in the run queue, that is, processes ready to run but not running. The following shows `uptime`'s output on a host named `marta`:

```
$ uptime
  2:51pm  up 1 day, 25 min,  3 users,  load average: 2.03, 2.10, 2.06
```

As you can see, the load average is 2.03 over the last minute, 2.10 during the last five minutes, and 2.06 during the last quarter hour. But, before you panic about the load average, you need to baseline it. *Baselining* means performing basic monitoring over a period of time to establish a system's normal usage profile. For example, you can create a cron job that runs `uptime` every 15 minutes and appends the output to a text file. After a week, you have a good idea of that system's typical usage.

On the other hand, one week's worth of data may not constitute an adequate sample of your site's typical data processing cycles. An accounting department's server, for example, is likely to be more heavily used at the end of standard accounting cycles, such as the end of the pay period, the month, the quarter, and the fiscal year. A back-end server for a point-of-sale (POS) system, likewise, routinely experiences its heaviest usage at the end of the business day when sales are tallied and summarized and during peak sales periods, such as the day after Thanksgiving and the week before Christmas. The point is that you have to spend some time developing an accurate picture of a system's normal usage before you can reasonably distinguish between normal but heavy usage and a real performance problem.

One shortcoming of uptime's reports is that it does not distinguish between high-priority jobs, such as interactive processes (a shell session, for example), and low-priority jobs, such as daemons or database servers. Moreover, uptime takes a snapshot at a given moment only, and usage can vary wildly. Consider uptime's report on marta load average 18 minutes after the first execution:

```
$ uptime
  3:09pm  up 1 day, 43 min,  3 users,  load average: 0.42, 0.52, 0.74
```

Because uptime is such a blunt tool, it is best used for obtaining an immediate snapshot of system performance and for trending the load average over a period of time as part of developing a comprehensive system usage profile.

The sar (system activity reporter) command is more informative because it samples CPU utilization a specific number of times over an interval defined in seconds. The simplest invocation is:

```
sar secs count
```

This command instructs sar to take count samples that are secs seconds apart. For example, the following sar invocation shows CPU usage sampled five times in five seconds:

```
$ sar -u 5 5

Linux 2.4.7-10 (marta.kurtwerks.com)    10/25/2001


03:09:56 PM       CPU      %user     %nice    %system      %idle
03:10:01 PM       all       9.20     89.20       1.60       0.00
03:10:06 PM       all      10.00     89.00       1.00       0.00
03:10:11 PM       all       0.00     99.60       0.40       0.00
03:10:16 PM       all       0.00     99.00       1.00       0.00
03:10:21 PM       all       0.00     99.80       0.20       0.00
Average:          all       3.84     95.32       0.84       0.00
```

The -u option tells sar to report on CPU utilization. %user indicates the percentage of time that the CPU spends executing user mode code (typically, application programs), %nice is the percentage of time the CPU spends executing user mode code with a nonzero nice priority, %system indicates the time spent executing kernel code (system calls), and %idle shows how much time the CPU is not doing anything.

As a general rule, if %system is high, application programs might be using system calls (kernel mode code) inappropriately. If %idle is high yet the load average as reported by uptime is significant (say, over 5), this suggests either an I/O problem or memory saturation (see the section titled "Monitoring Memory Utilization" for tips on how to identify memory saturation) — the CPU is idle because jobs are sitting in the run queue waiting for I/O to complete or for memory to be swapped back in from disk.

Configuring sar is simple enough. sar reads data from a log file (/var/log/sa/sadd by default, where dd is the current day). /usr/lib/sa/sadc, the system activity data collector, creates and maintains these log files. However, most sar implementations include two shell scripts /usr/lib/sa/sa1 and /usr/lib/sa/sa2 that front-end sadc. The simplest way to configure sar's data files is to create a system cron entry that calls sa1. As it happens, Red Hat has already configured sar for you. The file /etc/cron.d/sysstat is a system crontab entry that runs sa1 every 10 minutes, appending its output to the log file just mentioned:

```
*/10 * * * * root /usr/lib/sa/sa1 1 1
```

sa1 collects and stores data in a binary file format that sar reads. Bear in mind that the log files can grow quite large and that sadc can impose a noticeable performance impact depending on the command line options with which it is invoked.

If you prefer, you can use a graphical monitor to track the system's load status. xload is one such program, installed by default on any system with X11R6, including Red Hat Linux. Figure 20-1 shows a sample xload display.

Figure 20-1: xload shows the system load graphically.

xload's most useful options include the following:

- -scale *count* — The minimum number of lines displayed on the screen. Each line represents a load average value of 1.

- -update *secs* — The number of seconds between each update.

- -bg *color* — The color of the graph's background.

- -fg *color* — The color of the graph's foreground.

- -hl *color* — The color of any text and the scale lines.

The graph shown in Figure 20-1 was created by using the command `xload -scale 10 -update 1 -fg darkblue -hl tan`. You can see the scale lines, but, unfortunately, not the graph's dark blue color. The graph updates every second. The system was moderately loaded due to a kernel compilation running in the background — the graph shows a load average just over 6, which corresponds to the load average reported by `uptime`:

```
$ uptime
 3:57pm  up 1 day,  1:31,  2 users,  load average: 6.06, 5.05, 3.88
```

Although `xload` is visually appealing, it is, like `uptime`, a rather blunt tool that does not provide much detail. `xload` also consumes memory and CPU cycles that can be used by more important programs.

Monitoring Running Processes

The `ps` command is the weapon of choice for examining running processes. In terms of performance monitoring, the most useful set of command options to use is `-el` — that is, `ps -el`. Why `-el`? The `-e` option lists information on every running process and the `-l` option generates a long listing that displays information pertinent to performance monitoring and tuning (see Table 20-1). The following short listing illustrates the output of `ps -el` on `marta`:

```
$ ps -el
  F S   UID   PID  PPID  C PRI  NI ADDR    SZ WCHAN  TTY        TIME CMD
100 S     0   858     1  0  68   0   -   1554 do_pol  ?      00:00:00 gdm
000 S   500  1020     1  0  69   0   -    427 do_sel  ?      00:00:00 esd
040 S   500  1244     1  0  69   0   -    990 do_sel  ?      00:00:00 fetchmail
140 S     0  3914   858  0  69   0   -   1556 pipe_w  ?      00:00:00 gdm
100 S     0  3915  3914  0  69   0   -  15264 do_sel  ?      00:00:01 X
100 S    42  3920  3914  0  69   0   -   1762 do_pol  ?      00:00:00 gdmlogin
000 S    42  3921  3920  0  69   0   -   2128 do_pol  ?      00:00:00 xsri
040 S     0  5081     1  0  69   0   -    356 rt_sig  ?      00:00:00 ppp-watch
100 S     0  5083  5081  0  68   0   -    478 do_sel ttyS4   00:00:00 pppd
040 S     0  6170   757  0  68   0   -    400 pipe_w  ?      00:00:00 crond
040 S   500  6173     1  0  69   0   -    488 wait4   ?      00:00:00 seti.sh
000 R   500  6175  6173 48  75   1   -   4457   -     ?      04:50:05 setiathom
100 S     0  6176  6170  0  69   0   -   1370 pipe_w  ?      00:00:00 sendmail
040 S   500  6178     1  0  69   0   -    488 wait4   ?      00:00:00 seti.sh
```

The output was severely truncated to conserve space. Table 20-1 describes most of the fields shown in the listing.

TABLE 20-1 ps FIELDS RELEVANT TO PERFORMANCE MONITORING

Field	Description
F	Contains a value consisting of the sum of one or more hexadecimal values that describes the process's current status
S	Shows the process's current state (running, sleeping, and so forth)
UID	Lists the numeric user ID (UID) of the user who owns the process
PID	Lists the process's process ID (PID)
PPID	Lists the PID of the parent process
C	Shows the CPU utilization of the process
PRI	States the process's priority (higher numbers mean higher priority)
NI	Shows the process's nice value (higher numbers mean lower priority)
SZ	Lists how much swap space (virtual memory) the process requires
TTY	Names the terminal on which the process started (also known as the *controlling terminal*)
TIME	Summarizes the total CPU time (in hours and minutes) that the process has consumed
CMD	Displays the command that initiated the process

As a refresher, recall that the S field takes one of the following values:

◆ 0 – The process is currently executing on a CPU.

◆ S – The process is sleeping, waiting for another event to complete.

◆ R – The process is in the run queue (runnable) and is waiting to run.

◆ Z – The process is a zombie (it terminated, but its parent has not reaped its exit status).

◆ T – The process is stopped.

Here are some tips that help you correlate the output of the ps command with particular problems:

◆ Examine the PRI and the NI fields to locate processes that can run at lower priorities, and then use the nice or renice commands to modify their priorities. Alternatively, see if long-lived (long-running) or CPU-intensive processes can be scheduled to run at a time when the system is quiescent.

◆ Processes that remain stopped for long periods of time (a T in the S field) should be investigated and possibly killed.

◆ Similarly, long-running processes (see the TIME field) that consume significant CPU resources should be investigated, but bear in mind that they might simply require considerable computing horsepower. In the latter case, consider moving them to off-peak times, if possible.

◆ Processes consuming a great deal of memory, particularly swap space (see the SZ field), might have memory leaks and, when being swapped in and out, adversely impact performance.

◆ Sleeping processes (those with an S in the S field) might have I/O problems, or the I/O subsystem itself might be impaired. See "Monitoring Disk Usage and Performance," later in the chapter, for ways to diagnose and treat I/O problems.

The ps command really serves two purposes in performance monitoring and tuning. First, it provides clues about what process (or processes) might be causing the problem, which, in turn, suggests possible measures to alleviate the problem. Second, ps enables you to see whether the action you took solved the problem. After taking steps to discipline a wayward process, use ps -el again and evaluate the results. If the corrective measure worked, you have at least temporarily solved the problem. If not, try another tactic.

Monitoring Memory Utilization

Insufficient physical RAM and its corresponding problem, heavy swapping activity, profoundly erode system performance. The previous section suggested examining the amount of virtual memory (the value of the SZ field) that a process requires when diagnosing a system performance problem. The issue is that a process not currently running is not immediately accessible to the CPU. In some cases, its memory image is stored in RAM while other processes execute, so a short delay occurs when it is awoken to run. In other cases, especially on a busy system, either individual pages of the process's memory image or the entire process is swapped to disk, resulting in a significant delay when the process image is read back into RAM and prepared to run – disk I/O is almost always the weakest link in the system performance chain. The larger the amount of swap that is required, the greater the performance hit.

Linux allocates swap space on an as-needed basis, unlike some proprietary Unix versions (such as HP-UX) that allocate swap ahead of time in proportion to a program's actual memory requirements without regard to whether or not the program ever requires swap space.

Use the vmstat command to examine the virtual memory subsystem and isolate problems. vmstat reports a variety of statistics about the virtual memory subsystem, CPU load, and disk and CPU activity. Its general format is:

```
vmstat [secs [count]]
```

vmstat takes a total of *count* samples every *secs* seconds and displays its output to stdout.

```
$ vmstat 5 5
   procs                     memory    swap       io    system       cpu
 r  b  w   swpd   free   buff  cache  si  so   bi   bo   in   cs  us  sy  id
 2  0  0    792  58440  18868  45008   0   0    3    7  195  360  42   1  56
 2  0  0    792  58436  18884  45008   0   0    0   10  102   21 100   0   0
 2  0  0    792  58436  18884  45008   0   0    0    1  102   17  99   1   0
 2  0  0    792  58436  18884  45008   0   0    0    1  101   19  99   1   0
 2  0  0    792  58164  18884  45008   0   0    0    1  102   17  99   1   0
```

At first glance the information is hard to decipher. The first line of any vmstat report shows only summary information. Subsequent lines show the information that you use to track down memory problems. Before proceeding, though, look at Table 20-2 for an explanation of vmstat's output fields.

TABLE 20-2 vmstat OUTPUT FIELDS

Field	Description
procs	
r	The number of processes ready to run (in the run queue)
b	The number of processes blocked while waiting for some resources
w	The number of processes swapped out while waiting for some resources
memory	
swpd	The amount of swap space used in KB
free	The size of the unallocated memory store in KB
buff	The amount of memory used as a buffer in KB
cache	The amount of memory used as cache in KB

Continued

TABLE 20-2 vmstat OUTPUT FIELDS *(Continued)*

Field	Description
swap	
si	The amount of memory swapped in from disk in KB/sec
so	The amount of memory swapped out to disk in KB/sec
io	
bi	The number of blocks written to a block device in blocks/sec
bo	The number of blocks read from a block device in blocks/sec
system	
in	The number of device interrupts/sec
cs	The number of CPU process context switches in switches/sec
cpu	
us	The percentage of CPU time spent executing user code
sy	The percentage of CPU time spent executing system/kernel code
id	The percentage of CPU time spent idle

Of the fields listed in Table 20-2, those that refer to memory and swap space usage deserve special attention. When the amount of available swap space (shown in the swap column and displayed in kilobyte units) is low, this is an indication that the system is swapping heavily and likely is performing poorly. Use ps to identify the process or processes making heavy use of swap. In some cases, you might be able to tune the application itself to address the issue, but, more often than not, the permanent solution is adding RAM to the system.

If the w column is nonzero and the so and si columns indicate continuous swapping, start looking for processes consuming memory, particularly those with large virtual memory requirements. Watching the r and b columns over a period of time enables you to get some sense of how fast processes are moving through the queue. Except for long-running processes (easily identified using ps), the values in the r and b columns should stay low.

On systems that support it, the free command shows memory utilization, including swap usage and capacity. For example, the following command shows the output of the free command on a moderately loaded system:

```
$ free
              total       used       free     shared    buffers     cached
Mem:         191136     133768      57368        580      19216      45028
-/+ buffers/cache:       69524     121612
Swap:        253508        792     252716
```

At a glance, free gives you an informative snapshot of system memory usage. The first line following the header shows physical memory information (all information is in kilobytes), including the total amount of installed RAM, how much of it the kernel has allocated (but not necessarily used), how much RAM is free, how much RAM is configured as shared memory, and how much RAM is used for buffering and cache.

The second line shows memory usage adjusted for buffering. That is, free subtracts the amount of memory used for buffering and caching from the used column and adds it to the free column so that you get a more accurate picture of actual RAM usage as opposed to the kernel's allocation of RAM, which changes according to system usage and the load average. Note, for example, that if you subtract the buffers and cached values from the used value on the first line, you get 69,524 (133,768 – 19,216 – 45,028 = 69,524) and that adding buffers and cached to free yields precisely 121,612 (57,368 + 19,216 + 45,028 = 121,612).

The third line, finally, shows the amounts of swap space available, used, and free. As you can see, swap usage on this system was fairly low at the time the snapshot was taken.

If you prefer a graphical display, consider the System Monitor, shown in Figure 20-2, which is far more configurable and offers greater detail than xload. The System Monitor, basically an X version of the top utility discussed in the section titled "Tracking CPU Usage", is a real-time monitor and, as a result, can adversely affect the performance of the system it is monitoring. To start it, click Main Menu → Programs → System Monitor on the GNOME panel. The initial screen should resemble Figure 20-2.

To view the amount of actual physical memory used, click the Memory Usage (resident) tab. In addition to displaying the resident set sizes of processes, shown in Figure 20-3, GNOME System Monitor's memory usage display can also show the following:

◆ Shared memory usage by process

◆ Total memory usage by process

◆ Virtual memory usage by process

◆ Swap memory usage by process

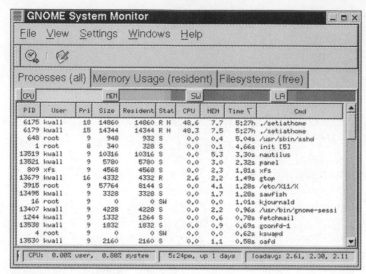

Figure 20-2: The main System Monitor screen

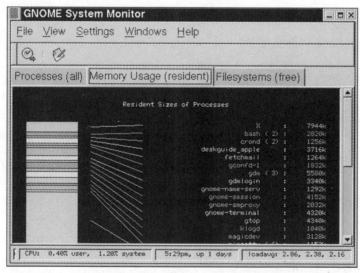

Figure 20-3: System Monitor's memory usage display

To change the view, click View on the menu bar and select the view you want. Figure 20-4 shows the menu from which you can select the different views.

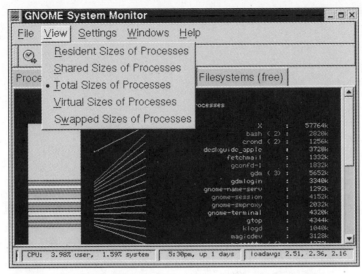

Figure 20-4: Use the View menu to select a different memory usage display.

Monitoring Disk Usage and Performance

Disk *usage* is straightforward to monitor using the df and du commands. df reports the amount of disk space that is available, and du reports the amount that is used. Table 20-3 lists useful options to df.

TABLE 20-3 df OPTIONS

Option	Description
-a	Includes empty file systems in the report
-h	Displays the report using human readable units
-k	Uses blocks of 1K
-l	Limits the report to local file systems
-m	Uses blocks of 1024K

Use df's -k option to see disk usage in kilobytes — for example:

```
$ df -k
Filesystem              1k-blocks       Used  Available Use% Mounted on
/dev/sda2                  959396     117364     793296 13% /
/dev/sda1                   21129       2997      17041 15% /boot
/dev/hdc1                 4076976    1203725    2662282 32% /home
none                        95568          0      95568  0% /dev/shm
/dev/sda3                 3153592    1638608    1354788 55% /usr
```

To make the display easier to read, you can use the -h option:

```
$ df -h
Filesystem      Size  Used Avail Use% Mounted on
/dev/sda2       937M  115M  774M  13% /
/dev/sda1        21M  3.0M   16M  15% /boot
/dev/hdc1       3.9G  1.2G  2.5G  32% /home
none             93M     0   93M   0% /dev/shm
/dev/sda3       3.0G  1.6G  1.2G  55% /usr
```

If you use the -l option, you list only the disk space that is physically located on your own system, not on NFS mounts or other disk drives that are accessed remotely. The -h option makes it amply clear how much space is available on each file system. All of the file systems are well under their maximum capacity.

To see how much disk space is in use, use the du command. Its basic syntax is

```
du [options] file
```

file can be a file system, a device, a directory, or a file. Useful values for *options* include:

- ◆ -d — Limits the report to the specified file system

- ◆ -h — Displays the report using human readable units

- ◆ -k — Prints the report using K units

- ◆ -m — Prints the report using MB unites

- ◆ -s — Reports only summary values

The default report, if no options are specified, shows usage statistics for each directory at or beneath *file*. For example, the following command shows du's default output:

```
# du /tmp
112      /tmp/.kde/tmp-localhost.localdomain
116      /tmp/.kde
4        /tmp/.X11-unix
4        /tmp/.font-unix
4        /tmp/.ICE-unix
12       /tmp/orbit-root
4        /tmp/.sawfish-root
12       /tmp/orbit-kwall
4        /tmp/.sawfish-kwall
4        /tmp/.esd
488      /tmp
```

The next command shows only a summary report for disk usage in /usr:

```
# du -s /usr
1605796 /usr
```

The next command shows the summary report but uses the -h option to print the report in more familiar notation and the -m option to use megabyte (MB) units:

```
$ du -smh /usr
1.6G     /usr
```

Disk I/O is the slowest part of a system. RAM and CPU speeds are hundreds of times faster than the fastest disk hardware. Fortunately, the Linux kernel and modern hard disks use software and hardware caches, read-ahead buffers, and delayed writes to offset and minimize this speed differential. Nevertheless, as a system administrator, you still need to know how to identify and address disk I/O problems. You will find it helpful to become familiar with the following terms, which are constantly used in performance-tuning literature:

♦ **Average seek time** – An estimated measure of how long an average seek operation takes

♦ **Maximum seek time** – The seek time between the two tracks that are farthest apart on a disk

♦ **Minimum seek time** – The seek time between two adjacent tracks

♦ **Queuing delay** – The delay that occurs while a disk controller identifies where on a disk to locate data to read or write

♦ **Rotational latency** – The delay that occurs while the disk spins into position underneath the read/write head, measured in revolutions per minute (RPMs)

◆ **Seek latency** – The delay that occurs while the disk's read/write head moves to the proper cylinder location over the disk

◆ **Seek time** – The time it takes to move the read/write head from one disk track to another

The most frequently used command for drilling down on I/O performance problems is iostat. Like vmstat, iostat's simplest invocation is:

```
iostat [seconds [count]]
```

seconds defines the interval between reports, and *count* specifies the number of reports. For example, the following command generates the default iostat report:

```
$ iostat
Linux 2.4.7-10 (marta.kurtwerks.com)    10/25/2001

avg-cpu:  %user   %nice   %sys   %idle
           2.02   52.99   1.01   43.97

Device:         tps   Blk_read/s   Blk_wrtn/s   Blk_read   Blk_wrtn
dev8-0         0.84         4.00        11.37     482868    1371784
dev22-0        0.48         0.41         1.68      49298     203210
```

The device listed under the Device column shows the physical device partitions in the format devm-n, where *m* is the major number and *n* is the minor number. In this case, dev8-0 maps to the first SCSI disk (/dev/sda), and dev22-0 maps to the second IDE disk (/dev/hdc). Table 20-4 shows iostat's output fields.

TABLE 20-4 iostat OUTPUT FIELDS

Field	Description
tps	The numbers of transfers (or I/O requests) per second sent to the disk
Blk_read/s	The number of blocks read from the device per second
Blk_wrtn/s	The number of blocks written to the device per second
Blk_read	The total number of blocks read
Blk_wrtn	The total number of blocks written

If you want to dig deeper into disk I/O performance, use the option -x with iostat and specify the disk or the partition in which you are interested. -x reports extended statistics on the I/O performance of the specified disks (or all disks if no disks are specified). The following command takes a snapshot of the activity on /dev/sda during a kernel compile (the -d option causes iostat not to print the CPU utilization summary):

```
$ iostat -d -x /dev/sda
Linux 2.4.7-10 (marta.kurtwerks.com)    10/26/2001


Device:  rrqm/s wrqm/s   r/s   w/s  rsec/s  wsec/s avgrq-sz avgqu-sz   await
svctm  %util
sda        0.27   0.79  0.31  0.59    4.64   11.07    17.45     0.29  322.27
48.97   0.44
```

How should you interpret iostat's output? Table 20-5 describes the meaning of each field.

TABLE 20-5 iostat EXTENDED DEVICE STATISTICS OUTPUT FIELDS

Field	Description
rrqm/s	The number of merged read requests per second
wrqm/s	The number of merged write requests per second
r/s	The number of read requests per second
w/s	The number of write requests per second
rsec/s	The number of sectors read per second
wsec/s	The number of sectors written per second
avgrq-sz	The average size (in sectors) of requests
avgqu-sz	The average queue length of the requests
await	The average time I/O waited to be served (in milliseconds)
svctm	The average time I/O requests required to complete (in milliseconds)
%util	Percentage of CPU consumed by I/O requests

Merged read and write requests occur when the multiple read and write requests, typically for contiguous or adjacent sectors of a disk, are coalesced into a single request, an attempt to optimize disk I/O. You want to see disk activity distributed roughly evenly across all the disks so that no single disk or controller is forced to handle the majority of I/O, a situation called an I/O *hot spot*. If you do identify such a hot spot, you may be able to resolve it by attaching the disk concerned to a different controller or moving all or part of the file system in question to another disk or perhaps both. When I/O waits (see the await field) start to climb and stay consistently high, resort to ps or vmstat to identify where the block is occurring and why. If the value of svctm is high, this means your disks are slow. On an IDE-based system, the %util field is significantly higher than on SCSI systems because IDE uses the CPU to process I/O requests, so one performance improvement can be to replace IDE disks with SCSI disks.

 A common disk layout for improving system performance generally is to install Linux on one disk and to place the swap partition on a separate disk. If you will be using a large database, such as Oracle or DB/2, follow the manufacturer's recommendations for organizing the database files across multiple disks and/or partitions.

Tracking CPU Usage

The best known utility for looking at CPU usage is the top utility, which displays the "top" CPU processes. top is a real-time monitor, meaning that it displays an ongoing list of the most CPU intensive processes running. The display is updated every five seconds by default, but you can change the default using a command line option. Indeed, most of top's functionality can be controlled using either command line options or dynamically using top's interactive interface. top's command line syntax is shown here, followed by Table 20-6, which describes its command line options and arguments.

top [-cCiqsS] [-d *delay*] [-p *pid*] [-n *num*]

TABLE 20-6 TOP COMMAND LINE OPTIONS

Option	Description
-c	Display the command line arguments used to invoke the process
-C	Display totals for CPU statistics on SMP machines
-d *delay*	Pause *delay* seconds between updates
-i	Ignore idle or zombie processes
-n *num*	Refresh the display *num* times, then exit

Option	Description
-p *pid*	Monitor processes with a process ID of *pid* (can be specified up to 20 times)
-q	Refresh constantly with no delay between updates
-s	Run in secure mode, disabling potentially dangerous interactive commands
-S	Show summary statistics for each process and its child processes (if any)

Invoked with no command line options, the default top display should resemble Listing 20-1.

Listing 20-1: The Default Top Display

```
11:06pm  up 7 days,  4:08,  2 users,  load average: 0.97, 0.88, 0.73
63 processes: 61 sleeping, 2 running, 0 zombie, 0 stopped
CPU states:  4.2% user,  2.7% system,  6.2% nice,  3.6% idle
Mem:   255580K av,  227732K used,   27848K free,    652K shrd,   15592K buff
Swap:  393348K av,    4748K used,  388600K free                 54500K cached
  PID USER     PRI  NI  SIZE  RSS SHARE STAT %CPU %MEM   TIME COMMAND
28543 lp        19   0  7944 7944   612 R    95.7  3.1   1:23 z53
28549 kwall     12   0  1048 1044   832 R     2.8  0.4   0:00 top
    1 root       8   0   152  104   100 S     0.0  0.0   0:04 init
    2 root       9   0     0    0     0 SW    0.0  0.0   0:01 keventd
    3 root      19  19     0    0     0 SWN   0.0  0.0   0:00 ksoftirqd_CPU0
    4 root       9   0     0    0     0 SW    0.0  0.0   0:04 kswapd
    5 root       9   0     0    0     0 SW    0.0  0.0   0:00 kreclaimd
    6 root       9   0     0    0     0 SW    0.0  0.0   0:00 bdflush
    7 root       9   0     0    0     0 SW    0.0  0.0   0:00 kupdated
    8 root      -1 -20     0    0     0 SW<   0.0  0.0   0:00 mdrecoveryd
   18 root       9   0     0    0     0 SW    0.0  0.0   0:04 kjournald
  139 root       9   0     0    0     0 SW    0.0  0.0   0:00 kjournald
  140 root       9   0     0    0     0 SW    0.0  0.0   0:03 kjournald
  141 root       9   0     0    0     0 SW    0.0  0.0   0:00 kjournald
  574 root       9   0   348  336   336 S     0.0  0.1   0:00 syslogd
  579 root       9   0   876  640   304 S     0.0  0.2   0:00 klogd
  599 rpc        9   0   396  384   384 S     0.0  0.1   0:00 portmap
  675 ntp        9   0  1920 1920  1728 S     0.0  0.7   0:02 ntpd
```

The first line shows the system uptime, just like the output of the uptime command. The next two lines of top's display summarizes CPU usage, one showing the total number of active processes, and the number that are sleeping, running, zombied, and stopped, and the next showing CPU utilization by percentage. A *zombie* is a process that terminated before its parent process could collect its exit status. Such processes are called *zombies* because they are dead processes that consume no resources (except for an entry in the kernel's process table) but still appear in process listings, such as the one that top displays. The fourth and fifth lines summarize current memory utilization using the same output as the free command. The sixth line is a header for the rest of the display. The balance of top's display shows the most CPU intensive tasks, sorted (by default) in decreasing order of CPU cycles they consume. Table 20-7 describes top's display fields.

TABLE 20-7 TOP DISPLAY FIELDS

Field	Description
PID	The process ID of each task
USER	The user name of the user that started the process
PRI	The process's execution priority
NI	The value used to modify the process's execution priority, relative to other processes with the same priority (PRI)
SIZE	The amount of memory the process requires
RSS	The amount of physical memory the process consumes
SHARE	The amount of shared memory the process uses
STAT	The process's current CPU state
%CPU	The percentage of total CPU time the process consumes
%MEM	The percentage of total physical memory the process uses
TIME	The total amount of CPU time that the process has been running
COMMAND	The command used to invoke the process, shown in parentheses if the task is currently swapped out

A process's CPU state can be D (uninterruptible sleep), R (running), S (sleeping), T (stopped or traced), or Z (zombie). If one of these CPU states is followed by <, the process has a negative nice value; if followed by N, it has a positive nice value; if followed by W, it is swapped out.

Finally, as mentioned at the beginning of this section, you can modify the sort order of the display, effectively causing top to use another criterion beside CPU utilization for the "top" CPU processes. While top is running, press the letter o or O, followed by one of the options in the following list to sort the display by that criterion:

- ◆ a or A — Sorts process by decreasing age

- ◆ m or M — Sorts processes by the physical memory consumed

- ◆ n or N — Sorts processes by numeric process ID

- ◆ p or P — Sorts processes by CPU usage

- ◆ t or T — Sorts processes by CPU time consumed

Listing 20-2 shows the same display as Listing 20-1, sorted by memory consumption rather than CPU usage:

Listing 20-2: top Display Sorted by Memory Consumption

```
11:06pm  up 7 days,  4:08,  2 users,  load average: 0.97, 0.88, 0.73
63 processes: 61 sleeping, 2 running, 0 zombie, 0 stopped
CPU states:  5.1% user,  1.8% system,  7.3% nice,  4.5% idle
Mem:   255580K av,  227732K used,   27848K free,     652K shrd,   15592K buff
Swap:  393348K av,    4748K used,  388600K free                  54500K cached
  PID USER     PRI  NI  SIZE  RSS SHARE STAT %CPU %MEM   TIME COMMAND
28543 lp        19   0  7944 7944   612 R    95.7  3.1  1:23 z53
  675 ntp        9   0  1920 1920  1728 S     0.0  0.7  0:02 ntpd
28549 kwall     12   0  1048 1044   832 R     2.8  0.4  0:00 top
  579 root       9   0   876  640   304 S     0.0  0.2  0:00 klogd
  574 root       9   0   348  336   336 S     0.0  0.1  0:00 syslogd
  599 rpc        9   0   396  384   384 S     0.0  0.1  0:00 portmap
    1 root       8   0   152  104   100 S     0.0  0.0  0:04 init
    4 root       9   0     0    0     0 SW    0.0  0.0  0:04 kswapd
   18 root       9   0     0    0     0 SW    0.0  0.0  0:04 kjournald
    2 root       9   0     0    0     0 SW    0.0  0.0  0:01 keventd
    3 root      19  19     0    0     0 SWN   0.0  0.0  0:00 ksoftirqd_CPU0
    5 root       9   0     0    0     0 SW    0.0  0.0  0:00 kreclaimd
    6 root       9   0     0    0     0 SW    0.0  0.0  0:00 bdflush
    7 root       9   0     0    0     0 SW    0.0  0.0  0:00 kupdated
    8 root      -1 -20     0    0     0 SW<   0.0  0.0  0:00 mdrecoveryd
  139 root       9   0     0    0     0 SW    0.0  0.0  0:00 kjournald
  140 root       9   0     0    0     0 SW    0.0  0.0  0:03 kjournald
  141 root       9   0     0    0     0 SW    0.0  0.0  0:00 kjournald
```

As you can see in Listing 20-2, changing the sort order of top's display makes it very easy to see which processes top the list, as it were, of the most memory intensive processes.

Monitoring Network Traffic

Network bottlenecks are highly visible. Moreover, the nature of a network makes troubleshooting performance problems rather difficult because any number of failure or bottleneck points could exist. The culprit could be network cards, cabling, bridges, routers, gateways, or firewalls. Worse still, on a TCP/IP Ethernet, *everyone* notices a network performance problem. Ethernet does not discriminate — if the network is congested, *everyone* suffers equally. From the administrator's point of view, network saturation translates into impatient users demanding a solution right now.

The first thing to check is raw packet traffic, which you can see using the netstat command and its -i option, which shows the TCP/IP traffic on all active network interfaces — for example:

```
$ netstat -i
Iface   MTU Met   RX-OK RX-ERR RX-DRP RX-OVR   TX-OK TX-ERR TX-DRP TX-OVR Flg
eth0   1500   0 5267273      0      0      0 6962122      0      0      0 BMRU
lo    16436   0   22003      0      0      0   22003      0      0      0 LRU
```

The output shows basic TCP/IP packet traffic for two interfaces, the loopback interface (lo0), and the Ethernet device (eth0). Table 20-8 describes the fields.

TABLE 20-8 netstat -i OUTPUT FIELDS

Field	Description
Iface	The name of the network interface
MTU	The maximum transmission unit, or packet size, of the interface
RX-OK	The number of incoming (received) packets since the interface was started
RX-ERR	The number of errors on incoming packets
RX-DRP	The number of incoming packets dropped
RX-OVR	The number of incoming packets that overran the input buffer
TX-OK	The number of outbound (sent) packets transmitted since the interface was started
TX-ERR	The number of errors on outbound packages since the interface was last started
TX-DRP	The number of outgoing packets dropped
TX-OVR	The number of outgoing packets that overran the output buffer

Ideally, the number of packets with errors (malformed, incomplete, or garbled packets) should be less than one percent. In the example output, 0 inbound errors on over 5 million received packets is perfect; the outbound traffic is also perfect. When outbound error rates increase, some sort of problem is occurring on your system; on the other hand, inbound errors, while problematic, rarely indicate problems on your system. That is, the problem is "out there."

To get a better idea of network saturation, use `netstat` without any options, as shown in the following example:

```
$ netstat
Active Internet connections (w/o servers)
Proto Recv-Q Send-Q Local Address          Foreign Address          State
tcp      0      0 marta.kurtwerks.c:34989 advent.kurtwerks.co:x11 ESTABLISHED
tcp      0      0 marta.kurtwerks.c:34984 advent.kurtwerks.co:x11 ESTABLISHED
tcp      0      0 marta.kurtwerks.c:34987 advent.kurtwerks.co:x11 ESTABLISHED
tcp      0      0 marta.kurtwerks.c:34986 advent.kurtwerks.co:x11 ESTABLISHED
tcp      0      0 marta.kurtwerks.c:34980 advent.kurtwerks.co:x11 ESTABLISHED
tcp      0      0 marta.kurtwerks.c:34982 advent.kurtwerks.co:x11 ESTABLISHED
tcp      0      0 marta.kurtwerks.c:34976 advent.kurtwerks.co:x11 ESTABLISHED
tcp      0      0 marta.kurtwerks.c:34979 advent.kurtwerks.co:x11 ESTABLISHED
tcp      0      0 marta.kurtwerks.c:34956 advent.kurtwerks.co:x11 ESTABLISHED
tcp      0      0 marta.kurtwerks.c:34968 advent.kurtwerks.co:x11 ESTABLISHED
tcp      0      0 marta.kurtwerks.c:34964 advent.kurtwerks.co:x11 ESTABLISHED
tcp      0      0 marta.kurtwerks.c:34966 advent.kurtwerks.co:x11 ESTABLISHED
tcp      0     20 marta.kurtwerks.com:ssh advent.kurtwerks.c:1246 ESTABLISHED
Active UNIX domain sockets (w/o servers)
Proto RefCnt Flags       Type       State         I-Node Path
unix  10     [ ]         DGRAM                     744    /dev/log
unix  3      [ ]         STREAM     CONNECTED      300563
unix  3      [ ]         STREAM     CONNECTED      300562
unix  3      [ ]         STREAM     CONNECTED      300561
```

The output is truncated to conserve space. A bare `netstat` command shows all active Internet connections for TCP, UDP, and UNIX domain sockets. You can use the `-t` and `-u` options to eliminate Unix sockets (that is, execute `netstat -t -u`) — Unix domain sockets handle only local network traffic, not connections between Internet hosts. The data that you are looking for here is nonzero values in the Send-Q column. If several connections have nonzero values in this column and the values are increasing, the network is saturated. To determine whether or not values in the Send-Q column are increasing, add the `-c` option to get a continuously updated display.

To check basic network connectivity, use the `ping` command. First, `ping` the local host by name (`ping localhost`) and by IP address (`ping 127.0.0.1`). Next, `ping` your host by hostname and IP address. If these `ping` commands work, networking is operable on the local system. On the other hand, if you can `ping` your own host by IP address but not by its name, make sure that you have the correct entry in /etc/hosts. Next, ping another system on your network, again by both name and IP address. Generally, if you can successfully ping any remote system by IP but not by name, you have a name server problem — make sure your name server is listed in /etc/resolv.conf. Finally, ping a system on another network (yes, by name and IP address). Successful pings of remote systems not on your network mean that you can at least reach the Internet. If a given remote system is inaccessible, it might not be up. If you cannot ping remote systems, make sure that you have a properly functioning name server and gateway, and make sure that the interface that you want to use is up and running. Similarly, netstat -nr checks both the kernel's routing tables and highlights invalid or incorrect DNS entries.

Keep the following admonition in mind: do *not* apply the tuning tips suggested in this chapter based on a single observation or on a small set of observations taken over a short period of time. Instead, endure user complaints about performance as well as management pressure to solve the problem long enough to develop a more comprehensive picture of the situation. Combining the data that you get from sar, vmstat, iostat, ps, and uptime yields a more accurate picture of overall system status and the problem domain, and thereby reduces the likelihood that you are chasing a red herring and that tuning one subsystem adversely affects another.

Similarly, rather than waiting until your end users or your managers are breathing down your neck, take advantage of cron and the command invocations that you have seen in this section to start creating a system usage profile. Doing so before a crisis yields several advantages. First, routine, automated monitoring makes it fairly simple to identify upward trends in usage and to schedule component upgrades or replacements before performance degradation becomes acute. Second, reviewing these reports gives you additional insight into how the system is used, which *does* make you a better administrator and helps you anticipate problems before they occur. Finally, intimate familiarity with how the system *usually* behaves causes unusual or atypical situations, such as sudden spikes in memory consumption or sharp increases in disk activity, to jump out at you. Ongoing monitoring gives you time to address a performance problem before it becomes acute and your telephone starts ringing.

Summary

In this chapter, you learned how to troubleshoot performance problems using some of the utility programs available in Red Hat Linux. You reviewed a general procedure to follow when tracking down problems and read about using the uptime command to take a quick snapshot of overall system performance. Next, you learned how to use the ps command to monitor running processes and how to isolate programs hogging memory using vmstat. You also began exploring the iostat command for monitoring disk performance and the df and du commands for reporting on disk space usage. Finally, you read about the top command for tracking CPU usage and how to identify network traffic problems using netstat.

Chapter 21

Administering Users and Groups

IN THIS CHAPTER

- ◆ Understanding the root account
- ◆ Implementing Sudo
- ◆ Creating and maintaining users and groups
- ◆ Managing disk usage with user and group quotas

THIS CHAPTER DISCUSSES the capabilities of the root account, explains how to use `sudo` to give normal users root capabilities on a limited and monitored basis, how to create and maintain user and group accounts, the Red Hat Linux user private group scheme, and how to implement user and group file system quotas to control and monitor disk space usage.

Understanding the Root Account

With very few and limited exceptions, the root or superuser account has unlimited power on any Linux or Unix system, and, in this respect, Red Hat Linux is no exception. The root account, or, to use the expression you see throughout this chapter, root, can access any file and modify any process. Indeed, it is for this reason that root is often called the *superuser* – root is effectively omnipotent.

The exceptions to root's capabilities are few. As explained in Chapter 7, root on an NFS client (that is, a system mounting an NFS exported file system from an NFS server) typically does *not* enjoy root privileges on the exported file system because the NFS server exports the file system using the `root_squash` option, which maps the root's UID and GID, 0, on the client system to the anonymous user. Keep in mind that this is the default behavior of the NFS server daemon (`exportfs`) and can be overridden using `no_root_squash` on the NFS server. This is one limit on root's power.

The ext2 and ext3 file systems also restrict root's power, although only slightly. The ext2 and ext3 file systems support a number of special file attributes, including immutability. Using the `chattr` utility, root can set a file's immutable attribute, which prevents *all* users, including root, from modifying the file – it cannot be deleted, renamed, or written to, and no link can be created to it until the immutable attribute is cleared. You guessed it — only root can set or clear a file's immutable attribute.

Finally, so-called Linux capabilities and Linux ACLs (Access Control Lists) are being developed that enable root's power with respect to process management and file access to be subdivided into more finely grained capabilities. Based on the IEEE's POSIX capabilities and first appearing in the 2.2 kernel, *Linux capabilities* (and, for that matter, POSIX capabilities) work by splitting root's traditional privileges into smaller sets of more specific privileges that can be enabled and disabled. Eventually, POSIX capabilities will also be applied to files in the file system.

The most immediately useful application is what is referred to as a *capability bounding set*, which defines a list of capabilities any process running on a Linux system can hold. If a capability does not appear in the bounding set, no process, regardless of how privileged it is, can exercise it. For example, you can disable kernel module loading by removing this capability from the bounding set. Although manipulating kernel capabilities is an advanced topic beyond this book's scope, you might find it interesting or useful, depending on your environment, to examine the Linux Kernel Capability Bounding Set Editor (LCAP), a tool that takes advantage of and manipulates POSIX capabilities. Its home page on the Web is `http://pweb.netcom.com/~spoon/lcap/`. Additional information about POSIX capabilities is available via FTP from the kernel source code repository at `ftp://linux.kernel.org/pub/linux/libs/security/linux-privs/`.

Implementing Sudo

Considering root's privileges, you can easily understand why root access on a Red Hat Linux system is carefully protected and the root password tightly guarded. Nevertheless, it is often desirable to grant privileges to a nonroot user that have traditionally been solely root's domain, such as printer management, user account administration, system backups, or maintaining a particular Internet service. Indeed, in many environments, subdividing system administration responsibilities is a necessity because the responsibilities of maintaining an active server in a large IT shop or a series of servers in an ISP can quickly overwhelm a single individual.

The problem in such a situation is clear: How do you grant administrative privileges to nonroot users *without* providing unfettered root access? In many situations, Sudo, a mnemonic for *superuser do*, is the solution. Sudo enables you to give specific users or groups of users the ability to run some (or all) commands requiring root privileges. Sudo also logs all commands executed, which allows you to maintain an audit trail of the commands executed. As the README in the source distribution states, Sudo's "basic philosophy is to give as few privileges as possible but still allow people to get their work done." Sudo's features include:

◆ Enabling the ability to restrict the commands a given user may run on a per host basis.

◆ Maintaining a clear audit trail of who did what using the system logger or Sudo's own log file. In fact, you can use Sudo in lieu of a root shell to take advantage of this logging.

◆ Limiting root-equivalent activity to a short period of time using timestamp based "tickets," thus avoiding the potential of leaving an active root shell open in environments where others can physically get to your keyboard.

◆ Allowing a single configuration file, /etc/sudoers, to be used on many machines, permitting both centralized Sudo administration and the flexibility to define a user's privileges on a per host basis.

After the configuration file has been created, a typical Sudo session proceeds as follows:

1. An authorized user prefixes the root command she wants to execute with sudo followed by a space, for example:

   ```
   $ sudo shutdown -h +5 "System halting for disk replacement"
   ```

2. Sudo prompts the user for her personal password (*not* the root password) and then checks the configuration file (/etc/sudoers) to make sure she has permission to run the given command on a given machine.

3. If the user is permitted to use that command, Sudo runs the command as root (or another user if specified), logs the details, and timestamps the Sudo session ticket.

4. If the user is *not* permitted to use that command, Sudo logs the attempt and exits. Sudo also logs problems and other invalid sudo uses.

5. After executing the first command, the user can use multiple sudo commands without being prompted for her password again. The session ticket expires five minutes after the last sudo command is issued, after which the user is again prompted for a password.

By default, sudo logs to /var/log/messages using the system logger (syslogd), but you can configure the system logger to log sudo-related messages to a different file. Sudo can even bypass the system logger completely and maintain its own log file. If Sudo is invoked by an invalid user, is invoked with an invalid command, or if other abnormal situations arise, Sudo notifies the root user (by default) via e-mail.

Sudo's configuration file is /etc/sudoers, which must be edited using visudo, part of the Sudo distribution. Using visudo is vital because it locks the /etc/sudoers to prevent simultaneous edits and validates the grammar and syntax in the configuration file, cowardly refusing to save changes if it believes it has detected an error.

Deciphering Sudo's configuration file

Sudo's configuration file, /etc/sudoers, is the key file. It contains three types of entries — alias definitions, privilege specifications, and global configuration defaults. *Alias definitions* are variables or placeholders that you can reuse throughout the configuration file. They come in four flavors: user aliases, command aliases, so-called runas aliases, and host aliases. The rationale for aliases is to simplify maintaining the configuration file — rather than editing multiple user or command lists when you update /etc/sudoers, you simply modify the appropriate alias and let sudo substitute the alias definition each place it is used. *Privilege specifications* define which users may execute what commands. *Global configuration defaults* are general settings that control sudo's overall behavior.

Instead of trying to understand sudoer's configuration syntax in the abstract, consider the following example that illustrates typical Sudo usage. Suppose you want to enable the users marysue and bubba to reset passwords for all users except root, which means that marysue and bubba need to be able to use the passwd command to set passwords for users other than themselves. Somehow, though, they must be prevented from changing the root password. As you know, the command for changing passwords is

```
passwd username
```

The general procedure is to use visudo to edit /etc/sudoers and create a *user alias* defining the users to whom you are granting access to one or more commands, a *command alias* that represents the command or commands to execute, a *host alias* to identify the host or hosts on which the named users are permitted to execute the named command (if necessary) a *runas alias* (again, if necessary) that identifies the user a command should run as, and a *user privilege specification* to connect the necessary aliases together to form a Sudo rule. The following procedure shows the specific steps to follow.

1. As the root user, start the edit session by executing visudo. Initially, the file should resemble Listing 21-1.

   Listing 21-1: Using visudo to Edit /etc/sudoers

   ```
   # sudoers file.
   #
   # This file MUST be edited with the 'visudo' command as root.
   #
   # See the sudoers man page for the details on how to write a
   sudoers file.
   #

   # Host alias specification
   ```

```
# User alias specification

# Cmnd alias specification

# User privilege specification
root    ALL=(ALL) ALL
```

The hash sign, #, prefixes a comment unless it is used in the context of a user name and is followed by one or more digits, for example, #502, in which case sudo interprets it as a UID.

2. Add the following line in the user alias section:

```
User_Alias PWADMIN=marysue,bubba
```

This statement defines a user alias named PWADMIN consisting of the accounts marysue and bubba.

3. Add the following line in the command alias section:

```
Cmnd_Alias PW=/usr/bin/passwd [A-z]*,!/usr/bin/passwd root
```

This statement defines a command alias named PW that has two components separated by a comma. Command aliases must include a full path specification and any arguments that you wish to permit to be invoked using sudo. The first component, /usr/bin/passwd [A-z]*, indicates that /usr/bin/passwd may be used with any argument that begins with the letters A–Z or a–z followed by zero or more characters. The second element uses the ! character to prevent /usr/bin/passwd from being used with an argument of root.

The character used as wildcards, permitted in both path name specifications and command arguments, are:

*	Matches any set of zero or more characters, but not a / in a path specification. That is, /usr/bin/* matches /usr/bin/bc, but not /usr/bin/filter/filter_innd.pl
?	Matches any single character
[...]	Matches any character in the specified range
[!...]	Matches any character *not* in the specified range
\x	Escapes the character x, including *, ?, [,], (,), @, !, =, :, ,, and \

4. Add the following line in the user specification section:

```
PWADMIN ALL = PW
```

This statement says that the PWADMIN users can use the PW command on all hosts (the ALL keyword). More generally, a user privilege specification takes the form

```
user_alias host_alias=[(runas_alias)] cmnd_alias[,...]
```

Note that the runas alias is not required and that you can specify multiple command aliases in the same entry if each is separated by a comma. In fact, it was not strictly necessary to create the user and command aliases, as the user privilege specification could have been written as follows:

```
marysue,bubba ALL=/usr/bin/passwd [A-z]*,!/usr/bin/passwd root
```

After these edits, /etc/sudoers should resemble the Listing 21-2.

Listing 21-2: /etc/sudoers after Edits to Enable marysue and bubba to Reset Passwords

```
# sudoers file.
#
# This file MUST be edited with the 'visudo' command as root.
#
# See the sudoers man page for the details on how to write a
sudoers file.
#

# Host alias specification

# User alias specification
User_Alias PWADMIN=marysue,bubba

# Cmnd alias specification
Cmnd_Alias PW=/usr/bin/passwd [A-z]*,!/usr/bin/passwd root

# User privilege specification
root    ALL=(ALL) ALL
PWADMIN ALL=PW
```

5. Save the changes and exit visudo.

6. As marysue or bubba, test the configuration to make sure that everything works as intended. The first test confirms that bubba can use passwd:

```
[bubba@localhost]$ sudo passwd gnuuser

We trust you have received the usual lecture from the local
System
Administrator. It usually boils down to these two things:
```

```
#1) Respect the privacy of others.
#2) Think before you type.

Password:
Changing password for user gnuuser
New password:
Retype new password:
passwd: all authentication tokens updated successfully
```

The next test demonstrates that members of the PWADMIN alias *cannot* change the root password:

```
[marysue@localhost]$ sudo passwd root
Sorry, user marysue is not allowed to execute
'/usr/bin/passwd root' as root on luther.
```

Sudo rules can be fine-tuned using flags and keywords in the configuration file. The source code directory for this chapter contains the sample.sudoers file shipped in Sudo's source code configuration. The file sample.sudoers contains many examples (with informative comments) that you can adapt to suit your own needs. In addition, the manual pages for sudo, visudo, and sudoers (man sudo, man visudo, and man sudoers) have complete information on the syntax and useful examples of configuring sudoers and using visudo.

Sudo configuration and usage tips

You should plan ahead for security, because sudo can be used to gain further power by obtaining root access. For example, if you enable users to run less as root, they could use its shell command, !, to run other commands as root or to view sensitive files, such as /etc/shadow. Indeed, the sudoers manual page cautions: "There is no easy way to prevent a user from gaining a root shell if that user has access to commands allowing shell escapes." In general, when configuring root command access using Sudo, adhere to the least-access principle, granting the minimum necessary privileges to accomplish a given task.

When using visudo, consider using its -s option, which enables a more rigorous level of syntax and grammar checking. In addition, do *not* give users permission to use visudo for two reasons: first, they can use vi's :! command to obtain a root shell, and, more importantly, it enables them to edit /etc/sudoers and alter its contents to give themselves unfettered root access and to disable logging.

Working With Users and Groups

Administering users and groups, or, more precisely, administering user and group *accounts*, is a fundamental Red Hat Linux system administration activity. Ordinarily, most people understand user accounts as accounts tied to a particular physical user. However, as you will see later in this chapter, Red Hat Linux systems also have *logical user accounts*, user accounts that can exist for particular applications, such as MySQL or PostgreSQL, or system functions, such as the mail and bin user accounts. Other than this distinction between real and logical user accounts, there are few substantive differences between actual and logical users. In particular, both actual and logical have user identification numbers (UIDs), numeric values that the kernel and many applications use instead of the account name. Ordinarily, each user account has a unique UID (on a given system), but this is not strictly required.

Unlike user accounts, group accounts always represent some sort of logical organization of users. Like user accounts, groups have group identification numbers, or GIDs, and it is common for users to be members of several groups. Groups are used to tie one or more users together in order to simplify administrative tasks. For example, an administrator can assign to a group permission to execute a certain application, and then add and delete users from that group, rather than giving individual users permissions, clearly a simpler, less labor-intensive way to handle access control. Similarly, file access can be controlled at the group level because files are assigned user and group owners when files are created and also carry separate read, write, and execute permissions for the file's owner, the group assigned to the file, and any other users on that host.

Because properly managing user and group accounts and assigning and revoking user and group permissions is so important on any Red Hat Linux system, this chapter spends a good deal of time examining the command line and GUI tools for doing so.

Understanding user private groups

Before delving into user and group administration tools, however, you need to understand the Red Hat Linux user private group (UPG) scheme, which makes Linux groups much easier to use. Although the UPG scheme does not add or change the normal Linux way of handling groups, it *does* introduce a new convention that is different from traditional Linux user and group idioms: when you create a new user, Red Hat Linux creates a unique group for that user. After you become accustomed to the user private group scheme, you will find that it is very natural to use and makes good sense.

The UPG scheme has the following salient characteristics:

◆ Each user has a primary group with the same name as the user account.

◆ Each user is the only member of her primary group.

◆ Each user's umask defaults to 002 — because every user has her own private group in the UPG scheme, the group protection afforded by the traditional Linux umask of 022 is unnecessary.

◆ Group-specific directories, such as project directories, have the set-GID (set group ID) bit enabled. If you set the set-GID bit on a directory, all files created in that directory have their group set to the directory's group

TIP   The default umask is set in /etc/profile.

For example, suppose the finance department maintains a large number of files in the /opt/finance directory and that many people work with these files on a daily basis. Using the UPG scheme, you would first create a group named, say, finance, use the chgrp command to change the group ownership on /opt/finance to the finance group, use the chmod command to enable the set-GID bit on /opt/finance, and then add the appropriate users to the finance group. As a result, all finance users can edit existing files in the /opt/finance directory. Similarly, when new files are created in the /opt/finance directory, the files are automatically assigned ownership by the finance group and all users who are members of the finance group can edit them without taking any special steps. Another benefit of the UPG scheme is that if you have users who work on multiple projects, they do not have to change their umask or group as they move from project to project (that is, directory to directory) because each main project directory's set-GID bit automatically sets the proper group for all files created in that directory and its subdirectories.

NOTE   Because each user's home directory is owned by that user and her private group, it is safe to set the set-GID bit on the home directory, but unnecessary. Why? By default, files are created with the primary group of the user; the set-GID bit is redundant with respect to a user's home directory and its subdirectories.

The following steps illustrate the scenario and process just described. The point of this exercise is to provide a concrete illustration of Red Hat Linux's UPG scheme, so I defer discussing the commands and their options until later in the chapter.

1. Create the finance group:

```
# /usr/sbin/groupadd finance
```

2. Change the group ownership of /opt/finance to the finance group to associate the directory contents with the finance group:

```
# /bin/chgrp -R finance /opt/finance
```

3. Add the proper users to the group (add the user bubba in this case):

```
# /usr/bin/gpasswd -a bubba finance
Adding user bubba to group finance
```

4. To enable the finance group's members to create, make the directory writeable by the group:

```
# /bin/chmod g+w /opt/finance
```

5. Set the set-GID bit on /opt/finance to cause newly created files in the /opt/finance tree to have finance group ownership:

```
# /bin/chmod g+s /opt/finance
```

After this command, the letter s appears where the group execute bit (denoted by the letter x) would ordinarily appear when you generate a long listing of /opt/finance's attributes:

```
ls -ld /opt/finance
drwxrwsr-x    4 root       finance        4096 Sep 23 21:49
/opt/finance/
```

With the default umask set to 002, files that bubba creates in /opt/finance are owned by the user bubba and the group finance, enabling other finance users to modify the file:

```
$ [bubba@localhost]$ touch /opt/finance/20010923
$ [bubba@localhost]$ ls -l /opt/finance/20010923
-rw-rw-r--    1 bubba      finance           0 Sep 23 22:15
/opt/finance/20010923
```

To summarize, the Red Hat Linux UPG scheme makes it trivial to create project groups that permit members of those groups to write files in the groups' common directory without unduly burdening users.

Adding, modifying, and deleting users

Although some administrators find the traditional command line tools for managing users and groups tedious or inconvenient to use, this chapter examines them in detail. For those readers who prefer GUI tools, the section titled "Using the Red Hat User Manager" covers Red Hat's User Manager tool, a GUI application for creating, modifying, and deleting both users and groups.

Table 21-1 lists the commands for adding, modifying, and deleting user accounts. They are discussed in detail in the following subsections.

TABLE 21-1 USER ACCOUNT ADMINISTRATIVE COMMANDS

Command	Description
chage	Changes password aging information
chsh	Changes the user's shell
passwd	Sets or changes user account passwords
newusers	Adds user accounts in batch
useradd	Adds new user accounts
userdel	Deletes user accounts
usermod	Modifies existing user accounts

Readers who may have used one version or another of an adduser script in earlier versions of Red Hat Linux, other Linux distributions, or various Unix versions, should note that Red Hat has replaced adduser with a symlink to /usr/sbin/adduser.

THE USER DATABASE FILES

In order to understand the following discussion, you need to know the format of the user database files, /etc/passwd and /etc/shadow. Each line in both files consists of colon-separated fields, one line per user. The format of the password file, /etc/passwd, is

username:password:uid:gid:gecos:directory:shell

Table 21-2 describes the fields in /etc/passwd.

TABLE 21-2 FIELDS IN THE PASSWORD FILE

Field	Description
username	The user's account name on the system
password	username's encrypted password or an x
uid	username's numeric UID (user ID)
gid	username's numeric primary group ID (group ID)

Continued

TABLE 21-2 FIELDS IN THE PASSWORD FILE *(Continued)*

Field	Description
gecos	An optional field used for informational purposes that usually contains *username*'s full name
home	*username*'s home directory
shell	*username*'s login shell

On Red Hat Linux systems (and most Linux systems these days), the actual password is stored in /etc/shadow, indicated by an x in the *password* field. Because /etc/passwd is readable by all users, storing even encrypted passwords in it makes password guessing easier. However, /etc/shadow is more secure because it is readable only by programs that run with root privileges, such as login and passwd. The sidebar "The Shadow Password System" discusses shadow passwords in greater detail.

The Shadow Password System

Red Hat Linux, like most, if not all, Linux and Unix systems, uses shadow passwords because they offer enhanced protection for your system's authentication files. During the installation of Red Hat Linux, shadow password protection for your system is enabled by default, as are MD5 passwords. MD5 passwords are an alternative and arguably more secure method of encrypting passwords because they are longer and use a stronger encryption method than the standard DES encryption used by the standard authentication utilities.

Shadow passwords offer a number of distinct advantages over the traditional password system, including:

♦ Improved system security by moving the encrypted passwords (normally found in /etc/passwd) to /etc/shadow, which is readable only by root

♦ Information concerning *password aging*, how long it has been since a password was last changed

♦ Control over how long a password can remain unchanged before the user is required to change it

♦ The ability to set and enforce a security policy using settings in /etc/login.defs, particularly concerning password aging

The shadow password suite contains a number of utilities that simplify working with shadow passwords and, if you wish, reverting to traditional password management. These utilities include:

◆ pwconv and pwunconv for switching from normal to shadow passwords and back, respectively

◆ pwck and grpck for verifying the contents and consistency of the password and group files, respectively, against their shadowed counterparts

◆ useradd, usermod, and userdel, the standard commands for adding, deleting and modifying user accounts

◆ groupadd, groupmod, and groupdel, the standard commands for adding, deleting, and modifying group accounts

◆ gpasswd, the standard command for administering the groups file, /etc/group

Strictly speaking *shell* identifies the program to run when a user logs in. If it is empty, /bin/sh is used. If it is set to a nonexistent executable or /bin/false, the user is unable to log in. An entry in /etc/passwd would resemble the following:

```
marysue:x:502:502:Mary Sue:/home/marysue:/bin/bash
```

In this entry, *username* is marysue, *password* is x, meaning it is stored in /etc/shadow, *uid* is 502, *gid* is 502, *gecos* is Mary Sue, *home* is /home/marysue, and *shell* is /bin/bash.

The *gecos* field is primarily of historical interest. *GECOS* is an acronym meaning General Electric Comprehensive Operating System and was renamed to GCOS when Honeywell purchased General Electric's large systems division. Dennis Ritchie, one of the creators of Unix, writes of it: "Sometimes we sent printer output or batch jobs to the GCOS machine. The gcos field in the password file was a place to stash the information for the $IDENT card. Not elegant."

In addition to storing the encrypted password, /etc/shadow stores password expiration information. Like /etc/passwd, fields are separated by colons. It contains the following fields, listed in the order in which they appear in /etc/shadow:

- ◆ The account name

- ◆ The account's encrypted password

- ◆ The number of days since 1 January 1970 that the password was last changed

- ◆ The number of days permitted before the password can be changed

- ◆ The number of days after which the password must be changed

- ◆ The number of days before the password expires that the user is warned

- ◆ The number of days after the password expires before the account is disabled

- ◆ The number of days since 1 January 1970 after which the account is disabled

- ◆ Reserved for future use

The entry from /etc/shadow that corresponds to the entry from /etc/passwd shown earlier is:

```
marysue:$1$EmRh1cmZ$gkXY3OH43D7NtpQXjm9FO1:11589:0:99999:7:::
```

Notice that the last three fields are empty. Rather than interpret these fields manually, you can use the chage command's -l option to obtain a friendlier display:

```
# chage -l marysue
Minimum:        0
Maximum:        99999
Warning:        7
Inactive:       -1
Last Change:            Sep 24, 2001
Password Expires:       Never
Password Inactive:      Never
Account Expires:        Never
```

chage does not display the fields in the order in which they appear in /etc/shadow.

ADDING USERS

The useradd command creates a new user account or, when invoked with the -D option, updates the default values applied to all new user accounts. useradd's syntax is shown in the following listing.

```
useradd [-c comment] [-d home] [-e expire_date] [-f n]
        [-g initial_group] [-G group[,...]]
```

```
        [-m [-k skel_dir] | -M] [-p passwd] [-s shell]
        [-u uid [ -o]] [-n] [-r] login
useradd -D [-g group] [-b home] [-f n] [-e expire_date]
        [-s shell]
```

As you can see in the syntax listing, useradd's only required argument is *login*, which identifies the user account to create. If no other command line options are specified, useradd uses built-in values and default values listed in /etc/login.defs (or, optionally, /etc/default/useradd if it exists). To view the current default values, invoke useradd with -D and no other arguments. The following short listing shows the defaults on a stock Red Hat Linux installation:

```
# useradd -D
GROUP=100
HOME=/home
INACTIVE=-1
EXPIRE=
SHELL=/bin/bash
SKEL=/etc/skel
```

Table 21-3 lists and briefly describes useradd's options.

TABLE 21-3 useradd COMMAND LINE OPTIONS

Option	Description
-c *comment*	Sets the comment (GECOS) field to *comment* (usually used for the full name associated with the account)
-d *home*	Sets the home directory to *home* (the default is to append *login* to /home)
-D	Displays or updates the default values used for the -d, -e -f, -g, and -s options
-e *expire_date*	Sets the account expiration date to *expire_date* in YYYY-MM-DD format (the default is no expiration)
-f *n*	Disables the account *n* days after the account password expires (the default value is −1, which disables this feature)
-g *initial_group*	Sets the primary login group name or GID (group ID) to *initial_group* (defaults to 100)
-G *group*	Adds the user to one or more *group*s (no default)

Continued

TABLE 21-3 useradd COMMAND LINE OPTIONS *(Continued)*

Option	Description
-m	Creates the home directory if it does not exist and copies any files in /etc/skel (see -k) to the newly created directory (by default, Red Hat Linux creates the home directory)
-M	Disables creation of the home directory even if the default behavior specified in /etc/login.defs requires creation of the home directory
-k *skel_dir*	Causes the file and directory structure in *skel_dir* to be created in the home directory (only valid with -m)
-p *passwd*	Specifies *passwd* as the encrypted password associated with the account
-s *shell*	Specifies the account's default shell
-u *uid*	Sets the account's UID (user ID) to *uid* (the default value is the next unused UID)
-o	Disables the requirement for unique UIDs (only used with -u)
-n	Disables use of the Red Hat Linux UPG scheme (a user private group will not be created)
-r	Creates a system account
login	Specifies the name of the account to create

To create the user joebob using useradd's default settings, then, execute the following command:

```
# useradd joebob
```

In addition to creating the home directory, /home/joebob in this case, useradd copies the file and directory structure of /etc/skel to the user's home directory. If -p *passwd* is omitted, the account is disabled, so be sure to use the passwd command (discussed shortly) to set the password for the new account. The command just shown adds the following entries to /etc/passwd, /etc/group, and /etc/shadow (the grep command is used to isolate the entries for joebob and adds the file names to the output):

```
# grep joebob /etc/passwd /etc/shadow /etc/group
/etc/passwd:joebob:x:503:503::/home/joebob:/bin/bash
```

```
/etc/shadow:joebob:!!:11589:0:99999:7:::
/etc/group:joebob:x:503:
```

Refer to the earlier discussion of the format of the password and shadow files to understand the meaning of the fields displayed from those files. Notice that the account has been disabled (the first ! in the password field) and that no password has been set, as indicated by the second ! in the password field. Bear in mind, too, that the entry in the group file represents the user private group created for joebob.

 Red Hat has modified the standard useradd command to support its UPG scheme.

The next command uses some of useradd's command line options to override the default values:

```
# useradd -c "Mary Sue" -e 2001-09-30 -f 3 -n  marysue
```

-c "Mary Sue" sets the comment (or GECOS) field to Mary Sue; -e 2001-09-30 sets the account's expiration date; -f 3 disables the account three days after the password expires (if it is not changed); and -n disables the UPG scheme. Here are the entries created for marysue in /etc/passwd, /etc/shadow, and /etc/group:

```
# grep marysue /etc/passwd /etc/shadow /etc/group
/etc/passwd:marysue:x:503:100:Mary Sue:/home/marysue:/bin/bash
/etc/shadow:marysue:!!:11589:0:99999:7:3:11595:
```

First, note that no entry appeared for /etc/group because -n prevented the creation of marysue's user private group. Instead, useradd used the default GID, 100, which corresponds to the users group. Also notice that the comment, Mary Sue, appears in the record added to /etc/passwd instead of the blank field (indicated by ::) for joebob. Finally, notice the slightly different entry added to /etc/shadow, reflecting the use of account expiration information.

To set or change an account password, use the passwd command. After creating a new account, you need to use passwd to set the account's password, unless you specified the encrypted password using useradd's -p option. passwd's syntax is quite simple:

```
passwd [-l] [-u [-f]] [-d] [-S] [username]
```

username indicates the user account on which to operate. If not specified, passwd operates on the current user's account. -l locks a user account by prefixing the password in /etc/shadow with !. -u, conversely, unlocks a user account. If the account password is *only* !, that is, it has no password, you must use the -f option to enable the account. -d disables a user account by removing the password, and -S shows the status of a user account (whether it is locked or not). Only the root user can use these options. In fact, normal users can only invoke passwd to change their own passwords. Only root can use any of passwd's command line options.

ADDING MULTIPLE USERS SIMULTANEOUSLY

In busy or large IT environments, system administrators often find themselves faced with the necessity of creating multiple user accounts. Using useradd to add one or two accounts is relatively simple, but it quickly becomes tedious if ten or twenty accounts need to be created. Fortunately, the shadow password suite includes the newusers utility, which can be used to create and update multiple user accounts. Its syntax is:

```
newusers userfile
```

userfile is the name of a text file consisting of lines in the same format as the standard password file, subject to the following exceptions:

- ◆ The password field appears as clear text — newusers encrypts it before adding the account

- ◆ pw_age: This field is ignored for shadow passwords if the user already exists.

- ◆ The GID can be the name of an existing group or a nonexistent GID. If the GID is the name of an existing group, the named user is added to that group, but if it is a nonexistent numeric value, a new group with the specified GID is created.

- ◆ If the specified home directory refers to a nonexistent directory, newusers creates the specified directory. Otherwise, ownership of the directory is set to that of the named user.

The following listing shows the contents of newusers.txt, which is passed to newusers to create three new user accounts, bubba, joebob, and marysue:

```
bubba:mypass:901:901:Bubba User:/home/bubba:/bin/bash
joebob:yourpass:902:902:Joe Bob:/home/joebob:/bin/bash
marysue:somepass:903:903:Mary Sue:/home/marysue:/bin/bash
```

After executing the command newusers newusers.txt, you will see the entries in /etc/passwd, /etc/group, and /etc/ shadow, as shown in Listing 21-3.

Listing 21-3: Entries in User Database Files after Using newusers

```
# tail -3 passwd
bubba:x:901:901:Bubba User:/home/bubba:/bin/bash
joebob:x:902:902:Joe Bob:/home/joebob:/bin/bash
marysue:x:903:903:Mary Sue:/home/marysue:/bin/bash
# tail -3 group
901:x:901:bubba
902:x:902:joebob
903:x:903:marysue
# tail -3 shadow
bubba:1Uv9E9KXbhuLY:11591:0:99999:7:::
joebob:1WFbzZpUa1z5g:11591:0:99999:7:::
marysue:1WrZ2DoIcmafo:11591:0:99999:7:::
```

MODIFYING AND DELETING USER ACOUNTS

To modify the account information set by useradd, use the usermod command. usermod accepts most of the same options as useradd plus two more, -L and -U. -L locks an account and -U unlocks an account. These options are comparable to the passwd command's -l and -u options. usermod's -l *login_name* option, not available with useradd, enables you to change an account name. usermod does not enable you to change the name of a user who is logged in.

Keep in mind some additional subtleties when you're using usermod. In particular, if you use -G to modify the list of supplementary or additional groups to which the user account belongs, if the user is currently a member of a group which is not listed, the user is removed from the unlisted group(s). If you use -l to change an account name, you need to update the name of the user's home directory manually to reflect the new login name. When you use usermod's -u option to change a user's UID, all files and directories rooted in the user's home directory are updated automatically to the new UID, but any files outside of the user's home directory must be altered manually. In addition, crontab files or at jobs must be updated manually; changes involving NIS must be made on the NIS server. If you do change the UID, ensure that no processes belonging to the named users are executing when the UID is changed. Similar caveats apply to changing the user account's GID (using -g).

To change user account expiry information, use the chage command. In general form, its syntax is

```
chage [options] username
```

chage supports the command line options shown in Table 21-4 in addition to the -l option mentioned previously. Normal (nonroot) users are permitted to use only the -l option and only for their own accounts.

TABLE 21-4 chage COMMAND LINE OPTIONS

Option	Description
username	Identifies the account on which to operate
-d *lastday*	Sets *lastday* as the number of days elapsed since 1 January 1970 that the account password was last changed (*lastday* may be specified in YYYY-MM-DD format)
-E *expireday*	Sets *expireday* as the number of days permitted to elapse after 1 January 1970 before the user account is disabled (*expireday* may be specified in YYYY-MM-DD format); a value of 0 disables account expiration
-I *inactivedays*	Sets *inactivedays* as the number of days permitted to elapse after the account password has expired before the account is disabled
-m *mindays*	Sets *mindays* as the number of days required to elapse before a user can change her password (a value of 0 permits changing the password at any time)
-M *maxdays*	Sets *maxdays* as the number of days permitted to elapse before a password must be changed
-W *warndays*	Set *warndays* as the number of days before password expiration during which the user is warned that her password is due to expire

Using the marysue account created previously, the following listing shows marysue's account expiration information:

```
# chage -l marysue
Minimum:        0
Maximum:        99999
Warning:        7
Inactive:       3
Last Change:            Sep 24, 2001
Password Expires:       Never
Password Inactive:      Never
Account Expires:        Sep 30, 2001
```

The next command uses some of the options Table 21-4 listed to modify marysue's expiry information, specifically, the minimum number of days between password changes (-m), the maximum number of days permitted to elapse before the password *must* be changed (-M), and the account's expiration date (-E):

```
# chage -m 5 -M 30 -E 0 marysue
# chage -l marysue
Minimum:           5
Maximum:          30
Warning:           7
Inactive:          3
Last Change:              Sep 24, 2001
Password Expires:         Oct 24, 2001
Password Inactive:        Oct 27, 2001
Account Expires:          Never
```

As you can see from the output of chage -l, marysue must wait 5 days between password changes, she must change her password every 30 days, and her account will never expire. Notice that changing the minimum and maximum values caused chage to display the dates on which the password expires and (oddly, because the inactivity date was not modified) the date on which the account becomes inactive if marysue fails to change her password.

To change a user's login shell, use the chsh command. Its syntax is:

```
chsh [-l] | [-s shell] username
```

shell is the shell to use and must be specified as a full path. *username* specifies the user account name to modify. To list the full path names of the available shells (from /etc/shells), specify -l.

> **TIP** You can also view the available shells by executing the command cat /etc/shells.

For example, to change the shell for marysue to the C shell, execute the following commands:

```
# chsh -l
/bin/bash2
/bin/bash
/bin/sh
/bin/ash
/bin/bsh
/bin/tcsh
/bin/csh
```

```
# chsh marysue
Changing shell for marysue.
New shell [/bin/bash]: /bin/csh
Shell changed.
```

The first command lists the available command so you can see the full path names. The second command changes marysue's shell. chsh prompts for the new shell after displaying the current shell in square brackets. If you do not specify a new shell, the shell remains unchanged. chsh fails if you do not provide an absolute path. You can also specify an arbitrary command name, which must be a full path, for the new shell, but if the command is not listed in /etc/shells, chsh displays a warning message before changing the shell, as shown in the following listing:

```
# chsh marysue
Changing shell for marysue.
New shell [/bin/csh]: /bin/false
Warning: "/bin/false" is not listed in /etc/shells
Shell changed.
```

Using chsh this way can disable a user's account because specifying a command that does not invoke a login shell prevents the login process from completing.

Finally, to delete a user account, use the userdel command. Its syntax is the simplest of all the user account administration commands you have seen so far:

```
userdel [-r] username
```

username indicates the user account to delete. The -r option causes userdel to delete the user's home directory, mail spool (/var/mail/*username*). If -r is omitted, only the account information is deleted from /etc/passwd, /etc/shadow, and /etc/group. Even if -r is used, any files owned by *username* not in /home/*username* must be searched for and deleted manually. One of the following commands can be used to accomplish this:

```
find / -user username -exec rm -rf {} \;
find / -user username | xargs rm -rf
```

The first command finds all files owned by *username*, beginning from the root (/) file system, and executes the rm -rf command for each file found. The second command pipes the output of the find command to xargs, which builds a command line using rm -rf and the file names generated by the find command. The second command may prove faster if *username* owns many files because the rm command is executed after the file name list has been generated, instead of iteratively, which is how the -exec argument find works. For more information about find and xargs, see their texinfo documentation (info find and info xargs) or their manual pages (man find and man xargs).

Adding, modifying, and deleting groups

As the section "Understanding User Private Groups" earlier in the chapter suggested, Red Hat Linux makes greater use of group accounts than other Linux distributions. So knowing how to add, modify, and delete group accounts is more important on Red Hat Linux systems than it is with other Linux distributions. Table 21-5 lists the commands used to add, modify, and delete group accounts. They are discussed in greater detail in the following subsections.

TABLE 21-5 GROUP ACCOUNT ADMINISTRATIVE COMMANDS

Command	Description
gpasswd	Sets group passwords and modifies group accounts
groupadd	Creates a new group account
groupdel	Deletes an existing group account
groupmod	Modifies existing group accounts

As with the discussion of the password file in the previous section, you will find the following discussion of working with group accounts less confusing if you understand the format of the group file, /etc/group. It has one entry per line, and each line has the format:

groupname:*password*:*gid*:*userlist*

- ◆ *groupname* is the name of the group
- ◆ *password* is an optional field containing the encrypted group password
- ◆ *gid* is the numeric group ID number
- ◆ *userlist* is a comma-separated list of the user account names that comprise the group

If x appears in the password field, nonmembers of the group cannot join it using the newgrp command. A typical entry in the group file might resemble the following:

admins:x:507:joebob,marysue,bubba

groupname is admins; *password* is empty, meaning no group password has been set; *gid* is 503; and *userlist* is joebob,marysue,bubba.

CREATING GROUPS

To create a new group, use the groupadd command. Its syntax is:

```
groupadd [[-g gid [-o]] [-r] [-f] groupname
```

groupname is the only required argument and must be the name of a nonexistent group. When invoked with only the name of the new group, groupadd creates the group and assigns it the first unused GID that is both greater than 500 and not already in use. Specify -f to force groupadd to accept an existing *groupname*. Use the -g *gid* option if you want to specify the new group's GID, replacing *gid* with a unique GID (use the -o option to force groupadd to accept a nonunique GID). To create system group, one that has special privileges, use the -r option.

The following command creates a new group named admins:

```
# groupadd admins
```

Here is the resulting entry created in /etc/group:

```
admins:x:507:
```

As this point, admins has no members and the password field has an x in it, meaning that no nonmembers (which is everyone at this point) except root can join the group using newgrp.

MODIFYING AND DELETING GROUPS

After creating a new group, you will likely want to add user accounts to it. Two commands modify group accounts, each serving different purposes. groupmod enables you to change a group's GID or name, and gpasswd enables you to set and modify a group's authentication and membership information. You should rarely need to change a group's name or GID, so I leave it to you to read the short manual page for groupmod. Here, I concentrate on gpasswd, which enables the root user to administer all aspects of a group account and to delegate some administrative responsibilities to a group administrator. To simplify the following discussion, I first explain the uses of gpasswd, *only* available to root, and then cover the gpasswd calls a group administrator can perform. As a result, keep in mind that root can administer all aspects of a group account.

From root's perspective, gpasswd's syntax is:

```
gpasswd [-A username] [-M username] groupname
```

Root can use -A *username* to assign *username* as *groupname*'s group administrator. -M *username* adds *username* to *groupname*'s membership roster. Assigning a group administrator using -A does not make the administrator a member of the group — you have to use -M to add the administrator as a member of the group.

Multiple *username*'s can be specified with -A and -M. The following command shows how to add marysue and joebob to the admins group:

 In order to use the -A option, the shadow group file, /etc/gshadow must exist. Read the subsection titled "Using a Shadowed Group File" to understand the implications of using shadowed group files.

```
# gpasswd -M marysue,joebob admins
```

After this change, the admins entries in /etc/group should resemble the following:

```
admins:!:507:marysue,joebob
```

Notice that adding users to the admins group account replaced x with ! in the password field, meaning that password-based access to the group (using newgrp) is disabled.

For group administrators, gpasswd's syntax is:

```
gpasswd [-R] [-r] [-a username] [-d username] groupname
```

gpasswd called with only *groupname* changes the group password. Once a group password is set, group members can still use newgrp to join the group without a password, but nonmembers of the group must supply the password. For example, the following commands show what happens when the user bubba uses newgrp to join the admins group after root sets a group password, which, for the record, is secret:

 newgrp *groupname* changes the group identification of the calling user to *groupname*. After calling newgrp successfully, file access permissions are calculated based on the new GID. If *groupname* is omitted, the GID is changed to the calling user's primary (login) GID.

```
$ newgrp admins
Password:
$ groups
admins bubba
```

By contrast, here is what happens when joebob, who *is* a member of admins, uses newgrp to join the admins group. Notice that joebob is not prompted for a password as bubba was:

```
$ newgrp admins
$ groups
admins joebob
```

Conversely, if no group password is set, *only* group members can use newgrp to join the group. To remove a group password, use the -r option. The next snippet shows what happens when bubba tries to join admins after the group password is removed. Keep in mind that the password field in the group file will be empty after the password is removed using -r:

```
$ newgrp admins
newgrp: Permission denied.
```

This time, bubba was not even prompted for a password. joebob, however, has no problem:

```
$ newgrp admins
$ groups
admins joebob
```

Calling gpasswd with the -R option disables access to a group using the newgrp command. Oddly, if you use this option, gpasswd places a ! in the password field in the group file, so nonmembers of the group get a password prompt but no password works.

To add a user to the group, a group administrator must use the -a *username* option. The -d *username* option removes a user from a group. The next example shows how to add and remove bubba using gpasswd's -a and -d options:

```
# gpasswd -a bubba admins
Adding user bubba to group admins
# grep admins /etc/group
admins:!:507:marysue,joebob,bubba
# gpasswd -d bubba admins
Removing user bubba from group admins
# grep admins /etc/group
admins:!:507:marysue,joebob
```

USING A SHADOWED GROUP FILE
Much of the behavior described in the previous subsection does not apply if the shadow group file, /etc/gshadow, is present. In particular, if the shadow group file is in use:

◆ Adding a group creates an entry for that group in the shadow group file that resembles the following:

```
admins:x:507:
admins:!::
```

◆ Adding a user to a group adds that user to both the standard group file and the shadow group file:

```
# gpasswd -M marysue admins
# grep admins /etc/group /etc/gshadow
group:admins:x:507:marysue
gshadow:admins:!::marysue
```

◆ The third field in the shadow group file holds the name of the group administrator, not the GID, if an administrator is added using gpasswd's -A username option:

```
# gpasswd -A marysue admins
# grep admins /etc/gshadow
admins:!:marysue:marysue
```

◆ A group administrator cannot join the group unless the administrator's account is also a member of the group. Similarly, a group administrator can add and delete her user account from the group without affecting her administrative function.

◆ Only group members can use newgrp to join the group. To put it another way, nonmembers of a group cannot use newgrp to join groups of which they are not members, even if they know the group password. In fact, passwords are irrelevant because they do not work for nonmembers and members do not need to use them.

Deleting a group is quite simple. Use the groupdel command, which takes no options except the name of the group to delete. For example, the following command deletes the admins group:

```
# groupdel admins
```

Those of you who find typing commands tedious, the next section shows you how to use User Manager, Red Hat's new GUI tool for administering user and group accounts.

Using the Red Hat User Manager

The Red Hat User Manager is a graphical tool for managing user and group accounts that replaces Linuxconf user and group management modules. To use it, you need to be logged in as root or know the root password. To start User Manager, click Main Menu → Programs → System → User Manager on the GNOME desktop, K → Red Hat →

System → User Manager on the KDE desktop, or execute the command redhat-config-users in a terminal window. The initial screen resembles Figure 21-1.

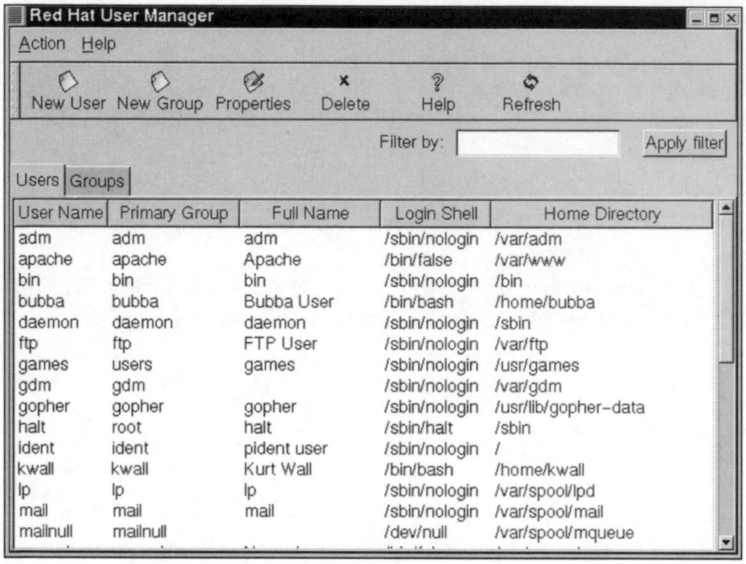

Figure 21-1: The main Red Hat User Manager dialog box

From this screen you can view, modify, and delete existing user and group accounts or create new ones. To reduce the list of displayed accounts or to search for a specific account, type the first few letters of an account name in the Filter by text box and click the Apply filter button. You can update most windows by clicking the Refresh button on the toolbar. To get context sensitive help, click the toolbar's Help button or, to view the entire User Manager manual, select Help → Manual from the toolbar.

CREATING USER ACCOUNTS

To add a new user

1. Click the New User button. The Create New User dialog box, as shown in Figure 21-2, appears.

Figure 21-2: Adding a new user

2. Type the new account name in the User Name text box.

3. Type the user's full name in the Full Name text box.

4. Type the user's password in the Password and Confirm Password fields. The password must be at least six characters.

5. Select a login shell. If you choose not to accept the default shell, select an alternative shell from the Login Shell drop-down box.

6. As noted earlier in this chapter, the default home directory is /home/*username*. You can change the home directory by editing the Home Directory text box or not create a home directory at all by unchecking the Create home directory check box.

7. To prevent creation of a user private group, remove the check from the Create new group for this user check box. A completed Create New User dialog box might resemble Figure 21-3.

Figure 21-3: A newly configured user account

8. Click OK to create the user.

MODIFYING AND DELETING USER ACCOUNTS

After you have created a user account, you can configure additional properties by clicking User Manager's User tab, selecting the user, and clicking the Properties button to open the User Properties dialog box. To add the user to additional groups, click the Groups tab (see Figure 21-4). Click the check box next to the groups of which the user should be a member, then click the Apply button.

Figure 21-4: Adding a user to additional groups

Other account data you can modify from the User Properties window includes the basic user information you supplied when you created the user (the User Data tab), account information (the Account Info tab), and password expiration information (the Password Info tab). On the Password Info tab, click the Enable account expiration check box to set the user account's expiration date if you want the account to expire on a certain date. To prevent this user account from logging in, place a check mark in the User account is locked check box.

Click the Password Info tab to view and change the account password expiration information (see Figure 21-5). The date that the user last changed her password appears across the top of the tab. Click Enable password expiration to force a password change after a certain number of days, and then enter the number of days between required password changes in the Days before change required text box. You can also set the number of days before the user can change her password, the number of days before the user is warned to change her password, and the number of days before the account becomes inactive. When you have finished modifying the user account properties, click OK to apply the changes and close the User Properties dialog box.

Figure 21-5: Modifying user account
password expiration information

Finally, to delete a user account click the account to delete on User Manager's Users tab and then click the Delete button.

CREATING GROUP ACCOUNTS

To add a new user group, click the New Group button. In the Create New Group dialog box (see Figure 21-6), type the name of the new group, and then click OK to create the group.

Figure 21-6: Adding a new group

MODIFYING AND DELETING GROUP ACCOUNTS

To view or modify the properties of an existing group, select the group to modify from the group list on the Groups tab and click the Properties button. The Group Properties dialog box, as shown in Figure 21-7, appears.

Figure 21–7: Modifying group properties

The Group Users tab (see Figure 21-8) displays the users that are members of the group. To add other users to the group, place a check mark next to the user account names in the list, and deselect account names to remove them from the group. Click OK to apply the changes and close the Group Properties box.

Figure 21–8: Modifying group properties

After you have finished adding or modifying user and group accounts, click Action → Exit to close the Red Hat User Manager.

Using File System Quotas

The aphorism "Disk space is cheap" has never been more true than it is today, when 20GB disk drives are standard equipment on new PCs and a 40GB disk drive can be purchased for $150. Unfortunately, just as the heralded paperless office has been answered by skyrocketing paper consumption, the proliferation of massive disk drives has been answered by ever-increasing pressures on disk space. For system administrators, one of the perennial challenges is managing disk space and making sure that no single user takes more than her fair share. The final section of this chapter shows you how to use the quota utilities to set, monitor, and enforce file system usage quotas for individual users and for groups of users. After you have performed the initial setup, managing file system usage with the quota suite is a largely automated task that leaves you free to concentrate on more pressing matters.

The programs you use to set and enforce disk usage quotas include the following:

- ◆ edquota — Sets, edits, and removes user and group file system quotas
- ◆ quota — Displays defined quotas and current file system usage
- ◆ quotacheck — Creates, checks, and repairs file system quota files
- ◆ quotaoff — Disables file system quotas
- ◆ quotaon — Enables file system quotas
- ◆ repquota — Summarizes and reports on quota utilization
- ◆ warnquota — Checks file system usage and sends email to users exceeding their assigned quotas

Note that quotas are set on a per file system basis, rather than per disk. You also must use disk blocks or disk inodes to set quotas, not the more familiar and more easily understood units of megabytes. Despite these inconveniences, however, the procedure for initializing quotas on file system is straightforward. Briefly, the steps to follow are:

1. Edit /etc/fstab to enable quotas on the desired file systems.
2. Create the quota accounting files on the root directory of each file system for which quotas are enforced.
3. Turn on quotas.
4. Set the desired file system quotas.
5. Review quota utilization regularly and frequently.

In the following subsections, you look at each of these steps and the commands to accomplish them.

Preparing the system for quotas

To prepare the system for quotas, the first step is to drop the system to single user mode. To do so, press Ctrl+Alt+F1 to flip over to the first virtual console and then log in as root. After you have logged in, execute the following command to bring the system down to single user mode:

```
# /sbin/telinit 1
```

The reason you should put the system into single user mode is to prevent logged in users from altering files and possibly losing data while you are setting up the quotas. Next, edit /etc/fstab and add the mount option usrquota to enable quotas for users, the mount option grpquota to enable quotas for groups, or both if you want to enable quotas for both users and groups. For example, the following line from /etc/fstab enables user quotas on the /home file system:

```
LABEL=/home    /home    ext3    defaults,usrquota    1 2
```

Note that mount ignores the usrquota keyword but that programs in the quota suite expect to see it in /etc/fstab.

Finally, execute the mount command using the remount option to update the kernel's mount table (/etc/mtab) with the quota option. For example, to activate quotas on the /home file system shown in the example, execute the following command:

```
# mount /home -o remount,rw
```

Creating the quota files

Now that the system is prepared, the next phase of the procedure for setting up quotas is to create the accounting files quota uses to monitor file system usage. There are two such files for each file system on which quotas are used, aquota.user if user quotas are enforced and aquota.group if group quotas are enforced. The quota accounting files are stored in the root directory of each file system. To create these accounting files, execute the quotacheck command, as shown in the following example:

```
# quotacheck -uv /home
quotacheck: Scanning /dev/hdc1 [/home] done
quotacheck: Checked 1158 directories and 24352 files
```

quotacheck scans the specified file system to determine its current usage and then writes this information into the quota accounting files. In the example shown, I have enabled only user quotas, so only the user quota file, /home/aquota.user, is created. quotacheck's -u option causes quotacheck to create (or check) only user quotas, and the -v option specifies verbose operation. /home, as you might guess, tells `quotacheck` which file system to scan. `quotacheck`'s most commonly used syntax is:

```
quotacheck [-bcgRuv] -a | filesys
```

filesys specifies the file system to check. If specified, `-a` instructs `quotacheck` to scan all mount file systems listed in `/etc/mtab` that are not NFS mounts. If `-a` is *not* specified, then *filesys* must be specified. Table 21-6 explains the other options.

TABLE 21-6 QUOTACHECK Options

Option	Description
-b	Make backup copies of quota files before overwriting old ones
-c	Ignore existing quota files
-g	Only check file system group quotas
-R	Used with -a, tells quotacheck not to check the root file system
-u	Only check file system user quotas, the default behavior if neither -g nor -u are specified
-v	Operate in verbose mode

Enabling quotas

After creating the quota accounting files, use the `quotaon` command to turn on quotas. `quotaon`'s invocation is simple

```
quotaon [-guv] -a | filesys
```

`quotaon`'s options have the same meaning as the corresponding options for `quotacheck` listed in Table 21-6. So, to turn on quotas for the `/home` file system used in this section, execute the following command:

```
# quotaon /home
```

Pretty easy, eh?

Setting and modifying quotas

At this point, you are finally ready to configure file system quotas because all of the preliminary setup is now complete. To set quotas, use the quota editor, `edquota`, which has the following syntax:

```
edquota [-ug] -t
edquota [-ug] account
```

The -u and -g options have the meaning listed in Table 21-6. The -t option in the first form of the command enables you to edit the time limits during which file system usage is permitted to be over quota, that is, to exceed the defined limits. Red Hat configures the default time limit, called a grace period, to seven days. To change this default value, execute the following command:

```
# edquota -u -t
```

By default, edquota uses the vi editor, so the resulting screen should resemble the following listing.

```
Grace period before enforcing soft limits for users:
Time units may be: days, hours, minutes, or seconds
  Filesystem              Block grace period      Inode grace period
  /dev/hdc1                     7days                   7days
```

To change the time limit, change the text that reads 7days to another value. You can use time units of seconds, minutes, hours, days, weeks, and months. So, for example, to set a time limit of three weeks, change the line that reads

```
  /dev/hdc1                     7days                   7days
```

so that it reads

```
  /dev/hdc1                     3weeks                  3weeks
```

After making the changes, save your changes and exit edquota using the standard vi keystrokes (:wq).

The second form of the edquota command enables you to set the actual file system usage limits. account must be the name of a user or group for which you are setting quotas. The following listing shows the edquota session for editing the user bubba's quotas. It was invoked using the command edquota -u bubba (the display may wrap on your system).

```
Disk quotas for user bubba (uid 500):
  Filesystem          blocks     soft     hard     inodes     soft     hard
  /dev/hdc1           950051        0        0      25020        0        0
```

The first column shows the file system(s) for which bubba has quotas; the second column shows the number of blocks bubba has used, followed by the soft and hard limits for block usage. The fifth column shows the number of inodes, or file system entries, bubba is currently using, followed by the soft and hard limits for inode usage. A *hard limit* is the absolute value beyond which file system usage is forbidden to go — once bubba reaches the hard limit, he will not be permitted to create any more files until he deletes enough files on the specified file system to go below his quota. A *soft limit*, on the other hand, is less restrictive than a hard limit — users (or groups) are permitted to exceed their soft limits for the grace period mentioned previously. After the grace period expires, however, no more files can be created until the user (or group) takes steps to reduce file system utilization below the soft limit.

How big is a block? It varies from system to system depending on the size of the underlying disk. On this system, a block is 1024K. To set bubba's quota, set the soft and hard limits for block usage to a nonzero value. For example, the following entry shows bubba's soft limit set to 960,000 blocks and his hard limit set to 975,000 blocks:

```
/dev/hdc1          950051   960000  975000      25020        0       0
```

After setting the limit, save your changes and exit edquota using the standard vi keystrokes (:wq).

TIP I strongly recommend not using inode limits. Each file a user creates requires *at least* one inode, so it is much easier to limit overall disk space usage than it is to limit the number of files a user can create.

Reviewing quota utilization

Reviewing and monitoring quota utilization is an ongoing process, but also easy to accomplish if you automate the process using a couple of cron jobs. One cron job should run the warnquota utility on a daily basis. The other cron job should run the repquota program, again on a daily basis. warnquota is a script that sends users a short e-mail message resembling that shown in Listing 21-4 if they are over quota.

Listing 21-4: Quota Exceeded Warning Message From warnquota

```
From: root@localhost
Reply-To:
Subject: Disk Quota usage on system
To: bubba@localhost.localdomain
Cc: root@localhost.localdomain

Hi,

We noticed that you are in violation with the quota system
```

Continued

Listing 21-4 *(Continued)*

```
used on this system. We have found the following violations:

                      Block limits            File limits
Filesystem        used    soft    hard  grace   used soft hard  grace
/dev/hdc1     +  960051  960000  975000 6days  25920   0     0

We hope that you will cleanup before your grace period expires.

Basically, this means that the system thinks you are using more disk space
on the above partition(s) than you are allowed.  If you do not delete files
and get below your quota before the grace period expires, the system will
prevent you from creating new files.


For additional assistance, please contact us at 800-GET-HELP
or via phone at 800-WHO-AREU.
```

The contact phone numbers, the subject line, and the CC list in warnquota's message can be customized by editing /etc/warnquota.conf, an example of which is shown in Listing 21-5. As shipped, the sendmail invocation defined by the MAIL_CMD line is incorrect, reading MAIL_CMD = "/usr/sbin/sendmail/.sendmail -t". Change it to read MAIL_CMD = "/usr/sbin/sendmail -t" instead, or warnquota will fail with an error message and the warning message will not be sent.

Listing 21-5: A Customized /etc/warnquota.conf File

```
MAIL_CMD = "/usr/sbin/sendmail -t"
FROM     = "root@localhost"
SUBJECT  = Disk Quota usage on system
CC_TO    = "root@localhost"
SUPPORT  = "800-GET-HELP"
PHONE    = "800-WHO-AREU"
```

warnquota generates its report by calling the quota program to check user quotas. You can use quota to check file system quota usage manually. quota's syntax is:

```
quota [-gus] user
```

The -g and -u options have the meaning shown in Table 21-6. Specifying -s tells quota to use more understandable units for displaying disk usage and limits. For example, the following command shows bubba's quota statistics:

```
# quota -s bubba
Disk quotas for user bubba (uid 500):
```

```
Filesystem  blocks   quota   limit   grace   files   quota   limit   grace
 /dev/hdc1   928M*    928M    939M    6days   25020       0       0
```

To see a complete list of quota statistics for all users and groups for a file system, use the `repquota` program, which accepts the same options as `quota` but requires a file system argument rather than a user argument. You can use the `-a` option to see a report for all file systems on which quotas are being used. The following command shows a `repquota` report for /dev/hdc1, using the `-s` option to display the output in units of megabytes:

```
# repquota -s /dev/hdc1
*** Report for user quotas on device /dev/hdc1
Block grace time: 7days; Inode grace time: 7days
                      Block limits            File limits
User          used   soft   hard  grace   used  soft  hard  grace
-----------------------------------------------------------------
root    --    579M      0      0           489     0     0
bubba   +     928M   928M   939M  6days   25020     0     0

Statistics:
Total blocks: 7
Data blocks: 1
Entries: 2
Used average: 2.000000
```

Summary

This chapter briefly recapped the power of the root account on a Red Hat Linux system and showed you how to delegate some of that power to nonroot users using Sudo. You also learned to create and manage user and group accounts using a variety of command line utilities and the new Red Hat User Manager graphical administration tool. Finally, you read how to prevent users and groups from monopolizing disk space and how to monitor system disk space utilization using the quota suite of programs.

Chapter 22

Backing up and Restoring the File System

IN THIS CHAPTER

◆ What should be backed up?

◆ Choosing media for backups

◆ Understanding backup methods

◆ Using backup tools

IN THIS CHAPTER you learn how to make backups of your files and restore damaged file systems from backups. It is important to make backups of the file system in order to avoid the loss of important information in the case of catastrophic hardware or software failure. An efficient backup and restoration process can minimize downtime and avoid the need to recreate lost work. In this chapter you learn how to choose a backup medium and how to use backup tools. Red Hat Linux provides several packages for dealing with backup and restoration of the file system. The `tar` and `dump` commands provide low-level interfaces to system backups. In addition, sophisticated backup tools such as Amanda can do automatic backups of multiple machines.

What Should Be Backed Up?

Determining what to back up on a particular machine depends largely on what data the machine contains and how the machine is used. However, there are some general guidelines that can be useful in determining what to back up.

Generally, temporary and cached files need not be backed up. The contents of the `/tmp` directory, for instance, are usually deleted when the machine is rebooted. Therefore it is alright to not back up these files. Also, the cache directory used by Netscape and found in users' `.netscape` directory is automatically regenerated by Netscape if it is deleted. You may find it worthwhile to investigate whether any other packages installed on the machine generate significant amounts of ignorable temporary data.

Depending on the situation, it may or may not be advisable to back up the machine's system files. If the machine is a standard installation of Red Hat Linux without any customizations or extra packages installed, the system files can be restored by reinstalling Red Hat Linux. The tradeoff is that reinstalling and reconfiguring a system probably takes more time and attention than restoring the file system from backup. However, this tradeoff may be worthwhile because of the amount of backup media that can be saved. In the particular case that a single Red Hat Linux installation is copied verbatim onto many machines, it may be appropriate to back up the system files of just one of the machines. If the system files are identical across machines, a single backup should restore all of them. In any case it is probably wise to back up at least the /etc directory of each machine. Probably the machines have at least some differing configuration information, such as network and hostname settings.

One other thing needs to be backed up, and indeed needs to be backed up via a special method: database files. Doing a straight tar from database files won't save you from a database crash, because the database files will all be in different states, having been written to backup when open. Oracle, Informix, Sybase, and so forth all allow the administrator to put the database tablespaces in backup mode. In backup mode, the data to be written goes to a memory cache rather than the file and transaction logs are updated only when the cache is flushed. This procedure slows things down but makes certain that the database will survive a crash.

The other aspect of the file system, other than the system files that need to be backed up, is the user files. Generally, all user files are stored in subdirectories of the /home directory. You should find it easy, therefore, to back up all user files at once. Even when the entire file system — both system and user files — is being backed up, you should still back them up separately. System and user files can have different relative priority depending on the situation. The user files are important because they may be irreplaceable, whereas many of the system files generally can be replaced by reinstalling Red Hat Linux. On the other hand, restoration of the system files is necessary for the machine to function and provide services, whereas the machine can be totally functional without restoration of the user files. Such priority considerations must be made when designing a backup strategy.

Give special thought to resources that do not easily fall into the system and user categories. Information stored in SQL databases, for instance, is often technically owned by root or by a special system user, but also often contains irreplaceable content entered by users. This kind of data can often be the most important to back up. You may find it beneficial to investigate which of the installed packages use this kind of data. Other examples besides databases are Web servers and mailing list archivers.

Choosing Media for Backups

A variety of backup mediums are available on the market today. Which backup medium you use depends on a number of factors and the particular needs of the situation. You should consider how often files are backed up, how long the backups need to last, how redundant the backups need to be, and how much money can be allocated to purchasing backup media. Table 22-1 provides a comparison of backup media.

TABLE 22-1 COMPARISON OF BACKUP MEDIA

Medium	Capacity	Reliability	Cost	Speed
Magnetic tape	High	High	Cheap	Slow
Writable CDs	Medium	Medium	Cheap	Fast
Hard drive	High	High	Expensive	Fast
Floppy disks	Low	Low	Cheap	Slow
DVD	High	High	Medium	Slow
Zip disks	Medium	Low	Medium	Slow
Flash ROM	Medium	High	Expensive	Fast
Removable hard drive (firewire)	High	High	Expensive	Fast
Removable hard drive (USB)	High	High	Expensive	Medium

Understanding Backup Methods

In order to save time and money in creating backups and restoring corrupted file systems and in purchasing backup media, it is important to institute a methodology for creating scheduled backups. The number of different backup methodologies is unlimited. How you should perform backups depends on the particular needs of your institution and computing infrastructure. The scheduling and type of backups depends on the type of backup media being used, the importance of the data, and the amount of downtime you can tolerate.

The simplest backup methodology is creating a full backup. A full backup copies the entire file system to the backup medium. This methodology can be good for small systems in which there is not much data to back up or systems in which the data is very important, is changing rapidly, and where historical snapshots of the system at different points in time are useful.

Performing frequent full backups has several disadvantages. Full backups take a long time to perform if there is a lot of data to back up or if the backup medium is slow. In order to get a clear snapshot of the system you may need to suspend the execution of processes that modify the file system while the backup process takes place. If backups take a long time, the downtime might be prohibitive. Full backups have no disadvantages when it comes to restoring an entire file system from backup. However, there is a disadvantage when restoring a partial file system from backup. If a sequential media such as magnetic tape is used, it must be searched sequentially in order to find the files that need to be restored. This process can cause a partial restoration to take as long as a full file system restoration in the worst case. Full backups also take significantly more space to archive than incremental backups. This situation is not too much of a disadvantage if you reuse the same backup media – you can just overwrite the old backup with the new one. However, it is often advisable to keep multiple generations of backups. Sometimes problems with the file system, such as corrupted or erased files, are not detected or reported immediately. If the file system is backed up once a day on the same backup tapes and an accidentally erased file is not found for two days, it cannot be recovered. On the other hand, if the file system is backed up once a week, any files lost between backups cannot be recovered. Keeping multiple full backups also has a disadvantage. If a full backup is made every day, the amount of archive media necessary to store it quickly becomes prohibitive.

The alternative to doing full backups is to do incremental backups. An incremental backup archives only the files that have changed or been added since the last backup. Incremental backups solve all of the disadvantages of full backups. Incremental backups are fast. In fact, the more often you do them, the faster they are because there is less to back up. Since the backups are smaller, searching from a given backup for a particular file is faster, thus making partial restorations faster if you need to restore from a particular known incremental backup archive. Because less is backed up each time, less media is used, so either less backup media needs to be bought or a longer history can be kept in the same amount of backup media. In the latter case, backups are more robust against lost or damaged files that are not discovered for a while.

Using incremental backups has disadvantages as well. While incremental backups are faster for retrieving individual files, they are slower for restoring entire file systems. To explain this problem, imagine that you have a week-long backup cycle. On the first day of the week you make a full backup. The rest of the week, you make an incremental backup. If a file system is erased accidentally on the last day of the week (right before a new full backup is to be made), you have to start at the last full backup and then load in a whole week of tapes in order to entirely restore the file system. If you made a full backup every day, you would have to load only the full backup and then you would be done restoring the file system.

When to use full backups and when to use incremental backups depends on the particular data stored on the machines, the way the machines are used, and how much money can be allocated to buying backup media. After you have decided on a backup methodology, you must configure your tools to use this methodology. Full and incremental backups can be implemented in scripts on top of the primitive backup tools such as tar. More advanced tools such as dump and Amanda have built-in support for backup levels and scheduling of various kinds of backups. Amanda even has a complex configuration language that lets you specify all kinds of details about the various types of backups you might want to do, the length of your backup cycle, and what files should be excluded from backup (such as private or temporary files).

Another thing to consider is the criticality of the system. If the system must be up at all times and downtime is a critical situation, then full backups are necessary in order to minimize downtime. One strategy for backing up critical machines is to create a separate volume group on mirrored disks solely for backups and use it as an intermediate area to copy files to prior to writing them to tape. A compressed tar file can be created on disk and then be written to tape faster than a normal tar file. Also, since a backup exists on disk, the tape archive is only used as a last resort if the disk archive fails. This strategy is similar to the one that the Amanda automated backup utility uses to take into account faulty backup devices or media. Even if the tape drive fails, the backup on disk can be written to tape when the problem has been solved.

Using Backup Tools

Red Hat Linux provides numerous tools for doing file system backups. There are tools for interacting with backup media, such as `ftape` for manipulating tapes drives, `cdrecord` for writing to CD drivers, and `mirrordir` for making backups to hard drives. Command line tools such as tar and dump allow for low-level control of file system backups and also easy automation through scripting. Using only shell scripts and periodic scheduling through cron jobs, you can develop a robust automated backup solution for many situations. Graphical tools also exist to create a more user-friendly interface to performing manual backups. Advanced backup tools exist which can be configured to fully automate the process of backing up multiple machines.

Command line tools

Red Hat Linux provides a number of command line tools for performing backups and restoring from backups. The tools for interacting directly with backup media are ftape, cdrecord, and mirror. The standard tools for creating archives are tar and dump for tape archives and mkisofs for CD archives. Each command provides a different interface and a number of options.

USING FTAPE
The ftape package is a collection of command line tools for accessing and managing magnetic tape drives. These utilities are useful if you are using tape drives to store your backups.

The `mt` command is used to scan, rewind, and eject magnetic tapes if you have an IDE drive. If you have a SCSI tape drive, the `st` command performs the same functions.

TESTING

You must be root in order to access the tape drives. As root, you can test a new magnetic tape by inserting it into the tape drive and then using the following command:

```
mt -f /dev/rft0 rewind
```

This command should rewind the magnetic tape. You can also format the magnetic tape with the command

```
ftformat -f /dev/rft0
```

However, many tapes come preformatted, so it is usually unnecessary to format new tapes.

USING THE CDRECORD PACKAGE

In order to make backups on CDs under Red Hat Linux, you need the cdrecord package to be installed. It contains several commands such as cdrecord, devdump, isodump, isoinfo, isovfy, and readcd. These commands are useful utilities for creating and managing writable CDs.

The cdrecord package requires that you have a SCSI CD drive. If you have an IDE CD drive, you must configure it to use SCSI emulation in order to use the cdrecord package.

The disadvantage to making backups on CD is that you must first create a CD image on the file system and then copy the CD image to the actual CD all in one step. This process requires that you have empty space on a single file system partition which is large enough to hold a CD image (up to 650MB). You create a CD image with the mkisofs command:

```
mkisofs -o /tmp/cd.image /home/blanu
```

This command makes a CD image file in the /tmp directory called cd.image. The CD image file contains all the files in the /home/blanu directory. You must have enough space to make the image file on the partition holding the /tmp directory. You can determine how much is free with the df command. You can determine how much space the image file is going to take up using the command du /home/blanu. By default, mkisofs preserves the ownership and permissions from the file system in the CD image.

In order to burn the image file to an actual CD, you must determine which SCSI device has the CD drive. If you don't actually have any SCSI drives and are using SCSI emulation with an IDE drive, the drive is probably on device scsi0. You can see what drives are on what SCSI devices with the following command:

```
dmesg | grep ^scsi
```

Next, you must determine which SCSI device ID the drive is using. You can find this with the following command:

```
cdrecord -scanbus
```

Next, you must determine the Logical Unit Number. If the device ID is zero, the Logical Unit Number should always be zero. You supply the SCSI device number, the device ID, and the logical unit number to the cdrecord command, in that order, as part of the dev option. A sample cdrecord command is as follows:

```
cdrecord -v dev=0,0,0 -data /tmp/cd.image
```

This command does not generally produce a bootable CD. In order for a CD to be bootable, the image file being recorded onto the CD needs to follow a specific format. Also, your BIOS must support booting from your particular CD-ROM. In order to produce a bootable image file, you need to follow several steps. First, you need to obtain a boot image. If you have a boot disk in the disk drive, the boot image can be written to a file with the following command:

```
dd if=/dev/fd0 of=boot.img bs=10k count=144
```

This command puts the boot image in the file boot.img. You must put this somewhere in the directory which you are going to put on the CD. In the example provided, you could create a directory /home/blanu/boot and place the file there. You also need to give mkisofs some extra parameters in order to have it create a bootable image.

```
mkisofs -r -b /home/blanu/boot/boot.img -c
/home/blanu/boot/boot.catalog -o /tmp/cd.image /home/blanu
```

The boot.catalog file does not need to already exist. It is generated by mkisofs. The command line option just tells mkisofs where in the image to store the generated file.

USING MIRRORDIR

The mirrordir command (in the mirrordir package) is a tool that enables you to easily back up a file system to an additional hard drive. In order to use mirrordir you must first mount the additional hard drive.

```
mount /dev/hdb1 /mnt
```

Then you can back up a given directory to the mounted hard drive using the mirrordir command.

```
mirrordir /home /mnt
```

The command backs up the /home directory, which contains all of the users' personal files, to the backup hard drive. You must get the order of the arguments correct. If the arguments were reversed, the /home directory would be overwritten with the contents of the backup hard drive, erasing valuable data. When executed, the mirrordir command makes the contents of the hard drive mounted on /mnt exactly identical to the contents of /home. All of the files are copied, and any files not present in /home are deleted. Subdirectories and their files are also copied.

To recover lost files if the partition containing /home crashes, the arguments to the mirrordir command are simply reversed. The following command overwrites the contents of /home with the contents of /mnt.

```
mirrordir /mnt /home
```

Note that any files extant in /home that are not also in /mnt are erased. Therefore, mirrordir is not useful for recovering individual files, but only in the situation where the entire directory, partition, or drive has been corrupted or erased.

If /home happens to be alone on a separate partition from the rest of the file system, you don't even need to restore the directory using mirrordir. The partition mounted on /mnt (in the example, /dev/hdb1) is an exact copy of the /home directory and so, in this case, an exact copy of that partition. So you can simply modify the /etc/fstab file and change the partition mounted under /home to be the partition where it is mirrored.

USING DUMP

The dump package consists of several commands for doing backup and restoration of the file system. The dump command is used to do backups of either entire partitions or individual directories. The restore command is used to restore an entire partition, individual directories, or individual files.

SYNTAX OF THE DUMP COMMAND   The first argument to the dump command is a list of options. Following that are all of the arguments required by the various options in the same order as the options were specified. The last argument is the file system to back up. Table 22-2 lists the available dump options.

TABLE 22-2 DUMP OPTIONS

Option	Meaning	Type
B	The number of records per volume.	Number
b	The number of kilobytes per dump record.	Number
h	The dump level at which to use nodump flags.	Number

Option	Meaning	Type
f	Name of file or device to write to.	Filename
d	Tape density.	Number
n	Tell dump to send a message when done.	None
s	Length of dump tape.	Number in feet
u	Record the date of this dump in /etc/dumpdates.	None
T	Add only files older than the given time.	Time (ctime)
W	List the file systems that need to be backed up.	None
w	List individual files that need to be backed up.	None
0-9	Specify a dump level of 0 through 9.	None

SAMPLE DUMP COMMAND

```
dump 0uf /dev/rft0 /dev/hda3
```

This command specifies that the file system on /dev/hda3 should be backed up on the magnetic tape on device /dev/rft0. It specifies that the backup should use backup level 0 (full backup) and write the time of the backup to the /etc/dumpdates file.

USING RESTORE

The restore command is used to retrieve files from the backups created with dump. You can use restore to restore an entire file system or you can use it to interactively select which files you want to restore.

The syntax for the restore command is the same as for the dump command, although it has different options. Table 22-3 lists the options.

TABLE 22-3 RESTORE OPTIONS

Option	Meaning	Type
r	Restore the entire dump archive	None
C	Compare the files on the file system to those in the dump archive	None

Continued

TABLE 22-3 RESTORE OPTIONS *(Continued)*

Option	Meaning	Type
R	Start the restore from a particular tape in a multivolume sequence	None
x	Extract only specified files	List of files
t	List the contents of the dump archive	List of files
I	Restore files in interactive mode	None
b	Block size of the dump in kilobytes	Number
D	Name of the file system to be compared against	File system
f	Name of the dump archive to restore from	Filename
h	Recreate directories but do not restore their contents	None
m	Extract files by inode number instead of name	None
N	Print file names rather than extracting them	None
s	Specify the tape number to start on when using the R option	Number
T	Specify where to write temporary files	Directory
v	Verbose mode	None
y	Do not prompt when bad blocks are encountered	None

RESTORING THE FILE SYTEM   In order to restore a damaged or erased file system you must first recreate the directory or partition that has been lost. If, for instance, you want to recreate the /home directory, which existed by itself on the /dev/hdb1 partition, you could use the following commands:

```
mkfs /dev/hdb1
mount /dev/hdb1 /home
```

Note that this command erases all of the data on the /dev/hdb1 partition. This method of restoration is useful only for restoring all of the files previously archived with dump. If any files have been added, modified, or deleted since the last backup, those changes are lost. Restoring individual files is covered in the section "Using Restore Interactively." Also, if mkfs is accidentally run on a different partition than the one meant to be restored, all of the data on the partition on which it is mistakenly run are irrevocably erased.

Restore must be run inside the directory that is going to be restored. So, restore can restore the /home directory with the following commands:

```
cd /home
restore rf /dev/rft0
```

The r flag tells restore to restore the entire archive rather than just some files. The f flag tells restore that the archive is located on the device /dev/rft0.

USING RESTORE INTERACTIVELY The restore command, in addition to being used to restore an entire file system, can also be used in an interactive mode, which enables you to restore individual files. The interactive mode is invoked as follows:

```
restore if /dev/rft0
```

This command runs restore in interactive mode and specifies that it should restore from the archive on the device /dev/rft0. The interactive mode enables you to type commands to restore in order to control its behavior. It includes the commands shown in Table 22-4.

TABLE 22-4 RESTORE COMMANDS

Command	Meaning
Add	Add a file or directory to the list of files to be extracted. If a directory is specified, all contained files, subdirectories, and files contained in subdirectories are extracted. File paths are relative to the current directory being viewed in the dump archive.
Cd	Change which directory within the dump archive is being viewed.
Delete	Remove a file or directory from the list of files to be extracted. If a directory is specified, all files in that directory, subdirectories, and files in subdirectories are removed from the list as well. Note that this does not affect what is stored in the dump archive, but rather which files are extracted during the restore.
Extract	Extract all of the files and directories currently in the list of files to extract and restore them in the file system.
help	List available commands.

Continued

TABLE **22–4** RESTORE COMMANDS *(Continued)*

Command	Meaning
ls	List the contents of the directory currently being viewed in the dump archive. If a directory is specified, the contents of the specified directory are listed rather than the contents of the current directory. Files and directories marked with * in the file listing are currently marked for extraction.
pwd	Print the path within the dump archive of the directory currently being viewed.
quit	Exit the restore program. No other actions are taken by restore.
setmodes	Rather than extract the files, set the permissions on the files in the file system so that they match the permissions of the files in the dump archive that are marked for extraction.
verbose	Switch verbose mode on or off.

USING TAR

Red Hat Linux includes the GNU version of tar. It includes some extensions to the older standard versions of tar, including multivolume archiving. Multi-volume archiving is an automated process in which tar prompts for new media to be inserted whenever it runs out of space. The tar program is a utility originally designed for making magnetic tape backups, but is useful for any kind of archiving purpose. When making archives, it is important to specify a leading ./ for files. That creates a relative path, which will be necessary when restoring the files later.

The tar command requires one command option followed by any number of optional options. Table 22-5 lists the command options.

TABLE **22–5** TAR OPTIONS

Command	Explanation
A	Append the contents of the given tar files to the specified tar archive.
D	Create a new tar archive and add the given files to it.
	Overwrite an existing tar archive. To append files use r or A.

Command	Explanation
D	Find differences between what's in the tar archive and what's in the file system.
R	Append the given files to the specified tar archive.
T	List the contents of the specified tar archive.
U	Append the given files to the specified tar archive, but only if they are newer than the files in the tar archive.
X	Extract the given files from the specified tar archive.

In addition to specifying a command, you must specify a device or file to act as the destination of the tar archive.

Advanced tools

This section discusses a number of advanced backup tools including AMANDA, the amdump test, pax, and taper.

USING AMANDA

The AMANDA (Advanced Maryland Automatic Network Disk Archiver) package is a set of tools for doing backups of multiple machines over the network. Using Amanda, you can configure your Red Hat Linux machine to be a backup server for the other machines in the network, including Windows systems. Amanda is included with Red Hat Linux 7.2. To use Amanda you should install the following packages:

```
Amanda
Amanda-client
Amanda-server
Gnuplot
```

You need to install the Amanda-server and gnuplot packages only on the machine that is going to be the backup server. However, you must install Amanda-client on any machine that you want to back up using Amanda. You must install the base Amanda package on both the client and server machines. The Amanda package contains several commands, shown in Table 22-6.

TABLE 22-6 AMANDA COMMANDS

Command	Use
Amdump	Normally executed periodically by a cron job, this utility is run on the Amanda server. It requests backups from the various Amanda clients.
Amflush	If amdump has trouble writing backups to tape, they are kept in temporary storage space on disk until the problem is corrected. After the problem is fixed, this command is run to write the data in the temporary storage space to the tapes.
Amcleanup	If the Amanda server crashes during the running of amdump, this utility should be run to cleanup after the interrupted amdump.
Amrecover	This utility provides a way to select which tapes should be used to recover files.
Amrestore	This utility is used to restore individual files or directories or entire partitions from Amanda backups.
Amlabel	This utility is used to write an Amanda label onto a tape. You must use this command to label tapes before they can be written to with amdump.
Amcheck	This utility should be run before amdump to verify that the correct tape is in the drive.
Amadmin	This utility does various administrative tasks.
Amtape	This utility is used for low-level tape control, such as loading and ejecting disks.
Amverify	This utility checks Amanda tapes for errors.
Amrmtape	This utility deletes a tape with a particular label from the Amanda tape database.
Amstatus	This utility reports on the current status of a running amdump program.

INSTALLING AMANDA   After installing the necessary RPMs, some additional installation is required to get Amanda running. You must create subdirectories in the /etc/Amanda and /usr/admn/Amanda directories for each backup schedule that you are going to run. For instance, if you plan to run a backup schedule called test, you must execute the following commands:

```
Mkdir -p /etc/Amanda/test
Mkdir -p /usr/admn/Amanda/normal
```

You also need to create some temporary space for Amanda to keep files, which it is in the process of backing up. So if, for instance, you want to create this space as a directory on your root partition, you can use the following command to make an `Amanda` directory:

`Mkdir /Amanda`

CONFIGURING AMANDA   To configure Amanda you must create an `Amanda.conf` file and put it in the subdirectory in `/etc/Amanda` that you created. So in the example, for instance, it would be called `/etc/Amanda/Amanda.conf`. The `Amanda.conf` file has many options, shown in Table 22-7, but has defaults for most of them.

TABLE 22-7 AMANDA.CONF OPTIONS

Option	Example	Meaning
org "name"	org "Tristero"	This option specifies the name used in reports generated by Amanda.
mailto "accounts"	mailto "root example"	This option specifies account names that Amanda should put in charge of the backup process.
dumpuser "account"	dumpuser "Amanda"	This option specifies the user account that the Amanda dump process should run as.
inparallel number	inparallel 5	This entry specifies the number of amdump processes that can run simultaneously.
netusage num unit	netusage 1000 Kpbs	This entry indicates the bandwidth that Amanda is allowed to consume while doing backups. It should be set such that even if all of the allocated bandwidth is consumed there is still enough bandwidth for other tasks that might operate at the same time as the Amanda backup process.

Continued

TABLE 22-7 AMANDA.CONF OPTIONS *(Continued)*

Option	Example	Meaning
dumpcycle num unit	dumpcycle 1 week	This option specifies the length of the backup cycle.
runspercycle num	runspercycle 7	This option specifies the number of backups that should be done during a single dump cycle. So with a dump cycle of 1 week and 7 runs per cycle, Amanda makes one full backup and 6 incremental backups every week.
tapespercycle num unit	tapespercycle 7 tapes	This option specifies how many tapes are available for use in a single backup cycle.
runtapes num	runtapes 1	This option specifies how many tapes are available for use in each backup.
tapedev "device"	tapedev "/dev/rft0"	This option specifies the device name of the tape device.

The `Amanda.conf` file also has some complex options, which consist of blocks with multiple subfields. The holdingdisk block defines a temporary storage space for holding data that is being backed up. You can define multiple holdingdisk blocks in a single file. The definition has the following format:

```
Holdingdisk name
{
      directory "name"
      use num unit
}
```

Example holdingdisk block:

```
Holdingdisk example
{
      directory "/example"
      use 4 Gb
}
```

The tapetype block defines a particular kind of magnetic tape that might be used in backups. It defines properties about the tape such as length and speed. The tapetype definition has the following format:

```
Define tapetype name
{
comment "freeform string"
length num unit
filemark num unit
speed num unit
}
```

Example tapetype definition:

```
Define tapetype EXAMPLE
{
comment "These are fictional numbers."
Length 5000 mbytes
Filemark 100 kbytes
Speed 500 kbytes
}
```

The interface block defines a particular network interface that can be used for communication between an Amanda server and client. The interface definition specifies how much bandwidth can be used on that particular network interface. The syntax of the definition is as follows:

```
Define interface name
{
comment "Freeform string"
use num unit
}
```

Example interface definition:

```
Define interface eth0
{
comment "This sets the bandwidth usage of the Ethernet network
interface"
use 500 kmps
}
```

The dumptype block defines a particular kind of dump. The entries in the disklist file refer to these definitions. A corresponding dumptype block must exist in the Amanda.conf file for it to be referenced in the disklist file. The dumptype block specifies certain properties of the kind of dump, such as which program to use for dumping, whether or not to compress backups, and files that should not be backed up.

The dumptype block has many options, shown in Table 22-8, which define how the dump works.

TABLE 22-8 DUMPTYPE OPTIONS

Option	Explanation
Auth	This option specifies which authorization method should be used between the client and the server. This option can be set to either "bsd" or "krb4" and defaults to "bsd".
Comment	This options is a freeform string and is ignored.
Comprate	This option specifies the compression rates for backed up files in terms of how the size of the compressed file should compare to the size of the uncompressed file. This option can either be a single value or two values separated by a comma. The first value specifies the compression rate for full backups. The second value specifies the compression rate for incremental backups and is assumed to be the same as the first value if omitted.
Compress	This option specifies the method to be used for compressing the data. The options are presented in the separate Table 22-9. The default compression type is "client fast."
Dumpcycle	This option specifies the number of days in the backup cycle. A full backup is preformed at the beginning of each backup cycle.
Exclude	This option specifies which files should not be included in the backup. This option works only when the backup program being used is tar. When used with dump or samba it is ignored. The possible values for exclude are either a quote wildcard pattern or else the list keyword followed by a quoted filename. If the list keyword is used, the filename should refer to a file on the client machine, which contains a list of wildcard patterns to match. Wildcard patterns are listed one per line. Any files matched by either the quoted patterns or any of the patterns in the specified file are excluded from the Amanda backups.
Holdingdisk	This option specifies whether or not the holding disk should be used for temporarily storing files that are going to be dumped. The default is "yes".

Option	Explanation
Ignore	This option specifies that this dump type should not actually be backed up even if the disklist file specifies that it should.
Index	This option specifies whether or not to keep an index of files that have been backup up. The default is "no".
Kencrypt	This option specifies whether or not the connection between the client and the server should be encrypted. The default is "no".
Maxdumps	This option specifies how many simultaneous instances of the amdump process can be run. The default is 1.
Priority	This option specifies the priority of the dump. When Amanda runs out of tape or is otherwise unable to write backups for some reason, all the data, which can be kept on the holding disk is put there in order of highest priority dump type to lowest priority. The possible values for the priority of a dump are "high," "medium," and "low." The default is "medium."
Program	This option specifies which program should be used for making the backup dump. The possible values are "DUMP" and "GNUTAR". The default is "DUMP." You must change this to "GNUTAR" if you wish to use the "exclude" option.
Record	This option specifies whether or not the date of the dump should be written to the /etc/dumpdates file. The default is "yes."
Skip-full	This option specifies that when Amanda is scheduled to do a full backup it should refrain from doing so. This option is useful if you want to use Amanda for incremental backups or to use some other method for full backups.
Skip-incr	This option specifies that when Amanda is scheduled to do an incremental backup it should refrain from doing so. This option is useful if you want to use Amanda for full backups but to use some other method for incremental backups or if you do not want to do incremental backups at all.
Starttime	This option specifies that the starting time of the dump should be delayed.
Strategy	This option specifies the dumping strategy that should be used for this kind of dump. The various available dump strategies are listed in Table 22-10. The default strategy is "Standard."

TABLE 22-9 AMANDA COMPRESSION TYPES

Type	Explanation
None	This option specifies that no compression should be used on Amanda backups.
Client best	This option specifies that the client should use the compression algorithm that results in the highest compression levels.
Client fast	This option specifies that the client should use the fastest compression algorithm.
Server best	This option specifies that the server should use the compression algorithm that results in the highest compression levels.
Server fast	This option specifies that the server should use the fastest compression algorithm.

TABLE 22-10 AMANDA DUMPING STRATEGIES

Strategy	Explanation
Standard	This option specifies that Amanda should use the standard dumping strategy, which includes both full and incremental backups.
Nofull	This option specifies that Amanda should use level 1 incremental backups always and never do full backups. This is useful when a set of machines all have the same base installation and setup with only minor differences that do not change rapidly. Amanda then saves space by backing up only the changes that occur over time.
Noinc	This option specifies that incremental backups should never occur and that Amanda should always do full backups. This is useful if it is important to make the restoration of a machine as swift and easy as possible. However, it makes backups much slower and requires much more storage space for the backups.
Skip	This option specifies that the dump type should never be backed up either with full backups or incremental backups. The dump type is ignored even if it occurs in the disklist file.

You need to adapt the Amanda.conf file to your system. Most notably you need to correctly specify the paths to the tape drive devices, the type of tape drives, and the path to the directory that Amanda can use as temporary space.

You must also create a disklist file that specifies which partitions to back up. In the example setup this file would be stored as /etc/Amanda/test/disklist.

The format of the disklist file is a series of entries, one per line, in the following format:

```
Hostname device dumptype
```

The disklist file has the arguments shown in Table 22-11.

TABLE 22-11 DISKLIST ARGUMENTS

Argument	Explanation
Hostname	This argument specifies the hostname of the Amanda client to be backed up. For the Amanda client to enable a connection from the Amanda server, the hostname of the Amanda server must be in that client's .amandahosts file.
Device	This argument specifies the name of the directory to be backed up.
Dumptype	This argument specifies the name of the dumptype definition in the Amanda.conf file which defines the properties associated with this type of dump.

The following is an example disklist file:

```
Blanu.net /home/blanu/public_html normal
Tristero.sourceforge.net /cvsroot/tristero incremental
Baldwinpage.com /var/www/htdocs/bruno/ normal
```

AMANDA CLIENT CONFIGURATION   In order to enable the Amanda backup servers to connect to the clients to request backups, you must create on each client an .amandahosts file in the /root directory of the machine. The file consists simply of the names of the server machines that are allowed to connect to the client in order to request backups.

Here is an example .amandahosts file:

```
Blanu.net
Thalassocracy.org
Tristero.sourceforge.net
Baldwinpage.com
```

You are wise to set the permissions of this file to 600 using `chmod`. That ensures that only root can modify the file and other users cannot add hosts to the file, thus bypassing the permission system and gaining access to the full file system.

PERFORMING BACKUPS WITH AMANDA   In order to perform a backup, you simply run `amdump` with the name of the backup that you want to run. The configuration information and list of partitions to back up are read from the configuration files in the particular subdirectory in `/etc/Amanda` that you created for this particular backup type.

AMDUMP TEST

The `amdump` commands then go through the list of the partitions specified in `amdump` and back up each of them, in order, to the tape drives specified in the associated `Amanda.conf` file. The partitions in the disklist file should be specified in order of importance so that in case of problems the most important files are more likely to have already been backed up. The results of the `amdump` operation, including any errors, are written to the `/usr/adm/Amanda/test` directory.

USING PAX

The pax tool is useful for converting between different archive formats. This capability is especially important in an environment where there may be different operating systems and distributions running in conjunction. Incompatibilities between the various tools and various versions of tools can be quite a hassle. Pax solves this problem by knowing how to read many versions of several different archiving formats. Table 22-12 lists the options you can use with pax.

TABLE 22-12 PAX OPTIONS

Option	Meaning
`-r`	Read files from archive.
`-w`	Write files to archive.
`-a`	Append files to an existing archive.
`-b blocksize`	Specify the size of a block of data in the archive. Block sizes must be a multiple of 512.
`-c`	Match all files except those with the specified pattern.
`-d`	Match wildcards against the file names only, rather than the complete path.
`-f`	Specifies the name of the archive file.

Option	Meaning
-I	Prompt to rename files when archiving.
-k	Do not overwrite existing files.
-l	Link files with hard links when in copying mode.
-n	Match only the first file that matches the supplied pattern.
-o options	Specifies a list of additional options that are specific to the archiving format.
-p string	Specifies file characteristics that should be retained on the archived versions of the files.
-s string	Specifies that the names of the files should be modified using the regular expression given in the argument string before the files are archived.
-t	Specifies that the access time information associated with the files that are being archived should be retained in the archived copies of the files.
-u	Specifies that pax should not overwrite files in the archive even if the files in the archive are older than the files specified to be archived.
-v	Specifies that pax should produce verbose output.
-x format	Specifies which format the archive should be in. The possible values for the format are cpio, bcpio, sv4cpio, sv4rc, tar, and ustar. The default format is ustar. When reading an archive instead of writing one, pax automatically determines the type of the archive, so this option is needed only when writing an archive.
-B number	Specifies the number of bytes in each volume of the archive. It is useful for creating multivolume archives on volumes with a known size such as CD-ROMs or floppy disks.
-D	Specifies that pax should not overwrite files in the tar archive with files supplied to be archived if the supplied files are older than the files already in the archive.
-E number	Specifies the number of times that pax should attempt to retry reading or writing an archive in the case of an error.

Continued

TABLE 22-12 PAX OPTIONS *(Continued)*

Option	Meaning
-G group	Specifies that only files in the given group should be written or read. The given group string is assumed to be a group name unless it starts with the "#" character, in which case it is assumed to be a group ID number.
-H	Specifies that only command-line symbolic links should be followed.
-L	Specifies that all symbolic links should be followed.
-P	Specifies that no symbolic links should be followed.
-T time	Specifies that only files with the given modification time should be read or written.
-U user	Specifies that only files owned by the given user should be written or read. The given user string is assumed to be a user name unless it starts with a "#" character, in which case it is assumed to be a user ID number.
-X	Specifies that directories should not be entered if the directory is on a different partition or device than the parent directory.

USING TAPER

The taper program is a graphical interface for backing up and restoring file systems under Red Hat Linux. The taper command is executed with the following syntax:

```
taper -T tapetype options device
```

The device is the name of the directory that you want to back up or restore. The tapetype should be from Table 22-13.

TABLE 22-13 TAPER TAPE TYPES

Tape Type Identifier	Description	Common Associated Device
z	Floppy tape driver	/dev/zftape
i	IDE tape driver	/dev/ht0
l	File	N/A

Tape Type Identifier	Description	Common Associated Device
f	Floppy tape driver	/dev/ftape
r	Floppy drive	/dev/fd0
s	SCSI tape drive	/dev/st0

The taper command has a number of options that can be specified at the command line, as shown in Table 22-14.

TABLE 22-14 TAPER OPTIONS

Name	Explanation
-T type	This option specifies the type of tape being used. The possible files for this option are enumerated and explained in the preceding table.
-f file	This option specifies that the given file should be used as the backup device and that the device can be considered to be a rewinding device.
-n file	This option specifies that the given file should be used as the backup device and that the device can be considered to be a nonrewinding device.
-b file	This option specifies that the given file should be used as the backup device and that the device can be considered both rewinding and nonrewinding.
+/-a	This option specifies that appending should be turned either on or off.
-A id	This option specifies that taper should print the differences between the given archive and the files currently on disk.
-c num	This option specifies that the given compression type should be used to compress files. The possible values are 0 to specify no compression, or 1, 2, or 3 to specify the level of compression.
+/-C	This option specifies that the prompt issued when a bad checksum is encountered should be turned on or off.
-d id	This option specifies that taper should print the directory of the archive with the given ID.
+/-D	This option specifies that taper either should or should not recursively descend into subdirectories.

Continued

TABLE 22-14 TAPER OPTIONS *(Continued)*

Name	Explanation
-F file	This option specifies files that should not be archived.
+/-h	This option specifies that soft links on the file system should be stored as either links or copies of the file in the archive.
-H num	This option specifies that taper should give the compressor the given number of minutes as a head start.
-i path	This option specifies the path to the archive information files.
+/-l	This option specifies that info files either should or should not be compressed.
-j num	This option specifies the device number of the proc file system.
-l file	This option specifies the name of the log file.
-m num	This option specifies the logging level. Possible values for this option are 0 for no logging through 4 for verbose logging.
-o num	This option specifies the level of file overwriting that should occur during restoration of a file system.
+/-O	This option specifies that taper either should or should not overwrite the tape if it already contains data.
-p file	This option specifies the name of the preference file that taper should use read preferences data from.
-q num	This option specifies which volume should be used for restoring the file system.
+/-Q	This option specifies that the tape drive either does or does not support fast `fsf`.
-r path	This option specifies the directory to which archived files should be restored.
-R list	This option specifies which directories should be excluded from backup or restoration.
-s num	This option specifies the level of pathname stripping that should occur.
+/-S	This option specifies that taper either should or should not set the block size before writing archives.
-t name	This option specifies the name of the archive.

Name	Explanation
+/-u	This option specifies that taper should use either incremental or full backups by default.
-v	This option specifies that taper should print its version information and then exit. If this option is specified, all other options are ignored.
-x num	This option specifies the size of the block that taper should use to write to the tape.
-X file	This option specifies which files should not be compressed.
+/-y	This option specifies that taper either should or should not sort directories.
+/-z	This option specifies that taper either should or should not prompt for confirmation when a directory is selected.
-Z num	This option specifies the size of the tape in megabytes.
-U file	This option specifies that taper should do an unattended backup of the given file.
+/-w	This option specifies that taper should restore either the most recent files or the selected files.
-?	This option specifies that taper should print usage information and then exit. If this option is specified, all other options are ignored.

As with all backup and restoration software, the `taper` command must be executed as root. It provides a curses-based interface that can be run from the console, from a remote login terminal via `ssh` or `telnet`, or under X in a shell such as `xterm` or `rxvt`.

Use the arrow keys to navigate the menus for the taper program. Use Enter to select a particular menu option or submenu. Press the *?* key to bring up the taper help screen.

In order to back up file systems using taper, select the Backup Module option from the taper main menu. You can then select files and directories on the file system that should be backed up to the device specified on the command line using the *I* key. Use the *F* key to finalize your backup file selections and begin writing the files to the backup medium. It is similarly easy to restore file systems by selecting the Restore Module option from the taper main menu. The taper program also has many options that can be set by selecting the "Change Preferences" option from the main taper menu. Make sure to also choose the Save Preferences menu option or your taper preferences exist for the current taper session only.

Summary

In this chapter you learned how to back up and restore your file system. You learned how to choose which files are important to back up and to choose a backup medium appropriate for the needs of your situation. You also learned how to use low-level archiving tools such as tar and dump to produce archives and file system data and to restore corrupted file system data from archives. In addition, you learned how to configure and use advanced archiving tools such as taper and Amanda.

Chapter 23

Installing and Upgrading Software Packages

IN THIS CHAPTER

◆ Using the Red Hat Package Manager

◆ Checking software versions

◆ Obtaining newer software

◆ Installing software

ONE OF LINUX'S most enjoyable qualities is the variety and number of software packages available for it. Even novice Linux users can download and install new or updated software with little or no difficulty using RPM, the Red Hat Package Manager. Blindly installing software, even on an RPM-based system, may cause problems, though, and in general the more you understand about software installation and maintenance, the more comfortable you will be with the process. This chapter provides detailed information and instructions for locating, downloading, building, and installing new and updated software. First, however, the chapter explains how to use RPM because it is the preferred tool for software management on Red Hat Linux systems.

Using the Red Hat Package Manager

RPM is a powerful software configuration manager and is the dominant tool for installing, removing, verifying, and updating software packages on Red Hat Linux systems. Red Hat Linux installs tools for using RPM at the command line and using a GUI. Although RPM is not the only software management option available, as you will see later in the chapter, it is the one most people use. This section describes how to use most RPM features. I cover some topics in greater detail in later sections of the chapter, though, so they are mentioned only briefly in this one. Most examples illustrate command line usage, but some show how to use Gnome-RPM, a GUI front end to RPM.

RPM consists of two components: a set of databases that store information about installed software and the programs that interface with the databases. It can work with binary and source packages. *Binary packages*, generally referred to simply as

RPMs, contain compiled software ready for installation. They use the file extension .rpm. *Source packages*, more often called source RPMs, are uncompiled packages used to create binary RPMs and have a .src.rpm file extension. Because RPM offers a rich feature set that makes it seem complex and difficult to learn to use, the following sections each explore one of RPM's modes, in order to simplify the discussion:

◆ General options

◆ Querying

◆ Package maintenance

◆ Package verification

◆ Package building

◆ Administrative options

◆ Miscellaneous options

The query functions can be used to obtain a considerable amount of information about installed software. Package maintenance enables package installation, removal, and upgrading. Package verification gives system administrators the ability to compare the present state of files installed by an rpm against information taken from the original package. The package building mode is used to build or rebuild rpms from source code. The administration and miscellaneous modes, finally, affect RPM itself, rather than software packages. They are used to fix possible database corruption and to determine RPM's general configuration.

General options

At the command line, the primary RPM command is rpm. In addition to the mode-specific command line options discussed in the following sections, rpm accepts the general command line options listed in Table 23-1.

TABLE 23-1 GENERAL RPM COMMAND LINE OPTIONS

Option	Description
-v	Displays basic information about the RPM operation's status.
-vv	Displays debugging information. Most useful to software packagers and RPM developers.
--quiet	Displays only error information.
--help	Shows a usage summary.

Option	Description
--version	Shows the RPM version number.
--justdb	Updates only the database, not the file system.

The -vv option may prove useful when troubleshooting package installation or removal that fails, but be prepared to sort through voluminous and frequently cryptic-looking output to find the information you need. --justdb causes RPM to perform a type of dry-run operation. The results of any operation, such as installing or removing an RPM, affect only RPM's databases; no files are added or removed from the file system. For example, the following command uses --justdb to delete the whois package from RPM's database without actually deleting the files:

```
# rpm --justdb -e whois
# rpm -q whois
package whois is not installed
# ls -l /usr/bin/whois
-rwxr-xr-x    1 root      root          7996 Feb 16 08:47 /usr/bin/whois
```

The second command uses the -q (query) option to see if the whois RPM is installed. As the output indicates, it is not in the database. But, the ls command shows that whois *is*, in fact, still installed. Only the RPM database changed, not the file system.

The rpm command supports more options than those listed in Table 23-1. To simplify the discussion, this chapter discusses only the most common and helpful options.

One common use of --justdb is to remove an RPM's entry from the database after the package has been upgraded using a non-RPM source, such as a tarball. In such cases, the RPM entry is invalid and needs to be removed without deleting the installed files.

Query mode

RPM's query mode is one of its most powerful, useful features. The general form of an RPM query is

```
rpm -q [queryoptions]
```

-q (or --query, if you prefer) specifies a query operation and *queryoptions* specifies what to query, the type of query, how it runs, or the format of its output. Most commonly, however, queries use the following general syntax:

```
rpm -q [queryoptions] package [...]
```

package names the RPM to query. Query multiple RPMs using a space-separated list of package names. Query mode's power comes at the cost of a long list of options for the *queryoptions* argument. The options fall into two broad categories. One group controls which package or packages to query, and the other defines what information to display. Table 23-2 lists many but not all of the options available in query mode. The Type column uses S to mark a package selection option and I to mark an information selection option. Unless mentioned otherwise, all options require at least one package name as an argument.

TABLE 23-2 RPM QUERY MODE OPTIONS

Option	Type	Description
-a	S	Query all installed RPMs. Does not require a package specification.
--whatrequires *capability*	S	Query all RPMs that need *capability* in order to function properly.
--whatprovides *capability*	S	Query all RPMs that provide *capability*.
-f *file*	S	Query the RPM that owns *file*. Does not require a package specification.
-g *group*	S	List the packages in the RPM group named *group*. Does not require a package specification.
-p *package [...]*	S	Query the *uninstalled* RPM named *package*.
-i	I	Display complete information about the queried RPM(s).
-R	I	List all RPMs on which the package depends.
--provides	I	List all of the capabilities the queried RPM(s) provides.
--changelog	I	Display change information about the queried RPM(s).

Option	Type	Description
-l	I	List all of the files stored in the RPM.
-s	I	For each file in the original RPM, display its state, which is one of `normal`, `not installed`, or `replaced`.
-d	I	List only the documentation files stored in the RPM.
-c	I	List only the configuration files stored in the queried RPM(s).
--dump	I	For each file stored in the queried RPM(s), display its path, size, modification time, MD5 checksum, permissions, owner, group, and whether it is a configuration file, documentation file, a device, or a symlink (must be used with -l, -c, or -d).
--last	I	Display the installation date and time of each RPM queried, starting with the most recently installed RPM.
--querytags	I	Print all known tags for use with the --qf option. Does not require a package specification.
--qf 'formatstring'	I	Create a customized output format for displayed information, using `formatstring` as the model.

As you can see in Table 23-2, RPM's query mode is extensive and flexible, allowing you to obtain any type of information the RPM databases store. Using the `--qf` option, in fact, you can create customized query output for use in reports and scripts. The next few sections demonstrate how to use many of these options. First, however, some of the option descriptions need additional elaboration. When using the `-f`, option, the `file` argument must be to a full path. That is, the command `rpm -qf /usr/bin/xmms` will show the name of the RPM that contains `xmms`; `rpm -qf xmms` will not. Finally, when specifying a package name with the `-p` option, you must use the complete RPM file name.

QUERYING PACKAGE DEPENDENCIES

The `--provides`, `-R`, `--whatrequires`, and `--whatprovides` options allow you to identify dependencies between packages. The `capability` argument represents the dependency itself, which is often the name of another RPM or the name of a particular file. RPM uses dependencies to maintain system integrity, so, for example, if one RPM requires something a second RPM provides, you cannot, in normal usage, delete the second RPM. To illustrate, to determine on what capabilities the RPM package depends, use the -R option as shown in the following command:

```
$ rpm -qR rpm
gawk
fileutils
textutils
mktemp
popt
glibc >= 2.1.92
db1 = 1.85
/bin/sh
...
```

The example output is truncated to preserve space. As the output shows, the RPM package requires, in part, the gawk capability and a glibc capability greater than or equal to version 2.1.92. In this case, the gawk capability is another RPM, and the glibc capability identifies the minimum acceptable version of glibc.

To identify what capabilities a package provides, use the --provides option:

```
$ rpm -q --provides rpm
librpm.so.0
librpmbuild.so.0
librpmio.so.0
rpm = 4.0.2-8
```

The first three lines state that RPM provides the capabilities (which are file names, in this case) librpm.so.0, librpmbuild.so.0, and librpmio.so.0. The last line shows both the version number of the rpm package itself and indicates that RPM is a capability of its own.

To determine what RPMs depend on a given capability, use --whatrequires *capability* to list all packages requiring *capability*. For example, the following command shows all the packages that require the RPM capability the RPM package provides. Although potentially confusing, keep in mind that the name of the package can be used as a capability.

```
$ rpm -q --whatrequires rpm
rpm-python-4.0.2-8
rhn_register-1.3.1-1
up2date-2.5.2-1
gnorpm-0.96-1
rpm-build-4.0.2-8
rpm-devel-4.0.2-8
```

The command output shows six packages requiring the rpm capability, including two packages that you might not suspect require it, rhn_register and up2date. Before you could remove the RPM package, therefore, you would have to remove the six packages that depend on it.

The options for querying RPM dependency information offer system administrators valuable information about the relationships between the many RPMs that constitute an installed Red Hat Linux system.

WHAT'S IN THAT RPM?

Naturally, it is often useful, or necessary, to find out the contents of an RPM, whether it is installed or not. A number of the options listed in Table 23-2 make this possible. The possibilities range from simply displaying the package name and version numbers all the way to detailed information about each file an RPM installs. In fact, you can list all installed RPMs using the -a option. Most queries, though, fall somewhere between these extremes and query a limited subset of packages or a limited selection of package characteristics or files.

The simplest query option, -q, shows only an RPM's name and version number, as the following command illustrates.

```
$ rpm -q whois
whois-1.0.6-1
```

If you want more — and more descriptive — information, add -i:

```
$ rpm -qi whois
Name        : whois              Relocations: (not relocateable)
Version     : 1.0.6                   Vendor: Red Hat, Inc.
Release     : 1                   Build Date: Fri 16 Feb 2001
Install date: Thu 24 May 2001     Build Host: porky.devel.redhat.com
Group       : Applications/Internet  Source RPM: whois-1.0.6-1.src.rpm
Size        : 38187                  License: LGPL
Packager    : Red Hat, Inc. <http://bugzilla.redhat.com/bugzilla>
Summary     : Internet whois/nicname client.
Description :
A whois client that accepts both traditional and finger-style queries.
```

The -i option results in a more comprehensive listing describing the RPM. Two of the entries may require additional explanation. The Group label organizes RPM packages by function. Descriptors, Applications and Internet in the example, are separated by / and become increasingly specific moving from left to right. Unfortunately, the values in the Group field are not standardized, and vary from vendor to vendor and even among RPM packagers. Browse the file /usr/share/doc/rpm-4.0.2/GROUPS to see the current list of groups that Red Hat uses (as of Red Hat Linux 7.1). The Relocations item indicates whether or not the RPM's base directory can be changed when it is installed. The whois package cannot be relocated. The next section, "Package installation and removal," explains more about RPM relocation.

To list all of the files in an installed RPM, use the -l option:

```
$ rpm -ql whois
/usr/bin/fwhois
/usr/bin/whois
/usr/share/doc/whois-1.0.6
/usr/share/doc/whois-1.0.6/COPYING.LIB
/usr/share/man/man1/fwhois.1.gz
/usr/share/man/man1/whois.1.gz
```

Gnome-RPM combines the functionality of the -i and -l options in a single command. Figure 23-1 shows the whois Package Info window in Gnome-RPM. To start Gnome-RPM from the GNOME desktop, select Main Menu → Programs → System → GnoRPM. To view the Package Info window for the whois RPM, click the + next to Applications to expand the tree, select Internet, scroll down until you find the icon for the whois RPM, select it, and then click the Query button on the toolbar or select Packages → Query from the menu.

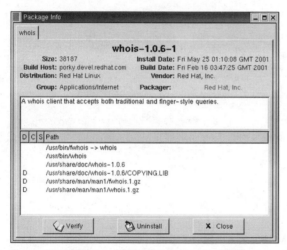

Figure 23-1: Gnome-RPM's Query command shows detailed information about the whois RPM.

Gnome-RPM presents the same information as the equivalent console command rpm -qli whois, save for one small difference, evident in the file list. The lower portion of the Package Info window includes three columns, labeled D, C, and S. A D in the first column means that the corresponding file is a documentation file, such as a man page or an application README. A C in the second column marks a configuration file. The third column resembles the functionality of the rpm command's -s option. R means the file has been replaced, N means the file was not installed, and S means the file is shared over a network. No letter indicates the file is normal, that is, that it has not changed since it was installed. As you can see in Figure 23-1, three of the whois files have a D tag, indicating that they are documentation files.

The -f *file* option approaches package listing from another direction. For any given file, you can find out which RPM installed it using -f *file*, where *file* contains the full path specification. The following command illustrates one way to use this option.

```
$ rpm -qf /usr/bin/find
findutils-4.1.6-2
```

Not much to it, right? Well, suppose you do not know the path to an application binary, just its name. In such a case, take advantage of shell commands and standard Linux utility programs. For example, the next command uses the which command and the Bash shell's command substitution to resolve a binary's name to a full path before invoking rpm:

```
$ rpm -qf $(which emacs)
emacs-X11-20.7-34
```

As you should recall from Chapter 20, the shell substitutes the value of $(which emacs), /usr/bin/emacs, before passing it to rpm -qf. The result is the same as the output of rpm -qf /usr/bin/emacs.

TIP By default, the which command works only with executable files available in the directories listed in the $PATH environment variable.

So far, every RPM query option discussed applies to installed packages. As it happens, many of them can be used on uninstalled packages, but only if the query specifies -p, which tells RPM to query an uninstalled package. Suppose, for example, you just downloaded the fortune-mod package, specifically, the fortune-mod-1.2.1-1.i386.rpm. To list its files, use -l, as explained earlier, and -p:

```
$ rpm -qpl fortune-mod-1.2.1-1.i386.rpm
/etc/profile.d/fortune.sh
/usr/bin/randstr
/usr/bin/rot
/usr/bin/strfile
/usr/bin/unstr
...
```

The output, truncated to conserve space, is identical to that of an installed package.

FORMATTING QUERY OUTPUT

Inveterate tweakers and hard-core customizers appreciate the `--qf` option because it allows custom formatting of query output. On the downside, it may not work with all query options, and RPMs rarely contain all of the information that can *potentially* be displayed. The general form of a query using query format strings is

```
$ rpm --qf 'formatstring' -q [queryoptions]
```

formatstring is the workhorse of custom query formatting. A *formatstring* must contain at least one tag; all other components are optional. Optional elements include literal text, directives to control the output's width and justification, control character sequences, output modifiers, and array iterators. A *tag* is a predefined token or symbol representing a piece of information. Examples include SUMMARY, DESCRIPTION, NAME, and VERSION, but there are many more; as of version 4.02-8, RPM understood 114 tags! Each tag must be embedded in a %{} construct, for example: %{SUMMARY} or %{NAME}.

TIP   Type `rpm --querytags` to view the entire list of tags RPM understands.

Note two details: First, *formatstring* should be delimited by single quotes ('), also called apostrophes or strong quotes, or by regular double quotes ("). Format strings used in shell scripts should be embedded between strong quotes to protect them from effects of shell expansion, described in Chapter 19. Secondly, make sure to type `--qf` (note the double dash); `-qf` means something else entirely, as you just read. To avoid confusion or the possibility of a typing error, consider using the long option `--queryformat`, a synonym of `--qf`.

CAUTION   The `rpm` man page mistakenly shows the short query formatting option as `-qf`. Be assured, the correct form is `--qf`.

To keep this chapter from turning into a book about RPM, it discusses only a few of the optional elements of a format string. The most important are directives to control the minimum width and justification of the displayed fields and escape sequences. To specify the width of a field, place a number between a tag's percent sign and its opening brace. By default, output is right justified, so to force left justification, prefix the field width with -. The escape sequences are the same as discussed in Chapter 20, such as \n for a newline and \t for a tab.

To illustrate, try the following examples and compare their output. The first example is the output of an unmodified query:

```
$ rpm -q setup db1 hdparm popt
setup-2.4.7-1
db1-1.85-5
hdparm-3.9-6
popt-1.6.2-8
```

You have seen this sort of query output already. It is simple and informative, but not terribly attractive. The next command uses two tags, NAME and VERSION, to specify the output fields:

```
$ rpm -q --qf '%{NAME}%{VERSION}' setup db1 hdparm popt
setup2.4.7db11.85hdparm3.9popt1.6.2$
```

Blech! This looks worse than the first example because all of the output runs together, including the command prompt. But it serves as a starting point. First, separate the fields using field width specifications:

```
$ rpm -q --qf '%-20{NAME}%10{VERSION}' setup db1 hdparm popt
setup      2.4.7db1      1.85hdparm      3.9popt      1.6.2$
```

Each NAME field has a width of 20 characters and is left justified. The VERSION column is 10 characters wide and is right justified (the default). Judicious use of the \t and \n escape sequences solves the jumbled output problem:

```
$ rpm -q --qf '%-20{NAME}\t%10{VERSION}\n' setup db1 hdparm popt
setup                    2.4.7
db1                      1.85
hdparm                    3.9
popt                    1.6.2
```

\t, the tab character, separates the name and version number fields, and \n, the newline, puts the command prompt back on its own line, where it belongs.

This short discussion is only a taste of the capabilities of query formatting. Nevertheless, it provides a solid foundation for creating richer, more visually appealing query output. It is also worth pointing out that the query format capability lets you create custom queries that simply are not possible using any other query option available. So, if you need RPM information you cannot obtain using the standard query options, use --qf to create a custom query that displays the information you need, and *only* that information.

Package installation and removal

Although RPM's query feature is one of its most powerful features, it earns its keep because of its package management features. This section summarizes how to install, remove, and upgrade software packages using RPM.

INSTALLING RPMS

The basic syntax for installing an RPM is

```
# rpm -i [options] package [...]
```

package is the complete name of the RPM to install and *options* refines the installation process. Table 23-3 lists commonly used *options* values. See the rpm man page for a comprehensive listing.

TABLE 23-3 COMMON RPM INSTALLATION OPTIONS

Option	Description
--force	Install the package even if it is already installed, install an older package version, or replace files already installed.
--h	Print up to 50 hash marks (#) to illustrate the progress of the installation.
--nodeps	Do not perform a dependency check before installing or upgrading a package.
--test	Do not install the package or update the database, just identify and display possible conflicts or dependency errors.
-v	Be slightly verbose and show some useful information during the installation.

Although they appear similar, --force and --nodeps serve different purposes. --nodeps only disables dependency checks. Use it only if you are certain that a dependency conflict will not cause problems later on. --force forces package installation regardless of all potential problems except for dependency violations. As a result, some situations may require using --force and --nodeps together. Common uses of --force include installing an older version of the same package (perhaps because the newer version is too buggy), reinstalling deleted files, and restoring altered files to their pristine state.

The following command demonstrates installing an RPM:

```
# rpm -ivh fortune-mod-1.2.1-1.i386.rpm
Preparing...              ########################################### [100%]
   1:fortune-mod          ########################################### [100%]
```

Figure 23-2 demonstrates using Gnome-RPM to install an RPM.

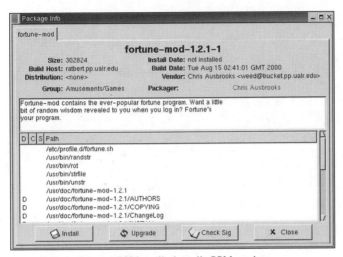

Figure 23-2: Gnome-RPM easily installs RPM packages.

The next example shows the error generated by trying to install a package already installed and how to use --force to ignore the error.

```
# rpm -ivh fortune-mod-1.2.1-1.i386.rpm
Preparing...              ########################################### [100%]
package fortune-mod-1.2.1-1 is already installed
# rpm -ivh --force fortune-mod-1.2.1-1.i386.rpm
Preparing...              ########################################### [100%]
   1:fortune-mod          ########################################### [100%]
```

--force caused RPM to ignore the conflict and perform the installation. To avoid encountering such conflicts, use the --test option, as shown in the next command, to perform a "dry run" installation to catch any problems:

```
# rpm -ivh --test fortune-mod-1.2.1-1.i386.rpm
Preparing...              ########################################### [100%]
package fortune-mod-1.2.1-1 is already installed
```

As you can see in the example, adding --test to the command line generated an error message. What you cannot see is that neither RPM's databases nor any files changed. Testing a package installation using --test is great protection against the heartburn caused by installing incompatible software.

UPGRADING RPMS

The options for upgrading existing RPMs come in two flavors, -U, for upgrade, and -F, for freshen. What is the difference between upgrading a package and freshening it? Upgrading a package, using -U, installs it even if an earlier version is not currently installed, but freshening a package, using -F, installs it only if an earlier version is currently installed. Other than this subtle but important difference, -U and -F are identical to -i, down to the options they accept (see Table 23-3). The following sequence of commands illustrates how to upgrade an RPM and the difference between the -U and -F options:

```
# rpm -Fvh fortune-mod-1.0-13.i386.rpm
# rpm -q fortune-mod
package fortune-mod is not installed
```

Hmm. Nothing happened. The rpm command line used -F, so it did not install the fortune-mod package because an earlier version did not exist.

```
# rpm -Uvh fortune-mod-1.0-13.i386.rpm
Preparing...                ########################################### [100%]
   1:fortune-mod            ########################################### [100%]
```

With -U, RPM "upgraded" the fortune-mod package even though an earlier version was not installed.

```
# rpm -Fvh fortune-mod-1.2.1-1.i386.rpm
Preparing...                ########################################### [100%]
   1:fortune-mod            ########################################### [100%]
```

This time, the freshen operation succeeded.

REMOVING RPMS

Removing or deleting RPMs and their contents is easy, perhaps frightfully so. The general form of the command is

```
rpm -e package [...]
```

package is the name, only, of the RPM to remove. Multiple packages can be removed simultaneously by listing each package on the command line. For example, the following command removes the fortune-mod and whois RPMs:

```
# rpm -e fortune-mod whois
```

Note that successful removal generates no additional output. Figure 23-3 illustrates using Gnome-RPM to remove the whois package:

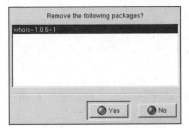

Figure 23-3: Using Gnome-RPM to remove an RPM package

To use Gnome-RPM to remove an RPM, locate the package using the main package browser window, click the Uninstall button, and then click the Yes button, as shown in Figure 23-3, to confirm the process.

Verifying RPMs

Verifying an RPM compares the current status of files installed by an RPM to the file information recorded at the time the RPM was installed, such as file sizes and MD5 checksum values, and reports any discrepancies. The general form of the verify command is

```
rpm -V package [...]
```

The -V option requests RPM to verify the status of files in package, the name of the RPM to verify. As with many other RPM operations, multiple packages can be verified simultaneously. Table 23-4 explains the file characteristics RPM evaluates when verifying an RPM.

TABLE 23-4 FILE INFORMATION EVALUATED DURING RPM VERIFICATION

Characteristic	Description
MD5 checksum	The file's MD5 checksum (calculated using the md5sum command)
File size	The file's size, in bytes
Modification time	The date and time the file was last modified
Device	The device file or files in the case of drivers and hardware devices

Continued

TABLE 23-4 FILE INFORMATION EVALUATED DURING RPM VERIFICATION
              (Continued)

Characteristic	Description
User	The file's owner, such as root or bin
Group	The file's group
Mode	The file's permissions and type

If none of the characteristics listed in Table 23-4 have changed for any of the RPM's files since they were installed, RPM displays no information, as the following example shows.

```
$ rpm -V whois
```

In this example, the rpm command generated no output save for the shell command prompt, so the whois package's files remain unchanged from their initial state at installation.

If, on the other hand, any of the tracked file characteristics have changed, the output will resemble the following:

```
$ rpm -V fortune-mod
S.5....T   /usr/bin/rot
.......T   /usr/bin/strfile
.....UG.   /usr/bin/unstr
.M......   /usr/man/man1/randstr.1
missing    /usr/man/man1/unstr.1
```

At the very least, it should be clear that something is up with the fortune-mod package. Each line out of the output consists of eight fields and a file name, separated by whitespace to format the output. Table 23-5 shows the keys for interpreting verification output.

TABLE 23-5 RPM VERIFICATION KEYS

Column	Value	Description
1	5	The MD5 checksum has changed
2	S	The file size has changed

Column	Value	Description
3	L	A symlink has changed (points to a different file)
4	T	The file's modification time has changed
5	D	The device designation has changed
6	U	The file's user (owner) has changed
7	G	The file's group has changed
8	M	The files mode (permissions or type) has changed
ANY	.	No change detected in the corresponding characteristic
ANY	?	This characteristic's current status could not be determined (usually because file permissions prevent reading the file)
N/A	missing	The corresponding file does not exist in its default location

Translating the admittedly cryptic output from the `rpm -V fortune-mod` command, then, you know the following:

♦ `/usr/bin/rot`'s file size, MD5 checksum, and modification time has changed

♦ `/usr/bin/strfile`'s modification time has changed

♦ `/usr/bin/unstr`'s user and group ownership has changed

♦ `/usr/man/man1/randstr.1`'s mode (either its permission bits, type, or both) has changed

♦ `/usr/man/man1/unstr.1` has been deleted, moved, or renamed

Figure 23-4 illustrates how Gnome-RPM presents the same information.

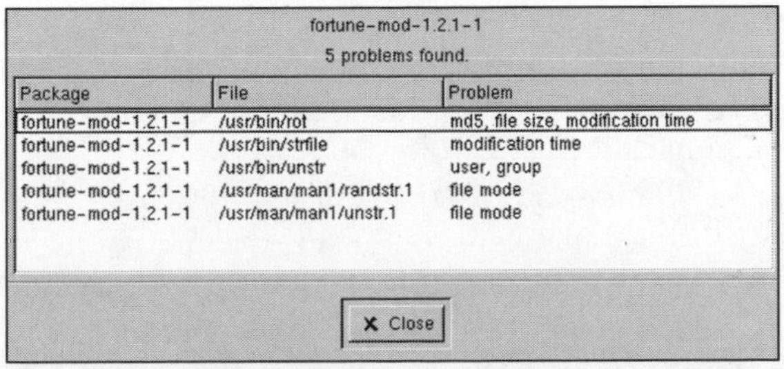

Figure 23-4: Gnome-RPM's verification screen for the fortune-mod package

Depending on the file and the local environment, some changes indicate a potential problem, but others do not. If a binary file's size, checksum, modification time, or user or group ownership has changed and you have not manually upgraded the package, this is cause for alarm because under normal circumstances, these characteristics do not change. That is, it is highly likely that the original file has been replaced or modified, perhaps by a cracker, and you should take steps to address this problem immediately. Exercise similar caution if a file is listed as missing. On the other hand, application and system configuration files, for example, files in the /etc directory and its subdirectories, change due to edits by administrators and system configuration tools.

Keeping a *handwritten* logbook that tracks changes to your system, such as installing, upgrading, and removing RPMs, is a very useful habit to acquire because it records each modification made to the system. It should be handwritten, rather than stored on the system, so that it is accessible even if the system is severely damaged.

In some situations, such as RPM verification reports, the logbook becomes an invaluable resource because you can compare log entries to the verification report to evaluate whether or not a reported discrepancy poses a security threat or is just the result of a long-forgotten file edit or package installation.

Unfortunately, it is impossible to define a general rule that distinguishes a legitimate change from a pernicious one. The best policy to follow is to know your system and to keep careful track of updates and changes so you can identify and respond quickly and appropriately to anomalous and potentially malicious modifications.

Building RPMs

Knowing how to create binary RPMs from source RPMs distinguishes knowledgeable Red Hat Linux administrators from novices. More importantly, it allows you to customize the software you install on your system. Among other things, compiling your own RPMs enables you to specify the CPU type on which the binary RPM will run, which can result in sometimes dramatic performance gains. The sections titled "Building and installing source RPMs" and "Using RPM with source tarballs" later in the chapter explore this process in greater detail, so this section highlights only the process and lists the available options.

Binary RPMs begin life as *source RPMs* — RPMs that consist of source code rather than compiled programs. As noted previously, the extension .src.rpm denotes a source RPM (referred to as SRPM hereafter). To install an SRPM, use the same -i option required when installing a binary RPM. For example, the command rpm -ivh /mnt/cdrom/SRPMS/anaconda-7.1-5.src.rpm installs the source files for the Red Hat Linux installation program, Anaconda. However, the SRPM is not installed into the active file system but into `/usr/src/redhat`, the area Red Hat sets aside for working with SRPMs.

Other RPM-based distributions use similarly named directories. For example, Caldera OpenLinux uses `/usr/src/OpenLinux` for its SRPM working area.

Similarly, RPM queries (using the `-q` option) do not report that SRPMs have been installed. Listing the contents of `/usr/src/redhat`, though, will confirm that the SRPM has been installed.

Once an SRPM is installed, build it using the `-b` option. The general form of the build command is

`rpm -b[stage] specfile [...]`

`specfile` is the name of *spec file*, a type of configuration file adhering to a strict format that tells RPM, among other things, how to compile the application, what the RPM's dependencies are, and where the resulting files should be installed. `stage` defines how far into the build process to go. For the purposes of this chapter, the most important stage is b, that is, `rpm -bb specfile`, which compiles the application, packages it into a binary RPM, and saves the RPM in a subdirectory of `/usr/src/redhat/RPMS`. Once the binary RPM builds successfully, install it as you would any other RPM. You will learn more about working with SRPMs in the section titled "Building and installing source RPMs."

RPM administrative commands

The last category of RPM commands affect RPM itself, rather than RPM packages or SRPMs. These commands are `--initdb`, `--rebuilddb`, and `--showrc`. The `--showrc` command, which accepts no arguments, displays RPM's configuration as determined by its primary configuration file, `/usr/lib/rpm/rpmrc`.

Customizing RPM's configuration and behavior is an advanced topic beyond this book's scope. For more detail, visit the RPM Web site at `http://www.rpm.org` or read Ed Bailey's excellent book, *Maximum RPM*. Although *Maximum RPM* describes an older RPM version, most of the information still applies to version 4, which ships with the current version of Red Hat Linux. Happily, *Maximum RPM* is currently being revised and much of the updated material is accessible through the RPM Web site.

Here is the part of the output produced by the `--showrc` option (the complete display is rather lengthy, so it has been trimmed to conserve space):

```
$ rpm --showrc
ARCHITECTURE AND OS:
build arch            : i386
compatible build archs: i686 i586 i486 i386 noarch
build os              : Linux
compatible build os's : Linux
install arch          : i686
install os            : Linux
compatible archs      : i686 i586 i486 i386 noarch
compatible os's       : Linux

RPMRC VALUES:
macrofiles            : /usr/lib/rpm/macros:/usr/lib/rpm/i686-linux/macros:/etc/
rpm/macros.specspo:/etc/rpm/macros.db1:/etc/rpm/macros:/etc/rpm/i686-linux/macro
s:~/.rpmmacros
optflags              : -O2 -march=i686
```

The section headed "ARCHITECTURE AND OS" lists RPM's idea of the system on which it is installed. The next section, "RPMRC VALUES" defines default values such as paths (`macrofiles`) and options to pass to the system compiler (`gcc`, in this case) when building software (`optflags`), and more. The complete output is over 10K of information, some of which is quite obscure and most of which is beyond this book's scope.

The `--rebuilddb` and `--initdb` commands perform maintenance on RPM's databases. Of the two, `--rebuilddb` is the most useful because it repairs a corrupt database and eliminates unused parts of the database. Hopefully, you will never encounter a message resembling "free list corrupt (42)" while using RPM but, if you do, execute `rpm --rebuilddb` to repair the problem. Parts of the RPM databases become unused, or empty, due to the type of database RPM uses, but this is only an issue for systems on which RPMs are very frequently added, removed, or upgraded.

The `--initdb` command creates a new RPM database. Naturally, any system that already has an RPM database does not need a new one, but, if you wish, you can use `--initdb` on such a system and it will not harm the existing RPM database.

TIP   Most users will never need to use either the `--initdb` or `--rebuilddb` commands.

This completes your tour of RPM. The next sections probe deeper into the subject of finding, building, and installing software.

Checking Software Versions

Before downloading and installing SuperWidget version 1.3.2-5, you may want to know what version is currently installed in order to avoid "upgrading" to an old, unstable, development, or possibly buggy version. Unfortunately, no single command for obtaining version information works for all software packages. Rather, a variety of methods exist. This section covers the most common methods for locating software version information.

On a Red Hat Linux system, the easiest way to identify software versions is to use RPM. Suppose, for example, you want to find out which version of Emacs, a popular editor, is installed on your system. As explained earlier in the chapter, use rpm's query option, -q. For example:

```
$ rpm -q emacs
emacs-20.7-34
```

The output indicates that the Emacs version is 20.7-34. What exactly does emacs-20.7-34 mean, though? RPM uses a standardized naming and version numbering scheme mirroring a very common approach used in the Linux development community. Its general format is *name-majornum.minornum[.patchnum]-buildnum*. Table 23-6 explains the meaning of each element in the format.

TABLE **23-6** COMMON VERSION NUMBERING ELEMENTS

Element	Interpretation
name	The name of the package (balsa, emacs, mozilla)
majornum	The primary version number; changes between major updates to the package.
minornum	The secondary version number; increments to reflect updates less dramatic than those indicated by *majornum*.
patchnum	The patch number; usually reflects only the application of bug fixes to a given version. Not all applications use *patchnum*.
buildnum	The build number; an RPM-specific feature indicating the packager's version.

So, the package name emacs-20.7-34 breaks down to the *name* emacs, the *majornum* 20, the *minornum* 7, no *patchnum*, and the *buildnum* 34. The build number means that it is the 34th version of Red Hat's Emacs 20.7 RPM.

TIP   Non-RPM software packages frequently use the same naming scheme as RPM.

If you do not want to use RPM, or for packages not installed using RPM, other options exist. Many applications accept command line options that cause them to display their version numbers. The most common such options are -v, -V, -version, and --version. Programs from the GNU project, in particular, almost always accept --version. For example, the next two examples pass -v and --version to mutt (a popular text-based e-mail client) and emacs, respectively, to obtain their version numbers:

```
$ mutt -v
Mutt 1.2.5i (2000-07-28)
Copyright (C) 1996-2000 Michael R. Elkins and others.
Mutt comes with ABSOLUTELY NO WARRANTY; for details type `mutt -vv'.
Mutt is free software, and you are welcome to redistribute it
under certain conditions; type `mutt -vv' for details.

System: Linux 2.4.2-2 [using slang 10402]
Compile options:
-DOMAIN
-DEBUG
-HOMESPOOL  -USE_SETGID  -USE_DOTLOCK +USE_FCNTL  -USE_FLOCK
+USE_IMAP  +USE_GSS  +USE_SSL  +USE_POP  +HAVE_REGCOMP  -
USE_GNU_REGEX
+HAVE_COLOR  +HAVE_PGP  -BUFFY_SIZE -EXACT_ADDRESS  +ENABLE_NLS
SENDMAIL="/usr/sbin/sendmail"
MAILPATH="/var/mail"
SHAREDIR="/etc"
SYSCONFDIR="/etc"
ISPELL="/usr/bin/ispell"
To contact the developers, please mail to <mutt-dev@mutt.org>.
To report a bug, please use the muttbug utility.

$ emacs --version
GNU Emacs 20.7.1
Copyright (C) 1999 Free Software Foundation, Inc.
GNU Emacs comes with ABSOLUTELY NO WARRANTY.
You may redistribute copies of Emacs
under the terms of the GNU General Public License.
For more information about these matters, see the file named
COPYING.
```

For better or worse, many applications display more information than simple version numbers, as the example demonstrates, but at least you get the information you sought.

 When invoked as discussed in this section, most applications display their version information and then exit. That is, they do not start.

Many X Window System applications use `-version` to show their version numbers. Similarly, almost every X application provides a dialog box (commonly accessible by selecting Help → About) that displays a version number. Figure 23-5, for example, shows GNOME Calendar's About dialog box, which includes version information.

Figure 23–5: GNOME Calendar's About
dialog box displays its version number.

If none of these suggestions work, try using `-help` or `--help` to generate a short usage summary that lists a program's options. If all else fails, read the package's documentation or manual page to find out how to access its version information, because it is very rare for an application, whether text mode or GUI, not to display version information.

Obtaining Newer Software

How and from where do you obtain newer software? There are many more options than can be covered here, so this section discusses the most common methods. The first step is to locate the software package you want. Then, of course, you have to download it.

The most popular sites for locating and downloading Linux software are the RPM repository at rpmfind.org, the application index at Freshmeat, and the Ibiblio

Web and FTP site. In addition, Gnome-RPM provides an interface that Red Hat has configured specifically for Red Hat Linux.

Using rpmfind.org

The rpmfind.org Web site is a huge repository of RPM-based software packages covering all the major distributions and many of the minor ones and spanning the entire range of application categories. It also lists RPMs by platform, such as Intel x86, SPARC, and Macintosh. Its finely tuned search engine makes it easy to find the RPM you want, or at least to reduce the possibilities from some 100,000+ to a more manageable figure.

To get started, point your Web browser at `http://www.rpmfind.net/` and then click the Go directly to the RPM database link at the top of the page. Click the Search link in the upper right-hand corner of the page, type **fortune-mod** in the text box, and then click the Search button to perform the search. The resulting page should resemble Figure 23-6.

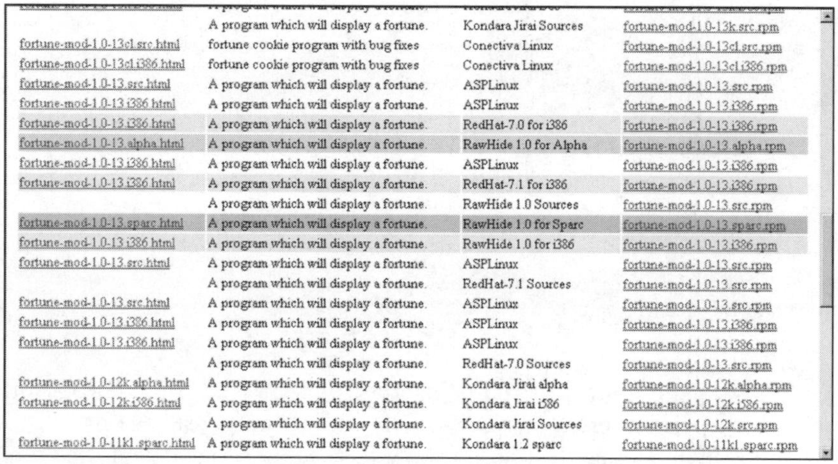

	A program which will display a fortune.	Kondara Jirai Sources	fortune-mod-1.0-13k.src.rpm
fortune-mod-1.0-13cl.src.html	fortune cookie program with bug fixes	Conectiva Linux	fortune-mod-1.0-13cl.src.rpm
fortune-mod-1.0-13cl.i386.html	fortune cookie program with bug fixes	Conectiva Linux	fortune-mod-1.0-13cl.i386.rpm
fortune-mod-1.0-13.src.html	A program which will display a fortune.	ASPLinux	fortune-mod-1.0-13.src.rpm
fortune-mod-1.0-13.i386.html	A program which will display a fortune.	ASPLinux	fortune-mod-1.0-13.i386.rpm
fortune-mod-1.0-13.i386.html	A program which will display a fortune.	RedHat-7.0 for i386	fortune-mod-1.0-13.i386.rpm
fortune-mod-1.0-13.alpha.html	A program which will display a fortune.	RawHide 1.0 for Alpha	fortune-mod-1.0-13.alpha.rpm
fortune-mod-1.0-13.i386.html	A program which will display a fortune.	ASPLinux	fortune-mod-1.0-13.i386.rpm
fortune-mod-1.0-13.i386.html	A program which will display a fortune.	RedHat-7.1 for i386	fortune-mod-1.0-13.i386.rpm
	A program which will display a fortune.	RawHide 1.0 Sources	fortune-mod-1.0-13.src.rpm
fortune-mod-1.0-13.sparc.html	A program which will display a fortune.	RawHide 1.0 for Sparc	fortune-mod-1.0-13.sparc.rpm
fortune-mod-1.0-13.i386.html	A program which will display a fortune.	RawHide 1.0 for i386	fortune-mod-1.0-13.i386.rpm
fortune-mod-1.0-13.src.html	A program which will display a fortune.	ASPLinux	fortune-mod-1.0-13.src.rpm
	A program which will display a fortune.	RedHat-7.1 Sources	fortune-mod-1.0-13.src.rpm
fortune-mod-1.0-13.src.html	A program which will display a fortune.	ASPLinux	fortune-mod-1.0-13.src.rpm
fortune-mod-1.0-13.i386.html	A program which will display a fortune.	ASPLinux	fortune-mod-1.0-13.i386.rpm
fortune-mod-1.0-13.i386.html	A program which will display a fortune.	ASPLinux	fortune-mod-1.0-13.i386.rpm
	A program which will display a fortune.	RedHat-7.0 Sources	fortune-mod-1.0-13.src.rpm
fortune-mod-1.0-12k.alpha.html	A program which will display a fortune.	Kondara Jirai alpha	fortune-mod-1.0-12k.alpha.rpm
fortune-mod-1.0-12k.i586.html	A program which will display a fortune.	Kondara Jirai i586	fortune-mod-1.0-12k.i586.rpm
	A program which will display a fortune.	Kondara Jirai Sources	fortune-mod-1.0-12k.src.rpm
fortune-mod-1.0-11k1.sparc.html	A program which will display a fortune.	Kondara 1.2 sparc	fortune-mod-1.0-11k1.sparc.rpm

Figure 23-6: rpmfind.net lists many fortune-mod RPMs.

As you can see in Figure 23-6, there are a number of fortune-mod RPMs available, so you could go back to the previous screen, refine the search criteria, and redo the search to reduce the number of results shown.

Selecting one of the listed RPMs takes you to its information page (see Figure 23-7). The information page includes a link to the package's home page, information about the listed RPM, and, most importantly, a download link.

Click the RPM file name at the top of the page (`fortune-mod-1.0.13.i386.rpm`, in this case) to download the RPM to your system.

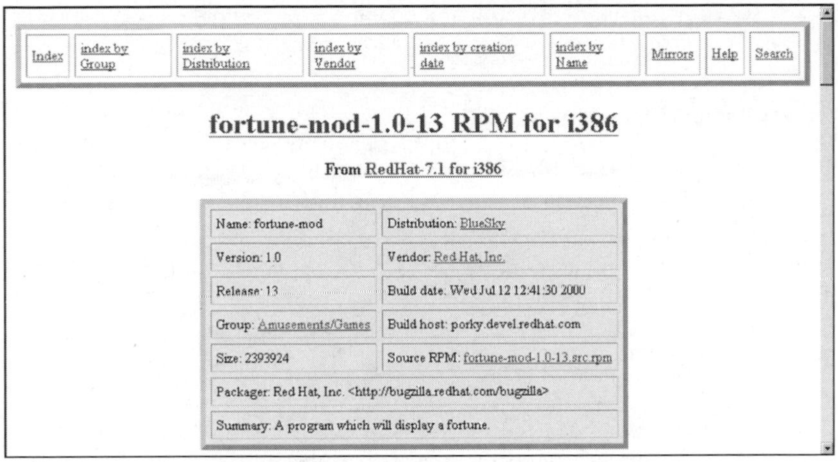

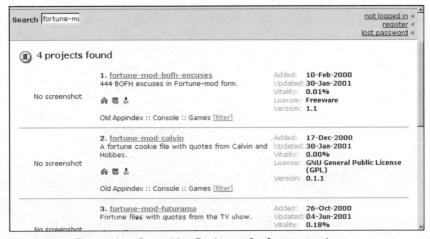

Figure 23-7: The information page for fortune-mod-1.0.13 at rpmfind.net

Using Freshmeat

Freshmeat, at `http://www.freshmeat.net/`, is a Linux and open source news and information site. It also maintains a large and actively-updated index of Linux and open source software. Although Freshmeat's database is not as large as rpmfind.net's, its search interface is simpler to use than rpmfind.net's and, in many cases, lists the application for which you are looking.

The search interface is available by typing the name, or part of it, in the Search text box and pressing Enter. For example, if you type **fortune-mod** and press enter, the resulting screen should resemble Figure 23-8.

Figure 23-8: The results of searching Freshmeat for fortune-mod

Freshmeat lists four packages. To download one of them, click the floppy disk icon.

Using Ibiblio.org

Ibiblio.org is arguably the sire of all of the Linux and open source software repositories currently available. It began life as Sunsite (strictly speaking, `ftp://sunsite.unc.edu/` and, after the World Wide Web became popular, `http://sunsite.unc.edu/`), one of a number of information repositories scattered throughout the world, hosted on hardware donated by Sun Microsystems (hence, the name) and provided as a public service by both Sun and the sites' administrators. In the late 1990s, the University of North Carolina renamed Sunsite to Metalab, and the URLs changed to `ftp://metalab.unc.edu/` and `http://metalab.unc.edu/`). In 1999, Metalab became Ibiblio.org, reflecting its phenomenal growth in size and popularity and its focus on providing the computing public at large access to a comprehensive store of information (and software) on a variety of topics.

Ibiblio.org (and its predecessors, Metalab and Sunsite) is a public repository for information of all sorts, not just downloadable software. For example, at the time this chapter was written, it featured an exhibit commemorating America's World War II veterans in honor of Memorial Day, including articles, photographs, and multimedia items. At the same time, Ibiblio.org hosted a stunning *55GB* of downloadable Linux software, and Linux software is only *one* of Ibiblio.org's software collections!

To access Ibiblio.org's Linux archive, point your Web browser at `ftp://www.ibiblio.org/pub/Linux/`. Browse through the archives at your leisure to locate the package that interests you. For example, a number of fortune packages reside in the `/pub/Linux/games/amusements/fortune` directory, as shown in Figure 23-9.

Figure 23-9 shows a portion of the fortune-related packages available in its Linux software archive. As usual, to download one to your system, click the corresponding link. If you are using the Netscape browser, it may be necessary to hold down the left Shift key and left click to download the archive file.

Ibiblio.org does not store RPM files in its standard Linux software archive. Rather, the preferred format is compressed tarballs. However, distribution-specific directories (stored under the `/pub/Linux/distributions` directory tree) do contain RPMs if the distribution in question is RPM-based (such as Red Hat Linux, Caldera OpenLinux, and Linux-Mandrake).

```
FTP directory /pub/Linux/games/amusements/fortune/ at www.ibiblio.org

Up to higher level directory

04/25/2001 10:12AM         1,229  !INDEX
04/25/2001 10:12AM         3,944  !INDEX.html
04/25/2001 10:12AM         1,926  !INDEX.short.html
02/11/1999 12:00AM            85  README
10/26/1998 12:00AM         4,953  fortune-0.2.tar.gz
04/25/2001 07:05AM         2,062  fortune-cs-1.4.README
04/25/2001 07:05AM         1,441  fortune-cs-1.4.lsm
04/25/2001 07:05AM       370,546  fortune-cs-1.4.tar.bz2
04/25/2001 07:05AM       475,791  fortune-cs-1.4.tar.gz
03/22/2000 12:00AM         1,292  fortune-fr-1411.lsm
03/22/2000 12:00AM        67,096  fortune-fr-1411.tgz
11/13/1990 12:00AM         1,796  fortune-it-1.51.lsm
11/13/1998 12:00AM       408,734  fortune-it-1.51.tar.gz
08/29/1997 12:00AM         7,381  fortune-mod-9708.README
08/29/1997 12:00AM     1,408,517  fortune-mod-9708.tar.gz
08/29/1997 12:00AM           705  fortune-mod.lsm
10/26/1998 12:00AM           429  fortune.lsm
12/17/1998 12:00AM        18,559  fortunes-hu-0.1.tar.gz
12/17/1998 12:00AM           433  fortunes-hu.lsm
01/25/1999 12:00AM           544  kfortune-1.3.lsm
01/25/1999 12:00AM       723,896  kfortune-1.3.tar.gz
```

Figure 23-9: Ibiblio.org's directory of Linux fortune packages

If you are uncertain about the contents of a particular directory or its subdirectories, the files !INDEX, !INDEX.html, !INDEX.short.html, and README in each directory describe, in varying levels of detail, the contents of each directory and, if applicable, its subdirectories. If you prefer not to browse Ibiblio.org's Linux archive directly, you can use its Linsearch interface, based on the Linux Software Map described in the next section, by pointing your browser at http://www. ibiblio.org/pub/Linux and selecting the Linsearch link.

 The Linux Software Map, less actively maintained than other sites discussed in this chapter, is a database of Linux software. It supports searches by keywords and titles and also lets you browse the entire database by application title.

Ibiblio.org's heyday as the authoritative Linux download site has passed, in large part because RPM has become the dominant software packaging system. Nevertheless, Ibiblio.org continues to cast a long shadow because it stores a truly staggering quantity of Linux software not yet (and which may never be) packaged in RPM format. Do not make the mistake of overlooking or disregarding Ibiblio.org when looking for a particular software package or when surveying the range of software available in a given category.

Using Gnome-RPM

Gnome-RPM, obviously, is not a software repository, but it does facilitate the process of finding and downloading updated RPMs. On Red Hat Linux systems connected to the Internet, Gnome-RPM is preconfigured to search a number of

standard Internet software repositories for Red Hat Linux-specific RPMs that are
newer than those currently installed on a given system. Figure 23-10 shows the
Preferences → Distributions window, which lists the paths and Internet sites
Gnome-RPM uses when searching for updated RPMs.

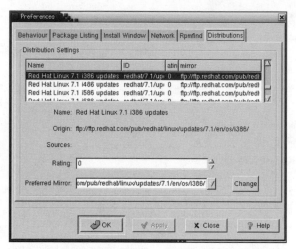

Figure 23-10: Gnome-RPM is configured automatically
to check for updated RPMs.

In fact, if you select Gnome-RPM's Web find button, it uses rpmfind to locate
packages to install on your computer by searching the Internet using the rpmfind
database. This combination of Gnome-RPM and rpmfind.net not only downloads
the RPM you specify, but also any additional required RPMs (dependencies).

Additional software repositories

In addition to the sites just described, the following Web sites offer Linux or open
source software for download:

- **Linux.com** — `http://www.linux.com/`
- **Linuxberg** — `http://www.linuxberg.com/`
- **GNU** — `http://www.gnu.org`

Linux.com is a popular news and information site, hosted by VA Linux, that also
contains some downloadable software, and links to much more. Linuxberg is part
of the Tucows software repository dedicated to Linux software. Like Tucows, and
unlike other Linux and open source software sites, Linuxberg is heavily commercially oriented. It is widely mirrored, however, so it may be easier to find most of
the popular Linux packages at a download site close to you. The GNU project's Web

site, naturally, is the host site for almost all of the packages sponsored by the GNU project. Like Linuxberg, it is widely mirrored, so you may get better download speeds if you locate a mirror close to you.

A final source for locating new or upgraded software is software developers. Many Linux developers maintain either entire Web sites or individual Web pages from which you can download their software packages and patches, report bugs, track package development, and subscribe or unsubscribe to package-related mailing lists.

Installing Software

After downloading either an RPM, SRPM, or a source archive such as a tarball, naturally, you will want to install it. The section titled "Using the Red Hat Package Manager" explained in detail how to install binary RPMs using the commands `rpm -i`, `rpm -U`, and `rpm -F`, so refer to that section if you need a refresher. This section shows you how to install software from source code, that is, to unpack, configure, build, and install a software package you download as uncompiled source code. Next, you will learn how to use RPM to build and install SRPMs, source RPMS, and how to use RPM to build software from tarballs.

Installing software from source

Before package management suites such as RPM became popular, you upgraded and installed software by downloading a *gzipped tarball* (a tar archive compressed using the `gzip` utility), unpacking it, configuring it by manually editing one or more header files or using a `configure` script that automatically customized the package to your system, executing `make` to build it, and then, more often than not, executing `make install` to install it. Despite RPM's popularity, a considerable amount of software still uses this approach, so this section walks you through the process to familiarize you with it. The method is much simpler than it might seem at first blush. The example used in this section configures, builds, and installs `bc`, an arithmetic processing language used in the text mode `dc` calculator.

CONFIGURING THE BUILD ENVIRONMENT

Implicit in the previous paragraph is the assumption that your system has a development environment installed. For end users and system administrators, a *build environment* consists of the compiler, gcc, and its supporting libraries, the `make` utility for automating compiler invocations, a few key development libraries (mostly consisting of header files), and the install utility for handling the details of copying files and assigning the proper ownership and setting file permissions appropriately.

During installation, select the development workstation option to install a complete development environment. Otherwise, make sure at least the following RPMs are installed on your system:

◆ gcc (for C programs)

◆ g++ (for C++ programs)

◆ make

◆ glibc-devel

◆ fileutils

◆ kernel-headers

◆ kernel-source

◆ gzip

◆ bzip2

◆ ncompress

◆ tar

Packages that have additional requirements usually state what they are, so read the package documentation to ensure your system has the required software.

UNPACKING THE SOFTWARE

After downloading the bc package (`bc-1.0.6.tar.gz` in this chapter's source code directory), move it to a location where it will not interfere with the system. For this example, I moved it to `/tmp`. After `cd`ing to `/tmp`, you can use one of two commands to decompress and unpack the archive. The first command combines decompression and unpacking the tar archive in a single command:

```
$ tar zxf bc-1.0.6.tar.gz
```

The z option uses `tar`'s built-in `gunzip` routine to decompress the file, x extracts the archive files, and f specifies the name of the file on which to operate. The second command you can use sends `gunzip`'s output to `tar`'s input using a pipe (|), that is:

```
$ gunzip -c bc-1.0.6.tar.gz | tar xf -
```

 TIP   If you want more feedback from either of these commands, use `tar`'s v option to cause it to display the files it is extracting from the archive.

gunzip's -c option sends the result of the decompression to standard output; using -f - with tar tells it to read its standard input; the pipe connects the two commands. In either case, you wind up with a directory named bc-1.0.6 in the current directory (/tmp, in this case). So, cd into bc-1.0.6 to proceed with configuring bc.

CONFIGURING THE SOFTWARE

Now that the bc package has been unpacked, the next step is to configure it for your system. In most cases, customizing a package for your system boils down to specifying the installation directory; but many packages, including bc, allow you to request additional customizations. Happily, this is an easy step.

bc, like numerous other software packages, uses a configure script to automate configuration and customization. A configure script is a shell script that makes educated guesses about the correct values of a variety of system-specific values used during the compilation process. In addition, configure allows you to specify the values of these same values, and others, by invoking configure with command line options and arguments. Values that configure "guesses" and that you pass to configure on its command line are normally written to one or more *Makefiles*, files that the make program uses to control the build process, or to one or more header (.h) files that define the characteristics of the program that gets built.

To see the items you can customize, execute ./configure --help in the base directory of the package you are building, as shown in Listing 23-1 (which has been edited to conserve space).

Listing 23-1: configure's **Command Line Options**

```
$ ./configure --help
Usage: configure [options] [host]
Options: [defaults in brackets after descriptions]
Configuration:
...
Directory and file names:
  --prefix=PREFIX          install architecture-independent files in PREFIX
                           [/usr/local]
  --exec-prefix=EPREFIX    install architecture-dependent files in EPREFIX
                           [same as prefix]
...
Host type:
  --build=BUILD            configure for building on BUILD [BUILD=HOST]
  --host=HOST              configure for HOST [guessed]
  --target=TARGET          configure for TARGET [TARGET=HOST]
Features and packages:
  --disable-FEATURE        do not include FEATURE (same as --enable-FEATURE=no)
  --enable-FEATURE[=ARG]   include FEATURE [ARG=yes]
  --with-PACKAGE[=ARG]     use PACKAGE [ARG=yes]
```

Continued

Listing 23-1 *(Continued)*

```
  --without-PACKAGE       do not use PACKAGE (same as --with-PACKAGE=no)
  --x-includes=DIR        X include files are in DIR
  --x-libraries=DIR       X library files are in DIR
--enable and --with options recognized:
  --with-pkg              use software installed in /usr/pkg tree
  --with-libedit          support fancy BSD command input
editing
  --with-readline         support fancy command input editing
```

The key options in Listing 23-1 are --prefix and the three under the heading --enable and --with options recognized, --with-pkg, --with-libedit, and --with-readline. --prefix enables you to specify an installation directory other than the default (indicated in brackets, []), /usr/local/. For this example, the root installation directory is /tmp/bctest, specified as --prefix=/tmp/bctest on configure's command line. The second group of command line options enable other features. This example uses --with-readline, which turns on support for the GNU readline library. The readline library enables command line editing inside the bc program, just as the Bash shell permits editing the shell command line.

After selecting the desired options, run configure with the appropriate options, as shown in the following example (again, the output has been edited to conserve space).

```
$ ./configure --prefix=/tmp/bctest --with-readline


creating cache ./config.cache
checking for a BSD compatible install... /usr/bin/install -c
checking whether build environment is sane... yes
checking whether make sets ${MAKE}... yes
checking for working aclocal... found
checking for working autoconf... found
checking for working automake... found
checking for working autoheader... found
checking for working makeinfo... found
checking for gcc... gcc
checking whether the C compiler (gcc  ) works... yes
...
checking for readline in -lreadline... yes
checking for readline/readline.h... yes
Using the readline library.
updating cache ./config.cache
creating ./config.status
creating Makefile
creating bc/Makefile
```

```
creating dc/Makefile
creating doc/Makefile
creating lib/Makefile
creating config.h
```

The lines beginning with `checking` indicate that `configure` is testing for the presence of a certain feature such as gcc. Because the command line specified `--with-readline`, the last two checking lines make sure the readline library is installed (`checking for readline in -lreadline... yes`) and that the appropriate header file, `readline.h`, is installed. Once all of the tests are completed, `configure` uses the test results to create a number of Makefiles and a header file. At this point, you are ready to build bc.

BUILDING THE SOFTWARE
To build bc, type **make** and press Enter. The following example shows the end of the build process's output:

```
$ make
...
gcc -DHAVE_CONFIG_H -I. -I. -I.. -I./.. -I./../h    -g -O2 -Wall -funsigned-char
-c dc.c
gcc -DHAVE_CONFIG_H -I. -I. -I.. -I./.. -I./../h    -g -O2 -Wall  funsigned-char
-c misc.c
gcc -DHAVE_CONFIG_H -I. -I. -I.. -I./.. -I./../h    -g -O2 -Wall -funsigned-char
-c eval.c
gcc -DHAVE_CONFIG_H -I. -I. -I.. -I./.. -I./../h    -g -O2 -Wall -funsigned-char
-c stack.c
gcc -DHAVE_CONFIG_H -I. -I. -I.. -I./.. -I./../h    -g -O2 -Wall -funsigned-char
-c array.c
gcc -DHAVE_CONFIG_H -I. -I. -I.. -I./.. -I./../h    -g -O2 -Wall -funsigned-char
-c numeric.c
gcc -DHAVE_CONFIG_H -I. -I. -I.. -I./.. -I./../h    -g -O2 -Wall -funsigned-char
-c string.c
gcc  -g -O2 -Wall -funsigned-char  -o dc  dc.o misc.o eval.o stack.o array.o
numeric.o string.o ../lib/libbc.a
make[2]: Leaving directory `/tmp/bc-1.06/dc'
Making all in doc
make[2]: Entering directory `/tmp/bc-1.06/doc'
make[2]: Nothing to be done for `all'.
make[2]: Leaving directory `/tmp/bc-1.06/doc'
make[2]: Entering directory `/tmp/bc-1.06'
make[2]: Leaving directory `/tmp/bc-1.06'
make[1]: Leaving directory `/tmp/bc-1.06'
```

Depending on the size and complexity of the program you are building, make's output might be extensive. In the example shown, you see the final compiler invocations and, most importantly, no errors. Accordingly, the next step is to test the build.

TESTING THE BUILD

Many programs, especially those from the GNU projects, include some sort of test suite to validate the program. The idea is to make sure the program works properly *before* installing it. In some cases, you execute the command make test to run the test suite. In other cases, as with bc, a special subdirectory of the build tree, conveniently named test or Test, contains the test suite. Each package handles testing slightly differently, so read the package documentation. In the case of bc, the test suite lives in a subdirectory named Test, and a shell script named timetest performs the actual test. In this case, timetest evaluates how long it takes bc to perform certain mathematical calculations, but it also serves to ensure that bc built properly. The following commands invoke bc's test suite:

```
$ cd Test
$ ./timetest
```

timetest takes at least ten minutes to run, so have a cup of coffee or whatever your favorite beverage is while the test runs. If no errors occur during the test, you are ready to install it.

INSTALLING THE SOFTWARE

In the case of bc, as with many, many other programs installed from source, installing the built and tested program is simply a matter of executing the command make install in the build tree's base directory (/tmp/bc-1.0.6, in this case). More complex programs might have additional commands, such as make install-docs to install only documentation, that break up the installation into more steps or that perform only part of the installation. Still other packages might use scripts to perform the installation. Regardless of the process, however, the goal is the same: install program executables and documentation in the proper directories, create any needed subdirectories, and set the appropriate file ownership and permissions on the installed files.

In the case of the bc package, the installation command is a simple make install, as shown in the following:

```
$ make install
...
/bin/sh ../mkinstalldirs /tmp/bctest/bin
mkdir /tmp/bctest
mkdir /tmp/bctest/bin
  /usr/bin/install -c  bc /tmp/bctest/bin/bc
...
```

```
make  install-man1
make[3]: Entering directory `/tmp/bc-1.06/doc'
/bin/sh ../mkinstalldirs /tmp/bctest/man/man1
mkdir /tmp/bctest/man
mkdir /tmp/bctest/man/man1
 /usr/bin/install -c -m 644 ./bc.1 /tmp/bctest/man/man1/bc.1
 /usr/bin/install -c -m 644 ./dc.1 /tmp/bctest/man/man1/dc.1
...
```

The output, edited to conserve space, shows the creation of the installation directory, /tmp/bctest (recall the --prefix=/tmp/bctest command line option passed to configure), a subdirectory for the binary (/tmp/bctest/bin) and the subdirectory for the manual pages, /tmp/bctest/man/man1. The output also shows the invocation of the install program that actually performs the installation. The -c option is ignored because it is used for compatibility with install programs used on proprietary Unix systems. The -m option sets the file permissions using the octal permission notation. So, -m 644 makes the files bc.1 and dc.1 (which are manual pages) read/write for the file owner and read-only for the file group and all other users.

For more information about the install program, read the manual page (man install) or the TeX-info page (info install).

At this point, package installation is complete. Although this example of building and installing a package from a source tarball is simple, the basic procedure is the same for all packages: unpack the source archive, configure it as necessary, build it, test the program, and then install it. One final exhortation before proceeding to the next section: *read the documentation*! Most software you obtain in source code form includes one or more files explaining how to build and install the software — I strongly encourage you to read these files to make sure your system meets all the prerequisites, such as having the proper library versions or other software components. The documentation is there to help you, so take advantage of it and save yourself some frustration-induced hair loss!

Building and installing source RPMs

In the simplest case, building and installing software from SRPMs requires one or possibly two commands. The same unpack/configure/build/install procedure described in the previous section takes place, but RPM handles each of these steps for you. In this section, you will learn how to use the two command cases (building and installing an RPM), how to invoke each step of the RPM build process, and how to use Gnome-RPM to build an SRPM.

As you learned in the section titled "Building RPMs," the general form of the command to build a binary RPM from a source RPM is

```
rpm -b[stage] specfile [...]
```

Any one of the values listed in Table 23-7 is a valid value of *stage*:

TABLE 23-7 VALID BUILD STAGES FOR RPM'S –b MODE

Stage	Mnemonic	Meaning
p	Prep	Unpacks the source code and applies any patches
l	List	Makes sure all the package files exist
c	Compile	Compiles the source code
i	Install	Installs the files
b	Binary	Builds only a binary RPM
s	Source	Builds only a source RPM
a	All	Builds both binary and source RPMs

Stages are executed in the order listed, and later stages require preceding ones, with one exception. That is, the l (list) step, for example, cannot be performed before the p (prep) stage, and the b (binary) stage happens after the p, l, c, and i (prep, list, compile, and install) stages have been completed. The exception is that building a source RPM (the s stage) does not require first building a binary RPM.

Note that the install stage of the RPM build process does not mean that files are moved into the working file system. Rather, files are "installed" in their proper paths underneath RPM's build directory. For example, if RPM's build directory is /var/tmp/myrpm, the files /usr/bin/foo and /usr/man/man1/foo.1 would be installed underneath /var/tmp/myrpm, so their complete paths would be /var/tmp/myrpm/usr/bin/foo and /var/tmp/myrpm/usr/man/man1/foo.1. This step is necessary because of the way binary RPMs are built and how RPM installs them.

The following two commands illustrate building the mount-2.10 binary RPM from its corresponding SRPM (and assumes the SRPM is already installed using the instructions in "Installing RPMs" earlier in the chapter).

```
# cd /usr/src/redhat/SPECS
# rpm -bb mount.spec
Executing(%prep): /bin/sh -e /var/tmp/rpm-tmp.59234
```

```
+ umask 022
+ cd /usr/src/redhat/BUILD
+ cd /usr/src/redhat/BUILD
+ rm -rf mount-2.10r
+ /bin/mkdir -p mount-2.10r
+ cd mount-2.10r
+ /usr/bin/bzip2 -dc /usr/src/redhat/SOURCES/util-linux-
2.10r.tar.bz2
+ tar -xf -
...
Wrote: /usr/src/redhat/RPMS/i386/mount-2.10r-5.i386.rpm
Wrote: /usr/src/redhat/RPMS/i386/losetup-2.10r-5.i386.rpm
Executing(%clean): /bin/sh -e /var/tmp/rpm-tmp.86539
+ umask 022
+ cd /usr/src/redhat/BUILD
+ cd mount-2.10r
+ rm -rf /var/tmp/mount-root
+ exit 0
```

The build process generates quite a bit of output, most of which was deleted in the output listing. The SPECS directory contains the spec (presumably, short for *specification*) files that control RPM's build process. The rpm command shown uses -bb to build a binary RPM using the instructions in the mount.spec file. As the initial few lines of output shows, RPM first decompresses the archive file, using bzip2 (which uses a more efficient compression algorithm than gzip), and unpacks the archived files using tar. Additional steps apply any necessary patches, configure the package as necessary, invoke the build process, and then "install" the files as explained previously. The following two lines appear near the end of the output listing:

```
Wrote: /usr/src/redhat/RPMS/i386/mount-2.10r-5.i386.rpm
Wrote: /usr/src/redhat/RPMS/i386/losetup-2.10r-5.i386.rpm
```

They indicate that RPM created two binary RPMs, mount-2.10r-5.i386.rpm and losetup-2.10r-5.i386.rpm, in the /usr/src/redhat/RPMS/i386 directory. First, how can one SRPM produce two binary RPMs? This is simply one of RPMs features. More importantly, *why* would it do so? Typically, one SRPM results in multiple binary RPMs because the binary RPMs are related, but not closely enough to put all of the programs into a single RPM. In this case, losetup and mount are related so the packager put them in the same SRPM. However, someone installing mount may not need or want losetup, so it was put in its own RPM.

 TIP You do not have to cd into the directory to build an RPM. You could just as well use a full path name in the command, for example, rpm -bb /usr/src/redhat/SPECS/mount.spec.

Once the packages are built, you can install them as you would any other binary RPM, as the following command illustrates:

```
# cd ../RPMS/i386
# rpm -ivh mount-2.10r-5.i386.rpm losetup-2.10r-5.i386.rpm
Preparing...              ########################################### [100%]
   1:losetup             ########################################### [ 50%]
   2:mount               ########################################### [100%]
```

You can also build an RPM in stages by specifying one of the earlier stages. Although this is typically an exercise package builders perform when debugging a binary RPM, you can do the same. For example, the following command executes only the prep (p) stage against the mount SRPM:

```
# rpm -bp mount.spec
```

The next command stops the process after the compile (c) stage:

```
# rpm -bc mount.spec
```

Again, using the build stages in this manner is not something end users usually need to do, but the capability is there. Note also that the results of one incomplete build invocation overwrite the results of a previous one. Thus, if you execute rpm -bp foo.spec, somehow change the unpacked files, and then execute another rpm -bp foo.spec, you will lose your changes.

Using RPM with source tarballs

As it happens, you can also use RPM to build binary RPMs from source tarballs. The key requirement is that the tarball *must* contain a spec file in order for RPM to know how to build the binary RPM. Software developers who are not familiar with RPM often provide a spec file in their source packages for the benefit of users who prefer to use RPM to build and install software. Indeed, this is a considerable benefit for users of RPM-based systems because building and installing source tarballs bypasses RPM completely — RPM does not track dependencies or requirements of packages installed from source tarballs, so using a spec file embedded in a tarball offers a very handy way to avoid this possibility.

To use this feature specify -t[stage] instead of -b[stage], where stage is one of the options listed in Table 23-7. So, for example, to build a binary RPM from util-linux-2.10r-5.tar.gz using an embedded spec file named util-linux.spec, use the following command line:

```
# rpm -tb util-linux-2.10r-5.tar.gz
```

This technique is especially useful if you would like to create an SRPM from a tarball for later reuse and, as noted, is an invaluable tool for maintaining an accurate an up-to-date RPM database.

Summary

This chapter covered a lot of territory. You learned how to use each of RPM's major operating modes, including querying the RPM database, installing, upgrading, and removing RPMs, and performing RPM maintenance. You also learned a variety of methods for obtaining the version information of installed software. The chapter also listed some popular software repositories and how to use them, and discussed a variety of methods for downloading software. Finally, you learned how to build and install software from source using both the traditional tools (`tar`, `gcc`, `make`, `install`) and RPM's higher level interface to these tools.

Part V

Security and Problem Solving

IN THIS PART:

Maintaining a secure system is a critical area of concern for system administrators. This part addresses security basics, local security, Internet security, and detecting intrusions. The final chapter provides solutions to problems you may encounter in your work as a system administrator.

Chapter 24

Security Basics

IN THIS CHAPTER

◆ Introducing basic security principles

◆ Thinking about security as loss prevention

◆ Understanding the cracker mind-set

◆ Formulating a security policy

◆ Finding additional security resources

◆ Creating a recovery plan

"Security isn't a tangible thing, it is applied psychology."
Alec Muffett, author of the `crack` *password cracking program*

BEFORE DIGGING INTO the practical, nuts and bolts, how-to, hands-on elements of system security, you need to understand the underlying principles of system security. Although the popular perception of security rightly focuses on fending off and recovering from deliberate, malevolent attempts to compromise a Linux system, security also involves protecting against accidents and establishing a recovery plan that restores an exploited or otherwise damaged system as quickly and as safely as possible. Moreover, the better you understand how crackers think and operate, the better you are able to protect your systems and your data from ne'er-do-wells. This chapter attempts to survey the basic principles that should inform any attempt to secure a Linux system and to describe the methods crackers use to defeat security measures.

Introducing Basic Security Concepts

The general subject of computer and network security is usually subdivided into two basic categories: host-based security, and network-based security. Most of the high-profile media attention of late has focussed on the latter, where blackhats and whitehats contend with each other for the public's attention. As a result host-based security often gets short-shrift, a circumstance the next chapter aims to rectify. Any given host can benefit from a number of measures that leave it far less likely to be the scene of a future compromise. Most of these measures are surprisingly simple, so much so that there is little excuse for not implementing at least some of them on practically every system in use within the organization.

Computer and network security is often a series of judgement calls and a matter of layering incremental defensive measures. The quality of these judgements can never exceed the importance an organization assigns to security matters. Ultimately, success or failure hinges on a series of value judgements of the worth of the organization's assets. Typically, system administrators cannot make these judgements because such decisions are properly the purview of management staff. Nevertheless, as a system administrator, you *can* help by clarifying exactly what assets are at stake, what threats they are under, and what defenses (along with their costs) are available. A great deal can be accomplished through effective marshalling of evidence; if you are willing to spend time working up your data into a form useful to your managers. Then they will be all the more likely to heed your opinions as to what is important and what isn't.

Network-based security is a huge topic, and only a few essentials can be covered here. As noted, keeping in the house what should not leave may turn out to be a greater challenge than keeping out what should not get in, and hopefully the reasons for that are clear in the chapter devoted to network security. The discussion of security topics finishes up with a chapter devoted to detecting intrusions. This subject spans both host- and network-based security, with different kinds of tools and different aims coming to the fore in each case. The question of how to respond once an intrusion has taken place is never an easy one, and I offer a few pointers in that area also.

What is the appropriate frame of mind for approaching the task of securing a computer network site? Paranoia is counter-productive because it wastes resources on inessentials. Panicky anxiety is not helpful either because it usually just produces paralysis, a fearful inability to act. Rather, the proper mindset to adopt is to seek the elusive middle of the road. A great deal of native curiosity about everything, compounded with *a degree* of suspicion and *a degree* of being somewhat on edge all of the time also helps. You should have a smidgen of pessimism too, a willingness not to be surprised when the worst possible outcome indeed becomes *the* outcome. Then the balancing act becomes how to avoid slipping backwards into general cynicism, which unfortunately lives just next door to paranoia. A passion for learning can carry you a long way because there is never a shortage of new things to learn in this neighborhood.

Security as loss prevention

Unfortunately, two dangerous misconceptions pervade the popular view of computer security. The first of these is that the only really secure computer is one not connected to any network. Nothing could be farther from the truth, as you learn when you read Chapter 25. The other mistaken belief is that computer security is primarily a matter of holding at bay legions of crackers, often referred to as *blackhats*. Although these personages have captured popular imagination, and some, such as Kevin Mitnick, have been romanticized as inequitably victimized antiheroes, don't be misled or deceived: the dollar losses attributable to cracker exploits are anything but romantic.

Data can be lost and services interrupted as a result of malicious action brought about by many others besides the cracker. At the top of the list might be the disgruntled former employee who, when discharged, carried several passwords out the door. Of course, it is not only former employees who can become disgruntled. Personnel still on the payroll can disseminate company data to the competition, or simply post it for the entire world to see. Indeed, keeping what belongs in-house actually *in the house* is much more likely to be more of a concern on an ongoing day-in, day-out basis than keeping the blackhats and script kiddies out. As for keeping the wrong people out, do not be misled by popular media to think that only mad scientists and rambunctious adolescents want to get in for the sake of the thrill or for subculture status that accrues to those who succeed with notorious *sploits*, as they are called in that subculture. Depending on the nature and value of the data and services comprising a given site's assets, attacks may be forthcoming from rather serious individuals, perhaps in the service of industrial or political espionage, and also to satisfy motives that remain unknown.

OOPS, I DIDN'T MEAN TO DO THAT
Accidents and mistakes account for a huge proportion of costs due to data loss and service interruptions. While some accidents or similar events appear to be outright negligence, more are simple mistakes born of ignorance, and even more still are outright mistakes. Attributing to malice what can instead be attributed to stupidity is often unwise. From the standpoint of a security administrator, or a system administrator charged with maintaining system security, the point is that the more randomness in an event, as opposed to deliberate intention on the part of a human being, the more difficult it is to defend against the given threat. For example, mechanical failures, which cannot be predicted with any degree of reliability, frequently can only be defended against by building redundancy into the hardware where feasible and desirable. Human error is another matter, in that it can be mitigated through training and anticipated to some degree, but only up to a certain point, beyond which even human error is as unpredictable as any machine's. Again, discussing how to anticipate and defend against both hardware failure and human fallibility occurs in the next chapter.

ACTS OF GOD, SO-CALLED
And what of flood, earthquake, civil insurrection and the like? How many threats found under the rubric "act of God" should fall into the purview of a computer security policy and security analysis? The answer here, as in many other places throughout this chapter, is, "It depends." On *what* does it depend? Until we arrive at a better understanding of exactly what the term "secure" means, it is difficult to say. The fundamental notion underlying all four security-related chapters in this book is that the definition of "secure" is not amenable to technical considerations only, but involves a number of factors any one of which at certain times can be assessed only via an act of *judgement*.

For now, though, the following definition should serve as a solid starting point. "Secure" should always be taken to mean *"strengthened with regard to this installation, configured in this manner, against these possible threats, as far as these data, operations, or services are concerned, as long as these specific measures and practices are adopted and maintained, according to the best of our knowledge of current realities, and in light of all sorts of unforeseen and unforeseeable contingencies."* You are correct if you observe that there are a lot of qualifications in this definition, but the temptation to oversimplify security concerns is widespread and, potentially, catastrophically costly.

As if to underline the second misconception mentioned earlier, that the task of the computer security analyst is mostly to fend off exotic hacker cult members, the Sans Institute recently compiled a list of "The Seven Worst Security Mistakes Senior Executives Make." It ranked relying primarily or solely on a firewall as number four on the list of seven. Computer security is much more than network security, and installing a given piece of firewall software never finishes the job of hardening a site, regardless of the claims made by the software vendor.

The last section of this chapter, "Finding Security-Related Resources," includes a link to the Sans Institute Web site.

Security: a distributed venture

Having just claimed that there is much more to computer security than network security, I must acknowledge that the Internet's phenomenal growth has put a whole new face on things. Using one compromised computer as a remote launch site for attacks on yet other computers is not a new technique – all self-respecting crackers leave back doors in all the machines they have compromised so that they can carry out further depredations from those machines rather than their own. The advent of distributed denial of service tools, which can trigger hundreds of these remote back doors simultaneously, has upped the ante so dramatically that it is no longer an overstatement to say that going online with an insecure machine makes one, at the very least, rather an irresponsible netizen. Even if, for the sake of argument, you could care less about the data you store or the operations you perform on your own system, if you connect to the Internet and pay no attention at all to what passes in and especially out of that system, then you increase the risk for everyone connected to the Internet. *That* is rather a new twist on netizenship, as it signals the beginning of the end of rugged individualism on the Internet.

Indeed, as broadband Internet access for individuals becomes the norm rather than the exception thanks to DSL and cable modems, some ISPs, bowing to consumer pressure, have rewritten their EUAs (End User Agreements) so that there is no longer explicit language forbidding the use of servers, such as Web and e-mail servers, on residential accounts. Instead, they contain vague mutterings about "excessive traffic" or "interfering" with others' use of the network. One consequence of this more relaxed (and, no doubt, profitable in the short term) attitude combined with the notion of irresponsible Internet citizenship was evident during the Code Red infestations of July and August 2001. Hundreds if not thousands of home users of cable networks, especially those with routable Internet addresses (as opposed to masqueraded or translated ones), provided an enormously fertile ground for Code Red traffic. For at least one cable system, the final solution was found only by shutting off port 80 (HTTP) on every residential account in the network. The resulting drop in ARP and HTTP traffic on that network was startling and virtually instantaneous.

The news here is not good, amounting to "ask not for whom the bell tolls." The mixture of elements is highly volatile: the Internet's future rests on increased security awareness in the face of the proliferation of insecure servers in the hands of everyday consumers hard wired to routable IPs in the presence of increasingly sophisticated worms, viruses, and trojans. In particular, one wonders how the implementation of the next generation Internet addressing scheme, IPv6, will fare under these increasingly bizarre conditions.

The fundamental mindset: shades of grey

The previous section suggested that security assessments, or the lack thereof, are fundamentally acts of judgement, rather than, say, evaluations based on the application of a discrete set of black and white rules. One might say that estimating the degree of a site's security is an analog, not a digital, process. That is, a site is not simply secure or insecure, but exists along a continuum ranging from less secure to more secure. This chapter dwells on this notion of security as an iterative process or a journey because security is radically different in kind from almost all the other parameters that a network operator might have to consider. You can quantify the traditional considerations of a system or network administrator, such as bandwidth, storage capacity, power requirements, CPU utilization, and you can evaluate in unambiguous terms the needs and capacities of a given system. Further, such evaluations can be the subject of comparisons from one system to another, or to a group of systems. Where security is concerned, though, you have no such luxury.

Secure and *insecure* are designations that have meaning *only* in a particular setting, under particular conditions, and, most importantly, only in light of specific decisions, usually made beforehand, about what constitutes acceptable levels of risk and acceptable tradeoffs between the cost of security measures and their anticipated benefits. Typically, managers make risk tolerance and cost/benefit analyses about the worth of assets, not engineers or consultants. The more deeply the system administrator comes to understand and embrace the conditions relevant to her site's security needs, the better she will be prepared to navigate the difficult, irksome, but all-important battleground where management and technical administration go head to head.

As a system administrator, particularly in a business or professional setting, your managers will likely put a lot of accountability but little responsibility in your hands. Being able to articulate clearly and convincingly that "intangible" quality Alec Muffett mentioned in the quote that opened this chapter, the nature of security matters, to your managers in terms that even they can grasp is your ace in the hole.

Not that there are any guarantees in these affairs, but if *you* are clear about the nature of the beast, you will be that much more likely to communicate that nature to those in authority, and communicate you must. Conversely, if you fail to comprehend the nature of the threat and how to meet it, you will not be able to convey this to your managers.

Understanding the enemy

One way to appreciate the psychological nature of the security game is to consider an imaginary attacker. Suppose this malevolent character possesses infinite technical skill; there is no firewall, no cryptography, and no operating system bag of tricks that this cyber-criminal cannot defeat *given enough time*. But, being human after all, there is only so much frustration the attacker can tolerate. Sooner or later one of two possible outcomes prevails: either the attacker succeeds, or the attacker moves on in search of easier, less frustrating prey. When this moment is reached in any given case is beyond anyone's guess, but one thing is certain: any attacker if delayed long enough will move on.

For some would-be assailants, this moment could come very early in the chase. It may arrive, for instance, when the blackhat determines that a given network's operating system is of a certain kind or that a network supports only encrypted traffic and none other. Because many of the most dangerous attacks do not come over the network wire, some intruders might be discouraged when they learn, for instance, that they cannot sweet-talk any receptionist, secretary, or telephone operator into giving them information about the network when they pose as a consultant. Well-trained staff are easy to spot; they always refer *all* questions or requests about the firm's computing systems to a full-time system administrator.

Visitors to a facility who are up to no good might lose interest when they notice that not one single monitor has a yellow sticky attached to it bearing a password. Perhaps they will notice that no computer in clear view seems to have a floppy drive installed. Maybe they have gone through the trash out back long enough to learn that only shredded paperwork (and no old computer manuals!) winds up there. You simply cannot predict what measure, when followed consistently, will prove to be the last straw that convinces a given marauder to move on. This is the point. As a system administrator charged with maintaining security on your systems, you are dealing with endless variations on shades of grey, and what might be appropriate 24 x 7 x 365 in one department would be ridiculous overkill in another.

Developing a Security Policy

An effective security policy will do several things, all related to the meaning of the term *secure* as used in this chapter. Recalling that definition, a security policy will reflect decisions made relative to factors that include:

1. The value of the organization's data, processes, and services to the organization, its customers, and to unknown others, such as potential customers, competitors, and business or strategic partners

2. The degree, intensity, and skillfulness of attacks that might be directed against that data, the business processes, and services

3. The costs of securing systems to various degrees of hardness commensurate with points 1 and 2, plus the costs of maintaining security at those levels

To begin, a security policy should state in concrete terms each of the items enumerated. This is a large task, even for a small organization, since smaller organizations generally have fewer resources that can be allocated to what might seem a non-productive and labor-intensive task. The tendency is to call in the consultant, but beware the software or hardware vendor who, coincidentally enough, offers security consulting along with those wares. Odds are you will buy a canned solution, and, probably worst of all, a false sense of security. Vendors target the anxiety that computer security concerns raise in most sensible people, and what all too many are selling is an emotional fix, a nice warm feeling of being safe now. This is not the mindset that should attend to security concerns. Somewhere between panic and complacency there is a proper middle ground wherein one is always a bit on edge, a bit skeptical about everything that parades before one's eyes, and always curious about the unusual.

Beware the security assertions ploy

Even if you avoid the canned solution approach, you ought to view other products in the security marketplace with extreme skepticism. Often the very term *security policy* suffers a supposed upgrade to security assertions. *Security assertions* are typically impressive looking documents, presented in designer three-ring binders emblazoned with rather attractive logos that contain little more than customized versions of the canned solution. The one-size-fits-all approach of the canned solution is not the problem here. Rather, the problem is that even though the specific operations of your organization have been worked into the contents, and some basic measures and practices spelled out, the net result remains a dead document that could very well migrate to the nether reaches of that bookcase behind you that holds catalogs and manuals from the past five years.

These security assertions are little more than expensive exercises in collective deniability. If security planning begins and ends with the three-ring binder, the result is fairly predictable. When trouble strikes and losses occur, the claim will be, "Well, we followed the security policy! It must be defective." Moreover, the consultants who authored the document will be well prepared to demonstrate how, within the terms of their consulting contract, they exercised due diligence preparing the security assertions, and could not possibly be held liable for what transpired. We have finally arrived at the crux of the matter, where management frequently draws the line and says, in so many words, "You've got to be kidding. There's no way we can budget any time or money for security planning as an ongoing continuous process. Either we have a plan, or we don't."

If this is management's mindset towards security, you would do well to learn so early in the game, for a couple of reasons. First, this is precisely the attitude that purveyors of canned solutions and fancy security assertions look for and hope to find as often as possible. It is their gravy train. Neither will they want to tell you up front that, where security policies are concerned, there is more to review and revise than an item on the agenda of a meeting that may or may not be held every month, if that often.

The bitter pill here, at least for those responsible for keeping costs in check, is this: a security policy is not an object, but a process. The three-ring binder ideally should be dog-eared and coffee-stain ridden. It should always be open on someone's desk. Indeed, periodically it ought to be reprinted so that all the notes placed in the margins can be made readable for everyone. *Antistasis*, or constant change, needs to be the spirit of a security policy. The good news is that since the recent high-profile exploits, typified by Code Red, you will not find it difficult to make the case that someone needs to constantly monitor not only the current state of threats and reported incidents, but also the latest information regarding newly discovered vulnerabilities and whatever fixes or patches that may have been released for them. With all these caveats in mind, you are ready to begin the initial how-to for security policies.

Creating the policy: a first iteration

The first task is to make lists, lots of lists. Make lists of assets, processes, services, threats, and costs. Why? So you know what you have to protect and, therefore, how stringent a security policy to create.

ASSETS

What assets need to be secured? This list should contain both objects (physical and virtual), and processes, that is, operations, services, tasks and the like. Examples of objects to include on this list are:

- ◆ Computer hardware
- ◆ Stored data and system backups
- ◆ Technical manuals
- ◆ Security documents, audit reports, and the security policy itself
- ◆ Equipment configuration records
- ◆ Original software media
- ◆ Power backup equipment
- ◆ Network cabling
- ◆ Keys

Some examples of processes and services are:

◆ Data processing and a statement of desired uptime

◆ E-mail communications (privacy, authenticity)

◆ Periodic data and system backups and the intervals at which they are performed

◆ Communication channels, such as telephone, fax, radio, or satellite, and a statement of desired uptime

◆ Software updates (upgrades, patches)

◆ Security reviews/audits

When you've completed your list, try to prioritize each item according to worth or value. You might consider an item's cost-of-replacement, including ancillary losses; that is, what will the loss of this item bring down with it? Also make a first *estimate* at ranking assets according to degree of exposure to loss; how at risk is each item currently, to the best of your knowledge?

THREATS

Listing potential threats is an endless affair, especially for one endowed with the degree of pessimism and fatalism (or paranoia) needed to make a good security officer. Examples of what might be on this list are:

◆ Loss of Internet connection

◆ Loss of power

◆ Computer failure (drives, power supply, boards, connectors, and so on)

◆ Network cable failure

◆ Theft of passwords — sure, you do not allow yellow stickies on monitors, but what about the 3 x 5 index cards taped to the underside of desk drawers?

◆ Script kiddies running a probe or attack script

◆ Skillful attacker attempting to gain root privilege

◆ Unauthorized person wandering into server room and trying Ctrl+Alt+Delete at the database server's system console

◆ Use of a system for unauthorized activity

◆ Personnel changes, especially key personnel — what and where *are* their passwords?

◆ Burglaries, fires, floods, tornadoes, hurricanes, earthquakes

◆ E-mail viruses/macros

- Release of confidential company information to a Usenet group

- Industrial espionage compromises proprietary company data

- Your site is targeted for a distributed Denial of Service attack

- Social engineering

- Bugs or other defects in mission critical proprietary or open source software

- Use of unauthorized — or worse, unknown — software, servers, and workstations

This list is never complete. As with the asset list, the list of possible threats should be ranked according to several different factors. What does the list look like ranked according to the worth, such as the replacement or repair cost, of the asset threatened? Next, try to rank the threats in order of their likelihood of occurrence. Essentially, one needs to wonder, "How realistic is this particular threat?"

Cataloging potential threats and assessing the value of the organization's assets can be a daunting task, so consider spreading the work of creating these lists over several weeks, during which you can invite different staff members to take a try at it. Your maintenance staff may be able to give you a best grasp of the reliability of the power supply from the pole in the street, as well as the physical security of the plant. On the other hand, third-shift system administrators can tell you whether or not the night cleaning staff props the back door open with a broom for hours at a time. Ask some of the administrative assistants in private and off the record exactly what kind of paperwork is shredded before being discarded. A security policy needs to reflect a rather complete picture of everything that transpires within the organization.

COSTS

Listing and prioritizing assets and threats and then comparing the lists will, over time, produce a cross tabulation of the most valuable assets that are at the greatest risk. At this point one can begin to assess the cost of implementing preventive *and* recovery measures. Also, getting the big picture into perspective should be near to hand, since now it ought to be evident that fire or the loss of key personnel can be far more damaging than a denial of service attack, the spread of a virulent virus, or a successful root compromise.

The goal of cost analysis is a set of data that can be presented to management so that *they* will be able to account for the expenditures you want them to authorize. The essential determination, for each threat and its target asset, is simplicity itself: which is larger, the value of an asset that is lost or the cost of avoiding that threat? The value of the asset should be prorated according to the probability that it will be in fact lost during a given time period plus the cost to replace it. After the most crucial threats — the ones most likely to occur and do the most damage — have been identified, cost/benefit figures can be produced for defending against them. Management needs to know they are getting the best value for each dollar they allot to security measures.

Trust Whom? Trust What?

One way to grasp the essentially incommensurable nature of risk in computer security considerations is to read Ken Thompson's classic paper "Reflections on Trusting Trust" in *Communications of the ACM*, vol. 27, No. 8, August 1984, pp. 761–763, online at `http://www.acm.org/classics/sep95/`. Thompson describes the construction of a compiler that, when used to build a new compiler, produces one that will, according to whether a given pattern is or is not matched in a piece of source code, introduce a given bug into the resultant binary. The bug could be a bug in the `login` command that enables a user named `dilbert` to login, for example. This evil compiler will always build a bona fide — but tainted — C compiler binary from pristine, unaltered compiler source code, and that build will not throw errors when the bug-introduction feature is compiled in.

The point? What source code and which binaries should you trust? Thompson offers this:

> "The moral is obvious. You can't trust code that you did not totally create yourself. (Especially code from companies that employ people like me.) No amount of source-level verification or scrutiny will protect you from using untrusted code. In demonstrating the possibility of this kind of attack, I picked on the C compiler. I could have picked on any program-handling program such as an assembler, a loader, or even hardware microcode. As the level of program gets lower, these bugs will be harder and harder to detect. A well installed microcode bug will be almost impossible to detect."

The idea here is not to instill panic, but to encourage a realistic grasp of the big picture. Here again, you are confronted with this fundamental truth: a skillful-enough attacker will *always* succeed if given enough time. There is no such thing as a site that has been secured, as if that is the end of it. One needs to be comfortable working with all those shades of grey. Only then will the method of building incremental layers of security, *some quite small in and of themselves*, make sense.

The policy itself

Thankfully, there is no one-size-fits-all recipe for creating the security policy itself. Some are quite short, laying out in essence the company's philosophy with regard to security, the orientation and fundamental working assumptions that ground all further security decisions and initiatives. Policies cast in this format are frequently published with extensive addenda that lay out standards and procedures on a more detailed level. Do not bury the principal security assertions in a maze of technical details.

I need to address one final essential ingredient of a good security policy. Such a policy must leave no doubt as to who is responsible for the safety of a given asset.

This element ought to be carefully worded, and the language of blame *must* be avoided. Every asset addressed in the policy needs to have an owner or a responsible party identified. Indeed, depending on the nature of the asset, there might be need for a chain of command. Simply indicating where the buck finally stops may not be sufficient; some of the intermediate stops might have to be enumerated. These types of questions merge imperceptibly into the domain usually covered by operations manuals, but there is no avoiding certain sorts of questions that arise regarding any asset or threat:

◆ In the absence of an asset's primary responsible party, who covers? Have the owners of the most valuable assets left documents or instructions indicating who should carry on and what must be done in their absence or incapacity?

◆ If a given threat appears to escalate, is there a clear point in that escalation when the asset's owner must be notified?

◆ Is there fuzziness about responsibility and authority? Is it clear who *must* do what, and who *can* do what?

◆ Documentation: of what, by whom, how often, reviewed by whom? Are we saving logs? Which ones? For how long?

◆ Periodic Security Audits: of what, how often, performed by whom, with what documentation, reported to whom?

Obviously this sort of thing can go on pretty much forever; there is no end to the questions that can be raised in a hypothetical vein. I have been stressing that security decisions are exercises of judgement rather than, say, logical conclusions derived from indubitable presuppositions. One such judgement will be about when the sort of questioning I have just indulged in should grind to a halt, at least as far as the preparation of the security policy is concerned. Of course, highly valued assets and credible threats merit answers carved in granite, as the saying goes. For instance, if only for purely academic reasons, you might want to ensure that the logs or databases produced by intrusion detection system (IDS) programs are saved for some considerable period of time. It is very early in the game of defending against distributed denial of server (DDoS) attacks, and it is easily within the realm of the feasible that IDS logs will prove valuable in learning more about the detection and analysis of such attacks. Similarly, some workstations ought to have their `syslog` facility configured to save considerably more `wtmp` files than is the default, with provision for backing up these files before they are rotated and/or deleted. A lot of common sense is called for: the system administrator certainly has enough tasks on any given day to make tweaking system logging settings on run-of-the-mill workstations a very low priority task indeed — which of course assumes you are clear on *which* workstations *are* run-of-the-mill!

Chapters 25 and 26 discuss IDS programs and DDoS attacks and how to defend against them.

Recovery plans

Many aspects of computer security get taken for granted, and recovery planning is one of them. Pursuing such a task can seem almost self-evident, but all too often the actual scenario is not thought through beyond, for example, a simplistic "reformat the drive and reinstall the system from the backup tape." Also, it is likely that recovery plans do not form part of the security policy *per se*, but rather belong in a standards and practices or policies and procedures manual. The owner of each asset ought to be responsible for seeing that an up-to-date and workable recovery plan is in place, and that it is available on-site to personnel faced with the job of implementing the plan should it become necessary.

Again, the emphasis on this facet of planning may appear unwarranted; it perhaps seems obvious that plans need to be kept up to date. One or two imaginary scenarios can help flesh out the possibilities here, and the need for attention to details. As the old saying goes, the devil is in the details, and that is perhaps nowhere more true than in the formulation of plans for recovering from disasters.

A hard drive on a key server crashes, rendering data irretrievable in the short term and the server useless until the disk is replaced. The plan might seem simple: replace the drive and get on with things. Simple, that is, to all except the weekend staff responsible for implementation! Some idle reflection easily turns up pitfalls, any one of which can delay the successful outcome of the plan:

◆ Is the make, model and part number of the drive documented anywhere, or will the box have to be opened and the drive pulled to find these things out?

◆ Is there a record of which vendor should be contacted for the replacement drive? Will the weekend staff know where this record is kept?

◆ Has anyone thought to check periodically whether the drive is still manufactured and still stocked by the vendor?

◆ Are the accounts with those vendors active? If not, who is going to pony up a company credit card? And can *that* person be reached on the weekend, and if not, who can?

Such problems arise with deadening regularity. In and of themselves, they are not insurmountable, but in the context of getting uptime back for a system that may be losing thousands of dollars for every hour of downtime, they become incredibly irksome hassles, to put it mildly. Ask the weekend staff.

Consider another all-too-common scenario: that hundred-year blizzard hits this year. A city plow takes out the pole in front of your building, and the power goes. For the sake of argument, assume your connectivity to the Internet backbone is still up, having been safely secreted underground, that you were generous in spending on UPS equipment, and that you even went the extra mile and bought enough on-site generator capacity to keep your primary server farm up and running. Here are some questions:

◆ Who owns a four-wheel drive vehicle? Since telephone poles are down all over the place, who has the cell phone numbers of those who *do* own four-wheel drive vehicles?

◆ Has a "phone tree" been set up to get news of the storm to the staff due in Monday morning? What about that office manager you fired last month? Is she still on the phone list?

◆ Is anyone charged with the job of testing that generator? Is there more than one person available who knows anything at all about it? Will you have the means to get that person to the job, if the need arises?

◆ As for the UPS's — is there provision for monitoring their condition? If so, have you followed up to ensure that monitoring has been documented?

◆ How much fuel for the generator have you planned on? How is it stored? Has the fire department been in for an inspection lately, or don't they know about that fuel storage? Have you wondered what your insurance carrier might have to say about that?

Yes, you are supposed to think these things through; that's why you get paid the big bucks, right?

You can easily see how at some point a bit of comic relief is needed. Once again, as a system or network administrator, you will find yourself confronted with problematic situations over which you had no authority, and over which in all likelihood you do not *want* any authority. Ideally, your expertise here will be, again, to communicate to management the nature of the problem, and if possible, quantify the cost/benefit picture for them. Thus, expending a lot of resources creating recovery plans for those assets already protected by elaborate defenses may not make as much sense as working on plans to recover those assets where the cost/benefit outcome went against a lot of protection.

Of course there will be key assets that merit both extensive recovery planning and defensive measures. The trick here is to realize that, *in general*, assets left unprotected because it would not be cost-effective to protect them will *probably* need more thorough recovery plans than those which have the benefit of expensive defensive measures. If this chapter has a moral, if you take nothing else away from it after reading it, this is it: the most weighty decisions are going to have to be *judgement calls.*

Social engineering

The cracker community sometimes refers to social engineering as *wetware hacking*, where wetware is cynical shorthand for human being. Unfortunately, the easiest point of entry in an organization that may budget tens or hundreds of thousands of dollars a year on the technical pursuit of computer security may be through an employee who has not been adequately educated in the ways of the digital confidence artist. Further, the really sly cracker knows that vulnerable employees are not found only in the word processing pool or answering the 800-number phone lines. A carefully crafted approach to middle or senior management can, if successful, reap huge rewards for the intruder.

WETWARE TECHNIQUES 101

At its simplest, social engineering could be nothing more profound than simply phoning someone with a question or two. Quite a few companies list employee's full names on their Web sites, so that even if confronted by one of those dreadful "If you know your party's extension you may dial it at any time; press the pound key for the company directory" recordings, a caller can get all sorts of people on the phone. Social engineers know that most people want to be helpful and want you to like them; this human characteristic is their stock-in-trade. Traditionally, confidence tricksters played on another human motive, greed; that is rarely helpful now to the social engineer because social engineering plays upon more contemporary anxieties: needing to be accepted and having self-esteem.

After you are on the phone talking to them, it can be all downhill: "Hello Shania, my name is Archibald, and I'm the new system administrator here at WidgetsGalore Inc. I'm having a lot of trouble getting oriented, so I need to check with everyone whether or not they're using the correct password for their accounts. So, if you don't mind, may I ask you what your password is? According to my records it's 'elvis'; is that right? Ok, thanks; and you're spelling that c-l-o-o-n-e-y, all lowercase? Thanks again. One last thing, your username is shaniat; is that correct? Thank you so very much; you've been very helpful. What's that? Oh, you're MORE than welcome. You sound like a very interesting person too. Let's do coffee sometime. Have a nice day."

A variation on this scenario might be for the social engineer to send an e-mail to anyone at your organization whose e-mail address falls into the wrong hands — and make no mistake, e-mail addresses are splattered all over the Web, as the proliferation of spam flooding your e-mail inbox should confirm. The e-mail could say something like: "Hello, I'm Archibald, the system administrator here at WidgetsGalore. We recently had a hacker break into our computer system, so we need to ask everyone to change their password. In the interest of increasing our network security, you have been assigned a new, special, randomly generated password. Your new password is: r578yw3r. Please open the settings menu on your workstation and change your password to this new one. Thank you so very much, and we are sorry for this disruption of your work day!"

Yes, both of these tactics have in fact worked, many times!

What's wrong with this picture? You cannot expect Shania to understand that Unix system administrators never need to ask anyone for their password. Nor can you expect Shania to know that Unix system administrators cannot (for the most part, there are exceptions) determine what password is currently being used on any account. More than likely these subtleties about Unix system administration are lost on quite a few middle managers. Create an education campaign, and build refresher courses into it. Mounting this campaign can be a tricky business, because few people consider themselves stupid and react poorly if made to feel so. Indeed, arguably the most frequent complaint lodged against "techie" system administrator types is that they do just that: talk down to staff members.

One approach is to focus the primary subject matter *on the network and system administrators themselves*. That is, educate staff as to just what the administrators do, what they are there for, in so many words. This approach keeps the focus off of the staff members; they feel less under the gun. Fewer sentences should begin with "You" and more should begin with "I" and "We." You can easily underestimate what effects can issue from such a shift in emphasis. People are, as a rule, sufficiently intelligent to draw conclusions if the data is presented clearly in a non-threatening way. Your presentation might go something like this:

"WidgetsGalore wants warm and helpful people representing the company on the front lines of the 800 number phones. That's why you are here, because you are that kind of person. It will not be news to you that not everyone who calls is in fact a good person. All you need to do is page us if you feel that a caller is asking just a few too many questions of too inquisitive a nature about the internal workings of the company, especially the company's computer and network facilities. Such a caller could seem to be an employee or even part of management; they might know that employee's name and quite a bit about the personal life of that employee. Remember, no employee or manager should ever call your number asking about computer accounts; every employee was given the phone numbers of the system administrator's office to use in the event there is a problem such as a lost password. Also, remember that *we* will never under any circumstances call you and ask you for your password or username."

ADVANCED WETWARE TECHNIQUES

The previous examples depicted the basic paradigms of social engineering. The possible variations are, obviously, endless. For instance, some crackers will go to extraordinary lengths to learn as much as possible about an employee, in order to pose either as that employee or as someone in that employee's life. Many companies post far too much information about their personnel on the Web. Usually this is an effort to impress potential clients with the quality of people working for the company.

For example, it is now trivial in many cases to gain in a very short time an astounding amount of information about someone's personal life: where they went to school, including graduate school, undergraduate, and high school. Given the ubiquity of Web sites and the astonishing amount of information available on the Web, alumni records can be searched for home addresses, maybe even home phone numbers. Depending on how illustrious a given employee is in her local community, a search of hometown newspaper articles can yield all sorts of personal goodies.

Remember that office paper shredder? Is it used? Some security policies require shredding anything from the office on paper that gets thrown into the trash. Why? Consider all those pink telephone message slips. Only one or two of those could give a bad person all the entrée they need to get a social engineering foot in the door.

When a cracker has enough information in hand, crafting a scenario around which to build a telephone calling campaign is trivial. Such a campaign might involve several calls to all sorts of places. It is not all that hard; use your imagination! Scenarios can be built around any sort of everyday "bump in the road" event: my car broke down, I missed the flight, the babysitter cancelled, my wife went to the ER, the police called, and I have to meet them at the office, the school nurse called, and I have to pick up my kid — right now, I forgot to pick up the laundry, my house burned down (probably too dramatic), my dog died, and so on *ad infinitum*. Given a talented, motivated social engineer, one who has done some homework, any one of these seemingly preposterous premises can be parlayed into a system compromise. It happens all too often. And it keeps happening. The end result is usually the same: someone is manipulated into being helpful, and information is given out over the phone that enables the cracker to gain the desired access.

Finding Security-Related Resources

Here are some organizations every security-minded person should know about, along with a brief list of readings.

Web sites

The following Web sites are some of the premier sources of security-related information on the World Wide Web.

- ◆ CERT

  http://www.cert.org/

  The CERT Coordination Center is the single most authoritative body that disseminates information concerning computer and network security. CERT engages in training and publishing, and maintains an important e-mail list for the circulation of security advisories and summaries. CERT advisories are issued as new vulnerabilities surface, but usually only when patches and/or workarounds have been made available for all effected systems. CERT does some of its most important work behind the scenes, gathering and collating incident reports, and analyzing vulnerabilities and exploits. CERT strives to maintain the highest possible standards of reliability in the information it releases.

◆ BugTraq

http://www.securityfocus.com/

To quote their Web site: "BugTraq is a full disclosure moderated mailing list for the *detailed* discussion and announcement of computer security vulnerabilities: what they are, how to exploit them, and how to fix them." Bugtraq thus has a different, but complementary, mission than CERT. Security items frequently first see the light of day on bugtraq. In general however the information found there is not as reliable as that issued by CERT. It comes in sooner, and as a consequence is likely to be a tad shaky at times.

◆ Sans

http://www.sans.org/

The Sans Institute's primary business is training and certification of security professionals, but they offer a large assortment of resources, including e-mail lists of various sorts. They also produce http://www.incidents.org, a site noteworthy for its Internet Storm Center. Sans is required reading for anyone charged with responsibility for security matters. They offer information of extremely high reliability, and are always abreast of the current security scene.

Recommended reading

Here are a few book-length studies of computer and network security:

◆ *Practical Unix and Internet Security* (O'Reilly, 1996), Simson Garfinkel and Gene Spafford

Some consider this book outdated, but it is still the granddaddy of all security books.

◆ *Security Engineering: A Guide to Building Dependable Distributed Systems* (Wiley, 2001), Ross Anderson

◆ *Real World Linux Security: Intrusion Prevention, Detection, and Recovery* (Prentice-Hall, 2000), Bob Toxen

Links

Just a sprinkling of various and sundry pages. All good stuff. Not necessarily Linux-specific. Not in any particular order. Check 'em all out!

- RobertGraham.com

  `http://robertgraham.com/`

  All kinds of really good security information

- Gibson Research Corporation

  `http://grc.com/`

  Steve Gibson's site contains a wealth of threat analyses and measures you can take to mitigate them.

- Security Archive

  `http://security-archive.merton.ox.ac.uk/`

  This archive combines postings to security-related mailing lists, including the Bugtraq, CERT, linux-security, linux-alert, rootshell, and security-discuss and security-audit mailing lists.

- 2600

  `http://www.2600.com/`

  Crackers stuff, but provides valuable information into the way that crackers think and operate.

- Whitehats

  `http://www.whitehats.com/`

  Whitehats.com is an online community resource for those — including network and security administrators — who are interested in network security.

Summary

This chapter staked out the basic lay of the land of computer security, and delineated its fundamental nature. Social engineering exemplifies the nature of the subject matter. Computer and network security is not primarily a technological challenge, but a managerial one. This fact can be either good news or bad news for the system administrator. The good news is that if one learns how to communicate effectively with management, there is at least the possibility that a really effective cooperation can be brought to bear on security issues. The bad news is that some organizations seem unable to come to terms with reality, regardless of how effectively that reality is conveyed to them. Any given system's degree of security will always lie on a continuum that ranges from less secure to more secure. Estimating the position of a given system on this continuum is an exercise in judgement, not the outcome of the application of a set of technical metrics.

Chapter 25

Implementing Local Security

IN THIS CHAPTER

- ◆ Exploring the nature of physical security

- ◆ Working with boot security

- ◆ Maintaining user and password security

- ◆ Securing file integrity

- ◆ Securing services

THIS CHAPTER ADDRESSES the security questions that fall into the *host-based security* category. The measures suggested here are not as flashy as their network-based cousins, but, in their own prosaic fashion they are no less necessary to the task of hardening a network installation.

Host-based security refers to two related activities:

- ◆ Defending against threats to a given individual computer that do not come in over the wire, but arise from how that particular host is used or misused, quite apart from any network connection it might have.

- ◆ Detecting at the level of that particular host's operation any evidence of compromise from any source, either local (host-based) or remote (network-based).

Network-based security, on the other hand, covered in the next chapter, refers to defending against any threat a given computer is exposed to as a result of being connected to a network, particularly those threats that might come in *via* a network (primarily the Internet). Network-based security also refers to protecting a connected group of hosts from threats that arise out of system-wide factors, such as the network's topology or layout, the design of its firewalls, proxies, and so-called demilitarized zones (DMZs), and the network's use of certain protocols, encryption and so forth.

A *DMZ* refers to one or more publicly accessible hosts that are outside the protected or private network and thus more exposed to attack by crackers and other Internet ne'er-do-wells.

As suggested in Chapter 24, on a dollar-for-dollar basis, losses due to incursions from remote sources on the Internet for the most part pale in comparison to the losses that issue from other, mostly internal or local sources. You can have the finest firewall or virtual private network technology money can buy, but your efforts are for naught if, for instance, password handling becomes sloppy. More than one high-profile commercial Web site co-location facility has suffered serious compromise because an administrator was less than scrupulous in safeguarding a password.

It is also worth repeating that, considered individually, some of the measures described in this chapter may seem, perhaps not trivial, but of very little conse- quence. Recall, however the point made repeatedly in the previous chapter: *there is no predicting at what point an intruder navigating a series of defensive measures grows weary of the chase and moves on to new targets.* An observant eye can quickly pick up many of the telltale signs that announce, "Here is an installation that suffers from careless site security." Conversely, a well-run site ought to broad- cast to all comers: "Don't even *think* about playing games here; you're wasting your time." The gestalt you want to accomplish can be created only by attending to one detail after another. In host-based security, vigilant monitoring is the nature of the beast.

Exploring the Nature of Physical Security

Physical security involves protecting a system, as much as possible, against the dif- ferent sorts of loss that might come about as a result of someone having physical access to your computer. Such losses come not only from the black hats, but also from others who might have a right to be in the building but who do not have any business touching a server or workstation. In a similar vein, physical security includes protecting against certain undesirable behaviors, whether mistaken or intentional, on the part of those who should be working at those machines.

Physical security ranks very near the top of any list of "Most Neglected Security Issues." It is potentially a huge subject because, depending on the value of the assets under consideration, it can extend from alterations of the power supply wiring inside a computer case to fundamental building construction considerations. Disabling the power and reset buttons on the front of a computer case can, in some situations, be thought of as part of physical security. At the other extreme, physical security might involve hiring a building inspector to survey the condition of a party, or shared, wall inside your building. Most of this spectrum is outside the scope of this chapter. The goal here is to raise consciousness regarding the potential scope of physical security concerns and to address a few selected measures that hopefully have wide applicability.

Building construction

Buildings new and old each have their own native pitfalls for a truly secure computer installation. Here are some examples of problem areas:

◆ The expensive new Halon fire extinguisher system is just great: it will not drown any electronic components. But what about the plumbing in the bathroom down the hall? How high off the floor should your servers be to stay above the high-water mark should a pipe burst?

◆ You have renovated a loft in an old mill building to house your new dot-com. What about the suspended ceilings? Do the new office partition walls extend only up to them, or do the walls connect to the old original ceiling? What about those raised floors beneath your feet? About those shared walls: you may be fairly certain they are intact in the floors you are occupying, where there is no evidence of alterations to the original wall, but has anyone gone into the basement and looked at them? From *both* sides? It is truly amazing how small a hole a dedicated person can pass through!

◆ You have refused to accept any "temporary" network cabling, right? Take the cost hit now and be certain all cables are at the very least in ordinary conduit. Do you have any really "fat pipes" (very high bandwidth) running out of the place? Consider the cost/benefit picture of putting them in pressurized double-walled conduit or some other type of armored protection.

◆ You have no control over your backbone connection once it hits the street, but what about that manhole in your company parking lot or the one in the corner behind the dumpster, where it cannot be visually checked from the street, or from the building? Odds are better than average that it is not locked and can be popped open with an ordinary pry bar.

◆ The salesman says the safe you bought to house your backup tapes is fireproof. What does "fireproof" mean in the safe business?

◆ As noted in Chapter 24, what about the night cleaning crew, and the back door they use?

The list is of course endless. Your site must undergo its own examination of conscience, so to speak, to determine whether or not it has kept faith with the organization's decisions about assets and their value. Clearly at some point, as the value of these assets rises, further costs have to be incurred because few technology-based companies have the requisite in-house civil, mechanical, and electrical engineering capabilities to see to it that faith is kept with those assets. If there is company data on a piece of tape that could do hundreds of thousands, if not millions of dollars, of damage should it fall into the wrong hands, how sane is it to keep that tape under conditions that have not had the best loss-protection engineering that money can buy?

Boot security

Perhaps "Reboot Security" would be a more apt title for this section. Alas, there are many ways to coax a computer into rebooting itself when only one is really wanted: a system administrator with the proper permissions or privileges, tradition-ally the superuser, who enters the command to do so. `shutdown`, `halt`, or `reboot` should not be commands available to every user with an account on the system. Nor should anyone strolling by the keyboard or computer case be able to easily accomplish these tasks. From the standpoint of the security administrator, it is pru-dent to assume that anyone with physical access to a computer will sooner or later, or, perhaps, sooner *rather than* later, gain root access to the machine. The aim here is push that event towards the "later" end of that scale.

Some of the vulnerability to unauthorized shutdown or reboot can be remedied only by changing the wiring of the power and reset switches inside the computer case, unless it happens to be a rack mounted unit, where the design has in all like-lihood taken care of these vulnerabilities. Rack mounts are of course easier to secure physically because their design permits building them into enclosures with no exposed power or data connectors.

THOSE OTHER DRIVES
Most PCs can boot from their floppy and CD-ROM drives, so you should think about how this vulnerability ought to be handled. For some machines it makes sense to simply remove the drives and replace them with blank panels. Many net-worked machines can do without a CD-ROM drive. As for the floppy drive, although it is useful for rebooting during a troubleshooting session, for some systems the tradeoff of the loss of this convenience is a good one. Nothing says, "Go away. You cannot get anywhere on this system." quite as persuasively as a computer case with no visible drive doors. Frequently, though, the easiest, although not the best, approach is to simply disable removable media drives from the system BIOS, and, depending on the particulars of the computer under consideration, install a BIOS password. The latter step might depend, for example, on the location of the computer, the kind of foot traffic common in that area, the value of the machine's contents or purpose, and the potential usefulness of its network connection to an intruder.

TIGHTENING UP RED HAT LINUX
Unfortunately, Red Hat Linux ships in a default condition that gives `poweroff`, `halt`, and `reboot` ability to any logged-in user. Happily, this condition is easily reversed with the following three commands:

```
# rm /etc/security/console.apps/poweroff
# rm /etc/security/console.apps/halt
# rm /etc/security/console.apps/reboot
```

You may prefer renaming these files to deleting them, so you have a reminder of taking them out of action. While you are at it, take a look at the other files in /etc/security/console.apps, keeping in mind their purpose: giving ordinary console users access to the commands with the same name as the files. You might want to think about removing more of these. Some of these do require the root password, but it is also worth finding out which ones, if only as an exercise in increasing your overall security consciousness.

The next thing to eliminate is the Ctrl+Alt+Delete method of rebooting. This procedure requires editing /etc/inittab. To eliminate *all* use of this keystroke combination, simply comment out the line that begins with ca:

```
# Trap CTRL-ALT-DELETE
#ca::ctrlaltdel:/sbin/shutdown -t3 -r now
```

This change does not take effect until you execute the following command:

```
# telinit q
```

You don't need to reboot. telinit can be thought of as "tell init" because it acts as a communication link to init. Notice the unusual syntax; there is no hyphen preceding q. Executed like this, with just the q, telinit prompts init to reread its /etc/inittab file.

If you are in the mood to be helpful, consider substituting another command for Ctrl+Alt+Delete, such as the following:

```
#Trap CTRL-ALT-DELETE
ca::ctrlaltdel:/bin/echo "Ctrl-Alt-Del has been disabled. Sorry."
```

This inittab entry can be fine-tuned so that only select users (and root, of course) can use the three-fingered salute. First, add the -a option to the command line in /etc/inittab:

```
# Trap CTRL-ALT-DELETE
ca::ctrlaltdel:/sbin/shutdown -a -t3 -r now
```

Next, create the file /etc/shutdown.allow containing the name of the user authorized to activate Ctrl+Alt+Delete. For instance:

```
# echo bubba > /etc/shutdown.allow
```

The behavior now is: if bubba or root is logged in on any console, then anyone currently logged in can use Ctrl+Alt+Delete. If you try this use of the -a option, be sure to test your results, because the logic is quirky and a bit counterintuitive. A safe bet is to make root the only user listed in /etc/shutdown.allow. Then, Ctrl+Alt+Delete is enabled only if root is logged in, a condition not satisfied by a merely mortal user employing su to become the root user.

X DISPLAY MANAGERS

If you opted for a graphical login screen, that is, one of the X display managers, xdm, gdm, or kdm (the choice depends on which desktop you selected when you installed Red Hat Linux), then you have to make some adjustments, or, perhaps better yet, back out of that login mode and revert to an ordinary virtual console login process. To back out, try simply changing the default runlevel in /etc/inittab from 5 to 3 and rebooting.:

```
id:3:initdefault:
```

Why disable the graphical login? X display managers typically exhibit two kinds of security problems. In some configurations, a menu of usernames (or faces) is presented, but this offers the whole wide world information it just does not need to have. There is simply no reason to offer a list of valid usernames to anyone, particularly the intrepid social engineer discussed in the previous chapter, who might happen by and do a bit of *shoulder surfing*, that is, look over someone's shoulder as they log in. Indeed, early in the development of the Unix password system, observant people noted that the login procedure inadvertently revealed to any user whether or not a given username was a valid user on the system. It did so because only the passwords of valid users would be compared via encryption to the contents of the /etc/passwd file. Checking passwords of only valid users produced a noticeable difference in the time required, say, for the login prompt to return after a valid user entered an incorrect password, compared to the time needed when an invalid username was followed by any password. The fix was obvious and it has stayed with us: the passwords entered for all usernames, valid and invalid, are sent through the same encryption and comparison process so no time differential appears between the two cases.

The thoughtful reader with experience on Unix and Linux systems rightfully and immediately asks, though, "What is the gain when any user on the system can simply execute the following command and get a listing of every directory under /home, and, hence of every valid user name on the system?"

```
$ cd
$ ls ../
```

The answer has two parts. First, it matters quite a bit less if user names are revealed to another user, who has a valid account and a password and is *already known to the system* than it does to reveal that information to someone who has no access at all (yet!). There are always users who insist on creating what are called *joeys*, users who use their user name, or simple-minded variations thereof, as their password. Here are a few of the common twists on this theme, taken from some of the rules used by crack, a password-guessing program discussed in greater detail later in the chapter.

◆ Reverse: "Fred" becomes "derF"

◆ Duplicate: "Fred" becomes "FredFred"

◆ Reflect: "Fred" becomes "FredderF"

◆ Reverse and then capitalize: "Fred" becomes "Derf"

Even a system with only a few user accounts is vulnerable to this sort of lapse. You are prudent to assume that sooner or later all that is needed to gain some kind of access to the system is a valid user name.

The other problem with the graphical login screen is that some X display managers offer reboot and shutdown as options to ordinary users. If you are confronted with a user who is really attached to the X-based login arrangement, then you ought to disable the provisions for halting or rebooting the system that are available in, for example, the gdm login screen under the System drop-down menu. To disable this misfeature, use the following procedure:

1. Start the GDM Configurator by clicking Main Menu → System → GDM Configurator. You need to enter the root password to get in if you are not already logged in as root. Figure 25-1 shows the initial screen.

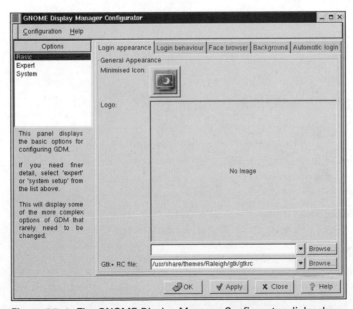

Figure 25-1: The GNOME Display Manager Configurator dialog box

2. Click the Login behavior tab (see Figure 25-2) and uncheck the check box labeled Show the 'system' menu, (for reboot, shutdown, etc.).

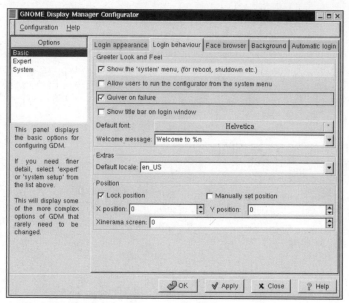

Figure 25-2: The GDM Configurator Login behavior tab

3. Click Apply.

4. Click OK.

5. Click Restart after logout (see Figure 25-3) to put the changes into effect.

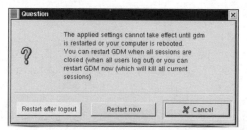

Figure 25-3: Click Restart after logout to activate the change.

Another method here is to use xdm instead of gdm or kdm. The simplest way to change the display manager is to edit /etc/X11/prefdm. If, for example, GNOME is the default desktop, look for the lines (about line 23) that resemble

```
if [ "$DESKTOP" = GNOME ]; then
    preferred=gdm
```

Change gdm to xdm, save the change, and end the edit session. Why use xdm? Because xdm's login screen is a simple, no-nonsense affair with edit boxes for only a user name and password.

Clicking the GNOME main menu button and selecting Logout brings up a dialog box with Reboot and Shutdown options; however, if the preceding steps have been taken, those two options should not have their intended effect, but instead bring back just one to the X display manager login screen. Be sure to test that this is *in fact* the case..

AUTOLOGOUT THE SUPERUSER

Here is a security measure that perfectly exemplifies the strategy of layering incremental levels of protection discussed in Chapter 24. As the system administrator you most likely find yourself using su to obtain root privileges on a fairly regular basis. Also on a fairly regular basis you probably get paged or otherwise called away from your desk for all manner of exigencies. Since it is never possible to predict how long your workstation will remain unattended, it is prudent to arrange for superuser console sessions to automatically log out after a certain period of inactivity.

In the Bash shell the environmental variable TMOUT sets this feature. In $HOME/.bash_profile put a line such as:

```
export TMOUT=300
```

This command sets a timeout of 300 seconds. It is helpful to add a reminder about the setting:

```
echo "Autologout set to 5 minutes!"
```

Users of the C shell (tcsh or csh) can put set autologout=5 in their $HOME/.cshrc file to achieve the same result. Unless otherwise set, tcsh's autologout defaults to sixty minutes, unless the shell detects that it is running in a windowed environment by testing whether or not environment variable DISPLAY is set.

While you have your $HOME/.bash_profile file open in an editor, turn off the $HOME/.bash_history file:

```
export HISTFILESIZE=0
```

Then delete the file ($HOME/.bash_history), if it exists, in your home directory.

WHEEL, SUDO, OR BOTH?

One handy security measure found on most Unix systems is not usually present or, if present, rarely used, on Linux computers: the wheel group. The theory is that making certain crucial system binaries only owner- and wheel group-executable, and then adding only certain users to the wheel group allows the administrator to exercise greater control over the use of superuser privileges. Red Hat Linux ships with a wheel group already created, so all that is needed is to change the ownership and permissions of whatever binaries you desire to place under the control of the wheel group. The following procedure illustrates the process using the su command:

```
# chgrp wheel /bin/su
# chmod 4750 /bin/su
# ls -l  /bin/su
-rwsr-x---  1  root  wheel       18452  Jul 23  12:23  /bin/su
```

Next, add the users you trust with the root password to the wheel group by editing /etc/group:

```
root:x:0:root
bin:x:1:root,bin,daemon
daemon:x:2:root,bin,daemon
sys:x:3:root,bin,adm
adm:x:4:root,adm,daemon
tty:x:5:
disk:x:6:root
lp:x:7:daemon,lp
mem:x:8:
kmem:x:9:
wheel:x:10:root,bubba,marysue,joebob
```

The sudo facility is quite a bit newer than the wheel group, and many administrators prefer it because of its greater flexibility and logging facilities. In its basic operation, sudo first prompts for the user's password (not the root password), and then grants that user superuser privileges for a default period of time, usually five minutes. sudo consults its configuration file, /etc/sudoers, to determine what privileges to grant which users when they invoke sudo.

/etc/sudoers must be edited with its own editor, visudo. visudo utilizes file locking during the edit and performs some syntax checking to minimize errors introduced during the editing session. sudo has a powerful configuration syntax and vocabulary, so you can probably create the necessary set or combination of users, groups of users, commands, groups of commands, and logging options to suit your needs very precisely with a properly constructed /etc/sudoers file. Here is a very simple example:

```
# Host alias specification
# User alias specification
User_Alias GOODGUYS = bubba, suzyque

# Command alias specification
```

```
# User privilege specification
root          ALL=(ALL) ALL
GOODGUYS      ALL=(ALL) ALL
%wheel        ALL=(ALL) ALL
```

This example grants root, bubba, suzyque, and all members of the wheel group complete root privileges. The possibilities are vastly more powerful than this example, and virtually every aspect of sudo's operation, and every compiled-in default, can be altered at run time by editing /etc/sudoers. Time spent with the man pages for sudo and /etc/sudoers is richly rewarded.

A one-size-fits-all solution for controlling access to superuser privileges does not exist. For many installations the relatively simple expedient of a wheel group suffices. Indeed, some will argue that, all other things being equal, simplicity should always carry the day. However some situations call for the increased flexibility of sudo. One example frequently cited is of a group of administrators charged with managing user accounts. These users do not need full superuser privileges, but do need access to a subset of superuser commands, such as useradd, passwd, and others needed to manage accounts.

The discussion of sudo in the context of controlling access to commands such as halt, reboot, and shutdown brings you squarely into the territory of this chapter's next section, which delves further into the management of user accounts and passwords.

Maintaining User and Password Security

The Sans Institute (http://www.sans.org/topten.htm) rates "User IDs, especially root/administrator with no passwords or weak passwords" eighth on its list of "The Ten Most Critical Internet Security Threats." Their trenchant one-paragraph summary cannot be improved upon:

> Some systems come with "demo" or "guest" accounts with no passwords or with widely-known default passwords. Service workers often leave maintenance accounts with no passwords, and some database management systems install administration accounts with default passwords. In addition, busy system administrators often select system passwords that are easily guessable ("love," "money," "wizard" are common) or just use a blank password. Default passwords provide effortless access for attackers. Many attackers try default passwords and then try to guess passwords before resorting to more sophisticated methods. Compromised user accounts get the attackers inside the firewall and inside the target machine. Once inside, most attackers can use widely-accessible exploits to gain root or administrator access.

Two points in that paragraph deserve reinforcement, because many computer users, including even very experienced ones, have never had reason or opportunity to encounter them.

♦ The ease of guessing passwords is truly astounding. Especially impressive are password *cracking* (guessing) programs such as crack or John the Ripper. While these programs basically do no more than guess passwords; they are *very* good at it.

♦ The use of administration or maintenance accounts, along with their default passwords, is truly ubiquitous in proprietary software, especially in database software. Anyone familiar with one installation finds easy entrée to other similar installations that have not been altered from the installation defaults.

After discussing password policy, I offer a few hints for managing user accounts in a security-conscious and conscientious fashion.

Passwords: theory and practice

Nostalgic, quaint, even quixotic, sentiments die hard. Only recently the operator of a rather substantial Unix site had to pull all of his public shell accounts off line due to a rather vicious compromise that mangled quite a few of those accounts. However, reading his commentary on the episode revealed that he clearly was taken aback by the fact that there are people who abuse the privilege of a free, public shell account, even to the extent of tampering with other folks' accounts.

The problem? The administrator had evidently clung to his origins in the early days of Unix, and part of that early Unix culture was a warm, collegial atmosphere in which trust, community, and mutual respect were assumed to be values shared by all users of the system. In those days, the likelihood of incurring community censure and opprobrium were (rightfully, at the time) thought to be adequate disincentives for keeping misbehavior in check. The possibility of deliberate malice was barely glimpsed, so much so that the first Unix implementations had no password facility at all! It was, in so many words, an "add-on."

To set a good password policy you need to make several decisions. First, will users be allowed to choose their own passwords? If so, what limits will you put on their freedom of choice? If not, how will you communicate passwords to users? Will they be able to select from a list of randomly generated passwords, and if so, is there such a thing as a random password generator? What are the pros and cons of randomly generated passwords?

Before you proceed any farther I *highly* recommended that you obtain, install, and take a few practice spins on one of the password crackers available for the Linux platform. Both crack and John the Ripper install fairly easily on any Linux system. These programs take advantage of a couple of linguistic and computing facts of life. First, there is nary a word in any dictionary of any language that has not been scanned into a digitally readable format. Both of these password cracking programs can utilize a huge array of these dictionary files. Second, some very clever programmers have taken it upon themselves to eat, sleep, and drink password guessing for many years now, so there are probably very few methods of permuting dictionary words that they have not thought of and programmed into their password guessing algorithms. If you thought it was pretty slick to spell your dog's name backwards with every other letter made uppercase, and every o transformed into a 0, think again! Such transformations are easy pickings for crack or John the Ripper.

John the Ripper can be downloaded from the Openwall Project's Web site at `http://www.openwall.com/john/`. crack is available via anonymous FTP from `ftp://ftp.cerias.purdue.edu/pub/tools/unix/pwdutils/crack/`.

The advent of shadow passwords, and improvements on the old DES encryption standard used by most Linux systems, made the work of password crackers more difficult. However, these enhancements have been paralleled by increases in computing horsepower and storage capacity. The point of trying out some of the password cracking programs is to drive home just how easy it is to guess passwords, especially short ones. The single greatest benefit of using the MD5 encryption algorithm now installed by default in Red Hat Linux is that passwords up to 255 characters long are now permitted; the old limit was eight. Given this fact it makes sense to think about imposing a minimum password length of greater than the typical six characters found on most systems. Required reading in this regard is the PAM documentation found on your Red Hat Linux installation in `/usr/share/doc/pam-0.75`. Be sure to look at the description of the cracklib module, which uses the same password guessing algorithms as the crack password guesser.

If you are confronted with an unfamiliar computer, you can easily determine if the standard Unix DES password encryption has been updated with MD5, Blowfish, or one of the other more advanced ciphers used for passwords. Look at the `/etc/shadow` file and count the number of characters in the encrypted password field, the first field following the user name. If there are thirteen characters, then you are dealing with the old DES encryption. DES-based passwords are limited to eight characters. Longer passwords are accepted by the system, but only the first eight characters are used. Consider upgrading such a system to MD5 as soon as possible. See Lance Spitzner's excellent paper "Armoring Linux" at his Web site, `http://enteract.com/~lspitz/linux.html`. Red Hat Linux systems can be upgraded via the command line utility setup, which runs Red Hat's Text Mode Setup Utility. The following procedure illustrates the process.

1. Log in or use su to become the root user.

2. Type setup, and press Enter. Figure 25-4 shows the initial screen.

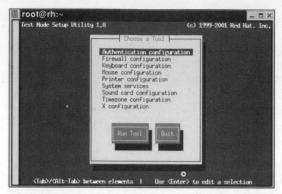

Figure 25-4: The Text Mode Setup Utility dialog box

3. Use the arrow keys to highlight Authentication configuration, press Tab to highlight the Run Tool button, and then press Enter.

4. Skip the User Information Configuration dialog box, pressing Tab until the Next button is highlighted, and then press Enter.

5. Figure 25-5 shows the Authentication Configuration dialog box. The Use Shadow Passwords option should be enabled. If not, press Space to place an asterisk (also called a *splat*) next to Use Shadow Passwords.

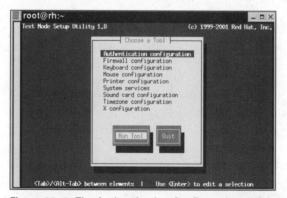

Figure 25-5: The Authentication Configuration dialog box

6. Press Tab to move the cursor to the Use MD5 Passwords option. Make sure it is enabled — if not, press Space to place a splat in the check box next to Use MD5 Passwords.

7. Press Tab until the OK button is highlighted and press Enter.

8. Highlight the Quit button, and press Enter again to exit the Text Mode Setup Utility.

Here is a fairly complete set of do's and don'ts for picking passwords. You can pass them on to your users, and then from time to time run crack or John on your own /etc/shadow file to detect any serious lapses in password selection. Only one moronic password puts the entire system at risk. Some of these rules are based on the rudiments of social engineering, described in the last chapter. Human nature being what it is, you can predict with a great deal of probability that left to their own devices your users gravitate towards passwords related to the eternal themes of sex, love, and money. Try to discourage this tendency if you can!

Now for *The Rules*. Do *not* use any of the following as a password:

◆ Your computer's host name or domain

◆ Your real name according to the computer, or any other such information kept in the password file

◆ The name of your pet or any family member's pet

◆ Your name or nickname, or any family member's name or nickname

◆ The name or nickname of a close friend, or anyone you work with or for

◆ The name of any fantasy, fictional, historical, mythological, or biblical character, book, or author

◆ The name of your operating system

◆ Anybody's name: first, middle or last or any proper name

◆ Any phone number or license plate

◆ Any part of your Social Security number

◆ Any username on the computer in any form (reversed, capitalized, doubled, and so on)

◆ Any place name

◆ Anybody's birthday

◆ Any part of your address, the name of your alma mater, or any other easily accessible information about you

◆ A password of all the same letters or numbers or a pattern of them

◆ Patterns of letters on the keyboard, such as qwerty

◆ Any word found in any dictionary of any language

◆ Any of the previous spelled backwards

◆ Any of the previous followed or prepended by a single digit

◆ Any of the previous modified by simplistic substitutions, such as certain numerals for letters, for example, 0 for O, 1 for l, 2 for Z, 3 for E, 5 for s or S, or 7 for L or T

Do try to:

- Create a password easy for you to memorize

- Use numbers, spaces, and punctuation marks

- Use both upper and lowercase letters

- Use special characters, avoiding @, #, and ?

- Never use less than seven characters

- Invent acronyms based on sayings familiar to you, for instance, "a fool and his money are soon parted" becomes, first, afahmasp, or afah$asp, or 1fAh$Asp.

One of the methods in the previous list, particularly the last one, results in a fairly easy to remember password that would give crack a run for its money.

ABOUT PASSWORD GENERATORS

The very notion of a password generator is problematic. Alec Muffett, crack's author, explains it like this in the documentation in the crack distribution (doc/appendix,v4.1.txt, to be precise):

> "You can't say that a certain method provides secure, random passwords, because, in defining an algorithm to create these passwords, you use only a subset of all the possible passwords that could ever exist. You have shrunk the "search space" for the passwords."

Simply put, using a password generator makes the work of password cracking programs simpler. With Muffett's caveat in mind, you should proceed very carefully if you decide to require users to choose from a set of generated passwords. A number of password generators are available for Linux, but some of them have had problems, and some of them are quite old. Unless you are an accomplished programmer and grasp the difficulties of random number generation, it is more than likely that the best solution is to enable users to create their own passwords, but aggressively restrict the parameters of that choice by using the PAM password modules, and follow that up with routine and frequent scans of your /etc/shadow file with crack or John the Ripper. Perhaps the single most important variable is the length of the password. Consider enforcing a minimum length of up to fourteen characters if you have followed the suggestion made a moment ago to use MD5 password authentication.

USING A PASSWORD GENERATOR

If you are still curious about password generators, install the expect RPM found on the Red Hat Linux FTP site. It installs the original examples written by expect's author, Don Libes, including his classic mkpasswd password generator. This password generator accepts command line arguments (which can be edited into the script itself) that control the length of the password generated, and its minimum number of upper and/or lowercase letters, numerals, and special characters. But interestingly enough, mkpasswd has come under scrutiny lately for the very reason alluded to previously, namely its method of randomizing the passwords it produces.

The bugtraq archive for the first two weeks of April 2001 contains some discussion of this problem and a proposed fix. This material is worthwhile reading, because it typifies the sort of limitation that regularly comes to light in the realm of security software. The constant development of PC hardware has put high-powered computing machinery in the hands of anyone who wants it, and this has brought to light many software shortcomings that, on older hardware, might have taken weeks or months if not years to detect. In the case of mkpasswd, after so many thousands of passwords it starts to repeat itself, turning out the same password more than once. This flaw was a consequence of how the random number generator was seeded, and mkpasswd is not by a long shot the only piece of software that has popped up with this particular shortcoming. A fix similar to that proposed on bugtraq has apparently been applied to the Red Hat version of mkpasswd found in the expect RPM (expect-5.32.2-64-386.rpm).

The bugtraq archive at http://www.securityfocus.com/ is one of the premier sites on the Web for security related issues.

Unfortunately the Red Hat version of mkpasswd does not process command line arguments properly, but this is quickly remedied. Comment out these first three lines from the version of /usr/bin/mkpasswd installed by Red Hat's RPM:

```
#!/bin/sh
# \
exec expect "$0" ${1+"$@"}
```

and insert above them, that is, as the first line in the script, the following line:

```
#!/usr/bin/expect --
```

USING AN ANALOG PASSWORD GENERATOR

Enticing a machine to behave in a truly random fashion is bound to be a challenge, since it goes completely against how we want machines to behave, that is, in a totally predictable manner. At least one method has been developed for using old-fashioned nonmechanical means of producing random events for generating random passwords. Actually, the Diceware (http://www.diceware.com/) method was designed for producing random passphrases for PGP, SSH, Tripwire, and related software, but it can be adapted to turn out passphrases of one word, that is, passwords. A *passphrase* is just that, a phrase used as a password, or, rather, *in place of* a password. All that is needed is a 6 x 6 matrix filled in like this:

```
  1  2  3  4  5  6
1 A  B  C  D  E  F
2 G  H  I  J  K  L
3 M  N  O  P  Q  R
4 S  T  U  V  W  X
5 Y  Z  0  1  2  3
6 4  5  6  7  8  9
```

Suppose your security policy requires ten-character passwords. Put fifteen pair of dice (thirty pieces) in a can, and, after closing the door and pulling the shades on the windows, roll the dice out onto your desk. Group the dice into ten groups of three each, and arrange each group of three in a row. Establish a convention for counting across each row, either right to left, or the reverse. Then simply use the first two dice in each group to identify a row/column pair in the matrix, and use the third die to modify the character found at that matrix location.

For instance, if the third die is even, then for a letter, make it uppercase; if odd, lowercase. If the row/column specifies a numeral, then if the third die is even use the numeral, if odd use a special character. A rule for picking the special character might be: use the character's position in the password to count across the row of number keys on your keyboard and use the special character at that location, skipping the @, #, and ? keys. For the next special character start counting at the next position on the keyboard. You can use endless variations on this example. This method is, admittedly, time consuming, and of course, cannot (or should not) be automated, but it produces highly random passwords that prove very difficult for any password cracker program to solve in a timely manner, that is, before the attacker gives up and moves on to other, arguably more fruitful targets.

The Diceware site also argues persuasively for moving away from passwords altogether. With modern cryptographic algorithms, such as MD5, Blowfish, and others (for instance, one derived from the John the Ripper password cracker), password length now accommodates passphrases. The rationale is that a good passphrase of several words is easier to remember and considerably harder to guess than the typical randomly generated password. Thus, passphrases answer one of the most frequent criticisms of the latter, that it is more likely to be written down, possibly even in a file kept on the computer. And, passphrases are useful in quite a few contexts other than just system access authentication. Symmetric (private key) encryption of files is available in the form of Phil Zimmerman's PGP (Pretty Good Privacy) and GNU's PGP cognate, GPG (GNU Privacy Guard). A good passphrase goes a long way toward ensuring the safety of files encrypted in this fashion.

Those pesky users

Administrative headaches seem to rise in direct, exponential proportion to the number of users on a system. Linux, taking its cue from its Unix forebears, has evolved an impressive array of tools and strategies for keeping track of users. This section can address only a few of the more important of these. The following list identifies a few simple commands for tracking user logins:

◆ users — prints a simple list of the usernames of everyone currently logged on. By default the list is derived from /var/run/utmp. For additional information, see the GNU texinfo pages for the shell-utils package (info shell).

◆ who — prints more data about currently logged-on users (also part of the GNU shell-utils package).

◆ last — prints data about current and recent logins. This data is also derived from /var/log/wtmp. Execute the command last reboot, for example, to view information about the last system reboots. See the last manual page for more information, as this command takes a number of useful options.

◆ lastlog —prints data from /var/log/lastlog about past and current logins. A good deal of system history is available via this command. man lastlog contains useful reference information.

Checking logs

Red Hat Linux routinely, and quietly, logs a huge amount of data during its ordinary operations. Due to the volume of information, the busy system administrator soon confronts the job of filtering the wheat from the chaff, that is, of finding ways to identify and focus on those logged events that deserve attention. Two utilities to a certain degree automate the job of scanning log files for unusual events, logwatch, and logcheck. logwatch is installed by default on Red Hat Linux systems, at least in its router/firewall flavor.

Key to using either of these utilities is setting a proper mail alias for root so that the utility mails its reports to a system administrator (you), not to root's mail spool. Edit the file /etc/aliases, paying particular attention to the following line at the bottom of the file:

```
# Person who should get root's mail
root:       bubba
```

After editing the file, execute newaliases to rebuild the alias database and update the running sendmail daemon with the new alias:

```
# newaliases
/etc/aliases: 41 aliases, longest 10 bytes, 404 bytes total
```

The exact output may vary somewhat on your system. Once this step is done, e-mail sent to the root user is redirected to the named user, bubba in this case.

logcheck and logwatch are similar in some respects but produce, at least in their default settings, fairly different reports. logcheck's configuration is simplicity itself, but, as usual with Linux and Unix software, the more complicated configuration of logwatch permits greater variation and finer control over the reports it generates. Red Hat's binary rpms install `logwatch` to run once daily; `logcheck` runs once every hour. Given the nature of each report, these are reasonable defaults, but they can be changed in the system cron settings. Listing 25-1 illustrates a typical `logcheck` report.

Listing 25-1: An example logcheck report

```
Security Violations
=-=-=-=-=-=-=-=-=-=
Sep  2 18:47:23 rh login(pam_unix)[11196]: authentication failure;
logname=LOGIN uid=0 euid=0 tty=tty3 ruser= rhost=  user=bubba
Sep  2 18:47:25 rh login[11196]: FAILED LOGIN 1 FROM (null) FOR
bubba, Authentication failure

Unusual System Events
=-=-=-=-=-=-=-=-=-=-=
Sep  2 04:02:08 rh syslogd 1.4.1: restart.
Sep  2 11:52:58 rh mc: /dev/gpmctl: No such file or directory
Sep  2 11:52:58 rh mc: /dev/gpmctl: No such file or directory
Sep  2 13:00:42 rh login(pam_unix)[2914]: session closed for user
 bubba
Sep  2 16:58:44 rh login(pam_unix)[867]: session closed for user
 root
Sep  2 18:44:58 rh su(pam_unix)[11519]: session opened for user
 root by wingnut(uid=502)
Sep  2 18:45:02 rh mc: /dev/gpmctl: No such file or directory
Sep  2 18:45:02 rh mc: /dev/gpmctl: No such file or directory
Sep  2 18:47:23 rh login(pam_unix)[11196]: authentication failure;
 logname=LOGIN uid=0 euid=0 tty=tty3 ruser= rhost=  user=bubba
Sep  2 18:47:25 rh login[11196]: FAILED LOGIN 1 FROM (null) FOR
 bubba, Authentication failure
Sep  2 18:47:32 rh login(pam_unix)[11196]: session opened for user
 bubba by LOGIN(uid=0)
Sep  2 18:47:32 rh  -- bubba[11196]: LOGIN ON tty3 BY bubba
Sep  2 18:50:46 clio login(pam_unix)[11439]: session opened for
 user bubba by LOGIN(uid=0)
Sep  2 18:50:46 rh  -- bubba[11439]: LOGIN ON tty4 BY bubba
Sep  2 18:59:16 rh mc: /dev/gpmctl: No such file or directory
Sep  2 18:59:55 rh last message repeated 2 times
Sep  2 18:52:13 rh sudo: ruptured : TTY=tty4 ; PWD=/home/bubba ;
 USER=root ; COMMAND=/bin/rpm -ivh logcheck-1.1.1-4.i386.rpm

From root  Sun Sep  2 19:07:50 2001
```

Several items of information can be gleaned from this report. First, bubba may be having some personal problems, or working too much overtime, since he seems a tad shaky when it comes to remembering his password. Then, Midnight Commander seems to want to find a particular device file for gpm; that might bear a little investigation, especially because gpm is not running on this system. Finally, you can see that bubba *could* recall his password long enough to use sudo to install the logcheck RPM.

Both logwatch and logcheck can be customized to widen or narrow the focus of their reporting. Typically, you want to narrow the focus in order to look at real or potential problems, not administrative noise. The needs of different systems dictate different emphases in what is included, and excluded, from a report. The logs on a server with few ordinary users other than its administrators does not need the same sort of vigilance as the logs on, say, a dial-up server host across the room that provides PPP connections to modem users dialing in from all over the place. Each of these log monitoring programs has its own strengths and weaknesses. One option very much worth trying is simply to run them both. After you review their reports for a week or so, you can make an informed decision about how they ought to be used on a production system.

Securing File Integrity

Tracking the behavior of users leads naturally to the next subject, file integrity security. Some of your users, inevitably, are interested in doing things such as removing all evidence of their movements from the logs that furnish logcheck and logwatch with raw data. A little familiarity with how rootkits do their work sheds immense light on the problem, and for this there is some wonderful data collected by the Honeypot Project, available on the Web at http://project.honeynet.org/. A *honeypot* is a networked host designed to appear vulnerable, and therefore potentially useful, to an attacker. It is a piece of bait, with a hook inside it. Once the attacker is inside the honeypot, his or her every move is recorded, and this data provides an accurate picture of current state-of-the-art cracking tools and methods. The series of white papers, "Know Your Enemy," provide an innovative look into cracker methods and are or should be required reading for anyone who takes system security seriously.

Basic to any attack seeking root privilege are certain file operations. Some files are added, some files are deleted, and some, especially certain crucial system binaries, are replaced with versions supplied by the intruder. These operations are done with sufficient finesse that frequently only a message digest, called a *hash*, of the file, betrays the file's surreptitious character when compared to a hash saved at an earlier time. Several techniques have evolved for taking cryptographic snapshots, rather like a fingerprint, of file systems and comparing the results of later snapshots to an earlier trusted version of the file system. Red Hat Linux ships with one of the oldest of these tools, also known as intrusion detection tools, Tripwire.

Using Tripwire

Tripwire grows on you, and that is a good thing because fine-tuning its policies to fit a particular computer is a trial-and-error process that takes a good deal of time. *Policy* is Tripwire's term for the collection of directories and files it should check when it is run, usually daily, as a cron job. The tuning aims at paring down this collection so that only alterations in really important directories are reported. It's important to keep the fluff level down; otherwise, one grows weary of reading through Tripwire's reports, and that of course is exactly when something bad happens. A couple of handy online Tripwire references are specifically aimed at a Red Hat Linux system:

- `http://www.redhat.com/support/manuals/RHL-7.1-Manual/ref-guide/ch-tripwire.html`

- `http://www.openna.com/community/articles/security/v1.3-xml/sysintegrity.html`

Different, but complementary, approaches are always sort of neat, and these two fit that mold.

Not for everybody, or every computer

Another consideration is where to deploy Tripwire, that is, on which workstations or servers. If a machine is used as a testbed for building complete distributions of Linux, or even substantial components of the Linux userland, then Tripwire overwhelms you with all the changes it reports every day as you rebuild the system, or parts of it. Actually, Tripwire probably does not belong on any workstation that sees intensive duty only as a developmental testbed. If the contents of that machine are that valuable, then by all means install Tripwire, but set up a chrooted environment in which to pursue the developmental work, and configure Tripwire to work around the chrooted directories. Or, work on a stand-alone machine, that is, one not connected to any network, use encrypted file systems, and put under lock and key in several locations daily backups of the file system. You can always find ways to bring adequate measures to bear, where *adequate* means, as explained in the previous chapter, "Commensurate with the dollar cost hit we will take if we lose the contents of this machine, especially if we lose it to the wrong people."

The point bears repeating: avoid at all costs running Tripwire in an environment where it throws a lot of false positives at you. You are only human, and you soon tire of Tripwire's reports on that machine, and that in turn impacts negatively your ability to read any Tripwire reports. It dulls your palate, so to speak. This human foible is a prime example of how security is in reality applied psychology, to cite yet again Alec Muffett's aphorism (See Chapter 24's introduction). Just as attackers, when not successful, tire and grow weary of the chase, so do defenders; *you can burn out*, and you do not need a pile of unread Tripwire reports to help get you there.

Setting up Tripwire

If you installed Tripwire when you installed Red Hat Linux (look for /etc/tripwire), there are a couple of tasks to perform manually before you can leave it to cron to run Tripwire daily. First, run the installation script, /etc/tripwire/twinstall.sh. This script creates the needed encryption keys (be ready to provide three good passphrases), and encrypt the key Tripwire configuration files, tw.cfg and tw.pol, from their text originals, twcfg.txt and twpol.txt. For now, do not delete the two source files when twinstall.sh finishes its run.

Unless you are familiar with Tripwire and its policy files, the best bet is to run the install script on the supplied twpol.txt. This gives you a feel for what Tripwire looks for, and how it behaves when it does not find something. Even your best first guess at a twpol.txt file needs to be tuned to get things right, so you might as well plunge in knowing that you are going to see Tripwire complain that it cannot find certain files on your computer. You see those complaints in the next step.

Run Tripwire in initialization mode, which starts its first trip through your file system, compares what it finds to what is in tw.pol, and creates and encrypts its first database, or snapshot, of the file system. As root, execute /usr/sbin/tripwire --init:

```
# /usr/sbin/tripwire --init
Please enter your local passphrase:
Parsing policy file: /etc/tripwire/tw.pol
Generating the database...
*** Processing Unix File System ***
### Warning: File system error.
### Filename: /usr/sbin/fixrmtab
### No such file or directory
### Continuing...
...
Wrote database file: /var/lib/tripwire/rh.kurtwerks.com.twd
The database was successfully generated.
```

Sit back and watch, because the initial database generation takes a few minutes. You see the odd error message when Tripwire doesn't find a file that tw.pol said would be there. This is nothing to worry about, and you fix this in the next two steps.

The next step is simply to run Tripwire --check mode, that is, manually run Tripwire in just the same way it runs daily by cron, /usr/sbin/tripwire -check.

```
# /usr/sbin/tripwire --check
Parsing policy file: /etc/tripwire/tw.pol
*** Processing Unix File System ***
Performing integrity check...
### Warning: File system error.
```

```
### Filename: /usr/sbin/fixrmtab
### No such file or directory
### Continuing...
...
Integrity check complete.
```

This time, you are likely to see a number of `No such file or directory` messages scroll past. When the program finishes, take a look at the reports Tripwire creates. You find them in `/var/lib/tripwire/report`:

```
# ls /var/lib/tripwire/report
rh.kurtwerks.com-20010905-143305.twr
```

Use the following Tripwire command to view the generated report, replacing the report name appropriately:

```
# twprint -m r --twrfile rh.kurtwerks.com-20010905-144.05.twr | less
```

Fine-tuning Tripwire

Now a bit of work needs to be done to get Tripwire's database and policy file in sync with the file system it is going to monitor. For the first report cycle or two or three, this updating is needed, but thereafter it ought to be only an occasional thing. Tripwire provides commands for this process.

At this point you've run a first integrity check and reviewed the report of that run. Assuming you have a very high degree of confidence in the state of your file system, you should now tell Tripwire, in so many words, "By the way, those things you thought were violations the first time around? They're not." Use Tripwire's `--update` mode to accomplish this:

```
# /usr/sbin/tripwire --update --twrfile /var/lib/tripwire/report/repname.twr
```

Replace *repname* with the name of the report you want to update. This step loads that report into the system editor (usually `vi` unless you have changed it). A check box containing an `x` (see Figure 25-6) appears next to every violation logged by Tripwire. Leave the box checked for every item you want Tripwire to *disregard* in the future; uncheck the check box for those items you want Tripwire to continue to view as violations.

In Figure 25-6, for example, removing the `x` from the box adjacent to `/var/lib/tripwire/rh.kurtwerks.com.twd` instructs Tripwire to flag this file in future integrity checks if it changes again.

At this point you will notice at least two things. First, a surprising number of files may change just in the ordinary course of the day's operations. Second, Tripwire continues to look for, and report as missing, quite a few files mentioned in its policy file. Accordingly, the task now is to edit that policy file, removing mention of files that will in all likelihood never exist on your system. If for some reason they are added to the file system at a later date, Tripwire certainly notifies you of their arrival!

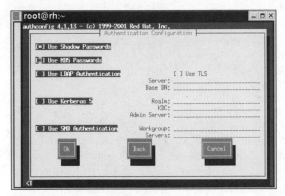

Figure 25-6: Editing the Tripwire report file

In your favorite editor, open /etc/tripwire/twpol.txt, and in another terminal view the latest report using the twprint command. Review every entry in the report that lists a file or directory "not found," and comment out the corresponding entry in twpol.txt. This can take some time, but it is only a one-time procedure. When you complete your edits, save the file and exit the editor. Then, execute the following command to create a new policy file:

```
# /usr/sbin/twadmin --create-polfile -S site.key /etc/tripwire/twpol.txt
```

Create a database from scratch whenever a new policy file is created. First, delete your old database and then initialize a new database:

```
# rm /var/lib/tripwire/luther.kurtwerks.com.twd
# /usr/sbin/tripwire --init
```

At this point the process repeats itself: run an integrity check, review the resultant report, run an update, and repeat the integrity check. At this point you should be able to settle down and see how Tripwire works as it is run out of its cron job every day. You probably want to try out Tripwire's interactive checking feature, which allows you to update your database as the integrity check is run. Most important is the better understanding you gain for how Tripwire works, and for how your computer works. Tripwire affords a unique perspective on the workings of your Linux system. On some hosts you may want to put fairly strong limits on what Tripwire inspects every day, on others you may want to leave Tripwire wide open.

Fine-tuning Tripwire for the particular host it is running on exemplifies the parameters that should guide all security policy: What is the value of the asset under protection? What threats will be leveled against that asset? What defensive resources are commensurate with that value, under those threats? In the event of loss, can the degree of damage be accurately assessed? Tripwire really comes into its own in the latter case, because an up-to-date Tripwire database can mean the difference between repairing some damage here and there, and tossing wholesale the entire contents of a file system. Time spent learning Tripwire in depth is indeed time well spent.

Summary

In this chapter you learned about host-based security, including securing your system against unauthorized reboots, configuring X display managers for better security, and making secure the building that houses a system. You also saw how to implement sturdier user and password security, including using password generators. After examining log checking tools, you learned how to configure and fine-tune Tripwire, a host-based intrusion detection system.

Chapter 26

Firewalls and Internet Security

IN THIS CHAPTER

♦ Limiting network services

♦ Understanding firewall theory, design, and configuration

CHAPTER 25 started the discussion of securing Red Hat Linux systems, focusing on measures most appropriate to securing workstations. This chapter continues that discussion by focusing on security measures that you should apply at the network level, that is, security measures that can protect entire networks of systems using a Red Hat Linux system as the barrier or fence between a protected internal network and the black hats that would like to compromise it.

Limiting Network Services

The first thing to do when securing a Red Hat Linux system is to identify what services are running, what services you need, and what services you do not need. Then you should disable the unneeded services. The term *services*, in this context, refers to the traditional server daemons and programs, such as Apache (the Web server), Sendmail (the mail server), TELNET, or the FTP server, and to lesser known access points, such as open ports for chargen, daytime, X, and so forth. To express it slightly differently, *services* refers to any process that listens on a network port or socket for requests for information or data.

From the point of view of the administrators trying to implement network-based security, they should also be able to determine who is doing what on the system, particularly via a network connection of some sort. This section and the next review some of the configuration files and tools that control running services, that enable you to turn services on and off at your discretion, and that empower you to find out what kind of system activity is taking place on your system, who is doing it, and from where the activity originates.

What services are running?

Like most Linux distributions, Red Hat Linux's default installation procedure leaves too many network services available. Of course, some services were enabled as a result of choices made during the installation process itself. Other services, however, seem simply to be enabled by default, that is, for no apparent reason. "For no apparent reason?" What do I mean by that? Many installations literally have *no* need to make *any* network services available. The typical workstation is probably in this category; it is a consumer of services, not a provider. For example, workstations ordinarily do not need to provide Web, e-mail, TELNET, or FTP services. In the course of this chapter you see how the effort to disable unneeded services works out in practice.

The first step towards limiting the availability of these services is finding out which ones are actively listening. This task is actually twofold, because a service running on a given host might be available to respond to requests originating from the host itself but not to requests from other systems that are connected to it. The potential for security weakness here arises from the fact that the service is on in the first place: Even though it is limited from responding to other hosts on the network by other features of the host's configuration, such as packet filtering or TCP wrappers, these methods of access control can be circumvented and thus become possible points of entry into the system. Therefore, the availability of services ought to be examined both internally and externally, that is, from inside the host itself, from inside the host's trusted network, and from outside the host's trusted network. Part, but not all, of the process of securing a network involves running a port scan from outside your network. The next few subsections explore a few utilities that come into play when performing these port scans — netstat, lsof, and nmap.

USING NETSTAT

netstat is a powerful utility for monitoring and reporting almost every aspect of the kernel's networking functionality and behavior. Most users are familiar with netstat's use to display the current routing table, as shown in the following command:

```
$ netstat -r
Kernel IP routing table
Destination     Gateway         Genmask         Flags   MSS Window  irtt Iface
192.168.1.0     *               255.255.255.0   U       40 0        0 eth0
127.0.0.0       *               255.0.0.0       U       40 0        0 lo
default         mambo.bernice   0.0.0.0         UG      40 0        0 eth0
```

A glimpse at netstat's man page conveys some idea of this command's many different uses, but for current purposes only one or two command line options are required, as listed in Table 26-1.

TABLE 26-1 netstat COMMAND LINE OPTIONS

Option	Description
-r	Displays the kernel routing table
-l	Displays only listening sockets

For instance, to display only listening sockets:

```
$ netstat -l
Active Internet connections (only servers)
Proto Recv-Q Send-Q Local Address          Foreign Address        State
tcp       0      0 *:http                  *:*                    LISTEN
tcp       0      0 *:ftp                   *:*                    LISTEN
tcp       0      0 *:ssh                   *:*                    LISTEN
tcp       0      0 *:https                 *:*                    LISTEN
Active UNIX domain sockets (only servers)
Proto RefCnt Flags     Type      State      I-Node Path
unix  2      [ ACC ]   STREAM    LISTENING  1139   /tmp/.font-unix/fs7100
```

The output from this command indicates that five servers are listening for requests on this host: http, a Web server, ftp, an FTP server, ssh, a secure shell server, https, a secure Web server, and the X font server. This display can be fine-tuned by protocol, showing, for instance, only Unix domain sockets (using the --unix argument with -l), or only Internet (TCP) sockets (using the --inet argument with -l):

```
$ netstat --unix -l
Active UNIX domain sockets (only servers)
Proto RefCnt Flags     Type      State      I-Node Path

unix  2      [ ACC ]   STREAM    LISTENING  1139   /tmp/.font-unix/fs7100


$ netstat --inet -l
Active Internet connections (only servers)
Proto Recv-Q Send-Q Local Address          Foreign Address        State
tcp       0      0 *:http                  *:*                    LISTEN
tcp       0      0 *:ftp                   *:*                    LISTEN
tcp       0      0 *:ssh                   *:*                    LISTEN
tcp       0      0 *:https                 *:*                    LISTEN
```

USING LSOF

This utility's name is an acronym for "list open files," and in Unix and Linux this means "list just about everything." Part of what distinguishes Unix and Unix-like operating systems from all others is that many diverse entities are handled as if they were files. The lsof man page lists a few of these. An "open file" might be a regular file, a directory, a block special file, a character special file, an executing text reference, a library, a stream, or a network file (Internet socket, NFS file, or UNIX domain socket).

The syntax for lsof is at least as arcane as netstat's, but as with that command only a small subset of lsof's options are needed to keep tabs on what services are running. With no options, lsof churns out an impressive amount of data (over sixteen hundred lines):

```
# lsof | wc -l
   1617
```

Again, as with netstat, the trick is to limit this output to what interests you, and the -i option starts you on this path; with it, lsof lists all Internet and x.25 network files:

```
[ruptured-duck@clio ruptured-duck]# lsof -i
COMMAND  PID  USER   FD    TYPE DEVICE SIZE NODE NAME
sshd     677  root    3u   IPv4    980       TCP *:ssh (LISTEN)
xinetd   696  root    3u   IPv4    999       TCP *:ftp (LISTEN)
httpd    750  root   16u   IPv4   1116       TCP *:https (LISTEN)
httpd    750  root   17u   IPv4   1117       TCP *:http (LISTEN)
X       9551  root    1u   IPv4  26045       TCP *:x11 (LISTEN)
httpd   9892  root   16u   IPv4   1116       TCP *:https (LISTEN)
httpd   9892  root   17u   IPv4   1117       TCP *:http (LISTEN)
httpd   9893  root   16u   IPv4   1116       TCP *:https (LISTEN)
httpd   9893  root   17u   IPv4   1117       TCP *:http (LISTEN)
httpd   9894  root   16u   IPv4   1116       TCP *:https (LISTEN)
httpd   9894  root   17u   IPv4   1117       TCP *:http (LISTEN)
httpd   9895  root   16u   IPv4   1116       TCP *:https (LISTEN)
httpd   9895  root   17u   IPv4   1117       TCP *:http (LISTEN)
httpd   9896  root   16u   IPv4   1116       TCP *:https (LISTEN)
httpd   9896  root   17u   IPv4   1117       TCP *:http (LISTEN)
httpd   9897  root   16u   IPv4   1116       TCP *:https (LISTEN)
httpd   9897  root   17u   IPv4   1117       TCP *:http (LISTEN)
httpd   9898  root   16u   IPv4   1116       TCP *:https (LISTEN)
httpd   9898  root   17u   IPv4   1117       TCP *:http (LISTEN)
httpd   9899  root   16u   IPv4   1116       TCP *:https (LISTEN)
httpd   9899  root   17u   IPv4   1117       TCP *:http (LISTEN)
```

This output can be filtered by host, service port or name, or protocol (TCP or UDP), for example:

```
# lsof -i:x11
COMMAND  PID USER   FD   TYPE DEVICE SIZE NODE NAME
X        9551 root    1u  IPv4 26045       TCP *:x11 (LISTEN)
# lsof -i:https
COMMAND  PID USER   FD   TYPE DEVICE SIZE NODE NAME
httpd    750 root   16u  IPv4 1116        TCP *:https (LISTEN)
httpd    9892 root  16u  IPv4 1116        TCP *:https (LISTEN)
httpd    9893 root  16u  IPv4 1116        TCP *:https (LISTEN)
httpd    9894 root  16u  IPv4 1116        TCP *:https (LISTEN)
httpd    9895 root  16u  IPv4 1116        TCP *:https (LISTEN)
httpd    9896 root  16u  IPv4 1116        TCP *:https (LISTEN)
httpd    9897 root  16u  IPv4 1116        TCP *:https (LISTEN)
httpd    9898 root  16u  IPv4 1116        TCP *:https (LISTEN)
httpd    9899 root  16u  IPv4 1116        TCP *:https (LISTEN)
```

netstat and lsof form a powerful team that can examine the workings of the kernel from many different angles. See, for instance, the discussion of using them together in lsof's documentation: /usr/share/doc//lsof-4.51/00QUICKSTART.

USING NMAP

No discussion of detecting network services would be complete without including nmap. Although usually mentioned in the context of probing remote hosts to determine their open ports, nmap can also port scan its own host. A simple port scan looks like this:

```
$ nmap -sT localhost

Starting nmap V. 2.54BETA22 ( www.insecure.org/nmap/ )
Interesting ports on mambo.bernice.org (127.0.0.1):
(The 1537 ports scanned but not shown below are in state: closed)
Port       State      Service
21/tcp     open       ftp
22/tcp     open       ssh
80/tcp     open       http
443/tcp    open       https
6000/tcp   open       X11
Nmap run completed -- 1 IP address (1 host up) scanned in 2 seconds
```

Regardless of the picture of a host's open services one gets from inside that host, the old attitude of "I'm from Missouri; show me!" applies where security is at stake.

After all of the commands just described, sooner or later one needs to assume a vantage point on a remote host and examine from there the state of your network's hosts and services. For that nmap is the ideal tool. Depending on how you configure your firewall, the simple ping scan just described may not be adequate to the task, but nmap is equipped to deal with those situations, which I discuss later in this chapter.

Stopping running services

You should be aware of two general issues regarding services, and, to carry forward a theme already broached in this section on security, neither issue can be resolved via solely technical considerations:

♦ What services should be running?

♦ What access should be allowed to services that are running?

Then, each case can be broken down further. The first question, what services should be running, also involves the more practical issue of *how* to control a given service, that is, how to turn it off and on. The basic answer is that services are controlled either through xinetd, with an initialization script in /etc/init.d/, or both. The follow-up question for the second issue, allowing access to running services, is how to control access to a given service. In this case, the answer is similar: access control is usually applied through xinetd, the access control files used by TCP Wrappers (/etc/hosts.allow and /etc/hosts.deny), or using a service's own access control facilities. Red Hat Linux installs xinetd, an enhanced version of inetd, which adds a great deal of flexibility and that might include features that are unfamiliar to users who have grown comfortable over the years with plain vanilla inetd and TCP Wrappers. Fortunately, the installation defaults selected for the various services and daemons that xinetd runs are such that the transition from inetd to xinetd need not be traumatic. Some services are started out of xinetd, and some are not. For the latter, chkconfig and its companion, ntsysv, form a dynamic duo for managing network services and other system daemons. chkconfig and ntsysv are essentially *run level editors*, tools that provide an interface to the slightly convoluted SystemV initialization script setup. chkconfig, a command line tool, is arguably the more powerful of the two programs, whereas ntsysv presents a simpler, more pleasant menu-driven console interface.

USING CHKCONFIG

chkconfig, in its basic use (chkconfig --list), lists each service named in /etc/init.d and whether that service is enabled (on or off) for each of the seven runlevels (0–6). It also lists each service handled by xinetd and whether that service is on or off. Here is a sample showing the current state of the host I have been using as an example. On this system, only sshd, httpd and ftpd are available to other hosts:

```
# chkconfig --list
ntpd         0:off   1:off   2:off   3:off   4:off   5:off   6:off
atd          0:off   1:off   2:off   3:off   4:on    5:on    6:off
keytable     0:off   1:on    2:on    3:on    4:on    5:on    6:off
rwhod        0:off   1:off   2:off   3:off   4:off   5:off   6:off
kdcrotate    0:off   1:off   2:off   3:off   4:off   5:off   6:off
syslog       0:off   1:off   2:on    3:on    4:on    5:on    6:off
gpm          0:off   1:off   2:on    3:off   4:on    5:on    6:off
kudzu        0:off   1:off   2:off   3:off   4:on    5:on    6:off
nscd         0:off   1:off   2:off   3:off   4:off   5:off   6:off
lpd          0:off   1:off   2:on    3:off   4:on    5:on    6:off
sendmail     0:off   1:off   2:on    3:on    4:on    5:on    6:off
autofs       0:off   1:off   2:off   3:off   4:on    5:on    6:off
snmpd        0:off   1:off   2:off   3:off   4:off   5:off   6:off
rhnsd        0:off   1:off   2:off   3:off   4:off   5:off   6:off
rawdevices   0:off   1:off   2:off   3:off   4:on    5:on    6:off
netfs        0:off   1:off   2:off   3:off   4:on    5:on    6:off
network      0:off   1:off   2:on    3:on    4:on    5:on    6:off
random       0:off   1:off   2:on    3:on    4:on    5:on    6:off
ipchains     0:off   1:off   2:on    3:on    4:on    5:on    6:off
apmd         0:off   1:off   2:on    3:off   4:on    5:on    6:off
iptables     0:off   1:off   2:on    3:off   4:on    5:on    6:off
isdn         0:off   1:off   2:on    3:off   4:on    5:on    6:off
identd       0:off   1:off   2:off   3:off   4:off   5:off   6:off
portmap      0:off   1:off   2:off   3:off   4:on    5:on    6:off
nfs          0:off   1:off   2:off   3:off   4:off   5:off   6:off
nfslock      0:off   1:off   2:off   3:off   4:on    5:on    6:off
radvd        0:off   1:off   2:off   3:off   4:off   5:off   6:off
crond        0:off   1:off   2:on    3:on    4:on    5:on    6:off
anacron      0:off   1:off   2:on    3:on    4:on    5:on    6:off
xfs          0:off   1:off   2:on    3:on    4:on    5:on    6:off
xinetd       0:off   1:off   2:off   3:on    4:on    5:on    6:off
ypbind       0:off   1:off   2:off   3:off   4:off   5:off   6:off
sshd         0:off   1:off   2:on    3:on    4:on    5:on    6:off
rstatd       0:off   1:off   2:off   3:off   4:off   5:off   6:off
rusersd      0:off   1:off   2:off   3:off   4:off   5:off   6:off
rwalld       0:off   1:off   2:off   3:off   4:off   5:off   6:off
vncserver    0:off   1:off   2:off   3:off   4:off   5:off   6:off
yppasswdd    0:off   1:off   2:off   3:off   4:off   5:off   6:off
ypserv       0:off   1:off   2:off   3:off   4:off   5:off   6:off
ypxfrd       0:off   1:off   2:off   3:off   4:off   5:off   6:off
httpd        0:off   1:off   2:off   3:on    4:off   5:off   6:off
squid        0:off   1:off   2:off   3:off   4:off   5:off   6:off
```

```
tux         0:off    1:off    2:off    3:off    4:off    5:off    6:off
rarpd       0:off    1:off    2:off    3:off    4:off    5:off    6:off
linuxconf   0:off    1:off    2:on     3:on     4:on     5:on     6:off
xinetd based services:
        chargen-udp:    off
        chargen:        off
        daytime-udp:    off
        daytime:        off
        echo-udp:       off
        echo:           off
        time-udp:       off
        time:           off
        sgi_fam:        off
        rsh:            off
        talk:           off
        finger:         off
        rexec:          off
        rlogin:         off
        ntalk:          off
        telnet:         off
        wu-ftpd:        on
        rsync:          off
        linuxconf-web:  off
```

That is an awful lot of information for one gulp, so it is handy to pipe the output through grep, looking for on. Because I eschew the use of X display managers and therefore in run level 3, you can make that 3:on. The following command illustrates the fine tuning of the command (note that id does not display the xinetd entries):

```
# chkconfig --list |grep 3:on
keytable    0:off    1:on     2:on     3:on     4:on     5:on     6:off
syslog      0:off    1:off    2:on     3:on     4:on     5:on     6:off
sendmail    0:off    1:off    2:on     3:on     4:on     5:on     6:off
network     0:off    1:off    2:on     3:on     4:on     5:on     6:off
random      0:off    1:off    2:on     3:on     4:on     5:on     6:off
ipchains    0:off    1:off    2:on     3:on     4:on     5:on     6:off
crond       0:off    1:off    2:on     3:on     4:on     5:on     6:off
anacron     0:off    1:off    2:on     3:on     4:on     5:on     6:off
xfs         0:off    1:off    2:on     3:on     4:on     5:on     6:off
xinetd      0:off    1:off    2:off    3:on     4:on     5:on     6:off
sshd        0:off    1:off    2:on     3:on     4:on     5:on     6:off
httpd       0:off    1:off    2:off    3:on     4:off    5:off    6:off
linuxconf   0:off    1:off    2:on     3:on     4:on     5:on     6:off
```

TIP   How can you determine the current run level? It might be 3, but if an X display manager is in use, it very well could be 5. Use the run level command as shown in the following example:

```
$ runlevel
N 3
```

runlevel returns the previous and current run levels. In cases in which there is no previous run level, run level displays an N, as shown in the example.

chkconfig has several modes of operation; the listing mode demonstrated just now is only one of them. Other modes enable chkconfig to add or delete services to the /etc/init.d startup hierarchy or to turn a given service on or off in any of the runlevels. This is a lot of control, most of which is not needed in the ordinary course of events. Only rarely is it necessary to alter the arrangement of symlinks in /etc/init.d — the installation defaults are perfectly adequate for all normal use. To start a service at boot time, or to prevent a service from starting at boot time, use the ntsysv utility, discussed in the next subsection.

NTSYSV

ntsysv provides an interface that permits any of the services listed by chkconfig to be turned on or off in the current run level, the run level in effect when ntsysv was launched. Other run levels can be similarly edited by passing their number(s) on the command line, but great care ought to be exercised in using this feature. As noted, it is the rare situation indeed that calls for altering the default run levels that the various services and daemons install for themselves.

The short answer to the question raised previously, "What services *should* be running?" is "None." If this seems to be an unduly harsh generalization, take another look at the question asked from the standpoint of understanding clearly what a host's role is. That is, "What services should be running?" arises only when there is fuzziness as to the role of a given host. Certainly, when setting up a Web server, one would never ask, "Should this host run httpd?" The point? *There is almost no need whatever to run a network service that the host is not designed to provide to other hosts.* For many computers (that is, workstations on a network), then, one can simply run ntsysv and click off everything except syslog, crond, and xinetd, which are almost always needed for proper functioning of the system as a whole.

This is of course not the end of the story. Rather, it is the starting point for adding any further services. For instance, Sendmail is not needed to get or send mail (indeed, even fetchmail is probably better off using procmail as its mail transport agent), but on the other hand it is not a bad idea to run Sendmail in the background using a -q 15m argument so that mail doesn't inadvertently get stuck in the queue forever. The basic method should be: begin by disabling everything except syslog, crond, and xinetd, and then enable other services where the need is clear and the security implications have been thoroughly examined.

Monitoring network traffic

Often a network or system administrator wants to quickly get a "look" at the actual network traffic on a given host. This desire could be the result of suspicious behavior of certain system functions or strange hardware performance. Indeed, any number of possible turns of events could raise the question, "What's on the wire?" When this happens one does not want to muck around in log files or in the reports generated by, say, intrusion detection system (IDS) software; a quick, direct, and immediate glimpse of traffic on the network is what is needed. The following subsections discuss several tools that should be on every system, tcpdump, trafshow, and snort.

TCPDUMP

tcpdump is the elder statesman of packet sniffers. In practice, it is often the first utility you turn to when you want to get a look at traffic on your network. The basic syntax for packet sniffing on a given interface is simple indeed (the actual IP addresses and hostnames have been obfuscated, which is the practice throughout this chapter):

```
# tcpdump -i eth1
tcpdump: listening on eth1
03:22:36.579707 arp who-has xx.yy.139.202 tell xx.yy.139.1
03:22:36.589707 arp who-has xx.yy.139.214 tell xx.yy.139.1
03:22:36.609707 arp who-has xx.yy.139.220 tell xx.yy.139.1
03:22:36.679707 cornfed.ruptured-duck.com.1025 > proxy1.big.huge_internet.domain:
16297+ PTR? aaa.bbb.67.10.in-addr.arpa. (44) (DF)
03:22:37.979707 arp who-has zz.qq.14.210 tell zz.qq.14.1
03:22:38.619707 arp who-has xx.yy.139.226 tell xx.yy.139.1
03:22:38.629707 arp who-has xx.yy.139.229 tell xx.yy.139.1
03:22:38.669707
8 packets received by filter
0 packets dropped by kernel
```

 You need to be root to perform the action shown in the section on tcpdump.

Ctrl+C kills the sniffing session. tcpdump is noteworthy for the binary file format it uses to store packets, known as *tcpdump format* and used by many network utilities including snort, which is discussed later in this section, and for its optional use of the Berkeley Packet Filter (BPF) language for specifying with dizzying precision exactly which packets ought to be sniffed and which simply ignored.

The following example directs tcpdump to listen for 100 packets (-c 100) on the eth1 interface (-i eth1) and store them in an output file named my_sniffed_packets in tcpdump format (-w my_sniffed_packets):

```
# tcpdump -c 100 -i eth1 -w my_sniffed_packets
```

The packets so collected can be played back using tcpdump and printed to the screen or redirected to a text file, as shown in the following example:

```
# tcpdump -r my_sniffed_packets > my_packets_text
```

Although the binary tcpdump format is faster and recommended for capturing packets on busy interfaces, tcpdump can redirect its output to text files. Its man page gives several examples and variations on these themes.

TRAFSHOW

trafshow produces a nice color coded display that updates in real time to reflect changes in the traffic across a given interface. The color coding is by network protocol, and hostname lookup can be toggled off and on without quitting the application. trafshow is ideal for running constantly in a small xterm in a corner of the display, perhaps with the window's sticky button on so it appears on every desktop (if you are using a window manager that supports multiple or virtual desktops).

SNORT

By design, snort is an Intrusion Detection System, but in its basic operation it is a handy packet sniffer with a few twists. Like tcpdump it can accept BPF packet specifiers, and it can write its packet capture to an output file using tcpdump's binary format. Also, like tcpdump, snort can replay a session by reading data from a tcpdump format data file. In the process, snort can apply, if need be, any of its IDS abilities to detect packets that match a given set of attack signatures.

Listing 26-1 shows a brief snort session that captures five packets. The options are: -i interface, -n packet count, -v verbose.

Listing 26-1: A Sample Snort Session

```
# snort -i eth1 -n 5 -v
Log directory =
        --== Initializing Snort ==--
Initializing Network Interface eth1
Decoding Ethernet on interface eth1
        --== Initialization Complete ==--
-*> Snort! <*-
Version 1.8.1-RELEASE (Build 74)
By Martin Roesch (roesch@sourcefire.com, www.snort.org)
```

Continued

Listing 26-1 *(Continued)*

```
09/10-11:54:04.219707 nn.m.192.223:61411 -> xx.yyy.213.167:554
TCP TTL:63 TOS:0x0 ID:41861 IpLen:20 DgmLen:40 DF
***A**** Seq: 0x218D4793  Ack: 0x9B5297  Win: 0x3EBC  TcpLen: 20
=+=+=+=+=+=+=+=+=+=+=+=+=+=+=+=+=+=+=+=+=+=+=+=+=+=+=+=+=+=+=+=+=+=+=+=+=+
09/10-11:54:04.309707 xx.yyy.213.167:554 -> 192.168.1.5:2401
TCP TTL:114 TOS:0x0 ID:37855 IpLen:20 DgmLen:694 DF
***AP*** Seq: 0x9B5297  Ack: 0x218D4793  Win: 0x1E56  TcpLen: 20
=+=+=+=+=+=+=+=+=+=+=+=+=+=+=+=+=+=+=+=+=+=+=+=+=+=+=+=+=+=+=+=+=+=+=+=+=+
09/10-11:54:04.329707 nn.m.192.223:61411 -> xx.yyy.213.167:554
TCP TTL:63 TOS:0x0 ID:41862 IpLen:20 DgmLen:40 DF
***A**** Seq: 0x218D4793  Ack: 0x9B5525  Win: 0x3C2E  TcpLen: 20
=+=+=+=+=+=+=+=+=+=+=+=+=+=+=+=+=+=+=+=+=+=+=+=+=+=+=+=+=+=+=+=+=+=+=+=+=+
09/10-11:54:04.409707 xx.yyy.213.167:554 -> 192.168.1.5:2401
TCP TTL:114 TOS:0x0 ID:14816 IpLen:20 DgmLen:694 DF
***AP*** Seq: 0x9B5525  Ack: 0x218D4793  Win: 0x1E56  TcpLen: 20
=+=+=+=+=+=+=+=+=+=+=+=+=+=+=+=+=+=+=+=+=+=+=+=+=+=+=+=+=+=+=+=+=+=+=+=+=+
09/10-11:54:04.409707 nn.m.192.223:61411 -> xx.yyy.213.167:554
TCP TTL:63 TOS:0x0 ID:41863 IpLen:20 DgmLen:40 DF
***A**** Seq: 0x218D4793  Ack: 0x9B57B3  Win: 0x39A0  TcpLen: 20
=+=+=+=+=+=+=+=+=+=+=+=+=+=+=+=+=+=+=+=+=+=+=+=+=+=+=+=+=+=+=+=+=+=+=+=+=+
========================================================================
Snort analyzed 5 out of 5 packets, dropping 0(0.000%) packets
Breakdown by protocol:                  Action Stats:
     TCP: 5          (100.000%)          ALERTS: 0
     UDP: 0          (0.000%)           LOGGED: 0
    ICMP: 0          (0.000%)           PASSED: 0
     ARP: 0          (0.000%)
    IPv6: 0          (0.000%)
     IPX: 0          (0.000%)
   OTHER: 0          (0.000%)
 DISCARD: 0          (0.000%)
========================================================================
Fragmentation Stats:
Fragmented IP Packets: 0           (0.000%)
    Fragment Trackers: 0
    Rebuilt IP Packets: 0
    Frag elements used: 0
Discarded(incomplete): 0
    Discarded(timeout): 0
  Frag2 memory faults: 0
========================================================================
TCP Stream Reassembly Stats:
        TCP Packets Used: 0           (0.000%)
         Stream Trackers: 0
```

```
        Stream flushes: 0
        Segments used: 0
Stream4 Memory Faults: 0
===============================================================================
Snort received signal 3, exiting
```

A Firewall Primer

The term *firewall* has suffered the fate of most creatures who gain too much popularity; it has become, if not debased, at least muddied as to its meaning. For some, a firewall is a software package they can install on a host, and, presumably, uninstall at some later date. The current rage for residential broadband Internet connections has spawned a huge market for such products; but to be fair, firewall software packages for heavy-duty server use in the back office have been around a long time indeed, predating their upstart home use cousins. In another common usage, the term denotes a particular host, typically one that sits between a more or less protected internal network and a more or less unprotected external network. These are often called *bastion hosts*.

For the purposes of this chapter, a *firewall* refers to a collection of hardware, software, and policy components designed to implement and safeguard certain relationships of trust between two networks. A dedicated firewall hardware component, for instance, might be a host containing no read/write storage capability, one that perhaps does not even have a hard drive. Firewall software comes in several flavors but this chapter focuses on two of these: packet filters, which examine network traffic at a very low level, and access controls, which permit or deny access based on high-level features such as the source or origin IP address or host name. I touch on firewall *policy* here only because it is part of the overall security policy of a site, a topic dealt with in Chapter 24.

Firewall policy

Three main topics deserve close attention under the rubric firewall policy:

- What gets in?
- What gets out?
- What face do you present to the world?

What gets in? What can you trust coming in from the "external world?" How do you need to specify it? By source? By protocol? By service (or port)? By content? Will these specifications vary over the course of a day? A week (or weekend)? Ever? To what extent do you fine-tune these specifications according to destination?

What gets out? All the glitz is expended on romanticizing cyber-criminals, as if they are the modern-day equivalent of the lone gunman in Dallas in 1963.

However, keeping out the black hats is easier than keeping in what needs to be kept in. Losses due to proprietary information being leaked into the wrong hands are difficult to assess because most businesses are loath — many of them have shareholders — to publicize the success of such exploits. Imposing draconian restrictions on access to your internal network from the outside is not going to stir up your users nearly as much as imposing similarly severe limits on their ability to contact hosts outside the internal net.

The previous two chapters repeatedly emphasized that, given a committed, concerted attack, *any* system can be exploited and any firewall can be breached. The reverse is also true: ultimately, if someone wants to get something out of a network, they will do so. For example, one can tunnel FTP via e-mail, provided one knows how. When data to which everyone has access cannot be prevented from leaving the internal network, the problem then becomes a matter of limiting access internally to certain online resources, and that in turn has immediate effects on productivity, to mention only the most obvious fallout. François-René Rideau, author of the Linux *Firewall Piercing mini-HOWTO* (`http://www.linuxdoc.org/HOWTO/mini/Firewall-Piercing.html`):

> "...the moral is: a firewall cannot protect a network against its own internal users, and should not even try to.
>
> "When an internal user asks your system administrator to open an outbound port to an external machine, or an inbound port to an internal machine, then you should do it for him. . . . For, unless he is so firewalled as to be completely cut off from the outside world, with no ssh, no telnet, no web browsing, no e-mail, no ping, no phone line, no radio, no nothing, then *the user can and will use firewall piercing techniques to access the machines he wants* . . . the net result for security will be an unaudited connection with the outside world. So either *you trust your users, after proper training and selection, or you shouldn't grant them access to the network at all. You can and you shall protect them from the outside world, but you can't protect them from themselves.*"

What face do you present to the world? Do you present your systems as an open book with ready access to your personnel and resources, or do you put on an electronic equivalent of the inscrutable poker face, revealing nothing beyond your mere presence? These questions are usually thought of as marketing issues, but they have security implications. Often there is a desire to be too open: "Hi, we're your friendly neighborhood online corporation; here is a list of all our employees along with their e-mail addresses." Probably too much information is made available in such an atmosphere, and that is a condition that itinerant social engineers never overlook. They are out looking right now!

The other extreme, the poker face, can backfire. If your online presence says in so many words: "This place is tight as a drum and I'm not about to change that for anybody, least of all for someone like you!" what you might in reality accomplish is attracting attention by communicating unmistakably that you want to avoid it or attracting the attention of the wrong people. The always elusive middle road needs to be sought here, as in most points of contact with other human beings.

Basic layout

Network layout, or *topology*, as it is often termed, is a sufficiently difficult and intricate topic that only a handful of ideas can be mentioned. The usual course of events is that a network or system administrator inherits a network already up and running. Occasionally the administrator may be consulted about the design of a new network that is being brought online; the admin may even have been hired to participate in this planning. Whatever the scenario, the next three sections describe features that need to be considered in virtually all network layouts, so it behooves administrators to be aware of the variety of approaches that are available in each scenario. The discussion is only of simple examples. Many network configurations and methodologies require that special attention be given to security questions. High availability networks, VLANs (Virtual Local Area Network), and VPNs (Virtual Private Network) are examples of increasingly popular network approaches that bring with them unique challenges for the security planner.

In rough overview, a generic firewall might look like Figure 26-1. The DMZ, or Demilitarized Zone, is home to hosts that provide publicly accessible services, such as the Web server, httpd, or the FTP server, ftpd. Systems that operate in the DMZ do not benefit from the protections afforded the internal, private LAN. Totally unfettered access is provided; the public can connect without navigating any security hurdles. The bastion host stands between systems in the DMZ and the protected internal LAN. The term *firewall* is usually applied to the bastion host, but it is more accurate to use this term to refer to all systems and software that stands between the protected network and the Internet.

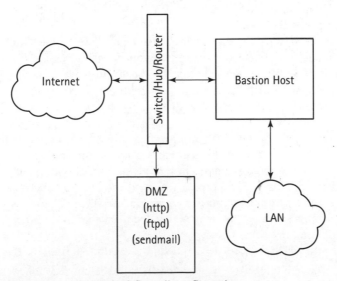

Figure 26-1: A standard firewall configuration

Designing the firewall

The distinguishing characteristic of the bastion host is that it runs absolutely no network services and runs only the absolute minimum of other services. In some formulations this means that not even the system logger, `syslogd`, or even the kernel logger, `klogd`, will be running. The bastion host has a single mission, access control, typically in the form of packet filtering. Network address translation (NAT), also known as *IP masquerading*, is commonly combined with the packet filtering role because the kernel facilities that implement packet filtering are ideally suited for the rewriting of packet headers that enables NAT. Another common compromise with the ideal of a completely service-free bastion host occurs when proxy services are located on this same host.

The idea of an empty bastion host can be expanded to include the complete absence of any writable media, such as disks, and further that the media that *is* present be composed of removable items, floppies or CD-ROMs. The administrator ought to be familiar with some of these products, since in the event of trouble it can be a Godsend to pop a bootable floppy disk or CD-ROM into the host and bring up a preconfigured packet filter that has been designed for just such an occasion. In particular, such removable emergency firewalls can be configured to log network activity on the bastion host on writable media housed in systems inside the protected LAN. Note that such an arrangement calls for a good deal of care, because the tradeoff for avoiding writable media on the bastion host necessitates establishing an additional connection to the internal network, that is, a connection other than the main one that is subject to the bastion host's access control enforcement. The additional connection can also be a trouble spot when laying out intrusion detection sensors: how should you make intrusion detection sensor logs available to hosts on the safe side of the bastion host?

Not all local networks need a DMZ standing between themselves and the Internet. If the local network does not provide any services for clients accessing the network from the Internet side of things, then there is no reason to leave any systems on the public or exposed side of the bastion. In particular, systems that store their incoming e-mail on a POP or IMAP host on another network have no need for a DMZ.

The exception to the rule is a DMZ with only one occupant, a host running an intrusion detection system (IDS) sensor. This IDS host can be a valuable addition to even the simplest network, and is perhaps the easiest way to avoid the problems that can arise when IDS is running on firewall host. The caveats alluded to concerning logging needs to be heeded, but putting an IDS sensor in the DMZ safeguards the firewall from the sorts of DOS attacks that may be leveled at hosts running IDS. A little division of labor goes a long way.

The type of DMZ illustrated in Figure 26-1 presupposes that sufficient IP addresses are available for services run out of the DMZ. Also, security for hosts in the DMZ calls for some special considerations, given their relatively unprotected status. Many of the points made concerning bastion hosts apply to DMZ hosts:

♦ They should run a minimum of services so that, for instance, the machine running `httpd` is not running `ftpd` also.

♦ These machines should have no ordinary user accounts, and as few administrative accounts as possible.

♦ Depending on the service made available by a given host, the host access control facility should be augmented with packet filtering.

♦ Keeping in mind that DMZ hosts are more likely to be compromised, host access control and packet filtering should pay particular attention to outbound traffic, the intent being to prevent use of the host as a remote platform for launching attacks on yet other hosts or networks.

♦ Access to machines in the DMZ from hosts on the internal, protected side of the firewall must be severely curtailed.

This last point about access to the DMZ hosts raises the important *policy* question: "What assets should be placed on DMZ hosts?" The answer here is rarely self-evident, because there are varying estimates within any organization as to the cost benefit breakdown of using, for instance, a Web server in the DMZ to host not only the resources that will be publicly available, but also private, internal Web assets. Is the situation such that an added Web server within the protected LAN is cost-effective? What about e-mail? If there is an SMTP host in the DMZ, should it handle mail destined for inside the organization?

Figure 26-2 illustrates another approach to designing the DMZ. Some of the questions just raised are technically easier to solve if the DMZ is put inside the firewall. Some additional complexity is introduced by the need for a third network interface.

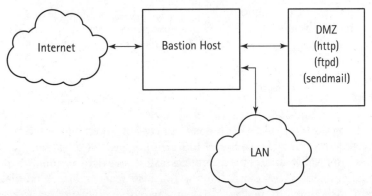

Figure 26–2: Placing a network DMZ inside a firewall

What is an IDS Sensor?

In the context of this discussion, an IDS Sensor is a host configured with special software and connected to an Ethernet segment whose interface device (NIC) is configured to transmit in promiscuous mode. The software is typically a package designed to sniff traffic on the segment and attempt to match up packets with known attack signatures. Like the firewall itself, these systems are fairly specialized, run no network services, have no ordinary user accounts, and in some cases have no writable media installed.

The rule of thumb for how many sensors to run is as many as possible. If limited to only one, then it should go outside the firewall. A sensor outside the firewall (in theory, at least) catches all attacks that reach the firewall. The firewall may prevent some attacks from completing the TCP handshake needed to actually enter the firewall; these putative attacks may not be seen by the sensor.

The main problem with sensors outside the firewall is so-called *false positive* responses, that is, responses that trigger the sensor outside the firewall but never develop into a full-fledged attack. A second sensor inside the firewall, or, in the case of the layout illustrated in Figure 26-1, inside the DMZ, deals less with background noise, and provides more useful information.

Finally, many security administrators prefer to monitor their IDS sensors via a second network interface card installed in each. Logging and analysis of all sensor output can then be centralized.

This approach allows hosts in the DMZ to be masqueraded (using network address translation), reducing the number of required IP addresses, theoretically, to one. On the other hand, if routable IP addresses are desired and available for DMZ hosts, then it may be convenient to place the DMZ and LAN on their own subnets.

Summary

This chapter showed you how to begin securing entire networks of computers using a Red Hat Linux system as a firewall. You learned how to determine what services are running and how to disable unnecessary services using a variety of tools that are part of a standard Red Hat Linux installation. You also read how to monitor incoming network connections to make sure that incoming connections from Internet hosts are not the precursors to concerted attempts to compromise the security of your internal network. Finally, you learned a bit of basic firewall theory. The introduction to firewalls prepared you for Chapter 27, which covers the business of detecting intrusions using ipchains and iptables.

Chapter 27

Detecting Intrusions

IN THIS CHAPTER

- ◆ Using Tripwire
- ◆ Using LogWatch
- ◆ Detecting intrusions with ipchains
- ◆ Detecting intrusions with iptables

THE PREVIOUS THREE CHAPTERS touched on some of this chapter's main topics, namely, detecting and blocking attempted intrusions of your Red Hat Linux-based network. This chapter revives and deepens these earlier discussions, describing methods for monitoring a Red Hat Linux system for attempted, potential, and actual security compromises using the tools available in a standard Red Hat Linux installation.

Understanding Host-Based Intrusion Detection Software

As used in this chapter, the phrase *host-based intrusion detection software* (IDS) refers to software packages that implement a variety of methods for monitoring a system for attempts to compromise it. One such method is file integrity software, such as Tripwire. As you learn in the section titled "Using Tripwire," file integrity packages create a database of key files and file systems on a host and then compare the results of frequent integrity checks to the attributes stored in the database. The reports generated highlight changes, which may or may not indicate that a system has been compromised. Other approaches to IDS include log monitoring tools such as LogWatch and real-time monitoring of incoming network traffic using a firewall implemented with ipchains or iptables. The sections titled "Using LogWatch," "Detecting Intrusions with ipchains," and "Detecting Intrusions with iptables" respectively, illustrate how to configure each of these tools to enhance the IDS component of your Red Hat Linux system's security.

Using Tripwire

As remarked in Chapter 25, Tripwire is not for everyone, that is, not every host on your network should be running or needs to run Tripwire. If the host is used for developmental work or as a testing platform, then it is likely that important system files are altered or replaced on a fairly regular basis. More generally, *any* system whose key system files and binaries are subject to frequent modification is unsuitable for IDS systems that rely on file integrity. This qualification notwithstanding, one central problem needs to be considered when deciding whether or not to install and run Tripwire on a given machine: without such a tool, it is impossible to prove that a system has *not* been compromised. This dilemma leaves you with few options for machines not so equipped if the suspicion or even slight likelihood of compromise is raised, and only one of those options, reformatting the hard drive, is safe. In some cases this is not a large problem, but in others, reformatting a drive is out of the question. Machines that are used to test operating system installation programs or otherwise used as laboratory testbeds barely notice that they are being reformatted, again, on any given day. Other systems, those with a fair amount of configuration detail implemented, are not so easy to replace, even with a decent set of backups. During and after an attack, a Tripwire check affords a degree of confidence when it is essential that time not be wasted on systems that are still intact.

 Tripwire is not the only file integrity software available for Red Hat systems. Another popular package is AIDE, an acronym for *Advanced Intrusion Detection Environment*. AIDE's home page on the Web is `http://www.cs.tut.fi/~rammer/aide.html`.

Tripwire helps ensure the integrity of critical system files and directories by comparing changes made to them relative to an initial baseline snapshot taken when Tripwire was first installed and initialized. These comparisons include file locations, creation and modification dates, file sizes, and other data. Tripwire can be configured to send alerts to designated users via e-mail if particular files are altered and to perform automated integrity checking via a cron job. Using Tripwire for intrusion detection and damage assessment also reduces the recovery time following a system compromise because it reduces the number of files you must restore to repair the system to a known secure state. For maximum reliability, install Tripwire and create the initial snapshot before the system is at risk from intrusion, that is, before it is connected to a network. The following steps outline how to install, initialize, and use Tripwire:

1. Install Tripwire, customize the policy and configuration files, and run the configuration script.

2. Initialize the Tripwire database of critical system files to monitor, based on the contents of the Tripwire policy file created in Step 1.

3. Run a Tripwire integrity check to compare the new database with the actual system files, looking for missing or altered files.

4. Examine the Tripwire report file and note integrity violations.

5. Take appropriate security measures if monitored files have been altered inappropriately. You can either replace the originals from backups or reinstall the affected programs.

6. Update the Tripwire database file. Valid integrity violations, such as intentionally edited files or updated programs, should be flagged to be ignored as violations in future reports.

7. Update the Tripwire policy file to change the list of files Tripwire monitors or to change how it treats integrity violations, regenerate a signed copy of the policy file, and then update your Tripwire database.

The following subsections detail how to perform each of these steps.

Installing Tripwire

The easiest way to install Tripwire is to install its RPM when you install Red Hat Linux. However, if you have already installed Red Hat Linux you can install the Tripwire RPM from the Red Hat Linux CD-ROM. Mount the Red Hat Linux CD-ROM and type the following command to install the binary RPM. The command assumes that /mnt/cdrom is the mount point for your CD-ROM drive, so adjust the path accordingly, if necessary.

```
# rpm -Uvh /mnt/cdrom/RedHat/RPMS/tripwire*
```

After installing the Tripwire RPM, read the release notes and README file located in /usr/share/doc/tripwire-version-number. These documents contain important information about the default policy file and other issues that you should know. Next, you must configure Tripwire for your system as outlined in the next section.

Configuring Tripwire

Configuring Tripwire consists of two steps, running the installation script, /etc/tripwire/twinstall.sh, and initializing the database. twinstall.sh prompts you to set passphrases, generates cryptographic keys that protect the Tripwire configuration and policy files, and then encodes and signs these files using the keys. Once encoded and signed, the configuration file (/etc/tripwire/tw.cfg) and the policy file (/etc/tripwire/tw.pol) generated by running the

twinstall.sh script should not be renamed or moved. If you modify the configuration or policy files after running the configuration script, you must rerun
twinstall.sh before initializing the database file. You *can* edit the configuration
and policy files *after* initializing the database file and running an integrity check,
however.

So, to perform the initial configuration, log in as root or use su - to become the
root user and execute the following command:

```
[root@luther root]# /etc/tripwire/twinstall.sh

The Tripwire site and local passphrases are used to
sign a variety of files, such as the configuration,
policy, and database files.

Passphrases should be at least 8 characters in length
and contain both letters and numbers.

See the Tripwire manual for more information.

Creating key files...
(When selecting a passphrase, keep in mind that good passphrases typically
have upper and lower case letters, digits and punctuation marks, and are
at least 8 characters in length.)
Enter the site keyfile passphrase: [Type the passphrase and press Enter]
Verify the site keyfile passphrase: [Retype the passphrase and press Enter]
Generating key (this may take several minutes)...Key generation complete.
(When selecting a passphrase, keep in mind that good passphrases typically
have upper and lower case letters, digits and punctuation marks, and are
at least 8 characters in length.)
Enter the local keyfile passphrase: [Type the passphrase and press Enter]
Verify the local keyfile passphrase: [Retype the passphrase and press Enter]
Generating key (this may take several minutes)... ...Key generation complete.

Signing configuration file...
Please enter your site passphrase: [Type the site passphrase and press Enter]
Wrote configuration file: /etc/tripwire/tw.cfg
A clear-text version of the Tripwire configuration file
/etc/tripwire/twcfg.txt
has been preserved for your inspection.  It is recommended
that you delete this file manually after you have examined it.


Signing policy file...
Please enter your site passphrase: [Type the site passphrase and press Enter]
Wrote policy file: /etc/tripwire/tw.pol
A clear-text version of the Tripwire policy file
```

```
/etc/tripwire/twpol.txt
has been preserved for your inspection. This implements
a minimal policy, intended only to test essential
Tripwire functionality. You should edit the policy file
to describe your system, and then use twadmin to generate
a new signed copy of the Tripwire policy.
```

Next, initialize the Tripwire database file by executing the command `/usr/sbin/tripwire -m i`. When initializing its database, Tripwire builds a collection of file system objects based on the rules in the policy file that serve as the baseline for integrity checks. As shown in the following, the database initialization requires you to enter the local passphrase you selected when you ran the `twinstall.sh` script (most of the output is deleted to save space):

```
# /usr/sbin/tripwire -m i
Please enter your local passphrase:
Parsing policy file: /etc/tripwire/tw.pol
Generating the database...
*** Processing Unix File System ***
### Warning: File system error.
### Filename: /usr/sbin/fixrmtab
### No such file or directory
### Continuing...
...
### Filename: /root/.pinerc
### No such file or directory
### Continuing...
Wrote database file: /var/lib/tripwire/luther.twd
The database was successfully generated.
```

This command can take several minutes to run and may generate a number of errors about missing files, such as the one shown in the example that you can safely disregard *this time* — in future reports, file integrity violations such as this should *not* be ignored because they may indicate a possible successful intrusion.

The final installation step is to run the first integrity check comparing the new Tripwire database to your system files by executing the following command and looking for errors in the generated report:

```
# /usr/sbin/tripwire -m c
Parsing policy file: /etc/tripwire/tw.pol
*** Processing Unix File System ***
Performing integrity check...
### Warning: File system error.
### Filename: /usr/sbin/fixrmtab
### No such file or directory
### Continuing...
```

```
...
138. File system error.
Filename: /root/.pinerc
No such file or directory

*** End of report ***
```

Tripwire 2.3 Portions copyright 2000 Tripwire, Inc. Tripwire is a registered trademark of Tripwire, Inc. This software comes with ABSOLUTELY NO WARRANTY; for details use—version. This is free software which may be redistributed or modified only under certain conditions; see COPYING for details.
All rights reserved.
Integrity check complete.

Selecting Passphrases

Tripwire files are signed or encrypted using cryptographic keys that protect the configuration, policy, database, and report files from being viewed or modified except by users who know the site and/or local passphrases. As a result, should intruders somehow obtain root access to your system, they can't alter the Tripwire files to hide their activities unless they know the passphrases.

Thus, selecting good passphrases is vitally important. Good passphrases have the following characteristics:

- They contain a mixture of upper and lowercase alphanumeric and symbolic characters, but do not use single or double quotes.

- They are between 8 and 1,023 characters in length.

- They are completely different from the root password for the system.

And good system administrators take the following precautions:

- Assign different passphrases for the site key and the local key.

- Store the passphrases in a secure location and *do not* store them on the system they protect, or someone who compromises the system may be able to discover and use them. As an additional precaution, you might want to save additional copies of the passphrases on a floppy disk that stays in a locked drawer.

The site key passphrase protects the site key, which is used to sign Tripwire configuration and policy files. The local key signs Tripwire's database and report files. Keep in mind that there is no way to decrypt a signed file if you forget your passphrase. If you forget the passphrases, the files are unusable and you have to run the configuration script again, which also reinitializes the Tripwire database.

Once you complete the initial integrity check, Tripwire has the baseline snapshot of your file system that it needs to check for changes to critical files. The integrity check can be time-consuming to execute because it compares the current, actual file system objects with their properties as recorded in its database – the more files it has to check, the longer the integrity check takes. As it executes, the check prints violations to stdout and to a report file that you can review using the twprint command.

You may find it helpful to know the locations of key Tripwire files and the names and functions of key Tripwire components. The following list shows this information:

- /etc/tripwire — Stores the local and site keys, the installation script, and the configuration and policy files

- /var/lib/tripwire — Stores the Tripwire database of your system's files (Tripwire's database files end with .twd)

- /var/lib/tripwire/report — Stores Tripwire reports (Tripwire's report files end with .twr)

- /usr/sbin — Stores the tripwire, twadmin, and twprint programs

After running the initial integrity check, update your Tripwire database to accept the violations found in the report. When executing the command to integrate valid violations into your database, be sure to use the most recent report. Type the following command (all on one line), where *reportname* is the name of the report to be used:

```
# tripwire -m u -r /var/lib/tripwire/report/reportname.twr
```

Tripwire shows you the particular report using the default text editor (vi, unless you have specifically set the EDITOR environment variable to something else or have edited /etc/tripwire/tw.cfg). Updates to the Tripwire database start with an [x] before the file name. If you want to exclude a valid violation from being added to the Tripwire database, remove the x from the box. To accept any files with an x beside them as changes, leave the x in the box. When you are done, save the file and exit the editor. When you attempt to exit the editor, you are asked to enter the local passphrase. After entering the correct passphrase, a new database file is written that includes the valid violations. The newly authorized integrity violations no longer show up as warnings when the next integrity check is run.

You also should change the files Tripwire records in its database or modify the severity in which violations are reported by editing the policy file, /etc/tripwire/twpol.txt. In particular, you might want to comment out files that do not exist on your system to prevent generating No such file or directory errors. For example, if your system does not have /usr/sbin/fixrmtab, tell Tripwire to ignore it by commenting out its line in twpol.txt:

```
#/usr/sbin/fixrmtab              -> $(SEC_CONFIG) ;
```

After editing the policy file, you have to generate a new signed policy file, /etc/tripwire/tw.pol, and generate an updated database file based on this policy information. Use the following command:

```
# twadmin -m P -S /etc/tripwire/site.key /etc/tripwire/twpol.txt
Please enter your site passphrase:
Wrote policy file: /etc/tripwire/tw.pol
```

After you create a new policy file, you must update the Tripwire database. The most reliable way to accomplish this is to delete the existing database and create a new database based on the new policy file. Use the following short procedure:

1. Delete the existing database:

   ```
   # rm /var/lib/tripwire/your.host.name.twd
   ```

2. Create a new database:

   ```
   # /usr/sbin/tripwire -m i
   ```

Once the new database has been created, rerun the first integrity check manually and view the contents of the resulting report, and then, if necessary, update the database.

Running Tripwire

Once the initial configuration is complete, running Tripwire largely consists of viewing and printing reports. The command for viewing and printing reports is twprint. Its syntax is:

```
twprint -m r [-c cfgfile] [-L localkey] [-t level] -r report
```

twprint -m r prints the report specified by -r report as clear text. -c cfgfile instructs twprint to use the configuration file cfgfile instead of the default configuration file (/etc/tripwire/tw.cfg). Similarly, -L localkey tells twprint to use the local key file specified by localkey instead of the default local key (/etc/tripwire/hostname-local.key). -t level, finally, sets the level of report detail to level, which must be a value between 0 (lowest detail) and 4 (most detail); the default level is 3. A typical twprint command line resembles the following:

```
# twprint -m r -r /var/lib/tripwire/report/reportname.twr
```

You can review previously saved reports at any time. To see the available reports, simply use ls to generate a listing of the available reports in /var/lib/tripwire/report. For example:

```
# ls /var/lib/tripwire/report
luther-20010925-042248.twr  luther-20010928-040443.twr
luther-20010926-042149.twr  luther-20010929-042941.twr
luther-20010927-040702.twr  luther-20010930-042119.twr
```

You can also use twprint to view the entire database or information about selected files in the Tripwire database. This procedure is useful for seeing what and how much information Tripwire is tracking with regard to your file system. twprint's sytnax for its database report mode is:

```
twprint -m d [-c cfgfile] [-L localkey] [-d database]
```

The -c and -L options have the same meaning they do when printing reports. -d *database* tells twprint to print the contents of the database file named *database*. To see information about a particular file that Tripwire is tracking, you can specify the full path to that file at the end of the command line shown. For example, the following command shows the database information for /boot/vmlinuz-2.4.9-13:

```
/usr/sbin/twprint -m d /boot/vmlinuz-2.4.9-13
Object name:  /boot/vmlinuz-2.4.9-13
```

```
Property:               Value:
------------            ----------
Object Type             Regular File
Device Number           2049
File Device Number      0
Inode Number            26
Mode                    -rw-r—r--
Num Links               1
UID                     root (0)
GID                     root (0)
Size                    618769
Modify Time             Fri 07 Sep 2001 12:27:01 AM MDT
Change Time             Fri 07 Sep 2001 12:27:01 AM MDT
Blocks                  1218
CRC32                   BkumMc
MD5                     A6rxQ2k+IsTOqZ4GN4zYHh
```

Detecting intrusions using Tripwire

I can provide a few tips here about how to respond to apparent file integrity violations. If you recently installed or upgraded an application, Tripwire (correctly) reports integrity violations for the new and upgraded files. In this case, update the database as described in the previous subsection to accept the changes. Similarly, if you have moved or removed an application or edited critical system files, update the database accordingly. However, if unauthorized changes are made to system files that generate integrity check violations, you should restore the original files from a backup or reinstall the program.

Additional Tripwire resources

For more information about Tripwire's capabilities and how to take advantage of them, refer to the installed documentation in /usr/share/doc/tripwire-2.3.1, especially for information about customizing the configuration and policy files. The manual pages for tripwire, twadmin, and twprint (man tripwire, man twadmin, and man twprint) are excellent resources for using these programs. Naturally, the Tripwire home page, http://www.tripwire.org/, is the authoritative source for Tripwire information, news, and updates.

Using LogWatch

LogWatch is a highly customizable and easy to use log monitoring system. It parses your system log files for a given period of time to create a report covering the areas that interest you. Its reports can be as succinct or as detailed as you want. By default, Red Hat configures LogWatch to run daily as a cron job (see /etc/cron.daily/00-logwatch), but it can also be run from the command line. The LogWatch executable is /usr/sbin/logwatch, a Perl script. Its syntax is:

```
logwatch [--detail level] [--logfile name] [--print] [--mailto addr]
[--archives] [--range range] [--save filename] [--service name]
```

As you can see from the syntax listing, logwatch can be run without any arguments, in which case, it uses the default values listed in /etc/log.d/logwatch. conf, which are defined in terms of the options listed in the syntax listing. Table 27-1 lists the options and their descriptions.

TABLE 27-1 LOGWATCH COMMAND LINE OPTIONS

Option	Description
--detail level	Defines the degree of report detail; level must be one of high, med, or low
--logfile name	Prints report based on the log specified in name; multiple names can be specified

Option	Description
--service *name*	Prints report for the service specified in *name*; multiple *name*s can be specified
--print	Displays report to stdout instead of sending e-mail
--mailto *addr*	E-mails report to the recipient specified in *addr*
--archives	Includes archived log files in the report in addition to current log files
--save *filename*	Saves the report to the file specified in *filename*
--range *range*	Defines the date on which to report; *range* must be one of yesterday, today or all

The default options and values in /etc/log.d/logwatch.conf are:

◆ mailto = root

◆ range = yesterday

◆ detail = low

◆ service = all

These options correspond to invoking logwatch using the following command:

```
# logwatch --mailto root --range yesterday --detail low --service all
```

LogWatch uses a set of filters, also written in Perl, for extracting information from the various log files on a Red Hat Linux system. These filters are stored in three separate directories:

◆ /etc/log.d/scripts/shared — Filters common to many services and/or logfiles.

◆ /etc/log.d/scripts/logfiles — Filters specific to just particular logfiles.

◆ /etc/log.d/scripts/services — Actual filter programs for the various services.

The list of services on which LogWatch can report can be determined by reviewing the list of files in /etc/log.d/conf/services, which contains configuration files defining how LogWatch processes the corresponding log entries. LogWatch currently processes log entries for the services listed in Table 27-2.

TABLE 27-2 SERVICES LOGWATCH MONITORS

automount	init	named	secure
cron	in.qpopper	pam	sendmail
ftpd-messages	kernel	pam_pwdb	sshd2
ftpd-xferlog	modprobe	proftpd-messages	sshd
identd	mountd	samba	syslogd

The type of information LogWatch reports varies from service to service and depends on the argument provided to the `--detail` option. For example, the log information generated for the `sendmail` service is the same for all values of `--detail`:

```
# logwatch --service sendmail --detail low --range today --print

################## LogWatch 2.1.1 Begin ####################

-------------------- sendmail Begin ----------------------
641360 bytes transferred
81 messages sent
-------------------- sendmail End ------------------------


####################### LogWatch End #######################
# logwatch --service sendmail --detail high --range today --print

################## LogWatch 2.1.1 Begin ####################

-------------------- sendmail Begin ----------------------
641360 bytes transferred
81 messages sent
-------------------- sendmail End ------------------------


####################### LogWatch End #######################
```

As you can see, LogWatch reports the same data for both `low` and `high`: the total number of bytes sendmail processed and the number of messages it sent. However, the story is different for the `kernel` service, as shown in the following:

TIP You can obtain more detailed information about mail traffic using the `mailstats` command. In order to use it, make sure that the file `/var/log/sendmail.st` exists. If it does not, execute `touch /var/log/sendmail.st` as the root user.

```
# logwatch --service kernel --detail low --range today --print

################## LogWatch 2.1.1 Begin #####################

###################### LogWatch End ########################
# logwatch --service kernel --detail high ==range today --print

################## LogWatch 2.1.1 Begin #####################


--------------------- Kernel Begin ------------------------

4 Time(s): Directory sread (sector 0x17) failed
2 Time(s): end_request: I/O error, dev 02:00 (floppy), sector 19
5 Time(s): end_request: I/O error, dev 02:00 (floppy), sector 23
1 Time(s): end_request: I/O error, dev 02:00 (floppy), sector 24
1 Time(s): end_request: I/O error, dev 02:00 (floppy), sector 26
1 Time(s): end_request: I/O error, dev 02:00 (floppy), sector 364
1 Time(s): end_request: I/O error, dev 02:00 (floppy), sector 372
1 Time(s): end_request: I/O error, dev 02:00 (floppy), sector 373
1 Time(s): end_request: I/O error, dev 02:00 (floppy), sector 400
1 Time(s): end_request: I/O error, dev 02:00 (floppy), sector 404
1 Time(s): floppy0: CRC error: track 0, head 1, sector 5, size 2
1 Time(s): floppy0: CRC error: track 0, head 1, sector 9, size 2
1 Time(s): floppy0: data CRC error: track 0, head 1, sector 17, size 2
4 Time(s): floppy0: data CRC error: track 0, head 1, sector 2, size 2
1 Time(s): floppy0: data CRC error: track 0, head 1, sector 6, size 2
1 Time(s): floppy0: data CRC error: track 0, head 1, sector 7, size 2
2 Time(s): floppy0: data CRC error: track 0, head 1, sector 9, size 2
1 Time(s): floppy0: sector not found: track 0, head 1, sector 2, size 2
1 Time(s): floppy0: sector not found: track 0, head 1, sector 3, size 2
1 Time(s): floppy0: sector not found: track 0, head 1, sector 5, size 2
10 Time(s): floppy0: sector not found: track 0, head 1, sector 6, size 2
1 Time(s): floppy0: sector not found: track 0, head 1, sector 7, size 2

--------------------- Kernel End --------------------------


###################### LogWatch End ########################
```

LogWatch's output when the detail level is high indicates that a disk used in the floppy drive is beginning to fail. To get the maximum benefit from LogWatch, consider changing the default detail level in /etc/log.d/logwatch.conf to high.

Detecting Intrusions with ipchains

After a thoughtfully designed and rigorously observed security policy, a packet filtering firewall, based on ipchains or iptables, is one of the strongest layers in a site's security. This section describes how to configure a firewall using *ipchains*, to facilitate detecting intrusion attempts. On its own, ipchains cannot detect intrusions *per se*. But if you use ipchains in conjunction with LogWatch or another log monitoring tool, you can determine what kind of intrusions blackhats are attempting, how often, on what ports, and so forth.

The key to using ipchains for intrusion detection is using its -l option to tell the kernel to log a packet that matches a rule. Although you would not ordinarily want to log packets, logging *denied* packets is a very useful way to get an idea of the kind of undesirable traffic coming into your system. For example, suppose you have the following rule:

```
# ipchains -l -A forward -i ppp0 -j DENY
```

As you should recall from Chapter 26, this ipchains invocation appends (-A) a rule to the forward chain (forward), directing that packets on the ppp0 interface (-i ppp0) to jump (-j) should be denied (DENY). The -l causes the kernel to log each packet matching this rule to the system log. The log entry resembles the following:

```
Oct  9 23:01:21 marta kernel: Packet log: forward DENY ppp0 PROTO=6
192.168.0.3:1896 207.46.131.71:80 L=40 S=0x00 I=55238 F=0x4000 T=127 (#1)
```

The log entry is intended more for networking gurus than for mere mortals, but, despite its opacity, it does contain useful information. It is designed to be terse, and contains technical information useful only to networking gurus, but it can be useful to the rest of us. It breaks down like so:

- forward is the chain containing the rule that matched the packet and generated the log entry.

- DENY (deny) is what the rule said to do to the packet.

- ppp0 is the interface name. The packet could be either an incoming or an outgoing packet because the forward chain contained the matching rule.

- PROTO=6 means that the packet used protocol 6, which maps to the TCP protocol (protocol 1 would be the ICMP protocol and 17 UDP).

◆ 192.168.1.3:1896 means that the packet's source IP address was 192.168.21.3, port 1896.

◆ 207.46.131.71:80 indicates that the packet's destination IP address was 207.46.131.71, port 80 (the HTTP port).

◆ L=40 means that the packet's total length was 40 bytes.

◆ S=0x00 tells you that the Type of Service (ToS) field was 0x00. Dividing this value (0) by 4 converts it to the ToS value ipchains uses, which, in this case, is still 0.

◆ I=55238 is the IP ID.

◆ F=0x4000 is the 16-bit fragment offset plus flags. A value starting with 0x4 or 0x5 means that the Don't Fragment bit is set.

◆ T=127 indicates that the packet's Time To Live (TTL) is 127. Recall from Chapter 26 that a packet's TTL usually starts at 15 or 255 and that it is decreased by 1 for each hop it takes.

◆ (#1) identifies the rule number that generated the log entry.

By default, ipchain's log messages go to /var/log/messages /var/log/messages. So, to detect attempted intrusions, add the -l option to each ipchains rule that you want to monitor, then configure LogWatch to use a high level of detail for kernel messages. That is, set detail = high in /etc/log.d/logwatch.conf. Now, when you run LogWatch, the kernel portion of the generated report should resemble the following:

```
# logwatch --server kernel --detail high --range today --print
-- ------------------ Kernel Begin ------------------------


Denied packets from host2.mydomain.dom (192.168.0.4).
  Port netbios-ns     (udp,ppp0,forward): 6 packet(s).
Total of 6 packet(s).

Denied packets from host1.mydomain.dom (192.168.0.3).
  Port domain   (udp,ppp0,forward): 42 packet(s).
  Port http     (tcp,ppp0,forward): 4 packet(s).
Total of 46 packet(s).



-------------------- Kernel End ------------------------
```

Notice how LogWatch summarizes the denied packet traffic on a per-host and per-port basis. For example, host1.mydomain.dom, at IP address 192.168.0.3, sent 42 packets to the domain port (these are probably DNS messages of some sort) using the UDP protocol on the ppp0 interface. The forward chain generated each of 42 log entries LogWatch detected. Although LogWatch's report provides a good deal of summary information, you might also want to analyze the traffic in detail. To do so, use a grep command to search for entries containing the string `Packet log` in the `/var/log/messages` file for the day in question. For example:

```
# grep 'Packet log' /var/log/messages
...
Oct 15 00:10:51 host2 kernel: Packet log: forward DENY ppp0 PROTO=17
192.168.0.4:137 198.60.22.2:137 L=96 S=0x00 I=3096 F=0x0000 T=127 (#1)
```

Based on the information generated by the combination of ipchain's `-l` option of LogWatch's reporting capability, you can decide how best to respond to attempts to access your network.

Detecting Intrusions with iptables

To detect intrusions using iptables, you can use the procedure described for ipchains, taking into account iptables' richer logging features. In particular, it enables you to use various options to control how iptables logs packets. This functionality is provided by the iptables log module, so, in keeping with iptables modular design, the first thing you have to do is make sure that the logging module is loaded. The easiest way to do this is to use `modprobe` to insert the module:

```
# modprobe ipt_LOG
```

After verifying that the module is loaded, modify your iptables rules to log traffic that should not get through. You can also set a prefix on these log entries to make them easy to identify and set a log level or facility (or both) to further refine the log entry and make it easy to identify in the system log.

The key components for intrusion detection using iptables are to use the new `LOG` target (`-j LOG`), the `--log-level` *level* option to set the logging level, and the `--log-prefix` *prefix* option to set the log entry prefix. Consider the following rule:

```
# iptables -A FORWARD -p tcp -j LOG --log-prefix "SAMPLE LOG RULE"
```

This rule appends a rule to the forward chain (`-A FORWARD`) that creates a log entry for TCP (`-p TCP`) packets traversing the forward chain, prefixing each entry with the string `SAMPLE LOG RULE`. The following log entry represents what such an entry might look like:

```
Oct 15 01:43:32 host2 kernel: SAMPLE LOG RULEIN=eth0 OUT=ppp0 SRC=192.168.0.3
DST=130.236.130.55 LEN=48 TOS=0x00 PREC=0x00 TTL=127 ID=30691 DF PROTO=TCP
SPT=2001 DPT=80 WINDOW=8192 RES=0x00 SYN URGP=0
```

Configure LogWatch using the same procedure described in the previous section to create a summary report listing the logged packet traffic.

Summary

This chapter described methods for monitoring a Red Hat Linux system for attempted, potential, and actual security compromises using the tools available in a standard Red Hat Linux installation. After learning how to configure Tripwire and interpreting its reports, you learned how to set up LogWatch to monitor log files for a wide variety of unusual conditions. You also learned how to log firewall activity, using both ipchains and iptables, and how to use LogWatch to monitor these log entries.

Chapter 28

Troubleshooting and Problem Solving

IN THIS CHAPTER

- ◆ Solving installation problems

- ◆ Solving file system problems

- ◆ Solving networking problems

- ◆ Solving boot problems

- ◆ Solving miscellaneous problems

DESPITE THE WORK AND TESTING that go into preparing each release of Red Hat Linux, unanticipated problems inevitably emerge. Most of these problems result from one of three situations:

- ◆ Testing Red Hat Linux for compatibility with every piece of hardware is simply not possible.

- ◆ Given the range of hardware available, any given combination of two components, for example, a SCSI disk controller and a SCSI disk, may result in subtle, but maddening incompatibilities.

- ◆ Due to the rapid rate of hardware revisions, drivers written for earlier revisions might not support the latest updates.

This chapter is intended to help you troubleshoot and, hopefully, solve the most common configuration challenges you might encounter installing and using Red Hat Linux. In particular, the sections in this chapter help you resolve problems related to installation, the file system, networking, and booting the system. A final section addresses a few common problems that do not fit into other categories.

Solving Installation Problems

The situations discussed in this section include problems with not being able to log in to the system after it has been installed, installing Star Office 5.2, the most common hardware-related gotchas, and installing Red Hat Linux on a laptop.

Unable to log in after installation

One of the most common problems when installing Red Hat Linux is not being able to log in after the post-installation reboot. If you did not create a user account during the installation, you must log in as root and create a user account. Similarly, if you forget the user account password you created during installation, log in as the root user and reset the password using this procedure:

1. At the console or in a terminal window, type the command passwd *user*, replacing *user* with the user account name.

2. Type a new password and press Enter.

3. Retype the password and press Enter.

4. Log out, and then log back in as the new user, providing the password you just set.

If you forget the root password, reboot and follow these steps:

1. Restart the system.

2. At the boot: prompt, type linux single and press Enter.

3. At the # prompt, type passwd root and follow the prompts to reset root's password.

4. Finally, type shutdown -r now; the system reboots and recognizes the new password.

Installing Star Office

Installing Star Office 5.2 from the Star Office 5.2 CD-ROM that comes with Red Hat Linux requires special handling. In particular, unlike most Linux CD-ROMs, the Star Office CD-ROM must be mounted with execute permissions. To do so, execute the following command as the root user, replacing /mnt/cdrom with your CD-ROM mount point:

```
# mount -o exec /dev/cdrom /mnt/cdrom
```

After the CD-ROM is mounted, you can execute the binary installation file using the `./command` notation. That is, after changing into the directory appropriate for your language (English, in this case), the command should resemble:

```
$ ./so-5_2-ga-bin-linux-en.bin
```

You should run the preceding command as a normal user, not root, so you do not have to be root to run the Star Office program.

Hardware-related installation problems

The tips in this section should help you solve the most common hardware-related problems people encounter when installing Red Hat Linux.

CANNOT RUN INSTALLATION PROGRAM ON IDE RAID CONTROLLER

The installation program is unable to install on drives attached to certain 3ware IDE RAID controllers, complaining that the attached drive has an invalid partition table. The solution is to download an updated installation disk. For a complete description of the problem and the steps to take to resolve it, see `http://www.redhat.com/support/errata/RHBA-2001-131.html`.

UNABLE TO MOUNT THE CD-ROM AFTER INSTALLATION

On some systems, the CD-ROM fails to mount after a new installation. Apparently, this is an installer bug. The symptom is that after completing a new installation or upgrading an existing Red Hat Linux installation, the `mount` utility issues an error message similar to `dev/cdrom not a valid block device`, followed by a failed mount and, in some cases, a system crash. To solve this problem, boot the system using the boot disk you created during installation, and then execute the following command as root:

```
# /sbin/depmod -ae
```

You should also download and install the latest kernel errata. For complete details, see the bug report and solution description in the document `http://www.redhat.com/support/errata/RHSA-2001-142.html`.

IDE CD-ROM NOT DETECTED

A similar CD-ROM installation problem is that an IDE CD-ROM is not detected, making CD-ROM installations impossible. The issue here is either that the CD-ROM is on an IDE channel that the system's BIOS does not know about, or that the kernel does not recognize the results of a hardware probe for IDE CD-ROMs. The ideal solution is to tell the kernel where to find the CD-ROM at the boot LILO `boot:` prompt using the following procedure.

TIP   You can also use this procedure if an IDE CD-ROM appears to lock up in the middle of an installation.

1. Boot the system using the boot disk you created for the installation.

2. When you see

   ```
   boot:
   ```

   or

   ```
   LILO:
   ```

   type `linux hdX=cdrom` and press Enter.

   X should be `a` or `b` if the CD-ROM is on the primary (first) IDE channel or `c` or `d` if the CD-ROM is on the secondary (second) IDE channel.

If the kernel *still* fails to recognize the CD-ROM and you have sufficient free disk space, you can attempt to install Red Hat Linux from the hard drive using the following procedure:

1. Make sure you have a DOS partition that is formatted as a FAT16 or FAT32 (DOS/Windows or Windows 95, respectively) partition.

2. Execute the following commands to copy the necessary files from the CD-ROM to the hard drive:

   ```
   mkdir C:\RedHat
   mkdir C:\RedHat\base
   mkdir C:\RedHat\RPMS
   mkdir C:\RedHat\instimage
   copy E:\RedHat\base C:\RedHat\base
   copy E:\RedHat\RPMS C:\RedHat\RPMS
   copy E:\RedHat\instimage C:\RedHat\instimage
   ```

   These commands assume your CD-ROM drive is the `E:` drive under DOS/Windows and that the free disk space exists on the DOS/Windows `C:` drive. Adjust the drive letters accordingly if necessary.

3. Start the installation using the boot disk you created earlier and, when prompted, select the hard drive installation method.

NO SOUND AFTER INSTALLATION

If you do not have sound support after installation, check the boot log (`/var/log/boot.log`) for messages resembling the following:

```
Nov 23 23:15:11 bubba rc.sysinit: Finding module dependencies:  succeeded
Nov 23 23:15:11 bubba modprobe: Using /lib/modules/2.4.7-10/misc/sound.o
Nov 23 23:15:11 bubba modprobe: insmod: a module named sound already exists
Nov 23 23:15:11 bubba rc.sysinit: Loading sound module (sb):  failed
Nov 23 23:15:11 bubba modprobe: insmod: insmod
/lib/modules/2.4.7-10/misc/sound.o failed
Nov 23 23:15:11 bubba modprobe: insmod: insmod sb failed
Nov 23 23:15:11 bubba rc.sysinit: Loading midi module (awe_wave):  succeeded
```

Next, use the `/sbin/lsmod` command to determine which, if any, sound modules are loaded. For example

```
# /sbin/lsmod
Module              Size  Used by
ide-cd             23628   0  (autoclean)
soundcore           2596   0  (autoclean) (unused)
lockd              31176   1  (autoclean)
sunrpc             52964   1  (autoclean) [lockd]
eepro100           19844   1  (autoclean)
agpgart            18600   0  (unused)
```

If the output resembles that shown, run the `sndconfig` sound card configuration program to set up your sound card.

SOLVING LAPTOP VIDEO PROBLEMS

Laptop installations are typically the most difficult type of installation to perform because the companies that build laptop computers often use proprietary hardware or modify standard PC components in order to shoehorn desktop PC functionality into the confines of a laptop or to meet weight, power, or functionality requirements. Aggravating such practical concerns, these engineering decisions are rarely publicly documented in order to protect trade secrets. As a result, you often have to use a trial-and-error method and rely on the experiences of others.

 A few laptop manufacturers actively support Linux. IBM, for example, preinstalls Linux on a select group of laptop computers, and certain dedicated Linux hardware vendors do the same. The lack of support *is* frustrating, but until manufacturers can be bothered to develop Linux drivers for their products at the same time as they develop Windows drivers, installing Linux on a laptop computer will continue to be a challenge.

While attempting a graphical Red Hat Linux installation from either the CD-ROM or a floppy disk, you may see the laptop screen go blank and you cannot

continue. In this case, attempting a text-based installation might work — trying to force a graphical installation rarely works if the installer cannot use your video hardware. With *some* laptops the graphical installer *might* work if you type the following parameter at the boot: prompt:

```
boot: linux vga=2
```

Similarly, you can try all of the possible VGA modes using the following parameter:

```
boot: linux vga=ask
```

Before giving up completely, have a look at the authoritative reference for Linux and laptops, the Linux Laptop Web site at http://www.cs.utexas.edu/users/kharker/linux-laptop/.

THE SIGNAL 7 AND SIGNAL 11 PROBLEM

Perhaps the most confusing problem people run into when installing Red Hat Linux is an error message resembling fatal signal 11 or fatal signal 7. Signal 11s and signal 7s are errors indicating a hardware problem in memory or on the system's data bus. Red Hat Linux does not cause such errors. Rather, it brings such problems to light because the Linux kernel typically pushes hardware to the fullest extent of its capabilities, much more so than DOS or Windows, often revealing substandard hardware.

How should you proceed? The first thing to do is check to see if you have the latest installation image from Red Hat. If the latest image still fails, the problem may be hardware related. Common suspects include bad RAM chips or defective CPU cache memory. Try turning off the CPU cache in the BIOS and see if the problem goes away. Likewise, try swapping memory around in the system's memory slots to see whether the error is slot or memory related. If that does not solve the problem, the Signal 11 Web site, http://www.bitwizard.nl/sig11/, may be able to help you. If all else fails, take the system to a computer repair shop and ask them to test the hardware, and emphasize that the RAM and possibly the CPU cache needs to be tested using a hardware tester.

Solving File System Problems

The tips in this section help you solve common problems you might encounter when working with Linux files and file systems.

Cannot delete a file

If you cannot delete, move, or rename a file, use the ls -l command to verify that you have permission to do so. If you receive an error message resembling rmdir:

`` `dirname' ``: `directory not empty` when using `rmdir` to delete a directory, either delete the files in the directory before retrying the `rmdir` command or use `rm -r` to delete the directory and its contents. For example

```
$ rmdir images
rmdir: `images': directory not empty
$ rm -r images
```

A common question is how to delete a file that has a name beginning with a minus (-). Suppose, for example, a file in your home directory is named `-foo`. The command `rm -foo` fails and generates the following error:

```
$ rm -foo
rm: invalid option -- o
```

This problem occurs because most Linux commands interpret a minus sign followed by a letter as a command option, and anything following that as an argument to the command. So, the argument to the `rm` command, `-foo`, looks like invalid syntax, not a filename. The solution is to use two minus signs (- -) between `rm` and `-foo`. Most Linux commands interpret two minus signs standing alone as the end of all options; everything afterward is interpreted as an argument. So, to remove the file named `-foo`, try `rm -- -foo`, as follows:

```
$ rm -- -foo
```

To delete a file that has a name beginning with -, you can also use the following:

```
$ rm -- "-foo"
```

Commands with multi-word arguments

If you pass an argument made up of multiple words to a command and get an error message stating, in part, `No such file or directory`, enclose the argument between weak quotes (" ") and try again. Remember that most shells use spaces and tab characters to distinguish between commands, options, and arguments. For example, the following command generates an error message before showing its result:

```
$ grep Kurt Wall /etc/passwd
grep: Wall: no such file or directory
/etc/passwd:kwall:x:500:500:Kurt Wall:/home/kwall:/bin/bash
```

Enclosing `Kurt Wall` within weak quotes solves the problem:

```
$ grep "Kurt Wall" /etc/passwd
/etc/passwd:kwall:x:500:500:Kurt Wall:/home/kwall:/bin/bash
```

Accessing Windows file systems

If you get an error message that the VFAT (Virtual File Allocation Table) file system, the Windows file system, is not supported when using the `mount` command to mount a DOS/Windows floppy disk, log in as the root user and execute the following command:

```
# /sbin/modprobe vfat
```

This command loads the necessary modules that Red Hat Linux needs in order to provide support for DOS/Windows file systems.

Working with floppy disks

If you get a `device busy` error message when trying to unmount a floppy disk with the `umount` command, make sure your current directory is not located on the floppy disk (use the `pwd` command). Red Hat Linux cannot unmount a file system or disk of any sort if a process is using it, which includes having a current working directory located anywhere on the file system.

If you cannot use the `cd` command to change your current working directory, execute the following command to see the process IDs (PIDs) of any processes using the mount point:

```
# fuser /file-system-name
```

Next, use the following command:

```
# ps -p pid
```

Replace *pid* with the PIDs from the previous command, to see what process or processes are still using the file system.

If you accidentally remove a floppy disk from a mounted drive without first unmounting it, in many cases you can simply reinsert the floppy disk and execute the appropriate `umount` command to unmount the drive properly.

Cannot mount a partition

If you are unable to mount one or more partitions after an upgrade, the problem could be due to the use of partition labels. Red Hat Linux uses partition labels to help prevent problems that occur when moving hard drives around in a system. For example, if / is on /dev/sdb and a new drive is added to the system with a lower SCSI ID, the drive that was previously /dev/sdb becomes /dev/sdc. This change causes the mount command to generate errors when it tries mount /. Partition labels address this problem because mount tries to mount the partition identified by its labels as / instead of trying to mount /dev/sdb1 and expecting it to be /. The idea is great in theory as long as you keep partition labels less than 16 characters. The Red Hat update site has a bugfix for the mount and e2fsprogs that fixes mount and e2fsprogs.

Avoiding file system checks at each system reboot

If you constantly have to run fsck each time you boot your system, the most likely suspect is that your partitions are not being unmounted properly when you last shut down the machine. The most important thing you can do is make sure that you are shutting down the machine properly. Shutdown is done through one of two methods:

◆ If you are in text mode — run level 3 — you should log in as root and type the following command:

```
# sync;sync;sync;shutdown -r now
```

◆ If you are using the graphical login — run level 5 — click System → Halt. Eventually, you see a line that reads Power Down, indicating it is safe to turn off the machine.

In either case, if you are running APM, Linux tries to stop the machine using the BIOS.

Getting a Zip drive to work

To get an Iomega Zip drive attached to a parallel port to work, use the following procedure:

1. Edit /etc/conf.modules and add the following lines:

```
alias parport_lowlevel parport_pc
alias scsi_hostadapter ppa
```

2. Log in as root and run the following command:

```
# modprobe ppa
```

If you are having problems with an IDE Zip drive, first check to make sure there is a disk in the drive and make sure you are mounting it as partition 4 instead of 1; for example, /dev/hdc4 instead of /dev/hdc1. The reason for this is that Macintosh uses partition 4 for its data partition and has problems if data is on another partition.

Solving Networking Problems

If you are unable to access hosts on a network, make sure you have at least one name server listed in /etc/resolv.conf. If an external system cannot connect to your system, remember the order in which the hosts.allow and hosts.deny files are read and applied. The program that starts Internet services consults /etc/hosts.allow first. If TCP wrappers does not find a matching rule, it applies the first matching rule, if any, in /etc/hosts.deny. If neither file contains a match, access is granted.

If you performed an upgrade of Red Hat Linux from an earlier version, it may appear that the upgrade did not preserve the contents of your network service configuration files. This is not the case, however. The configuration files were renamed with the extension .rpmsave and can be found in the network service's directory. For example, you might find that the old /etc/httpd/conf/httpd.conf file was renamed /etc/httpd/conf/httpd.conf.rpmsave. Changes should be copied to the new version of the configuration file.

- ◆ Files with a .rpmorig extension are configuration files not in an RPM package that was upgraded or installed.

- ◆ Files with a .rpmsave extension are configuration files that were in an RPM package that was upgraded or installed.

- ◆ Files with a .rpmnew extension indicates the new version of a file installed by an upgraded package.

Affected network services configuration files include, but are not limited to:

- ◆ /etc/httpd/conf/httpd.conf

- ◆ /etc/samba/smb.conf

- ◆ /etc/sendmail.cf

- ◆ /etc/named.conf

- ◆ /etc/dhcpd.conf

To avoid unfortunate accidents and needless panic or confusion, remember to back up your data before upgrading or installing the latest version of Red Hat Linux.

Chapter 22 shows you how to back up your Red Hat Linux system.

Getting online with a modem

If you are having trouble getting your modem to work, first verify that it is supported by checking the Hardware Compatibility List at `http://hardware.redhat.com/`. Next, see if the modem is being detected by the system and make sure that it does not conflict with other resources. You can check this using the following commands:

```
#.cat /proc/ioports
0000-001f : dma1
0020-003f : pic1
0040-005f : timer
0060-006f : keyboard
0070-007f : rtc
00a0-00bf : pic2
00c0-00df : dma2
00f0-00ff : fpu
0170-0177 : ide1
01f0-01f7 : ide0
0220-022f : soundblaster
02f8-02ff : serial(auto)
0330-0333 : MPU-401 UART
0376-0376 : ide1
03c0-03df : vga+
03f6-03f6 : ide0
03f8-03ff : serial(auto)
d000-d07f : eth0
d800-d807 : ide0
d808-d80f : ide1
# cat /proc/interrupts
          CPU0
0:     1296380        XT-PIC  timer
1:       30736        XT-PIC  keyboard
2:           0        XT-PIC  cascade
5:           1        XT-PIC  soundblaster
8:           1        XT-PIC  rtc
0:       73593        XT-PIC  eth0
2:      159669        XT-PIC  PS/2 Mouse
3:           1        XT-PIC  fpu
4:      246863        XT-PIC  ide0
5:      584998        XT-PIC  ide1
NMI:         0
```

One example of a resource conflict is that your modem and some other device share an interrupt. COM1 (/dev/ttyS0) and COM3 (/dev/ttyS3) try to share the same interrupt unless told otherwise. Eliminate the conflict by setting a jumper for one of the devices that causes it to use another IRQ. Next, use `minicom` to see if you can communicate with the modem. The following Web pages help you configure a PPP connection:

- ◆ http://www.redhat.com/support/docs/tips/PPP-Client-Tips/ PPP-Client-Tips.html

- ◆ http://www.redhat.com/support/docs/tips/Network-Config-Tips/ Network-Config-Tips.html

If `setserial` shows your modem's UART as `unknown`, as you see in the following example, the kernel has not detected your serial port or the modem attached to it:

```
/dev/ttyS2, UART: unknown, Port: 0x03f8, IRQ: 10
```

This problem usually occurs because your PC's BIOS is set up to expect a Plug and Play (PnP) operating system. To solve the problem, reboot the PC and, as it powers up, press the key that permits you to access the system's BIOS. Typically, this is a function key, such as F2, but the exact key depends on your PC's BIOS. In the setup screen, locate the option for PnP operating system (often labeled "Plug & Play O/S") and turn off that option. Then save the BIOS settings and exit. Doing so causes the PC to reboot. This time, when Red Hat Linux boots, the kernel should be able to detect the PC's serial port correctly.

If your serial ports are correctly detected but the modem does not respond, make sure that `/dev/modem` is linked to the proper device file in `/dev`. An unresponsive modem is especially common with PCI modem cards, which typically do not use COM1 (`/dev/ttyS0`) or COM2 (`/dev/ttyS1`) by default. For example, suppose `dmesg | grep ttyS` shows the following:

```
ttyS02 at port 0x6800 (irq = 10) is a 16550A
```

In this case, execute the following command to make sure that `/dev/modem` is linked to the proper device file:

```
# ln -sf /dev/ttyS2 /dev/modem
```

If your modem does not appear to be detected, use the Windows Device Manager to obtain the modem's IRQ and I/O address, and compare those values to the values the `setserial` command reports for that port.

At present, some modems simply do not work with Linux. These are so-called "WinModems," which, in order to function, rely on the Windows operating system and a special, Windows-specific device driver. WinModems, also called *software modems*, rely on a device driver, rather than hardware, to function. In this case, your only recourse is to replace the modem with a hardware modem.

If you can connect to your ISP but are unable to surf the Web, or Netscape complains that it cannot connect to remote hosts, the problem is most likely unconfigured or misconfigured DNS (Domain Name Server) information. You need to specify your ISP's DNS servers in the `/etc/resolv.conf` file. Contact your ISP for this information and edit the file to include those settings. For example:

```
search example.com
nameserver 24.8.89.15
nameserver 24.8.89.16
```

What to do when the boot process hangs

A network problem exists if your system boots but then seems to hang when starting `sendmail`, the Sendmail daemon; `httpd`, the Apache Web server daemon; or `smb`, the Samba daemon. The most common cause is that Linux cannot resolve the host name to an IP address. The apparent hang is a pause while the kernel waits for the name resolver to time out — the boot process *will* eventually complete. To solve this problem, wait until you can log in, then log in as root to investigate and solve the problem. If you are attached directly to a network with a functioning DNS server, make sure the file `/etc/resolv.conf` has the correct values for your system's DNS server(s). Make sure that the values are correct. If you are using Red Hat Linux on a system attached to a network without a DNS server, or if your Red Hat system is destined to be the DNS server, edit the `/etc/hosts` file and insert your system's IPaddress and name to have the host name and IP address so that the lookups occur correctly. The format of the `/etc/hosts` file is:

```
127.0.0.1        localhost.localdomain localhost
192.168.0.1      bubba.somedomain.com bubba
```

Replace `bubba.somedomain.com` with the proper name of your system and the IP address with the IP address of your system.

Using two Ethernet cards

To use two Ethernet cards in your Red Hat Linux system, first ensure that both cards are supported. Next, if the two cards use different drivers, you need to set up the second network interface and edit the `/etc/modules.conf` file to load the proper driver for the second card. If the two cards use the same driver, you may need to recompile your kernel, but several modules now allow for multiple cards. It may be that you just need to use boot arguments, such as:

```
boot: linux ether=11,0x300,eth0 ether=5,0x340,eth1
```

This option can be made permanent so that you do not have to reenter it every time your system boots. See the LILO configuration option `append=` in the `lilo.conf` man page. The Ethernet HOWTO is an excellent source of information

for configuring multiple Ethernet cards in the same system. It can be found at
http://www.redhat.com/mirrors/LDP/HOWTO/Ethernet-HOWTO.html.

Solving Boot Problems

If you try to shut down or reboot your Red Hat Linux system using the commands
reboot, halt, shutdown -r now, or shutdown -h now and the shutdown process
starts to execute correctly but then the display blanks and the system hangs, the
only way to recover is to power cycle the system and then try some of the following
workarounds. The problem is that at the point the system appears to hang, control
of the hardware has been handed back from Linux to the firmware — it is up to the
firmware (software embedded in key system hardware components) to reboot the
system correctly. Fortunately, Linux enables you to select multiple ways to reboot
the system in order to fix, or at least sidestep, buggy or broken BIOSes or hardware.

At the LILO: boot prompt, you can specify:

reboot=X,Y

X can be one of hard or bios.

- ◆ hard — Uses the CPU's reset instruction to restart the system.
- ◆ bios — Uses a BIOS routine (sometimes called a *BIOS vector*) to restart the system.

Y can be one of warm or cold.

- ◆ warm — A *warm boot* is the type of reboot invoked when you press Ctrl+Alt+Delete.
- ◆ cold — A *cold boot* is the type of boot invoked by power cycling the system.

So if you boot with the following command, Linux reboots by the BIOS vector
with a warm reboot:

LILO: linux reboot=bios,warm

The goal is to find the right combination of X and Y that triggers the bugs in the
system BIOS. Once you have found this magic sequence, use LILO's append= option
to pass these parameters to the kernel each time you boot the system by adding it
to /etc/lilo.conf as shown in the following example:

append="reboot=bios,warm"

Rerun /sbin/lilo -v to write the change to your boot device.

If your system installed without incident until it tried to write LILO information to the MBR (Master Boot Record), at which point the installer complained that it could not write to the MBR, the MBR may be locked by the BIOS. You need to access your system's BIOS and verify that the MBR is not write-protected. Similarly, disable any virus scan enabled in the BIOS that may interfere with writing to the MBR. If neither of these situations applies, you may already have another boot loader in the MBR that conflicts with LILO. If you know the MBR is not write-protected, try the following steps to install LILO to the MBR:

1. Boot the system to Linux. If your system cannot boot into Linux from the hard drive, boot using your boot floppy.

2. Type `vmlinuz root=/dev/hdXX` at the `LILO:` prompt, replacing `hdXX` with the correct location of your Linux root partition.

3. When your system is finished booting, log in as root and check `/etc/lilo.conf` to make sure everything is correct. An example `/etc/lilo.conf` is shown in the following listing:

```
boot=/dev/hda
map=/boot/map
install=/boot/boot.b
prompt
timeout=50
message=/boot/message
default=linux

image=/boot/vmlinuz-2.4.7-10
    label=linux
    initrd=/boot/initrd-2.4.7-10.img
    read-only
    root=/dev/hda5
```

Type `man lilo.conf` for more information about configuring `/etc/lilo.conf`.

4. When you are sure that `/etc/lilo.conf` is properly configured, execute the following command to test the configuration:

```
# /sbin/lilo -v -v -t
```

If you receive any errors, stop and verify that `/etc/ lilo.conf` file is correctly configured. If the `lilo` command works correctly, remove the `-t` option and rerun the command:

```
# lilo -v -v
```

5. Finally, reboot the system:

```
# sync;sync;sync;shutdown -r now
```

These steps install LILO to your MBR properly and enable you to boot without using a boot disk.

If you have trouble booting Windows from your second hard disk /dev/hdb after installing Red Hat Linux on the first hard disk, /dev/hda, the problem is that Windows expects to boot from the first hard disk. The symptom of this problem is that if you select Windows at the boot prompt, all you see is:

```
Starting....
```

Then the system locks up. To fix this problem, trick Windows into believing that it is the first drive in the system by modifying the /etc/lilo.conf file so that the entry for Windows looks like the following:

```
other=/dev/hdb1
    label=dos
    table=/dev/hdb
    map-drive = 0x80
    to = 0x81
    map-drive = 0x81
    to = 0x80
```

Rerun LILO so that your changes take effect:

```
#/sbin/lilo -v -v
```

Another common LILO problem is seeing only the following when the system boots:

```
LI
```

This means that LILO is having problems loading itself. A couple of possible situations may be causing this. You may have installed LILO above cylinder 1024 on your hard drive. (The kernel needs to reside entirely below cylinder 1023 on the drive.) If this is the case, you need to create a /boot partition that resides in these limits, and then reinstall LILO. You may also need to go into your system's BIOS and make certain that logical block addressing (LBA) mode is enabled. If LBA is off, you need to repartition and reinstall.

To remove LILO from the MBR, you can use one of the following commands. From Linux, execute the following command to replace the MBR with an earlier saved version of the MBR:

```
# /sbin/lilo -u
```

From DOS, Windows 95, or Windows NT you can use the `fdisk` command to create a new MBR using the `/mbr` option. This rewrites the MBR to boot only the primary DOS partition:

```
fdisk /mbr
```

Solving Miscellaneous Problems

The tips suggested in this section address the hodgepodge of problems and challenges you might face using Red Hat Linux.

Getting sound to work

If you are having trouble getting sound to work in Red Hat Linux, you usually need only log in as root and run the `sndconfig` command. If this does not work, some of the methods suggested next may help you narrow down or solve the problem.

Disable Plug and Play on the card via jumpers or card configuration tools that work from Windows or DOS.

If `sndconfig` is not configuring the sound card correctly, or at all, try:

```
# /usr/sbin/sndconfig --noautoconfig
```

This command lets you manually specify the plug and play values for the card. The values from Windows probably works if it is the only plug and play device in the machine, but examine the output from the following four commands to make sure you are not running into a resource conflict with another device in the system:

```
$ cat /proc/interrupts
$ cat /proc/ioports
$ cat /proc/dma
$ cat /proc/pci
```

You can also try using `sndconfig`, and then edit `/etc/modules.conf` to use the correct values. Your `/etc/modules.conf` will have a couple of lines that resemble the following:

```
alias sound sb
options sb irq=7 io=0x320 dma=3,5
```

After editing `/etc/modules.conf`, reload the sound modules using the following commands:

```
# /etc/rc.d/init.d/sound stop
# /etc/rc.d/init.d/sound start
```

Finally, you can also edit `/etc/modules.conf`, delete any lines that refer to your sound card, reboot, and then try to use `sndconfig` again to configure your sound card.

If none of the previous steps work, you can try using the `isapnptools` programs as shown in the following procedure:

1. Execute the following command as root:

   ```
   # /sbin/pnpdump > /etc/isapnp.conf
   ```

   The `pnpdump` command probes the system to see what plug and play devices are installed and generates a template file named `/etc/isapnp.conf` that the plug and play configuration tool, `isapnp`, reads.

2. Edit `/etc/isapnp.conf` to select a set of resources that do not conflict with other devices in the system.

3. Execute the following command to set up your plug and play devices:

   ```
   # /sbin/isapnp /etc/isapnp.conf
   ```

If this does not work, edit `/etc/isapnp.conf` and adjust the values to fit those of your card. The file format is pretty cryptic, so you may want to check the ISA PNP Tools Web page at `http://www.roestock.demon.co.uk/isapnptools/` for more information.

If the card is not a plug and play card *and* you know its settings, you can set them manually by editing `/etc/modules.conf`. For example

```
alias sound sb
alias midi opl3
options opl3 io=0x388
options sb io=0x220 irq=5 dma=1,3 mpu_io=0x330
```

You may need to go through one or more of these procedures several times to get good values. Essentially, this trial-and-error process is what `sndconfig` does automatically, but, unfortunately, `sndconfig` does not work for all sound cards.

Using screensavers and power management

To disable screen blanking, turn off your screen saver. In text mode, the kernel turns on the screen blanker after 15 minutes, but you can disable this using the following command:

```
# setterm -powersave off -blank 0
```

If you hear disk drives speed up or other sounds, this is most likely APM (Advanced Power Management) starting up the system after idle time. You can disable APM from starting at boot time by logging in as root and typing `ntsysv`. Deselect APM, exit `ntsysv`, and reboot the machine. APM is one of the few Red Hat Linux services that require a system restart to make it take effect — APM is a low-level kernel function, so a full reset is needed.

Starting the X Window System

What should you do if you run `startx` and get a black screen? To get out of the black screen mode, try pressing Ctrl+Alt+Backspace. This keystroke combination causes the X server to exit if possible. If it does not work, reboot the system and reconfigure the X Window System using `Xconfigurator` after making sure that all your video hardware is compatible. You may want or need to obtain the latest version of XFree86 from `http://www.redhat.com/support/errata/`. Upgrading X is fairly simple, but an upgrade HOWTO is available at the Red Hat Web site at `http://www.redhat.com/support/docs/howto/XFree86-upgrade/XFree86-upgrade.html`.

If you get an error message resembling `errno 111` when you run `startx`, an X client (any X program except the X server itself running on your XFree86 X system, such as terminal window or even the window manager) tried to connect to the X server but failed to do so for some reason. Unfortunately, you ordinarily see only the last few lines of the error message. To see the complete message, execute the following command:

```
$ X -probeonly >& startx.out
```

This command creates a file named `startx.out` that contains the complete error message. Review the text of the error message carefully for clues concerning the real problem X is having.

Summary

This chapter offered numerous tips and techniques for overcoming commonly encountered problems installing, configuring, and using Red Hat Linux. You first read how to solve installation problems, such as not being able to use some RAID cards and not being able to mount a CD-ROM after the post-installation reboot. Next, you learned how to work around problems accessing files and using Windows file systems. After you explored ways to resolve difficulties getting online using a modem, you read how to disable power management and how to work through problems starting the X Window System.

Appendix

What's on the CD-ROM?

IN THIS APPENDIX

♦ System requirements

♦ What's on the CD?

♦ Troubleshooting

THIS APPENDIX provides you with information about the contents of the CD-ROM that accompanies this book. (For the latest and greatest information, please refer to the README file located at the root of the CD-ROM.)

System Requirements

Make sure that your computer meets the minimum system requirements listed in this section. If your computer doesn't match up to most of these requirements, you may have a problem using the contents of the CD:

♦ PC with a Pentium processor running at 120 MHz or faster

♦ At least 64MB of RAM installed on your computer

♦ Ethernet network interface card (NIC)

♦ Modem with a speed of at least 28,800 bps

♦ A CD-ROM drive

 You can use a Windows or Macintosh system for viewing the PDF version of the book and reading the Links document. The programs included with the disc, with the exception of Adobe Acrobat, are intended to be used on a system running Red Hat Linux.

What's on the CD?

The following sections provide a summary of the software and other materials on the CD.

Sample code

All examples from the book, including code listings and samples, are on the CD in the folder named "Author."

Links

The CD also includes a file containing all of the links referenced in the book. From this file, you can click the listed link and, assuming you're connected, go to that location on the Internet.

While we have made every effort to ensure that the links listed in the Links file are valid at the time of publication, Web addresses sometimes change. In some instances, a link listed in the file may be broken or may not take you to the desired site.

Applications

The CD contains several network utility and security-related programs. Using these programs, you can analyze your network, determine your system's vulnerabilities, and fix the problems you might discover. The following applications are on the CD:

ADOBE ACROBAT READER
This program is used to view and print files stored in Adobe PDF format. Look for more information about Adobe Acrobat at www.adobe.com.

ETHEREAL
Ethereal is a network protocol analyzer for Unix and Linux systems. You can use Ethereal to examine data from a live network or from a saved file. You can find more information about Ethereal at www.ethereal.com.

LOGCHECK
Logcheck is a program that can identify problems and security violations in your logfiles and automatically send the details to you in an e-mail. You can obtain more information about Logcheck at www.psionic.com/abacus/logcheck.

NET-SNMP

net-snmp provides tools and libraries relating to the Simple Network Management Protocol, including an extensible agent, an SNMP library, tools to request or set information from SNMP agents, and tools to generate and handle SNMP traps. For information about net-snmp, go to `http://sourceforge.net/projects/net-snmp`.

NMAP

Nmap is a port-scanning program. Use Nmap to search for one or more hosts on a network to determine the services offered, operating system used, and type of firewall on the searched host. You can also obtain information on many other items. For more about Nmap, go to `www.insecure.org/nmap`.

SAINT

SAINT is an acronym for Security Administrator's Integrated Network Tool. This program can be used to test various areas of network security. For more information about SAINT go to `www.wwdsi.com/saint/`.

Shareware programs are fully functional trial versions of copyrighted programs. If you like particular programs, register with their authors for nominal fees and receive licenses, enhanced versions, and technical support. *Freeware programs* are free copyrighted games, applications, and utilities. Unlike shareware, these programs do not require a fee or provide technical support. *GNU software* is governed by its own license, which is included inside the folder of the GNU product. See the GNU license for more details.

Trial, demo, or evaluation versions are usually limited either by time or functionality (such as being unable to save projects). Some trial versions are sensitive to system date changes. If you alter your computer's date, the programs "time out" and are no longer functional.

Electronic version of Red Hat Linux Networking and System Administration

The complete text of this book is on the CD in Adobe's Portable Document Format (PDF). You can read and search through the file with the Adobe Acrobat Reader (also included on the CD).

Troubleshooting

If you have difficulty installing or using any of the materials on the companion CD, try the following solutions:

◆ **Turn off any antivirus software that you may have running.** Installers sometimes mimic virus activity and can make your computer incorrectly believe that it is being infected by a virus. (Be sure to turn the antivirus software back on later.)

◆ **Close all running programs.** The more programs you're running, the less memory is available to other programs. Installers also typically update files and programs; if you keep other programs running, installation may not work properly.

◆ **Consult the ReadMe.txt.** Please refer to the README file located at the root of the CD-ROM for the latest product information at the time of publication.

If you still have trouble with the CD, please call the Wiley Customer Care phone number: 800-762-2974. Outside the United States, call 317-572-3993. You can also contact Wiley Customer Service by e-mail at techsupdum@ wiley.com. Wiley provides technical support only for installation and other general quality control items; for technical support on the applications themselves, consult the program's vendor or author.

Index

Symbols and Numerics

B

continued

continued

continued

continued

continued

continued

continued

continued

continued

W

warm boot, 780

warnquota, 607, 611–613

Washington, University of. *See* Pine e-mail program; WU-FTPD

weak quotes ("), 506, 507, 773–774

Web browser
  kernel, upgrading through, 426–429
  Microsoft networks, running, 215
  Mozilla, 394
  Red Hat Network, using through, 413–418

Web pages
  Apache, 369
  updating, 387, 394–396

Web resources, security, 701–703

Web server. *See* Apache Web server

Web sites, addresses listed
  Apache information, 366, 369, 376
  applications on CD, back-of-the-book, 788–789
  Filesystem Hierarchy Standard (FHS), 71
  firewall piercing, 744
  hardware issues, 19, 31, 769, 772, 780
  Internet Software Consortium, 274
  kernel source code, 426
  NcFTPd, 303
  NFS (Network File System), 179
  NIS (Network Information Service), 190
  password cracking program, 717
  password generators, 721
  Plug and Play Tools, 784
  POSIX, 576
  ProFTPD, 303
  Red Hat installation manual, 27
  Red Hat Network, registering, 404
  Red Hat package repositories, 666, 667, 668, 670

rootkits, 725

Samba, 210

security, 22, 726, 750, 758

Zip drives, configuring and using, 445

Web sites, software updates
  Apache Web server, 372
  Freshmeat, 667–668
  Gnome-RPM, finding through, 669–670
  GNU project, 670–671
  Ibiblio.org, 668–669
  Linuxberg, 670
  Linux.com, 670
  most popular, 665–666
  rpmfind.org, 666–667

wetware hacking, 699–701

wheel group, boot security, 713–715

while loop, 523, 526–527

Whitehats, 703

wildcards
  archive files, 636
  Bash, 504–508

Windows (Microsoft). *See also* Samba
  boot disk, creating, 31–32
  boot loader, 100
  mixed networks, security, 19
  monitors, setting up, 54
  networks, connecting, 209
  starting, 44

Windows (Microsoft) file systems
  access problems, 774
  described, 72, 81
  kernel, customizing, 451

Windows printers (Microsoft), enabling, 230–232

WinModems, 778

WKS, 289

workstations
  booting diskless, 302
  client/server networking, 18

Wiley Publishing, Inc.
End-User License Agreement

READ THIS. You should carefully read these terms and conditions before opening the software packet(s) included with this book "Book". This is a license agreement "Agreement" between you and Wiley Publishing, Inc. "WPI". By opening the accompanying software packet(s), you acknowledge that you have read and accept the following terms and conditions. If you do not agree and do not want to be bound by such terms and conditions, promptly return the Book and the unopened software packet(s) to the place you obtained them for a full refund.

1. **License Grant.** WPI grants to you (either an individual or entity) a nonexclusive license to use one copy of the enclosed software program(s) (collectively, the "Software" solely for your own personal or business purposes on a single computer (whether a standard computer or a workstation component of a multi-user network). The Software is in use on a computer when it is loaded into temporary memory (RAM) or installed into permanent memory (hard disk, CD-ROM, or other storage device). WPI reserves all rights not expressly granted herein.

2. **Ownership.** WPI is the owner of all right, title, and interest, including copyright, in and to the compilation of the Software recorded on the disk(s) or CD-ROM "Software Media". Copyright to the individual programs recorded on the Software Media is owned by the author or other authorized copyright owner of each program. Ownership of the Software and all proprietary rights relating thereto remain with WPI and its licensers.

3. **Restrictions On Use and Transfer.**

   (a) You may only (i) make one copy of the Software for backup or archival purposes, or (ii) transfer the Software to a single hard disk, provided that you keep the original for backup or archival purposes. You may not (i) rent or lease the Software, (ii) copy or reproduce the Software through a LAN or other network system or through any computer subscriber system or bulletin-board system, or (iii) modify, adapt, or create derivative works based on the Software.

   (b) You may not reverse engineer, decompile, or disassemble the Software. You may transfer the Software and user documentation on a permanent basis, provided that the transferee agrees to accept the terms and conditions of this Agreement and you retain no copies. If the Software is an update or has been updated, any transfer must include the most recent update and all prior versions.

4. **Restrictions on Use of Individual Programs.** You must follow the individual requirements and restrictions detailed for each individual program in Appendix of this Book. These limitations are also contained in the individual license agreements recorded on the Software Media. These limitations may include a requirement that after using the program for a specified period of time, the user must pay a registration fee or discontinue use. By opening the Software packet(s), you will be agreeing to abide by the licenses and restrictions for these individual programs that are detailed in Appendix and on the Software Media. None of the material on this Software Media or listed in this Book may ever be redistributed, in original or modified form, for commercial purposes.

5. **Limited Warranty.**

   (a) WPI warrants that the Software and Software Media are free from defects in materials and workmanship under normal use for a period of sixty (60) days from the date of purchase of this Book. If WPI receives notification within the warranty period of defects in materials or workmanship, WPI will replace the defective Software Media.

   (b) WPI AND THE AUTHOR OF THE BOOK DISCLAIM ALL OTHER WARRANTIES, EXPRESS OR IMPLIED, INCLUDING WITHOUT LIMITATION IMPLIED WARRANTIES OF MERCHANTABILITY AND FITNESS FOR A PARTICULAR PURPOSE, WITH RESPECT TO THE SOFTWARE, THE PROGRAMS, THE SOURCE CODE CONTAINED THEREIN, AND/OR THE TECHNIQUES DESCRIBED IN THIS BOOK. WPI DOES NOT WARRANT THAT THE FUNCTIONS CONTAINED IN THE SOFTWARE WILL MEET YOUR REQUIREMENTS OR THAT THE OPERATION OF THE SOFTWARE WILL BE ERROR FREE.

   (c) This limited warranty gives you specific legal rights, and you may have other rights that vary from jurisdiction to jurisdiction.

6. **Remedies.**

   (a) WPI's entire liability and your exclusive remedy for defects in materials and workmanship shall be limited to replacement of the Software Media, which may be returned to WPI with a copy of your receipt at the following address: Software Media Fulfillment Department, Attn.: *Red Hat linux Networking and System Administration,* Wiley Publishing, Inc., 10475 Crosspoint Blvd., Indianapolis, IN 46256, or call 1-800-762-2974. Please allow four to six weeks for delivery. This Limited Warranty is void if failure of the Software Media has resulted from accident, abuse, or misapplication. Any replacement Software Media will be warranted for the remainder of the original warranty period or thirty (30) days, whichever is longer.

(b) In no event shall WPI or the author be liable for any damages whatsoever (including without limitation damages for loss of business profits, business interruption, loss of business information, or any other pecuniary loss) arising from the use of or inability to use the Book or the Software, even if WPI has been advised of the possibility of such damages.

(c) Because some jurisdictions do not allow the exclusion or limitation of liability for consequential or incidental damages, the above limitation or exclusion may not apply to you.

7. **U.S. Government Restricted Rights.** Use, duplication, or disclosure of the Software for or on behalf of the United States of America, its agencies and/or instrumentalities "U.S. Government" is subject to restrictions as stated in paragraph (c)(1)(ii) of the Rights in Technical Data and Computer Software clause of DFARS 252.227-7013, or subparagraphs (c) (1) and (2) of the Commercial Computer Software - Restricted Rights clause at FAR 52.227-19, and in similar clauses in the NASA FAR supplement, as applicable.

8. **General.** This Agreement constitutes the entire understanding of the parties and revokes and supersedes all prior agreements, oral or written, between them and may not be modified or amended except in a writing signed by both parties hereto that specifically refers to this Agreement. This Agreement shall take precedence over any other documents that may be in conflict herewith. If any one or more provisions contained in this Agreement are held by any court or tribunal to be invalid, illegal, or otherwise unenforceable, each and every other provision shall remain in full force and effect.

GNU General Public License

Version 2, June 1991

Preamble

The licenses for most software are designed to take away your freedom to share and change it. By contrast, the GNU General Public License is intended to guarantee your freedom to share and change free software--to make sure the software is free for all its users. This General Public License applies to most of the Free Software Foundation's software and to any other program whose authors commit to using it. (Some other Free Software Foundation software is covered by the GNU Library General Public License instead.) You can apply it to your programs, too.

When we speak of free software, we are referring to freedom, not price. Our General Public Licenses are designed to make sure that you have the freedom to distribute copies of free software (and charge for this service if you wish), that you receive source code or can get it if you want it, that you can change the software or use pieces of it in new free programs; and that you know you can do these things.

To protect your rights, we need to make restrictions that forbid anyone to deny you these rights or to ask you to surrender the rights. These restrictions translate to certain responsibilities for you if you distribute copies of the software, or if you modify it.

For example, if you distribute copies of such a program, whether gratis or for a fee, you must give the recipients all the rights that you have. You must make sure that they, too, receive or can get the source code. And you must show them these terms so they know their rights.

We protect your rights with two steps: (1) copyright the software, and (2) offer you this license which gives you legal permission to copy, distribute and/or modify the software. Also, for each author's protection and ours, we want to make certain that everyone understands that there is no warranty for this free software. If the software is modified by someone else and passed on, we want its recipients to know that what they have is not the original, so that any problems introduced by others will not reflect on the original authors' reputations.

Finally, any free program is threatened constantly by software patents. We wish to avoid the danger that redistributors of a free program will individually obtain patent licenses, in effect making the program proprietary. To prevent this, we have made it clear that any patent must be licensed for everyone's free use or not licensed at all.

The precise terms and conditions for copying, distribution and modification follow.

TERMS AND CONDITIONS FOR COPYING, DISTRIBUTION AND MODIFICATION

0. This License applies to any program or other work which contains a notice placed by the copyright holder saying it may be distributed under the terms of this General Public License. The "Program", below, refers to any such program or work, and a "work based on the Program" means either the Program or any derivative work under copyright law: that is to say, a work containing the Program or a portion of it, either verbatim or with modifications and/or translated into another language. (Hereinafter, translation is included without limitation in the term "modification".) Each licensee is addressed as "you".

   Activities other than copying, distribution and modification are not covered by this License; they are outside its scope. The act of running the Program is not restricted, and the output from the Program is covered only if its contents constitute a work based on the Program (independent of having been made by running the Program). Whether that is true depends on what the Program does.

1. You may copy and distribute verbatim copies of the Program's source code as you receive it, in any medium, provided that you conspicuously and appropriately publish on each copy an appropriate copyright notice and disclaimer of warranty; keep intact all the notices that refer to this License and to the absence of any warranty; and give any other recipients of the Program a copy of this License along with the Program.

   You may charge a fee for the physical act of transferring a copy, and you may at your option offer warranty protection in exchange for a fee.

2. You may modify your copy or copies of the Program or any portion of it, thus forming a work based on the Program, and copy and distribute such modifications or work under the terms of Section 1 above, provided that you also meet all of these conditions:

   a) You must cause the modified files to carry prominent notices stating that you changed the files and the date of any change.

   b) You must cause any work that you distribute or publish, that in whole or in part contains or is derived from the Program or any part thereof, to be licensed as a whole at no charge to all third parties under the terms of this License.

   c) If the modified program normally reads commands interactively when run, you must cause it, when started running for such interactive use in the most ordinary way, to print or display an announcement including an appropriate copyright notice and a notice that there is no warranty (or else, saying that you provide a warranty) and that users may redistribute the program under these conditions, and telling the user how to view a copy of this License. (Exception: if the Program itself is interactive but does not normally print such an announcement, your work based on the Program is not required to print an announcement.)

These requirements apply to the modified work as a whole. If identifiable sections of that work are not derived from the Program, and can be reasonably considered independent and separate works in themselves, then this License, and its terms, do not apply to those sections when you distribute them as separate works. But when you distribute the same sections as part of a whole which is a work based on the Program, the distribution of the whole must be on the terms of this License, whose permissions for other licensees extend to the entire whole, and thus to each and every part regardless of who wrote it.

Thus, it is not the intent of this section to claim rights or contest your rights to work written entirely by you; rather, the intent is to exercise the right to control the distribution of derivative or collective works based on the Program.

In addition, mere aggregation of another work not based on the Program with the Program (or with a work based on the Program) on a volume of a storage or distribution medium does not bring the other work under the scope of this License.

3. You may copy and distribute the Program (or a work based on it, under Section 2) in object code or executable form under the terms of Sections 1 and 2 above provided that you also do one of the following:

   a) Accompany it with the complete corresponding machine-readable source code, which must be distributed under the terms of Sections 1 and 2 above on a medium customarily used for software interchange; or,

   b) Accompany it with a written offer, valid for at least three years, to give any third party, for a charge no more than your cost of physically performing source distribution, a complete machine-readable copy of the corresponding source code, to be distributed under the terms of Sections 1 and 2 above on a medium customarily used for software interchange; or,

   c) Accompany it with the information you received as to the offer to distribute corresponding source code. (This alternative is allowed only for noncommercial distribution and only if you received the program in object code or executable form with such an offer, in accord with Subsection b above.)

The source code for a work means the preferred form of the work for making modifications to it. For an executable work, complete source code means all the source code for all modules it contains, plus any associated interface definition files, plus the scripts used to control compilation and installation of the executable. However, as a special exception, the source code distributed need not include anything that is normally distributed (in either source or binary form) with the major components (compiler, kernel, and so on) of the operating system on which the executable runs, unless that component itself accompanies the executable.

If distribution of executable or object code is made by offering access to copy from a designated place, then offering equivalent access to copy the source code from the same place counts as distribution of the source code, even though third parties are not compelled to copy the source along with the object code.

4. You may not copy, modify, sublicense, or distribute the Program except as expressly provided under this License. Any attempt otherwise to copy, modify, sublicense or distribute the Program is void, and will automatically terminate your rights under this License. However, parties who have received copies, or rights, from you under this License will not have their licenses terminated so long as such parties remain in full compliance.

5. You are not required to accept this License, since you have not signed it. However, nothing else grants you permission to modify or distribute the Program or its derivative works. These actions are prohibited by law if you do not accept this License. Therefore, by modifying or distributing the Program (or any work based on the Program), you indicate your acceptance of this License to do so, and all its terms and conditions for copying, distributing or modifying the Program or works based on it.

6. Each time you redistribute the Program (or any work based on the Program), the recipient automatically receives a license from the original licensor to copy, distribute or modify the Program subject to these terms and conditions. You may not impose any further restrictions on the recipients' exercise of the rights granted herein. You are not responsible for enforcing compliance by third parties to this License.

7. If, as a consequence of a court judgment or allegation of patent infringement or for any other reason (not limited to patent issues), conditions are imposed on you (whether by court order, agreement or otherwise) that contradict the conditions of this License, they do not excuse you from the conditions of this License. If you cannot distribute so as to satisfy simultaneously your obligations under this License and any other pertinent obligations, then as a consequence you may not distribute the Program at all. For example, if a patent license would not permit royalty-free redistribution of the Program by all those who receive copies directly or indirectly

through you, then the only way you could satisfy both it and this License would be to refrain entirely from distribution of the Program.

If any portion of this section is held invalid or unenforceable under any particular circumstance, the balance of the section is intended to apply and the section as a whole is intended to apply in other circumstances.

It is not the purpose of this section to induce you to infringe any patents or other property right claims or to contest validity of any such claims; this section has the sole purpose of protecting the integrity of the free software distribution system, which is implemented by public license practices. Many people have made generous contributions to the wide range of software distributed through that system in reliance on consistent application of that system; it is up to the author/donor to decide if he or she is willing to distribute software through any other system and a licensee cannot impose that choice.

This section is intended to make thoroughly clear what is believed to be a consequence of the rest of this License.

8. If the distribution and/or use of the Program is restricted in certain countries either by patents or by copyrighted interfaces, the original copyright holder who places the Program under this License may add an explicit geographical distribution limitation excluding those countries, so that distribution is permitted only in or among countries not thus excluded. In such case, this License incorporates the limitation as if written in the body of this License.

9. The Free Software Foundation may publish revised and/or new versions of the General Public License from time to time. Such new versions will be similar in spirit to the present version, but may differ in detail to address new problems or concerns.

Each version is given a distinguishing version number. If the Program specifies a version number of this License which applies to it and "any later version", you have the option of following the terms and conditions either of that version or of any later version published by the Free Software Foundation. If the Program does not specify a version number of this License, you may choose any version ever published by the Free Software Foundation.

10. If you wish to incorporate parts of the Program into other free programs whose distribution conditions are different, write to the author to ask for permission. For software which is copyrighted by the Free Software Foundation, write to the Free Software Foundation; we sometimes make exceptions for this. Our decision will be guided by the two goals of preserving the free status of all derivatives of our free software and of promoting the sharing and reuse of software generally.

NO WARRANTY

11. BECAUSE THE PROGRAM IS LICENSED FREE OF CHARGE, THERE IS NO WARRANTY FOR THE PROGRAM, TO THE EXTENT PERMITTED BY APPLICABLE LAW. EXCEPT WHEN OTHERWISE STATED IN WRITING THE COPYRIGHT HOLDERS AND/OR OTHER PARTIES PROVIDE THE PROGRAM "AS IS" WITHOUT WARRANTY OF ANY KIND, EITHER EXPRESSED OR IMPLIED, INCLUDING, BUT NOT LIMITED TO, THE IMPLIED WARRANTIES OF MERCHANTABILITY AND FITNESS FOR A PARTICULAR PURPOSE. THE ENTIRE RISK AS TO THE QUALITY AND PERFORMANCE OF THE PROGRAM IS WITH YOU. SHOULD THE PROGRAM PROVE DEFECTIVE, YOU ASSUME THE COST OF ALL NECESSARY SERVICING, REPAIR OR CORRECTION.

12. IN NO EVENT UNLESS REQUIRED BY APPLICABLE LAW OR AGREED TO IN WRITING WILL ANY COPYRIGHT HOLDER, OR ANY OTHER PARTY WHO MAY MODIFY AND/OR REDISTRIBUTE THE PROGRAM AS PERMITTED ABOVE, BE LIABLE TO YOU FOR DAMAGES, INCLUDING ANY GENERAL, SPECIAL, INCIDENTAL OR CONSEQUENTIAL DAMAGES ARISING OUT OF THE USE OR INABILITY TO USE THE PROGRAM (INCLUDING BUT NOT LIMITED TO LOSS OF DATA OR DATA BEING RENDERED INACCURATE OR LOSSES SUSTAINED BY YOU OR THIRD PARTIES OR A FAILURE OF THE PROGRAM TO OPERATE WITH ANY OTHER PROGRAMS), EVEN IF SUCH HOLDER OR OTHER PARTY HAS BEEN ADVISED OF THE POSSIBILITY OF SUCH DAMAGES.

*****END OF TERMS AND CONDITIONS*****

How to Apply These Terms to Your New Programs

If you develop a new program, and you want it to be of the greatest possible use to the public, the best way to achieve this is to make it free software which everyone can redistribute and change under these terms.

To do so, attach the following notices to the program. It is safest to attach them to the start of each source file to most effectively convey the exclusion of warranty; and each file should have at least the "copyright" line and a pointer to where the full notice is found.

This is free software, and you are welcome to redistribute it under certain conditions; type `show c' for details.

The hypothetical commands `show w' and `show c' should show the appropriate parts of the General Public License. Of course, the commands you use may be called something other than `show w' and `show c'; they could even be mouse-clicks or menu items-whatever suits your program.

You should also get your employer (if you work as a programmer) or your school, if any, to sign a "copyright disclaimer" for the program, if necessary. Here is a sample; alter the names:

```
Yoyodyne, Inc., hereby disclaims all copyright
interest in the program `Gnomovision'
(which makes passes at compilers) written
by James Hacker.

1 April 1989
Ty Coon, President of Vice
```

This General Public License does not permit incorporating your program into proprietary programs. If your program is a subroutine library, you may consider it more useful to permit linking proprietary applications with the library. If this is what you want to do, use the GNU Library General Public License instead of this License.